T0321971

Advancing Cloud Database Systems and Capacity Planning With Dynamic Applications

Narendra Kumar Kamila
C.V. Raman College of Engineering, India

A volume in the Advances in Data Mining and
Database Management (ADMDM) Book Series

www.igi-global.com

Published in the United States of America by
    IGI Global
    Information Science Reference (an imprint of IGI Global)
    701 E. Chocolate Avenue
    Hershey PA, USA 17033
    Tel: 717-533-8845
    Fax: 717-533-8661
    E-mail: cust@igi-global.com
    Web site: http://www.igi-global.com

Library of Congress Cataloging-in-Publication Data

Names: Kamila, Narendra Kumar, 1967- editor.
Title: Advancing cloud database systems and capacity planning with dynamic
    applications / Narendra Kumar Kamila, C.V. Raman College of Engineering,
    India, [editor].
Description: Hershey, PA : IGI Global, Information Science Reference, [2017]
    | Series: Advances in data mining and database management (ADMDM) book
    series | Includes bibliographical references.
Identifiers: LCCN 2016052518| ISBN 9781522520139 (hbk) | ISBN 9781522520146
    (ebook)
Subjects: LCSH: Data warehousing--Planning. | Cloud computing. | Database
    security.
Classification: LCC QA76.9.D37 A355 2017 | DDC 005.74/5--dc23 LC record available at https://lccn.loc.gov/2016052518

This book is published in the IGI Global book series Advances in Data Mining and Database Management (ADMDM) (ISSN: 2327-1981; eISSN: 2327-199X)

British Cataloguing in Publication Data
A Cataloguing in Publication record for this book is available from the British Library.

For electronic access to this publication, please contact: eresources@igi-global.com.

Advances in Data Mining and Database Management (ADMDM) Book Series

David Taniar
Monash University, Australia

ISSN:2327-1981
EISSN:2327-199X

MISSION

With the large amounts of information available to organizations in today's digital world, there is a need for continual research surrounding emerging methods and tools for collecting, analyzing, and storing data.

The **Advances in Data Mining & Database Management (ADMDM)** series aims to bring together research in information retrieval, data analysis, data warehousing, and related areas in order to become an ideal resource for those working and studying in these fields. IT professionals, software engineers, academicians and upper-level students will find titles within the ADMDM book series particularly useful for staying up-to-date on emerging research, theories, and applications in the fields of data mining and database management.

COVERAGE

- Predictive analysis
- Association Rule Learning
- Decision Support Systems
- Factor Analysis
- Customer Analytics
- Data Mining
- Educational Data Mining
- Quantitative Structure–Activity Relationship
- Cluster Analysis
- Enterprise systems

IGI Global is currently accepting manuscripts for publication within this series. To submit a proposal for a volume in this series, please contact our Acquisition Editors at Acquisitions@igi-global.com or visit: http://www.igi global.com/publish/.

Titles in this Series

For a list of additional titles in this series, please visit: www.igi-global.com

Intelligent Multidimensional Data Clustering and Analysis
Siddhartha Bhattacharyya (RCC Institute of Information Technology, India) Sourav De (Cooch Behar Government Engineering College, India) Indrajit Pan (RCC Institute of Information Technology, India) and Paramartha Dutta (Visva-Bharati University, India)
Information Science Reference • copyright 2017 • 450pp • H/C (ISBN: 9781522517764) • US $210.00 (our price)

Emerging Trends in the Development and Application of Composite Indicators
Veljko Jeremic (University of Belgrade, Serbia) Zoran Radojicic (University of Belgrade, Serbia) and Marina Dobrota (University of Belgrade, Serbia)
Information Science Reference • copyright 2017 • 402pp • H/C (ISBN: 9781522507147) • US $205.00 (our price)

Web Usage Mining Techniques and Applications Across Industries
A.V. Senthil Kumar (Hindusthan College of Arts and Science, India)
Information Science Reference • copyright 2017 • 424pp • H/C (ISBN: 9781522506133) • US $200.00 (our price)

Social Media Data Extraction and Content Analysis
Shalin Hai-Jew (Kansas State University, USA)
Information Science Reference • copyright 2017 • 493pp • H/C (ISBN: 9781522506485) • US $225.00 (our price)

Collaborative Filtering Using Data Mining and Analysis
Vishal Bhatnagar (Ambedkar Institute of Advanced Communication Technologies and Research, India)
Information Science Reference • copyright 2017 • 309pp • H/C (ISBN: 9781522504894) • US $195.00 (our price)

Effective Big Data Management and Opportunities for Implementation
Manoj Kumar Singh (Adama Science and Technology University, Ethiopia) and Dileep Kumar G. (Adama Science and Technology University, Ethiopia)
Information Science Reference • copyright 2016 • 324pp • H/C (ISBN: 9781522501824) • US $195.00 (our price)

Data Mining Trends and Applications in Criminal Science and Investigations
Omowunmi E. Isafiade (University of Cape Town, South Africa) and Antoine B. Bagula (University of the Western Cape, South Africa)
Information Science Reference • copyright 2016 • 386pp • H/C (ISBN: 9781522504634) • US $210.00 (our price)

Intelligent Techniques for Data Analysis in Diverse Settings
Numan Celebi (Sakarya University, Turkey)
Information Science Reference • copyright 2016 • 353pp • H/C (ISBN: 9781522500759) • US $195.00 (our price)

www.igi-global.com

701 E. Chocolate Ave., Hershey, PA 17033
Order online at www.igi-global.com or call 717-533-8845 x100
To place a standing order for titles released in this series, contact: cust@igi-global.com
Mon-Fri 8:00 am - 5:00 pm (est) or fax 24 hours a day 717-533-8661

Editorial Advisory Board

Table of Contents

Detailed Table of Contents

Chapter 1
Sathiyamoorthi V, Sona College of Technology, India

It is generally observed throughout the world that in the last two decades, while the average speed of computers has almost doubled in a span of around eighteen months, the average speed of the network has doubled merely in a span of just eight months! In order to improve the performance, more and more researchers are focusing their research in the field of computers and its related technologies. Data mining is one such area that extracts useful information from the huge amount of data present in the dataset. The discovered knowledge can be applied in various application areas such as marketing, fraud detection and customer retention in product based companies and so on. It discovers implicit, previously unknown and potentially useful information out of dataset. Recent trends in data mining include web mining where it discovers knowledge from web based information to improve the page layout, structure and its contents.

Chapter 2
Atefeh Khosravi, The University of Melbourne, Australia
Rajkumar Buyya, The University of Melbourne, Australia

Cloud computing provides on-demand access to computing resources for users across the world. It offers services on a pay-as-you-go model through data center sites that are scattered across diverse geographies. However, cloud data centers consume huge amount of electricity and leave high amount of carbon footprint in the ecosystem. This makes data centers responsible for 2% of the global CO_2 emission. Therefore, having energy and carbon-efficient techniques for resource management in distributed cloud data centers is inevitable. This chapter presents a taxonomy and classifies the existing research works based on their target system, objective, and the technique they use for resource management in achieving a green cloud computing environment. Finally, it discusses how each work addresses the issue of energy and carbon-efficiency and also provides an insight into future directions.

Chapter 3

Marcus Tanque, Independent Researcher, USA

Cloud computing consists of three fundamental service models: infrastructure-as-a-service, platform-as-a service and software-as-a-service. The technology "cloud computing" comprises four deployment models: public cloud, private cloud, hybrid cloud and community cloud. This chapter describes the six cloud service and deployment models, the association each of these services and models have with physical/virtual networks. Cloud service models are designed to power storage platforms, infrastructure solutions, provisioning and virtualization. Cloud computing services are developed to support shared network resources, provisioned between physical and virtual networks. These solutions are offered to organizations and consumers as utilities, to support dynamic, static, network and database provisioning processes. Vendors offer these resources to support day-to-day resource provisioning amid physical and virtual machines.

Chapter 4

Rashmi Rai, Birla Institute of Technology, India
G. Sahoo, Birla Institute of Technology, India

The ever-rising demand for computing services and the humongous amount of data generated everyday has led to the mushrooming of power craving data centers across the globe. These large-scale data centers consume huge amount of power and emit considerable amount of CO_2. There have been significant work towards reducing energy consumption and carbon footprints using several heuristics for dynamic virtual machine consolidation problem. Here we have tried to solve this problem a bit differently by making use of utility functions, which are widely used in economic modeling for representing user preferences. Our approach also uses Meta heuristic genetic algorithm and the fitness is evaluated with the utility function to consolidate virtual machine migration within cloud environment. The initial results as compared with existing state of art shows marginal but significant improvement in energy consumption as well as overall SLA violations.

Chapter 5

Suvendu Chandan Nayak, C. V. Raman College of Engineering, India
Sasmita Parida, C.V. Raman College of Engineering, India
Chitaranjan Tripathy, Veer Surendra Sai University of Technology, India
Prasant Kumar Pattnaik, KIIT University, India

The basic concept of cloud computing is based on "Pay per Use". The user can use the remote resources on demand for computing on payment basis. The on-demand resources of the user are provided according to a Service Level Agreement (SLA). In real time, the tasks are associated with a time constraint for which they are called deadline based tasks. The huge number of deadline based task coming to a cloud datacenter should be scheduled. The scheduling of this task with an efficient algorithm provides better resource utilization without violating SLA. In this chapter, we discussed the backfilling algorithm and its different types. Moreover, the backfilling algorithm was proposed for scheduling tasks in parallel. Whenever the application environment is changed the performance of the backfilling algorithm is changed.

The chapter aims implementation of different types of backfilling algorithms. Finally, the reader can be able to get some idea about the different backfilling scheduling algorithms that are used for scheduling deadline based task in cloud computing environment at the end.

Chapter 6

Thangavel M., Thiagarajar College of Engineering, Madurai, India
Varalakshmi P., Anna University, India
Sridhar S., M. Kumarasamy College of Engineering, India
Sindhuja R., Thiagarajar College of Engineering, India

Cloud computing has given a bloom to the technical world by providing various services. Data storage is the essential factor for the users who are having or working with lots and lots of data. Cloud data storage becomes the only way to store and maintain the large data, which can be accessed from anywhere and anytime. The open nature of cloud computing leads to some security issues. With respect to the cloud data storage, the Cloud Service Provider (CSP) has to provide security for the data outsourced. Data owner will be concerned on the data correctness after outsourcing into the cloud. To verify the data correctness, ensuring the state of data at the cloud data storage is needed, which is performed with the help of a Trusted Third Party Auditor (TTPA). Data owner can also perform the verification task, but it leads to computation cost and communication costs in huge amount. This survey gives a brief on public auditing schemes to explore what are all the system models designed by various researchers.

Chapter 7

Prashant Sangulagi, BKIT, India
Ashok V Sutagundar, Basaveshwar Engineering College, India

Sensor Cloud is one of the attractive trend in present world. Sensor cloud is a combination of wireless sensor network and cloud computing. Due to the lack of battery energy and bandwidth the sensor nodes are incapable to store and process large data. Hence storing raw data is a challenging task. The sensor cloud comes into existence to accomplish multiple tasks that are not possible with existing sensor network. In sensor cloud the sensed data are processed and stored in the clouds and data can be accessed anywhere and anytime. Maintaining the resources and providing the resources to end users is a challenging task in sensor cloud. This chapter will brief the architecture of sensor cloud, application of sensor cloud in various sector, advantages of using sensor cloud compared to existing networks and management of resources in sensor cloud.

Chapter 8

Sathiyamoorthi V., Sona College of Technology, India

It is generally observed throughout the world that in the last two decades, while the average speed of computers has almost doubled in a span of around eighteen months, the average speed of the network has doubled merely in a span of just eight months! In order to improve the performance, more and more researchers are focusing their research in the field of computers and its related technologies. Internet is one such technology that plays a major role in simplifying the information sharing and retrieval. World

Wide Web (WWW) is one such service provided by the Internet. It acts as a medium for sharing of information. As a result, millions of applications run on the Internet and cause increased network traffic and put a great demand on the available network infrastructure.

Chapter 9

Raghvendra Kumar, LNCT College, India
Prasant Kumar Pattnaik, KIIT University, India
Priyanka Pandey, LNCT, India

Large companies have different methods of doing this, one of which is to run sales simulations. Such simulation systems often need to perform complex calculations over large amounts of data, which in turn requires efficient models and algorithms. This chapter intends to evaluate whether it is possible to optimize and extend an existing sales system called PCT, which is currently suffering from unacceptably high running times in its simulation process. This is done through analysis of the current implementation, followed by optimization of its models and development of efficient algorithms. The performances of these optimized and extended models are compared to the existing one in order to evaluate their improvement. The conclusion of this chapter is that the simulation process in PCT can indeed be optimized and extended. The optimized models serve as a proof of concept, which shows that results identical to the original system's can be calculated within < 1% of the original running time for the largest customers.

Chapter 10

Balamurugan Balusamy, VIT University, India
Nadhiya S, VIT University, India
Sumalatha N, VIT University, India
Malathi Velu, RGM College of Engineering and Technology, India

In earlier days, people ran their applications or programs on a physical computer or a server. Cloud computing is a kind of Internet-based computing, where shared resources, data and information are provided to computers and other devices on-demand. Many business organizations were moving towards cloud because it provides flexibility, disaster recovery, security, collaboration etc., Relational Databases ruled the IT Industries for almost 40 years. Limitations of relational database lead to the rise of cloud database. A cloud database is a database that typically runs on a cloud computing platform. Cloud databases are on the rise as more and more businesses look to capitalize on the advantages of cloud computing to power their business applications. Cloud databases are mainly used in data mining, data warehousing and business intelligence. This chapter deals with different types of cloud database and how database influence capacity planning.

Chapter 11

Marcus Tanque, Independent Researcher, USA

In recent decades, vendors developed technology infrastructure solutions to integrate with enterprises and consumers' mobile devices. Hybrid development platforms are solution architecture designed to enhance developers' capabilities and provide organizations as well as customers the level of services to support mobile devices capabilities. Hybrid development platform solutions are easy to deploy at various enterprises. These capabilities can be distributed to/or integrated with mobile devices as agile applications and system interfaces. Hybrid mobile devices are designed to further provide users with enhanced technology solutions: cloud computing, big data, the Internet, physical and/or virtual network systems. The development of hybrid mobile platforms provides developers with advanced technology capabilities, necessary for supporting mobile devices once deployed to the marketplace. Technical and security features affecting the development and security of mobile devices are also discussed in this chapter.

Chapter 12

Cloud computing is the fastest growing technology in today's world. Cloud services provide pay as go models on capacity or usage. For providing better cloud services, capacity planning is very important. Proper capacity planning will maximize efficiency and on the other side proper control over the resources will help to overcome from attacks. As the technology develops in one side, threats and vulnerabilities to security also increases on the other side. A complete analysis of Denial of Service (DOS) attacks in cloud computing and how are they done in the cloud environment and the impact of reduced capacity in cloud causes greater significance. Among all the cloud computing attacks, DOS is a major threat to the cloud environment. In this book chapter, we are going to discuss DOS attack in the cloud and its types, what are the tools used to perform DOS attack and how they are detected and prevented. Finally it deals with the measures to protect the cloud services from DOS attack and also penetration testing for DOS attack.

Chapter 13

Cloud computing is recently emerging technology, which provides a way to access computing resources over Internet on demand and pay per use basis. Cloud computing is a paradigm that enable access to shared pool of resources efficiently, which are managed by third party cloud service providers. Despite of various advantages of cloud computing security is the biggest threat. This chapter describes various security concerns in cloud computing. The clouds are subject to traditional data confidentiality, integrity, availability and various privacy issues. This chapter comprises various security issues at different levels in environment that includes infrastructure level security, data level and storage security. It also deals with the concept of Identity and Access Control mechanism.

Chapter 14

It is generally observed throughout the world that in the last two decades, while the average speed of computers has almost doubled in a span of around eighteen months, the average speed of the network has doubled merely in a span of just eight months! In order to improve the performance, more and more researchers are focusing their research in the field of computers and its related technologies. Data Mining is also known as knowledge discovery in database (KDD) is one such research area. The discovered knowledge can be applied in various application areas such as marketing, fraud detection, customer retention and production control and marketing to improve their business. It discovers implicit, previously unknown and potentially useful information out of datasets. Recent trends in data mining include web mining where it discovers knowledge from web based information to improve the page layout, structure and its content thereby it reduces the user latency in accessing the web page and website performance.

Cloud computing is a technology that offers an enterprise model to provide resources made available to the client and network access to a shared pool of configurable computing resources and pay-for-peruse basis. Generally, a session is said to be the collective information of an ongoing transaction. This package is typically stored on the server as a temporary file and labeled with an ID, usually consisting of a random number, time and date the session was initiated. That session ID is sent to the client with the first response, and then presented back to the server with each subsequent request. This permits the server to access the stored data appropriate to that session. That, in turn allows each transaction to be logically related to the previous one. Session hijacking is the common problem that is experienced in the cloud environment in which the session id is gained and information is gathered using the session ID compromising its security. This chapter covers session hijacking and the countermeasures to prevent session hijacking.

Foreword

The advent of cloud computing and big data analytics has revolutionized society and better management of the data for sustainability of next generation lives. Although cloud computing and big data are complementary, forming a dialectical relationship, today's job market requires IT professionals to understand theory of cloud computing and have hands-on skills for developing real-world database systems. However, coverage of these two topics in integrated manner is limited in the literature. To bridge the gap, *Advancing Cloud Database Systems and Capacity Planning With Dynamic Applications* explains how to take advantage of the cloud environment to develop fully functioning database systems without further additional investments in IT infrastructure.

The book begins by providing readers with the required foundation in database systems and cloud-based database development techniques and followed by concepts and applications.

I appreciate the efforts made by Prof. Kamila to compile the book on pertinent areas of cloud computing and big data analytics. The topics covered include resource management, dynamic virtual machine management, cloud platforms and infrastructure, cloud services, energy and carbon-aware management of geo-distributed cloud data centers, big data optimization in cloud environment, privacy & security and some applications. He has meticulously collated the articles, reviewed and put them in appropriate order for the benefit of readers. I am sure readers will benefit from the knowledge presented in the book.

Rajkumar Buyya
The University of Melbourne, Australia

Preface

Three IT initiatives are currently popular in every organization across the globe: cloud computing, big data analytics and Internet of Things (IoT). Cloud computing and big data are complementary, forming a dialectical relationship. Cloud computing and the Internet of Things' widespread application is people's ultimate vision, and the rapid increase in big data is a thorny problem that is encountered during development. Cloud computing is a trend in technology development, while big data is an inevitable phenomenon of the rapid development of a modern information society. In the other hand, big data analytics offers the promise of providing valuable insights that can create competitive advantage, spark new innovations, and drive increased revenues. As a delivery model for IT services, cloud computing has the potential to enhance business agility and productivity while enabling greater efficiencies and reducing costs. But, Internet of Things refers to scenarios where network connectivity and computing capability extends to objects, sensors and everyday items not normally considered computers, allowing these devices to generate, exchange and consume data with minimal human intervention. There is, however, no single, universal definition. The concept of combining computers, sensors, and networks to monitor and control devices has existed for decades. The recent confluence of several technology market trends, however, is bringing the Internet of Things closer to widespread reality. These include Ubiquitous Connectivity, Widespread Adoption of IP-based Networking, Computing Economics, Miniaturization, Advances in Data Analytics, and the Rise of Cloud Computing. IoT implementations use different technical communications models, each with its' own characteristics. Four common communications models described by the Internet Architecture Board include: *Device-to-Device, Device-to-Cloud, Device-to-Gateway*, and *Back-End Data-Sharing*. These models highlight the flexibility in the ways that IoT devices can connect and provide value to the user. However, this edited book deals with cloud database systems with capacity planning and big data/big data analytics. And cloud computing is core to cloud database systems.

Cloud computing and big data analytics, both technologies continue to evolve. Organizations are moving beyond questions of what and how to store big data to address how to derive meaningful analytics that respond to real business needs. As cloud computing continues to mature, a growing number of enterprises are building efficient and agile cloud environments, and cloud providers continue to expand service offerings. Speculation says that all IT organizations look for cloud computing as the structure to support their big data projects. Big data environments require clusters of servers to support the tools that process the large volumes, high velocity, and varied formats of big data. The outbreak of big data is a thorny problem encountered in social and informatization development. Because of the growth of data traffic and data volume, data formats are now multisource and heterogeneous, and they require real-time and accurate data processing. Big data can help us discover the potential value of large amounts of data. Traditional IT architecture is incapable of handling the big data problem, as there are many bottlenecks, such as: poor scalability; poor fault tolerance; low performance; difficulty in installation, deployment, and maintenance; and so on. Because of the rapid development of the Internet of Things, the Internet, and mobile communication network technology in recent years, the frequency and speed of data transmission has greatly accelerated. This gives rise to the big data problem, and the derivative development and deep recycling use of data make the big data problem even more prominent. Clouds are already deployed on pools of server, storage, and networking resources and can scale up or down as needed. Cloud computing offers a cost-effective way to support big data technologies and the advanced analytics applications that can drive business value.

As a new computing model, Cloud computing has gained great momentum in both academia and industry. Governments, research institutions, and industry leaders are actively trying to solve the growing computing and storage problems in the Internet age using Cloud computing. In addition to Amazon Web Services (AWS), Google's App Engine, and Microsoft's Windows Azure Services—along with other commercial cloud platforms—there are also many open-source Cloud computing platforms, such as: OpenNebula, Eucalyptus, Nimbus, and OpenStack. Each platform has its own significant features and constantly evolving community. AWS is the most popular Cloud computing platform. The most distinct features of its system architecture are open data, functioning via Web Service interfaces, and the achievement of loose-coupling via Service Oriented Architecture.

At the same time, big data processing needs the support of cloud data centers that have large-scale physical resources and Cloud computing platforms that have efficient resource scheduling and management. Cloud computing management platforms can: provide flexible and efficient deployment, operation, and management environments for large data centers and enterprises; support heterogeneous underlying hardware and operating systems with virtualization technology; provide applications with cloud resource management solutions that are secure, high performance, highly extensible, highly reliable, and highly scalable; reduce the costs of application development, deployment, operation, and maintenance; and improve the efficiency of resource utilization. This book focuses cloud database system taking big data into consideration.

The area cloud computing and big data analytics play a major role in daily life and it's importance is increasing day by day. Without research, technology does not carry any meaning. Similarly, without information and engineering the word "grow" has no existence in every field of life. Technology makes life better and smoother. To achieve that objective we have to value the potential global contribution of our researchers. Every day new inventions are coming to limelight enriching human life. The above topic tells about the latest development of cloud database systems which is essential to inform and educate the demand of global scientists and human being as well. Hence, our endeavor is to capture new inventions and present those to the researchers at large.

It gives me immense pleasure to introduce this collection of chapters, *Advancing Cloud Database Systems and Capacity Planning With Dynamic Applications*, to the readers of the book series. The objective of this book is to bridge the existing gap in literature and comprehensively cover the system, processing and application aspects of cloud computing and big data analytics. Due to rapid developments in specialized areas of cloud computing and big data, this book takes on the form of a contributed volume where well known experts address specific research and application problems. It presents the state of the art as well as the most recent trends both in theory and applications. It serves the needs of different readers at different levels. It can be used as stand-alone reference for masters, researchers and practitioners. For example, the researcher can use it as an up-to-date reference material since it offers a broad survey of the relevant literature. Finally, practicing engineers may find it useful in designing and implementing various cloud database system tasks.

This book purports to serve as a research reference book in the area of cloud computing and big data analytics by providing useful cutting edge research information to the students, researchers, scientists, engineers and other working professionals in this area. The book provides the latest research trends and concepts to develop new methodologies and applications in the area of resource allocation, resource management, dynamic virtual machine management, cloud platforms and infrastructure, energy and carbon-aware management of geo-distributed cloud data centers, big data optimization in cloud environment and its applications. In addition, the book also incorporates chapters related to new challenging application area of cloud computing and big data analytics. Above all, each and every chapter is designed in such a way as to incorporate the latest literature review, methods and models, implementation, experimental results, performance analysis, conclusion, future work and the latest relevant references.

Besides huge applications of the subject cloud computing and big data analytics in diversified fields, several challenges are coming into picture in the new millennium based on different applications and geographical locations. Such challenges are of different types like privacy and security, data integration, cloud capacity planning, data virtualization, mining and visualization, predictive analytics in the cloud, big data processing algorithms and machine learning for information extraction, etc.

Theory and applications are both important in cloud computing and cloud database systems with capacity planning. They are treated equally well in this book on a pragmatic basis. Here different types of problems of scientists and engineers are addressed concerning cloud database systems with cloud computing. The book comprises chapters contributed by highly qualified and diverse group of authors.

I am very grateful to the researchers who offered their services in making the book effective and scientific.

It is my pleasure to present this book which includes selected chapters of internationally recognized authors on cloud database systems, cloud computing and related areas. The book is intended to provide a forum for researchers, educators and professionals to share their discoveries and innovative practices with others and to explore future trends and applications in the field of cloud database systems and its future trends. However, this book will also provide a forum for dissemination of knowledge on both theoretical and applied research on the above areas with an ultimate aim to bridge the gap between these coherent disciplines of knowledge. This forum accelerates interaction between the above bodies of knowledge, and fosters a unified development in the next generation cloud database systems and application.

The broad spectrum of this book includes the topics:

- Information Systems Applications,
- Artificial Intelligence,
- Database Management,
- Information Storage and Retrieval,
- Data Mining and Knowledge Discovery,
- Algorithm Analysis and Problem Complexity,
- Big Data Architectures,
- Cloud Capacity Planning,
- Cloud Database Systems (NoSQL, NewSQL, and Hybrid),
- Cloud Platforms and Infrastructures,
- Data Integration as a Service,

- Data Mining and Predictive Analytics in the Cloud,
- Data Virtualization and Governance,
- Statistical, Mathematical, and Dynamical Properties of Big Data,
- Machine Learning for Information Extraction,
- Distributed Systems and Cloud Computing for Big Data,
- Big Data Applications,
- Big Data Security and Privacy,
- Big Data Management,
- Big Data Processing Algorithms,
- Big Data Search, Mining and Visualization,
- Big Data Applications for Business, Government, and Society,
- Multimedia Big Data,
- Big Data Communication,
- And Related Topics.

ORGANIZATION OF THE BOOK

The book, *Advancing Cloud Database Systems and Capacity Planning With Dynamic Applications*, provides an overview of recent research developments in the field of cloud database systems and its applications. This book contains 15 chapters starting from basic concept level to research and application level.

The first chapter discusses the fundamentals of data mining and data warehousing techniques, tools and methodologies to solve different kinds of problems being generated day by day in order to extract valuable information for future development of the mankind.

Atefeh and Buyya in second chapter titled "Energy and Carbon-Aware Management of Geo-Distributed Cloud Data Centers: State of the Art and Future Directions" have addressed a taxonomy and classified the existing research works based on their target system, objective, and the technique they use for resource management in achieving a green cloud computing environment. Finally, this chapter discusses how each work addresses the issue of energy and carbon-efficiency and also provides an insight into future directions. These challenges have motivated many researchers to work in this area.

The third chapter talks about Cloud service models as designed to power storage platforms, infrastructure solutions, provisioning and virtualization. Cloud computing services are developed to support shared network resources, provisioned between physical and virtual networks. These solutions are offered to organizations and consumers as utilities, to support dynamic, static, network and database provisioning processes. Vendors offer these resources to support day-to-day resource provisioning amid physical and virtual machines.

In contrast, Chapter 4 gives overview about the consumption of huge amount of power by large scale data centers and generation of considerable amount of carbon dioxide. The authors have tried to solve this problem by using utility functions, which are widely used in economic modeling for representing user preferences. This approach also uses Meta heuristic genetic algorithm and the fitness is evaluated with the utility function to consolidate virtual machine migration within cloud environment. Their results show the significant improvement in energy consumption over the existing methodologies.

Chapter 5, "Resource Allocation Policies in Cloud Computing Environment," attempts to discuss the task scheduling algorithms for better resource utilization without violating service level agreement

(SLA). The authors have developed different backfilling algorithms for task scheduling scalable to cloud computing environment and implemented. Based on the result it works well.

In Chapter 6, the authors have demonstrated an overview on public auditing schemes to explore the system models designed by various researchers to provide security when data outsourced. This book chapter aims to discuss some security issues concerned to cloud data storage in cloud computing environment. The cloud service provider has to verify the data correctness by trusted third party auditor (TTPA) while outsourcing takes place. Although it leads to computation cost and communication costs in huge amount, it is essential due to open nature of cloud. Moreover, the authors have tried their best to discuss different standards.

In Chapter 7, Sangulagi et al. have discussed about the processing and storing of sensed data in cloud. In general due to the lack of battery energy and bandwidth the sensor nodes are incapable to store and process large amount of data which is a challenging task. The sensor cloud comes into existence to accomplish multiple tasks that are not possible with existing sensor network. In sensor cloud the sensed data are processed and stored in the clouds and data can be accessed anywhere and anytime. Maintaining the resources and providing the resources to end users is a challenging task in sensor cloud. This chapter talks about the architecture of sensor cloud, application of sensor cloud in various sectors, advantages of using sensor cloud compared to existing networks and management of resources in sensor cloud.

Chapter 8 presents challenges and issues in information retrieval system. When the average speed of computers has almost doubled in a span of around eighteen months, the average speed of the network has doubled merely in a span of just eight months. In order to improve the performance, the author has used different techniques for web based information retrieval system. The author has also tried his best to show the pros and cons of the techniques used with sufficient justification.

Chapter 9 intends to evaluate whether it is possible to optimize and extend an existing sales system called *Patent Customer Treaty* (PCT), which is currently suffering from unacceptably high running times in its simulation process. This is done through analysis of the current implementation, followed by optimization of its models and development of efficient algorithms. The performances of these optimized and extended models are compared to the existing one in order to evaluate their improvement. The conclusion of this chapter is that the simulation process in PCT can indeed be optimized and extended.

Whereas, Chapter 10 presents Cloud Database Systems- NoSQL, NewSQL and Hybrid. In this chapter, the authors have discussed the limitations of relational database over cloud database. A cloud database is a database that typically runs on a cloud computing platform. Cloud databases are on the rise as more and more businesses look to capitalize on the advantages of cloud computing to power their business applications. Cloud databases are mainly used in data mining, data warehousing and business intelligence. This chapter deals with different types of cloud database and how database influence capacity planning.

In Chapter 11, the author has presented the challenges and opportunities of developing hybrid mobile devices. In recent decades, vendors developed technology infrastructure solutions to integrate with enterprises and consumers' mobile devices. Hybrid development platforms are solution architecture designed to enhance developers' capabilities to provide organizations and customers the level of services to support mobile devices capabilities. These solutions are easy to deploy at various enterprises. These capabilities can be distributed to/or integrated with mobile devices as agile applications and system interfaces. Hybrid mobile devices are designed to also provide users with enhanced technology solutions: cloud computing, big data, the Internet, physical and/or virtual network systems. In general, the development of hybrid mobile platforms provides developers with advanced technology capabilities, necessary for supporting mobile devices once deployed to the marketplace. Technical and security features affecting the development and security of mobile devices are also discussed in this chapter.

However, Chapter 12 presents a literature survey on denial of service attacks over cloud environment. Cloud services provide pay as go models on capacity or usage. For providing better cloud services, capacity planning is very important. Proper capacity planning maximizes efficiency and on the other side proper control over the resources helps to overcome from attacks. As the technology develops in one side, threats and vulnerabilities to security also increases on the other side. A complete analysis of Denial of Service (DOS) attacks in cloud computing and how are they done in the cloud environment and the impact of reduced capacity in cloud causes greater significance. Among all the cloud computing attacks, DOS is a major threat to the cloud environment. In this chapter, the authors have discussed DOS attack in the cloud and its types, tools used to perform DOS attack and how they are detected and prevented. Finally it deals with the measures to protect the cloud services from DOS attack and also penetration testing for DOS attack.

Chapter 13 tells us about security aspects in cloud. The goal of this chapter is to present an intensive study of various security concerns in cloud computing. Cloud computing is recently emerging technology which provides a way to access computing resources over Internet on demand and pay per use basis. Cloud computing enables access to shared pool of resources efficiently that are managed by third party cloud service providers. Despite of various advantages of cloud computing security is the biggest threat. This chapter comprises various security issues at different levels in environment which includes infrastructure level security, data level and storage security. It also deals with the concept of Identity and Access Control mechanism.

In Chapter 14, the author has discussed the recent trend in data mining include web mining where it discovers knowledge from web based information to improve the page layout, structure and its content thereby it reduces the user latency in accessing the web page and website performance.

But the objective of Chapter 15 is to know about session hijacking over cloud environment. Generally, a session is said to be the collective information of an ongoing transaction. This package is typically stored on the server as a temporary file and labeled with an ID, usually consisting of a random number, time and date the session was initiated. That session ID is sent to the client with the first response, and then presented back to the server with each subsequent request. This permits the server to access the stored data appropriate to that session. That, in turn allows each transaction to be logically related to the previous one. Session hijacking is the common problem that is experienced in the cloud environment in which the session id is gained and information is gathered using the session ID compromising its security. This chapter discusses session hijacking and the countermeasures to prevent session hijacking.

This edited book has specific salient features. They are:

- It deals with important and timely topic of emerging relationship between cloud computing technology and big data analytics in unattended area.
- It presents research findings and materials authored by global experts in the field.
- It serves as a comprehensive source of information and reference material on the topic cloud database systems.
- It presents latest development of the topic related to cloud computing and big data analytics.
- It presents the research findings in well organized and structured manner.
- Even though it is not a text book, it can serve as a complete reference material for both cloud computing and big data analytics.

- It can certainly be used as one for graduate courses and research oriented courses dealing with cloud database management system.
- It can serve as light house of knowledge in cloud computing research lab including data science lab.

This comprehensive and timely publication aims to be an essential reference source, building on the available literature in the field of cloud computing and big data analytics to boost further research in this dynamic and challenging field. It is expected that this text will provide the resources necessary for technology developers, scientists and manufacturer to adopt and implement new inventions across the globe.

In short, I am very happy with both experience and end product of our sincere efforts. It is certain that this book will continue as an essential and indispensable resource for all concerned for coming years.

Narendra Kumar Kamila
C. V. Raman College of Engineering, India

Acknowledgment

The editor would like to thank each one of the authors for their contributions. My sincere gratitude goes to the chapter's authors who contributed their time and expertise to this book. They are all models of professionalism, responsiveness and patience with respect to my cheerleading and cajoling. The group efforts that created this book are much larger, deeper and of higher quality than that any individual could have created. Each and every chapter in this book has been written by a carefully selected distinguished specialist, ensuring that the greatest depth of understanding be communicated to the readers. I have also taken time to read each and every word of every chapter and have provided extensive feedback to the chapter authors in seeking to make the book perfect. Owing primarily to their efforts I feel certain that this book will prove to be an essential and indispensable resource for years to come.

The editor also wishes to acknowledge the valuable contributions of the reviewers regarding the improvement of quality, coherence, and content presentation of chapters. Most of the authors also served as referees; we highly appreciate their double task.

Finally, the editor would like to thank all members of IGI Global publication for their timely help; constant inspiration and encouragement with friendly support make me able to publish the book in time.

Narendra Kumar Kamila
C. V. Raman College of Engineering, India

Chapter 1
Fundamentals of Data Mining and Data Warehousing

Sathiyamoorthi V
Sona College of Technology, India

ABSTRACT

It is generally observed throughout the world that in the last two decades, while the average speed of computers has almost doubled in a span of around eighteen months, the average speed of the network has doubled merely in a span of just eight months! In order to improve the performance, more and more researchers are focusing their research in the field of computers and its related technologies. Data mining is one such area that extracts useful information from the huge amount of data present in the dataset. The discovered knowledge can be applied in various application areas such as marketing, fraud detection and customer retention in product based companies and so on. It discovers implicit, previously unknown and potentially useful information out of dataset. Recent trends in data mining include web mining where it discovers knowledge from web based information to improve the page layout, structure and its contents.

INTRODUCTION

Data mining is the process of nontrivial extraction of implicit, previously unknown and potentially useful information from the raw data present in the large database (Jiawei et al. 2006). It is also known as Knowledge Discovery in Databases (KDD). Data mining techniques can be applied upon various data sources to improve the value of the existing information system. When implemented on high performance client and server system, data mining tools can analyze large databases to deliver highly reliable results. It is also described that the data mining techniques can be coupled with relational database engines (Jiawei et al. 2006).

Data mining differs from the conventional database retrieval in the fact that it extracts hidden information or knowledge that is not explicitly available in the database, whereas database retrieval extracts the data that is explicitly available in the databases through some query language. Based on the fact that, a certain degree of intelligence is incorporated in the system, data mining could further be viewed as a branch of artificial intelligence and thus, it could be treated as an intelligent database manipulation

DOI: 10.4018/978-1-5225-2013-9.ch001

system. Dunham et al. (2006) have explained that data mining is an interdisciplinary field that incorporates concepts and techniques from several disciplines such as statistics, neural networks and machine learning in the process of knowledge discovery.

Data warehousing is the location where it stores subject oriented and task relevant data for an organization decision support system. It contains data that are most important and relevant to decision making process. Hence, this chapter describes the functionality of data mining and data warehousing system with its applications. Also, it focuses on Web mining where it addresses the issues and challenges present in it. Finally, it describes the integration technique where data mining and data warehousing system can be combined for an effective functionality.

As data mining is an interdisciplinary field, it uses algorithms and techniques from various fields such as statistics, machine learning, artificial intelligence, neural networks and database technology. The most commonly used methods that assist in data mining tasks are (Jiawei et al. 2006) given below:

- **Artificial Neural Networks (ANN):** A non-linear predictive model comprises of different layers namely input, hidden and output layers that learn through training and resemble biological neural network in a structure.
- **Decision Tree:** A tree structure comprises of nodes and branches and represents a set of decisions. A node in decision tree represents conditions and branches of outcome. These decisions generate rules for the classifications of a dataset. Specific decision tree method includes classification and regression trees.
- **Genetic Algorithm (GA):** This Evolutionary optimization technique uses operators such as genetic combination, mutation, and natural selection in a design-based concept of evolution. This can be applied to optimization problem that either maximize or minimize the given objective function.
- **Nearest Neighbor Method:** A technique that classifies each record in a dataset based on a combination of the classes of 'k' records that are most similar to its historical dataset. Sometimes called as the K-Nearest Neighbor (KNN) technique.
- **Rule Induction:** This is the extraction of useful if-then rules from the dataset.

BACKGROUND

It is described that data mining can be viewed as a crucial step in knowledge discovery process which is shown in Figure 1. It is composed of various phases such as,

- Pre-processing
- Data Mining
- Pattern Extraction
- Pattern Evaluation
- Knowledge Presentation

The data preprocessing phase devises the data to be in a format that are suitable for further data mining operations. Data cleaning removes noise, inconsistent data, and irrelevant data that are present in the data sources. Since the input database could be composed of data that arrives from multiple sources, data integration is employed to integrate data from those sources. Data mining phase identifies the specific data mining tasks that employs intelligent methods and extracts knowledge. The resulting knowledge or patterns are evaluated for usability in the pattern evaluation phase. The last step of KDD process is the presentation of discovered knowledge in a user friendly and user understandable format referred to as the knowledge presentation phase (Jiawei et al. 2006). Data mining system could be categorized into the following dimensions (Jiawei et al. 2006).

- Kinds of databases to be mined
  - This includes whether it uses relational, transactional, object-oriented, object-relational, active, spatial, time-series, text, multi-media, heterogeneous, legacy, WWW and so on.
- Kinds of knowledge to be discovered,
  - This includes whether it applies characterization, discrimination, association, classification, clustering, and trend, deviation and outlier analysis and so on.
- Kinds of techniques utilized,
  - This includes type of techniques it employed such as database oriented, data warehouse, machine learning, statistics, visualization, neural network and so on.
- Kinds of applications adapted.
  - This includes application areas such as retail, telecommunication, banking, fraud analysis, stock market analysis; Web mining, Web log analysis and so on.

Data Mining Tasks

In general, data mining tasks can be broadly classified into either descriptive or predictive (Jiawei et al. 2006). Descriptive data mining tasks are those that provide description or characterization of properties of the input database. Predictive data mining tasks are those that provide inference on input data to arrive at hidden knowledge and to make interesting and useful predictions. Some of the data mining tasks and its categorization are given below.

- Classification [Predictive]
- Clustering [Descriptive]
- Association Rule Mining [Descriptive]
- Sequential Pattern Discovery [Descriptive]
- Regression [Predictive]
- Deviation Detection [Predictive]

Data sources for mining knowledge can vary depending on the type of data present in the database. Typical data sources are:

- Spatial data base
- Text database
- Multimedia database
- Web database
- Relational database
- Bioinformatics like DNA database
- Time series database and so on

Figure 1. Steps in KDD process

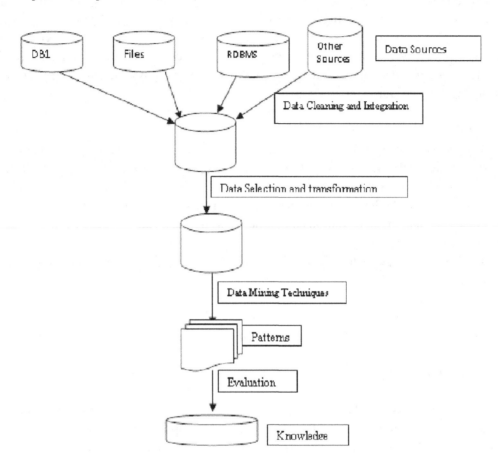

As mentioned earlier, data mining is an interdisciplinary field which utilizes the domain knowledge, skills, tools and techniques from several other fields such asDatabase, Data Statistics, Machine Learning, Information Retrieval, Data Visualization and other disciplines as well which is shown in Figure 2.

DATA MINING TASKS

Classification

It is one of the data mining techniques used for data analysis and used to construct the classification model. It is used to predict future trends analysis. It is also known as supervised learning.

The classification models used to predict categorical class labels whereas and prediction models predict continuous valued.

For example, classification model for bank is used to classify bank loan applications as either safe or risky one. A prediction model is used to predict the potential customers who will buy computer equipment given their income and occupation.

Some other examples of data analysis task of classification are given below.

Figure 2. Data mining as inter-Disciplinary field

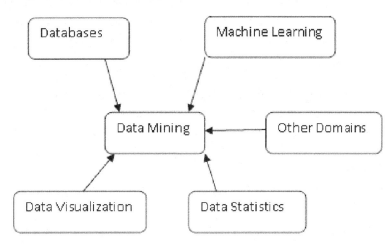

- A bank loan officer wants to analyze the data in order to predict which loan applicant is risky or which are safe.
- A marketing manager at a company needs to analyze a customer with a given profile, who will buy a new computer as shown in Figure 3.

In both the cases, a model is constructed to predict the categorical labels. These labels are risky or safe for loan application and yes or no for marketing data.

Working Principles

It is the task of building a model that describe and distinguish data class of an object. This is used to predict class label for an object where class label information is not available (Jiawei et al. 2006). It is an example of learning from samples. The first phase called model construction is also referred to as

Figure 3. Data mining task classification

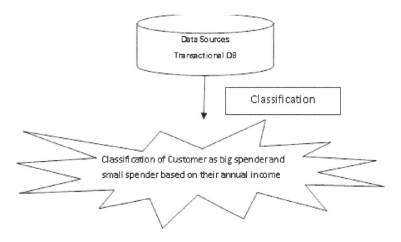

training phase, where a model is built based on the features present in the training data. This model is then used to predict class labels for the testing data, where class label information is not available. A test set is used to determine the accuracy of the model. Usually, the given data set is divided into training and test sets, with training set used to construct the model and test set used to validate it.

Decision trees are commonly used to represent classification models. A decision tree is similar to a flowchart like structure where every node represents a test on an attribute value and branches denote a test outcome and tree leaves represent actual classes. Other standard representation techniques include K-nearest neighbor, Bayesians classification algorithm, if-then rules and neural networks (Jiawei et al. 2006). It is also known as supervised learning process. Effectiveness of prediction depends on training dataset used to train the model.

The classification is two steps process. They are:

- **Phase I**: Building the Classifier(Training Phase)
- **Phase II**: Using Classifier (Testing Phase)

Training and Testing Phase

This is the first step in classification and in this step a classification algorithm is used to construct the classifier model shown in Figure 5. The model is built from the training dataset which contain tuples called records with the associated class labels. Each tuple presents in the training dataset is called as category or class.

Consider that training dataset of a bank_loan schema contains value for the following attributes.

<Name, Age, Income, Loan_decision>

and class label here is Loan_decision and possible class label are risky, safe and low_risky. Say for an example, classification algorithm uses ID 3 then classification model is the decision tree which is shown below Figure 4. A decision tree is a tree that includes a root node, branches and leaf nodes. Each internal node denotes a test on an attribute, each branch denotes the outcome of the test, and each leaf node holds a class label. The node without parent is the root node. Nodes without children is called leaf node and it represents the outcome.

Once the decision tree was built, then it uses the IF-THEN rules on nodes present in the node to find the class label of a tuple in the testing dataset.

May be following six rules are derived from the above tree.

1. If Age=young and Income=low then Loan_decision= risky
2. If Age=Senior and Income=low then Loan_decision= risky
3. If Age=Middle_Aged and Income=low then Loan_decision= risky
4. If Age=young and Income=High then Loan_decision= Safe
5. If Age=Middle_Aged and Income=High then Loan_decision=Safe
6. If Age=Senior and Income=High then Loan_decision= Low_risky

Once the model is built then next step is testing the classifier using some sample testing dataset which is shown above figure. Here, the testing dataset is used to measure the accuracy of classification model

Figure 4. Decision tree

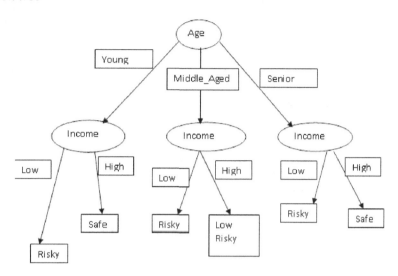

Figure 5. Training process of classification

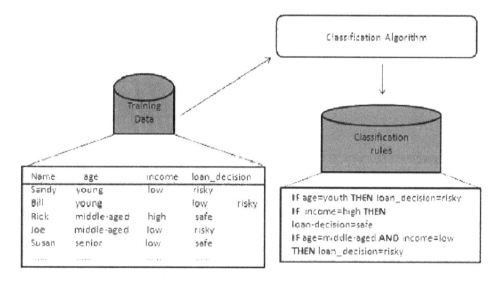

shown in Figure 6. There are two different metrics such as precision and recall used for measuring accuracy of a classification model.

Prediction

Data mining is an analytic process designed to explore data for consistent patterns or systematic relationships among variables and then to validate the findings by applying the detected patterns to new subsets of data. (Jiawei et al. 2006) uncover that the predictive data mining is the most common type of data mining and it has the most direct business applications. Example is shown in Figure 7. The process of predictive data mining task consists of three stages:

Figure 6. Testing process of classification

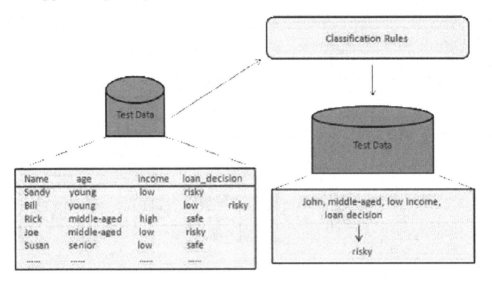

Figure 7. Data mining task prediction

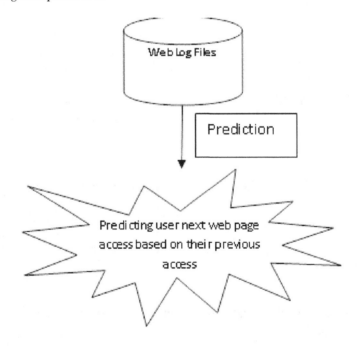

- Data exploration
- Model building
- Deployment

Data Exploration usually starts with data preparation which may involve data cleaning, data transformations, selecting subsets of records and feature selection. Feature selection is one of the important operations in the exploration process. It is defined as reducing the numbers of variables to a manageable range if the datasets are with large number of variables performing some preliminary feature selection operations. Then, a simple choice of straightforward predictors for a regression model is used to elaborate exploratory analyses. The most widely used graphical and statistical method is exploratory data analysis. Model building and validation steps involve considering various models and choosing the best one based on their predictive performance. Deployment is the final step which involves selecting the best model in the previous step and applying it to a new data in order to generate predictions or estimates of the expected outcome.

Both classification and prediction are used for data analysis but there exist some issues dealing with preparing the data for data analysis. It involves the following activities:

- **Data Cleaning**: Data cleaning involves removing the noisy, incomplete and inconsistent data and methods for handling missing values of an attribute. The noisy data is removed by applying smoothing techniques such as binning and then problem of missing values is handled by replacing a missing value with most commonly occurring value for that attribute or replacing missing value by mean value of that attribute or replacing the missing value by global constant and so on.
- **Relevance Analysis**: Datasets may also have some irrelevant attributes and hence correlation analysis is performed to know whether any two given attributes are related or not. All irrelevant attributes are removed.
- **Normalization**: Normalization involves scaling all values for given attribute in order to make them fall within a small specified range. Ex. Min_Max normalization.
- **Generalization**: It is data generalization method where data at low levels are mapped to some higher level there by reducing the number of values of an attributes. For this purpose we can use the concept hierarchies. Example is shown in Figure 8 below.

Figure 8. Generalization of days

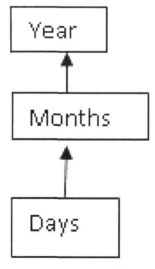

Clustering

Clustering is the process of grouping of objects into classes of similar objects based on some similarity measures between them (Sathiyamoorthi & Murali Baskaran 2011b). It is unsupervised leaning method. Each cluster can be represented as one group and while performing cluster analysis, first partition objects into groups based on the similarity between them and then assign the class labels to those groups. The main difference between clustering and classification is that, clustering is adaptable to changes and helps select useful features that distinguish objects into different groups. Example of clustering is shown in Figure 9.

Applications of Cluster Analysis

- Clustering is used in many different applications such as market research, pattern recognition, data analysis and image processing.
- It helps marketing manager to discover distinct potential buyers from the customer base. Also, it helps in characterizing the customer groups based on their purchasing patterns and select target audience for the current products.
- In biology department, it helps to deriving plant and animal taxonomy, categorizing genes with similar functionalities and gaining insight into structures inherent to populations and so on.
- In spatial database application, it helps in identification of areas of similar land and groups the houses in a city based on the house type, house value, and geographic location and so on.
- In web based application, it helps in categorizing the similar documents on the web for information retrieval.
- It used in outlier detection applications such as detection of credit card fraud and fraud transaction and so on.
- In general, in data mining clustering acts as a tool for gaining knowledge about distribution of data and observes characteristics of each cluster.

Figure 9. Data mining task clustering

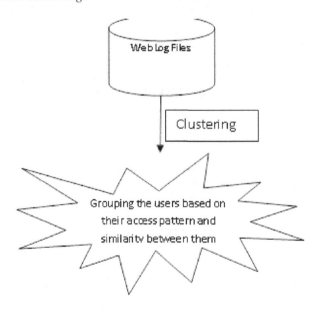

Issues Related to Clustering

- **Scalability**: Clustering algorithms should be scalable and can handle large databases.
- **Ability to Deal with Different Kinds of Attributes:** Clustering algorithms should be in such a way that it should be capable of handling different kinds of data such as numerical data, categorical, and binary data and so on.
- **Discovery of Clusters with Attribute Shape**: Clustering algorithms should be capable of producing clusters of arbitrary shape using different measures.
- **High Dimensionality:** Clustering algorithm should be designed in such way that it should be capable of handling both low as well as high dimensional data.
- **Ability to Deal with Noisy Data**: Data sources may contain noisy, missing or erroneous data. So presence of these data may leads too poor quality clusters. Hence clustering algorithm should be designed in such way that it should handle noisy, missing and error data and produce high quality clusters.
- **Interpretability**: The results of clustering should be readable, interpretable, comprehensible into different form and useful to the end users.

Types of Clustering

- Partitioning Method
- Hierarchical Method
- Density-based Method
- Grid-Based Method
- Model-Based Method
- Constraint-based Method

Partitioning Method

Given a database of 'n' objects and then the partitioning algorithm groups the objects into 'k' partition where $k \leq n$. Each group should have at least one object. Also, objects in the same group should satisfy the following criteria.

- Each group contains at least one object.
- Each object must belong to exactly one group.
- Objects within clusters are highly similar and objects present in the different clusters are highly dissimilar.
- Kmeans algorithm is the most popular algorithm in this category. It works as follows.
- For a given number of partitions (say K), the Kmeans partitioning will create an initial partitioning representing K clusters using some distance measure.
- Then it uses the iterative technique to improve the partitioning by moving objects from one group to other. The problem with Kmeans algorithm is that K (number of partition) value is fixed before executing cluster and it does not change.
- Another algorithm is Kmedoid which is an improvement of Kmeans algorithm and provides better performance.

Hierarchical Clustering

In this method, it tries to create a hierarchical decomposition of given objects into various groups. There are two approaches used here for decomposition.

- Agglomerative Approach
- Divisive Approach

In agglomerative approach, clustering starts with each object forming a different group. Then, it keeps on merging the objects that are close to one another into groups. It repeats it until all of the groups are merged into one or until the termination condition holds. It is also known as bottom-up approach.

In divisive approach, clustering starts with all the objects representing a single cluster as a root. In each iteration, it tries to split the cluster into smaller clusters having similar i.e. objects that are close to one another. It proceeds towards down and split the cluster until each object in one cluster or the termination condition holds. This method is inflexible means that once a merging or splitting is done then it cannot be undone. It is also known as top-down approach.

Density-Based Clustering

It is based on the concept of density i.e. each clusters should have minimum number of data objects within the cluster radius. Here a cluster is continuing growing as long as the density in the neighborhood exceeds some threshold.

Grid-Based Clustering

In this clustering, the objects together form a grid. The object space is quantized into finite number of cells that form a grid structure. The main advantage of this approach is that it produces the cluster faster and takes less processing time.

Model-Based Clustering

In this approach, a model is used to build each cluster and find the best fit of data object for a given clusters. This method locates the clusters by using the density function. It reflects spatial distribution of the data objects among the clusters. It determines the number of clusters based on statistics, taking outlier or noise into account. Also, it yields robust clustering algorithm.

Constraint-Based Clustering

In this approach, the clustering is performed by incorporating the user and application constraints or requirements. Here, a constraint is the user expectation or the properties of desired clustering results. It is so interactive since constraints provide an interactive way of communication with the clustering process. Constraints can be specified by the user or by the application.

Association Rule Mining

As defined by (Jiawei et al. 2006), an association rule identifies the collection of data attributes that are statistically related to one another. The association rule mining problem can be defined as follows: Given a database of related transactions, a minimal support and confidence value, find all association rules whose confidence and support are above the given threshold. In general, it produces a dependency rule that predicts an object based on the occurrences of other objects.

An association rule is of the form X->Y where X is called antecedent and Y is called consequent. There are two measures that assist in identification of frequent items and generate rules from it. One such measure is confidence which is the conditional probability of Y given X, Pr(Y|X), and the other is support which is the prior probability of X and Y, Pr(X and Y) (Jiawei et al 2006). It can be classified into either single dimensional association rule or multidimensional association rule based on number of predicates it contains (Jiawei et al. 2006). It can be extended to better fit in the application domains like genetic analysis and electronic commerce and so on. Aprior algorithm, FP growth algorithm and vertical data format are some of the standard algorithm used to identify the frequent items present in the large data set (Jiawei et al. 2006).

Algorithms used for association rule mining are given below.

- Aprior algorithm
- FP-Growth
- Vertical Data format algorithm

Applications of Data Mining

Data mining applications include (Sathiyamoorthi & Murali Baskaran 2010b),

- Market Basket Analysis and Management
  - Helps in determining customer purchase pattern i.e. what kind of consumer going to buy what kind of products.
  - Helps in finding the best products for different consumers. Here prediction is a data mining technique used to find the users interests based on available data.
  - Performs correlations analysis between product and sales.
  - Helps in finding clusters of consumers who share the same purchase characteristics such as user interests, regular habits, and monthly income and so on.
  - Is used in analyzing and determining customer purchasing pattern.
  - Provides multidimensional analysis on user data and support various summary reports.
- Corporate Analysis and Risk Management in Industries
  - It performs cash flow analysis and prediction, contingent claim analysis to evaluate assets.
  - Where it summarizes and compares the resource utilization i.e. how much resources are allocated and how much are currently available. it, helps in production planning and control system
  - Current trend analysis where it monitors competitors and predict future market directions.
- Fraud Detection or Outlier Detection

- ○ It is also known as outlier analysis which is used in the fields of credit card analysis and approval and telecommunication industry to detect fraudulent users.
  - ○ In communication department, it helps in finding the destination of the fraud call, time duration of the fraud call, at what time the user made a call and the day or week of the calls and so on.
  - ○ It helps in analyzing the patterns that are deviating from the normal behavior called outlier.
- Spatial and Time Series Data Analysis
  - ○ For predicting stock market trends and bond analysis
  - ○ Identifying Areas that Shares Similar Characteristics
- Image Retrieval and Analysis
  - ○ Image segmentation and classification
  - ○ Face recognition and detection
- Web Mining
  - ○ Web content mining
  - ○ Web structure mining
  - ○ Web log mining

The most emerging research area is Web mining which is discussed in the next section.

WEB MINING

In today's Internet scenario, WWW plays a significant role in retrieving and sharing information. Hence, WWW becomes a huge repository of data. As a result, it is difficult for data analyst or end users to analyze the entire data and to discover some useful information. To overcome these troubles, data mining can be applied for knowledge discovery in WWW. To discover knowledge from Web, Web mining is used. Web mining is broadly categorized into three major areas such as Web Content Mining; Web Structure Mining and Web Log Mining or Web Usage Mining (Srivastava et al. 2000; Zaiane 2000).

Web Content Mining is the part of Web Mining which focuses on the raw information available in Webpages (Kosala & Blockeel 2000). Data source mainly consists of textual data present in the Webpages. Mining is based on content categorization and content ranking of Web pages. Web Structure Mining is a Web Mining task which deals with the structure of the Websites. The data source consists of structural information present in Webpages that are hyperlinks. The mining includes link-based categorization of Webpages, ranking of Webpages through a combination of content and structure (Brin & Pange 1998), and reverse engineering of Website models. Web Usage Mining (WUM) is another Web Mining task which describes knowledge discovery from Web server log files. The source data mainly consist of the raw text file that is stored in Web server when a user accesses the Webpage. It might be represented either in Common Log Format (CLF) or in Extended Common Log Format (ECLF). It includes Web personalization, adaptive Websites, and user modeling. In this research work, WUM is used to optimize the existing Web caching technique. It is noted that Research in Web Usage Mining started in late 1990's according to Srivastava et al. (2000), Mobasher et al. (2002), Cyrus et al (1997) and Feng et al. (2009). Web Usage Mining is also known as Web log mining wherein it relies on the information present in the Web log file produced by the Web servers. Web log files are raw text file which needs certain preprocessing methods before applying the data mining techniques. Hence, the next subsection gives an overview of Web log mining and its applications.

Web Log Mining

Who's coming to your site? What are they doing there? Where are they coming from? Answers to these questions are recorded in raw log file.

It provides necessary information to enhance the performance of WWW. Web usage mining, an application of data mining technique is used to discover pattern from Web sources. These discovered patterns are used to understand and to serve the need of Web-based system in a better way. Hence, prior to applying data mining techniques, Web log files require certain kind of preprocessing activities that must be performed on raw text file called Web server log.

Web usage mining is defined as the automatic discovery of useful patterns from Web server log (Sathiyamoorthi, 2016). In this, knowledge discovery process and pattern analysis focus on Web user access data. The browsing behaviors exhibited by different users are captured in access log by the server. Most systems use log data as their data source. In this thesis, the usage data represents the access log recorded in proxy server that records information about user navigation to different Websites.

The basic steps involved in WUM are (Sathiyamoorthi & Murali Baskaran 2011a):

1. Data Collection
2. Data Preprocessing
3. Pattern Extraction
4. Pattern Analysis and Visualization
5. Pattern Applications

Data sources used for WUM can be collected from three different locations (Srivastva et al. 2000) as is given below.

- **Server-Level**: It stores data about the requests that are activated by different clients. It keeps track of multiple users' interest on a single Website. The main drawback is that log files must be secured since it contains some sensitive information about the users. Further, it does not contain information about cached pages.
- **Client-Level**: The browser itself will send some information to a repository regarding the user's access. This is achieved by using an adhoc browsing application or through client-side applications that can run on standard Web browsers. It requires the design team to develop special software and deploy it along with the end users' browsers.
- **Proxy-level**: It collects the information about user's browsing behavior and recorded at proxy server log. It keeps track of multiple users' interest on several Websites. It is used only by the users whose requests are passed through the proxy.

Need for Data Pre-Processing

In the present internet scenario, there has been barely credible growth of Web in terms of users and Webpages. It is vital for the Website owners to better understand their customer's need; provide better services and to improve the Website quality. Due to these reasons, a huge amount of data related to the users interactions with the Websites were recorded in the Web server access log (Navin et al. 2011). Thus, Web access log plays a predominant role to predict the user access pattern, by pre-fetching and caching of Web data for better performance.

Web log files contain raw data, which needs certain kind of pre-processing activities prior to data mining techniques. Most of the recorded data present in the Web log are irrelevant and incomplete to accomplish data mining tasks. Hence, the task in Web usage mining is data pre-processing activities which prepares data for data mining tasks.

On Web usage data, different data mining techniques such as association rule, clustering, classification and so on can be applied in order to discover hidden patterns. This discovered knowledge is useful in applications such as System improvement, Website modification, Business intelligence, etc. The following section presents a detailed research works on Web log mining.

Research Progress in Web Log Mining

Many researchers have focused on Web Usage Mining in recent years (Srivastava et al. 2000; Mobasher et al. 2002; Sathiyamoorthi & Muralibaskaran 2013). Web mining is concerned as extracting knowledge from Web data (Etizoni 1996). It can be categorized into different areas as follow; Web content mining, Web structure mining and Web usage mining. Web usage mining is the application of data mining techniques to large Web data repositories (Cooley et al. 1997). Data is collected in the Web server whenever user accesses the Website and is represented in standard formats.

The standard log format called Common Log File (CLF) consists of IP address, access date and time, request method (GET or POST), URL of page accessed, transfer protocol, success return code or in Extended Common Log File (ECLF) format (Cooley et al. 1999). As raw data collected from the Web server is incomplete and also limited fields are required for pattern discovery, preprocessing is necessary to discover access pattern. Once the raw log data is preprocessed, different data mining techniques like statistical analysis, association rules, sequential mining and clustering can be applied to discover patterns.

The basic steps in data preprocessing are user identification, page identification, session identification and page view identification (Cooley et al. 1999). The authors have also proposed some heuristics to deal with the difficulties involved in these tasks. Joshi and Krishnapuram (2000) have compared time-based and referrer-based heuristics for session identification process. The authors also state that a heuristic-based approach depends on the Website design and on the length of visit. Fu et al. (2000) have discussed the possibility of merging and analyzing multiple server log files.

Various techniques have been used from the fields like statistics, machine learning, data mining and pattern recognition in order to discover patterns from Web usage log (Cooley et al 1999). Data mining tools have also been widely used to analyze and perform statistical analysis such as most visited Web-pages, average daily hits, etc. These tools are mainly used to analyze Web traffic and server loads. Joshi and Krishnapuram (2000) have used association rules to discover patterns where it considers each URL as an item and identifies the relationships between them with the given support and confidence value. The sequential analysis is used by Fu et al (2000), to predict the user's future access, based on the past access sequence. Another data mining technique called clustering is used to form clusters based on the similarity present in the user access pattern by Srivastva et al (2000).

In yet another work (Berendt et al. 2002), the authors have compared time-based and referrer-based heuristics for visits reconstruction. Marquardt et al (2004) have developed and used the Web usage mining application that is specific to e-learning domain.

Applications of Web Usage Mining

Web Usage Mining has been considered with great importance and hence many researchers have started focusing on this for better Web utilization. The significance of this research work can be better realized through the following research scope and findings.

Web Usage Mining is well explained by Facca and Lanzi (2005), Srivastava et al (2000). Both of them have described it in their research and business communities' perspective.

Web personalization is a technique which delivers personalized Web content depending on the user profile or user needs. It includes, a recommender system explained (Jaczynski & Trousse 1998, Mobasher et al. 2000) and an adaptive Website (Velasquez et al. 2004; De et. al 2004).

A recommender system suggests possible links to the user based on the access history. The adaptive Website is the one which adapts itself for each user visiting the Website in order to deliver the personalized content. Personalization is achieved by keeping track of the previously accessed Webpages for E-Commerce applications (Pirolli et al. 1996).

The appearance of a Website, in terms of both content and structure, is the most important factor to be considered in many applications like product catalog for E-Commerce. Web usage mining provides detailed information regarding user behavior and it can help Website designers to redesign their Website based on it. In adaptive Website (Anderson 2002; Perkowitz & Etzioni 1998), the structure of a Website changes dynamically based on the user access patterns discovered from server logs. Site improvement may be achieved either by modifying the logical structure or the physical structure of the Website depending on the access patterns of the Website users. Some of the important works related to web usage mining is tabulated below with its merits and demerits.

Research Works on Web Prefetching

Response time and performance are the two important factors that play major role in determining user satisfaction (Sathiyamoorthi & Murali Baskaran 2012a). This is mainly helpful for services like Web-based applications, databases and networks, etc. Similar qualities are been expected from the users of Web services. To enhance the performance, Web log mining could provide the key to understand Web traffic behavior by developing policies for Web caching and network transmission (Anderson et al. 2002).

Web caching represents another possibility for improving the quality of a Website as the pages are delivered to the users in a faster way (Podlipnig & Boszormenyi 2003). Users are less likely to spend time on a slow Website. By using the results of a WUM system, a Web caching system turns capable to predict the user's next request by loading it into a cache. Thus, the speed of page retrieval from a Website is improved as the user will not wait for the page to be loaded from the server. Information about how customers use a Website is central for the marketers of retailing business. Alex and Mulvenna (1998), Srivastava et al (2000) have discussed a knowledge discovery process to discover marketing intelligence from Web data (Sathiyamoorthi & Murali Baskaran 2012b).

Some of the research work on web usage mining is tabulated in Table 1. From this, it is also observed that both the techniques would improve the performance by reducing server load and latency in accessing

Table 1. Literature support for formulation of research problem

Base papers	Authors	Issue and Inference
1. Web user clustering and its application to pre-fetching using ART neural networks	Rangarajan et al (2004)	It presents a pre-fetching approach based on ART1 neural network. It does not address the issues while integrating Web caching and Web pre-fetching
2. Integrating Web caching and Web pre-fetching in Client-Side Proxies	Teng et al (2005)	Have proposed pre-fetching approach based on association rule. They have proposed an innovative cache replacement policy called (Integration of Web Caching and Pre-fetching (IWCP). They have categorized Web objects into implied and non-implied objects.
3. A clustering-based pre-fetching scheme on a Web cache environment	Pallis et al (2008)	Proposed a graph-based pre-fetching technique. Have used DG for pre-fetching. It is based on association rule and it is controlled by support and confidence. Moreover they have used traditional policies in Web cache environment and didn't address issues while integrating these two.
4. Intelligent Client-side Web Caching Scheme Based on Least Recently Used Algorithm and Neuro-Fuzzy System	Ali and Shamsuddin (2009)	It uses the neuro-fuzzy system to classify a Web object into cacheable or un-cacheable objects. It has LRU algorithm in cache to predict Web objects that may be re-accessed later. Training process requires long time and extra computational cost. It ignored the factors such as cost and size of the objects in the cache replacement policy
5. A survey of Web cache replacement strategies	Podlipnig and Böszörmenyi (2003)	The authors have reviewed and presented an overview of various page replacement policies. It is observed that GDSF perform better in Web cache environment. They also have presented merits and demerits of various page replacement policies.
6. A Keyword-Based Semantic Pre-fetching Approach in Internet News Services	Ibrahim and Xu (2004)	It predicts users' future access based on semantic preferences of past retrieved Web documents. It is implemented on Internet news services. The semantic preferences are identified by analyzing keywords present in the URL of previously accessed Web. It employs a neural network model over the keyword set to predict user future requests.
7. A Survey of Web Caching and Pre-fetching	Waleed et al (2011)	The authors have discussed and reviewed various Web caching and Web pre-fetching techniques. It is observed that most of the pre-fetching techniques discussed here were focusing on single user which will ultimately reduce server performance if number of users increase. Moreover, in recent year's data mining plays a major role in Web pre-fetching areas and most of the data mining-based approach uses association rule mining.

Webpages. However, if the Web caching and pre-fetching approaches are integrated inefficiently then this might causes huge network traffic; increase in Web server load in addition to the inefficient use of cache space (Waleed et al. 2011). Hence, the pre-fetching approach should be designed carefully in order to overcome the above said limitations. Therefore, the importance of Web usage mining to optimize the existing Web cache performance has been realized.

DATA WAREHOUSE

A data warehouse contains a subject oriented, integrated, time variant and nonvolatile data for organizational effective decision-making. It supports analytical reporting, structured, ad hoc queries and decision making. It has following characteristics.

- **Subject Oriented**: Means that it containing relevant and useful data for timely decision making under different sections

- **Integrated**: It is an integrated data source which collects data from various heterogeneous data sources such as relational databases, flat files and mapped under a unified schema.
- **Time Variant**: It contains current and up-to-date historical data.
- **Non-Volatile**: It is permanently stored data i.e. data is not removed when database modification such as insertion or deletion. The data warehouse is separated from the organizational database thereby it reduces the frequent changes. Any changes in the operational database are not reflected to the data warehouse.

DATA WAREHOUSE CONSTRUCTION

The process of building data warehouse consists of following steps and shown in Figure 10.

- **Data Collection:** Where data are collected from various data sources which are geographically distributed across the world
- **Data Cleaning**: Where it removes noise, irrelevant and inconsistent data present in the collected data
- **Data Integration:** Where it integrates various data sources into a single unified schema and provide a consistent view of data warehouse
- **Data Transformation:** Formatting the data in accordance to the data warehouse schema and architecture

Figure 10. Data warehouse construction

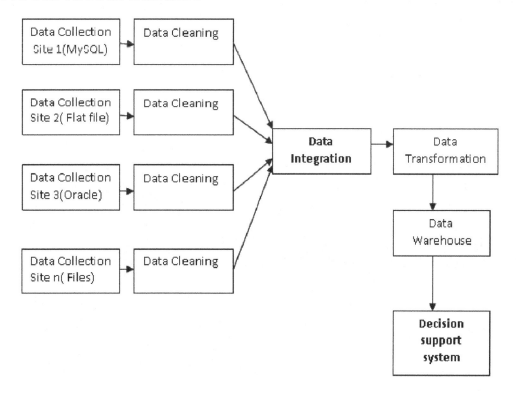

COMMUNICATION BETWEEN DATA WAREHOUSE AND DATA SOURCES

To communicate with the various heterogeneous data sources following two approaches are used. There are,

- Query Driven Approach
- Update Driven Approach

Query-Driven Approach

In this approach, mediators are used on the top of many heterogeneous data sources for transforming the data between the data warehouse and the client data source. These mediators are acting as an inter-mediatory for data communication to bridge communication gap between the client and data warehouse.

- When a query is issued to data sources, the mediator retrieves the metadata from the local data source that is used to translate the given query into the query that is appropriate to execute in that local source.
- Then, the translated query is send to the query processor engine which executes the query and retrieves the data from that source.
- Finally, resultant data are collected from various data sources and merged then transformed for the original query.
- The main drawback of this approach is that it takes longer time to communicate with different data sources and to get actual data from there. If there is any communication delay or problem with the computer network then retrieval of data is impossible. So, it is not suitable for timely decision making system and hence rarely used.

Update-Driven Approach

In this update-driven approach, rather than issuing a query to various heterogeneous data sources to collect the data on demand basis, the information from multiple heterogeneous data sources are pushed and combined under unified schema called as data warehouse. It uses processes called data cleaning, integration and transformation in advance. Here, the data is collected and stored in a place called data warehouse well in advance. Further, it is used for direct querying and analysis of data by the top level manager to make an effective decision. Also, it contains up-to-date information for decision making.

- It is suitable for quick and timely decision making and provides high performance.
- Communication delay and network problems can be avoided in transferring data.
- Quick feedback to all the departments is possible

INTEGRATION OF DATA MINING SYSTEM WITH A DATA WAREHOUSE SYSTEM

There is various integration strategies are possible which are based on whether it uses the underlying concepts or functionality of the underlying database or data warehouse system. Based on this, it is classified as follows.

- **Non-Coupling:** Data mining system is not integrated with any of the database or the data warehouse system components and all are working as independent parts. Hence, there is no communication with the other system. It is mainly used for designing new data mining system which focuses on research and development of various data mining techniques for knowledge discovery. Most of the scientists are using this type of system.
- **No Coupling**: Data mining system does not utilize functionalities of a data mining or data warehousing system. It only fetches the data from a particular data source called files, processes it by using some data mining techniques and then stores the results in another file. Here, typical data source will be the operating system files which are used for storing input and output.
- **Loose Coupling**: The data mining system may use some of the functionalities of an underlying database and data warehouse system. It fetches the data from the particular database or from data warehouse and then process it using data mining system. It stores the results back to the database or in the warehouse for future reference.
- **Semi−tight Coupling**: The data mining system is coupled with the database or the warehouse for fetching and storing the data. In addition to that, an efficient implementation of a few data mining task primitives can be derived from the underlying database.
- **Tight Coupling**: The data mining system is smoothly integrated into the database or data warehouse system. Also, data mining is treated as one of the subsystems and used as one of the functional component of an information processing system. It fully dependent on data warehouse or data base for their functionalities.

Figure 11 shows the integration of data mining system with data warehousing in an organization. The organizational decision support system uses the data mining techniques to make an effective and timely decision. In this Figure 11, data mart is a component that contains data that is specific to the given department (Sathiyamoorthi & Murali Baskaran 2010b).

FUTURE RESEARCH DIRECTIONS

As the user datasets containing the privacy information should not be exposed to the outside world then privacy preserving data mining techniques can be applied in order to hide some personal information about the users. Also, evolutionary optimization techniques can be applied in order to optimize the data mining system further. Moreover, a hybrid approach out of existing algorithms can be tried out for the process that requires two or more techniques. Data mining system can also be used to extend the performance of Content Distribution Network (CDN) server and Enterprise Resource Planning (ERP) system for an effective content distribution and decision making process. This system can also be used in the application areas where Web search, access and retrieval are involved, such as Predicting user purchase

Figure 11. Integration of data warehouse with data mining system

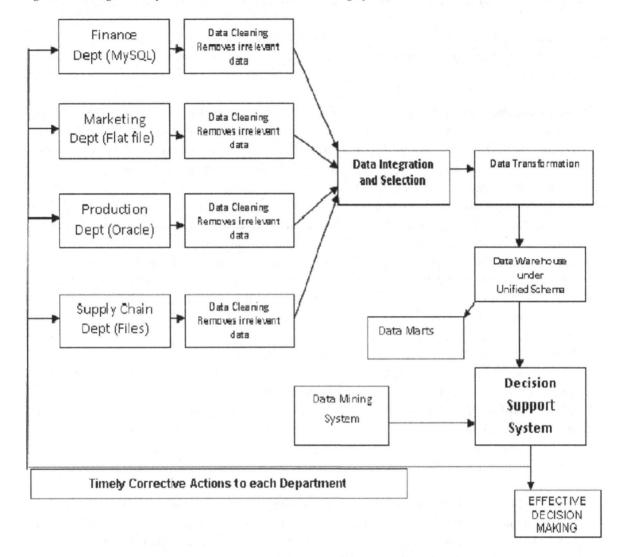

pattern of commodities in E-Commerce Website, redesigning of a site according to user interest. Nowadays, big data is a field that is emerging rapidly and lot of research work is progressing in this field.

CONCLUSION

Due to the presence of huge volume of data and noisy data, it is impossible for a human being to analyze and retrieve some useful knowledge out of it. Hence, data mining plays a vital role in knowledge discovery from huge datasets. From this extensive survey, it is understood that data mining plays a vital role and helps in discovering knowledge from huge dataset. This chapter discussed the basic concepts, techniques and importances of data mining in KDD process and the construction of a data warehousing system. Also, it narrated and underlined the importance of certain data mining techniques in various fields or domains like web mining. Though data is retrieved from data sources, they need to undergo a data preprocessing step where removal of irrelevant and inconsistent content takes place. Hence, data preprocessing was discussed. Through the preprocessing approach, data is prepared for data mining tasks. This chapter also gave an overview of Web mining and its applications in order to improve the website performance.

REFERENCES

Ali, W., & Shamsuddin, S. M. (2009). Intelligent Client-Side Web Caching Scheme Based on Least Recently Used Algorithm and Neuro-Fuzzy System. In *sixth International Symposium on Neural Networks, Lecture Notes in Computer Science (LNCS)*. Springer-Verlag Berlin Heidelberg. doi:10.1007/978-3-642-01510-6_9

Anderson, C. R. (2002). *A Machine Learning Approach to Web Personalization* (Ph. D. Thesis). University of Washington.

Berendt, B., Mobasher, B., Nakagawa, M., & Spiliopoulou, M. (2002). The Impact of Site Structure and User Environment and Session Reconstruction in Web usage analysis. *Proceedings of the forth Web KDD 2002 Workshop at the ACM – SIGKDD Conference on Knowledge Discovery in Databases (KDD 2002)*, 159-179.

Brin, S., & Pange, L. (1998). The Anatomy of a Large-scale Hyper Textual Web Search Engine. *Computer Networks and ISDN Systems*, *30*(1-7), 107–117. doi:10.1016/S0169-7552(98)00110-X

Cooley, R., Bamshed, M., & Srinivastava, J. (1997). Web Mining: Information and Pattern Discovery on the World Wide Web. In *International conference on Tools with Artificial Intelligence*. IEEE. doi:10.1109/TAI.1997.632303

Cooley, R., Mobasher, B., & Srinivastaa, J. (1999). Data Preparation for Mining World Wide Web Browsing Patterns. *Journal of knowledge and Information Systems*, 78-85.

Cyrus, S., Zarkessh, A. M., Jafar, A., & Vishal, S. (1997). Knowledge discovery from Users Web Page Navigation. In *Workshop on Research Issues in Data Engineering*. Data mining tutorial retrieved from www.tutorialspoint.com/data_mining/notes

De, P. B., Aroyo, L., & Chepegin, V. (2004). The Next Big Thing: Adaptive Web-Based Systems. *Journal of Digital Information*, *5*(1), 22–30.

Dunham, M. H. (2006). *Data Mining Introductory and Advanced Topics* (1st ed.). Pearson Education.

Etizoni, O. (1996). The World Wide Web: Quagmire or Gold Mine. *Communications of the ACM*, *39*(2), 65–68. doi:10.1145/240455.240473

Facca, F.M., & Lanzi, P. L. (2005). Mining Interesting Knowledge from Web logs: A Survey. *International Journal of Data and Knowledge Engineering*, *53*(3), 225-241.

Feng, W., Man, S., & Hu, G. (2009). *Markov Tree Prediction on Web Cache Pre-fetching. Software Engineering, Artificial Intelligence (SCI)* (Vol. 209, pp. 105–120). Berlin: Springer-Verlag.

Fu, Y., Sandhu, K., & Shih, M. (2000). A Generalization-Based Approach to Clustering of Web Usage Sessions. *Proceedings of the KDD Workshop on Web Mining, 1836*, 21-38.

Ibrahim, T. I., & Xu, C. Z. (2004). A Keyword-Based Semantic Pre-fetching Approach in Internet News Services. *IEEE Transactions on Knowledge and Data Engineering, 16*(5), 601–611. doi:10.1109/TKDE.2004.1277820

Jaczynski, M., & Trousse, B. (1998). WWW Assisted Browsing by Reusing Past Navigations of a Group of Users. *Proceedings of the Advances in Case-Based Reasoning, Forth European Workshop, 1488*, 160-171.

Jiawei, H., Micheline, K., & Jian, P. (2006). *Data Mining Concepts and Techniques*. Pearson Education.

Joshi, A., & Krishnapuram, R. (2000). On Mining Web Access Logs. *ACM SIGMOD Workshop on Research Issues in Data Mining and Knowledge Discovery*, 63- 69.

Koskela, T.J., Heikkonen, & Kaski, K. (2003). Web cache optimization with nonlinear model using object feature. *Computer Networks Journal, 43*(6), 805-817.

Marquardt, C., Becker, K., & Ruiz, D. (2004). A Pre-processing Tool for Web Usage Mining in the Distance Education Domain. *Proceedings of the International Database Engineering and Application Symposium (IDEAS)*, 78-87.

Mobasher, B., Dai, H., Luo, T., & Nakagawa, M. (2002). Discovery and Evaluation of Aggregate Usage Profiles for Web Personalization. *Data Mining and Knowledge Discovery, 6*(1), 61–82. doi:10.1023/A:1013232803866

Navin, K., Tyagi, & Solanki, A.K. (2011). Analysis of Server Log by Web Usage Mining for Website Improvement. *International Journal of Computer Science Issues, 7*(4).

Pallis, G., Vakali, A., & Pokorny, J. (2008). A Clustering-Based Pre-Fetching Scheme on A Web Cache Environment. ACM Journal Computers and Electrical Engineering, 34(4).

Perkowitz, M., & Etzioni, O. (1998). Adaptive Web Sites: Automatically Synthesizing Web Pages. *AAAI '98/IAAI '98: Proceedings of the Fifteenth National/Tenth International Conference on Artificial Intelligence/Innovative Applications of Artificial Intelligence*, 727-732.

Pirolli, P., Pitkow, J., & Ramna, R. (1996). Extracting Usable Structure from the Web. CHI – 96, 118-125.

Podlipnig, S., & Boszormenyi, L. (2003). A Survey of Web Cache Replacement Strategies. *ACM Computing Surveys, 35*(4), 374–398. doi:10.1145/954339.954341

Rangarajan, S.K., Phoha, V.V., Balagani, K., Selmic, R.R., & Iyengar S.S. (2004). Web User Clustering and its Application to Pre-fetching using ART Neural Networks. *IEEE Computer*, 45-62.

Sathiyamoorthi, V. (2016). A Novel Cache Replacement Policy for Web Proxy Caching System Using Web Usage Mining. *International Journal of Information Technology and Web Engineering, 11*(2), 12–20. doi:10.4018/IJITWE.2016040101

Sathiyamoorthi, V., & Murali Bhaskaran, V. (2010a). Data Preparation Techniques for Mining World Wide Web through Web Usage Mining-An Approach. *International Journal of Recent Trends in Engineering, 2*(4), 1–4.

Sathiyamoorthi, V., & Murali Bhaskaran, V. (2010b). Data Mining for Intelligent Enterprise Resource Planning System. *International Journal of Recent Trends in Engineering*, 2(3), 1–4.

Sathiyamoorthi, V., & Murali Bhaskaran, V. (2011a). Improving the Performance of Web Page Retrieval through Pre-Fetching and Caching. *European Journal of Scientific Research*, 66(2), 207–217.

Sathiyamoorthi, V., & Murali Bhaskaran, V. (2011b). Data Pre-Processing Techniques for Pre-Fetching and Caching of Web Data through Proxy Server. *International Journal of Computer Science and Network Security*, 11(11), 92-98.

Sathiyamoorthi, V., & Murali Bhaskaran, V. (2012a). A Novel Approach for Web Caching through Modified Cache Replacement Algorithm. *International Journal of Engineering Research and Industrial Applications*, 5(1), 241–254.

Sathiyamoorthi, V., & Murali Bhaskaran, V. (2012b). Optimizing the Web Cache Performance by Clustering Based Pre-Fetching Technique Using Modified ART1. *International Journal of Computers and Applications*, 44(1), 51–60.

Sathiyamoorthi, V., & Murali Bhaskaran, V. (2013). Novel Approaches for Integrating MART1 Clustering based Pre-Fetching Technique with Web Caching. *International Journal of Information Technology and Web Engineering*, 8(2), 18–32. doi:10.4018/jitwe.2013040102

Srivastava, J., Cooley, R., Deshpande, M., & Tan, P. N. (2000). Web Usage Mining: Discovery and Applications of Usage Patterns from Web Data. *SIGKDD Explorations*, 1(2), 12–23. doi:10.1145/846183.846188

Teng, W., Chang, C., & Chen, M. (2005). Integrating Web Caching and Web Pre-fetching in Client-Side Proxies. *IEEE Transactions on Parallel and Distributed Systems*, 16(5), 444–455. doi:10.1109/TPDS.2005.56

Velasquez, J., Bassi, A., Yasuda, H., & Aoki, T. (2004). Mining Web Data to Create Online Navigation Recommendations.*Proceedings of the Fourth IEEE International Conference on Data Mining (ICDM)*, 551-554. doi:10.1109/ICDM.2004.10019

Waleed, A., Siti, M. S., & Abdul, S. I. (2011). A Survey of Web Caching and Pre--fetching. *International Journal on Advances in Soft Computing and Application*, 3(1).

KEY TERMS AND DEFINITIONS

Association Rule: Given a database of related transactions, a minimal support and confidence value, it will find all association rules whose confidence and support are above the given threshold. In general, it produces a dependency rule that predicts an object based on the occurrences of other objects.

Classification: It is the process of building a model that describes the class for an object. The main purpose of this model is, to predict the class label of an object. Classification model is built based on the training datasets and tested using testing datasets where testing datasets contain objects whose class label are unknown or to be predicted.

Clustering: Cluster analysis refers to grouping of objects that are similar to each other. Here objects that are highly similar form a cluster. Here various measures are used to find the similarity between objects.

Data Cleaning: it is the process of removing irrelevant, inconsistent and incomplete attribute values from the dataset. It is used to select task relevant data from huge dataset.

Data Mining: It is also known as knowledge Discovery in Database (KDD) is the process of extracting implicit, previously unknown and potentially useful information out of database.

Data Warehousing: A data warehouse contains a subject oriented, integrated, time variant and nonvolatile data for organizational effective decision-making.

Normalization: Normalization involves scaling all values for given attribute in order to make them fall within a small specified range.

Outlier Analysis: it is used to predict an object that deviates from the group of objects called outlier. It is mainly used in fraud detection.

Prediction: It is used to predict unknown value from the given set of data. Regression analysis is a statistical methodology that is used to predict numeric value which is based on either linear regression or non-linear regression.

Chapter 2
Energy and Carbon Footprint-Aware Management of Geo-Distributed Cloud Data Centers:
A Taxonomy, State of the Art, and Future Directions

Atefeh Khosravi
The University of Melbourne, Australia

Rajkumar Buyya
The University of Melbourne, Australia

ABSTRACT

Cloud computing provides on-demand access to computing resources for users across the world. It offers services on a pay-as-you-go model through data center sites that are scattered across diverse geographies. However, cloud data centers consume huge amount of electricity and leave high amount of carbon footprint in the ecosystem. This makes data centers responsible for 2% of the global CO_2 emission. Therefore, having energy and carbon-efficient techniques for resource management in distributed cloud data centers is inevitable. This chapter presents a taxonomy and classifies the existing research works based on their target system, objective, and the technique they use for resource management in achieving a green cloud computing environment. Finally, it discusses how each work addresses the issue of energy and carbon-efficiency and also provides an insight into future directions.

INTRODUCTION

In recent years the use of services that utilize cloud computing systems has increased greatly. The technology used in cloud is not new and its main goal is to deliver computing as a utility to users. Cloud computing consists of virtualized computing resources inter-connected through a network, including private networks and the Internet. Over the years since its formation, different definitions for cloud

DOI: 10.4018/978-1-5225-2013-9.ch002

computing have been proposed. According to the definition by the National Institute of Standards and Technology (NIST) (Mell and Grance, 2011): "Cloud computing is a model for enabling ubiquitous, convenient, on-demand network access to a shared pool of configurable computing resources (e.g., networks, servers, storage, applications, and services) that can be rapidly provisioned and released with minimal management effort or service provider interaction. This cloud model is composed of five essential characteristics, three service models, and four deployment models". The three service models provided by the cloud providers are Infrastructure, Platform, and Software as a Service.

Cloud computing delivers service, platform, and infrastructure services to users through virtual machines deployed on the physical servers. Virtualization technology maximizes the use of hardware infrastructure and physical resources. Hardware resources are the servers located within the data centers. Data centers are distributed across the world to provide on-demand access for different businesses. Due to the distributed nature of cloud data centers, many enterprises are able to deploy their applications, such as different services, storage, and database, in cloud environments. By the increase of demand for different services, the number of data centers increases as well; which results in significant increase in energy consumption. According to Koomey (2008) energy usage by data centers increased by 16% from the year 2000 to year 2005. Energy consumption of data centers almost doubled during these five years, 0.5% and 1% of total world energy consumption in 2000 and 2005, respectively. Hence, during the recent years there has been a great work on reducing power and energy consumption of data centers and cloud computing systems. Recently, considering data centers carbon-efficiency and techniques that investigate cloud data centers energy sources, carbon footprint rate, and energy ratings have attracted lots of attention as well. The main reasons for considering carbon-efficient techniques are increase in global CO_2 and keeping the global temperature rise below 2°C before the year 2020 (Baer, 2008).

In the rest of the chapter, the authors provide an in-depth analysis of the works on energy and carbon-efficient resource management approaches in cloud data centers, based on the taxonomy showed in Figure 1. The authors explore each category and survey the works that have been done in these areas. A summary of all the works is given in Table 1.

Figure 1. Taxonomy of energy and carbon-efficient cloud computing data centers

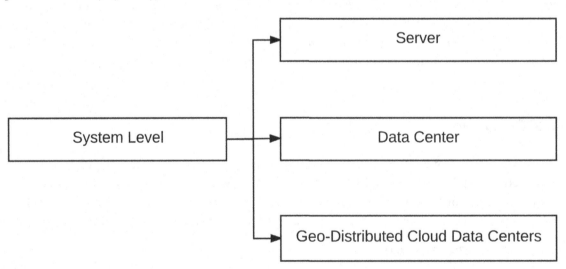

Table 1. Summary of various techniques for energy and carbon-efficient resource management in cloud data centers

Project Name	Goal	Architecture	Technique	Carbon-Aware
Dynamic right-sizing on-line algorithm, Lin. et al. (2011)	Minimize energy consumption and total cost	Single data center	Online prediction algorithms for the number of required servers for the incoming workload	No
Green open cloud framework, Lefevre et al. (2010)	Minimize energy consumption	Single data center	Predict the number of switched-on servers through providing in-advance reservation for users	No
Prediction-based Algorithms, Aksanli et al. (2011)	Maximize renewable energy usage and minimize number of job cancellation	Single data center	Use prediction-based algorithms to run the tasks (mainly batch jobs) in the presence of renewable energies	Yes
GreenSlot scheduler, Goiri et al. (2011)	Maximize renewable energy usage and minimize cost of using brown energies	Single data center	Prediction-based algorithms for the availability of solar energy and suspending the batch jobs in the absence of green energy	Yes
Multi-dimensional energy-efficient resource allocation (MERA) algorithm, Goudarzi et al. (2012)	Minimize energy consumption and maximize servers' utilization	Single data center	VM placement heuristic to split the VMs and place them on a server with the least energy consumption	No
Multi-objective VM placement, Xu et al. (2010)	Minimize power consumption, resource wastage, and the maximum temperature on the servers	Single data center	Data center global controller places the VMs based on a multi-objective algorithm to provide balance between power consumption and temperature	No
Green SLA service class, Haque et al. (2013)	Explicit SLA to guarantee a minimum renewable energy usage to run the workload	Single data center	Power distribution infrastructure to support the service and optimization based policies to maximize cloud provider's profit while meeting user's green SLA requirements	Yes
Cost-aware VM placement problem (CAVP), Chen et al. (2013)	Minimize the operating cost	Distributed data centers	VM Placement using meta-heuristic algorithms, considering different electricity prices and WAN communication cost	No
Energy model for request mapping, Qureshi et al. (2009)	Minimize electricity cost	Distributed data centers	Request routing to data centers with lower energy price using geographical and temporal variations	No
Free Lunch architecture, Akoush et al. (2011)	Maximize renewable energy consumption	Distributed data centers	VM migration and execution between data center sites considering renewable energy availability	Yes
Energy and carbon-efficient cloud architecture, Khosravi et al. (2013)	Minimize carbon footprint and energy consumption	Distributed data centers	VM placement heuristics to place the VM on the data center/cluster with the least carbon footprint and energy consumption and on the server with the least increase in power consumption	Yes
Framework for load distribution across data centers, Le et al. (2009)	Minimize brown energy consumption and cost	Distributed data centers	User request is submitted to the data center with access to the green energy source and least electricity price	Yes
Geographical load balancing (GLB) algorithm, Liu et al. (2011)	Minimize brown energy consumption	Distributed data centers	Use the optimal mix of renewable energies (solar/wind) and energy storage in data centers to eliminate brown energy consumption	Yes
Online global load balancing algorithms, Lin et al. (2012)	Minimize brown energy consumption and cost	Distributed data centers	Route requests to the data centers with available renewable energy using online algorithms	Yes
GreenWare middleware, Zhang et al. (2011)	Maximize renewable energy usage	Distributed data centers	Submit the requests to the data center site with available renewable energy, while meeting provider's budget cost constraint	Yes

continued on following page

Table 1. Continued

Project Name	Goal	Architecture	Technique	Carbon-Aware
Environment-conscious meta-scheduler, Garg et al. (2011)	Minimize carbon emission and maximize cloud provider profit	Distributed data centers	Near-optimal scheduling policies to send HPC applications to the data center with the least carbon emission and maximum profit, considering application deadline	Yes
Carbon-aware green cloud architecture, Garg et al. (2011)	Minimize energy consumption and carbon footprint	Distributed data centers	Submit the user requests to the data center with the least carbon footprint, considering user deadline	Yes
MinBrown workload scheduling algorithm, Chen et al. (2012)	Minimize brown energy consumption	Distributed data centers	Copy the data in all the data centers, then based on the request deadline and the data center with least brown energy consumption executes the request	Yes
Federated CLEVER-based cloud environment, Celesti et al. (2013)	Minimize brown energy consumption and cost	Distributed data centers	Allocate the VM request to the cloud data center with the highest amount of photovoltaic energy and lowest cost	Yes
Temperature-aware workload management, Xu et al. (2013)	Minimize cooling energy and energy cost	Distributed data centers	Joint optimization of reducing cooling energy by routing requests to the site with lower ambient temperature and dynamic resource allocation of batch workloads due to their elastic nature	No
Provably-efficient on-line algorithm (GreFar), Ren et al. (2012)	Minimize energy cost	Distributed data centers	Use servers' energy efficiency information and places with low electricity prices to schedule batch jobs and if necessary suspending the jobs	No
Optimization-based framework, Le et al. (2010)	Minimize cost and brown energy consumption	Distributed data centers	Distribute the Internet services to the data centers considering different electricity prices, data center location with different time zones, and access to green energy sources	No
Dynamic load distribution policies and cooling strategies, Le et al. (2011)	Minimize cost	Distributed data centers	Intelligent placement of the VM requests to the data centers considering data centers geographical location, time zone, energy price, peak power charges, and cooling system energy consumption	No
Online job-migration, Buchbinder et al. (2011)	Minimize cost	Distributed data centers	On-line migration of running jobs to the data center with lowest energy price, while considering transport network costs	No
Spatio-temporal load balancing, Luo et al. (2015)	Minimize cost	Distributed data centers	Route the incoming requests to the data centers considering spatial and temporal variation of electricity price	No
Data centers' intelligent placement, Goiri et al. (2011)	Minimize cost, energy consumption, and carbon footprint	Distributed data centers	Find the best location for data center, considering location dependent and data center characteristics data	Yes
GreenNebula, a prototype for VM placement that follows-the-renewables, Berral et al. (2014)	Minimizing data center and renewable power plant building costs	Distributed data centers	Find the best geographical location to build data centers and renewable power plants and migrate the VMs, whenever necessary, to use a certain amount of renewables (solar or wind)	Yes

ENERGY EFFICIENCY IN SERVERS

Servers are the physical machines that run the services requested by users on a network. Servers are placed in a rack and any number of racks can be used to build a data center. Servers along with cooling systems and other electrical devices in the data centers consume 1.1-1.5% of the global electricity usage (Koomey, 2007). Hence, power and energy management of servers by the increase in users' demand for computing resources is irrefutable. Figure 2 shows a classification of techniques that are used in

Figure 2. Server level energy and carbon-efficient techniques

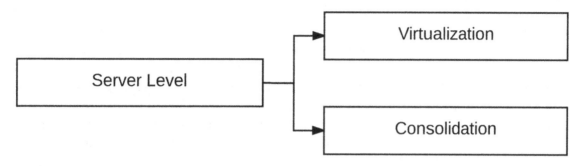

data center servers to reduce energy consumption. Virtualization and consolidation are two well-known strategies that make the data center servers energy-aware. These are two powerful tools that are applied in cloud data center servers in order to reduce energy consumption and accordingly carbon footprint.

Virtualization

Virtualization technology is the main feature of data center servers that leads to less energy consumption (Brey & Lamers, 2009). By having virtualized servers and resources, and using virtualization technology several virtual machines (VMs) can be built on one physical resource. Three types of virtualization that are widely used in data centers are hardware, software, and operating system virtual machines. The VMs run on the servers share the hardware components, that helps the operators to maximize server's utilization and benefit from the unused capacity. By maximizing server's utilization, huge savings in cost and energy consumption of data centers will be made. Decrease in data centers costs and energy consumption is not the only advantage of using virtualization technology. As the average life expectancy of a server is between three to five years, data and applications need to be consolidated and migrated to another server. Virtualization helps these two techniques to be done faster and with less cost and energy.

Consolidation

Server consolidation technique benefits from emerging of multi-core CPUs and virtualization technology. It's aim is to make efficient usage of computing resources to reduce data centers cost and energy consumption (Srikantaiah, Kansal, & Zhao, 2008). Consolidation is used when the utilization of servers is less than the cost associated to run the workloads (energy cost to run servers and cooling cost for data center servers). By using consolidation, servers can combine several number of running VMs and workloads from different servers and allocate them on a certain number of physical servers. Therefore, they can power-off or change the performance-level of the rest of physical servers and reduce the energy consumption, cost, and carbon footprint.

ENERGY EFFICIENCY IN DATA CENTERS

This section gives an overview of the researches that have been done at data center level to improve carbon and energy-efficiency of cloud data centers. An extensive taxonomy and survey of these techniques is done by Beloglazov, Buyya, Lee, and Zomaya (2011). Most of the works within a data center focuses on reducing energy consumption, which can indirectly result in carbon footprint reduction as well. Figure 3 classifies different approaches that have been taken for single data center. Some approaches use server level techniques (virtualization and consolidation) to migrate the current workload (user applications or virtual machines) and turn-off unused servers. Moreover, a provider could use the incoming workload pattern to place user request in the best suited cluster and server (and virtual machine for user applications) with less increase in energy consumption and carbon footprint.

Migration

Using virtualization, data center workloads migrate between servers. VM migration is the process of moving a running virtual machine from its current physical machine to another physical machine. Migration should be done in a way that all the changes be transparent to the user and the only change that user may encounter is a small increase in latency for the running VM or application.

Migration allows a virtual machine to be moved to another physical server so that the source physical server could be switched off or be moved to a power saving mode in order to reduce the energy consumption. VM migration in cloud data centers could be done off-line or live (Harney, Goasguen, Martin, Murphy, & Westall, 2007). There has been a great amount of work done in this area try to identify the VMs on the servers with low utilization that could be migrated, so that the provider can put the unused servers in idle or power-off state.

Figure 3. Data center level energy and carbon-efficient techniques

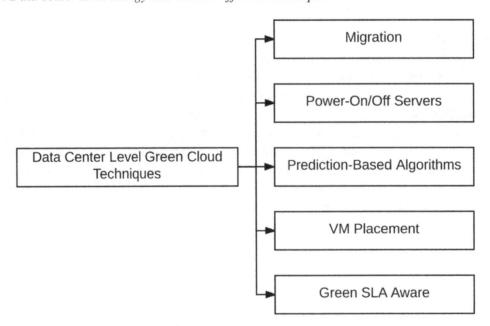

Power-On and Off Servers

When in an idle state data centers consume around half the power of their peak utilization and power state (Barroso & Holzle, 2007). There are technologies that try to design data center servers so that they just consume power in the presence of load, otherwise they go to a power saving mode. Work that is done by Lin, Wierman, Andrew, and Thereska (2011) uses a dynamic right-sizing on-line algorithm to predict the number of active servers that is needed by the arriving workload to the data center. Based on the experiments that are done in Lin et al. (2011) dynamic right-sizing algorithm can achieve significant energy savings in the data center. We should consider that this requires servers to have different power modes and be able to transit to different states while still keeping the previous state. Moving the system to different power consumption modes is a challenging problem and requires dynamic on-line policies for resource management.

Green Open Cloud (GOC) is an architecture which is proposed by Lefèvre and Orgerie (2010) on top of the current resource management strategies. The aim of this architecture is to switch-off unused servers, predict the incoming requests, and then switch-on required servers on the arrival of new requests. GOC proposes green policies to customers in the way that they can have advance resource reservation and based on this knowledge cloud provider could estimate how many servers, and when they should be switched-on. Using this framework and strategy, they were able to save a considerable amount of energy on cloud severs.

Prediction-Based Algorithms

Aksanli, Venkatesh, Zhang, and Rosing (2012) used the data from solar and wind power installations in San Diego (MYPVDATA) and National Renewable Energy Laboratory (NREL), respectively to develop a prediction-based scheduling algorithm to serve two different types of workloads, web-services and batch-jobs. The main goal of this model was to increase the efficiency of the green energy usage in data centers. Based on the experiments of the proposed model, the number of tasks that were done by the green energy resources increased and the number of works that were terminated because of the lack of enough green energy resources decreased. This model uses a single queue per server for web services which are time sensitive applications, and for the batch-jobs it uses the Hadoop which is the general form of Map-Reduce framework.

GreenSlot scheduler (Goiri t al., 2011) also proposes a scheduling and prediction mechanism to efficiently use the green energy sources. Goiri et al. (2011) consider solar as the main source of energy and smart grid, known as brown energy, as the backup power source for the data center. The main objective of GreenSlot is to predict the availability of solar energy two days in advance so that it can maximize the use of green energy and reduce the costs associated with using brown energy. GreenSlot uses the suspension mechanism when there is not enough green energy available and based on the availability of enough solar energy it resumes the jobs. According to the experimental results that are presented in comparison with other conventional scheduling mechanisms, like backfilling scheduler (Mu'alem & Feitelson, 2001), GreenSlot scheduler can significantly increase the use of green energy for running batch-jobs and decrease the brown energy costs, which leads to less carbon footprint and moving towards a sustainable environment. Unlike web-service jobs which are time-sensitive batch-jobs are compute intensive and the deadline is not critical as web-service jobs, so the suspension will not affect the user quality of service (QoS) parameters.

VM Placement

Users send their requests to the cloud Infrastructure as a Service (IaaS) providers in the form of VMs. Goudarzi and Pedram (2012) presented a VM placement heuristic algorithm to place the VMs in physical servers in a way to reduce data centers energy consumption. The algorithm receives the VM requests and splits each VM into several copies and places them on servers. Each copy of VM gets the same amount of physical memory but with different CPUs. The total summation of assigned CPUs for copies of a VM request will be equal to the required CPU by the VM at the time of arrival to the data center. The proposed algorithm, which is known as MERA (Multi-dimensional Energy-efficient Resource Allocation), receives the VM requests and after a certain time epoch places the VMs on the servers and calculates the consumed energy. Then, it splits the VMs and places the copies on servers and recalculates the energy consumption. Based on the calculated energies the algorithm makes decision whether to split and replicate VMs or not. This algorithm tries to increase the servers' utilization while decreasing the energy consumption without considering the physical characteristics and energy related parameters of servers and data centers. Moreover, it does not perform the VM placement dynamically. The algorithm receives a group of VMs and after a certain time epoch performs VM placement. In addition, inter-communication between replicated VMs could lead to bottleneck and high energy consumption. Finally, in the placement all VMs are treated the same. As all the replicated VMs get the same amount of physical memory, whilst for memory-intensive VMs this could result to shortage in resources and it is better to make balance between CPU intensive and memory intensive VM requests.

The work done by Xu and Fortes (2010) addresses the problem of data centers VM placement with the objective to simultaneously minimize resource wastage, power consumption, and maximum temperature of the servers. They used a genetic algorithm on the global controller of the data center to perform the VM placement. The global controller receives the VM requests and then based on a multi-objective VM placement algorithm assigns each VM to a server. This algorithm, same as the previously discussed work, performs VM placement after receiving all the VM requests, which is not in a dynamic manner. Moreover, the algorithm makes balance between power consumption and temperature. Therefore, it uses more servers to distribute the load and avoid hotspots in the data center. This might cause more carbon footprint as more servers will be used and more electricity will be consumed.

Green SLA Aware

Due to the high energy consumption by cloud data centers and climate concerns, cloud providers do not just rely on the electricity coming from brown energy sources. They have their own on-site green energy sources or draw it from a nearby power plant. Moreover, enterprises and individuals demand for quantifiable green cloud services. Haque, Le, Goiri, Bianchini, and Nguyen (2013) propose a new class of cloud services that provides a specific service level agreement for users to meet the required percentage of green energy used to run their workloads. They undertake a new power infrastructure in which each rack can be powered from brown or green energy sources. The optimization policies have the objective of increasing the provider's profit by admitting the incoming jobs, with Green SLA requirements. If cloud provider cannot meet the requested percentage of green energy to run the job should pay penalty to the user, which means decrease in the total gained profit of running jobs. The type of green energy used by Haque et al. (2013) in the data center is solar energy and they predict the availability and amount of solar energy based on the method proposed in Goiri et al. (2012). The experiments carried in their work are based on comparison with greedy heuristics, and they show that optimization based policies outperform the greedy ones. Furthermore, among optimization based policies cloud provider can decide whether wants to increase the number of admitted jobs or violate less Green SLAs.

In the calculated total cost to run the admitted jobs in the work by Haque et al. (2013), it is not clear that whether it is the cost to run the servers or the total cost in the data center, including overhead energy cost as well. This is important because overhead energy is dependent on the data center power usage effectiveness (PUE) and this varies by the change in the data center total utilization and ambient temperature (Rasmussen, 2007; Goiri, Le, Guitart, Torres, & Bianchini, 2011). Therefore, the calculated value for profit in the optimization based policies would vary based on the two aforementioned parameters for different jobs with different configuration requirements and also time of the day.

ENERGY EFFICIENCY IN GEOGRAPHICALLY DISTRIBUTED DATA CENTERS

Applying different policies to switch-off and on servers and placing user requests within a data center could lead to reduce in energy consumption. But still these are not enough to solve the problem of high energy consumption and carbon footprint by cloud data centers.

By increasing the use of cloud computing services that leads to increase in energy consumption and carbon footprint in the environment, some cloud providers decided to use green energy as a secondary power plant. Therefore, the need to have a scheduling policy to select the data center site to run the user request based on the energy source is necessary. Moreover, data center selection based on considering different data centers energy efficiency, as it has a direct effect on total carbon footprint, reduces energy consumption and carbon dioxide in the ecosystem. This section explores different energy and carbon-efficient approaches have been taken across distributed cloud data centers. Some of the applied techniques are the same as single data center level, but with considering factors to select the data center site before cluster and server selection. Figure 4 shows the taxonomy of different approaches taken at multi data center level with different optimization objectives, such as minimizing cost, energy consumption, carbon emission, and maximizing renewable energy consumption.

Figure 4. Multi data center level energy and carbon-efficient techniques

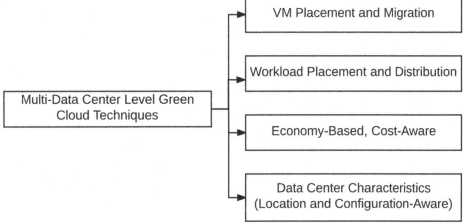

VM Placement and Migration

Research works in this area consider initial placement of a VM and further monitoring of the running VM to meet the optimization objective. Virtual machine (VM) placement in a geographically distributed data center environment requires selection of a data center and a server within the data center based on the optimization objective and data centers characteristics. Moreover, after the VM placement considering the future state of the host data center and other data centers, cloud provider can perform VM live migration to move the VM to another data center with preferable parameters. There are a few research works that consider these two techniques.

Chen, Xu, Xi, and Chao (2013) developed a model for optimal VM placement considering a cloud provider with distributed data center sites connected through leased/dedicated lines. They introduce a cost-aware VM placement problem with the objective of reducing operational cost as a function of electricity costs to run the VMs and inter-data center communication costs. For this purpose, they take advantage of variable electricity costs at multiple locations and wide-area network (WAN) communication cost to place the VMs using a meta-heuristic algorithm. Similarly, Qureshi, Weber, Balakrishnan, Guttag, and Maggs (2009) try to minimize electricity cost of running the VMs by initially placing the VMs into data centers with low spot market prices. They take advantage of spatial and temporal variations of electricity price at different locations.

Akoush, Sohan, Rice, Moore, and Hopper (2011) propose an architecture known as Free Lunch to maximize renewable energy consumption. They consider having data center sites in different geographical locations in such a way to complement each other in terms of access to renewable energy (solar and wind) by being located in different hemisphere and time zone. The architecture considers pausing VMs execution in the absence of renewable energy or migrating the VMs to another data center site with excess renewable energy. The proposed architecture provides a good insight to harness renewable energy by having geo-distributed data center sites with dedicated network. However, this model has technical challenges and limitations dealing with VM availability, storage synchronization, VM placement and migration that have been pointed out in their work.

Work done by Khosravi, Garg, and Buyya (2013) addresses the problem of energy consumption and carbon footprint of distributed cloud data centers by proposing a novel framework and algorithm for VM placement. This system model uses a component known as Cloud Information Service (CIS) in order to get the data centers' information and updates to perform the scheduling algorithm. The information a data center sends to the CIS consists of data center's available resources, energy and carbon related parameters, such as power usage effectiveness, carbon footprint rate/s (a data center might use more than one energy source), and servers' proportional power as a metric related to the CPU frequency and utilization. The cloud broker, as the interface between users and cloud provider, uses this information to perform a dynamic two-level scheduling algorithm. The algorithm places the VM in the data center/cluster with the least carbon footprint and energy consumption (first level), and in the server with the least increase in the power consumption (second-level), while meeting the users' quality of service in terms of number of rejected VMs. The proposed algorithm reduces the carbon footprint and energy consumption considerable in comparison to other competing algorithms.

Workload Placement and Distribution

A large body of literature recently focused on reducing energy consumption and energy costs by load placement and distribution across geographically distributed data centers.

Le, Bianchini, Martonosi, and Nguyen (2009) proposed a framework to reduce cost and brown energy consumption of cloud computing systems by distributing user requests across data center sites. This is the first research that considers load distribution across data center sites with respect to their energy source and cost. The framework is composed of a front-end that receives user requests and based on a distribution policy forwards the requests to the data center site with less cost and more available green energy sources. The request distribution policy sorts the data center sites based on the percent of the load that could be completed within a time period and minimum cost to run the requests. The evaluation results show that by knowing data centers' electricity price (constant price, dynamic, or on/off-peak prices) and base/idle energy consumption of the servers', significant improvements in cost reduction will be made. Moreover, being aware of the energy sources (green or brown) in the data centers could lead to less brown energy usage with a slight increase in the total cost.

Zhang, Wang, and Wang (2011) use the idea of distributing the load among a network of geographically distributed data centers to maximize renewable energy usage. They proposed a novel middleware, known as GreenWare, that dynamically conducts user requests to a network of data centers with the objective of maximizing the percentage of renewable energy usage, subject to the cloud service provider cost budget. Experiment results show GreenWare could significantly increase the usage of renewable energies, solar and wind with intermittent nature, whilst still meeting the cost budget limitation of the cloud provider.

Following the idea of reducing brown energy consumption in data center sites, Liu, Lin, Wierman, Low, and Andrew (2011) proposed the geographical load balancing (GLB) algorithm. The algorithm takes advantage of diversity of data center sites to route requests to the places with access to renewable, solar and wind, energy sources. Considering the unpredictable nature of renewable energy, specially wind, GLB algorithm finds the optimal percentage of wind/solar energies to reduce the brown energy consumption and carbon footprint. Moreover, the authors consider the role of storage of renewable energies, when they are not available in data centers in reducing brown energy usage. Based on the experiments, by using even small-scale storage in the data centers, the need for brown energy will decrease and in some cases even will be eliminated. A question that might rise with Liu et al. (2011) work is the carbon footprint caused by the batteries in a long-term period, since renewable energy storage in the data center sites is done through reserving them in the form of batteries. Lin, Liu, Wierman, and Andrew (2012) extended the GLB algorithm to reduce the total cost along with reducing the total brown energy consumption for geographically distributed data centers. They compared their proposed algorithm with two prediction-based algorithms with a look-ahead window, known as receding horizon control (RHC) a classical control policy and an extension of RHC known as averaging fixed horizon control (AFHC) (Kwon & Pearson, 1977). The analytical modelling and the simulations carried, based on real workload traces, show that GLB algorithm can reduce the energy cost by slightly increase in network delay. Moreover, it can eliminate the use of brown energy sources by routing user requests to the sites where wind/solar energy is available.

Garg, Yeo, Anandasivam, and Buyya (2011) proposed an environment-conscious meta-scheduler for high performance computing (HPC) applications in a distributed cloud data center system. The meta-scheduler consists of two phases, mapping the applications to the data center and scheduling within a data center. They treat the mapping and scheduling of applications as an NP-hard problem with the objective to reduce carbon emission and increase the cloud provider profit at the same time. They run different experiments in order to find the near optimal solution for this dual objective problem. The parameters taken into account in the simulations and scheduling algorithms are data centers' carbon footprint rate, electricity price, and data center's efficiency. The simulations carried for high urgent applications (with short deadlines) and different job arrival rates help the cloud providers to decide for each application which scheduling algorithms should be used in order to meet the objective of reducing the carbon emission or maximizing the profit. Moreover, they proposed a lower bound and an upper bound for the carbon emission and profit, respectively. Another work done by Garg, Yeo, and Buyya (2011) addresses the issue of energy efficiency of ICT industry, specially data centers. The main focus of this work is to reduce the carbon footprint of running workloads on data centers by proposing a novel carbon-aware green cloud architecture. This architecture consists of two directories, which imposes the use of green energy by data centers while meeting users and providers' requirements. In this framework, cloud providers should register their offered services in the aforementioned directories, and the users should submit their requests to the data centers through the Green Broker. The scheduling mechanism used in the broker, Carbon Efficient Green Policy (CEGP), chooses the cloud provider based on the least carbon footprint while considering users QoS parameters. The performance evaluation results of the proposed framework and policy in comparison with a traditional scheduling approach shows that CEGP can achieve a considerable reduction in energy consumption and carbon footprint in the ecosystem. However, this algorithm does not work dynamically. It receives all the job requests and based on the jobs deadline assigns them to the data center with the least carbon footprint. Moreover, it only considers high performance computing applications (non-interactive workloads) with predefined deadlines at the time of submission.

Chen, He, and Tang (2012) use the idea of geographically distributed data centers to increase usage of green energy and reduce brown energy consumption in data centers. They proposed a workload scheduling algorithm, called MinBrown, that considers green energy availability in different data centers with different time zones, cooling energy consumption for data centers based on outside temperature and data center utilization, incoming workload changes during time, and deadline of the jobs. The workload used to run the simulation is HPC jobs with sufficient slack time to allow advanced scheduling. The algorithm copies all the data in all the data centers and based on the least consumed brown energy executes the task. Based on the simulation results, the MinBrown algorithm reduces brown energy consumption in comparison to other competitive algorithms. The idea of replicated data in distributed data center sites itself results to high energy consumption that is not considered in Chen et al. (2012) work. Moreover, assignment of the jobs and tasks are based on the availability of green energy, that does not consider communication between tasks of the same job and jobs of the same workload. Finally, the scheduler does not consider an efficient resource assignment within a data center in a way to reduce the need for future consolidation of the running jobs.

The idea of federation of cloud providers can be useful for relocation of computational workload among different providers in a way to increase the use of sustainable energy. Celesti, Puliafito, Tusa, and Villari (2013) take advantage of a federated cloud scenario to reduce energy costs and CO_2 emissions. They consider cloud providers' data centers are partially powered by renewable energies along with getting the required electrical energy from electrical grids. The main contribution of their work is based on the approach of moving the workload towards the cloud data center with most available sustainable energy. This is inspired by the fact that if a provider generates more green energy than its need, it would be difficult to store the exceeded amount in batteries or put it in public grids; therefore, the easiest way is to relocate the workload to the site with the excess renewable energy. The architecture is based on an Energy Manager, that is known as CLoud-Enabled Virtual Environment (CLEVER). By applying CLEVER-based scenario, the VM allocation would be based on the energy and temperature driven policies. The energy manager in the architecture receives different data centers' information, such as temperature, sun radiation, energy grid fare, photovoltaic energy, cost, and data centers' PUE and number of available slots or physical resources, and based on this data assigns VMs to the site with the most sustainable energy and least cost.

Celesti et al. (2013) work increases the use of sustainable energies and it is based on the availability of the photovoltaic (PV) energy. When a site has a high value for the PV energy, the outside temperature would be higher and this will increase the need for more energy for the cooling, and as a result higher PUE value. Relying only on the amount of used PV in the system is not enough for a green and sustainable system. Cloud providers should consider the whole picture and take into account all the parameters that affect the total CO_2 emission. Moreover, Celesti et al. (2013) assume that each new VM request would be replicated in all the federated providers. Considering the consumed energy for this replication and the effect of network distance are also important that should be considered by the time of system design.

Xu, Feng, and Li (2013) take advantage of diversity in data centers location to route the incoming workload with the objective of reducing the energy consumption and cost. They studied the effect of ambient temperature on the total energy consumed by cooling system, which is 30% to 50% of the total energy consumption of data centers (Pelley, Meisner, Wenisch, & VanGilder, 2009; Zhou et al., 2012). Energy consumption often is modelled as a constant factor, which is an over-simplification of what is happening in reality. Xu et al. (2013) considered partial PUE (power usage effectiveness) to participate cooling systems' energy along with the servers' total energy consumption. Through using partial PUE data centers can route the workload to the sites that use outside air cooling and reduce considerable amount of energy consumption. Moreover, they took advantage of having two types of incoming requests to manage the resources and reduce the energy consumption. The proposed model does not only depend on the energy consumed by interactive workload form users, instead it reduces energy costs by allocating capacity to the batch workloads, which are delay tolerant and can be run at the back-end of the data centers. The proposed joint optimization approach could reduce cooling energy and overall energy cost of data centers.

However, the proposed partial PUE only considers the energy consumed by cooling system as the total overhead energy in the data center. Based on the introduced definition by Xu et al. (2013), PUE is mainly dependent on the ambient temperature, while IT load of the data center is the second important factor affecting the PUE (Rasmussen, 2007). Finally, source of the energy used to generate the electricity and its carbon footprint is not considered. This is important because as mentioned earlier reducing energy cost does not necessarily lead to reduce in the carbon footprint in the environment.

Economy-Based, Cost-Aware

Cost associated with energy usage in large data centers is a major concern for the cloud providers. Large data centers consume megawatts of electricity, which leads to huge operational costs. Work done by Ren, He, and Xu (2012) takes advantage of different electricity prices in different geographical locations and over time to schedule batch jobs on the servers in scattered data centers. Their proposed online optimal algorithm, known as GreFar, uses servers' energy efficiency information and locations with low electricity prices to schedule the arrived batch jobs from different organizations. GreFar's key objective is to reduce energy cost, while assuring fairness considerations and delay constraints. The scheduling is based on a provably-efficient online algorithm, that schedules the jobs according to the current job queue lengths. Based on the simulation results, GreFar online algorithm can reduce system cost, in terms of a combination of energy cost and fairness, in comparison to the offline algorithm that has knowledge of system's future state. The algorithm's main contribution is to serve the jobs when the electricity price is low or there are energy-efficient servers in the system. To accomplish this objective, it queues jobs and suspends low priority jobs whenever the electricity price goes up or there are not enough efficient servers in the system. This approach is not applicable for interactive jobs and web requests that are time sensitive and need to be served immediately from the queue and also cannot be suspended. Moreover, the cloud provider does not consider the cost of the transmission network and its energy consumption at the time of data center selection to submit the job request.

Le, Bianchini, Nguyen, Bilgir, and Martonosi (2010) take advantage of capping the brown energy consumption to reduce the cost of serving Internet services in data centers. They proposed an optimization-based framework to distribute requests among distributed data centers, with the objective to reduce costs, while meeting users' service level agreement (SLA). The main parameters that affect the site selection by the framework are different electricity prices (on-peak and off-peak loads), different data centers location with different time zones, data centers with access to green energy sources, which enables the data center to have a mixture of brown and green energy. The front-end of the framework performs the site selection and optimization problem for the arrived requests periodically, in contrast to heuristic algorithms, which are greedy and select the best destination for each request that arrives (Qureshi et al., 2009). The optimization framework uses load prediction by Auto-Regressive Integrated Moving Average (ARIMA) modeling (Box, Jenkins, Reinsel, & Ljung, 2015) and simulated annealing (SA) (Brooks & Morgan, 1995) to predict the load for the next epoch (one week) and schedule the requests. This approach helps the front-end to decide about the power mixes at each data center for the next week, unless a significant change occurs in the system and predictions. Le et al. (2010) use simulation and real system experiments with real traces to evaluate their proposed framework and optimization policy. The evaluation results show that by taking optimization policy and using workload prediction, diversity in electricity price, taking benefit of brown energy caps, and use of green energy sources significant savings in cost related to the execution of Internet services in distributed data centers would be made. The framework assumes that all the received requests from the users are homogeneous. While in the real systems this is not the case and having heterogeneous requests and distributing them in a way to reduce resource wastage is very difficult and itself results to huge energy consumption and accordingly high costs. Moreover, it focuses on the electricity prices in different locations without considering the carbon footprint rate of the sources. Since some brown energy sources, which are cheap and lead to reducing the system overall cost, may lead to huge amount of carbon dioxide in the ecosystem.

The other work by Le et al. (2011) investigates different parameters that affect the electricity costs for geographically distributed data centers with the focus on IaaS services that run HPC workloads. According to their proposed cost computation framework for the data centers, there are two important parameters that affect the total cost, energy consumed to run the service and the cost for the peak power demand. The provider can reduce the consumed energy by selecting the sites with off-peak period electricity prices, lower outside temperature, and lower data center load, so that the energy used for cooling would be low. Because as the data center temperature rises, the provider needs to use chillers to reduce temperature, which increases the energy consumption dramatically. In order to show this relation, they used a simulation model for the data center cooling system. Based on the simulation model, increase in the outside temperature and data center load forces the providers to use the chillers in order to keep the data center cool. This simulation has been carried with real workload traces from the Feitelson (2007), Parallel Workloads Archive. Le et al. (2011) compared their two proposed algorithms, cost-aware and cost-aware with migration, with baseline policies. Based on the results, considering above mentioned factors can reduce the energy cost of data centers. Moreover, predicting the need to use the chillers for system cooling and considering the transient cooling prevents the data center from overheating and would not let spikes in the temperature.

Le et al. (2011) conducted sensitivity analysis to investigate the effect of parameters, such as predicting the run-time of the jobs, the time to migrate the jobs, outside temperature, price of the energy in a region, and size of the data center on the total cost of the data center. According to the simulation results, in order to maximize the cost-saving all the electricity-related parameters should be considered in job placement in the system. One of the shortcomings of this work, similar to the previously discussed work, is not considering the source of electricity. As some brown energy sources with high carbon footprint might be cheaper and more desirable to run the services. Moreover, as the temperature changes during the day and the consumed energy for cooling changes consequently; PUE should be modelled as a dynamic parameter instead of having a constant value per data center. Considering network distance and the energy consumption of intra and inter-data centers will also affect the total cost.

Work by Buchbinder, Jain, and Menache (2011) has also the objective of reducing energy cost for a cloud provider with multi data center sites but with a different approach. They perform on-line migration of running batch jobs among data center sites, taking advantage of dynamic energy pricing and power availability at different locations, while considering the network bandwidth costs among data centers and future changes in electricity price. The total cost in their model, is the cost of energy to run the jobs at the destined data center plus the bandwidth cost to migrate the data. To attain an optimal algorithm with lower complexity comparing the optimal off-line solution, Buchbinder et al. (2011) proposed an efficient on-line algorithm (EOA) with higher performance comparing to the greedy heuristics that ignore the future outcomes. The calculated cost in their work is based on the data centers' operational cost, which focuses on the energy consumption by servers and transport network. However, a considerable part of the energy consumed by a data center is related to the overhead energy, such as cooling systems. Moreover, the objective of reducing the energy cost and routing the jobs to the data center with lowest cost without considering the energy source might lead to increase in the carbon footprint in the environment. The migration of running jobs in this work is in the context of batch jobs, which are delay tolerant in comparison to user interactive requests such as web requests that are delay sensitive. Therefore, the applicability of this algorithm should be investigated for other workloads and user requests in a cloud computing environment. Similarly, work by Luo, Rao, and Liu (2015) leverages both the spatial and temporal variation of electricity price to route the incoming requests between geographically distributed data centers targeting energy cost minimization.

Data Center Characteristics (Location and Configuration-Aware)

There are several works try to make data centers energy and carbon-efficient by reducing the number of active servers or run the virtual machines and applications on the physical machines with the least energy consumption and carbon footprint rate. However, geographical location of the data center has a direct impact on the amount of consumed energy that leads to CO_2 emission in the ecosystem. Work done by

Goiri et al. (2011) considers intelligent placement of data centers for Internet services. Their goal is to find the best location for data center site to minimize the overall cost and respect users' response time, consistency, and availability. They classified the parameters that affect data centers overall cost into location dependent and data center characteristics data.

The location dependent data specifies the data center's distance to the network backbones, power plants, and the CO_2 emission of the power plant. Moreover, it includes the electricity, land, and water price. The last and one of the most important factors related to the location is the outside temperature. Since, when the temperature goes high the need for cooling increases as well. Cooling system is an important parameter in the data centers, which its energy consumption increases as outside temperature increases. Indeed, high temperature leads to need for more chillers and more chillers increases data center's total energy consumption. This situation eventually leads to higher PUE and energy consumption, which indirectly increases carbon footprint. Goiri et al. (2011) propose a framework to find the most optimum location for the data center to minimize the total costs. Explicit decrease in data center's cost, leads to indirect decrease in energy consumption and carbon footprint.

In order to increase the use of renewable energies, Berral et al. (2014) propose a framework to find the best location to site the data centers and renewable power plants, solar and wind in their work. In the meantime, their objective is reducing total cost for building these infrastructures to support cloud HPC services with different amounts of renewable usage. Berral et al. (2014) divided the costs of building green cloud services into capital (CAPEX) and operational (OPEX) costs and CAPEX itself is divided to costs dependent and the costs that are independent to the number of servers to be hosted. Independent CAPEX costs are cost of bringing brown energy to the data center and connecting to the backbone network. Land cost, building green power plants, cooling infrastructure, batteries, networking equipment, and servers are part of the dependent CAPEX costs. Costs incurred during the life cycle of the data center, such as network bandwidth and amount of brown energy usage are part of the OPEX. Brown energy consumption is the total energy needed by the servers and overhead parts, such as cooling and networking, minus energy derived from renewables. To calculate the overhead energy, Berral et al. (2014) use PUE as a parameter related to the location temperature. It should be noted that temperature is not the only parameter that affects PUE, data center load is also an important parameter that changes PUE value (Rasmussen, 2007).

In order to take the most of the generated renewable energy in different data centers, Berral et al. (2014) compare different approaches such as net metering, which is directing the excess renewable energy into the grid and mix it with brown energy, using batteries and having storage for renewables or not having any storage and migrating the load to the sites with available solar or wind. One of the shortcomings of their work is neglecting the network delay and amount of energy consumed due to VM migration, as the data centers are scattered at different geographical locations. Moreover, all the data in this system are replicated at all the sites, which itself imposes overhead and increases energy consumption.

CONCLUSION AND FUTURE DIRECTIONS

In this chapter, the authors studied the research works in the area of energy and carbon footprint-aware resource management in cloud data centers. They first had an overview on the existing techniques in green cloud resource management with the focus on a single server and a single data center and the limitations facing these techniques, specially not being able to harvest renewable energy sources at different locations.

The authors then focused more specifically on the works considering geo-distributed cloud data centers, as nowadays most of the big cloud providers have data centers in different geographical locations for disaster recovery management, higher availability, and providing better quality of experience to users.

A large body of literature in the context of distributed data centers considers assigning resources to the arrived requests in such a way to minimize brown energy consumption. They use different techniques such as applying VM placement heuristics, workload scheduling, and targeting data centers with the most available renewable energy. These works explicitly consider access to renewable energy sources to minimize brown energy consumption and carbon footprint. However, some of the research works achieve energy efficient resource management through minimizing cost and the cost of brown energy usage, which indirectly could lead to less carbon footprint in the ecosystem.

Research in the area of energy and carbon-efficient resource management in data centers is still an important field of work. Apart from the surveyed techniques in this chapter, there are still areas that can be pursued by researchers. VM migration across data center sites to harvest the renewable energy sources is still at its early stages. First of all, it is important to study the effect of minimizing brown energy usage and carbon cost versus network cost and delay imposed due the data transfer over the network. Selecting the VMs to migrate depending on the application running on top of the VM with respect to users' service level agreement is also another area of future study.

There are studies that consider storing excess renewable energy in batteries to use at times of the day that renewable sources are not available. Since main cloud providers started to build their own on-site renewable energy sources and having large scale renewable energy power plants, studying the cost-effectiveness of storing the renewable energy for future usage and contributing to the electrical grid is an important area for future study.

REFERENCES

Akoush, S., Sohan, R., Rice, A. C., Moore, A. W., & Hopper, A. (2011). Free Lunch: Exploiting Renewable Energy for Computing. HotOS, 13, 17.

Aksanli, B., Venkatesh, J., Zhang, L., & Rosing, T. (2012). Utilizing green energy prediction to schedule mixed batch and service jobs in data centers. *SIGOPS Operating Systems Review, ACM, 45*(3), 53–57. doi:10.1145/2094091.2094105

Baer, P. (2008). *Exploring the 2020 global emissions mitigation gap. Analysis for the Global Climate Network*. Stanford University, Woods Institute for the Environment.

Barroso, L. A., & Holzle, U. (2007). The case for energy-proportional computing. *IEEE Computer, 40*(12), 33–37. doi:10.1109/MC.2007.443

Beloglazov, A., Buyya, R., Lee, Y. C., & Zomaya, A. (2011). A taxonomy and survey of energy-efficient data centers and cloud computing systems. *Advances in Computers, 82*(2), 47-111.

Berral, J. L., Goiri, Í., Nguyen, T. D., Gavalda, R., Torres, J., & Bianchini, R. (2014). Building green cloud services at low cost.*34th International Conference on Distributed Computing Systems (ICDCS)*, 449-460. doi:10.1109/ICDCS.2014.53

Box, G. E., Jenkins, G. M., Reinsel, G. C., & Ljung, G. M. (2015). *Time series analysis: forecasting and control*. John Wiley & Sons.

Brey, T., & Lamers, L. (2009). Using virtualization to improve data center efficiency. *The Green Grid, Whitepaper, 19*.

Brooks, S. P., & Morgan, B. J. (1995). Optimization using simulated annealing. *The Statistician, 44*(2), 241–257. doi:10.2307/2348448

Buchbinder, N., Jain, N., & Menache, I. (2011). Online job-migration for reducing the electricity bill in the cloud. *International Conference on Research in Networking*, 172-185. doi:10.1007/978-3-642-20757-0_14

Celesti, A., Puliafito, A., Tusa, F., & Villari, M. (2013). Energy Sustainability in Cooperating Clouds. CLOSER, 83-89.

Chen, C., He, B., & Tang, X. (2012). Green-aware workload scheduling in geographically distributed data centers. *4th International Conference on Cloud Computing Technology and Science (CloudCom)*, 82-89. doi:10.1109/CloudCom.2012.6427545

Chen, K. Y., Xu, Y., Xi, K., & Chao, H. J. (2013). Intelligent virtual machine placement for cost efficiency in geo-distributed cloud systems. *International Conference on Communications (ICC)*, 3498-3503. doi:10.1109/ICC.2013.6655092

Feitelson, D. (2007). *Parallel workloads archive*. Academic Press.

Garg, S. K., Yeo, C. S., Anandasivam, A., & Buyya, R. (2011). Environment-conscious scheduling of HPC applications on distributed Cloud-oriented data centers. *Journal of Parallel and Distributed Computing, 71*(6), 732–749. doi:10.1016/j.jpdc.2010.04.004

Garg, S. K., Yeo, C. S., & Buyya, R. (2011). Green cloud framework for improving carbon efficiency of clouds. *European Conference on Parallel Processing*, 491-502. doi:10.1007/978-3-642-23400-2_45

Goiri, I., Le, K., Guitart, J., Torres, J., & Bianchini, R. (2011). Intelligent placement of datacenters for internet services. *31st International Conference on Distributed Computing Systems (ICDCS)*, 131-142. doi:10.1109/ICDCS.2011.19

Goiri, Í., Le, K., Haque, M. E., Beauchea, R., Nguyen, T. D., Guitart, J., & Bianchini, R. (2011). GreenSlot: scheduling energy consumption in green datacenters. *Proceedings of International Conference for High Performance Computing, Networking, Storage and Analysis*, 20. doi:10.1145/2063384.2063411

Goiri, Í., Le, K., Nguyen, T. D., Guitart, J., Torres, J., & Bianchini, R. (2012). GreenHadoop: leveraging green energy in data-processing frameworks. *Proceedings of the 7th ACM european conference on Computer Systems*, 57-70. doi:10.1145/2168836.2168843

Goudarzi, H., & Pedram, M. (2012). Energy-efficient virtual machine replication and placement in a cloud computing system. *5th International Conference on Cloud Computing (CLOUD)*, 750-757. doi:10.1109/CLOUD.2012.107

Haque, M. E., Le, K., Goiri, Í., Bianchini, R., & Nguyen, T. D. (2013). Providing green SLAs in high performance computing clouds.*International Green Computing Conference (IGCC)*, 1-11. doi:10.1109/IGCC.2013.6604503

Harney, E., Goasguen, S., Martin, J., Murphy, M., & Westall, M. (2007). The efficacy of live virtual machine migrations over the internet.*Proceedings of the 2nd international workshop on Virtualization technology in distributed computing*, 8. doi:10.1145/1408654.1408662

Khosravi, A., Garg, S. K., & Buyya, R. (2013). Energy and carbon-efficient placement of virtual machines in distributed cloud data centers.*European Conference on Parallel Processing*, 317-328. doi:10.1007/978-3-642-40047-6_33

Koomey, J. G. (2007). *Estimating total power consumption by servers in the US and the world*. Academic Press.

Koomey, J. G. (2008). Worldwide electricity used in data centers. *Environmental Research Letters. IOP Publishing*, 3(3), 034008

Kwon, W., & Pearson, A. (1977). A modified quadratic cost problem and feedback stabilization of a linear system. *IEEE Transactions on Automatic Control*, 22(5), 838–842. doi:10.1109/TAC.1977.1101619

Le, K., Bianchini, R., Martonosi, M., & Nguyen, T. D. (2009). Cost-and energy-aware load distribution across data centers. Proceedings of HotPower, 1-5.

Le, K., Bianchini, R., Nguyen, T. D., Bilgir, O., & Martonosi, M. (2010). Capping the brown energy consumption of internet services at low cost.*International Green Computing Conference*, 3-14. doi:10.1109/GREENCOMP.2010.5598305

Le, K., Bianchini, R., Zhang, J., Jaluria, Y., Meng, J., & Nguyen, T. D. (2011). Reducing electricity cost through virtual machine placement in high performance computing clouds.*Proceedings of International Conference for High Performance Computing, Networking, Storage and Analysis*, 22. doi:10.1145/2063384.2063413

Lefèvre, L., & Orgerie, A. C. (2010). Designing and evaluating an energy efficient cloud. *The Journal of Supercomputing*, 51(3), 352–373. doi:10.1007/s11227-010-0414-2

Lin, M., Liu, Z., Wierman, A., & Andrew, L. L. (2012). Online algorithms for geographical load balancing.*International Green Computing Conference (IGCC)*, 1-10.

Lin, M., Wierman, A., Andrew, L. L., & Thereska, E. (2013). Dynamic right-sizing for power-proportional data centers. *Transactions on Networking (TON), IEEE/ACM*, 21(5), 1378-1391.

Liu, Z., Lin, M., Wierman, A., Low, S. H., & Andrew, L. L. (2011). Geographical load balancing with renewables. *Performance Evaluation Review*, 39(3), 62–66. doi:10.1145/2160803.2160862

Luo, J., Rao, L., & Liu, X. (2015). Spatio-Temporal Load Balancing for Energy Cost Optimization in Distributed Internet Data Centers. *IEEE Transactions on Cloud Computing*, 3(3), 387–397. doi:10.1109/TCC.2015.2415798

Mell, P., & Grance, T. (2011). *The NIST definition of cloud computing*. NIST special publication, 800, 145.

Mualem, A. W., & Feitelson, D. G. (2001). Utilization, predictability, workloads, and user runtime estimates in scheduling the IBM SP2 with backfilling. *IEEE Transactions on Parallel and Distributed Systems*, *12*(6), 529–543. doi:10.1109/71.932708

MYPVDATA Energy Recommerce. (n.d.). Retrieved from https://www.mypvdata.com/

National Renewable Energy Laboratory (NREL). (n.d.). Retrieved from http://www.nrel.gov/

Pelley, S., Meisner, D., Wenisch, T. F., & VanGilder, J. W. (2009). Understanding and abstracting total data center power.*Workshop on Energy-Efficient Design*.

Qureshi, A., Weber, R., Balakrishnan, H., Guttag, J., & Maggs, B. (2009). Cutting the electric bill for internet-scale systems. ACM SIGCOMM Computer Communication Review, 39(4), 123-134. doi:10.1145/1592568.1592584

Rasmussen, N. (2007). Electrical efficiency measurement for data centers. *White paper, 154*.

Ren, S., He, Y., & Xu, F. (2012). Provably-efficient job scheduling for energy and fairness in geographically distributed data centers.*32nd International Conference on Distributed Computing Systems (ICDCS)*, 22-31. doi:10.1109/ICDCS.2012.77

Srikantaiah, S., Kansal, A., & Zhao, F. (2008). Energy aware consolidation for cloud computing.*Proceedings of the conference on Power aware computing and systems*, 10, 1-5.

Xu, H., Feng, C., & Li, B. (2013). Temperature aware workload management in geo-distributed datacenters.*Proceedings of the 10th International Conference on Autonomic Computing (ICAC)*, 303-314. doi:10.1145/2465529.2465539

Xu, J., & Fortes, J. A. (2010). Multi-objective virtual machine placement in virtualized data center environments.*Int'l Conference on Green Computing and Communications (GreenCom) & Int'l Conference on Cyber, Physical and Social Computing (CPSCom), IEEE/ACM*, 179-188. doi:10.1109/GreenCom-CPSCom.2010.137

Zhang, Y., Wang, Y., & Wang, X. (2011). Greenware: Greening cloud-scale data centers to maximize the use of renewable energy.*International Conference on Distributed Systems Platforms and Open Distributed Processing, ACM/IFIP/USENIX*, 143-164. doi:10.1007/978-3-642-25821-3_8

Zhou, R., Wang, Z., McReynolds, A., Bash, C. E., Christian, T. W., & Shih, R. (2012). Optimization and control of cooling microgrids for data centers.*13th Intersociety Conference on Thermal and Thermomechanical Phenomena in Electronic Systems (ITherm)*, 338-343. doi:10.1109/ITHERM.2012.6231449

Chapter 3
Cloud–Based Platforms and Infrastructures:
Provisioning Physical and Virtual Networks

Marcus Tanque
Independent Researcher, USA

ABSTRACT

Cloud computing consists of three fundamental service models: infrastructure-as-a-service, platform-as-a service and software-as-a-service. The technology "cloud computing" comprises four deployment models: public cloud, private cloud, hybrid cloud and community cloud. This chapter describes the six cloud service and deployment models, the association each of these services and models have with physical/virtual networks. Cloud service models are designed to power storage platforms, infrastructure solutions, provisioning and virtualization. Cloud computing services are developed to support shared network resources, provisioned between physical and virtual networks. These solutions are offered to organizations and consumers as utilities, to support dynamic, static, network and database provisioning processes. Vendors offer these resources to support day-to-day resource provisioning amid physical and virtual machines.

INTRODUCTION

In recent years, cloud computing has transformed the way information technology organizations and consumers conduct business. This technology revolution is attributable to the Information Technology (IT) democratization of physical and virtual platforms or network infrastructure solutions. Cloud computing is a pervasive technology that many organizations and consumers continue to adopt. In the cloud, deployment models are adopted as integrated solution architecture to interface with other cloud- based technologies: virtualization, cyber-physical systems, data analytics, big data, Internet of things, artificial-predictive intelligence, cybersecurity. In this chapter other useful solutions required to make more efficient the production time, enhance productivity and improve operation's performance are discussed. The integration of cloud computing with other technology solutions has improved the consumption of

DOI: 10.4018/978-1-5225-2013-9.ch003

technology services i.e., forecasting, aggregating hardware and software performance for emergency response time, and the adoption of innovative business models. Vendors examine the transformation of traditional IT systems to leading-edge cloud-based, as a complex process for enhancing involved policy implementation. The adoption of cloud solutions is often supported by analytical and practical procedures needed to balance all-inclusive cloud implementation processes (Buyya, Ranjan, Rodrigo, & Calheiros, 2010; Gartner, 2012; Buyya, Ramamohanarao, Leckie, Calheiros, Dastjerdi, & Versteeg). In recent times, the provisioning of cloud service and deployment models has advanced significantly. Despite vendor's adoption of database-as-a-Service/DBaaS, the industry has developed assorted methods to support enterprise IT network infrastructure solutions (Ko, Ahn, & Shehab, 2009; Vozmediano, Montero, & Llorente, 2011). Aside from these developments, more security solutions are developed to protect organizations and consumers' IT resources (Stanton et al., 2005; Ko, Ahn, & Shehab, 2009; Alhazmi, & Shami, 2014). IT experts continue to research on measures to enable the integration of native computer solutions with cloud computing systems i.e., hardware, software, data and user-users (Grance & Mell, 2011; Ross, 2010; Buyya, Ranjan, Rodrigo, & Calheiros, 2010; Ko, Ahn, & Shehab, 2009; Vozmediano, Montero, & Llorente, 2011). The transformation of these solutions is vital for leveraging day-to-day IT operations and provide essential strategies organizations need for adopting, configuring and deploying integrated computer systems (Lease, 2005). The adoption and implementation of cloud-based solutions are key of deploying IT resources for diverse enterprises (Grance & Mell, 2011; Gentry, 2009). In general, Service level agreements (SLAs) are fundamental business methods every organization would require, to assess its economic growth (Alhazmi & Shami, 2014). Lacking proper security standards commonly can affect the adoption/deployment of cloud computing resources. This could also expose network infrastructure solutions to cyber related vulnerabilities (Lease, 2005; Buyya, Ranjan, Rodrigo, & Calheiros, 2010; Gartner, 2012; Gartner, 2009; Alhazmi & Shami, 2014). Vendors must to develop customized solutions, to properly mitigate malicious cyber-attacks. Besides, this chapter aims to emphasize on areas affecting the virtualization and provisioning of cloud-based services. These services comprise: IaaS, SaaS, PaaS, DBaaS, public cloud, private cloud and hybrid cloud. The three NIST certified cloud computing services discussed in this chapter are: PC, PC and HC (Ross, 2010; Gartner, 2012; Amazon, 2012; Bruening & Treacy, 2009; Ko, Ahn, & Shehab, 2009; Alhazmi & Shami, 2014).

BACKGROUND

For nearly a decade, industry has implemented XaaS or EaaS as "anything/everything-as-a-service" service model. XaaS and/or EaaS is an emerging cloud service model developed to interact with related technology-based services and business processes. This cohesive model is designed to interact with cloud computing services: infrastructure-as-a-service, platform-as-a-service and software-as-a-service. These solutions are carefully selected to interface with the following deployment models: public cloud, private cloud, hybrid cloud and community cloud (Grance & Mell, 2011). The need for industry to adopt XaaS/EaaS is to supplement organization and customer's cloud platform specifications (Grance & Mell, 2011; Toosi, Calheiros, & Buyya, 2014). XaaS/EaaS is defined as a collection of cloud services: IaaS, IaaS and SaaS. This term includes other industry-based cloud services i.e., communication as a service, monitoring-as-a-Service. Vendors have developed software/hardware products and related XaaS capabilities/services to interact with related service-centric solutions (Buyya, Ranjan, Rodrigo, & Calheiros, 2010; Toosi, Calheiros, & Buyya, 2014). This include a variety of capabilities needed to enable XaaS/EaaS solutions as delivered utilities (Toosi, Calheiros, & Buyya, 2014). Vendors designed XaaS/EaaS solutions to serve the customer's needs, address any deficiencies between legacy network infrastructure solutions and state-of-the-art cloud business models (Buyya, Ramamohanarao, Leckie, Calhieros, Dastjerdi, & Versteeg, 2015). Vendors define public cloud as pay-as-you-go or pay-per-use model. XaaS features consist of (Toosi, Calheiros, & Buyya, 2014; Alhazmi & Shami, 2014):

- High Scalability
- Multitenancy
- Online Provisioning
- Automated Provisioning
- Try and Purchase
- Device Independence (e.g., which in numerous instances, allows users to acquire software despite the type of device they are using)
- Location Independence
- Term-based Billing
- Pay-per-use Models

XaaS/EaaS services consist of: (Buyya, Ranjan, Rodrigo, & Calheiros, 2010; Gartner, 2012; Toosi, Calheiros, & Buyya, 2014)

- **Business Process**: Offered by third party cloud or managed service providers
- **Communication**: Type of service offerings Cisco, Hewlett-Packard, Microsoft, usually deliver to many customers, as a service utility
- **Identify**: Cloud services that (OpenID, Google, FB, Salesforce), deliver to many clients
- **Security**: Defined as Symantec cloud services deployed to enterprise IT infrastructure solutions
- **Software**: Delivered by Salesforce, Workday and Netsuite
- **Database**: Service made available to customers (e.g., MongoDB, Clustrix)
- **Platform**: Cloud services provided by VMforce, Google AppEngine, Salesforces
- **Infrastructure**: Provided by Amazon, Rackspace
- **Monitor**: Often delivered by Logic Monitor

XaaS/EaaS model is a business enabler offering agile cloud solutions to support organization and customer's requirements as well as enhance business values (Buyya, Ramamohanarao, Leckie, Calhieros, Dastjerdi, & Versteeg, 2015). These characteristics are based on cloud-based platforms, infrastructure solutions and/or process elements required for supporting dynamic, static, network and database provisioning processes (Buyya, Ranjan, Rodrigo, & Calheiros, 2010; Buyya, Ramamohanarao, Leckie, Calhieros, Dastjerdi, & Versteeg, 2015; Toosi, Calheiros, & Buyya, 2014). The process also redefines the crucial method for multi-tier server operation, virtualization, sustainability, scalability and load balancing. Analytical and responsive procedures are needed to support these processes when deployed to the cloud. The provisioning of these resources has altered the way physical and virtual machines frequently interface, distribute and process data (Ross, 2010; Gartner, 2012; Amazon, 2012; Lease, 2005; Stanton et al., 2005; Alhazmi & Shami, 2014). Besides, this chapter explains different concepts of cloud computing service and deployment models, benefits and limitations. Thereby the manuscript aims to provide measures for supporting the adoption of cloud architecture solutions in support of the public and private sector. The chapter also explains the benefits and limitations cloud computing presents, to organizations, consumers, data center evolutions & trends, continuous monitoring of network infrastructure services (Lease, 2005; Stanton et al., 2005). These cloud-based solutions are selected to provide optimal research directions and recommendations for the body of knowledge (Buyya, Ranjan, Rodrigo, & Calheiros, 2010; Buyya, Ramamohanarao, Leckie, Calhieros, Dastjerdi, & Versteeg, 2015). The improvement of storage, data, protection and privacy preservation, yet has elevated interest among software developers, IT engineers and management (Lease, 2005; Toosi, Calheiros, & Buyya, 2014; Messmer, 2009). These analyses are associated with multidisciplinary technical procedures. These processes are developed to minimize and/ or address any security threats, affecting the public and private sector (Grance & Mell, 2011). Such level of threats can influence how organizations and customers conduct business (Stanton et al., 2005; Lease, 2005; Ko, Ahn, & Shehab, 2009).

MAIN FOCUS OF THE CHAPTER

The chapter focuses on topics affecting the provisioning of cloud computing platform solutions (Buyya, Ranjan, Rodrigo, & Calheiros, 2010; Gartner, 2012; Alhazmi, & Shami, 2014). Each of these sections/ subsections are viewed as accentuated areas supporting service and deployment models. The chapter also different aspects such as the database systems, virtualization technology, security techniques and how physical and virtual systems can easily scale (Ross, 2010; Buyya, Ranjan, Rodrigo, & Calheiros, 2010; Buyya, Ramamohanarao, Leckie, Calhieros, Dastjerdi, & Versteeg, 2015). Cloud technology solutions are key factors affecting the provisioning of physical, virtual server infrastructure and data (Lease, 2005; Stanton et al., 2005; Alhazmi & Shami, 2014).

Cloud Architecture Models and Key Areas of Functionality

Cloud-based technology is an emerging technology built with key capability solutions to increase productivity (Stanton et al., 2005). Cloud-based solutions consist of: cloud-based services, dynamic and static provisioning. These solutions are frequently deployed to increase organization and consumer's productivity (Grance & Mell, 2011; Messmer, 2009). The following is a set of cloud architectural models and functional concepts (Gartner, 2009; Gartner, 2012; Buyya, Ramamohanarao, Leckie, Calhieros, Dastjerdi, & Versteeg, 2015):

- **Amazon ECS**: Simple storage and relational databases services for enterprises
- **Cloud Service Alliance**: Enterprise security based
- **Cisco**: IT data centers and networks
- **IBM**: Cloud service management
- **Storage Networking Industry Association**: IT cloud storage
- **Windows Azure**: Microsoft data center applications

For many years, cloud computing technology has played a major role in fulfilling IT organizations and consumers requirements. Below are commercial benefits cloud computing offers to various organizations and customers. These services are provided by major vendors (Alhazmi & Shami, 2014):

- **Amazon** (e.g., Amazon EC2)
  - ○ *Infrastructure-as-a-Service*
- **Microsoft** (i.e., Window Azure, Google App Engine)
  - ○ *Platform-as-a-Service*
- **Google** (e.g., Google Apps)
  - ○ *Software-as-a-Service*
- **SalesForce** (e.g., SalesForce.com)
  - ○ *Software-as-a-Service*

Virtualization and Migration

The term "virtualization" was originally introduced in 1960s. At that juncture this term "virtualization" was adopted, to define virtual machines also known as pseudo-machines. The activities executed by virtualization technology are called platform or server virtualization. Vendors describe virtualization as a technology developed to support software, operating systems, performing parallel activity(ies), independently from other programs and/or applications. In general, platform virtualization is described as a process through which various activities are performed by the computer hardware over a host and/ or control program. In platform virtualization, a computer software is responsible for assigning a host machine. As a consequence, the role host machine is to emulate events within the network infrastructure environments. In platform virtualization, VMs are designed to perform several process activities for the guest software, despite independent ability these machines have, to support any functions/requests beyond the user's applications. Thereby host computers are designed to provide operating systems with a wide -range of activities. In VM environment the software component is responsible for directly perform any required computing activities. These applications often run on a physical machine. There is a set of strict registration cloud administrators must enforce when initiating requests/transactions between virtual and physical machines. The following functions: network access, display of any applications, keyboard request/related activities to disk storage are managed and restricted to various security levels e.g., those performed by host processor or system-memory (Oracle, 2016; Cisco, 2011; RedHat, 2016). All guest machines are restricted from retrieving computer applications or related peripheral devices. This includes any subclass of system built-in capabilities lacking hardware access policy for the virtualization host (Oracle, 2016; Cisco, 2011; RedHat, 2016). The following are important details involving virtualization technology as relate to IT organizations: server or hardware consolidation/migration, reduction of energy consumption/ratio, adequate control or inspection of VMs from assigned external entity, instead of internal administrator, who often are responsible for provisioning existing VMs without acquiring new hardware/software. These actions can be performed by relocating/migrating single/multiple VMs from physical to virtual environments, physical-to-physical, virtual-to-virtual, etc (Oracle, 2016; Cisco, 2011; RedHat, 2016). Vendors such as Red Hat, Cisco, Oracle have also adopted virtualization technology as a utility to support data centers/network infrastructure solutions. This includes the adoption of cutting-edge hypervisor hardware and software (Oracle, 2016; Cisco, 2011; RedHat, 2016).

The technology industry, refer to hypervisor as an interface application layer designed to support other hardware devices on the network i.e., server, storage, applications as well as related operating systems e.g., "guest" system (Oracle, 2016; Cisco, 2011). If associated activities are performed on computer/ machine residing in the same physical system environment, either the operating system or guest is described as a "host" computer. For many years, there has been false technical impression in the public and public sector which led to whether the process of virtualizing machines between physical to virtual environments is cost-effective or not (Oracle, 2016; Cisco, 2011; RedHat, 2016). Such conjectures have concluded that virtualization can be a complex solution to implement. Since then, vendors have encouraged decision makers to conduct a wide-ranging analysis of alternatives on IT organizations' anticipated return-on-investment/ROI, prior to deciding whether it is reasonable migrating their physical resources i.e., applications, storages, servers and database systems to virtual environments (Cisco, 2011; Oracle, 2016; RedHat, 2016). Other studies similarly have provided cost savings benefits for virtualizing platforms and network infrastructure solutions from physical to virtual locations. When conducting the ROI analysis, decision makers should consider the following factors e.g., decide whether it is feasible making a compelling management decision, to support an organization's business requirements: less power consumption, minus maintenance, adequate lifecycle of installed software or applications, forecast cost association and space limitation. Similar studies have also confirmed that virtualization involves numerous procedures. These processes can be determined as follows (Oracle, 2016; Cisco, 2011; RedHat, 2016):

- **Full Virtualization**: The practice which includes hardware capabilities initiated by a single or various processor(s). This allows guest(s) operating systems to access resources running on the host physical system. Through this concept new virtual system(s) also can be created known as "virtual machines" (Oracle, 2016; Cisco, 2011; RedHat, 2016). VMs are designed to provide guest operating system(s) and support required to perform further activities, whether the guest VM systems are aware or not of any other instances running on a virtual environment. In Red Hat Enterprise Linux environment hypervisor(s) are designed to support full-virtualization events
- **Para-Virtualization**: A set of applications and information patterns, available to the virtualized guest system. This process requires modification of software running on a particular machine e.g., guest. The process generally allows the guest machine to consume para-virtualized settings. A complete Kernel is required in virtualized-environment e.g., Xen para virtualized guest system, drivers for the input/out devices (Oracle, 2016)
- **Software Virtualization**: There is a degree of limitation in virtualization technology, which consist of machine activities and performance degradation. This is attributable to binary translation/resolution forcing the system to perform leisurely. The Red Hat Enterprise Linux does not support software virtualization

Migration

Migration is a practice of relocating guest virtual systems from single-to-single or single-to-multiple host computers. This method requires that VMs often run in a simulated/physical environment. In VM environment the migration process involves (Oracle, 2016; Cisco, 2011; RedHat, 2016):

- **Off-Line Migration**: The guest virtual machine(s) does/do not perform its/their activities on the network, while the off-line migration is in progress. Any machine selected as part of the off-line migration must immediately be removed or its activities should be suspended from execution of normal operations within the network. The complete process of migration is thereafter performed by the image of virtual machines' memory, to assigned host destination machine(s) (Oracle, 2016; Cisco, 2011; RedHat, 2016). As a result, the designated VM restarts its activities, after the migration process is complete; in so doing deployed system(s) will automatically resume their typical operations. The memory attached to a particular VM will independently restart its activities within the network

- **Live Migration**: The process which begins by migrating an active VM from physical to virtual network environment or assigned destination host. Then the migration process is selected to move VM memory onto disk volumes residing in a particular machine (Oracle, 2016; Cisco, 2011; RedHat, 2016). During the migration process, live blocks are required to support all systems activities

Virtualization Security Features

For many years, both the public and private sectors have developed security solutions to protect physical and virtual machines. Listed are software security tools already available in industry for IT organizations use: SELinux, sVirt. Following are limitless advantages of migrating virtual machines: load balancing, upgrades of host machines, energy-saving, geographic relocation of VMs (Oracle, 2016; Cisco, 2011; RedHat, 2016).

Capacity Planning and Management

The need for planning and managing cloud-based services is crucial on how customers commonly adopt and/or deploy these models. The deployment of cloud services normally is designed to determine, how responsive computer processes can be (Buyya, Ranjan, Rodrigo, & Calheiros, 2010; Gartner, 2012). SLAs are key for an effective deployment of cloud technology solutions (Buyya, Ranjan, Rodrigo, & Calheiros, 2010; Buyya, Ramamohanarao, Leckie, Calhieros, Dastjerdi, & Versteeg, 2015; Gartner, 2012). The cloud capacity and infrastructure management encompass the following characteristics or models (Gartner, 2009; Gartner, 2012):

- Network Model
- Compute Model
- Storage Model
- Data Center Facilities
- Cloud Platform Capacity
- Demand Forecasting
- Procurement

Cloud computing has altered how IT and business resources are managed (Leighton, 2009). According to Gartner survey, cloud computing is a paradigm that advances IT and business operations (Gartner Hype-Cycle, 2012; Oracle, 2016). These resources are required to balance capital and operational expenditures. Infrastructure management and platform are indispensable when deploying IT resources (Price, 2008; Oracle, 2016; Cisco, 2011; Oracle, 2016). Quite the opposite, cloud computing is a technology developed for delivering software applications and processes, needed to support platform provisioning (Badger, Grance, Patt-Corner, & Voas, 201; Price, 2008; Alhazmi & Shami, 2014). Cloud computing services are designed to interact with virtualization technology: hypervisors, VMware, vSphere and Hyper-V provide resourceful, flexible management and load balancing for virtual machines (Oracle, 2016; Cisco, 2011). Commodity hardware and software appliances are fundamental cloud resources designed to support the enterprise deployment of cloud resources (Alhazmi, Abusharkh, Ban, & Shami, 2014). Both hardware and software solutions are designed to provide a flexible and efficient management between legacy and modern systems (Buyya, Ranjan, Rodrigo, & Calheiros, 2010; Grance & Mell, 2011; Buyya, Ramamohanarao, Leckie, Calhieros, Dastjerdi, & Versteeg, 2015).

In the 1990s vendors began adopting open-source software to support organization and consumer's operation requirements (Buyya, Ranjan, Rodrigo, & Calheiros, 2010; Gartner, 2012; Buyya, Ramamohanarao, Leckie, Calhieros, Dastjerdi, & Versteeg, 2015; Oracle, 2016). In consequence of deployment of open-source software as a product, now organizations have the option to acquire and customize desired applications, required to interact with other IT infrastructure capabilities (Lease, 2005; Grance & Mell, 2011; Alhazmi, et al, 2014). In part, integrated solutions are simplified applications designed to provisioning and enabling dynamic computer as well as server scalability (Lease, 2005; Alhazmi & Shami, 2014; Alhazmi & Shami, 2014; Oracle, 2016; Cisco, 2016). Server virtualization and infrastructure performance are technologies developed to provide self-regulating automation process, multi-tenancy and system resiliency for delivering results to the end-users. Network infrastructure solutions are deployed to provide data centers virtualized network resources, strengthen IT organizations' effectiveness and productivity (Grance & Mell, 2011; Bruening & Treacy, 2009; Oracle, 2016; Cisco, 2011; RedHat, 2016).

PROVISIONING PHYSICAL AND VIRTUAL NETWORKS

Physical and virtual networks concepts date back to traditional and interconnected complex systems deployed to various geographic locations. There are two types of virtual network provisioning: adaptive and initial virtual network provisioning (Oracle, 2016). Adaptive virtual network provisioning is the process of maintaining and managing agile computer resources residing on various network systems (Alhazmi & Shami, 2014; Oracle, 2016). This concept is adopted to support virtual network topologies required to parsing/distributing resources for various physical or virtual computer systems (Vaquero et al., 2009; Vouk, 2008; Chowdhury, Rahman, & Boutaba, 2012; Metzler, 2011; Oracle, 2016; Oracle, 2016; Cisco, 2011; RedHat, 2016).

Database Provisioning

Provisioning is a process that enables agility of IT systems for organizations and consumers. This method is designed to satisfy organizations and customers' requirements. Database provisioning consist of several network resources residing between physical and virtual machines (Badger et al., 2011; Garfinkel, & Shelat, 2003). Thus resource pooling is a major factor in the provisioning of cloud assets (Badger et al., 2011; Alhazmi & Shami, 2014). There are two types of provisioning (dynamic and static). Dynamic provisioning is a self-governing process developed to increase system capacity for multi-layer cloud-based applications. These applications allow for increased system performance (Sen & Sengupta, 2005; Garfinkel & Shelat, 2003; Alhazmi & Shami, 2014; RedHat, 2016). Despite various methods required to support the performance process for larger disk state, database provisioning remains a complex practice. Virtual machines can create a bottleneck when performing functional/intensive compute workload if not correctly configured (Biggs & Vidalis, 2009; Amazon, 2012). There is a difference between database and the legacy web server provisioning. Thereby the need for replicating large workload manually is one of the reasons why database provisioning has transformed from the traditional to automated concept (Badger et al., 2011; Alhazmi & Shami, 2014). A successful provisioning of database requires that system administrators, first define the amount of time required to replicate/synchronize disk state and imagine each replica online. This is attributable to the workload being processed and storage engine configuration (Sen & Sengupta, 2005; Bruening & Treacy, 2009; Alhazmi & Shami, 2014). The following areas are fundamentals for system administrators to know during database, network, dynamic, and static provisioning in the cloud (Biggs & Vidalis, 2009; Buyya, Ranjan, Rodrigo, & Calheiros, 2010; Gartner, 2012; Alhazmi & Shami, 2014; Oracle, 2016; RedHat, 2016; Cisco, 2011):

- When to provision
- How to provision
- Prototype implementation
- Evaluating public, private cloud, hybrid cloud, community cloud platforms

In database provisioning replication is a crucial concept that organizations and consumers must comply with. How data is backed up, restored and/or snapshot could determine the homogenous configuration of database systems in interconnected clusters (Biggs & Vidalis, 2009; Gartner, 2012; Buyya, Ranjan, Rodrigo, & Calheiros, 2010; Badger et al., 2011; Chor et al., 1998).

Network Function Virtualization

Network Function Virtualization (NFC) is a process that commonly manages and supports virtualized technology solutions. In NFV, middleboxes resources are distributed to various networks through software versa hardware-based solutions. In recent years, vendors have designed middleboxes technology to replace NFV (Chowdhury, Rahman, & Boutaba, 2012; Oracle, 2016). In essence, the software was developed to take precedency of provisioning network solutions through commoditized and hardware-based solutions (Chowdhury, Rahman, & Boutaba, 2012; Alhazmi, et al, 2014; Oracle, 2016). These functions are designed to reducing cost and providing responsive processes. Despite the fact much research has been conducted as part of NFV, cloud vendors have elected new technology solutions such as service functions chains and software-defined network solutions (Oracle, 2016; Alhazmi, & Shami, 2014). New investigations indicate that the number of middleboxes deployed to various networks i.e., Internet service providers and data centers parallels to that of physical routers dispersedly in the enterprise (Chowdhury, Rahman, & Boutaba, 2012; Oracle, 2016; Houidi et al., 2010).

Network Provisioning

Provisioning is a process that integrates network infrastructure solutions and streamlines the time system administrators need to deploy, configure, maintain and manage services within the multi-tenancy cloud environments. The main goals for network provisioning are (Oracle, 2016; Cisco, 2011; RedHat, 2016): Reducing latency, increasing throughput and allowing for effective, efficiency, automated and repeatable infrastructure management (Biggs & Vidalis, 2009; Leighon, 2009; Buyya, Ranjan, Rodrigo, & Calheiros, 2010; Oracle, 2016). In these scenarios, the traditional network security systems i.e., firewall, intrusion detection/protection systems, web application firewalls can be displayed as middleboxes (Alhazmi, et al, 2014; Oracle, 2016). The configuration of these systems frequently occurs inside and outside network boundaries. Attributable to continuous adoption of cloud computing technology, innovated network systems are deployed to support the migration of enterprise IT and related multi-tenancy solutions (Chowdhury, Rahman, & Boutaba, 2012; Alhazmi & Shami, 2014; Oracle, 2016). Both physical or virtual networks are designed to perform provisioning process of resources for user's specifications. In physical and virtual networks, the provisioning process involves (Alhazmi, et al, 2014; Chowdhury, Rahman, & Boutaba, 2012; Alhazmi & Shami, 2014; Oracle, 2016):

- Resource and Advertisement
- Resource Discovery and Matching
- Physical and Virtual Network Embedding
- Physical and Virtual Network Binding

Physical and virtual networks are generally deployed and managed as cloud computing technology solutions (Alhazmi & Shami, 2014). These technology solutions 'physical and virtual networks' are designed to satisfy the consumer and organization's requirements. Generally, these networks are divergently distributed via a dynamic provisioning process (Vaquero et al., 2009; Vouk, 2008; Houidi, Louati, Zeghlache, Papadimitriou, & Mathy, 2010). Such activities are attributable to asymmetrical deviations, which could conceivably affect the following: stream of traffics and physical assets. The below Figure 1 outlines different specifications of the virtual network provisioning (Chowdhury, Rahman, & Boutaba, 2012; Alhazmi, et al, 2014; Alhazmi & Shami, 2014; Houidi et al., 2010).

Figure 1. Provisioning of virtual networks
Source: https://orbi.ulg.ac.be/bitstream/2268/126822/1/adaptive_embedding_VISA10.pdf

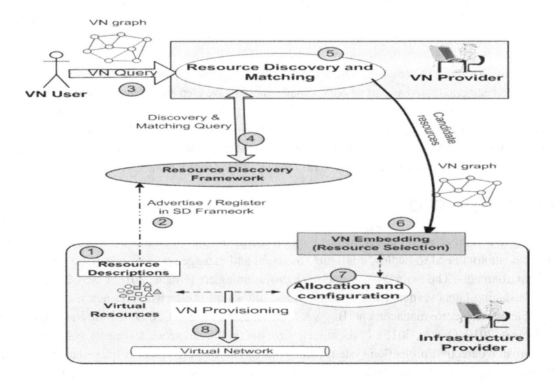

Service Function Chaining

Service Function Chaining (SFC) is a technology that still in its emerging phase. Generally, Service Function Chains (SFCs) are deployed to support the functionality of network devices: firewalls, load balancers are logical functioning (Chowdhury, Rahman, & Boutaba, 2012; Oracle, 2016; Houidi et al., 2010). By and large, SFCs are central technology solutions developed to defining and instantiating network systems as well as interacting with the network (Chowdhury, Rahman, & Boutaba, 2012; Oracle, 2016). SFCs provides data traffic flows through selected service functions. The delivery of end-to-end services can only be processed through the aid of several provision functions. Application-specific service functions are illustrated as hypertext transfer protocols/HTTP header manipulation (Alhazmi & Shami, 2014; Oracle, 2016). Tenants are responsible for delivering service functions (Chowdhury, Rahman, & Boutaba, 2012). This process is described as shared concept involving several groups or users assigned to a single or multiple networks (Vaquero et al., 2009; Vouk, 2008; Chowdhury, Rahman, & Boutaba, 2012; Alhazmi & Shami, 2014; Houidi et al., 2010).

Software-Defined Networking

This network function is a utility designed to streamline SFC embedded technologies (Oracle, 2016). In recent years, vendors have designed software-defined networking/SDN technology as technology to balance NFV and SFC features. The main purpose of this new technology discovery aim at providing efficiency for the flow of data being transported over end-to-end physical and virtual networks (Chowdhury, Rahman, & Boutaba, 2012; Oracle, 2016). In the cloud, NFV and SDN technology solutions are designed with flexible, responsive and sustainable solutions. These solutions are intended to guarantee that instances of virtual network functions are deployed into diverse enterprise IT infrastructures. The end-to-end paths are preconfigured within network systems, to expedite data flow through various network functions (Chowdhury, Rahman, & Boutaba, 2012; Alhazmi, et al, 2014; Houidi et al., 2010).

Network Virtualization Forces

System architects use network virtualization forces to re-examine assumptions when designing network topologies (Houidi et al., 2010). In virtualized network traffic flow and server performance occur faster than in usual external network hardware environment i.e., physical server network interface controller/card, physical switches and routers (Cisco, 2016). The ability to set up and modify virtualized network topologies may disrupt organizational structures dedicated to separate computer, storage and network management (Oracle, 2016; Cisco, 2011; Houidi et al., 2010).

Topology Dependencies

Topology dependencies are services required to deploy single or multiple networks. The process of various cloud services is often by specific, physical and virtual networks. These solutions are called hybrid network topologies. In the virtual local area network or vLANs the firewalls are deployed to normalize the flow of network traffic (Chowdhury, Rahman, & Boutaba, 2012; Alhazmi, et al, 2014). If a firewall is deployed or positioned on a particular network segment through the process of vLAN foundation, data flow is predetermined by the selected path required to balance the traffic flow in the direction of the firewall device. This topology dependence is needed to further enforce upon certain restrictions on functions such as service delivery mechanisms (Chowdhury, Rahman, & Boutaba, 2012; Alhazmi & Shami, 2014). Network operator is prevented from making use of its service resources or decreasing elasticity (Chowdhury, Rahman, & Boutaba, 2012; Houidi et al., 2010). New service functions, such as firewalls are designed with other collation of topology variations tagged to the front and back of each service function. This model allows for complex network changes and device configuration. If properly configured, the firewall will guarantee all traffics sent through meet certain security measures (Chowdhury, Rahman, & Boutaba, 2012; Alhazmi, et al, 2014; Oracle, 2016).

Vendor's Contribution

In recent years, the public and private sectors have experienced seismic shift in operation's activities. Business owners are now able to deploy additional cloud services with better cost-savings. Customers prefer to adopt leased, customized commodity hardware, and application appliances in IT infrastructure environment (Amazon, 2012; Buyya, Ranjan, Rodrigo, & Calheiros, 2010; Buyya, Ramamohanarao, Leckie, Calhieros, Dastjerdi, & Versteeg, 2015; Badger et al., 2011).

CLOUD COMPUTING

The National Institute for Standards and Technology, describes cloud computing as (Badger, Grance, Patt-Corner, & Voas, 2011; Grance & Mell, 2011; Buyya, Ramamohanarao, Leckie, Calhieros, Dastjerdi, & Versteeg, 2015): "a model for enabling convenient, on-demand network access to a shared pool of configurable computing resources (e.g., networks, servers, storage, applications and services) that can be provisioned and released with economical management efforts or service interaction". The advancement of cloud computing solution architecture comprises the following asymmetrical process: networks, inter-networks "Internet", world wide web, grid computing and cloud computing ((Badger, Grance, Patt-Corner, & Voas, 2011). See Figure 2.

Figure 2. Cloud computing evolution and trends
Source: http://ir.lib.uwo.ca/cgi/viewcontent.cgi?article=3713&context=etd

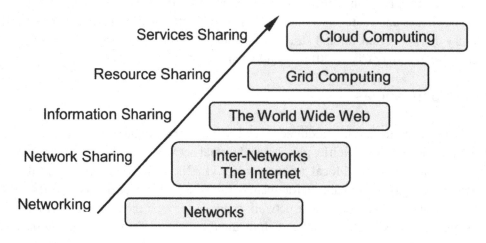

BENEFITS OF PUBLIC AND PRIVATE CLOUD COMPUTING SERVICES

In the public and private sector cloud service providers and/or managed service providers' responsibilities aim to provide key solutions for supporting IT organizations and consumers' day-to-day operations. These service/product offerings are based on selected paradigms organizations and consumers require to achieve business or market demands. Public cloud comprises larger scale services focusing on broader technical standards such as open source solutions (Buyya, Ranjan, Rodrigo, & Calheiros, 2010; Buyya, Ramamohanarao, Leckie, Calhieros, Dastjerdi, & Versteeg, 2015; Pearson, & Charlesworth, 2009; Torry Harris, n.d.). Public cloud services focus on rapid and effective deployment. Cloud service providers are responsible for hardware maintenance and application pooling in support of platform deployment and infrastructure delivery service (Buyya, Ranjan, Rodrigo, & Calheiros, 2010; Gartner, 2015; Gartner, 2012; Blaze et al., 2009). Private cloud services are deployed to specific organizations, where services are directed to organization's capabilities and business trends (Pearson & Charlesworth, 2009; Oracle, 2016; Cisco, 2011; RedHat, 2016). Organizations have far-reaching proprietorship of private cloud and their services (Torry Harris, n.d.). This allows private cloud service providers to specifically tailor their services to conform with customer's requirements. Despite the need for more bandwidth, organizations and consumers are doubting of deploying resources to the cloud, due to security and privacy (Buyya, Ranjan, Rodrigo, & Calheiros, 2010; Buyya, Ramamohanarao, Leckie, Calhieros, Dastjerdi, & Versteeg, 2015; Zhang & Joshi, 2009; Torry Harris, n.d.).

Cloud-Based Architecture

Cloud computing is one of the fastest growing technology developed to support cloud-based service and delivery models (Lease, 2005). The need for resource-sharing, scalability, responsiveness, availability, real-time disposition of resources in the cloud is essential. This process has significant impact on the way IT organizations determine their operations, system performances and upgrades (Ross, 2010; Buyya, Ranjan, Rodrigo, & Calheiros, 2010). Each of these components can be managed, provisioned, deployed and decommissioned through utility-based consumption and allocation model. Cloud architectures are designed to support compute modules (Sen & Sengupta, 2005). These solutions are deployed to data centers for enhancing performance and streamlining provision time as well as restrict access to unauthorized individuals (Buyya, Ramamohanarao, Leckie, Calhieros, Dastjerdi, & Versteeg, 2015; Gartner, 2012; Buyya, Ranjan, Rodrigo, & Calheiros, 2010). There are six key cloud technology features that describe the resource management between cloud services and legacy computing systems: (CSA Security Guidance, 2009)

- Abstraction of Infrastructure(s)
- Resource Democratization
- Service-oriented Architecture
- Elasticity
- Dynamism
- Utility Model of Consumption, Allocation

The basics of cloud-based architecture discussed in this chapter are envisioned to leverage cloud deployment models (Lease, 2005). Cloud deployments models are designed to integrate resources and maintain some level of data provisioning with assigned service models (i.e., IaaS, PaaS, SaaS, DaaS). These analytical solutions entail (Lease, 2005; Buyya, Ramamohanarao, Leckie, Calhieros, Dastjerdi, & Versteeg, 2015; Alhazmi & Shami, 2014):

- Ability to define infrastructure, deployment, skill reduction, capital and operational expenditures, prior to deploying IT resources
- Understanding of data elasticity and resource-processing to determine deployment demands, maintenance and improve bandwidth allowing for scalable system performance
- How to mitigate internal resource capabilities, to sustain compliance, threat management, governance, and related security requirements
- The need to systems with more resources and processes required to support data sources
- Design agile and faster IT solutions, procurement of enhanced prototypes with cost-effective processes

Public Network Systems

Public network systems are technology specifications that can be integrated with public network systems via the Internet. This includes assorted data sources, application services and users. Public network systems consist of exterior bases such as the N data collected to support big data analytics efforts on the Internet. The functions in these components are comprise of: domain network system servers, firewalls, content delivery networks (Gartner, 2012; Buyya, Ranjan, Rodrigo, & Calheiros, 2010; Buyya, Ramamohanarao, Leckie, Calhieros, Dastjerdi, & Versteeg, 2015).

Cloud Data Sources

There are several data sources in the cloud. These data sources include big data systems and data analytics solutions. How investment and risk management can be evaluated often can influence the deployment of cloud data sources in the enterprise. These components comprise the three original characteristics: velocity, volume, variety, and data discrepancy. The data resources, enterprise applications, and cloud user capabilities comprise (Buyya, Ramamohanarao, Leckie, Calhieros, Dastjerdi, & Versteeg, 2015; Gartner, 2009; Gartner, 2012):

- Machine and Sensor Data
- Image and Video
- Social Data
- Internet Data
- Third Part Data
- Self-service
- Visualization
- Edge Services
- Domain Name System Server
- Content Delivery Networks
- Firewalls
- Load Balancer

Cloud Service Providers

For numerous years, cloud service providers have played a vital role in the management of cloud resources. The decision to provisioning resources over the cloud is determined by the administrators assigned to data centers. These components comprise the following (Buyya, Ramamohanarao, Leckie, Calhieros, Dastjerdi, & Versteeg, 2015; Gartner, 2009; Ross, 2010; Amazon, 2012; Alhazmi, & Shami, 2014):

- Data Integration
- Data Repositories
- Streaming Computing
- Transformation, Connectivity

Cloud Elasticity, Fast Provisioning and Scalability

Public and private clients are now able to deploy IT resources needed, to support the enterprise IT infrastructure community at a viable, scalable and reasonably priced rates, without experiencing any system downtime. Storage capacity, allocated time, unlimited demand of resources and data availability are key factors that decide the adoption and/or deployment of resources in the cloud (Ross, 2010; Buyya, Ranjan, Rodrigo, & Calheiros, 2010; Buyya, Ramamohanarao, Leckie, Calhieros, Dastjerdi, & Versteeg, 2015; Everett, 2009). A fast provisioning between physical and virtual servers reduces capital and operational expenditures. Attributable to the implementation of cloud-based solutions, users now appreciate the self-autonomy of data, continuous availability of resources, accessibility of information, fast provisioning, enhanced security, et al (Amazon, 2012; Biggs & Vidalis, 2009; Everett, 2009; Alhazmi & Shami, 2014).

Cloud Elasticity

In cloud elasticity computers are programmable to interact with any changes that can be made affecting the workloads. These changes are expected when an autonomous resource provisioning and de-provisioning process occur within the network infrastructure environments. Autonomous resource provisioning and de-provisioning process occur to guarantee data is extracted and/or processed allowing for computer resources to be distributed consistent with the user's needs.

Cloud Provisioning

Cloud provisioning is a process that selects which applications and services to be made available in the public cloud. This process comprises the resources that stay on-premises behind the firewall or in the private cloud. The method is designed to share resources stored on the service provider's data center and make these assets accessible to customers at the same time (Molnar & Schechter, 2010; Alhazmi & Shami, 2014). In cloud provisioning, providers are responsible for evaluating and determining any acceptance of requests made by customers (Alhazmi & Shami, 2014). Such processes are done by creating a number of virtual machines to support the client's requests. This method is needed to deliver an array of cloud computing services to customers (Molnar & Schechter, 2010; Alhazmi & Shami, 2014). In the provisioning sequence, desired solutions or methods are targeted at arraying and incorporating cloud services as well as deployment models (Gellman, 2009, Leavitt, 2009; Alhazmi & Shami, 2014). Cloud computing provisioning comprises: server, user, database, network, self-service mobile subscriber, Internet access and mobile content provisioning (Zetter, 2010; Grance & Mell, 2011; Gruschka & Iacono, 2009; Molnar & Schechter, 2010; Zimory, 2009). The provisioning of cloud computing solutions helps integrating policies, techniques and IT objectives for related sourcing cloud services, along with other technology solutions. These services or solutions are provided by both cloud service provider and managed service provider (Ross, 2010; Badger, Grance, Patt-Corner, & Voas, 2011; Pearson, 2009; Shacham & Waters, 2009). Cloud computing provisioning consists of tagging, dispensing and making available IT assets to support organizations' day-to-day operations (Pearson, 2009). When customers initiate requests to cloud service providers or managed service providers and these requests are accepted; for that reason, an applicable number of virtual machines and resources must be identified and made accessible to support such an operation (Ross, 2010; Gartner, 2012; Badger, Grance, Patt-Corner, & Voas, 2011; Grance & Mell, 2011; Gellman, 2009; Alhazmi & Shami, 2014).

Cloud provisioning is the provisioning or sharing of requested resources from the Internet service provider to IT organizations or customers. These activities are performed when the customer and/ or an IT organization submits the request to the ISP for approval. Once the approval is reviewed and processed, the provisioning of data or resources is granted. Cloud provisioning is performed through a proportionate assistance of virtual provisioning cloud administrators and/or virtual provisioning operators, who are responsible to monitor and regulate user requests. VMs are responsible for provisioning or distributing resources between ISPs and identified customers, from whom respective requests were generated. Vendor's Technologies such as Amazon EC2, Microsoft Azure, Google Engine Manager and IBM SoftLayer are used to provisioning or distributing data from several ISPs to elected IT organizations or customers. During cloud provisioning the following specifications are monitored: virtualization system abstraction; VM reuse and configuration, controlled lease time, programmed cost regulation, improved service catalog interface, role-based access, the need for dedicated service portals, complete integration of serviceNow platform.

CRITERIA FOR EFFECTIVE PUBLIC AND PRIVATE SECTOR CLOUD ADOPTION

The adoption of cloud computing services is a major topic in many public and private sectors. The adoption of cloud computing consists of the below six major criteria. These point of reference underline the main criteria for effective public and private sector cloud computing adoption (Buyya, Ranjan, Rodrigo, & Calheiros, 2010; Buyya, Ramamohanarao, Leckie, Calhieros, Dastjerdi, & Versteeg, 2015; Sims, 2009; Grance & Mell, 2011; Ristenpart et al., 2009). The six criteria comprise (Grance & Mell, 2011; Gartner, 2012):

- **Agility:** A service that is applied to dynamic infrastructure management "orchestration". The service allows agile deployment and system scalability. Agile services are designed to reduce the deployment of solutions, while providing sustained time management
- **Security:** Consist of trusted and secure cloud-based services required to apply the defense-in-depth measures. These measures are vital in preventing information disclosure to unauthorized users. This service is provided to prevent, repudiate and minimize data tampering and guarantee infrastructure integrity

- **Dependability:** This service guarantees for streamlined performance and reliability, compliance and service level agreement
- **Open:** This service is designed to implement benchmarks needed to advance interoperability, portability, through mixed conditions
- **Transparent:** This service offers the public and private sector alongside stakeholders, the ability to parallel, monitor, and audit balancing books
- **Aware:** Designed for capitalizing on several embedded service offerings in the cloud infrastructure. These services are hosted and provisioned to assorted computing systems. When provisioned, users are able to access these services in real-time

Enterprise Network Systems

Enterprise networks are applications required to transport complex business solutions over the Internet. These systems support IT platforms and network infrastructure solutions. The services are designed to support data storage and network systems in the enterprise. Comparatively, enterprise network systems involve the following components (Ross, 2010; Gartner, 2012; Buyya, Ramamohanarao, Leckie, Calhieros, Dastjerdi, & Versteeg, 2015; Amazon, 2012):

- Reference Data
- Master Data
- Transitional Data
- Application Data
- Log Data
- Enterprise Content Data
- Historical Data

Cloud Computing Service Models

Consistent with NIST the following are three government approved cloud computing service models (Badger, Grance, Patt-Corner, & Voas, 2011; Bruening & Treacy, 2009):

- **IaaS**: A method through which vendors could manage the system performance 'power' and the amount of storage, to support customers in the public and private sector. This service is capable of providing the performance and storage required to house data
- **PaaS**: Services to users via the cloud services. These services can be developed and provisioned in real-time and/or through a configuration-based system
- **SaaS**: Pay-per-use application services to diverse IT and business communities. This application can be leased from cloud service providers. Users benefit by leasing the services from cloud service providers, rather than managing application resources in-house. Salesforce, Zoho, Google, Amazon, Yahoo are demonstrated examples of SaaS

Managing IT resources is challenging and requires continuous planning, sustainable capital resources and operational assets necessary, to scale cloud-based infrastructure and platforms. IT issues must be resolved prior to adopting cloud-based solutions (Armbrust et al., 2009; Buyya, Ramamohanarao,

Figure 3. Cloud service models
Source: http://www.thbs.com/downloads/Cloud-Computing-Overview.pdf

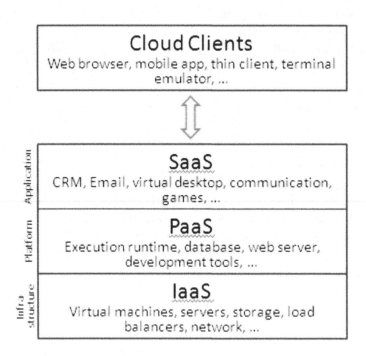

Leckie, Calhieros, Dastjerdi, & Versteeg, 2015). These models influence application, server and network provisioning. These models enable users the tools necessary to forecast the provisioning of computing resources, needed to produce desirable results in the workplace (Lease, 2005; Torry Harris, n.d.). Technical experts select the best strategies, to support enterprise IT infrastructure. These strategies are key in reducing redundancy other business and technical constraints (Armbrust et al., 2009; Buyya, Ranjan, Rodrigo, & Calheiros, 2010; Torry Harris, n.d.). The below Figure 3 describes the cloud service models and respective characteristics (Alhazmi & Shami, 2014).

CLOUD DEPLOYMENT

Cloud Computing Deployment Models

models are infrastructure-based. The models are developed to store and protect data. When engineered with service models, these solutions are capable of storing, provisioning and supplying larger data loads from/to various data center end points in real-time (Armbrust et al., 2009; Buyya, Ranjan, Rodrigo, & Calheiros, 2010; Buyya, Ramamohanarao, Leckie, Calhieros, Dastjerdi, & Versteeg, 2015; Torry Harris, n.d.):

- **Private Cloud**: The cloud-based solutions are delivered to single or multiple organizations exclusively. As such, every organization has the autonomous right to manage its provisioned solutions

- **Public Cloud**: This cloud-based technology allows users the ability to manage resources via the cloud service providers. Cloud-based services may be sold individually, despite the availability of these solutions that can be provisioned to enterprises and their respective users
- **Hybrid Cloud**: These are cloud-based solutions provisioned from physical and virtual data centers. The data stored in private servers is shared with several users residing in the public domain to guarantee end-users have the policy and rights to access data through selective provisioning
- **Community Cloud**: Cloud-based solutions provisioned to support single or multiple communities. Despite complex provisioning, this service is offered to support the public and private sector users. These services are frequently monitored by a single and/or multiple cloud service providers

Cloud Computing and Database Platforms

These cloud-based database central mechanisms are key in providing the public and private sector with assets needed to support their day-to-day operations. Below is a list of vendor's approved cloud-based platforms (Gartner, 2009; Gartner, 2012):

- Amazon Web Services - Elastic Compute Cloud
- Oracle Cloud Solutions
- Hewlett Packard Cloud Services
- IBM Cognitive Cloud
- Cisco Platforms
- Microsoft Cloud Services
- Intel Cloud Services
- Google Cloud Services
- Yahoo Cloud Services
- Government Cloud
- Dell Cloud

The below Figure 4 illustrates the four cloud computing deployment models.

Public Sector

Cloud computing technology has transformed how public sector adopts and deploys cloud services. Such technical deviations have affected the way cloud services are delivered in both physical and virtual environments. How cloud services are deployed often guarantees the availability, agility, scalability, reliability, dependency, sustainability and overall security of network infrastructure solutions (Grance & Mell, 2011). Lacking such services could influence how resources are deployed in various organizations (Lease, 2005). These resources consist of: servers, compute nodes, network appliances, applications, storage and network systems. Public clouds comprise broad-spectrum computing systems (Buyya, Ranjan, Rodrigo, & Calheiros, 2010; Gartner, 2012; Buyya, Ramamohanarao, Leckie, Calhieros, Dastjerdi, & Versteeg, 2015). Apart from these adoptions and security barriers, vendors believe that improved security best practices are required to address any level of threats or vulnerability concerns, minimize capital expenditures and operational expenditures (Grance & Mell, 2011; Gartner, 2012; Buyya, Ramamohanarao, Leckie, Calhieros, Dastjerdi, & Versteeg, 2015). The benefits cloud computing offers to

Figure 4. Cloud computing deployment models
Source: www.csrc.nist.gov/groups/SNS/cloud-computing/index.html

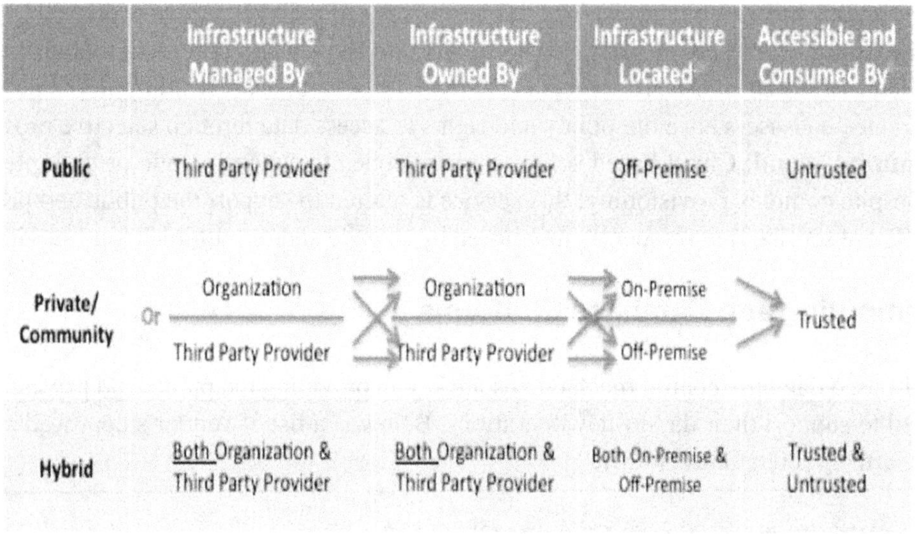

	Infrastructure Managed By	Infrastructure Owned By	Infrastructure Located	Accessible and Consumed By
Public	Third Party Provider	Third Party Provider	Off-Premise	Untrusted
Private/ Community	Or Organization / Third Party Provider	Organization / Third Party Provider	On-Premise / Off-Premise	Trusted
Hybrid	Both Organization & Third Party Provider	Both Organization & Third Party Provider	Both On-Premise & Off-Premise	Trusted & Untrusted

information technology engineers and managers in the public-sector are fundamental to organizations' mission-critical and operational posture (Buyya, Ranjan, Rodrigo, & Calheiros, 2010; Gartner, 2012; Buyya, Ramamohanarao, Leckie, Calhieros, Dastjerdi, & Versteeg, 2015). In an organization the adoption of virtual desktop services is envisioned to redefine the posture and how the public sector may benefit from this technology. The provisioning of agile, available, scalable, reliable and secure desktop applications encourages probe of new practical solutions. On occasion Chief Information Officers (CIOs) benefit from the deployment of cloud-based solutions. The solutions are designed to administrate the trade-offs and balance IT resources after being deployed to the cloud (Buyya, Ranjan, Rodrigo, & Calheiros, 2010; Stanton et al., 2005; Buyya, Ramamohanarao, Leckie, Calhieros, Dastjerdi, & Versteeg, 2015; Golden 2009). Cloud computing technology guarantees the scalability of systems in multi-tenant environments. Public sector requires more bandwidth to support the provisioned workload (Grance & Mell, 2011; Stanton et al., 2005; Buyya, Ranjan, Rodrigo, & Calheiros, 2010; Buyya, Ramamohanarao, Leckie, Calhieros, Dastjerdi, & Versteeg, 2015). Capital and operational expenditures are key factors for determining bandwidth cost apportionment in the cloud. The lack of suitable asset scalability in the cloud is critical to how systems respond and execute each task in the physical and virtual environment (Grance & Mell, 2011; Golden, 2009).

Private Sector

The adoption or deployment of cloud services in the private sector is essential to several IT organizations. The benefits can be determined by the economic growth opportunities, trade-offs, cost-effectiveness, enhanced security, economies of scale and new policies. Cloud computing offers information technology engineers, managers and organizations an integrated computing architecture. This architecture is designed to support system interoperability and dependency. Integrated computing architecture is the model through which consumers in the private sector describe the need to select several resources from several distributed computing environments (Buyya, Ranjan, Rodrigo, & Calheiros, 2010; Gartner, 2012; Buyya, Ramamohanarao, Leckie, Calhieros, Dastjerdi, & Versteeg, 2015). This model allows for provisioning and balancing management resources and ensures these solutions are central factors on how resources are deployed and secured. How such resources are distributed to consumers is based on higher provisioning practices required to support multiple-tier cloud platforms. Users are able to access and share data from virtual sources via the Internet (Buyya, Ranjan, Rodrigo, & Calheiros, 2010; Buyya, Ramamohanarao, Leckie, Calhieros, Dastjerdi, & Versteeg, 2015; Lease, 2005). Aside from several advantages customers have in the private sector, managers are inclined to reevaluate capital and operational expenditures, when adopting cloud services. How much budget an organization has would certainly determine the agility, reliability, scalability and dependability of services in the cloud. Security, agility, reliability, scalability and reliability always regulate the level of complexity designers, developers, information technology engineers and managers would need, when adopting/deploying cloud services (Alhazmi & Shami, 2014). Cloud computing technology is designed and deployed to support small, medium and large scale business communities. With cloud computing technology, businesses could scale to larger computer environments without significant capital and operational costs (Grance & Mell, 2011).

Data Integrity and Protection

Data integrity involves the complexity and consistency required to attribute a validity and accurateness of data composition. This process involves data back-ups and archives. Customers in the public and private sectors seek solutions to maintain record retention trends. These trends include the metadata needed to reconstruct attributes. Record-keeping procedures are accentuated concepts, which organizations implement to protect data from being corrupted or compromised (Buyya, Ramamohanarao, Leckie, Calhieros, Dastjerdi, & Versteeg, 2015; Sen & Sengupta, 2005; Alhazmi & Shami, 2014). In the public and private sector decision markers, put into effect security policies and procedures to protect organizations' data. Such procedures are necessary to protect IT infrastructure resources in the public private sector.

In recent years, there has been significant issues affecting data integrity and how organizations must conform to security requirements (Sen & Sengupta, 2005; Gartner, 2009; Gartner, 2012). Lacking security best practices in customized commodity e.g., hardware and software peripherals is a key factor to infrastructure security (Badger et al., 2011). Both the public and private sector are facing numerous challenges, when preparing to adapt new cloud computing solutions in on-premises or off-premises. Vendors working on optimum solutions required to redefine these security issues. The provisioning of physical and virtual machine systems is an essential topic to public and private customers (Sen & Sengupta, 2005; Buyya, Ranjan, Rodrigo, & Calheiros, 2010; Buyya, Ramamohanarao, Leckie, Calhieros, Dastjerdi, & Versteeg, 2015). Prior studies indicate the need for vendors to develop advanced solutions to moderate these technology limitations is fundamental. To attract a large number of customers in the public and private sectors an important determination in industry must be adopted whether by researching, developing solutions, and upgrading the existing hardware/software to attract the client's interest (Ross, 2010; Buyya, Ranjan, Rodrigo, & Calheiros, 2010; Buyya, Ramamohanarao, Leckie, Calhieros, Dastjerdi, & Versteeg, 2015). The primary tasks of data centers comprise the following (Buyya, Ramamohanarao, Leckie, Calhieros, Dastjerdi, & Versteeg, 2015; Amazon, 2012; Biggs & Vidalis, 2009; Buyya, Ranjan, Rodrigo, & Calheiros, 2010; Alhazmi & Shami, 2014):

- **Provisioning**: A process of deploying network equipment, via virtualized servers
- **Management**: A method that could influence on both strategic and operational decisions. After selected hardware is deployed and/or configured system administrators and engineers must begin monitoring or maintaining the management of the IT environment
- **Orchestration**: A process for managing data center infrastructure explicitly, servers, storage and others. The synchronization of computing systems for example storage and associated network equipment is what defines the orchestration process in the network environment

DATA CENTER EVOLUTION AND TRENDS

In recent decades, data centers experienced legacy "client-server" technology transformations. Business needs increased, due to the adoption of physical and virtual data centers (Grance & Mell, 2011; Song, Wagner, & Perrig, 2000; Kant, 2009). Data centers are designed to fulfil business or client requirements. The process involves agility, efficiency, scalability, availability, fast provisioning and virtualization (Kant, 2009). Server virtualization is designed to provide IT managers with the tool needed to tackle various IT challenges such as minimize capital and operational expenditures (Grance & Mell, 2011; Shin & Ahn, 2005; Takabi, Joshi, & Ahn, 2005; Kant, 2009). The integration of compute infrastructure, self-governing tools, and management systems has yield significant effects between services and infrastructure (Grance & Mell, 2011; Buyya, et al, 2015; Petry, 2007; Song, Wagner, & Perrig, 2000). Figure 5 describes the data center evolution and trends (Alhazmi & Shami, 2014; Kant, 2009).

Figure 5. Data center evolution and trends
Source: http://bnrg.cs.berkeley.edu/~randy/Courses/CS294.S13/1.3.pdf

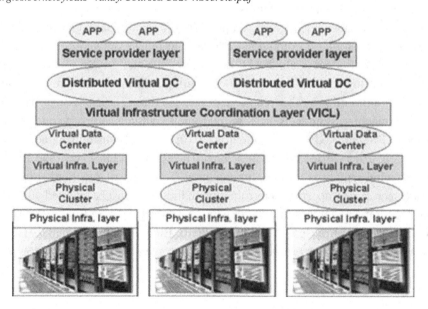

Aside from these trends in cloud technology, data centers require high performance computing infrastructure to operate (Golden, 2009). Despite these processes and configuration theories, programing developers, engineers and managers in both public and private sectors are concerned about the lack of expertise to support the IT network infrastructure (Grance & Mell, 2011; Lease, 2005; Golden, 2009; Kant, 2009). To improve the IT infrastructure performance, reduce any constraints in data center operations, vendors must develop enterprise solutions, responsive processes and best practices (Grance & Mell, 2011; Gartner, 2012; Buyya, Ranjan, Rodrigo, & Calheiros, 2010; Buyya, Ramamohanarao, Leckie, Calhieros, Dastjerdi, & Versteeg, 2015; Oracle, 2016; Cisco, 2011; Kant, 2009).

Data Center Automation

In recent years, data center automation has regained its market presence in the public and private sectors (Ross, 2010). Vendors are committed to develop optimal cloud-based platforms that is, virtualization, provisioning and synchronization to sustain such enterprise transformation. For instance, demilitarized zones in the cloud environment have proven automated data centers are more agile, secure, reliable, scalable and cost effective (Leighon, 2009; Badger et al., 2011). Virtualization occurs at (Grance & Mell, 2011; Gartner, 2012; Ross, 2010; Alhazmi & Shami, 2014; Kant, 2009):

- System Level (i.e., Java Virtual Machine or .NET CLRs)
- Machine Level (e.g., VMware, Citrix)
- Network Level (e.g., Virtual Private Networks)
- Database Level (e.g., Delphix)
- Entire data center level (e.g., Nutanex)
- Cloud Computing level (i.e., public, private and hybrid cloud; IaaS, PaaS, SaaS)

Data Center Security Challenges

Lacking security procedures to protect data centers' core infrastructure and resources could result in major challenges for organizations and customers. Data centers are one of the major targets hackers could launch cyber-attacks against. There are many methods hackers or intruders use to gain access beyond organization's security perimeters. Such process can be accomplished by a series of exploitations intruders frequently perform in an effort to increase access to the network infrastructure solutions (Lease, 2010; Takabi, Joshi, & Ahn, 2005). As a result of these types of threats, decision makers in the public and private sector urge vendors, to improve their solutions designed to deter, retract and defend organizations' vital resources (Gartner, 2012; Buyya, Ranjan, Rodrigo, & Calheiros, 2010; Buyya, Ramamohanarao, Leckie, Calhieros, Dastjerdi, & Versteeg, 2015; Sinclair, & Smith, 2008). Vendors are designing front-line solutions e.g., VMware NSX, to support customer's enterprise IT resources. VMware NSX is a tool required to provide network virtualization resources on data centers. Thus VMware is a trusted solution designed to provide detection, analytics and responsive controls required for protecting the infrastructure network resources. In part, VMware is a tool designed with cutting-edge features and/ or capabilities to thwart vulnerabilities and threats. Additionally, the features are needed to detect and prevent malware propagation inside data centers and related cloud-based platforms (Sen & Sengupta, 2005): hypervisors, virtual switches. The NSX distributed firewalls are programmable applications that inspect horizontal traffic (end-to-end) amid VMware systems deployed in the data centers (Sinclair & Smith, 2008).

Data Center Virtualization

In recent years, VMware products have transformed virtualization. As a consequence, virtualization is a theory that has existed for many decades (Oracle, 2016; Cisco, 2011, RedHat, 2016). In the past VMware technology was incorporated by industry, to ensure that high performance computers can process large quantity of data (Oracle, 2016; Cisco, 2011). Nearly ten years ago, industry reinstated the virtualization technology, to guarantee for system, storage and network convergence as well as real-time resource provisioning. The lack of improved security measures has encouraged vendors to adopt newer solutions to improve the security of IT platform and infrastructures (Buyya, Ranjan, Rodrigo, & Calheiros, 2010). For instance, virtualization technology is a modeling for which virtualized systems are adopted (Alhazmi & Shami, 2014; Oracle, 2016; Cisco, 2011). These virtualized systems were designed to support analytic performance models: server consolidation, virtual machine monitor, transaction processing monitor, batching, testing, hardware performance, mapping of virtual to physical disks, central processing unit/ CPU processing, workload variance, load balancing, legacy application stance (Biggs & Vidalis, 2009). The management and optimization of virtualization systems i.e., oracle/Sun Microsystems virtual box, IBM, and VMware products is/are essential on how customers manage IT resources (Biggs & Vidalis, 2009). Virtualization is an enabling platform that simplifies IT resources. This process mostly provides a higher level of abstraction (Leighon, 2009). Abstraction simplifies system's operation, while disconnecting physical dependences (Buyya, Ranjan, Rodrigo, & Calheiros, 2010; Oracle, 2016; Cisco, 2011).

Desktop Virtualization

The outright concept involving desktop virtualization remains a major challenge to numerous IT organizations and consumers. In desktop virtualization the limited management of applications through IT enterprise is prodigious to cloud administrators and developers. Such challenges are prone to significant increase of applications needed to preserve IT organizations' production, business continuity operations and corporate growth opportunities and/or margins (Metzler, 2011; Oracle, 2016; Cisco, 2011; RedHat, 2016). The operational constraints have compelled IT organizations to implement daily project/operational functions that are outside of their regular business missions and scopes. Beneath is a list of extra activities that organizations need perform to sustain their operational postures (Metzler, 2011; Oracle, 2016; Cisco, 2011):

- Provisioning new requests or desktop systems
- Repairing desktop machines along with random updates of software
- Guarding platforms and complex infrastructure from unsolicited users
- Providing continuous service desk support to sustain infrastructure environment and platform performance
- Conforming with inner organization requirements, code of practice and guidelines as relating to the PC environment & measurability or continuous monitoring against both inside and outside threats

Network Virtualization

The integrated method network virtualization offers to public and private sectors is key in defining organization success. The benefit of the operating system provisioned techniques allows for the creation and configuration of virtual networks that can be separated from regular physical network. Physical networks are used as a backbone to forward packets on the networks (Oracle, 2016; Cisco, 2011; RedHat, 2016). In essence, virtual networks are comprised of a single or multiple systems using VMs and zones with one or more network interface(s). These interface(s) are configured through a physical network interface card or vNIC (Oracle, 2016). Whether are located on the same network or dispersed locations vNIC are capable to seamlessly communicate. This process allows VMs to talk to each other, while connected to a same host machine (Oracle, 2016; Cisco, 2011). In network virtualization the convergence of hardware and software resources e.g., physical and virtual resources is vital to the organization's day-to-day operations (Oracle, 2016). In network virtualization multiple VMs have the ability to perform multiple or simultaneous activities in a single physical machine (Oracle, 2016). The concept also allows for VMs to run independently on several instances as well as performing functions on a single physical machine (Oracle, 2016; Cisco, 2011). Virtualization technology provide servers, firewalls, routers, switches the ability to run independently. This exempts organizations from acquiring or procuring extra network hardware (Metzler, 2011; Oracle, 2016; Cisco, 2011). For several decades, network virtualization has been used in the following technology scenarios (Oracle, 2016; Cisco, 2011): production, testing, prototyping, designing, and deployment of novel solutions. Network virtualization consists of the following (Metzler, 2011; Oracle, 2016; Cisco, 2011):

- **Platform Virtualization**: (e.g., assert and network virtualization)
- **Network Virtualization**: (e.g., virtualized process that supports external and internal compute methods)
- **Wireless Virtualization**: (e.g., spectrum distribution, infrastructure and air crossing point virtualization). This process is parallel to network virtualization. In the wired virtualization, many Internet service providers are accountable for the day-to-day operations of their corresponding physical network infrastructure solutions. Wireless network virtualization includes physical wireless systems, for instance radio assets, which can be abstracted or secluded to support frequent virtual machines
- **Peripheral "External" Virtualization**: Single or multiple local networks known as LANs. Generally, the LANs are segmented into virtual network platforms needed to perform various activities in support of larger network systems e.g., data centers
- **Inner "Internal" Virtualization**: Designed to syndicate one or more software containers (e.g., Xen hypervisor control programs or quasi crossing points); for example, the virtual network interface controllers. The goal is to interact with physical networks with software. Internal virtualization is designed to augment one or multiple systems' performance through the process of segregating applications to various dispersed containers or virtual crossing points

In recent years, vendors e.g., Citrix, Microsoft, Vyatta have manufactured computer-generated systems and protocol stacks. The purpose of these virtual networks and protocol stacks is designed to converge complex solutions: routers, firewalls and virtual private network utilities (Buyya, Ranjan, Rodrigo, & Calheiros, 2010). These functions are then combined with Citrix NetScaler load balancer, outlet repeaters e.g., Wide Area Networks (WAN) optimizers as well as Secure Socket Layers (SSLs) for virtual private network systems (Buyya, Ranjan, Rodrigo, & Calheiros, 2010). OpenSolaris networks comprise virtualized systems designed to providing load balancing between VPNs, LANs and WANs. This model is described as "network in a box" technique designed to support the x86 systems. Any of these containers can seamlessly perform in wide-ranging operating systems/machines (i.e., Microsoft windows, Linux). These operating systems are also designed to interact with network interface controllers. This process is performed through a sustained availability, applicability and operation computerization of resources deployed to the physical and virtual environments (Lease, 2005; Oracle, 2016; Cisco, 2011). VMware solutions are designed to provide the industry, public and private sector customers with the capability needed, to redefine virtualized infrastructure-based technology postures. In general, VMware is a reliable solution that delivers scalable support to diverse clients in the public and private sectors (Buyya, Ranjan, Rodrigo, & Calheiros, 2010; Grance & Mell, 2011; Gartner, 2012; Buyya, Ramamohanarao, Leckie, Calhieros, Dastjerdi, & Versteeg, 2015; Oracle, 2016; Cisco, 2011).

Virtualization Challenges

In modern days, server infrastructure, resource-enablement, optimization, and dynamic dataload management are perceived as key challenges for the overall process (Buyya, Ranjan, Rodrigo, & Calheiros, 2010; Buyya, Ramamohanarao, Leckie, Calhieros, Dastjerdi, & Versteeg, 2015; Ross, 2010). Virtualization overhaul occurs when the network fails to perform its activities (Oracle, 2016; Cisco, 2011). This also arises when hardware components require immediate remediation to prevent further outage. Such activities include the reliability, cost-effectiveness (Oracle, 2016; Cisco, 2011). There are five types of hardware virtualization: complete virtualization/virtual machine model, partial virtualization, storage virtualization and client virtualization. The following is a list of some of the challenges that virtualization technology poses to IT organizations (Oracle, 2016; Cisco, 2011; Rajalakshmi, Srinandhini, & Uma, 2015):

- **Argumentative Management of vSwithes**: A method of managing vSwitch systems or virtualized network assets. This concept comprises a single or multiple application-based computer-generated switches. Yet this model is designed to boost one or more network layers to data center or local area network settings. The overall process can be challenging when assigned to administrators its yielding a degree of system anomalies e.g., from planning, executing and system degradation
- **Failure of System Structure and Monitoring Tools**: The range of tasks or activities assigned to the administrators can be prodigious to network configuration and divergences. Often such deviations, can range from system configuration process that administrators require to ensure/guarantee for data center's agility and optimum performance. Lacking such practical network functions could result in noticeable dynamic network degradation and/or virtual machine performance
- **Multiple Hypervisors and Difference in Functionality**: For several years, VMware was the main vendor for hypervisors in wide-reaching technology or computer/hardware industry. VMware remains one of the few technology leading companies in the designing of hypervisor hardware/software. Recently, there has been other vendors i.e., Citrix, Red Hat and Microsoft that also have launched similar versions of hypervisor hardware and storage systems. In recent years, some of these vendors have designed and transformed their respective versions of hypervisor hardware and software applications i.e., Xen, Kernel-based virtual machines and Hyper-V

- **Virtual Machine-to-Virtual Device Traffic Flow Discernibility**: The initial product of vSwitches was designed with limited or inadequate network traffic flow features. By contrast, the physical access switches are designed with limited features. Such technical limitations are due to the lack of security features, to support all server-domain activities within the virtualized network environment

- **Dynamic Infrastructure Management**: The process encompassing the dynamic virtualized network settings. Active infrastructure administration is a process which administrators bank on from complex scalability vantage point, to unified domain name system, dynamic host configuration protocol and Internet process address management solutions. DNS, DHCP or IPAM are protocols designed to aggregate database resources. The process is designed to prevent system administrators from managing records located in various sites without prior permission

- **Multiple Troubleshootings on a Per-Virtual Device Source**: In recent years, IT organizations have adopted other computing performances known as "n-tier" applications. The four-tier application consist of: web servers, application servers, database servers and web browsers. In the past, the performance of these applications was infrequent to the organization's efficiency. Lacking collaboration among cloud administrators, end-users and/or managers could affect the organization's day-to-day operations and productivity

- **Distributed Virtual Switching**: This process includes vSwitches built with merged system boards. This process also allows for the adaptation and administration of vSwitches' control planes with contiguous alterations with virtual server systems

- **Planning and Provisioning**: In planning and provisioning of resources adaptive and provisioning methods are required to support everyday tasks performed manually. Some of these tasks are now provisioned through a unique physical or dynamic controller. This is also viewed as a capacity designed to support virtualization services. Yet, more than half of IT organizations are beginning to espouse desktop virtualization in their respective industries. The concept further advances organization's productivity, and lessening capital or operational expenditures e.g., procedures, policies, and security specifications needed to maintain data center functionality, while providing robust information protection. Consequently, there are two rudiments of desktop virtualization processes: client-side application to desktop virtualization and server-side application to desktop virtualization

- **Server Resources Over Subscription**: As virtual machines escalate, the return-on-investment aligned with the server virtualization has an affinity to spiral as well. This is viewed as a balanced flow of both virtual machines and the CPU sequences allowing for the increase of traffic flow via application-based virtual switches: the complex the percentage rotation of physical machines or CPUs with ability to sustain the VMs application performance

- **Edge Virtual Bridges**: Eccentric procedures developed to support this model and sustain the edge virtual bridges. This method further segments multiple network devices through various virtual software-based topology

- **Physical Network Reconfiguration to Provision VM Migration**: The dependency of on-demand computing staging for virtual machines and/or physical servers can be resolute by data centers' dispersed locations. Recently, vendors have designed better virtual server management systems, to support the migration process of virtual machines. In recent decade, pervasive challenges in the quality of service, access control lists and firewalls have resulted in insufficient transferal of

Figure 6. Hardware virtualization process
Source: http://www.ijircce.com/upload/2015/october/69_A%20Technical.pdf

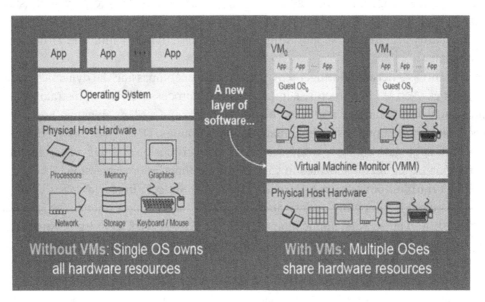

VM systems, to new locations. Yet cloud administrators are concerned with the amount of time required to physically configure and/or migrate VMs

- **Varying Network Plan Enforcement**: Traditional vSwitches are designed with limited hardware/software specifications, needed to support large data capacities and traffic flow as well as providing suitable computational mechanisms between segmented and virtual data centers. This includes VLANs, the quality of service and/or far-reaching access control lists. In the event that some of these capabilities are to be supported by vSwitches, administrators are responsible for physically configuring each machine. The process is performed through virtual server management application console. The anticipated features must be configured and/or attuned to support the physical access switches. This diagram (Figure 6) displays a wide-ranging virtualization processes.

In the network infrastructure layer, virtualization process is performed beyond the server hardware (Gorelik, 2013). The migration of CC technology enables data centers, the ability to interact with multi-tenant virtual systems (Grance & Mell, 2011; Buyya, Ranjan, Rodrigo, & Calheiros, 2010; Buyya, Ramamohanarao, Leckie, Calhieros, Dastjerdi, & Versteeg, 2015). Virtualization management overhaul is a range of architecture solutions that consists of: (Grance & Mell, 2011; Ross, 2010; Grance & Mell, 2011; Buyya, Ranjan, Rodrigo, & Calheiros, 2010; Buyya, Ramamohanarao, Leckie, Calhieros, Dastjerdi, & Versteeg, 2015; Cisco, 2011; Oracle, 2016; RedHat, 2016; Rajalakshmi, Srinandhini, & Uma, 2015)

- VMware ESX/GSX Server(s)
- VMware Virtual Machine File System(s)
- VMware Virtual Symmetric Multi-Processing
- VirtualCenter Management Server(s)
- Virtual Infrastructure Client

- Virtual Infrastructure Web Access
- VMware VMotion
- VMware High Availability
- VMware Distributed Resource Scheduler
- VMware Consolidated Backup(s)
- VMware Infrastructure SDK
- Citrix–Xen
- Citrix (i.e., Xenserver and Xensource)
- Microsoft (i.e., Microsoft Hyper-V "formerly known as windows server virtualization")
- Oracle (i.e., Virtual Machines)
- Novel
- Read Hat
- Parallels
- Amazon
- GoGrid
- IBM
- Joyent
- Carpathia
- Rackspace
- Hewlett Packard
- NetApp
- Cisco

In recent decades, vendors have developed security solutions to address challenges affecting the day-to-day performance of both private and public sector's data centers (Sen & Sengupta, 2005; Gorelik, 2013). These security solutions are developed to scan, detect and analyze any connections between processes and hypervisors (Takabi, Joshi, & Ahn, 2005). The solutions consist of the following components (Gartner, 2012; Buyya, Ramamohanarao, Leckie, Calhieros, Dastjerdi, & Versteeg, 2015; Rajalakshmi, Srinandhini, & Uma, 2015; Chen, n.d.; Gorelik, 2013):

- Secure Virtual Machine(s)
- Analysis and Inspection Engine
- Centralized Management Components

The below Figure 7 describes the core architecture concept of VMware NSX virtualization architecture (Chen, n.d.; Gorelik, 2013).

Dynamic Applications

Dynamic applications are programing languages designed to perform several tasks on the network. Dynamic applications consist of: server, network, platform, container-level and database scalability (Buyya, Ranjan, Rodrigo, & Calheiros, 2010; Gartner, 2012; Gorelik, 2013). Scalability is a capability that consists of networks, systems and processes. This capability is deployed to support customer's day-to-day operations. These capabilities are developed to support large amount of workloads (Gartner, 2012; Buyya,

Figure 7. VMware NSX virtualization architecture
Source: http://www.mit.edu/~caoj/pub/doc/jcao_j_netsec.pdf

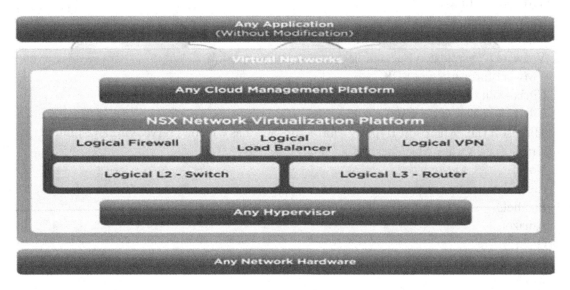

Ranjan, Rodrigo, & Calheiros, 2010; Buyya, Ramamohanarao, Leckie, Calhieros, Dastjerdi, & Versteeg, 2015). Dynamic applications are defined as the base of advanced network computing resources. In the cloud, scalability plays a key role; particularly on how services, platforms and infrastructure share data in real-time (Itani, Kayssi, & Chehab, 2009). The following is a list that integrates numerous scalability models involving dynamic applications (Gartner, 2012; Ross, 2010; Buyya, Ramamohanarao, Leckie, Calhieros, Dastjerdi, & Versteeg, 2015; Gorelik, 2013):

- Server Scalability
- Network Scalability
- Platform Scalability
- Container-level Scalability
- Database Scalability

Dynamic scalability was added to the evolution of virtual machine technology. While scalability resource management is the process that emphasizes the application program interface unchanging activities, protocol dependency and the need for other toolkits is/are necessary to develop software applications designed to balance network, server and storage workload. Cloud services: IaaS, PaaS, SaaS cannot provide system performance to assigned platforms: public cloud, private cloud, hybrid cloud and cloud computing. Customers in the public and private sector must invest in prime IT solutions, required to perform cloud services that is, agile, reliable, scalable and sustainable.

Cloud Security and Privacy

Advanced solutions to support security of cloud infrastructure and platforms are key resources to public and private sectors (Sen & Sengupta, 2005). Lacking these solutions could affect the overall functionality of IT network infrastructure. Grance & Mell (2011) argued that vendors must develop viable techni-cal solutions to moderate existing security breaches in the enterprise. In the public and private sector, security challenges are paramount (Takabi, Joshi, & Ahn, 2005). There is a lack of security solutions, to address the level of threats affecting the cloud service providers, services, and infrastructure (Buyya, Ranjan, Rodrigo, & Calheiros, 2010; Sen & Sengupta, 2005; Buyya, Ramamohanarao, Leckie, Calhieros, Dastjerdi, & Versteeg, 2015; Itani, Kayssi, & Chehab, 2009). IT vendors must discuss these security challenges affecting the physical and virtual infrastructure (Sen & Sengupta, 2005). In the public and private sector customers are skeptical in granting cloud service providers complete access, to data stored in their enterprise IT infrastructure e.g., the physical and virtual servers, networks or storage systems. This uncertainty is due to frequent security threats organizations have dealt with over the course of years (Sen & Sengupta, 2005; Gartner, 2012; Buyya, Ranjan, Rodrigo, & Calheiros, 2010). There is a need for trusted connectivity between physical and virtual infrastructure. This need consists of end-to-end 'trusted' encryption solutions, designed to avert or minimize security breaches in the cloud (Sen, 2010b; Oracle, 2016). When vendors develop security solutions, cloud service providers have equal responsibility to improve security measures i.e., policies and guidelines necessary to secure data in the cloud (Takabi, Joshi, & Ahn, 2005). There is a need for vendors to develop robust data-mining applications systems (Buyya, Ranjan, Rodrigo, & Calheiros, 2010; Buyya, Ramamohanarao, Leckie, Calhieros, Dastjerdi, & Versteeg, 2015; Gartner, 2012). These systems can be used to detect and prevent malware from dissemi-nating in the cloud. Apache Hadoop is an open source software application designed to support storage and distributed provisioning of data to various compute clusters. In this instance, commodity hardware act as independent frameworks designed to support, prevent any latency, during hardware performance (Sen, 2010c; Sen, 2010b; Buyya, Ranjan, Rodrigo, & Calheiros, 2010; Buyya, Ramamohanarao, Leckie, Calhieros, Dastjerdi, & Versteeg, 2015; Itani, Kayssi, & Chehab, 2009). In the cloud, legacy security methods and network firewalls do not interact (Sen, 2010b). Elastic perimeters or 'boundaries' are needed in the enterprise in tandem with outside legacy firewalls (Alhazmi, & Shami, 2014). Cloud devices are designed to provide seamless access and share data located in the outer boundary of the demilitarized zone and firewalls (Armbrust et al., 2009; Takabi, Joshi, & Ahn, 2005). The use of these advanced security models or controls is designed to guarantee security for the physical and virtual infrastructure (Buyya, Ranjan, Rodrigo, & Calheiros, 2010; Gartner, 2012; Alhazmi, & Shami, 2014). The security of physical infrastructure requires a broader concept and newer solutions, benchmarks and end-to-end multi-tier infrastructure encryption methods. The need for policies, new methods and security controls is necessary to protect data, applications, services, end-point devices and related infrastructure (Armbrust et al., 2009; Buyya, Ranjan, Rodrigo, & Calheiros, 2010; Buyya, Ramamohanarao, Leckie, Calhieros, Dastjerdi, & Versteeg, 2015). For many years, vendors have developed security solutions to satisfy cus-tomer's technical and business demands. These demands include, but are not limited to the following areas (Sen, 2010c; Sen, 2010b; Alhazmi, et al, 2014; Alhazmi & Shami, 2014):

- Security of data stored in data centers worldwide
- Developing encryption, security solutions or techniques to guarantee for continuity of operations on the physical and virtual networks
- Security of transitory data between single and multiple network systems
- Authentication of users, application, network, server, and storage systems
- Develop proven security solutions, to detect, prevent, and repudiate any vulnerabilities or threats found on the physical and virtual IT infrastructure

- Develop methods for data aggregation in several storage systems
- Address any regulatory, policy, and other related legal issues affecting the public and private sector enterprise IT infrastructure
- Data sanitization between cloud service providers and customer's physical or virtual systems i.e., servers, networks, applications and storage
- Develop measures to address, prevent, repudiate, deter and/or manage incident response issues

The need for training, retaining and employing other security experts is crucial. In view of that, any current or imminent threats to the cloud can be mitigated, if vendors invest more resources, to research and come with robust security solutions (Sen, 2010c; Buyya, Ramamohanarao, Leckie, Calhieros, Dastjerdi, & Versteeg, 2015).

Virtualized Cloud-Based Platforms and Applications

In the cloud, the virtual process allows for elastic and balanced utilization of resources in real-time. Overall, public and private sector customers benefit from the adoption and deployment of virtualized solutions in IT infrastructure environment. The consumption of electricity and space-cooling are core factors users often seek to deploy virtualized on physical and virtual data centers (Amazon, 2012; Gartner, 2012). Subsequent to the adoption of 'virtualization' there has been shifts in IT infrastructure and applications (Sen & Sengupta, 2005; Gartner, 2012). These are integral and/or enabling processes through which services and platforms benefit from the unified and/or distributed IT environment. Vendors developed virtualization technology to support and augment cloud solutions. Virtualization is designed to transform applications and network platforms' interaction in real-time. This technology is also designed to provide load balancing and resource sharing. Virtualization allows for the incorporation of physical and virtual servers in a unique operational disposition (Ross, 2010). Virtualization and cloud technology are key resources to support the customer's IT infrastructure. This technology permits the migration of legacy physical servers to modern virtual single or multiple server farms physically dispersed throughout the world (Amazon, 2012; Alhazmi & Shami, 2014).

Virtual Disks Structures

Virtual disks are categorized as virtual drives are applications mechanisms designed to compute such system functions/actions. These activities are supported by disk storage devices. Disk storages are hardware components or peripheral devices e.g., electronic, magnetic, optical disk, virtual disk or hard disk drives designed to store, record and process data. Often virtual disks are stored inside of virtual machines/ computer hardware virtualization (Metzler, 2011; Oracle, 2016; Cisco, 2011). As hardware platforms virtual drives provide consistent abstractions needed to boot up operating systems. In virtualization, the physical description of any computer hardware platform is hidden from the actual end-users. Such activity, provides the user with an abstraction of computer platform. Virtual drives comprise of: disk image, logical disk, and random-access memory/RAM disk (Metzler, 2011; Oracle, 2016; Cisco, 2011). In hardware virtualization, virtual drives are implemented by VMs. This process duplicates the function a physical machine would require to implement (e.g., ordinary computer). Alike physical computer, VMs require virtual disks or a disk image to run. By contrast, in network boot administrators must add more virtual drives for any computer activity to initiate. Virtual optical drives are used to transfer data between optical and hard disk drives. System administrators have the choice to use optical disk drives, as these devices provide faster disk transfer time than CDs or DVDs (Metzler, 2011; Oracle, 2016; Cisco, 2011).

Cloud Storage

Cloud storage involves virtual machines that are physically dispersed through several data centers in the world. These virtual machines share data storage pools. As such, virtualized storage systems are hosted by cloud service providers, and in large data centers throughout the world. Cloud service providers must require users to store data in leased data centers. Virtual machines access data from servers located in multiple infrastructures (Buyya, Ranjan, Rodrigo, & Calheiros, 2010; Buyya, Ramamohanarao, Leckie, Calhieros, Dastjerdi, & Versteeg, 2015; Gartner, 2012). In the public and private sectors, customers must lease the amount of storage needed to support the day-to-day business and IT operations. Whether in the public or private cloud, organizations are not required to deploy additional servers in respective premises (Gorelik, 2013). Instead, these storage devices are deployed to data centers that are sustained by the cloud service providers. Even with the geographic locations that cloud storages are located, the off-shore costs are much lower than the leasing rates in the United States (Buyya, Ramamohanarao, Leckie, Calhieros, Dastjerdi, & Versteeg, 2015; Gartner, 2012; Gorelik, 2013). Faster storage systems allow users to conduct incremental and regular backups of data. In the event that users are in need of more storage, proper requests must be made to cloud service providers for approval (Gorelik, 2013). Cloud service providers are responsible for allocating extra space to accommodate their customers' needs. This gives users the flexibility needed to divert their attention to other business missions (Gartner, 2012; Buyya, Ranjan, Rodrigo, & Calheiros, 2010). Figure 8 describes virtualized cloud-based platforms and applications (Gorelik, 2013).

Figure 8. Virtualized cloud-based platforms and applications
Source: http://web.mit.edu/smadnick/www/wp/2013-01.pdf

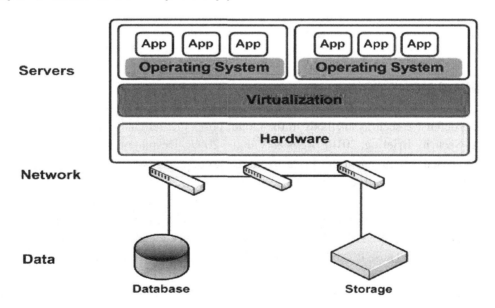

Data Model

The two types of cloud database systems discussed are: relational database management system, non-relational and/or NoSQL databases among others are very prevalent to how organization provision and share data. Each vendor adapts to its zest of database systems, which are supported in the cloud (Buyya, Ranjan, Rodrigo, & Calheiros, 2010; Gartner, 2012). These database systems contain the following (Gartner, 2009; Gartner, 2012; Gorelik, 2013):

- Oracle Database
- Microsoft Database
- Apache Cassandra
- IBM DB2
- Sybase

These databases are deployed in the cloud as virtual machine images or DaaS to support the customer-based infrastructure. Databases are difficult to maintain and/or scale, due to complexity and performance that are not suited to cloud environments. Non-relational databases otherwise known as NoSQL consist of: (Gartner, 2012; Gorelik, 2013).

- Apache Cassandra
- CouchDB
- MariaDB
- MongoDB

These databases are capable to scale over cloud platforms and infrastructure. NoSQL databases have compatible features, to support heavy read/write workloads. NoSQL databases are scaled without any point of failure or interruption through performance (Gartner, 2012). The embedded rewrite of application code is designed around SQL data models. NoSQL are scalable with complete rewritable application code to boost databases' performance (Buyya, Ramamohanarao, Leckie, Calhieros, Dastjerdi, & Versteeg, 2015; Amazon, 2012; Itani, Kayssi, & Chehab, 2009).

CONTINUOUS MONITORING

Implementing defensive security methods in the cloud, poses greater challenges to public and private sector (CPNI Security Briefing, 2010; Biggs & Vidalis, 2009). Despite numerous security perimeters between cloud-based systems and users, there are numerous other types of vulnerabilities and threats affecting IT platforms and infrastructure (CPNI Security Briefing, 2010). Cloud services and applications are exposed to external and internal attacks. These attacks and threats may be minimized, prevented and repudiated, if vendors invest adequate resources to support public and private sector customers (Biggs & Vidalis, 2009; Badger et al., 2011). Continuous development or integration of security tools is found in the trusted solutions. These trusted solutions include: vulnerability scans, cyber risk management, identity management access/risk and end-to-end security. Such solutions are designed provide layers of security to physical and virtual platforms (Sen & Sengupta, 2005; Emig et al., 2007; Schubert, Kipp,

& Wesner, 2009). The need for federated and integrated cloud-based solutions is designed to provide management security tools, needed to obviate and deter unauthorized/authorized individuals' from accessing private-private sector IT assets/resources (CPNI Security Briefing, 2010). In the public and private sector customers are concerned on how cloud service providers/vendors secure consumers' data (Sen & Sengupta, 2005); CPNI Security Briefing, 2010; Schubert, Kipp, & Wesner, 2009). These concerns are as follows (Biggs & Vidalis, 2009; Gartner, 2012; Ross, 2010):

- Define security benchmarks and related policy requirements
- Conduct routine due-diligence and due-process on platforms and infrastructure
- Manage cloud-based supplier's risks, network vulnerabilities and system threats

The following security fundamentals are critical to public and private sector's IT infrastructure and platforms (Amazon, 2012; Biggs & Vidalis, 2009; Buyya, Ranjan, Rodrigo, & Calheiros, 2010; Buyya, Ramamohanarao, Leckie, Calhieros, Dastjerdi, & Versteeg, 2015; Badger et al., 2011; Bruening & Treacy, 2009):

- Legacy security issues and concerns
- Current and imminent issues
- Cloud service provider's data access, security and monitoring

This Figure 9 illustrates the theoretical method of database management systems.

These applications and/or platforms are designed to reduce redundancy, fault-tolerance, scalability, latency, machine-image, federation, enhanced encryption methods, democratization, self-autonomy, real-time data sharing, fast provisioning, system agility, no single point of failure, backup/disaster recovery,

Figure 9. Process for database management system
Source: https://www.google.com/search

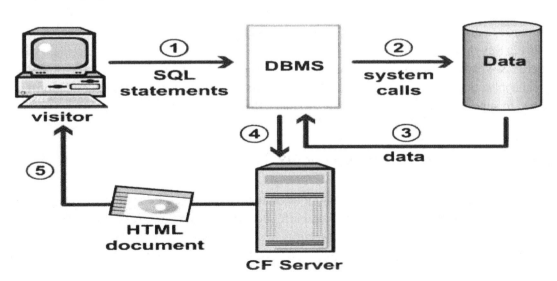

security, clustering, and elasticity solutions (Amazon, 2012; Biggs & Vidalis, 2009; Buyya, Ranjan, Rodrigo, & Calheiros, 2010; Joshi et al., 2004).

Database Management Systems

In recent years, cloud database systems have gained a lot of attention in the public and private sector (Amazon, 2012). The adoption of amazon web services-elastic compute cloud has spun web-based applications and integrated solutions. Web-based applications and network platforms are easy to deploy, due to such evolution (Badger et al., 2011).

Database System Replication

In databases, replication is defined as a process/component that shares data between computers and servers (Badger et al., 2011). Redundant resources are software and hardware components. These computer resources are deployed to improve, maintain and orchestrate the fault-tolerance posture and display data in real-time. In the replicated environment, data is stored in several computers for continuous task processing (Sen & Sengupta, 2005). Replication is a very fundamental concept for all database systems (Joshi et al., 2004). IT professionals and vendors agree that the process of replicating database systems is a very complex task (Biggs & Vidalis, 2009; Amazon, 2012; Gartner, 2012; Gartner, 2009). For many years, vendors have designed database solutions to support the replication process between instances and incremental business environments. In essence, database tables are separated from several objects to allow data residing in the back-end database and/or network server environment (i.e., network-based, Internet, and intranet). This process is developed to guarantee that database queries, forms, reports, macros and modules activities are executed in the front-end database and/or end-user computer (Sen, 2010c; Biggs & Vidalis, 2009; Badger et al., 2011; Chen et al., 2010).

Oracle Cloud-Based Enterprise Solutions

Enterprise manager is a solution platform that provides engineering and infrastructure concepts needed, to optimize IT customer services and operational capacities. These IT solution architectures, though, are required to decrease cost complexity, capital and operational outlays (Sen & Sengupta, 2005; Gartner, 2012; Buyya, Ranjan, Rodrigo, & Calheiros, 2010; Buyya, Ramamohanarao, Leckie, Calhieros, Dastjerdi, & Versteeg, 2015). These solutions are incorporated as enterprise manager, virtual machine and real application cluster or architecture. Both the enterprise manager and backbone-platform yet are designed to support many Oracle technologies (Badger et al., 2011; Oracle, 2016).

SOLUTIONS AND RECOMMENDATIONS

Cloud computing technology offers a range of advantages to current and/or future adopters (Biggs & Vidalis, 2009; DeCandia et al., 2007). Attributable to such benefits, vendors are committed to researching and improving existing cloud solutions and security best practices, to meet organizations and customers' business/operation's requirements (Lease, 2005; Buyya, Ranjan, Rodrigo, & Calheiros, 2010; Badger et al., 2011). IT and cloud experts anticipate that continued research in cloud computing technology will give rise to diverse discoveries of topics such as, data science, big data/predictive analytics, data mining, data-warehousing and others. Any advent research areas including cyber security and computer forensics must benefit from basis of prior cloud computing research findings (Grance & Mell, 2011; Buyya, Ramamohanarao, Leckie, Calhieros, Dastjerdi, & Versteeg, 2015; Biggs & Vidalis, 2009; Badger et al., 2011; Garfinkel & Shelat, 2003).

FUTURE RESEARCH DIRECTIONS

The future direction of this research aims to produce significant conclusions for the academic, public and private sectors. This study builds on the body of knowledge required, to advance the functionality of cloud solutions, improve physical, virtual machine performance, software, hardware scalability and the way programming language (i.e., *PHP, Python, HTML, Java, Visual Basic, C Shell, C++)* interaction in the enterprise. In essence the goal of this chapter is to provide fundamental or depth of expertise for technology novices, junior, expert IT professionals and/or vendors (CPNI, 2010). The chapter further delineates and/or improves on parallel technology essentials necessary, to support the deployment of cloud solutions (Sen & Sengupta, 2005; Buyya, Ramamohanarao, Leckie, Calhieros, Dastjerdi, & Versteeg, 2015). The ability to solve daily management and technical issues organizations and consumers deal with will be determined by different trends of cloud computing technology (Bruening & Treacy, 2009; Chen et al., 2010). These trends include big data analytic solutions, storage capacity, agility, robust of IT systems and program language solutions needed to leverage the performance of physical and virtual machines (Sen & Sengupta, 2005; Biggs & Vidalis, 2009; Buyya, Ranjan, Rodrigo, & Calheiros, 2010; Badger et al., 2011; Blaze et al., 2009; CPNI, 2010; Chen et al., 2010; Lowensohn & McCarthy, 2009).

CONCLUSION

In present years, cloud computing transformed the way customers in the public and private sector view IT technology. Presently, more organizations are adopting and deploying cloud computing solutions (Leighon, 2009; Bruening & Treacy, 2009; Chow et al., 2009). The flexibility, scalability, fast provisioning, elasticity, availability, encryption-based solutions, sustainability, improved security, reliability, redundancy, fault tolerance no single point of failure and latency encouraged customers to migrate enterprise IT resources from the legacy to modern data center infrastructure and platforms (Sen & Sengupta, 2005; Biggs & Vidalis, 2009; Chor et al., 1998; Chow et al., 2009; Gajek et al., 2009). Cloud computing is the next technology frontier in the innovation of information and communications technology (ICT). Vendors define cloud computing as a transformative leap for the physical and virtual network systems besides data centers. Cloud services and deployment models are selected as crucial service assets (Chor et al., 1998; DeCandia et al., 2007). While CIOs measure cloud computing as a progressing paradigm, customers need its resources, to support business transformation and system scalability (Lease, 2005; Sen & Sengupta, 2005; Buyya, Ranjan, Rodrigo, & Calheiros, 2010; Biggs & Vidalis, 2009; Chor et al., 1998).

REFERENCES

Alhazmi, K., Abusharkh, M., Ban, D., & Shami, A. (2014). A map of the clouds: Virtual network mapping in cloud computing data centers.*IEEE Canadian Conference on Electrical and Computer Engineering.* doi:10.1109/CCECE.2014.6901053

Alhazmi, K., Abusharkh, M., Ban, D., & Shami, A. (2014). *Drawing the Cloud Map: Virtual network embedding in cloud computing Environment. IEEE Systems Journal.*

Alhazmi, K. M. (2014). *Online Virtual Network Provisioning in Distributed Cloud Computing Data Centers.* Electronic Thesis and Dissertation Repository. Paper 2319. Retrieved from: http://ir.lib.uwo.ca/cgi/viewcontent.cgi?article=3713&context=etd

Alhazmi, K., & Shami, A. (2014). *A Greener Cloud: Energy Efficient Provisioning for Online Virtual Network Requests in Cloud Data Centers.* IEEE International Conference on Communications (ICC).

Alliance for Telecommunications Industry Solutions. (n.d.). Retrieved from: http://www.atis.org

Amazon S3 Availability Event. (2008). Retrieved from: http://status.aws.amazon.com/s3-20080720.html

Amazon Auto Scaling. (n.d.). Retrieved from: http://aws.amazon.com/autoscaling/

Armbrust, M., Fox, A., Griffith, R., Joseph, A. D., Katz, R. H., Konwinsky, A., . . . Zaharia, M. (2009). *Above the Clouds: A Berkley View of Cloud Computing.* Technical Report No. UCB/EECS-2009-28, Department of Electrical Engineering and Computer Sciences, University of California at Berkley. Retrieved from: http://www.eecs.berkeley.edu/Pubs/TechRpts/2009/EECS-2009-28.pdf

Association for Retail Technology Standards (ARTS). (n.d.). Retrieved from: http://www.nrf-arts.org

Badger, L., Grance, T., Patt-Corner, R., & Voas, J. (2011). *Draft Cloud Computing Synopsis and Recommendations.* National Institute of Standards and Technology (NIST) Special Publication 800-146. US Department of Commerce. Retrieved from: http://csrc.nist.gov/publications/drafts/800-146/Draft-NIST-SP800-146.pdf

Bertion, E., Paci, F., & Ferrini, R. (2009). *Privacy-preserving digital identity management for cloud computing. IEEE Computer Society Data Engineering Bulletin.*

Biggs & Vidalis. (2009). Cloud Computing: The Impact on Digital Forensic Investigations. *Proceedings of the 7th International Conference for Internet Technology and Secured Transactions* (ICITST'09), 1-6.

Blaze, M., Kannan, S., Lee, I., Sokolsky, O., Smith, J. M., Keromytis, A. D., & Lee, W. (2009). Dynamic Trust Management. *IEEE Computer, 42*(2), 44–52. doi:10.1109/MC.2009.51

Bruening, P. J., & Treacy, B. C. (2009). *Cloud Computing: Privacy, Security Challenges.* Bureau of National Affairs.

Buyya, R., Ramamohanarao, K., Leckie, C., Calhieros, N., Dastjerdi, A., & Versteeg, S. (2015). *Big Data Analytics-Enhanced Cloud Computing: Challenges, Architectural Elements, and Future Directions.* Retrieved from: http://arxiv.org/abs/1510.06486

Buyya, R., Ranjan, R., Rodrigo, N., & Calheiros, R. N. (2010). InterCloud: Utility-oriented federation of cloud computing environments for scaling of application services. In *Proceedings of the 10th International Conference on Algorithms and Architectures for Parallel Processing, 6081*, 13–31.

Center for the Protection of Natural Infrastructure. (2010). *Information Security Briefing on Cloud Computing, March 2010*. Retrieved from: http://www.cpni.gov.uk/Documents/Publications/2010/2010007-ISB_cloud_computing.pdf

Chen, Y., Paxson, V., & Katz, R. H. (2010). What's New About Cloud Computing Security? Technical Report UCB/EECS-2010-5. Berkeley, CA: EECS Department, University of California. Retrieved from http://www.eecs.berkeley.edu/Pubs/TechRpts/2010/EECS-2010-5.html

Chen, Z., Dong, W., Li, H., Cao, L., Zhang, P., & Chen, X. (n.d.). *Collaborative network security in multi-tenant data center for cloud computing*. Retrieved from: http://www.mit.edu/~caoj/pub/doc/jcao_j_netsec.pdf

Chor, B., Kushilevitz, E., Goldreich, O., & Sudan, M. (1998). Private Information Retrieval. *Journal of the ACM, 45*(9), 965–981. doi:10.1145/293347.293350

Chow, R., Golle, P., Jakobsson, M., Shi, E., Staddon, J., Masuoka, R., & Molina, J. (2009). Controlling Data in the Cloud: Outsourcing Computation without Outsourcing Control. In *Proceedings of the ACM Workshop on Cloud Computing Security (CCSW'09)*. ACM Press. doi:10.1145/1655008.1655020

Chowdhury, M., Rahman, R. M, & Boutaba, R. (2012). Vineyard: Virtual network embedding algorithms with coordinated node and link mapping. *IEEE/ACM Transactions on Networking, 20*(99), 206–219.

Cisco. (2011). *Virtual Machine Networking: Standards and Solutions*. San Jose, CA: Cisco.

Cloud Security Alliance (CSA)'s Security Guidance for Critical area of Cloud Computing. (2009). CSA. Retrieved from: https://cloudsecurityalliance.org/csaguide.pdf

DeCandia, G., Hastorun, D., Jampani, M., Kakulapati, G., Lakshman, A., Pilchin, A., & Vogels, W. et al. (2007). Dynamo: Amazon's Highly Available Key-Value Store.*Proceedings of the 21st ACM SIGOPS Symposium on Operating Systems Principles,* 205-220. doi:10.1145/1294261.1294281

Desisto, R. P., Plummer, D. C., & Smith, D. M. (2008). *Tutorial for Understanding the Relationship between Cloud Computing and SaaS*. Stamford, CT: Gartner.

Emig, C., Brandt, F., Kreuzer, S., & Abeck, S. (2007). Identity as a Service- Towards a Service-Oriented Identity Management Architecture. *Proceedings of the 13th Open European Summer School and IFIP TC6.6 Conference on Dependable and Adaptable Network and Services*, 1-8.

Everett, C. (2009). Cloud Computing- A Question of Trust. *Computer Fraud & Security,* (6), 5-7.

Gajek, S., Jensen, M., Liao, L., & Schwenk, J. (2009). Analysis of Signature Wrapping Attacks and Countermeasures. *Proceedings of the IEEE International Conference on Web Services*, 575-582. doi:10.1109/ICWS.2009.12

Garfinkel, S., & Shelat, A. (2003). Remembrance of Data Passed: A Study of Disk Sanitization Practices. *IEEE Security and Privacy, 1*(1), 17–27. doi:10.1109/MSECP.2003.1176992

Gartner. (2009). *Gartner Says Cloud Consumers Need Brokerages to Unlock the Potential of Cloud Services*. Retrieved from http://www.gartner.com/it/page.jsp?id=1064712

Gartner Hype-Cycle. (2012). *Cloud computing and Big data*. Retrieved from http://www.gartner.com/technology/research/hype-cycles/

Gellman, R. (2009). *Privacy in the Clouds: Risks to Privacy and Confidentiality from Cloud Computing*. World Privacy Forum (WPF) Report. Retrieved from: http://www.worldprivacyforum.org/cloudprivacy.html

Gentry, C. (2009). Fully Homomorphic Encryption Using Ideal Lattices.*Proceedings of the 41st Annual ACM Symposium on Theory of Computing,* 169-178. doi:10.1145/1536414.1536440

Golden, B. (2009). *Capex vs. Opex: Most People Miss the Point about Cloud Economics*. Retrieved from: http://www.cio.com/article/484429/Capex_vs._Opex_Most_People_Miss_the_point_About_Cloud_Economic

Gorelik, E. (2013). *Cloud computing models* (Master's Thesis). Massachusetts Institute of Technology, MIT Sloan School of Management. Retrieved from: http://web.mit.edu/smadnick/www/wp/2013-01.pdf

Grance, T., & Mell, P. (2011). The NIST definition of cloud computing. (NIST Publication No. NIST SP- 800-145). Washington, DC: US Department of Commerce. Retrieved from http://csrc.nist.gov/publications/drafts/800-146/Draft-NIST-SP800-146.pdfhttp://www.nist.gov/manuscript-publicationsearch.cfm?pub_id=909616

Gruschka, N., & Iacono, L. L. (2009). Vulnerable Cloud: SOAP Message Security Validation Revisited. *Proceedings of IEEE International Conference on Web Services,* 625-631. doi:10.1109/ICWS.2009.70

Harris, T. (n.d.). *Cloud computing. An Overview*. Retrieved from: http://www.thbs.com/downloads/Cloud-Computing-Overview.pdf

Houidi, I., Louati, W., Zeghlache, D., Papadimitriou, P., & Mathy, L. (2010). *Adaptive virtual network provisioning*. Retrieved from: https://orbi.ulg.ac.be/bitstream/2268/126822/1/adaptive_embedding_VISA10.pdf

Itani, W., Kayssi, A., & Chehab, A. (2009). Privacy as a Service: Privacy-Aware Data Storage and Processing in Cloud Computing Architectures.*Proceedings of the 8th IEEE International Conference on Dependable, Automatic and Secure Computing,* 711-716. doi:10.1109/DASC.2009.139

Joshi, J. B. D., Bhatti, R., Bertino, E., & Ghafoor, A. (2004). Access Control Language for Multi-domain Environments. *IEEE Internet Computing, 8*(6), 40–50. doi:10.1109/MIC.2004.53

Kant, K. (2009). *Data center evolution. A tutorial on state of the art, issues, and challenges*. Intel Corporation. Retrieved from: http://bnrg.cs.berkeley.edu/~randy/Courses/CS294.S13/1.3.pdf

Kaufman, L. M. (2009). Data Security in the World of Cloud Computing. *IEEE Security and Privacy, 7*(4), 61–64. doi:10.1109/MSP.2009.87

Ko, M., Ahn, G.-J., & Shehab, M. (2009). Privacy-Enhanced User-Centric Identity Management.*Proceedings of IEEE International Conference on Communications,* 998-1002.

Lease, D. R. (2005). Factors influencing the adoption of biometric security technologies by decision-making information technology and security managers (Capella University). ProQuest Dissertations and Theses. Retrieved from http://search.proquest.com/docview/305359883?accountid=27965

Leavitt, N. (2009). Is Cloud Computing Really Ready for Prime Time? *IEEE Computer, 42*(1), 15–20. doi:10.1109/MC.2009.20

Leighon, T. (2009). *Akamai and Cloud Computing: A Perspective from the Edge of the Cloud*. White Paper. Akamai Technologies. Retrieved from http://www.essextec.com/assets/cloud/akamai/cloudcomputing-perspective-wp.pdf

Lowensohn, J., & McCarthy, C. (2009). *Lessons from Twitter's Security Breach*. Retrieved from: http://news.cnet.com/8301-17939_109-10287558-2.html

Messmer, E. (2009, October 21). Gartner on Cloud Security: 'Our Nightmare Scenario is Here Now'. *Network World*. Retrieved from: http://www.networkworld.com/news/2009/102109-gartner-cloud-security.html

Metzler, J. (2011). *Virtualization: Benefits, Challenges and Solutions*. Riverbed Technology. Retrieved from: http://www.stotthoare.com.au/sites/default/files/files/1_16100_WhitePaper_VirtualizationBenefits_by_Webtorials.pdf

Molnar, D., & Schechter, S. (2010). Self-Hosting vs. Cloud Hosting: Accounting for the Security Impact of Hosting in the Cloud. *Proceedings of the Workshop on the Economics of Information Security*. Retrieved from: http://weis2010.econinfosec.org/papers/session5/weis2010_schechter.pdf

Oracle. (2016). *Management Network Virtualization and Network Resources in Oracle Solaris* (11.3 ed.). Reston, VA: Oracle.

Pearson, S. (2009). Taking Account of Privacy when Designing Cloud Computing Services.*Proceedings of the ICSE Workshop on Software Engineering Challenges of Cloud Computing*, 44-52. doi:10.1109/CLOUD.2009.5071532

Pearson, S., & Charlesworth, A. (2009). Accountability as a Way Forward for Privacy Protection in the Cloud.*Proceedings of the 1st International Conference on Cloud Computing*, 131-144. doi:10.1007/978-3-642-10665-1_12

Petry, A. (2007). *Design and Implementation of a Xen-Based Execution Environment* (Diploma Thesis). Technische Universitat Kaiserslautern.

Price, M. (2008). The Paradox of Security in Virtual Environments. *IEEE Computer, 41*(11), 22–38. doi:10.1109/MC.2008.472

Rajalakshmi, A., Srinandhini, S., & Uma, R. (2015). *A technical review on virtualization technology*. Retrieved from: http://www.ijircce.com/upload/2015/october/69_A%20Technical.pdf

RedHat. (2016). *Advantages and Misconceptions of Virtualization*. Raleigh, NC: RedHat.

Ristenpart, T., Tromer, E., Shacham, H., & Savage, S. (2009). Hey, You, Get Off of My Cloud: Exploring Information Leakage in Third-Party Compute Clouds.*Proceedings of the 16th ACM Conference on Computer and Communications Security,* 199-212. doi:10.1145/1653662.1653687

Rochwerger, R., Caceres, J., Montero, R. S., Breitgand, D., & Elmroth, E. (2009). The RESERVOIR Model and Architecture for Open Federated Cloud Computing. *IBM Systems Journal, 53*(4), 4:1–4:11. doi:10.1147/JRD.2009.5429058

Ross, V. W. (2010). *Factors influencing the adoption of cloud computing by Decision making manager.* (Capella University). ProQuest Dissertations and Theses. Retrieved from http://search.proquest.com/docview/305262031?accountid=27965

Schubert, L., Kipp, A., & Wesner, S. (2009). Above the Clouds: From Grids to Service- Oriented Operating Systems. In Towards the Future Internet- A European Research Perspective (pp. 238-249). Amsterdam: IOS Press.

Sen, J. (2010b). An Intrusion Detection Architecture for Clustered Wireless Ad Hoc Networks.*Proceedings of the 2nd IEEE International Conference on Intelligence in Communication Systems and Networks*, 202-207. doi:10.1109/CICSyN.2010.51

Sen, J. (2010c). A Robust and Fault-Tolerant Distributed Intrusion Detection System.*Proceedings of the 1st International Conference on Parallel, Distributed and Grid Computing*, 123-128. doi:10.1109/PDGC.2010.5679879

Sen, J., Chowdhury, P. R., & Sengupta, I. (2006c). A Distributed Trust Mechanism for Mobile Ad Hoc Networks.*Proceedings of the International Symposium on Ad Hoc and Ubiquitous Computing,* 62-67. doi:10.1109/ISAHUC.2006.4290649

Sen, J., Chowdhury, P. R., & Sengupta, I. (2007). A Distributed Trust Establishment Scheme for Mobile Ad Hoc Networks.*Proceedings of the International Conference on Computation: Theory and Applications*, 51-57. doi:10.1109/ICCTA.2007.3

Sen, J., & Sengupta, I. (2005). Autonomous Agent-Based Distributed Fault-Tolerant Intrusion Detection System.*Proceedings of the 2nd International Conference on Distributed Computing and Internet*, 125-131. doi:10.1007/11604655_16

Sen, J., & Sengupta, I. (2005). Autonomous Agent-Based Distributed Fault-Tolerant Intrusion Detection System. In *Proceedings of the 2nd International Conference on Distributed Computing and Internet Technology,*125-131. doi:10.1007/11604655_16

Sen, J., Sengupta, I., & Chowdhury, P. R. (2006a). A Mechanism for Detection and Prevention of Distributed Denial of Service Attacks.*Proceedings of the 8th International Conference on Distributed Computing and Networking,* 139-144. doi:10.1007/11947950_16

Sen, J., Sengupta, I., & Chowdhury, P. R. (2006b). An Architecture of a Distributed Intrusion Detection System Using Cooperating Agents.*Proceedings of the International Conference on Computing and Informatics*, 1-6. doi:10.1109/ICOCI.2006.5276474

Sen, J., Ukil, A., Bera, D., & Pal, A. (2008). A Distributed Intrusion Detection System for Wireless Ad Hoc Networks. *Proceedings of the 16th IEEE International Conference on Networking*, 1-5. doi:10.1109/ICON.2008.4772624

Shacham, H., & Waters, B. (2008). Compact Proofs of Retrievability. *Proceedings of the 14th International Conference on the Theory and Application of Cryptology and Information Security*, *5350*, 90-107. doi:10.1007/978-3-540-89255-7_7

Shin, D., & Ahn, G.-J. (2005). Role-Based Privilege and Trust Management. *Computer Systems Science and Engineering*, *20*(6), 401–410.

Shin, D., & Ahn, G. J. (2005). Role-Based Privilege and Trust Management. *Computer Systems Science and Engineering*, *20*(6), 401–410.

Sims, K. (2009). *IBM Blue Cloud Initiative Advances Enterprise Cloud Computing*. Retrieved from: http://www-03.ibm.com/press/us/en/pressrelease/26642.wss

Sinclair, S., & Smith, S. W. (2008). Preventive Directions for Insider Threat Mitigation Using Access Control. In Insider Attack and Cyber Security: Beyond the Hacker. Springer.

Song, D., Wagner, D., & Perrig, A. (2000). Practical Techniques for Searches on Encrypted Data. *Proceedings of the IEEE Symposium on Research in Security and Privacy*, 44-55.

Song, D., Wagner, D., & Perrig, A. (2000). Practical Techniques for Searches on Encrypted Data. *Proceedings of the IEEE Symposium on Research in Security and Privacy*, 44-55.

Sotomayor, B., Montero, R. S., Llorente, I. M., & Foster, I. (2009). Virtual Infrastructure Management in Private and Hybrid Cloud. *IEEE Internet Computing*, *13*(5), 14–22. doi:10.1109/MIC.2009.119

Stanton, J. M., Stam, K. R., Mastrangelo, P., & Jolton, J. (2005). Analysis of end user security behaviors. *Computers & Security*, *24*(2), 124–133. doi:10.1016/j.cose.2004.07.001

Takabi, H., Joshi, J. B. D., & Ahn, G.-J. (2010). Security and Privacy Challenges in Cloud Computing Environments. *IEEE Security and Privacy*, *8*(6), 24–31. doi:10.1109/MSP.2010.186

Toosi, A. N., Calheiros, R. N., & Buyya, R. (2014). Interconnected Cloud Computing Environments: Challenges, Taxonomy, and Survey. *ACM Comput. Surv.*, *47*(1), Article 7.

Vaquero, L. M., Rodero-Merino, L., Caceres, J., & Linder, M. (2009). A Break in the Clouds: Towards a Cloud Definition. *Computer Communication Review*, *39*(1), 50–55. doi:10.1145/1496091.1496100

Vouk, M. A. (2008). Cloud Computing – Issues, Research and Implementations. *Proceedings of the 30th International Conference on Information Technology Interfaces*, 31-40.

Vozmediano, R. M., Montero, R. S., & Llorente, I. M. (2011). Multi-Cloud Deployment of Computing Clusters for Loosely-Coupled MTC Applications. *IEEE Transactions on Parallel and Distributed Systems*, *22*(6), 924–930. doi:10.1109/TPDS.2010.186

Zetter, K. (2010). Google hackers Targeted Source Code of More Than 30 Companies. *Wired Threat Level*. Retrieved from: http://www.wired.com/threatlevel/2010/01/google-hackattack/

Zhang, Y., & Joshi, J. (2009). *Access Control and Trust Management for Emerging Multidomain Environments.*In S. Upadhyay & R. O. Rao (Eds.), *Annals of Emerging Research in Information Assurance, Security and Privacy Services* (pp. 421–452). Emerald Group Publishing.

Zimory Gmb, H. (2009). *Zimory Distributed Cloud-Whitepaper.* Retrieved from: http://www.zimory.de/ index.php?eID=tx_nawsecuredl&u=0&file=fileadmin/user_upload/pdf/Distributed_Clouds_Whitepaper.pdf&t=1359027268&hash=93c5f42f8c91817a746f7b8cff55fbdc68ae7379

KEY TERMS AND DEFINITIONS

Cloud Provisioning: A process that selects applications and services to be made available in the public cloud.

Full Virtualization: The practice which includes hardware capabilities initiated by a single or various processor(s).

Migration: A practice of relocating guest virtual systems from single-to-single or single-to-multiple host computers.

Network Virtualization: The method of delivering hardware and software network resources and software into an exclusive, application-based or physical as well as virtual network solutions.

Provisioning: A process of deploying network equipment and/or making available network resources via virtualized servers.

Para-Virtualization: Best described as a set of applications and information patterns that are made available to the virtualized guest system.

Software Virtualization: The limitation of software virtualization is that, all machine activities/ performance degrade, due to binary translation or resolution that force the system to run slowly.

Virtual Machines: A process that takes place on physical machines that use applications designed to provide functioning background. The software is designed to run or host a guest operating system.

Virtualization: A central physical configuration of several technologies. This includes the method of building virtual rather than physical system(s) in the network e.g., hardware platform, operating system, storage device or other related network resources.

Chapter 4
Advances in Dynamic Virtual Machine Management for Cloud Data Centers

Rashmi Rai
Birla Institute of Technology, India

G. Sahoo
Birla Institute of Technology, India

ABSTRACT

The ever-rising demand for computing services and the humongous amount of data generated everyday has led to the mushrooming of power craving data centers across the globe. These large-scale data centers consume huge amount of power and emit considerable amount of CO2.There have been significant work towards reducing energy consumption and carbon footprints using several heuristics for dynamic virtual machine consolidation problem. Here we have tried to solve this problem a bit differently by making use of utility functions, which are widely used in economic modeling for representing user preferences. Our approach also uses Meta heuristic genetic algorithm and the fitness is evaluated with the utility function to consolidate virtual machine migration within cloud environment. The initial results as compared with existing state of art shows marginal but significant improvement in energy consumption as well as overall SLA violations.

INTRODUCTION

With the advancements in computing power and the rapid increase in computing services being delivered as a utility to the consumer, there is a paradigm shift towards cloud computing technologies (Armbrust et al., 2010; Bilal et al., 2013; Foster et al., 2008). Big and small organizations, businesses as well as individual users have started relying on cloud services instead of building and managing their own data centers for fetching the required services. As a result of which there has been sharp increase in the number of large scale data centers across globe. For example, there are more than 454,000 servers for Amazon EC2 and it is steadily increasing every year (Amazon data centre size, 2012).

DOI: 10.4018/978-1-5225-2013-9.ch004

The number of datacenters is growing at a steady pace as per the recent forecast by CISCO and the cloud workload will be almost triple from 2013 to 2018.However the work load in traditional data centers will decline as per the survey due to increasing virtualization in cloud environment (Cisco Global Cloud Index, 2013).

These large-scale data centers consume humongous amount of energy leading to huge operating costs and also contribute significantly towards the global CO2 emission. According to (Koomey, 2011), the total energy consumption by data centers will persist to grow at a past pace until unless some sophisticated energy efficient measures are deployed. Thus, reducing the energy usage in cloud data centers have become a prime concern across the globe, both for the sake of cloud providers benefit and the greener environment.

Reduction in high energy usage involves eliminating the energy waste that happens at various levels of cloud data center environment. At the hardware level the energy usage can be minimized by improving the physical infrastructure of data centers while at software level optimizing various resource allocations and scheduling algorithms can reduce the energy wastage. Latest and advanced designed data centers have resulted in drastic increase in infrastructure efficiency. For example, the social media giant Facebook's data center located at Oregon has successfully achieved a PUE (Power Usage Effectiveness) of 1.08, this ratio (Open Compute Project, 2015) clearly indicates that roughly 91% of the data center's energy is used by the computing resources. Another very recent announcement made by Facebook is the newest datacenter at Fort Worth, Texas which is expected to be one of the most advanced and efficient datacenter that will use 100% renewable energy.

At software level the inefficient usage of computing resources accounts for the maximum amount of energy waste. As per the analysis of more than 5000 servers for a period of six months it was noted that the server utilization barely ever reached full potential although servers were not kept idle. These servers mostly operated at almost 10-50% of their complete capacity which caused added cost towards maintenance and management of over-provisioned servers leading to increased TCO i.e. Total Cost of Ownership (Barroso and Holzle, 2007). Hence underutilized servers are detrimental both from cost as well as energy usage perspective.

Our work mainly focuses on improving the energy usage at software level specifically the virtual machine migration level. The main contributions of this chapter are the following.

1. A Utility function based Meta heuristic for the efficient management of virtual machine migration which significantly reduces the energy consumption in a cloud environment.
2. An elaborate simulation and performance evaluation through a different set of experiments conducted for 10 simulation days.

The remainder of the chapter is organized as follows. In Section 2 we discuss the related work. In Sections 3 and its subsections we present the preliminaries of our work where we have defined in detail the main idea behind the whole VM consolidation problem along with our meta heuristic approach. In section 4 various algorithms for the cost model development have been proposed continuing with performance evaluation in Section 5 and analysis of the obtained experiment results in Section 6. The last section discusses the future research directions and concludes the work.

RELATED WORK

Creating high efficiency of power in virtual data centers has already become a critical issue. Towards this end, several methods have been proposed.

To our knowledge, the initial work to manage power efficiently in virtual data centers was done by (Nathuji and Schwan, 2007), where a Virtual Power Management approach (VPM) for VM consolidation was proposed. The VPM supports the remote and independent operation assumed by guest VMs running on virtualized platforms, and makes it possible to control and globally coordinate the effects of the varied power management polices applied by guest VMs to virtualized resources.

Different from the VPM, (Stoess et al., 2007) presented a framework for energy management in modular and multi-layered operating system structures which provides a unified model for VM consolidation.

Similar works may be found in (Kansal et al., 2010 and Oh et al., 2011) For performance-driven workload consolidation in virtual environment, (Verman et al., 2008) proposed architecture of power-aware application consolidation framework (pMapper), which can include several scenarios including power and performance management using Virtualization. It also offers a practical solution i.e. power minimization subjected to a fixed performance requirement.

Srikantaiah (Srikantaiah et al., 2008) deliberated the inter-relationships among energy consumption, resource utilization, and performance of consolidated workloads. And they modeled the consolidation problem as a modified multi-dimensional bin-packing problem. Cardosa (Cardosa et al., 2009) presented a unique suite of techniques for VM consolidation in data centers taking benefit of the min–max and shared features intrinsic in Virtualization. The techniques delivers a smooth mechanism for energy-performance tradeoffs in data centers running heterogeneous applications, wherein the amount of resources allocated to a VM can be adjusted based on the available resources, power costs, and application utilities. The similar works can be found in Gong and Gu (2010), Goudarzi and Pedram (2012), Bila et al. (2012). However, the above researches are workload dependent, whereas our research is workload independent and can be deployed in any generic Cloud environment. There are other works that treat VM consolidation as a multi-objective optimization problem or use prediction to minimize the number of running servers for energy aware. Xu (Xu et al., 2010) proposed an improved genetic algorithm with fuzzy multi objective evaluation for VM consolidation, which got better energy-performance tradeoffs than other approaches. Duy (Duy et al., 2010) integrated a neural network predictor into a Green scheduling algorithm to forecast future resource requirements based on historical data, which made energy saving by turning off unused servers.

Since most of the VM consolidation approaches are limited to single resource and hard to distribute, Feller (Feller et al., 2011) modeled the VM consolidation problem as an instance of the multi-dimensional bin-packing problem and designed a nature-inspired VM consolidation algorithm based on Ant Colony Optimization (ACO). Compared with one frequently applied algorithm (i.e. First-Fit Decreasing), the ACO-based approach achieves better energy-performance tradeoff and can be implemented in a fully distributed environment.

The similar works can be found in the work done by Mills et al. (2011), Bobroff et al. (2007) Borgetto et al. (2012), Lovsz et al. (2012). Dupont (Dupont et al., 2012) proposed a flexible and energy-aware framework for VM consolidation in a data center. The central element of the framework is an optimizer which deals with Service Level Agreement (SLA) requirements, the inter-connection among diverse data centers and energy consumption. Finally, experimental results demonstrated that the framework achieved a good energy-performance tradeoff.

Anton (Anton et al., 2012) defined an architectural framework and principles for energy-aware Cloud computing, and developed algorithms for energy-aware mapping of VMs to appropriate Cloud resources in addition to dynamic VM consolidation. The process of the VM consolidation is as follows: firstly, set a fixed upper utilization threshold for hosts in data centers; secondly, review each host's utilization for a period of time. If it exceeds the threshold, it is denoted as overload; finally, choose VMs from those overload hosts to migrate. However, the fixed threshold is not appropriate for virtual environment with variable workloads. Therefore, they illustrated that VM consolidation should be optimized continuously in an online manner due to the variability of workloads experienced by modern applications. Then, they suggested new adaptive heuristics for dynamic VM consolidation based on the analysis of historical data. Experimental results show that the distribution and selection algorithms can save energy considerably. However, we think that the SLA violation and energy consumption produced by the framework can be further improved upon.

We have summarized the key work done so far in the area of virtual machine consolidation problem in the Table 1.

Table 1. Related work in the area of VM consolidation

Author	Model
1. Nathuji and Schwan, 2007	A Virtual Power Management approach (VPM) for VM consolidation was proposed. The VPM supports the remote and independent operation assumed by guest VMs running on virtualized platforms, and makes it possible to control and globally coordinate the effects of the varied power management polices applied by guest VMs to virtualized resources.
2. Stoess et al., 2007	Presented a framework for energy management in modular and multi-layered operating system structures which provides a unified model for VM consolidation.
3. Verman et al., 2008	Proposed architecture of power-aware application consolidation framework (pMapper), which can include several scenarios including power and performance management using Virtualization. It also offers a practical solution i.e. power minimization subjected to a fixed performance requirement.
4. Srikantaiah et al., 2008	Deliberated the inter-relationships among energy consumption, resource utilization, and performance of consolidated workloads. And they modeled the consolidation problem as a modified multi-dimensional bin-packing problem.
5. Cardosa et al., 2009	Presented a unique suite of techniques for VM consolidation in data centers taking benefit of the min–max and shared features intrinsic in Virtualization. The techniques deliver a smooth mechanism for energy-performance tradeoffs in data centers running heterogeneous applications, wherein the amount of resources allocated to a VM can be adjusted based on the available resources, power costs, and application utilities.
6. Xu et al., 2010	Proposed an improved genetic algorithm with fuzzy multi objective evaluation for VM consolidation, which got better energy-performance tradeoffs than other approaches.
7. Duy et al., 2010	Integrated a neural network predictor into a Green scheduling algorithm to forecast future resource requirements based on historical data, which made energy saving by turning off unused servers.
8. Feller et al., 2011	Modeled the VM consolidation problem as an instance of the multi-dimensional bin-packing problem and designed a nature-inspired VM consolidation algorithm based on Ant Colony Optimization (ACO). Compared with one frequently applied algorithm (i.e. First-Fit Decreasing), the ACO-based approach achieves better energy-performance tradeoff and can be implemented in a fully distributed environment.
9. Dupont et al., 2012	Proposed a flexible and energy-aware framework for VM consolidation in a data center. The central element of the framework is an optimizer which deals with SLA requirements.
10. Anton et al., 2012	Defined an architectural framework and principles for energy-aware Cloud computing, and developed algorithms for energy-aware mapping of VMs to appropriate Cloud resources in addition to dynamic VM consolidation. The process of the VM consolidation is as follows: firstly, set a fixed upper utilization threshold for hosts in data centers; secondly, review each host's utilization for a period of time. If it exceeds the threshold, it is denoted as overload; finally, choose VMs from those overload hosts to migrate. However, the fixed threshold is not appropriate for virtual environment with variable workloads.

PRELIMINARIES

Utility Functions

Utility functions are used in consumer behavior theory to describe user preferences. While in computer science area they are used in autonomic computing where they capture the agent's preferences for self –resilient systems. In such autonomic systems, the agent can either be a human or software whose preferences are defined in terms of utility functions. They are a popular approach for depicting an agent or user's preferences in autonomic systems as they provide a lucid and uncomplicated basis for taking decisions (Kephart & Das, 2007). According to the work on autonomic systems (Ranjan et al., 2012),autonomic management is one of the most desirable attribute for any large scale dynamic infrastructure like cloud. Due to the unpredicted and dynamic nature of cloud environment, the scheduling and management of resources can be seen as a self-optimized and self-managed problem as the data center manager is responsible for managing the resources like VMs according to demand. Autonomic systems are deemed as self-managing that is they are self-regulating, self-improving, self-protecting and self-healing (Buyya et al., 2012).

In real world computing scenarios the autonomic computing problems are solved using one among the three types of policies called as action policies (also known as rule-based),goal policies and utility functions. The differences in these policies along with examples can be illustrated as in the following Figure 1.

Action policies or the rule-based policies are classically represented in the form of IF (condition) THEN (action), where the condition is the current state of the system. The heuristics based approach presented in the work by (Beloglazov, & Buyya, 2012) and (Beloglazov et al., 2012) utilized action policies for the adaptive cloud scheduling problem.

Figure 1. Policies with examples

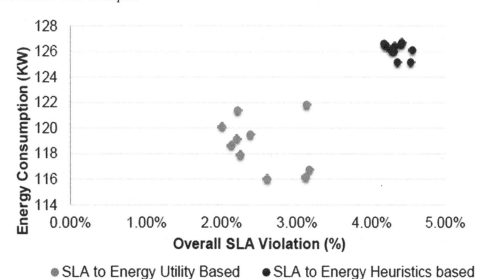

However, the goal based policies specify the desired outcome instead of specifying the task in the beginning unlike the action policies. As illustrated in the example, these policies specify the goal in the beginning and the system will strive to reach for the goal. Essentially the goal based policies carry out a sort of binary categorization against the state of the system and this categorization will be either accepted or rejected according to the goal policy.

Likewise, utility function policies can be seen as an extension of goal policies, where the desired state needn't be specified in advance. In contrast to goal policies, the desired state is computed by repeatedly selecting the state with the highest utility from the feasible ones. This means that utility functions do not perform any kind of classification done in goal policies. Example for utility function in the figure 1 shows solving the same problem previously solved by action and goal policies. The utility function specifies the self-managing policy adopted for the adaptive cloud scheduling problem.

The overall goal of the utility is maximizing the benefit of the adaptive allocation of VMs by minimizing energy consumption and minimizing any sources of violation to the negotiated SLA. As a result, the properties of the utility function will be the total amount of energy consumption (E) and the percentage of SLA violation (SLAV). The high-level definition of the utility of the assignment of the VMs list to the hosts list is formulated as follows in Equation 1:

$$(a,t) = PredictedEnergyCo(a,t) + PredictedViolationCost(a,t) + PDMCost(a,t) \tag{1}$$

Where **a** is a vector representing the assignment of the list of VMs to the hosts list in the datacenter; **t** is the total time of this assignment which is the same as the time of the scheduling interval; *PredictedEnergyCost(a,t)* is the cost of energy consumed due to the assignment. Any violation in the SLA will expose the cloud provider to a penalty which should be paid to the cloud users. In this utility definition, there are two different violation costs that are going to be computed, the first one is *PredictedViolationCost(a,t)* which represents the cost of SLA violation and is computed by counting the number of VMs that are in violation due to the assignment. The second source of violation is the *PDMCost(a,t)* which is the penalty due to the degradation in VMs' performance resulting from the migration of VMs among hosts. Maximizing the utility is achieved by minimizing the sources of cost defined by the different parameters in the utility definition in Equation 1. Therefore, the utility should be expressed by an inverse relationship with the summation of different costs. This makes the final definition of the utility function be as follows in equation 2.

$$Utility(a,t) = \frac{1}{PredictedEnergyCost(a,t) + PredictedViolationCost(a,t) + PDMCost(a,t)} \tag{2}$$

The total energy cost in the datacenter will be the summation of the predicted energy cost per host. The algorithms for calculating the predicted energy cost, the predicted violation cost and the cost of performance degradation due to migration are all shown in the cost model development, section 4, and its sub-sections.

Optimization Algorithm

The aim of this optimization algorithm is to find a good assignment which is rated against the utility function described above. It involves searching for an optimized assignment among all the candidate assignments while evaluating the fitness of the assignment against the utility function. A genetic algorithm (GA) is a meta-heuristic approach for optimizing a combinatorial problem (Holland, 1992). It is considered as a powerful stochastic optimization and search technique based on the Darwin's principle of natural selection (Gen & Cheng, 2000). A genetic algorithm facilitates the exploration of a large search space by iteratively evolving a number of candidate solutions towards the global optimum. The GA initially generates a random population of chromosomes which act as the seed for the search. The algorithm then performs genetic operations such as crossover and mutations to iteratively obtain successive generations of these chromosomes. The crossover operator takes a pair of parent chromosomes and generates an offspring chromosome by crossing over individual genes from each parent. This helps potentially combine partial solutions from the parents into a single offspring. Further, the mutation operator is used to randomly alter some parts of a given chromosomes and advance the search by possibly avoiding getting stuck in a local optimum. The algorithm then applies a selection operator which picks the best chromosomes from the entire population based on their fitness values and eliminates the rest. This process is repeated until a stopping criterion, such as a certain number of iterations or the convergence of a fitness value, is met (Kumbhare et al., 2015). We adapt GA to our optimization problem by defining these domain-specific data structures and operators also show the design requirements of each of these components for finding an efficient assignment for the utility based VM migration problem.

Representation Design

The representation design for our problem will be a vector of m elements, where each element represents a VM and the value of that element is the ID of the host to which the VM is assigned. Figure 2; show the representation of the solution vector of our problem.

Figure 2. Solution Vector

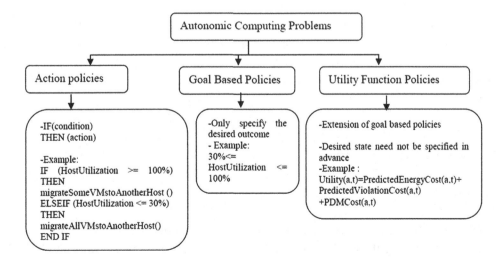

According to the research problem, the representation in Figure 2 is simple and represents the solution efficiently.

Initial Population

For the genetic algorithm to work there should be a way for creating an initial population of solutions to the problem. The initial population consists of a number of individuals where each individual is considered a candidate solution to the problem. In this work, the individual will be a vector of elements, where each element represents a VM and the value of that element is the ID of the host to which the VM is assigned as exhibited in Figure 2. The initial population will be randomly generated based on the output of the initial allocation.

Evaluation/Fitness Function

Each individual "candidate solution" will be evaluated against the fitness "objective" function. In this work, the fitness function is actually the utility function defined in Section 3. A higher fitness means a better result as the goal is to maximize the utility of the assignment.

Genetic Operators

A genetic operation performs some stochastic transformations to generate new individuals "offspring". These transformations are mutation and crossover. The mutation function creates new individuals or structures by making changes in one or more gene values in a single individual. These new individuals are similar to current individuals with changes resulting from a pre-defined probability. The mutation is used to make changes to the population from one generation to another. In this work, there is two different mutation probabilities. The first one is MUTATION_PROBABILITY_DURING_INIT which defines the probability of changing a VM-to-host mapping when building the initial population. The second is MUTATION_PROBABILITY which defines the probability of changing a VM-to-host mapping during generations. The values of those two mutation probabilities should be selected carefully as they are crucial for the genetic algorithm. The crossover function creates new individuals by trying to combine good parts of two individuals. The crossover probability should be tuned carefully for helping in producing better assignment. In the implementation, NEW_CROSSOVER_GENES_RATIO parameter is used for specifying how many new crossover gene pairs to generate in each iteration. A new population is formed by selecting the more fit individuals from the parent population. After the specified number of generations, the algorithm converges to the best individual which hopefully represents a robust solution to the problem.

COST MODEL DEVELOPMENT

Predicted Energy Cost Calculation

The total energy cost can be predicted once the total energy consumption in known. There are various methods used for calculating the total energy consumption as described in the work by (Beloglazov et al., 2012). Accordingly, there are two ways for calculating energy consumption, firstly by defining a suitable power model and secondly using the real data given by SPECpower_ssj2008 benchmark. Modeling power consumption of a server due to the advent of multiple core CPUs and virtualization, is an intricate research problem. Additionally, the work (Beloglazov et al., 2012) we have been referring to has also taken the real power consumption data hence we have taken the same approach to maintain the uniformity. We have taken two configurations of servers in our experiments and the result is published in March 2012 first one is Dell Inc. PowerEdge R620 (Intel Xeon E5-2670, 2.6 GHz, 8 Core, 24 GB) and the second one is Dell Inc. PowerEdge R720 (Intel Xeon E5-2670, 2.6 GHz, 8 Core, 24 GB). Table 2 shows the power consumption by the chosen servers at different workload levels in Watts.

Predicted Energy Cost Algorithm

The energy cost is calculated on the basis of the predicted CPU utilization which is calculated using the power model described in the previous section. The power model is calculated using the real data from industry as given in the Table 2. The algorithm for calculating the predicted energy cost is given in the Table 2. It first of all calculates the utilization of all physical machines based on the CPU utilization. The algorithm is implemented in cloudSim and hence pm.getUtilization() method returns the CPU utilization in MIPS(Millions instruction per second). After the predicted utilization of each PM, for every physical machine in the assignment list it finds the power consumed by per physical machine. The algorithm in Table 3 returns the total energy cost.

Table 2. Power consumption percentage at different workload

Server	0%	10%	20%	30%	40%	50%	60%	70%	80%	90%	100%
Dell PowerEdgeR620	54.1	78.4	88.5	99.5	115	126	143	165	196	226	243
Dell PowerEdgeR620	51.0	75.0	84.5	95.0	110	120	137	159	187	217	231

Table 3. The energy cost calculator algorithm

Algorithm: The Energy Cost Calculator
Input: Allocation a, Scheduling Interval t
Output: Cost of total energy consumed
1. Calculate the predicted utilization of all PMs
2. **for** each PM in the assignment list **do**
Calculate the power consumed per PM
Calculate the Total Power Consumed by all PMs
Total Energy Cost = Total Power Consumed * ENERGY_COST_PER_SEC * t;
3. **return** Total Energy Cost

Predicted SLA Violation Cost

The quality of service (QoS) is one of the crucial concerns of the cloud computing users which are usually fulfilled in terms of SLAs. When working in Software as Service (SaaS) layer SLAs can be expressed in terms of maximum response time, minimum bandwidth, minimum throughput, etc. which are delivered to the users by the application. These parameters are dependent on the type of application or the workload and hence can't be used to define SLAs in Infrastructure as a Service (IaaS) model of cloud. Therefore we have used the SLA metrics which are workload independent as described in the work (Beloglazov, 2012).According to this the SLAs are generated whenever the performance delivered by the virtual machine is lower than its capabilities. In our work, we have taken two sources of SLA violation, firstly when the host is over utilized and secondly the violation caused during the migration of VMs. More detail calculation of these two SLAs violation is described in the following algorithm in Table 4 for SLA violation calculation.

Table 4. The SLA violation cost calculator algorithm

Algorithm: The SLA Violation Cost Calculator
Input: Allocation a, Scheduling Interval t
Output: Cost of SLA violation
1. **for** each PM in the assignment list a **do**
VMList= list of VMs from a in PM
VMList=sort VMList by demand
demand=sum of demands in VMlist
supply= get Total MIPS of the PM
2. **While** demand is greater than supply
violation = violation +1
demand= demand-VMList
3. violationCount +=violation
4. return violationCount*SLA_Cost_Per_Sec*t

Table 5. The PDM violation cost calculator algorithm

Algorithm: The PDM Violation Cost Calculator
Input: Allocation a, Scheduling Interval t
Output: Cost of PDM violation
1. **for** each vm in the assignment list
2. **if** the VM is migrated
3. migrationTime= VM.get MIPS/pm.getBW()
4. **return** pdmViolationCost += migrationTime * PDM_COST_PER_SEC

Predicted PDM Violation Cost

This PDM violation is the second type of violation which occurs during actual virtual machine migration and so the violation is dependent upon the total time required for finishing the migration task successfully. If the migration takes more time to happen then the performance would deteriorate and hence the name performance degradation due to migration (Beloglazov, 2013). The algorithm 3 calculates the PDM violation cost depending on the migration time. The required migration time is calculated by virtual machine capability in MIPS divided by the network bandwidth. The cost is subsequently in Table 5 calculated by multiplying migration time by the cost of PDM.

With the above description of the cost models for calculating the three required costs, the definition of Utility Function is now complete. This utility Function has been used in this work to search for an appropriate assignment of virtual machine which is the ultimate goal of our proposed work.

Performance Evaluation

In this section the effectiveness of our proposed utility function based method for dynamic resource provisioning has been tested using extensive experiments. The results of our approach are compared with the already existing heuristics based approach (Beloglazov, 2013; Beloglazov, 2012). In their work the authors have used various heuristics for solving the virtual machine consolidation problems and their findings indicate the LRR (local regression robust) as the most effective heuristic for virtual machine overload detection. Additionally, the MMT (minimum migration time) for the virtual machine selection was deemed to be most effective among other proposed heuristics. Hence, we have compared our utility based approach with the heuristics that have used MMT for selecting the VMs and LRR for detecting the host overload as when combined they produced best outcomes for the given heuristics. To compare our approach with heuristic based approach we have used certain performance metrics to examine the efficacy of the proposed approach in contrast with other existing approaches. Energy Consumption and Overall SLA violation are the two metrics used by the heuristic based work and so we have used to the same metrics. Energy consumption denotes the total amount of energy consumed by all the hosts, its lower value is indicative of greater utility in our approach. Hence, for our case lower the energy consumption better is the VM assignment. The overall SLA violation is another metrics that we have focused upon. The SLA is deemed to be violated when the requested resource like CPU MIPS is less than whatever is agreed upon in the SLA contract. The main cause behind this violation is either the host over-utilization or the migration of VMs

Experiments Setup

In this section, we have discussed in detail the experiments that were conducted using the CloudSim toolkit for evaluation and comparison purposes. The analysis of the results follows each of the experiments. For all of the following experiments, randomly generated cloudlets using the CloudSim toolkit are used for representing the application's workload to the VM. The length of each cloudlet is 2500 multiplied by the SIMULATION_LIMIT. The SIMULATION_LIMIT represents how long the simulation works. For all of the following experiments, the simulation works for one day. The adaptive scheduling algorithm runs every 5 minutes (300 seconds) which represent the scheduling interval. The performance evaluation was based on three different sets of experiments with three different configurations. The whole setup can be seen in Figure 3.

Figure 3. Performance evaluation setup

Host4	Host1	Host1	Host9	......	......	......	......	......	Hosti
VM1		VM2		VM3		VM3		VMm	

Experiment 1: Configuration 1(50PMs & 50VMs)

In the Experiment 1 with Configuration 1, the number of physical machines (PM) is 50 and the number of virtual machine (VM) is also 50. The key objective of the Experiment 1 was to demonstrate the effectiveness of the utility based approach in slightly loaded data centers where both the number of physical as well as virtual machines is same. Table 6, shows the values of the performance metrics that resulted from deploying the utility based approach after running the experiment 10 different times.

Similarly, Table 7 shows the performance metrics for heuristic based approach after running the experiment 10 times.

Figure 4 shows the scatter plot for the results found in Table 6 and Table 7 for the configuration 1 of experiment 1. The X-axis shows the percentage of overall SLA violation and the Y-axis shows the amount of energy consumption in Kilowatt-hour (kWh). Through the graph it is shown that the utility based approach performs better than the heuristic based approach both in terms of energy consumption and SLA violation.

The average results from both the Tables 6 and Table 7 shows the energy consumption as 31.902 and 35.172 kWh, respectively. This shows that the utility based approach out performs the heuristic approach by almost 10%.

Table 6. Utility based approach

No. of Physical Machines (PMs)	No. of Virtual Machines	No. of VM Migrations	No. of Host Shutdowns	Energy consumption (Kw)	Overall SLA Violation (%)
50	50	312	42	32.13	1.75%
50	50	351	40	33.05	2.67%
50	50	360	43	32.12	2.63%
50	50	390	41	31.68	1.65%
50	50	320	40	29.83	2.15%
50	50	400	40	34.07	3.32%
50	50	215	40	31.55	3.52%
50	50	375	41	30.65	1.56%
50	50	420	39	34.02	2.43%
50	50	415	40	29.92	1.57%

Table 7. Heuristic based approach

No. of Physical Machines (PMs)	No. of Virtual Machines (VMs)	No. of VM Migrations	No. of Host Shutdowns	Energy consumption (Kw)	Overall SLA Violation (%)
50	50	2827	827	35.15	3.96%
50	50	2792	801	34.52	3.85%
50	50	3029	815	34.84	3.35%
50	50	2850	821	35.01	3.18%
50	50	2872	823	35.43	3.80%
50	50	2919	802	35.28	3.24%
50	50	2962	805	35.06	3.56%
50	50	2815	789	35.78	3.35%
50	50	3003	870	35.28	3.26%
50	50	2999	806	35.37	3.66%

Figure 4. Result of experiment 1 and configuration 1

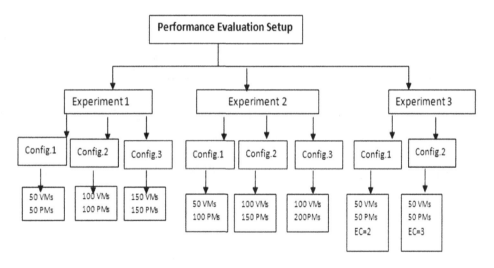

Experiment 1: Configuration 2(100PMs & 100VMs)

In the experiment 1 with configuration 2 the number of physical machines (PM) is 100 and the number of virtual machine (VM) is also 100. Table 8, shows the values of the performance metrics that resulted from deploying the utility based approach after running the experiment 10 different times. Table 9 shows the performance metrics for heuristic based approach.

Figure 5 shows the result of experiment 1 and configuration 2 in a scatter plot. The performance metrics have been taken from Table 5 and Table 6 where the average energy consumption for utility based approach is 64.124 while in case of heuristics based approach it is 67.75. Similarly, the overall SLA violation in case of utility based approach is 2.66% while the same for heuristics based approach is 4.07%. Both these results are indicative of the effectiveness of the utility based approach.

Table 8. Utility based approach

No. of Physical Machines (PMs)	No. of Virtual Machines (VMs)	No. of VM Migrations	No. of Host Shutdowns	Energy consumption (Kw)	Overall SLA Violation (%)
100	100	1334	84	63.44	1.83%
100	100	1345	90	63.02	2.62%
100	100	1402	91	64.41	2.61%
100	100	1645	85	61.99	3.33%
100	100	1456	87	63.71	2.43%
100	100	1543	94	64.95	2.40%
100	100	1443	95	65.41	3.99%
100	100	987	92	66.53	2.59%
100	100	1481	93	62.7	2.60%
100	100	1425	88	65.08	2.15%

Table 9. Heuristics based approach

No. of Physical Machines (PMs)	No. of Virtual Machines (VMs)	No. of VM Migrations	No. of Host Shutdowns	Energy consumption (Kw)	Overall SLA Violation (%)
100	100	7120	1719	66.94	4.15%
100	100	6794	1617	67.52	4.19%
100	100	6921	1703	67.98	4.10%
100	100	6886	1644	67.52	4.23%
100	100	7100	1720	68.24	3.96%
100	100	7022	1681	67.8	4.07%
100	100	7036	1714	67.91	4.00%
100	100	6874	1661	67.72	3.97%
100	100	7105	1711	68.13	4.05%
100	100	7176	1715	67.74	4.02%

Experiment 1: Configuration 3(100PMs & 100VMs)

In the experiment 1 with configuration 3 the number of physical machines (PM) is 150 and the number of virtual machine (VM) is also 150. Table 10, shows the values of the performance metrics that resulted from deploying the utility based approach after running the experiment 10 different times. Table 11 shows the performance metrics for heuristic based approach.

Figure 6 shows the result of experiment 1 and configuration 3 in a scatter plot where the values for the performance metrics are taken from Table 10 and Table 11.The average of energy consumption for utility based approach is 96.675 kWh while the same result for heuristics based approach is 101.43kWh. The SLA violation for utility based approach is 2.49% while for the heuristics based approach it is 4.20%.

Figure 5. Result of experiment 1 and configuration 2

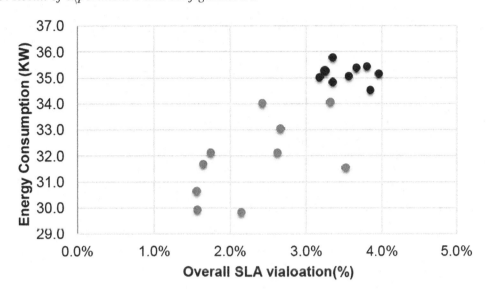

● SLA to Energy Utility Based   ● SLA to Energy Heuristics based

Table 10. Utility based approach

No. of Physical Machines (PMs)	No. of Virtual Machines (VMs)	No. of VM Migrations	No. of Host Shutdowns	Energy consumption (Kw)	Overall SLA Violation (%)
150	150	1654	130	100.51	2.51%
150	150	1759	121	100.52	2.20%
150	150	1702	136	98.4	2.31%
150	150	1755	89	94.61	2.57%
150	150	1759	76	92.62	2.21%
150	150	1722	81	97.89	2.13%
150	150	1593	85	96.91	2.11%
150	150	960	109	97.29	2.53%
150	150	1220	111	93.35	3.31%
150	150	1133	126	94.65	3.01%

This difference in both the performance metrics is a clear indication of the effectiveness of the utility based approach.

Experiment 2: Configuration 1(100PMs & 100 VMs)

This configuration of the datacenter is exactly same as the one presented in experiment 1 configuration 2.

Table 11. Heuristics based approach

No. of Physical Machines (PMs)	No. of Virtual Machines (VMs)	No. of VM Migrations	No. of Host Shutdowns	Energy consumption (Kw)	Overall SLA Violation (%)
150	150	10763	2523	101.27	4.42%
150	150	11190	2605	102.15	4.14%
150	150	10853	2556	101.83	4.12%
150	150	11249	2472	101.11	4.11%
150	150	10766	2433	100.53	4.44%
150	150	11193	2476	100.82	4.04%
150	150	10573	2503	101.03	4.11%
150	150	11192	2605	102.11	4.14%
150	150	11362	2566	101.42	4.22%
150	150	11227	2579	102.03	4.23%

Figure 6. Result of experiment 1 and configuration 3

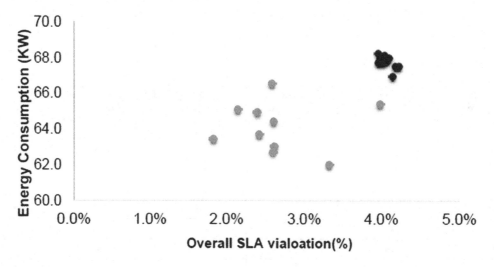

● SLA to Energy Utility Based   ● SLA to Energy Heuristics based

Experiment 2: Configuration 2(100PMs & 150VMs)

In the experiment 2 with configuration 2, the number of physical machines (PM) is 100 and the number of virtual machine (VM) is 150. Table 12, shows the values of the performance metrics that resulted from deploying the utility based approach after running the experiment 10 different times. Table 13 shows the performance metrics for heuristic based approach.

Figure 7 shows the result of experiment 2 and configuration 2 in a scatter plot. The performance metrics have been taken from Table 12 and Table 13 where the average energy consumption for utility based approach is 94.645kWh while in case of heuristics based approach it is 100.891kWh. Similarly,

Table 12. Utility based approach

No. of Physical Machines (PMs)	No. of Virtual Machines (VMs)	No. of VM Migrations	No. of Host Shutdowns	Energy consumption (Kw)	Overall SLA Violation (%)
100	150	1015	75	92.3	2.75%
100	150	800	71	94.93	1.91%
100	150	932	72	92.32	2.85%
100	150	777	76	94.85	2.52%
100	150	1013	73	87.73	3.24%
100	150	898	71	90.81	2.11%
100	150	795	72	95	2.98%
100	150	1816	75	99.25	2.86%
100	150	1636	77	100.69	2.84%
100	150	1813	81	98.57	1.85%

Table 13. Heuristics based approach

No. of Physical Machines (PMs)	No. of Virtual Machines (VMs)	No. of VM Migrations	No. of Host Shutdowns	Energy consumption (Kw)	Overall SLA Violation (%)
100	150	11135	2477	100.17	4.03%
100	150	11073	2464	100.72	4.56%
100	150	11412	2467	100.96	4.41%
100	150	11395	2478	101.82	4.34%
100	150	11277	2459	100.74	4.33%
100	150	11125	2484	100.77	4.61%
100	150	11283	2477	101.34	4.42%
100	150	11386	2502	100.49	4.17%
100	150	10899	2463	100.87	4.24%
100	150	11123	2490	101.03	4.31%

the overall SLA violation in case of utility based approach is 2.59% while the same for heuristics based approach is 4.34%. Both these results are indicative of the effectiveness of the utility based approach.

Experiment 2: Configuration 3(100PMs & 200VMs)

In the experiment 2 with configuration 3, the number of physical machines (PM) is 100 and the number of virtual machine (VM) is 200. Table 14, shows the values of the performance metrics that resulted from deploying the utility based approach after running the experiment 10 different times. Table 15 shows the performance metrics for heuristic based approach.

Figure 8 shows the result of experiment 2 and configuration 3 in a scatter plot where the values for the performance metrics are taken from Table 14 and Table 15. The average of energy consumption for

Figure 7. Result of experiment 2 and configuration 2

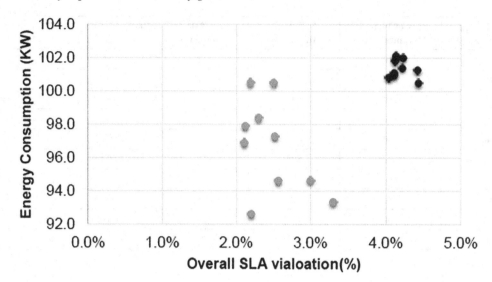

Table 14. Utility based approach

No. of Physical Machines (PMs)	No. of Virtual Machines (VMs)	No. of VM Migrations	No. of Host Shutdowns	Energy consumption (Kw)	Overall SLA Violation (%)
100	200	1075	70	121.83	3.13%
100	200	1138	64	116.02	2.61%
100	200	1232	62	118.66	2.13%
100	200	1150	66	116.73	3.17%
100	200	1023	61	117.91	2.25%
100	200	1328	66	116.13	3.11%
100	200	1064	63	119.16	2.21%
100	200	869	69	119.48	2.39%
100	200	1005	60	120.11	2.01%
100	200	945	62	121.36	2.22%

utility based approach is 118.739kWh while the same result for heuristics based approach is 126.137 kWh. The SLA violation for utility based approach is 2.52% while for the heuristics based approach it is 4.35%. This difference in both the performance metrics is a clear indication of the effectiveness of the utility based approach.

Table 15. Heuristics based approach

No. of Physical Machines (PMs)	No. of Virtual Machines (VMs)	No. of VM Migrations	No. of Host Shutdowns	Energy consumption (Kw)	Overall SLA Violation (%)
100	200	12411	2397	126.59	4.40%
100	200	12436	2366	126.42	4.31%
100	200	12251	2323	125.16	4.53%
100	200	12041	2378	126.62	4.17%
100	200	12274	2376	126.49	4.19%
100	200	12522	2380	126.01	4.30%
100	200	12306	2363	126.13	4.55%
100	200	11968	2301	126.09	4.26%
100	200	12481	2392	126.71	4.41%
100	200	12269	2304	125.15	4.35%

Figure 8. Result of experiment 2 and configuration 3

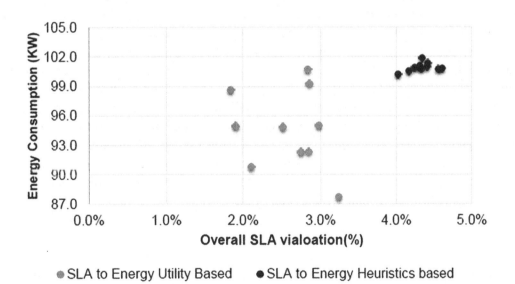

● SLA to Energy Utility Based   ● SLA to Energy Heuristics based

PERFORMANCE ANALYSIS

In slightly loaded datacenters, any increase in the number of VMs accompanied with an increase in the number of hosts with the same percentage, using either the utility or heuristics based approaches, results in the following: The amount of energy consumed increases by a percentage that is slightly less than the percentage of the increase in the number of VMs. The percentage of SLA violations remains approximately at the same level without any substantial changes.

In more loaded datacenters, using either the utility or heuristics based approach; any increase in the number of VMs almost produces the same results found in slightly loaded datacenters. This means that there will be an increase in the energy consumption with a percentage that is somewhat less than the percentage of increase in the number of VMs. However, the percentage of SLA violations approximately remains in the same range. Increasing energy cost in the utility based approach by 50% results in an increase in the percentage of SLA violations by about 45%. Nonetheless, there is only about 10% decrease in energy consumption. This result, emphasis on the importance of thoroughly determining the cost of energy and violations. All the foregoing experiments showed that the utility based approach is more efficient than the heuristics based approach, on average; as it produced less energy consumption besides minimizing the percentage of SLA violations. However, there are notable variations in the values of the performance metrics among the different runs of the same experiment compared to the consistency in the results of the heuristics based approach.

CONCLUSION AND FUTURE WORK

Nowadays, there is a tremendous demand for cloud computing services. As a consequence, cloud providers built gigantic datacenters to meet this high demand of cloud services. These gigantic datacenters consume enormous amounts of energy that badly affect the environment and increase the operational costs of the datacenter. Adaptive cloud scheduling techniques are essential for saving energy consumption and creating green cloud computing environments. Adopting the adaptive cloud scheduling techniques are useful for the cloud providers, cloud consumers and the environment.

Creating an adaptive cloud scheduling strategy means creating a self-managing datacenter that dynamically reacts to changes in the cloud environment. Self-managing computing systems can be built using rule-based policies, goal policies or utility functions. This research work used utility functions to create a self-managing cloud datacenter that dynamically assigns VMs-to-hosts according to resource utilization. The aim of this research was, designing, implementing and evaluating an adaptive cloud scheduling strategy based on utility functions. The utility function was represented as the inverse of the summation of the energy cost, violation cost and the cost of performance degradation due to migration (PDM). In this study, experiments had been conducted to compare between the effectiveness of the action-based "heuristics-based" policies and utility functions.

By and large, the results showed that utility based approach implemented in this work is more efficient than the heuristics based approach in saving energy consumption and minimizing the percentage of SLA violations. These results of the utility based approach are encouraging; however, more future work is required in different directions as described in the following section. The conducted experiments demonstrated that, heuristics based approach adapts whenever there is a problem, host overload or host under-load. On the contrary, the utility based approach adapts if it identified a solution that is predicted to be better.

Future Work

In this work, utility functions along with genetic algorithms are used for the adaptive VMs-to-physical hosts scheduling. Due to time and scope limitations, the approach depended upon CPU as the only resource for this scheduling problem. However, there are many other resources and environment parameters that should be taken into consideration to produce more realistic results. The following sub-sections discuss the future work and ideas.

1. **Improving the Cost Model:** Work is needed for improving the effectiveness of the cost model. This work should be in the area of calculating the predicted violation cost. The first idea for improving the predicted violation cost is through the implementation of the Markov chain that will anticipate future CPU utilization, and this might help in minimizing SLA violations. Moreover, further study needs to be performed for finding a concrete relationship between cost of energy and cost of the violation.

2. **Considering all Computing Resources:** Although, the CPU consumes most of the server's power; all other host and network resources should be involved in the adaptive assignment of VMs-to-hosts in cloud computing environments. Examples of these resources are the memory, network bandwidth, storage and the number of CPU cores. In general, cloud providers use centralized disk storage to ease live migration of VMs between physical machines. Thus, disk storage could be excluded from the resources involved in the adaptive scheduling.

3. **Multi-Objective Optimization:** In this study, the fitness function has been expressed as a utility with one objective, maximizing the profit. However, what would be results if we expressed the problem as a multi-objective optimization problem? This multi-objective optimization problem should consider minimizing energy consumption together with minimizing SLA violation.

REFERENCES

Armbrust, M., Stoica, I., Zaharia, M., Fox, A., Griffith, R., Joseph, A. D., & Rabkin, A. et al. (2010). A View of Cloud Computing. *Communications of the ACM*, *53*(4), 50–58. doi:10.1145/1721654.1721672

Barroso, L.A., & Holzle, U. (2007). The case for energy-proportional computing. *Computer*, *40*(12), 33–37. doi:10.1109/MC.2007.443

Beloglazov, A. (2013). Energy-efficient management of virtual machines in data centers for cloud computing.

Beloglazov, A., Abawajy, J., & Buyya, R. (2012). Energy-aware resource allocation heuristics for efficient management of data centers for Cloud computing. *Future generation computer systems*, *28*(5), 755–768.

Beloglazov, A., & Buyya, R. (2012). Optimal online deterministic algorithms and adaptive heuristics for energy and performance efficient dynamic consolidation of virtual machines in cloud data centers. *Concurrency and Computation*, *24*(13), 1397–1420. doi:10.1002/cpe.1867

Beloglazov, R.A., & Buyya, R. (2012). Optimal online deterministic algorithms and adaptive heuristics for energy and performance efficient dynamic consolidation of virtual machines in cloud data centers. *Concurrency and Computation*, *24*(13), 1397–1420. doi:10.1002/cpe.1867

Bila, N., & Lara, E. D. et al.. (2012). Jettison: efficient idle desktop consolidation with partial VM migration.*Proceeding EuroSys'12 proceedings of the 7th ACM European conference on computer systems* (pp. 211–224). New York: ACM. doi:10.1145/2168836.2168858

Bobroff, N., Kochut, A., & Beaty, K. (2007) Dynamic placement of virtual machines for managing SLA violations. *Proceedings of the 10th IFIP/IEEE international symposium on integrated network management IM '07*, Munich (pp. 119–128).

Buyya, R., Calheiros, R.N., Li, X., & Computing, A.C. (2012). Open Challenges and Architectural Elements. *Proceedings of theThird International Conference on Emerging Applications of Information Technology (EAIT)*. doi:10.1109/EAIT.2012.6407847

Cardosa, M., Korupolu, M.R., & Singh, A. (2009). Shares and utilities based power consolidation in virtualized server environments. Proceedings of the IFIP/IEEE international symposium on integrated network management, Long Island (pp. 327–334).

Cisco. (n. d.). Cisco Global Cloud Index: Forecast and Methodology, 2013–2018 (whitepaper).

Cisco. (2011). Cisco Global Cloud Index "Growth in data center electricity use 2005 to 2010." (Tech. Report). Analytics Press.

Dupont, C., & Schulze, T., Giuliani, G., Somov, A., & Hermenier, F. (2012). An energy aware framework for virtual machine placement in cloud federated data centres. *Proceedings of the 3rd international conference on future energy systems: where energy, computing and communication meet e-Energy'12*. New York: ACM.

Duy, T. V. T., Sato, Y., & Inoguchi, Y. (2010). *Performance evaluation of a green scheduling algorithm for energy savings in Cloud computing. Proceedings of the 2010 IEEE international symposium on parallel and distributed processing, workshops and Phd forum* (pp. 1–8). Atlanta: IPDPSW. doi:10.1109/IPDPSW.2010.5470908

Borgetto, D., Casanova, H., Da Costa, G., & Pierson, J. M. (2012). Energy-aware service allocation. Future Generation Computer Systems, 28(5), 769–779.

Feller, E., Rilling, L., & Morin, C. (2011). Energy-aware ant colony based workload placement in Clouds. *Proceeding GRID'11 proceedings of the 2011 IEEE/ACM 12th international conference on grid computing* (pp. 26–33). IEEE Computer Society, Washington, DC, doi:10.1109/Grid.2011.13

Foster, I., Zhao, Y., Raicu, I., & Lu, S. (2008). Cloud computing and grid computing 360-degree compared. *Proceedings of the Grid Computing Environments Workshop GCE'08*. IEEE.

Gen, M., & Cheng, R. (2000). *Genetic algorithms and engineering optimization*. John Wiley & Sons.

Gong, Z.H., & Gu, X.H. (2010). PAC: pattern-driven application consolidation for efficient Cloud computing. *Proceeding MASCOTS' 10 proceedings of the 2010 IEEE international symposium on modeling, analysis and simulation of computer and telecommunication systems* (pp. 24–33). doi:10.1109/MASCOTS.2010.12

Goudarzi, H., & Pedram, M. (2012). Energy-efficient virtual machine replication and placement in a Cloud computing system. *Proceedings of the2012 IEEE fifth international conference on Cloud computing*, Honolulu (pp. 750–757). doi:10.1109/CLOUD.2012.107

Holland, J. H. (1992). *Adaptation in Natural and Artificial Systems*. Cambridge, MA, USA: MIT Press.

Huanliu. (2012, March 13). Amazon data centre size. Retrieved from http://huanliu.wordpress. com/2012/03/13/amazondata-center-size/

Kansal, A., Zhao, F., Liu, J., Kothari, N., & Bhattacharya, A.A. (2010). Virtual machine power metering and provisioning. *Proceeding SoCC'10 proceedings of the 1st ACM symposium on Cloud computing* (pp. 39–50). New York: ACM. doi:10.1145/1807128.1807136

Kephart, J. O., & Das, R. (2007). Achieving self-management via utility functions. *IEEE Internet Computing, 11*(1), 40–48. doi:10.1109/MIC.2007.2

Koomey, J. G. (2007). *Estimating total power consumption by servers in the US and the world.* Lawrence Berkeley National Laboratory, Tech. Rep.

Kumbhare, A. G., Simmhan, Y., Frincu, M., & Prasanna, V. K. (2015). Reactive Resource Provisioning Heuristics for Dynamic Dataflows on Cloud Infrastructure. *IEEE Transactions on Cloud Computing, 3*(2), 105–118.

Lovsz, G., Niedermeier, F., & Meer, H. D. (2012). Performance tradeoffs of energy-aware virtual machine consolidation. *Cluster Computing.*

Mills, K., Filliben, J., & Dabrowski, C. (2011). Comparing VM-placement algorithms for on-demand Clouds. *Proceedings of the2011 IEEE third international conference on Cloud computing technology and science (CloudCom),* Athens (pp. 91–98). doi:10.1109/CloudCom.2011.22

Nathuji, R., & Schwan, K. (2007). Virtualpower: coordinated power management in virtualized enterprise systems. *ACM SIGOPS Oper. Syst. Rev., 41*(6).

Oh, F.Y.K., Kim, H.S., Eom, H., & Yeom, H.Y. (2011). Enabling consolidation and scaling down to provide power management for Cloud computing. *Proceeding HotCloud'11 proceedings of the 3rd USENIX conference on hot topics in Cloud computing.*

Bilal, K., Manzano, M., Khan, S.U., Calle, E., Li, K., & Zomaya, A.Y. (2013). On the Characterization of the Structural Robustness of Data Center Networks. *IEEE Transactions on* Cloud Computing, *1*(1), 1–1.

Open Compute Project. (n. d.). Energy efficiency. Retrieved from http://opencompute.org/about/energy-efficiency/

Ranjan, R., Buyya, R., & Parashar, M. (2012, June). Autonomic Cloud Computing: Technologies, Services, and Applications. *Concurrency and Computation: Practice and Experience, 24*(9), 935-937.

Srikantaiah, S., Kansal, A., & Zhao, F. (2008). Energy aware consolidation for Cloud computing.*Proceedings of the 2008 conference on power aware computing and systems,* San Diego (p. 10).

Standard Performance Evaluation Corporation. (2012). SPECpower_ssj2008 Results res2012q1. Retrieved from http://www.spec.org/power_ssj2008/results/res2012q1/power_ssj2008-20120306-00434.html

Stoess, J., Lang, C., & Bellosa, F. (2007). Energy management for hypervisor-based virtual machines. *Proceeding ATC'07 USENIX annual technical conference on proceedings of the USENIX annual technical conference.*

Verman, A., Ahuja, P., & Neogi, A. (2008). pMapper: power and migration cost aware application placement in virtualized systems. *Proceeding middleware '08 proceedings of the 9th ACM/IFIP/USENIX international conference on middleware* (pp. 243–264). New York: Springer.

Xu, J., & Fortes, J. A. B. (2010). Multi-objective virtual machine placement in virtualized data center environments. Proceedings of the 2010 IEEE/ACM international conference on green computing and communications and international conference on cyber, physical and social computing, Hangzhou (pp. 179–188). doi:10.1109/GreenCom-CPSCom.2010.137

Chapter 5
Resource Allocation Policies in Cloud Computing Environment

Suvendu Chandan Nayak
C. V. Raman College of Engineering, India

Sasmita Parida
C. V. Raman College of Engineering, India

Chitaranjan Tripathy
Veer Surendra Sai University of Technology, India

Prasant Kumar Pattnaik
KIIT University, India

ABSTRACT

The basic concept of cloud computing is based on "Pay per Use". The user can use the remote resources on demand for computing on payment basis. The on-demand resources of the user are provided according to a Service Level Agreement (SLA). In real time, the tasks are associated with a time constraint for which they are called deadline based tasks. The huge number of deadline based task coming to a cloud datacenter should be scheduled. The scheduling of this task with an efficient algorithm provides better resource utilization without violating SLA. In this chapter, we discussed the backfilling algorithm and its different types. Moreover, the backfilling algorithm was proposed for scheduling tasks in parallel. Whenever the application environment is changed the performance of the backfilling algorithm is changed. The chapter aims implementation of different types of backfilling algorithms. Finally, the reader can be able to get some idea about the different backfilling scheduling algorithms that are used for scheduling deadline based task in cloud computing environment at the end.

INTRODUCTION

Cloud computing is the leading booming technology for delivery of reliable, secure, fault-tolerant, sustainable, and scalable computational services to the end-users. Cloud computing is nothing but taking services that are "cloud services" and moving them outside an organizations firewall on shared systems (Mell & Grance, 2009). These applications and services are accessed via the web, instead of your hard drive. Cloud service providers offer elastic, on-demand, and measured infrastructure, platforms and software services. On-demand facility of virtualized resources as service is offered using virtualization in cloud computing without any delay (Kumbhare et al., 2015).

DOI: 10.4018/978-1-5225-2013-9.ch005

Cloud computing is typically classified based on either their deployment or service models represents cloud models based on the NIST definition framework (Mell & Grance, 2009). Cloud deployment models can be classified as private, public, community, and hybrid cloud. According to IDC (Calheiros & Buyya, 2014), the most beneficial aspects of using cloud include fast and easy deployment, the pay-per-use model, and reduction of in-house IT costs. In the public cloud, tenants have control over the OS, storage and deployed applications. Resources are provisioned in different geographic regions (Calheiros & Buyya, 2014). In the public cloud deployment model, the performance of an application deployed in multiple regions is a matter of concern for organizations. Proof of concepts in the public cloud environment gives a better understanding, but cost a lot in terms of capacity building and resource usage even in the pay-per-use model.

For implementation of such characteristics on cloud systems is under consideration, but it is required timely, iteratively, and controllable methodologies for the evaluation of newly developed cloud applications and policies before actual development of cloud products (Venkatesan et al., 2013). As the utilization of real test beds samples limit the experiments to the scale of the test bed performances and their results are an extremely difficult to undertake, simulate which may be used in future. The service model of cloud computing is shown in Figure 1. The service model mainly includes three types of services such as: Software as a Service (SaaS), Platform as a Service (PaaS) and Infrastructure as a Service (IaaS). Basically, for SaaS belongs to software. PaaS deals with a platform for the user application which is cost effective for the user without cloud computing and IaaS include both software and hardware resources (Kumbhare et al., 2015).

Cloud computing infrastructures and application services, allowing its users to focus on specific system design issues that they want to investigate, without getting concerned about the low level details related to cloud-based infrastructures and services. Simulation of cloud environments and applications to evaluate performance can provide useful insights to explore such dynamic, massively distributed, and scalable environments cloud to host applications (Parida & Nayak, 2013). The cloud creates complex provisioning, deployment, and configuration requirements. Mainly cloud computing is the collection

Figure 1. Different service models in cloud computing

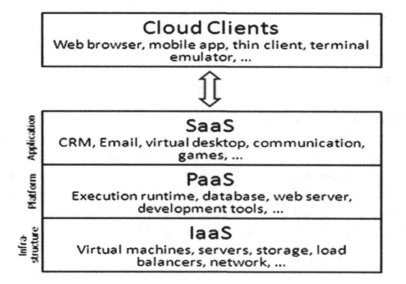

of datacenters which provides virtual machines(VM) and each data center has a collection of physical machines (Nayak & Tripathy, 2016). Here, each physical machine has its own resources with a fixed or scalable amount such as CPU, main memory, storage area, I/O and bandwidth. When a request is sent by the end user to the datacenter, then the virtual machine (VM) is created according to the request of the physical machine (Nayak & Tripathy, 2016). The main challenging issue is the creation of different of virtual machines in a physical machine to execute the user's request as showed in Figure 2.

A virtual machine is software for computer that behaves like a physical computer, runs an operating system and applications from remote side. The virtual machine is comprised of a set of specifications and configuration files which are backed by the physical resources of a host (Bichler et al., 2006). Every virtual machine has virtual devices that provide the same functionality as physical hardware, and have additional benefits in terms of portability, manageability and security (Di et al., 2015). Virtual machines are the key component in a virtual infrastructure. Every virtual machine has CPU, memory and disk as resources. A virtual machine is associated with a particular datacenter, host, cluster, or resource pool. Basically, in cloud computing the virtual machines are associated with the datacenters.

Due to the insufficient resources, mostly it is very difficult to successfully execute all the user's requests at a particular instant. For that we have follow different resource allocation mechanisms and some scheduling policies, methods or algorithms which are very much efficient to process all the users' requests. As observed in (Sotomayor et al., 2009) resource allocation model is broadly divided into three categories:

1. Data Center Processing Resource Allocation
2. Data center Network Resource Allocation
3. Energy Efficient Data Center Resource Allocation

The user is unknown about the physical machine. The user request which is called the lease consists of different parameters like CPU Time, Main memory, Storage area. To schedule resources different models and algorithms are proposed. Basically, the resource allocation is done in terms of leases. Haizea lease manager is most popular in cloud computing (Sotomayor, 2009).

Figure 2. VMs created in physical machines

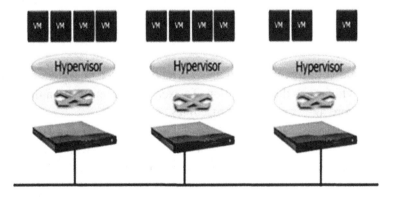

Connected to Physical machines

BACKGROUND

To understand deadline based task scheduling in any meaningful way, it is necessary for a computer scientist to understand some basic terminology. In this chapter a short and basic introduction to the fundamentals and relevant to task scheduling in cloud computing is given which are illustrated below. When the user sends a request to execute an application through the cloud then that application is sent to data center where actual physical machine which handles the request. After that it allocates one or more than one Virtual machine to run the application (Lai, 2013). Thus, the resource allocation policies are required for proper utilization of resources. Resource allocation management is one of the most important problems in cloud computing. However, it is a very challenging issue to efficiently design resource scheduling algorithms and implement them (since general scheduling problem is NP complete problem) (Nayak & Tripathy, 2016).

For distributed cloud systems a network aware resource allocation is proposed (Di et al., 2015). In this paper the authors minimized the maximum distance, latency between the selected data centers. If a user has to run a large task which needs more than one virtual machine then there is solution by Haizea resource manager. Haizea also provides an efficient resource allocation for advanced reservation and deadline sensitive type of leases. Another type of leasing is Capacity leasing in cloud systems which is discussed in (Sotomayor et al., 2009) by using the Open Nebula engine. In (Sotomayor, 2009) some more types of resource leasing and the art of suspending virtual machines are briefly discussed. Sotomayor also discussed resource leasing by combining batch execution and using virtual machines (Lai, 2013).

In Haizea model different types of resource scheduling algorithms are proposed basing upon lease management. By considering different specific subsystems of Large Scale and Distributed Systems, such as (Nathani et al., 2012) on the basis of performance of memory systems, or it only deal with one or two specific SLA parameters. Petrucci et al. (Tsafrir et al., 2005) and Lindsay (Lindsay et al., 2011) discussed one general resource management constraint and Khanna et al. (Shmueli, 2003) also discussed only on response time and throughput during resource scheduling. Moreover, Haizea is an open-source VM-based lease management architecture (Wong & Goscinski, 2007) which provides the following features:

- Haizea is a resource manager depending on scheduling of resources.
- Haizea uses different types of leases: Each lease is some form of contract where one party agrees to provide a set of resources to another party.
- Haizea is VM-based: Haizea's scheduling algorithms are managed different virtual machines, by considering all the extra operations (and overhead) involved in managing VMs.
- Haizea is an open source.

Haizea architecture allows different types of leases which are listed below. Here each lease is considered as the user request which runs the application. To execute that application these leases need either one virtual machine or more number of virtual machines.

- **Advance Reservation Leases** *:* This types of leases or tasks need resources at a specific time. The resources are needed to allocate at a particular time. There is a large time gap between the request and execution.

- **Immediate Leases** : These types of leases need the resources at right now. If the sufficient resources are not available then the request is rejected. Though the leases required resources immediately it is called immediate lease.
- **Best - Effort Leases** : These are the types of leases which will wait in a queue until resources become available. It means that when the resources will be free it will be allocated to the leases as soon as possible.
- **Deadline Sensitive** : Except the above three types of leases one more type of lease is possible in the cloud computing that is called deadline sensitive leases. In these types of leases, some more parameter constraints are associated like deadline. Whenever a best-effort lease is associated with a deadline for the resource and the lease should be scheduled within it. This type lease has specific start Time, end Time (deadline), duration. If the cloud provider can provide resources in this stipulated time duration then the lease is accepted otherwise it is rejected.

The Haizea architecture is shown in Figure 3 where the user requests are in the form of lease. Once a requested lease is accepted by the scheduler then it cannot be rejected anymore. Here, the scheduler plays a vital and important role as it is tries to accommodate newly arrived leases as much as possible within some specific time but not always. The scheduler has to check whether the already accommodated leases are still comfortably able to run successfully or not. Haizea follows simple resource allocation mechanisms to schedule the deadline sensitive leases. First, it tries to find out a single slot within the start Time and end Time of the given lease. By which the lease can be allocated with the requested resources for the user. If no such type of time slot not found by the scheduler then that lease will be rejected.

Figure 3. The Haizea architecture

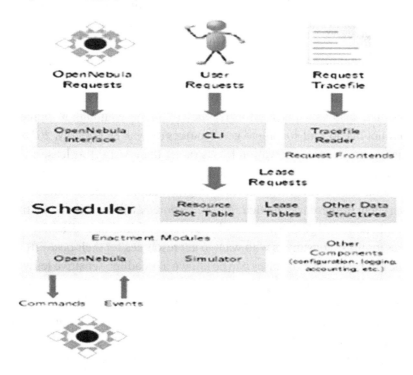

MAIN FOCUS OF THE CHAPTER

Resource allocation algorithms for scheduling which can handle a variety of usage scenarios. Typically, the user's requests may arrive and leave at any point of time and also a user may make requests for more resources according to the need as time and lease progresses. User may change need of specific amount of resources for the application in a cloud which can be given for some specific amount of time. Thus, for every resource there is a start time and given end time (deadline) which has to be considered. This above type of requirement can be handled by Haizea in the form of a deadline sensitive lease. When there is a request of deadline sensitive lease comes to Haizea, it first tries to find out a single slot which can provide the required resources within the specific time duration. If Haizea model can find such type of a time slot, then it accepts the newly arrived deadline sensitive lease. On the other hand if it cannot find such type of a single slot then Haizea reschedules already accommodated deadline sensitive leases and apply best effort leases. For this, first of all it finds which leases can be rescheduled and then how they can be rescheduled again. For rescheduling, the leases which are having start time or end time greater than or equal to the start time of a newly arrived lease are considered. Once these leases are found and fixed, Haizea adds the newly arrived deadline sensitive lease to the list (Feitelson, 2001) for scheduling.

Further, we move forward with deadline sensitive lease scheduling with best effort lease management. Along with the swapping and backfilling algorithm with its different modifications, we discussed the performance enhancement of deadline sensitive algorithms.

UNDERSTANDING OF DEADLINE SENSITIVE

Moreover, we considered the lease parameters are number of nodes means number of virtual machines, physical resource for each node like CPU utilization and Main Memory, start time, duration and end time which is called deadline. In Haizea model a lease object is maintained to store lease's information after receiving the lease from a user. Then the scheduler tries to schedule this lease.

Haizea has several scheduling and resource allocation which specify how Haizea selects resources and schedules the leases. There is no guarantee that a submitted best-effort lease will get resources to complete the processing within a certain time limit. If the system is flooded with lots of advance reservation and immediate leases then best effort leases will not have enough resources to run on. The best-effort leases may not like to wait so long to get resources (Nayak & Tripathy, 2016). They will start submitting their requests as advance reservation leases rather than best-effort leases, to be assured that the submitted requests will be completed within a certain time limit. As a result, the system will have more advance reservation leases which will increase fragmentation of free resources. As there are less best-effort leases, very few of these fragmented unused resources will be utilized by them.

Thus, the system utilization will go down. To handle such type of situations, deadlines can be associated with best-effort leases for those consumers who want to get resources for their best-effort leases within a specific range of time limit. This type of leases can be known as deadline sensitive leases where deadline lease parameter is added (Nayak & Tripathy, 2016). Generally, Deadline sensitive leases are considered to be preemptive scheduling but there is a limitation. It is preemptive only if the scheduling algorithm of Haizea can assure that it can be completed before its deadline. S,o it will assure consumers that their request will be completed within a certain time limit. There are several other options by which one can modify the scheduling algorithms, such that when backfilling algorithm and swapping are to be used?

In cloud computing the service provider needs to utilize the resource in an efficient way whereas the user needs the task should be completed in the time line. Moreover, the service provider also needs to compute more number of users' request by which the revenue can be maximized. These things can be achieved by designing a good scheduler which will fulfill the above benefits for both user and service provider. In real time, most of the user requests are bounded with a time constraint to finish the execution. The user request will be computed with sufficient demanded resources (Nayak & Tripathy, 2016).

Representation

Deadline sensitive tasks or leases have number of dependent parameters such as arrival time, start time, execution duration, deadline to finish the execution and the resource parameter that is number of nodes(VMs) to compute the application. We can represent a deadline sensitive task T is below:

$$T = \{n, AT, ST, E, D\} \tag{1.1}$$

In Equation 1.1, we defined a deadline sensitive task T in five tuple form. The parameters are described as:

n = Number of nodes a task needs to execute the application. In real time scenario most of the task execution is parallel, for which we need more number of nodes in the physical machine. Here the node means the number of virtual machines (VMs) required for computing the user application.

AT = Arrival time of the task. This parameter specifies the time when the user request is made. In cloud computing the user request are mainly different types as we discussed in section 2.

ST = Start time, this is the actual time when the application starts execution. The task gets n number of nodes at this time, not before it.

E = Execution duration, this is the time period where n number of nodes are allocated to the task T. When the E is lapsed the n number of nodes is released from the task T.

D = Deadline, It is a time constraint which specifies a task T must be executed for the time E with n number of required nodes. It is very important that the task should be schedule within D.

The deadline D of a task T must satisfy the conditions:

- $D \geq ST + E + \delta$ (1.2)

Where δ is any integer value. It represents the gap time or extra time associated to the task. We can called tolerate factor.

if $\delta = 0$ then Equation1.2 can be expressed as:

$$D = ST + E$$

At this case the task is considered as hard deadline sensitive task. The existing algorithms may not give a better scheduling where resources can be utilized more. The scheduling of hard deadline sensitive task is beyond in this chapter.

- Slack Value (SV) specifies, whether the task is considered as a deadline sensitive task or an advance reservation task (Nathani et al., 2012), (Nayak & Tripathy, 2016).

$$SV = \frac{D - ST}{E} \tag{1.3}$$

In Equation 1.3, the SV is derived and defined by the system administrator. If it is greater than the lower bound slack value, then the lease is considered as deadline sensitive lease and must be scheduled. In this article we considered the lower slack value is 1.1 (Nathani et al., 2012).

OpenNebula supports deadline sensitive task which is called deadline sensitive lease. As we discussed Haizea is a lease manger to schedule these leases or tasks. The backfilling algorithm is mostly used to schedule deadline sensitive tasks in OpenNebula. Except backfilling other algorithms are also used in some scenario. In this article, we mainly focused on different scheduling algorithms used in Haizea. Moreover, we also discussed different types of backfilling algorithm and its challenges for scheduling deadline sensitive leases. Table 1 shows the deadline sensitive tasks with suitable parameters.

Table 1 shows the deadline sensitive tasks or leases. The table contains four tasks with their required parameter value according to the Equation 1. Here the maximum number of VMs required is 4 by lease number 4. So, we consider scheduling the tasks shown in Table 1 the physical machine creates maximum 4 VMs. In Haizea at time slots t_i the possible free VMs is four for Table 1. The VMs are available from 12.00 PM to 1.50 PM with different time slots.

In general, the VMs are available from the min (ST) to max (D). It is also required that all the deadline sensitive tasks should be sorted according to their start time (ST) in ascending order. It means that one task cannot be scheduled if it is not sorted. This mechanism restricts dynamic scheduling. Details of scheduling of deadline sensitive tasks using different algorithms are discussed in the below section.

Table 1. Deadline sensitive task information (Nayak & Tripathy, 2016)

Lease no.	Nodes	Submit time (AM)	Start Time (PM)	Duration	Deadline (PM)
1	2	11.10	12.00	20	12.30
2	3	11.20	12.00	40	01.00
3	2	11.30	12.00	50	01.50
4	4	11.40	01.00	20	01.50

Different Scheduling Mechanisms

In this section, we discussed some mechanisms to schedule deadline sensitive tasks with suitable illustrations. Mainly we focused backfilling algorithm. The backfilling algorithm is an optimized First Come First Serve (FCFS) algorithm. It is widely used in number of production systems. There is number of discussions carried out by the researchers but till it is a challenging one to schedule deadline sensitive tasks in cloud computing environment. Before discussing backfilling algorithm let us discuss some earlier scheduling algorithms implemented in Haizea. The algorithms that are discussed in this article are FCFS, Swapping and Backfilling algorithm with different modification.

FCFS

FCFS is a simple scheduling algorithm. It is used in the most of the systems for some specific requirements. In cloud computing service provider prefers parallel execution of the tasks for better utilization of resources. For better understanding let us consider the Table 1 to schedule the tasks. The task1(T1) needs two VMs at time 12.00PM. According to the principle of FCFS T1 will execute for the duration of 20 minutes at 12.00PM with its required VMs that is 2 out of 4 VMs. No other task is selected to be executed along with T1 for 20 minutes, even if T2 has ST=12.00PM and required VMs is 3. Because tasks are non-primitive in FCFS and T2 need to be executed for 40 minutes. So the parallel execution is not possible. Two VMs are wasted at for the duration of 20 minutes from 12.00PM to 12.20PM. The scheduling result of the Table 1 is shown in the Figure 4.

As the Figure 4 shows, only three tasks are able to schedule.T1 at 12.00 PM by duration of 20 minutes, T2 at 12.20 PM by duration of 40 minutes and T3 at 1.00PM by duration of 50minutes, whereas,

Figure 4. Task scheduling using FCFS

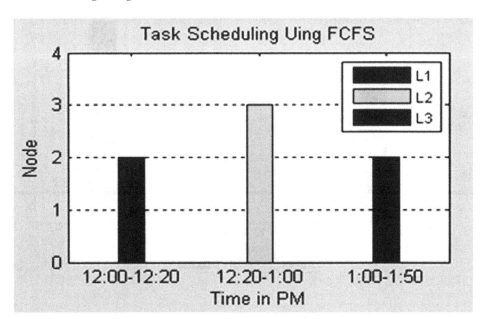

task T4 could not be able to meet its deadline and get rejected. But according to the Equation 1.3 T4 should be scheduled. Moreover, parallel execution is not supported by FCFS, for which other algorithms are proposed.

Swapping

The swapping algorithm performs better scheduling than the FCFS in some scenario not all time. But for the tasks shown in Table 1, the scheduling result is same as FCFS which is shown in Figure 5. The principle of swapping algorithm specifies that two consecutive leases can be swapped if and only if, the first lease has requested fewer resources than the second lease and after swapping they must finish their execution within their deadline.

The leases or tasks T2, T3 and T4 are scheduled and able to meet their respective deadlines. But T1 get rejected because T2 has more number of required resources than T1. So T1 and T2 swapped according to the principle of swapping algorithm. After execution of T2, T1 cannot be scheduled at 12.40PM, because couldn't meet its deadline. So it is rejected. If we considered the number of tasks scheduled which is same in both FCFS and Swapping, but in some scenario swapping performs better scheduling than FCFS. So Haizea uses swapping in some scenario. The above two algorithms are non-preemptive in which tasks are rejected while most of the resources are not utilized. For better resource utilization number of preemptive algorithms is proposed. Among these backfilling algorithm is one of them. It is widely used in different production systems.

Figure 5. Task scheduling using swapping

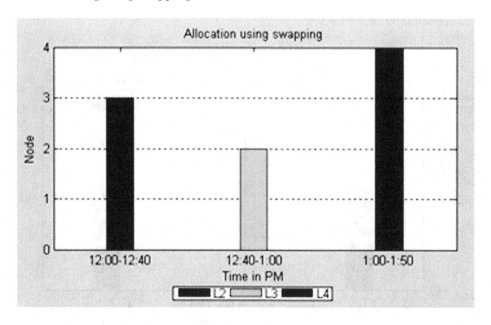

Backfilling Algorithm

In backfilling, short tasks are allowed to execute ahead of their time given slots provided that they should not be delayed by previously queued tasks. For this type of algorithm, the users are required to provide some information like how long the task will run to complete, starting time and deadline in terms of time. Here, if the next queued task cannot run because sufficient resources are not available, then the scheduler never continues rather it scans the queue, and again selects the next shorter task which may utilize the available resources (Tsafrir et al., 2005).

The backfilling algorithm improves FCFS. It increases the resource utilization of the physical system meanwhile decreases the average waiting time of the task. It allows other short task to be executed by allocating required resources if the first task is at the first position in the queue of the scheduler. It is essential to know the maximum execution time for each of the task by backfilling algorithm. Backfilling allows to schedule the short task first to improve the response time and resource utilization (Lindsay et al., 2011). There are different types of backfilling algorithms which are discussed below (Shmueli, 2003).

Easy Backfilling

EASY backfilling takes a more aggressive approach and allows jobs to skip ahead provided that they do not delay just the job at the head of the queue (Wong & Goscinski, 2007). It was developed for the IBM SP2 super computer. It allows the first job in the queue to reserve its required resources. Easy backfilling is more aggressive in nature to increase resource utilization. But the main disadvantage is that it does not guarantee that a task is not delayed by another one submitted later. EASY backfilling was selected for system performance evaluation when static workloads of parallel jobs are executed on a computer cluster. EASY backfilling provides better opportunities for jobs to be backfilled especially if the number of jobs in the waiting queue is large. The policy of Easy backfilling is as below. Only parallel tasks are considered.

1. Tasks are submitted by users and they are stored according to their start time.
2. Tasks are represented by number of nodes required, start time, execution duration and deadline.
3. A scheduling decision is made at min (start time) in the cluster.
4. The queue-priority policy and the computer-allocation policy of the scheduler are set by the administrator of the cluster.

Conservative Backfilling

In the backfilling algorithm, resources are reserved for each task, when it is inserted into the job queue. The task will be executed if there are enough nodes, are available. Otherwise the job has to wait and later arriving small job will be executed if enough nodes for that job are available (Feitelson, 2001). Conservative backfilling is assumed in the literature although it seems not to be used. The conservative backfilling mainly focused to check that it does not delay any previous job in the queue for which it is called "conservative" backfilling.

The advantage is of conservative backfilling is that it allows scheduling decisions to be made upon job submitted, and thus has the capability of predicting when each job will run and giving users execution guarantees (Feitelson, 2001). The user can then plan based on these guaranteed response times.

To perform resource allocations, conservative backfilling maintains two data structures. One is the list of queued jobs and the times at which they are expected to start execution. The other is a profile of the expected processor usage at future times. When a new job arrives, the following allocation is executed. Conservative backfilling maintains a profile provides a tentative schedule for all queued deadline tasks. Each task start time serves as a reservation, a time in which the job is guaranteed to start. Newly arriving jobs are placed into this profile at the earliest possible time that does not interfere with any other job (Rajbhandary et al., 2013). The steps of conservative backfilling algorithm are as follows:

1. **Step 1**: Select the anchor point
   a. Scan the tasks and find the slot where sufficient VMs are available for the
      i. task T_i. This is called anchor point.
   b. Continue scanning from anchor point until the task T_i completes its execution and release the VMs.
   c. If not, return to the tasks set and scan to find the next suitable anchor point
2. **Step 2**: Update the log book of the tasks to reflect the allocation of VMs to the tasks from the anchor point.
3. **Step 3**: If the task's anchor is the current time, start it immediately.

Slack Based Backfilling

The slack-based backfilling algorithm consists of two parts which apply at task-submission time and at task-scheduling time. The task-scheduling time for considering relaxed ordering is exclusively the back-filling time, i.e. in each scheduler invocation, tasks are first filled in regularly (Tsafrir & Feitelson, 2006). However, backfilling then not only relaxes the rules in regards to delays in other waiting jobs but looks at the overall situation and attempts to find the best group of tasks to be backfilled rather than making decisions one-by-one as most other schedulers do. The basic backfilling approach used for estimations for fair start time and as a default (if no combination meeting the criteria can be found) is conservative backfilling. The backfilling approach supports two possible objectives:

1. **Action at Job-Submission Time**
   a. Calculate the fair start time
   b. Apply FCFS with conservative backfilling where the task is not backfilled, place all the tasks which should packed into machine.
   c. Schedule the task T_i
2. **Action at Job-Scheduling Time**
   a. Select the task with required nodes from waiting queue.
   b. Apply following conditions to achieve the objectives
   c. Try backfilling with different combination of tasks
   d. Evaluate each solution based upon the criteria
   e. Calculate the corresponding delay for non-scheduled tasks
   f. Select the best solution.

Selective Backfilling

In conservative backfilling a task affects other categories of tasks. Due to the constraints of the schedule by the reservations of all waiting tasks conservative backfilling performs less backfilling. Tasks do not easily backfill, they might have to wait till they get to the head of the queue before they get a reservation (Srinivasan, 2002). Selective backfilling algorithm focused to obtain the best characteristics from both strategies while avoiding the drawbacks of conservative backfilling. The main idea is to provide reservation for resources selectively, only to those tasks that are waited a long time in the queue. The number of reservations of resources is limited. The amount of backfilling is greater than conservative backfilling but by assuring reservations to tasks after a limited wait.

The motivation of selective backfilling algorithm is: a task does not get a reservation until its expected slowdown exceeds some threshold, whereupon they get a reservation (Srinivasan, 2002). Depending upon the tasks can be allocated; the allocation of resources to the task is based upon the threshold value. The mostly needy task gets the resources due to threshold. It is more challenging one to set the threshold for a system in cloud computing. This threshold value is called threshold of starvation. In the selective backfilling algorithm, a single starvation threshold is used for all categories of tasks. In real time, different tasks categories have different slowdowns, so another variant of selective reservations is evaluated to allocate resources where a better resource utilization can be achieved. To schedule these tasks different starvation thresholds were used for different tasks categories.

Relaxed Backfilling

In deadline based on task the execution duration is specified by the user, which specifies how much time the task needs to utilize the resources. The resources are allocated in such way that without delaying other jobs. A rational assumption is that users would be motivated to provide accurate estimates to have a better chance to make their jobs be backfilled. However, empirical studies of traces from sites using backfilling show that user estimates are generally inaccurate (Li et al., 2011).

Relax-based scheduling algorithms provide benefits by providing accurate runtime estimation. The scheduling results compared with user-specific runtime estimate, as the runtime estimations of tasks become accurate. The average waiting time and the average bounded slowdown of tasks decrease. These values don't increase sharply as the value of reservation depth increases. The performance of the task does not depend on the reservation deep heavily when the runtime estimates are accurate i.e., the performance differences between EASY backfill and conservative backfill are not so good (Ward et al., 2002).

Relaxed backfilling does not seek better performance improvements in all scenarios. The performance metrics do not change with a fixed tendency as the slack factor and/or the reservation depth change (Li et al., 2011). Relaxed backfilling shows a better performance improvements for all traces based on reservation depth value. As the degree of relaxation increases, relaxed backfilling poses more improvements during the allocation of resources. The drawback of relaxed backfilling is that when the scheduler gives a larger pool of backfill tasks. It is difficult to select the lower priority tasks which are scheduled earlier and the priority scheme may be undermined. Moreover, the observed improvement in overall wait time may have come at the expense of high priority jobs (Ward et al., 2002).

Multiple-Queue Backfilling

Multiple-queue backfilling was proposed by Lawson and Amirin (Lawson & Smirni, 2002). In multiple queue backfilling algorithm each task is given to a queue in order with its running time where each queue is given to the partition of the parallel system and the only tasks of this queue can be scheduled. In the multiple-queue backfilling the average task job slowdown is reduced because the scheduler automatically changes the system parameters with respect to change of task parameters. The multiple-queue backfilling algorithm is inspired for distributed servers that strongly encourage separation of tasks according to execution duration.

The physical machine is divided into multiple disjoint partitions in order to VMs by tasks according to their execution duration. As time evolves, the partitions may exchange resources so that free resources in one partition can be used for backfilling in another partition (Lawson & Smirni, 2002). If a task in a certain cluster and cannot begin executing due to insufficient of resources, then the task is migrated to other cluster if there sufficient resources. For this purpose, cluster boundary becomes dynamic, allowing the system to adapt itself to changing workload conditions. Each cluster contains its own separate queue of tasks. The task is placed into the queue in a cluster according to the task priority. If the task has low priority, it is placed at the tail of the queue. If the task has high priority, it is placed in the queue after all previously queued high priority tasks in the cluster but before the first low priority task in the cluster. The basic steps used to implement multiple-queue are as follows for (all high priority jobs in order of arrival, then all low priority jobs in order of arrival):

Step 1: $p \leftarrow$ Cluster in which task belongs

Step 2: $pivot_p \leftarrow$ first job in queue in cluster C

Step 3:   *pivot start time*$_p$ ←earliest time when sufficient are available for *pivot*$_p$ without delaying any other pivot of equal or higher priority

Step 4: $idle_p$ ←currently free resources in cluster C

Step 5: $extra_p$ ←free resources in cluster C at *pivot start time*$_p$ not used by *pivot*$_p$

Step 6:   if task is *pivot*$_p$ then follow the steps

   a.   if current time equals *pivot start time*$_p$

   b.   if required, allocate resources from other cluster to cluster K

   c.   start task immediately

Step 7:   else

   a.   if the task requires $\leq idle_p$ and will finish by *pivot start time*$_p$, start task immediately

   b.   else if the task requires $\leq \min\{idle_p, extra_p\}$, start task immediately

   c.   else if the task requires $\leq$ ($idle_p$ plus some combination of idle/extra resources from other cluster) in such way that no pivot is delayed

   d.   allocate necessary resources from other cluster to cluster C

   e.   execute task immediately

A queue is assigned to each task according to its execution duration time. In cloud computing a non-overlapping cluster of resources to the queue in which a task can be executed with its required resources. The clusters change dynamically, with intension of task arrival and availability of resources. Table 2 shows a comparison of some of the mostly used parallel algorithms. Except these algorithms researchers have also proposed some modified algorithms for parallel scheduling in cloud computing environment.

Table 2. Comparison of parallel algorithms

Algorithm	Scheduling Parameters	Performance
1. Backfilling Algorithm	Execution duration, priority of task in the queue	Shortest tasks are over ahead to improve response time and resource utilization
2. Conservative Backfilling Algorithm	Arrival time of task, reservation for all tasks, estimated execution duration for each task	improves resource utilization
3. EASY Backfilling	Run time of a task	maximum execution time of task
4. Flexible Backfilling	execution duration, deadline time, number of resources	Shortest task will be executed first in the queue. Resource utilization is improved
5. Multiple Queue Backfilling	Task priority, task reservation, arrival time, execution duration	Reservation cost reduced and on demand in nature

Basically, researchers focused on the performance of these algorithms in cloud computing for better resource utilization. Moreover, modified algorithms are also considered in the research area to overcome the black holes of these algorithms.

CASE STUDIES

Backfilling Algorithm

In this case study, we considered the set of tasks which are deadline based tasks with their required parameters as showed in Table 1. These tasks are scheduled using FCFS and swapping algorithm. The scheduling results are shown in the Figure 4 and 5 respectively. As we observed that only three tasks are scheduled using swapping. The L4 could not be able to meet its deadline, whereas using backfilling algorithm L4 is scheduled along with other tasks as showed in the Figure 6

Figure 6. Task scheduling using backfilling algorithm

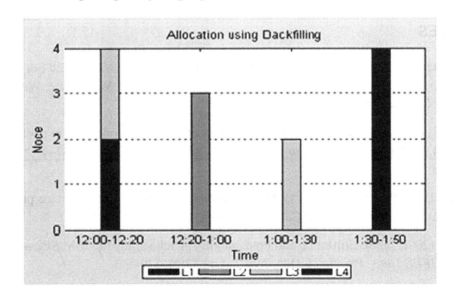

In Table 1, four tasks are considered and all are deadline sensitive tasks. Task 1, 2, 3 have the same starting time that is 12.00 PM. Maximum 4 number of VMs are created in the physical machine. All these tasks are queued in scheduler. So the 1st task will be scheduled to be executed at 12.00 PM with 2VMs as it requires. The execution duration of T1 is 20 minutes from 12.00 PM to 12.20 PM. Out of 4 VMs 2 VMs are occupied by T1. The rest of the 2VMs should be allocated to next task T2 in the queue. But T2 requires 3 VMs, which is more than the available VMs. Though backfilling provides the better resource utilization, it will find the next suitable task in the queue which is T3. So task T3 will be executed in parallel with task T1 for the duration of 20 minutes out of its execution duration as showed in the Figure 6.

After execution of 20 minutes, system time reached to 12.20 PM. At this time, there are two tasks in the queue T2 and T3, whereas T1 deleted from the queue though its execution is completed. Among the task T2 and T3 the task T2 requires 3 VMs for the duration of 40 minutes and its deadline is 1.00 PM where T3 requires to executed for its rest of 30 minutes from 50 minutes but its deadline id 1.50 PM. If the scheduler schedules the task T3 then task T2 could not meet its deadline. Moreover, T2 requires 3 VMs as compared with T3. So, the T3 will be scheduled in the time slots from 12.20 PM to 1.00 PM. Now at time 1.00 PM the task T3 which is backfilled will be executed and then T4 as showed in the Figure 6. Here all the tasks of Table 1 are scheduled and able to meet their deadline.

CONCLUSION

Backfilling algorithms have been proposed for parallel scheduling. As we discussed it provides better resource utilization. In cloud computing resource utilization is very much essential. Researchers are focusing to propose different modified version of backfilling algorithm for cloud computing environment. In this chapter, we have discussed the basic principles of simple backfilling algorithm by a case study. We also discussed how it is more essential in deadline based task scheduling in cloud computing. However, other case studies may be carried out and discussed in different environment of cloud computing in the future.

REFERENCES

Bichler, M., Setzer, T., & Speitkamp, B. (2006). Capacity Planning for Virtualized Servers. *Proceedings of theWorkshop on Information Technologies and Systems (WITS)*, Milwaukee, Wisconsin, USA. Social Science Network.

Calheiros, R. N., & Buyya, R. (2014). Meeting deadlines of scientific workflows in public clouds with tasks replication. *IEEE Transactions on Parallel and Distributed Systems, 25*(7), 1787–1796. doi:10.1109/TPDS.2013.238

Di, S., Kondo, D., & Wang, C. L. (2015). Optimization of composite cloud service processing with virtual machine. *IEEE Transactions on Computers, 64*(6), 1755–1768.

Feitelson, D.G. (2001, June). Utilization and Predictability in Scheduling the IBM SP2 with backfilling 1 Introduction. *IEEE Trans. Parallel & Distributed Syst., 12*(6), 529-543.

Kumbhare, A. G., Simmhan, Y., Frincu, M., & Prasanna, V. K. (2015). Reactive Resource Provisioning Heuristics for Dynamic Dataflows on Cloud Infrastructure. *IEEE Transactions on Cloud Computing*, *3*(2), 105–118. doi:10.1109/TCC.2015.2394316

Lai, J. K. 2013. Truthful and Fair Resource Allocation [Doctoral dissertation]. Harvard University. Retrieved from http://nrs.harvard.edu/urn-3:HUL.InstRepos:11108713

Lawson, B. G., & Smirni, E. (2002, March). Multiple-queue Backfilling Scheduling with Priorities and Reservations for Parallel Systems. *Performance Evaluation Review*, *29*(4), 40–47. doi:10.1145/512840.512846

Li, B., Li, Y., He, M., Wu, H., & Yang, J. (2011). Scheduling of a Relaxed Backfill Strategy with Multiple Reservations. *Proceedings of the Parallel and Distributed Computing, Applications and Technologies (PDCAT)International Conference*. IEEE.

Lindsay, A. M., Galloway Carson, M., Johnson, C.R., Bunde, D.P., & Leung, V.J. (2011). Backfilling with guarantees granted upon job submission. In *Euro-Par'11 Parallel Processing* (pp. 142-153). Springer. doi:10.1007/978-3-642-23400-2_14

Mell, P., & Grance, T. (2009). Effectively and Securely Using the Cloud Computing Paradigm. NIST, Information Technology Laboratory. Retrieved from https://www.cs.purdue.edu/homes/bb/cs590/handouts/Cloud_NIST.pdf

Nathani, A., Chaudhary, S. & Somani, G. (2012). Policy based resource allocation in IaaS cloud. *Future Generation Computer Systems,* *28*(1), 94–103. Retrieved from at:.10.1016/j.future.2011.05.016

Nayak, S. C., & Tripathy, C. (2016). Deadline sensitive lease scheduling in cloud computing environment using AHP. *Journal of King Saud University - Computer and Information Sciences*. doi:10.1016/j.jksuci.2016.05.00

Parida, S., & Nayak, S. C. (2013). An algorithm that earning users' trust on cloud. *Proceedings of the2013 Fifth International Conference*Advanced Computing (ICoAC*)*. IEEE.

Rajbhandary, A., Bunde, D. P., & Leung, V. J. (2013). Variations of Conservative to improve fairness. *Proceedings of the17th Workshop on Job Scheduling Strategies for Parallel Processing (JSSPP)*. Springer.

Shmueli, E. (2003, June). Backfilling with Lookahead to Optimize the Packing of Parallel Jobs.

Sotomayor, B., Montero, R.S., Llorente, I.M., & Foster, I. (2009). Resource Leasing and the Art of Suspending Virtual Machines. *Proceedings of the 2009 11th IEEE International Conference on High Performance Computing and Communications* (pp. 59–68).

Sotomayor, B. 2009. The Haizea Manual. Retrieved from http://haizea.cs.uchicago.edu/haizea_manual.pdf

Srinivasan, S. (2002). Selective Reservation Strategies for Backfill Job Scheduling £ 2 Background and Workload Characterization. *Proceedings of the8th International Workshop, JSSPP* (pp. 55-71). Springer.

Tsafrir, D., Etsion, Y., & Feitelson, D. G. (2005). Backfilling using runtime predictions rather than user estimates (tech. report). Hebrew University of Jerusalem. Retrieved from http://leibniz.cs.huji.ac.il/tr/acc/2005/HUJI-CSE-LTR-2005-5_pred+schedulers.pdf

Tsafrir, D., & Feitelson, D. G. 2006. The dynamics of backfilling: Solving the mystery of why increased inaccuracy may help.*Proceedings of the 2006 IEEE International Symposium on Workload Characterization IISWC '06* (pp. 131–141). doi:10.1109/IISWC.2006.302737

Venkatesan, S., Basha, M.S.S., Vaish, A., & Bhavachelvan, P. (2013). Analysis of accounting models for the detection of duplicate requests in web services. Journal of King Saud University - Computer and Information Sciences, 25(1), 7–24. doi:10.1016/j.jksuci.2012.05.003

Ward, W.A., Jr., Mahood, C.L., & West, J.E. (2002). Scheduling Jobs on Parallel Systems Using a Relaxed Backfill Strategy. *Proceedings of the8th International Workshop JSSPP* (pp. 88-102). Springer. doi:10.1007/3-540-36180-4_6

Wong, A.K.L., & Goscinski, A.M. (2007). Evaluating the EASY-Backfill Job Scheduling of Static Workloads on Clusters. *Proceedings of the2007 IEEE International Conference onCluster Computing.*

Chapter 6
Privacy Preserving Public Auditing in Cloud: Literature Review

Thangavel M.
Thiagarajar College of Engineering, Madurai, India

Varalakshmi P.
Anna University, India

Sridhar S.
M. Kumarasamy College of Engineering, India

Sindhuja R.
Thiagarajar College of Engineering, India

ABSTRACT

Cloud computing has given a bloom to the technical world by providing various services. Data storage is the essential factor for the users who are having or working with lots and lots of data. Cloud data storage becomes the only way to store and maintain the large data, which can be accessed from anywhere and anytime. The open nature of cloud computing leads to some security issues. With respect to the cloud data storage, the Cloud Service Provider (CSP) has to provide security for the data outsourced. Data owner will be concerned on the data correctness after outsourcing into the cloud. To verify the data correctness, ensuring the state of data at the cloud data storage is needed, which is performed with the help of a Trusted Third Party Auditor (TTPA). Data owner can also perform the verification task, but it leads to computation cost and communication costs in huge amount. This survey gives a brief on public auditing schemes to explore what are all the system models designed by various researchers.

INTRODUCTION

Computing technologies like distributed, parallel, mobile, grid and cloud computing become essential to process huge data in an effective manner. In the recent trends, Cloud Computing is a key computing technology for everyone in the world today, because of enormous computing resources and services are available in pay per use model. Cloud computing is a technology enabling ubiquitous on demand access to a shared pool of configurable computing resources. It also has issues such as disaster recovery, abuse and nefarious use, malicious insiders, shared technology, etc. Data security issues in cloud computing

DOI: 10.4018/978-1-5225-2013-9.ch006

are serious in many faces. Once the user outsource the data in the cloud, then the access to that data is done by any computing devices like laptop, mobile and other devices, which is allowed with a valid identity. If the data revealed by anonymous users, then in such cases sometimes even malicious insiders give the data to the competitors.

Ensuring privacy of outsourced data and the correctness of the data are considered to be a serious issue in cloud services. The availability of data is ensured by performing data duplication in different cloud servers. Maintenance of this duplicated data such as regular data updates in a dynamic form is harder to achieve. As per the researcher's statement, the privacy preservation can be achieved using appropriate cryptographic techniques. Correctness of the data at cloud storage should be ensured to provide a reliable service delivery to users. This requires data auditing through cryptographic hashing techniques. In case of data availability, replica placement leads to difficulty in achieving the dynamicity of data. Data update and maintenance is harder in this situation. So, there is a need to overcome these problems with the appropriate techniques, in order to provide a reliable, guaranteed service delivery to the cloud users and data owners.

The survey concise the methodologies followed in the existing system or technique. Identification of problems in the existing system and the performance of that system are reviewed. The auditing task performed with the help of TTPA involves challenge and response actions. This task may be handled by the data owner, but the cost required to run the system is very large.

Integrity

In general, the state of the data needs to be consistent. Once the data is outsourced from the user, it is uploaded to the server safely. The uploaded data has been modified only by the person who is authorized or owner of that data. The unnecessary modification need to be blocked. So, the integrity of the data is needed to be verified for certain time intervals.

Cloud Based Auditing

Verifying the data integrity is a major task when considering the data amount and its location. Huge amount of data in a place may lead to such violations. Periodic verification of the data will give a success to the system. It also ensures the reliable service delivery. To verify the data integrity various cryptographic mechanisms are used. If the size of the data to verify is huge, then it is hard to perform by a normal user, since normal user can have limited number of hardware resources. This situation brings a Trusted Third Party Auditor (TTPA) to perform auditing which is also called as public auditing (Figure 1). In Cloud, public auditing is done by the TTPA where he initially gets the request from the Data Owner or the Client to perform auditing for the specific file or blocks of a file. He also receives the metadata to compute a challenge to the cloud server. Based on the proposed algorithm or scheme the challenge is created and imposed to the cloud server. The cloud server then generates the proof, as a response to the challenge for the requested file or blocks to be verified and sends it to the TTPA. The TTPA compares the result obtained from the computation on proof with the values received from the Data Owner and generates the result to the Data Owner denoting whether the data is verified and correct or it has been modified.

The public auditing or integrity verification by the third-party auditor will overcome the resource overhead issues of cloud user. It also ensures the integrity of the data with such additional supports.

Figure 1. Public auditing of the data stored in cloud

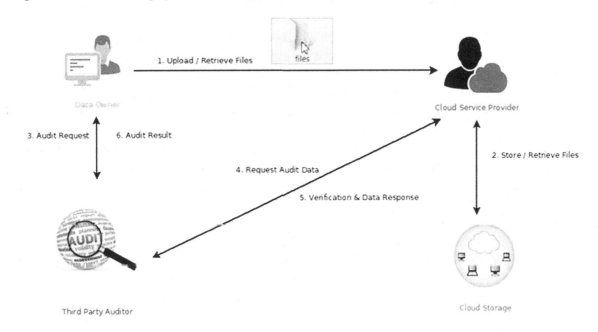

BACKGROUND

The data stored in the cloud server who holds all the control over the data need to store and maintain the data in a secured manner. To ensure the integrity of the data that it has not been modified by any adversary or due to any attacks or any data loss occurred by the cloud service provider. The need of integrity verification of the data stored in cloud storage by the Data Owner is to protect and prevent the data from unintended users. The privacy of the data as well as the Data Owner has to be preserved. It means that the data in cloud could contain personal details, social security numbers, health records or any sensitive data that becomes more valuable when it is into the hands of the competitor or attacker of the Data Owner who could cause harm to the Data Owner by monetary or reputation oriented commitments or personal gain of an attacker. Thus, auditing or checking of the data for its correctness and being assured that data has not been modified by anyone is done. Since not all the Data Owners are capable with large amount of resources to audit all the data in cloud, the Data Owner gives the responsibility of auditing the data to a TTPA. The third-party auditor performs auditing of the data in cloud on behalf of the Data Owner and gives the result back for further actions. The TPA gets the request from Data Owner and challenges for a file to the cloud server and cloud server generates the proof and sends to TPA. TPA verifies the values computed from both Data Owner and cloud server and generates the final integrity result. Mostly, in public auditing digital signatures are used for integrity verification. It works in such a way that the original data is performed hashing through any cryptographic hash function or hashing algorithm and the hash values are altogether signed or encrypted with the private key of the sender and sent to the receiver. The receiver uses the public key of the sender and retrieves the hash value and also computes the hash values of the encrypted blocks and compares the resulted hash values bit by bit to ensure they are equal denoting data is intact or else not. These concepts have been modernized in algorithmic approaches by various researchers and applied the same for public auditing of the data stored in cloud.

STATE-OF-ART OF PUBLIC AUDITING IN CLOUD

C. Wang et al. (2010) initiated the concept of publicly auditable secure cloud data storage services. The usage of cloud data storage is increased because of the user dependency in the data maintenance. Enterprises need to fulfill the customers need on time with efficient data management services. Cloud data storage is the key for the users in urge of data outsourcing. To do this work securely it is necessary to ensure the data security after outsourcing it. Public auditing is a mechanism provided to verify the data storage security in the public storage. Trusted users who have the knowledge to do the verification are performing the verification. The data owner gives the task to the external verifier to save the computation time at his side. This makes the data owner having more trust into the service provider. The author noted many real-time incidents on behalf of the secure cloud storage service. The concept of cryptographic techniques is not suitable for this situation. It is not possible to download the entire data for each time to do the verification. A person doing this task specifically for secure cloud data storage is a Third-Party Auditor (TPA). The Third-Party Auditor is doing the auditing task of verifying the integrity of the outsourced data. The report generated by the TPA gives the actual status of the data at the cloud storage.

There are some requirements for doing this public auditing for the outsourced data at the cloud storage. First is to minimize the overhead while performing the auditing. Second is the privacy of data, at the time of auditing. Third is to provide access to the user for performing any operations with the outsourced data. Fourth is the external verifier has the chances to do multiple tasks simultaneously. Existing methods in this arena follows some cryptographic primitives, some systematic models, some frameworks and some models. In case of data size is huge hash tree (Merkle, 1980) concepts are used. This hash tree was constructed using the hash values. The hash values of the file are used to construct the tree with smaller hashes at the leaves in the tree as child nodes. This will finally make a tree with a root node value. The root node value is used for performing the verification.

With the above approaches, there is a need for the user to download the data from the cloud storage. So, there is another concept with the use of MAC keys. The data owner has to compute such MAC keys for the whole data and store as metadata with the cloud service provider. When verification is performed the verifier asked the CSP to give a fresh keyed MAC value. The value is compared with the locally stored MAC. Each time the CSP needs to compute and give a fresh MAC key value. This is restricted in terms of number of times the calculation is done. A file is restricted with a certain number of MAC key values. By doing verification with these MAC key values the time and cost are saved. In this approach a verifier can recompute another set of MAC values. Data owner need to update the MAC values at the server side. It could cause in terms of performance issue. By doing this task, it may not support data dynamics because the keys are for the files which are already stored in the cloud storage. Homomorphic authenticator is another technique which is used for reducing the online burden of data owner (Shah et al., 2008; Curtmola et al., 2008). The metadata values are computed from aggregated set of values. In this data block is divided with a common set of blocks. The data blocks are computed with a signature for each of its own value. The blocks and the signature values are stored. The verifier can ask the cloud service provider to provide the signature values of particular file blocks. The CSP response by aggregated set of signature values to the verifier. In this approach, there is a chance for the verifier can regenerate the data from the signature values. So, this technique works well in encrypted format data only.

The random masking of blocks could ensure the block request at verification. Data operations performed by block level could improve and support the data dynamics. It can be formulated as block level insertion, updation, deletion and modification. The concept of Merkle Hash Tree (MHT) is used for supporting this requirement. The calculation of root node and the leaf nodes auxiliary authentication information is a formidable task. It requires huge communication cost and introduce newer vulnerabilities to violate data privacy. To overcome this MHT concept is linked with the homomorphic authenticator based technique. It supports operations of individual blocks. Bilinear signature is a technique used by the TPA to do multiple auditing tasks at a time. Each auditing task is considered and aggregated with signatures.

There is no mechanism to verify the actors involved in this scenario, any entity can be a malicious at any point of time. All such tasks are lacking their capacity in terms of time consideration. Performance and time are the issues in this area. The regulatory and compliance are ensuring such security of the outsourced data. Through this analysis a secure model is needed for the cloud data storage.

Q. Wang et al. (2011) described about the public verification and dynamics nature of data for the cloud computing storage security. The Classic Merkle Hash tree is used for providing salient features in public verification and the data dynamism. Existing models using the concept of Provable Data Posses sion (PDP) and Proof of Retrievability (PoR) to achieve data dynamics (Ateniese et al., 2007; Shacham et al., 2008). These models have the lacking in security concerns.

In public verification, any user owns the public key can be a verifier for the data integrity. To overcome the issue of signature index calculation for the data blocks each time, the index information is removed from the existing model. Calculation of hash value for each message blocks is done only with the information about the data is known. At each time of protocol execution, the tags need to be authenticated.

There are six algorithms defined for this auditing model. The algorithms are, KeyGen, SigGen, GenProof, VerifyProof, ExecUpdate, VerifyUpdate. During the setup phase the KeyGen and SigGen algorithms are performed. Public and Private key of data owner are generated by KeyGen algorithm. Signature values for the file bocks are generated and Merkle Hash Tree is constructed using the computed signature values. The client stores the file, signatures and hash value of the root node in MHT at server side.At integrity verification GenProof and VerifyProof are executed. In GenProof the cloud service provider has receiving a challenge from the verifier as random blocks signatures needed.

The cloud service provider provides the nodes auxiliary information to construct root node in MHT, hash values of blocks, aggregated signatures. With the provided values verifier compares the root hash value of MHT. If it is matched the verification is success otherwise it is not.

Dynamic operations of data are performed with block level operations as data insertion, updation, modification and deletion. The author performed security analysis by theorem proofs for Computational Diffie Hellman. Performance Analysis is performed by comparing the computation complexity at each actor's side and the cost required to do each task. The concentration is only on the public verification with data dynamics. There is no concentration given on the data privacy at this work.

C. Wang et al. (2012) proposed a public auditing system model for data storage security in cloud computing. The problem taken here is the auditor can perform the audit task without local copy of data and it never gives an online burden to user, this process doesn't bring newer vulnerabilities to this area. This model uses the concept of public key based homomorphic authenticator with random masking technique. They reviewed some existing models are using the public key based homomorphic authenticators. This technique is vulnerable to data loss. The external auditor can reveal the user data based on the linear combination of blocks. So, the author applied a random masking concept with the above technique. Related works of this paper finds information as follows. It is the first work to involve Provable Data Possession (PDP) in public auditing to ensure the possession of data at untrusted storage. This work is based on RSA based homomorphic authenticators. This scheme requires linear combination of data blocks. This leads to privacy issues. It uses Proof of Retrievability (PoR) concept used with spot checking and error correcting codes. This ensures possession of data and Retrievability. In this scheme the number of times to perform the audit task is limited and the construction of Merkle Tree construction applicable only to encrypted data (Ateniese et al., 2007) uses the PoR scheme with BLS construction. This also leads privacy issues (Ferrara et al., 2009). a scheme based on encryption and hash values is described (Shah et al., 2007; Chang et al., 2008) but this works only for encrypted data files. Author proposed a dynamic version of the previous PDP scheme. It supports symmetric key cryptography and encrypted data files only for limited number of audits (Ateniese et al. 2008).

The author stated that none of the literature review papers are fulfils the required scenario of public auditing. Four algorithms were mentioned to perform the public auditing task. Each of these algorithms is describe the task of public auditing scheme as a series steps.

KeyGen algorithm is used to generate the keys that are required to do the public auditing task. It takes some input parameters such as generators, prime value and others. Then it generates public and private key pairs.

SigGen algorithm is used to generate signatures which are for data privacy. The outcome of this algorithm avoids the data given to the auditor for auditing. Because some models designed as the auditors are requiring the copy of data. This algorithm will generate signatures for a block or set of blocks based on the user input. After getting the output from this algorithm the signature values are stored with the data in the cloud.

GenProof algorithm is used to generate proof for the requested audit task based on the details given by the auditor. This algorithm calculates hash values and aggregated signatures. A PseudoRandomFunction (PRF) is used with algorithm to generate random elements. The details got from the algorithm are hash value, signature value and random element. These details are given to the auditor.

VerifyProof algorithm is used to audit the data which are requested by the auditor based on the user requirement. Once the auditor get the required details then he immediately use this algorithm to verify the data correctness. The auditor perform comparison between the data given by the previous algorithm with the given user details.

This model is based on two basic schemes. The scheme functionalities are enhanced in this model. The schemes are:

- Pre-computed (Message Authentication Code) MAC and data files stored in the server. Set of secret keys are given to the auditor. The auditor requires some selected data blocks and its MAC values from the server. It gives an easier task because the selected blocks verification is easier than entire data verification. This introduces problems which is the auditor request data blocks for verification. It leads to privacy issues. Performance overhead are introduced such as time delay, bandwidth.
- The second scheme is an extension to the above scheme as, random message authentication code keys are chosen and MAC values are computed for the whole file block. For every audit the auditor may give some MAC keys to the server and request fresh keyed MAC values. This scheme has the problem as the keys are only fixed. It requires re-computation and re-publishing of keys. Auditor must update the status of each audit. These schemes support only with static data.

This model supports batch auditing task by utilizing the technique of bilinear aggregate signature (BLS). Based on this server sends an aggregated signature with each user id mentioned values to the auditor. The auditor checks the signatures by the user id attached. The corruption of any portion in this response will lead a mismatch. So, the author further mentioned a technique based on divide and conquer approach which is recursive one. The responses are divided into two equal halves and find which is invalid and re perform the audit as individual user data audit. The author proves some theorems for storage correctness guarantee, privacy preserving guarantee, and security guarantee for batch auditing.

Performance analysis of this work are done by measuring the cost of privacy preserving guarantee, batch auditing efficiency, sorting out invalid responses, computation time and communication complexity. The author concluded that this work is full- fledged for public auditing. The future work as extend this scheme to work in multi user setting. No error correction measures are defined in this paper. The author concentrates only on the data privacy. The public key based homomorphic authenticator with random masking technique is to overcome the linear data block identification. But not the auditing task is strengthened in terms of performance and security.

Q. Wang et al. (2012) solve the problem in public auditing and support of dynamics in remote data storage in cloud. Modified classic merkle hash tree is constructed for block tag authentication of file. For multi user data auditing, bilinear aggregate signature is used. Some existing system models are designed for checking the integrity of static data files in remote data storage (Atenicse et al., 2007: Juels et al., 2007; Shacham et al., 2008; Schwarz et al., 2006; Ateniese et al., 2008). In the case of dynamic data storage and updates the schemes are not efficient and security loopholes may arise (Ateniese et al., 2007). In the Provable Data Possession (PDP) scheme the number of queries to perform dynamic data operation is limited. The same work followed has limitation of partial support in data dynamics. Data block is identified by using a sentinel value based on the Proof of Retrievability (PoR) concept (Juels et al., 2007). Dynamic provable data possession model is proposed to support the provable updates for the data storage by using the rank based authenticated skip lists. The PDP model (Ateniese et al., 2007) utilized by eliminating the tag information and uses authenticated skip list data structure for updates verification procedure. But the efficiency is still not improved. This work has used with several system models but the scheme has limited number of operations and dynamic operations are not supported. It is based on block tag information instead of index value used in the existing schemes (Ateniese et al., 2008; Juels et al., 2007; Shacham et al., 2008). By the block tag information operation on block doesn't affect other blocks. So, the dynamicity of data is achieved. Classic merkle hash tree (Merkle, 1980) is reconstructed by select the blocks from the left to right sequence and compute root based on this sequence. So the leaf nodes are determined uniquely for operations. KeyGen, SigGen, GenProof, VerifyProof, ExecUpdate, VerifyUpdate are the six algorithms used. To overcome the problem of MAC and Signature based solutions the author went to public key based homomorphic authenticator to perform multiple auditing tasks simultaneously. Data dynamics is performed using the ExecUpdate and VerifyUpdate.

ExecUpdate is performed by the client using the File F, aggregated signature and update is a request message for modification. Update consists of Modification operation, position of block, updated message, and updated signature. The server replaces the updated block, signature, hash value and generates a new root in (Merkle Hash Tree) MHT. CSP sends a response as auxiliary authentication information, hash value of message, signature value, and the updated root. The client executes VerifyUpdate using the response send by the CSP. Then generates new root using the aggregated signature and hash value of message then perform authentication on the root value. If update is correct, proceed otherwise reject it. The client generates a new metadata and sends it to CSP for update.

At the same time dynamicity is achieved for insertion and deletion. Batch auditing task is performed by the use of (Boneh-Lynn-Shacham) BLS based aggregation signature. The author proves their work using theorem and mathematical proofs. Comparison of the work is performed with the others by using time complexity term taken by the operations such as public audit, server computation, communication cost etc., Performance analysis is shown that the scheme take merely same or less time than other works. The use of homomorphic authenticator may lead to regeneration of linear blocks by the verifier. They concentrate on the data dynamics operations as a feature. Error correction mechanism such as erasure codes is not provided.

C. Wang et al. (2012) proposed a model for the problem of public auditing mechanism by utilizing the homomorphic token with data dynamic operations and multiple auditing tasks. The author introduces a mechanism called distributed erasure coded data. This erasure correcting code used in file distribution process gives against byzantine servers (Castro et al., 2002). This scheme works with less communication overhead compared to other schemes. In data error localization the identification of server which is misbehaving. Generalized framework for existing framework via different PoR model is given as theoretical study matters (Curtmola et al., 2008). BLS based homomorphic authenticator with merkle hash tree is proposed (Wang et al., 2011) by the combination of two existing models. Another skip list based scheme is defined to provide provable data possession with full data dynamics support (Erway et al., 2009). Incremental cryptography provides a set of cryptographic building blocks such as hash, MAC and signature functions for integrity verification in dynamic data. But this scheme requires maintaining a local copy of data for verification (Bellare et al., 1994). Another scheme provided for ensure data possession for multiple replicas maintained at distributed storage system. The PDP scheme extended to cover multiple replicas. No need to encode each replica separately (Curtmola et al., 2008). By using erasure codes a backup scheme on P2P mechanism is followed to disperse data files blocks of data files across m+k peers using (m,k) erasure code. To verify the integrity peer requests, random blocks from their backup peers by using a separate keyed hash values attached on each block. It detects loss of data from free riding peers. It doesn't ensure all data are changed (Lillibridge et al., 2003). An RSA based hash defined to verify the integrity. It ensures data possession in peer-to-peer file sharing networks. It is not possible for large size files (Filho et al., 2006). A scheme proposed by applying encryption to the data. Pre computed hash keys are given to the auditor for verifying the integrity. It works only for encrypted data files and the auditors maintain their state for a long time (Shah et al., 2011; Rivest, 2007) Erasure codes and block level file integrity checks ensure the integrity of files in distributed servers (Schwarz et al., 2006).

Previous work (Erway et al., 2009) of the author gives the storage and auditing process. In this work the author gives more importance to error detection and correction. The user computes a set of verification tokens for individual vectors. Each token covers a subset of data block in random number. Token Precomputation, Correctness Verification and Error Localization, FileRetrieval and ErrorRecovery are the algorithms concentrated by the author. The algorithms are separately defined and used for error localization and recovery. The work is by utilizing the PRP and PRF. Data dynamics is achieved by block level insertion, deletion and modification. The work fully depends on the erasure correcting code to give a guarantee on the data. The scheme is proved by security analysis as detection probability against data modification where the identification probability of misbehaving server's security strength against a worst case scenario file and the performance evaluation is done for file distribution preparation, challenge token computation.

Worku et al. (2013) proposes privacy preserving public auditing protocol that prevents from any internal and external attacks and also assures the integrity of the data stored in cloud. The proposed framework has four algorithms such as KeyGen, SigGen, ProofGen and VerifyProof. In KeyGen algo-

Figure 2. Signature based auditing

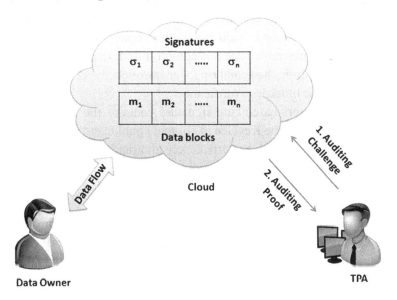

rithm, a security parameter is used to create a private - public key pair. It is also used to provide audit delegation to TPA to get authorized from the CSP.

In SigGen, a randomized algorithm is used to create a set of signatures for every file block using the secret key and the input file. A tag is generated to identify the blocks uniquely. In ProofGen phase, a proof for the challenge given on the specific set of signatures of a corresponding file is generated by the cloud server as shown in Figure 2.

In VerifyProof phase, the TPA or the user on receiving the proof computed by the cloud server checks with the signature and challenge and outputs the result as either True or False, where the former denotes data is verified for its correctness whereas the latter denotes that the data has been modified or lost. Here, the cloud server uses a random value to blind the original data from the TPA.

This framework also supports batch auditing where the challenges are aggregated from the request of multiple users. The server randomly selects files from each user request to compute a blinding factor and generates the proof, which is verified by the TPA for integrity verification. This approach has resulted with preserving the privacy of the user data as well as it has contributed with minimum computational overhead and communication overhead as it uses BLS short signatures where less data is communicated during both data outsourcing and retrieval.

B. Wang et al. (2014) proposed a public auditing mechanism for shared data in the cloud storage. The public auditing mechanism is described with the concept of ring signatures to generate the metadata needed for verifying the correctness of shared data. The identity of the signer for every block is kept private to avoid the problems from the external verifiers. In normal case the data verification is done by downloading the data from the server and calculating the hash values for it. The calculated hash values are compared with pre-stored hash values. But this approach is not suitable for cloud data storage services. The existing models to verify the outsourced data integrity are not suitable for the shared data storage services (Bellare et al., 1999; Jackobsson et al., 1999; Kubiatowiz et al., 2009; Maheswari et al., 2000; Boneh et al., 2001; Golle et al., 2001). The scheme provided to support public auditing, correctness, unforgeability and identity privacy. Identity privacy is achieved with various mechanisms in some models as to use a globally shared private key with a group of users. The computation of key for each time a user relieving from the group introduces overhead issues. The usage of proxy to perform the middle tasks is allowed but it is vulnerable once it is compromised. Homomorphic authenticators based ring signature scheme is derived from the actual ring signature scheme (Wang et al., 2003). It supports to preserve the identity as well as block less verification.

The homomorphic authenticators based ring signature contains the algorithms such as, KeyGen, RingSign, RingVerify. The user runs the KeyGen to compute public and private key pairs. In RingSign the user computes the ring signature with the private key and randomly chosen blocks. In RingVerify user uses the public key with the blocks, then computes the signature. Compare the signature values to verify it. Security analysis for these Homomorphic authenticators based ring signature is performed with four theorem proofs.

In the public auditing mechanism or concept the author runs five algorithms as KeyGen, SigGen, Modify, ProofGen and ProofVerify. In KeyGen the user computes the public and private key pairs needed for verification. Additionally, the user generates a public aggregate key by the random elements of global parameters. In SigGen algorithm each block signature values are computed by using the private key and with the blocks of the file. Aggregated signature is calculated by using the aggregated blocks and with the public aggregate key. Modify algorithm is run three levels as insert, update and delete. To insert a new block the identifier for the newer block has computed. The signature for the blocks is updated in the storage. The total number of blocks in the shared data storage is increased by one. If any blocks want to be deleted from the storage the id and the signature are located. Then the number of blocks in the storage is decreased by one. To update a newer block to the data storage the signature for the block to update is computed and stored in the storage. The total value of the file blocks remains same.

To perform the integrity verification for the outsourced data the cloud service provider runs the ProofGen algorithm. The verifier sends a challenge to the CSP as number of blocks needed from a particular set and a random value. The CSP generates the proof by calculating the aggregated signature. The verifier runs the ProofVerify algorithm to verify the proof. With public aggregate key and with the aggregate signature the proof has been verified. Security analysis of this public integrity verification is done with three theorem proofs.

In batch auditing the algorithms used are BatchProofGen and BatchProofVerify. In BatchProofGen the verifier needs to generate the challenge which is same as sent in the ProofGen of public integrity verification. Once receiving the challenge the cloud service provider returns the proof as aggregated signature. The verifier runs the BatchProofVerify to verify the proof given by the cloud service provider. By using the private key the signatures are computed and compared. Security analysis of this batch auditing is done with two theorem proofs. Performance analysis is done in terms of computation and communication cost. By the usage of ring signatures with the homomorphic authenticators it is possible to verify the integrity of the outsourced data without retrieving the actual data from the server. Traceability and data freshness are considered as future scope for extending this work.

C. Liu et al. (2014) proposed a public auditing framework for dynamic big data storage on cloud to support efficient verifiable fine grained updates. In the existing models the authorization or authentication of the verifier at the cloud service provider is still open. It makes anyone with some necessary details can request auditing. Some works support the data updates for the fixed size blocks by utilizing the BLS signatures, if the block size is dynamic in nature, the scheme doesn't support it. The author utilizes the Merkle Hash Tree into a Ranked Merkle Hash Tree to support efficient dynamics operations of data.

The actors involving in this process can authorize each other. There are some schemes defined for supporting data dynamics. The works are with random masking technology and to ensure the TPA cannot infer any information from this. But the cost required for storage and communication are comparatively huge. A rank based merkle hash tree is introduced in which each level of the tree such each node of the tree is assigned with a particular rank value. Each node contains a hash value and a rank. Compare to the binary tree this merkle hash tree contains two leaf nodes for the non-leaf nodes at each level. Parent node is constructed at each level by performing concatenation between the leaf nodes.

Block level operations in fine grained updates are performed by Partial Modification, whole block Modification, block Deletion, block Insertion, and block Splitting. The algorithms used with this framework are KeyGen, FilePreProc, Challenge, Verify, GenProof, PerformUpdate and VerifyUpdate. During the Setup phase KeyGen and FilePreProc are performed. The KeyGen algorithm outputs the public and private key pairs for signing. In FilePreProc the file is divided into set of blocks, signatures are calculated for divided set of blocks and for the entire file. The construction of ranked merkle hash tree is done with the hash values. The root node value is computed and file tag information is generated. The file tag contains the name, number of blocks and signature values. In verifiable data updation the algorithms applied are PerformUpdate and VerifyUpdate. UpdateReq is sent from user to cloud service provider. Then PerformUpdate algorithm is run by the CSP. The UpdateReq contains the type of operation such as PartialModification or Whole block Modification. The cloud service provider will update the data blocks by message, root node value and signature values. Once it is done the cloud service provider respond to the client by $P_{update.}$. Once receiving the P update the client runs VerifyUpdate with the received value and by using the public key. The client computes the root value and its hash value then perform comparison between these values. If all are true, the update is success. To verify the integrity of the outsourced data the following algorithms are performed as GenChallenge, GenProof and Verify. TPA runs the GenChallenge algorithm to request the TPA for public auditing. TPA sends challenge message with signature, ID assigned to the TPA and a random set of file blocks. Cloud service provider received the challenge from the TPA and runs the GenProof algorithm to generate the proof.

From the GenProof algorithm the cloud service provider respond to the TPA as Proof P. The cloud service provider verifies the TPA by the VID sent and with the signature sent. Upon successful receiving of Proof the TPA runs Verify algorithm. This algorithm runs by public key, challenge and with the proof received. The TPA computes the hash values and compares the root node value in the ranked Merkle hash tree. Fine-Grained Dynamic data updates are proved with a theorem. Security analysis is performed for each level by utilizing the theorems and definitions. There performance analysis is not explicitly done but the experimental evaluation is performed. This scheme shows that the fine grained updates in the big data applications are possible with security. Future scope is to ensure the confidentiality and the availability of data at the server side storage.

B. Wang et al. (2013) proposed a system model for public auditing of shared data with efficient user revocation in the cloud data storage. In the shared data storage, if a user revoked from a group it is need to sign the data blocks which are already signed by the revoked user. It is performed by the actual data is downloaded from the server and the resigning is done at user revocation. To overcome the problems in this user revocation the concept of proxy re signatures is used. In this the cloud will perform the resign of blocks instead of the user can doing this task. The shared data integrity is preserved by the signature attachment with the data where the signature is calculated by any user in the group. A user acts as a group manager to provide keys to the other users. Once a user leaves from the group, the signature generated by the user is revoked by the group manager. A common group key is shared between the group, and the key is used to sign each block of data. If a user leaves from a group, a new key is calculated and shared among the group. The system is designed to provide the following properties such as Correctness, Efficient and Secure User Revocation, Public Auditing and scalability. The homomorphic authenticators based signature scheme run with the following algorithms as KeyGen, ReKey, Sign, ReSign, and Verify. Public and Private key pairs are generated with the KeyGen algorithm. Resigning of key is done by running the ReKey algorithm. With the private key and the block to store, sign algorithm is performed. ReSign algorithm is used for signing a particular block using proxy. A particular block is verified with the public key, block value, block identifier and signature. Two theorems are shown the security analysis of this resigning process. The public auditing mechanism is performed with the algorithms KeyGen, ReKey, Sign, ReSign, ProofGen, ProofVerify. The public and private key pairs are generated and a list of user is generated and maintained by the user in a group. ReKey is performed by the cloud. In Sign private key and block identifier are used to generate the signature. In ReSign the public key, signature block, block identifier are used to generate the signature. Once it is done the user list has been updated. If a TPA wants to perform verification then ProofGen algorithm is performed. TPA sends an audit message to the cloud service provider. The cloud service provider sends the proof as signature for the requested blocks. With the received proofs the TPA compares the signatures and gives the result to the owner. The scheme is shown with security and performance analysis at each level.

Yuan et al. (2015) proposed a public integrity auditing model dynamic data sharing with multiuser modification. The model supports multi user modification, public auditing, error detection, user revocation as well as less communication and computation overhead. The existing models supports only single data owner files auditing. Some models are defined to support the multi user data. Any user can access the data at any time. But computational cost required is high and no error detection mechanism with less probability. There are some challenges in this area are an aggregation of tags with user read, write operations require each time a new set of tags and secret keys. This limits the scalability. So sharing of secret key is needed to overcome it. Revocation is a challenging issue in such security model. A PoR scheme proposed in both public and private model with a constant communication overhead. It utilizes algebraic property of polynomial (Yuan et al., 2013). By utilizing oblivious RAM a private PoR model with the support of data dynamics is derived (Cash et al., 2013). An auditing scheme derived for shared data by using ring signature based homomorphic authenticators. User revocation is not attained in this model and the overhead is increase in cost (Wang et al., 2012). The extension of the above scheme with user revocation is defined by utilizing tag and key based concept. It is possible to get the keys of user at the time of revocation. It doesn't ensure batch auditing (Wang et al., 2013). This work has two models as basic system model and threat model. In the system model, the entities are cloud server, group user and third party auditor. A master user is for a number of users on each group. The tag are generated by the master user. Shamir's secret sharing mechanism (Merkle, 1980) is utilized with user revocation. By this, an advanced user revocation model is designed. It has the algorithms such as setup, key generation, update, challenge, prove and verify. It is also defined for batch processing as batch challenge, batch drive and batch verify. Performance evaluation is performed for the factors of communication cost, update, user revocation, real time auditing of single file, and real time auditing of multiple files. This work overcomes and gives the public data auditing mechanism for multi user modification data files. The advanced user revocation method is an extra feature. It ensures error detection and resist the impersonation attack. Also batch auditing support model is defined. Authentication and aggregation of tags are used for data blocks aggregation. So the verification is easily done as aggregated one by the verifier. The author concludes that the model provides a solution for public auditing of multi data that requires less resource overhead.

Liu et al. (2015) considers that the process of public auditing without the authentication of the blocks enables the cloud service provider to create a fake proof for the third party auditor that passes the auditing process without having the intact data in cloud storage. To protect data from dishonest storage servers and to reduce the communication overhead due to the update operations performed in all replicas which is caused by updating a single block of data, a novel public auditing scheme using Authenticated Data structure (ADS) is proposed. It is based on the concept of Merkle hash tree that is constructed not only based on the file but also depends on its replicas as well as the cryptographic hash function. It involves the process of key generation, file pre-processing, data updates and verification and auditing of replicas. In this approach, initially the user and the cloud service provider decide the parameters and the hash function. To generate the keys, the client generates a primitive root of a residual set and generator value for a group. The value of generator to the power of primitive root value is considered as public key and the primitive root as secret key. Another key pair having a secret key and public key is chosen for computing the signature. Then the client stores the files as blocks in the cloud. To do so, client makes indices to the number of replicas and computes random values to form blocks. Then the Multi Replica-Merkle Hash Tree (MR-MHT) is constructed with the replica blocks. Root value of the tree is found in such a way that every node holds the value of the hash of that block, level of the node, maximum number of nodes that could be reached to leaf node and the binary value denoting left or right of the sub-tree. Using these values, signature is computed with the secret key. The authenticator value is computed for all the blocks. At last, the block, authenticator and signature are uploaded to the cloud server.

To perform updates on blocks, every time the client computes the new block values and sends to the server. Client sends the request to server mentioning the type of update as modification, insertion or deletion along with the block number and updated block. The server updates the level of the node for every insertion and deletion whereas the auxiliary information remains the same for the non-leaf nodes. On receiving the request, the server locates the corresponding sub tree and updates the root hash value and sends newly computed values to client. Client verifies with the existing values and the newly sent root value if they are equal then the blocks are said to be updated. In performing auditing, the TPA sends the challenge request with signature, block indices and random values to server that verifies the signature and computes proof with the hash of blocks, auxiliary information, authenticator value and signature that is sent to the TPA. The TPA then verifies root value, signature and authenticator value to uniquely identify the block and if all verifications are passed then data is said to be intact. Thus, auditing of multiple replicas in the cloud storage is performed. The auditing of multiple replica yields the drawback of data confidentiality as the data has not been encrypted and additional communication overhead is caused during the retrieval of data.

J. Wang et al. (2015) addresses the issues of cloud service provider who try to send an incomplete query result or a wrong query result in order to save the bandwidth or due to any resource constraints. In performing auditing process, the original data getting tampered by the third party auditor or by an adversary is protected. The handling of dynamic verification of the entire database based on the audit request is performed. In the proposed framework, initially the data owner generates master key from which three keys are created and one is used for encryption process and two keys are shared to the authenticated users. The bloom filter tree with hash functions for attributes are initialized and sent to the Arbitration center (similar to TPA).

The Data owner then finds the hash value of the attribute with total number of tuples considered and the computed hash values are placed in leaf nodes of the Merkle hash tree. The root node holds the hash value of the entire record. Encryption of every attribute is done with the key and a search tag is generated from the key and cipher text. The cipher text is sent with the signature of root value and bloom filter to CSP. To retrieve the data, the user sends the request to CSP. On verifying the signature, CSP returns the cipher text to user. User further sends the cipher text to Owner and he decrypts and sends the original message to the user. The user checks for integrity of the result and in case of error it reports the AC as reject or else it sends a message as accept after verifying the signature. Auditing process prevents the exposure of the sensitive data to cloud service provider and also protects from TPA. It checks for completeness and correctness of data retrieved as records or tuples from the cloud storage. It evaluates the strategy through security analysis and performance analysis to ensure less overhead to the Data owner.

Tian et al. (2016) derived a two dimensional data handing mechanism with dynamic hash table (DHT). It is given to the third party auditor for protecting the data process for dynamic auditing. The public key based homomorphic authenticator with random masking is utilized for privacy preservation and BLS signature used for batch auditing task. Auditing the data by the data owner is directly performed between the user and the CSP (Sebe et al., 2008; Juels et al., 2007). This requires relatively lower cost. But in case of huge size data it leads to overhead. Encryption is followed to ensure the privacy of outsourced data (Sebe et al., 2008). At the time of verifying this data, there is a chance for leaking the data content (Wang et al., 2010). An index hash table based public auditing scheme is storing the hash table information at the auditor place. So, the cloud service provider doesn't face such issues or overheads. This reduces computation overheads. This index hash table also provides a support for data dynamicity. The update operation is inefficient due to the structure of index hash table (Zhu et al., 2013). Compared to MHT and scheme of skip list, this DHT gives less communication and computation overhead. On the auditing process performed by the auditor, it is difficult to handle multiple auditing at a same time (Wang et al., 2010; Cash et al., 2013; Zhu et al., 2012). To overcome this aggregation of different data block tags produced from different users are making as single and verify it.

Dynamic Hash Table (DHT) is designed with the advantage of linked list. It is a two-dimension structure model containing file and block elements. Each file element has index number, file identifier and pointer for indicating the array elements. DHT performs file level and block level operations. Each file can have one or more number of blocks. It requires very less time for searching at the time of verification process. The dynamic data verification with privacy preservation involves setup and verification phases. In setup, key initiation, data initiation, signature generation and tag generation are performed. In verification, the flow follow as file identifier check, challenge, proof generation and proof check. Dynamic updates and batch verification models are defined with series of steps. The security analysis is performed for proving the unforgeability, resist to replacing attack, and replay attack. Computation cost at the time of setup, verification, update, batch auditing is reduced than the reviewed works. The author concluding that this work has provided with DHT which completely reduces the cost of computation at server side. Multiple auditing task aggregates BLS signature techniques from bilinear maps to perform the task at the same time. Signature of data blocks are aggregated as a single one. So, it reduces the communication cost at the verification process. This scheme proposed a hash table technique based on indexed hash table. This gives efficient data blocks updation at the time of multiple user data maintenance and the public key based homomorphic location authenticators with random masking technique ensure the data privacy. BLS signatures are provided to support aggregated tasks. It gives a newer model which overcomes the existing techniques with fewer overheads. Calculation of hash values in the DHT has taken some time in case of data size is huge with multiple user requests. So, it gives such overhead issues.

More et al. (2016) proposed a framework for public auditing that involves Data owner, cloud server and TPA. It is ensured that TPA gets zero knowledge of the data being audited. Initially, the Data owner splits the file into blocks and encrypts the blocks using AES algorithm. Then, the hash values of the blocks are generated using SHA-2 algorithm. All the hash values of the blocks are concatenated together and a signature is generated on this concatenated hash value. The Data owner stores the encrypted blocks in the cloud storage. For data auditing, the TPA receives the computed signature from the Data owner and the encrypted blocks from the cloud storage. It then computes the hash values of the blocks and the signature of the concatenated blocks. It is then compared with the signature received from the Data owner for integrity verification and generates the results to the Data owner. Though integrity is maintained, the transfer of original encrypted blocks for auditing to TPA may lead to retrieval of original data as well as it increases the communication cost and overhead to the Data owner.

Li et al. (2016) proposes two privacy-preserving public auditing protocols with lightweight computations that are able to be performed in less powerful user devices. It addresses various issues such as cloud service providers who remove the stored user data that has not been used for a long time, curious TPA who try to attain the knowledge of the user data at the time of auditing. It also addresses handling of multiple audit requests simultaneously. The overhead causing complexity in the update operations like modification, insertion or deletion operations are addressed for light weight computational power devices.

The solution approach is that, if the input is smaller in size, the basic protocol is implemented otherwise the improved protocol is used. Consider the smaller input message as a Telephone number. The basic protocol involves various phases as follows:

- **Globe Setup**: The Trusted Authority (TA) generates the global parameters. The security parameter is chosen as input to generate two generators using the bilinear map having two groups. A hash function and a secure signature scheme are chosen. It generates a private-public key pair.
- **User Setup**: The User's public and private key, certificates are generated by the TA. The User generates full private key and full public key and receives a certificate signed by the TA using his secret key.
- **OffTagGen**: The User generates the offline tags. The User chooses some random values and generates a finite number of offline tags that are stored locally with the user.
- **OnTagGen**: User generates online tags from the offline tags when data is to be outsourced. The file to be sent is split into blocks. For each block the unused tuples in the local storage of the user is used to generate online tags. They are computed to generate the final tag of the file which is sent along with the filename to CSP and sends the signature, file name and tags to TPA. TPA checks whether the signature is valid and CSP also checks whether the online/offline signature of the file is valid.
- **Audit**: Third Party Auditor sends a challenge to CSP. CSP generates the response and sends to TPA. TPA checks for correctness. The TPA chooses certain blocks and computes values based on the indices of the blocks and constructs the challenge with the filename, indices and the computed values then sends to CSP. On receiving the challenge CSP generates the proof by hiding the block value to TPA. Then TPA computes the values and checks whether the data is intact or not.
- **Batch Audit**: TPA receives multiple audit tasks. It behaves the same as auditing but instead it takes multiple files of multiple users simultaneously and performs computation.

User performs operations such as, modification, insertion and deletion. In modification, the user modifies the file. The user chooses an unused tuple and generates an online tag and sends the modified block with file name, tags, signature and time stamp to the CSP. CSP verifies the signature of the auxiliary information and the tags. On being valid it updates the blocks and sends the updated signature to TPA. When TPA receives, it checks for signature validation and updates the tags and sends the intact information status to CSP and user. Similarly, insertion and deletion is performed.

In Improved Protocol, Merkle Hash Tree is used in every process where the leaf stores the hash values of the online tags. The signature of the root hash value is used to check for integrity whereas the operations performed in every phase remains the same. The experiment shows that the overhead and time taken to perform operations is quite low when compared to another research work as shown in Figure 3.

SUMMARY

The cloud service provider needs to provide a reliable service delivery to their customers. So, the correctness of data needs to be known and it is verifiable by the data owner at any point of time. This verification task is given to the Third Party auditor, who will perform the auditing task. This process also introduces vulnerabilities as such what details are needed to be given to the TPA for verification. The details which are given to the TPA doesn't give any clue about the actual data. There are some models defined for the public auditing of cloud data storage. See Table 1.

All schemes are based on the setup of four basic algorithms such as setup, challenge, generate proof, and verify proof. These four algorithms are used for verifying the correctness of data residing at cloud data storage. The existing schemes are providing solutions on the basis of signatures and key generation mechanisms. By this schemes, data stored in the cloud are in original format. No mechanisms are provided to address this issue. Preferred encryption techniques are not mentioned for the cloud data. The

Figure 3. Time taken to generate tags for varying number of blocks

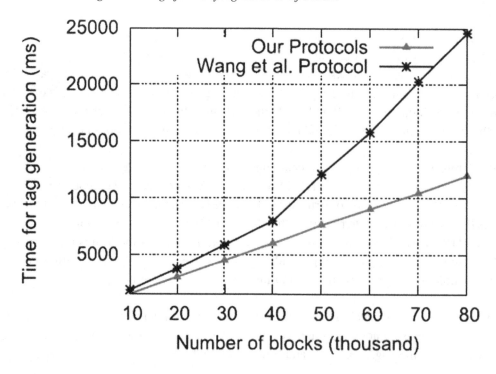

authorization of auditor is not followed in many schemes and the followed schemes are not strong. It is a semi trusted concept. Constructing a tree using hash values and verifying the root value is a technique followed in many systems. Hash tree construction, replicas, regeneration of code takes more computation time and it is vulnerable in some cases.

Most schemes perform auditing tasks only for the block of files. No full auditing concepts are mentioned. Mentioned system models are failure in performance issues. In some models the identity of user is secured for securing the confidential data files like government data. But the technique such as proxy based solution is not providing support. Proxies are vulnerable as it is easily compromised by an attacker. Maintaining these proxy servers is a harder task as what data given to the proxy, how the communication happen over the proxy setup is needed.

DISCUSSION AND ANALYSIS

From the analysis of the various research works discussed in this chapter, it is evident that every approach is different from each other but still the objective to ensure integrity of the data remains the same. Different parameters are compared based on the complexity and the cost incurred to achieve more security with reduced complexity. Those parameters involved in performance evaluation are communication

Table 1. Comparison of public auditing schemes in cloud

Comparison factor / Paper	C. Wang et al. (2010)	Q. Wang et al. (2011)	C. Wang et al. (2012)	Q. Wang et al. (2012)	C. Wang et al. (2012)	B. Wang et al. (2013)	C. Liu et al. (2014)	B. Wang et al. (2014)	J. Yuan et al. (2015)	H. Tian et al. (2016)
Authentication	No	Yes	Yes	Yes	No	Yes	Yes	Yes	Yes	Yes
Availability	No	No	No	No	No	No	No	No	No	No
Protocol	No	PDP POR	No	No	PRP	No	No	No	No	No
Technique	No	No	PKHVARM	BLS	Homomorphic token	Homomorphic authenticator based ring signatures	Tags	Homomorphic authenticators	Tags	Dynamic Hash Table
External auditor	Yes	Yes	Yes	Yes	Yes	Yes	Yes	Yes	Yes	Yes
Encryption	No	No	Yes	Yes	Yes	Yes	Yes	Yes	Yes	Yes
Data structure concept	Yes	Merkle Hash Tree	No	Modified merkle hash tree	No	Merkle hash tree	Ranked merkle hash tree	No	No	Dynamic hash values
Signature	No	Yes	Yes	Yes	Yes	Yes	Yes	Yes	Yes	Yes
Functions	Yes	No	PRF	No	PRF	No	No	No	Yes	No
Dynamism	Yes	Yes	No	Yes	Yes	Yes	Yes	Yes	No	Yes
Batch auditing	Yes	Yes	Yes	Yes	Yes	Yes	Yes	Yes	Yes	Yes
Error localization	No	No	No	No	Yes	No	No	No	Yes	No
Data recovery	No	No	No	No	Yes	No	No	No	No	No

overhead, computational overhead and time taken to perform auditing of the data blocks, to perform data dynamics operation like insertion, deletion and modification, in addition to it also finds the cost incurred to store, retrieve and verify the computed hash values for error localization and correction. From the theoretical study of the performance analysis, the computational complexity gets increased in utilizing multiplicative and exponential operations. When the local copy data of huge size is transferred between the stakeholders for integrity verification, it increases the communication overhead by continuously utilizing the maximum bandwidth. Similarly, when a small update in a block causing additional update to the entire tree of file blocks happens, it contributes greatly towards computational complexity and computational cost. The storage overhead occurs in scenario where the metadata gets increased in volume to verify the single piece of data at anytime required. Thus, an approach has to be framed that keeps an efficient trade-off between the utmost security and minimum cost with reduced complexity.

SOLUTIONS AND RECOMMENDATIONS

Cloud data storage and the correctness of stored data are the important considerations in the cloud arena. It is observed that public auditing schemes provide a verification mechanism for the storage data correctness. The existing system models are defined with various solutions such as cryptography based solutions, data structure based solutions, signature based solutions, key updation based solution, proxy based solution, and function models based solutions. Each model gets defined with its own concept. As a separate model defined or used, it is not possible to satisfy the problem in this public auditing. A model needed with a collaboration of two or more schemes. At each level a separate methodology is need to be defined for satisfying the security constraints. The cost and complexity mainly applies on the operations of data dynamics as well as data transferred between entities for integrity verification. Thus the metadata and the data used to perform these functionalities have to be handled in smaller size without compromising security objectives. It could certainly reduce the communication cost and overhead. At the same time, the computations should be able to be performed on the data with the anytime available sufficient resources to reduce the computation cost and overhead for the stake holders like Data owner, Third party auditor and cloud storage server.

FUTURE RESEARCH DIRECTIONS

Based on the analysis of the existing schemes, it is clear that the existing schemes are providing a limited security model for public auditing of data storage. To overcome these issues, a newer framework would be designed by providing security primitives at each level. The future framework of the auditing model will be designed and it would be completely new to this arena that holds the efficiency regarding performance and security analysis. The framework should be feasible to handle data of any size, to preserve the privacy of the data and to audit the replicas of the original file blocks for complete integrity verification. Data dynamics and batch auditing should reduce the communication cost and overhead in order to meet out its significance on implementation. It shall also meet the requirements to be adopted for real time scenario that allows to be deployed for real time implementations involving TPA for auditing. Even techniques could be proposed that satisfies the above solutions without involving any third-party auditor for integrity verification. Meanwhile, it should also be easy for the data owner to verify integrity of the data along with the cloud storage server without any overhead and security issues.

CONCLUSION

Digital data world has started to incorporate and maintain the data in the cloud data storage. Cloud data storage model helps the user to store their data without worrying about the maintenance of the data. But the data stored in the cloud data storage has the possibility of being accessed and modified in some cases such as attacks. So, it is mandatory to verify the correctness of the outsourced data. This is done by Trusted Third Party Auditor. TTPA performs verification tasks and gives the result to the Data owner. But this scheme also has some constraints or limitations to provide a secure auditing system. The Data owner can perform this task on his own but due to the time and resource required to do this task is not enough for the user, it is done by the TTPA. The existing models define various solutions or schemes to perform auditing process. But no such solutions are effective and efficient in terms of cost, security and performance. From this survey, existing system models followed for the auditing task and the problems with the models are identified. Based on the identification, the criteria to design a secure data auditing framework is studied that suits the purpose of performing an auditing task in the cloud data storage with utmost efficiency in terms of performance and security.

REFERENCES

Allmydata Inc. (2001). Unlimited Online Storage and Backup. Retrieved from http://allmydata.com

Amazon.com. 2009. Amazon Web Services (AWS). http://aws.amazon.com

Ateniese, G., Burns, R., Curtmola, R., Herring, J., Kissner, L., Peterson, Z., & Song, D. (2007). Provable data possession at untrusted stores. Cryptology ePrint Archive. Retrieved from http://eprint.iacr.org/

Ateniese, G., Pietro, R.D., Mancini, L.V., & Tsudik, G. (2008). Scalable and Efficient Provable Data Possession. *Proceedings of Fourth International Conference on. Security and Privacy in Communication Networks SecureComm '08* (pp. 1-10). doi:10.1145/1460877.1460889

Bellare, M., & Goldreich, O. (1992). On defining proofs of knowledge. In E.F. Brickell (Ed.), Advances in Cryptology – CRYPTO '92, (pp. 390–420). Springer.

Bellare, M., Goldreich, O., & Goldwasser, S. (1994). Incremental Cryptography: The Case of Hashing and Signing. *Proceedings of 14th Annual International Cryptology Conference: Advances in Cryptology CRYPTO '94* (pp. 216-233).

Bellare, M., & Miner, S. (1999). A forward-secure digital signature scheme. In Advances in Cryptology CRYPTO'99 (pp. 431-448). doi:10.1007/3-540-48405-1_28

Blum, M., Evans, W. S., Gemmell, P., Kannan, S., & Naor, M. (1994). Checking the correctness of Memories. *Algorithmica*, *12*(2/3), 225–244. doi:10.1007/BF01185212

Boneh, D., Gentry, C., Lynn, B., & Shacham, H. (2003). Aggregate and Verifiably Encrypted Signatures from Bilinear Maps.*Proceedings of 22nd International Conference on Theory and Applications of Cryptographic techniques Eurocrypt'03* (pp. 416-432). doi:10.1007/3-540-39200-9_26

Boneh, D., Lynn, B., & Shacham, H. (2001). Short Signatures from the Weil Pairing. *Proceedings of Seventh International Conference on Theory and Application of Cryptology and Information Security: Advances in Cryptology ASIACRYPT '01* (pp. 514-532). doi:10.1007/3-540-45682-1_30

Bowers, K.D. Juels, A. & Oprea, A. (2008). Proofs of Retrievability: Theory and Implementation. Cryptology ePrint Archive.

Cash, D., Kp, A., & Wichs, D. (2013). *Dynamic proofs of retrievability via oblivious ram. In Advances in Cryptology: EUROCRYPT 2013, LNCS* (pp. 279–295). Springer. doi:10.1007/978-3-642-38348-9_17

Castro, M., & Liskov, B. (2002). Practical Byzantine Fault Tolerance and Proactive Recovery. *ACM Transactions on Computer Systems*, *20*(4), 398–461. doi:10.1145/571637.571640

Chang, E. C., & Xu, J. (2008). Remote Integrity Check with Dishonest Storage Server.*Proceedings of 13th European Symposium on Research in Computer Security ESORICS '08* (pp. 223-237). doi:10.1007/978-3-540-88313-5_15

Clarke, D. E., Suh, G. E., Gassend, B., Sudan, A., vanDijk, M., & Devadas, S. (2005). Towards constant bandwidth overhead integrity checking of untrusted data. *Proceedings of the IEEE Symposium on Security and Privacy'05* (pp. 139–153). doi:10.1109/SP.2005.24

Curtmola, R., Khan, O., Burns, R., & Ateniese, G. (2008). MR-PDP: Multiple-Replica Provable Data Possession.*Proceedings of IEEE 28th International Conference on Distributed Computing Systems ICDCS '08* (pp. 411-420).

Deswarte, Y., Quisquater, J. J., & Saidane, A. (2003). Remote Integrity Checking. *Integrity and Internal Control in Information Systems*, *6*, 1–11.

Dodis, Y., Vadhan, S., & Wichs, S. (2009). Proofs of Retrievability via Hardness Amplification.*Proceedings of the Sixth Theory of Cryptography Conference on Theory of Cryptography TCC '09* (pp. 109-127).

Dwork, C., Goldberg, D., & Naor, M. (2003). On memory-bound functions for fighting spam. In D. Boneh, (Ed.), CRYPTO '03 (pp. 426–444). Springer. doi:10.1007/978-3-540-45146-4_25

Erway, C., Kupcu, A., Papamanthou, C., & Tamassia, R. (2009). Dynamic provable data possession.*Proceedings of the 16th ACM conference on Computer and Communications Security: CCS'09* (pp. 213-222).

Ferrara, A. L., Greeny, M., Hohenberger, S., & Pedersen, M. (2009). Practical short signature batch verification.*Proceedings of CT-RSA, LNCS* (pp. 309–324). Springer. doi:10.1007/978-3-642-00862-7_21

Filho, D.L.G., & Barreto, P.S.L.M. (2006). Demonstrating Data Possession and Uncheatable Data Transfer. IACR Eprint archive.

Golle, P., Jarecki, S., & Mironov, I. (2002). Cryptographic primitives enforcing communication and storage complexity. In M. Blaze (Ed.), Financial Cryptography '02 (pp. 120–135). Springer.

Golle, P., & Mironov, I. (2001). Uncheatable distributed computations. In D. Naccache (Ed.), CT-RSA '01 (pp. 425–440). Springer. doi:10.1007/3-540-45353-9_31

Hendricks, J., Ganger, G., & Reiter, M. (2007). Verifying Distributed Erasure-Coded Data.*Proceedings of 26th ACM Symposium on Principles of Distributed Computing PODC '07* (pp. 139-146).

Hwang, M., Lu, J., & Lin, E. (2003). A Practical (t, n) Threshold Proxy Signature Scheme Based on the RSA Cryptosystem. *IEEE Transactions on Knowledge and Data Engineering, 15*(6), 1552–1560. doi:10.1109/TKDE.2003.1245292

Jakobsson, M., & Juels, A. (1999). Proofs of work and bread pudding protocols. In B. Preneel (Ed.), *Communications and Multimedia Security* (pp. 258–272). Kluwer.

Juels, A., & Kaliski, J. S. (2007). PoRs: Proofs of Retrievability for Large Files.*Proceedings of 14th ACM Conference Computer and Communication Security CCS '07* (pp. 584-597) doi:10.1145/1315245.1315317

Kallahalla, M., Riedel, E., Swaminathan, R., Wang, Q., & Fu, K. (2003). Plutus: Scalable secure file sharing on untrusted storage. *Proceedings of the 2nd USENIX conference on File and Storage Technologies FAST' 03* (pp. 29–42).

Kher, V., & Kim, Y. (2005). Securing distributed storage: Challenges, techniques, and systems. *Proceedings of the ACM Workshop on Storage security and survivability StorageSS '05* (pp 9–25). doi:10.1145/1103780.1103783

Kubiatowicz, J., Bindel, D., Chen, Y., Czerwinski, S., Eaton, P., Geels, D., & Zhao, B. et al. (2000). Oceanstore: An architecture for global-scale persistent storage. *SIG PLAN Notices., 35*(11), 190–201. doi:10.1145/356989.357007

Li, J., Krohn, M., Mazieres, D., & Shasha, D. (2004). Secure untrusted data repository (SUNDR). *Proceedings of 6th conference on symposium on Operating System Design & Implementation OSDI '04* (pp. 121–136).

Li, J., Zhang, L., Liu, J. K., Qian, H., & Dong, Z. (2016). Privacy-Preserving Public Auditing Protocol for Low-Performance End Devices in Cloud. *IEEE Transactions on Information Forensics and Security, 11*(11), 2572–2583. doi:10.1109/TIFS.2016.2587242

Libert, B & Vergnaud, D. (2011). Unidirectional Chosen-Ciphertext Secure Proxy Re-Encryption. *IEEE Transactions on Information Theory, 57*(3), 1786-1802.

Lillibridge, M., Elnikety, S., Birrell, A., Burrows, M., & Isard, M. (2003). A Cooperative Internet Backup Scheme.*Proceedings of USENIX Annual Technical Conference: General Track* (pp. 29-41)

Liu, C., Ranjan, R., Yang, C., Zhang, X., Wang, L., & Chen, J. (2015). Mur-DPA: Top-Down Levelled Multi-Replica Merkle Hash Tree Based Secure Public Auditing for Dynamic Big Data Storage on Cloud. *IEEE Transactions on Computers, 64*(9), 2609–2622. doi:10.1109/TC.2014.2375190

Liu, C., Ranjian, R., Zhang, X., Yang, C., Georgakopoulos, D., & Chen, J. (2013). Public Auditing for Big Data Storage in Cloud Computing - A Survey. *Proceedings of 16th IEEE International Conference on Computational Science and Engineering CSE* (pp. 1128-1135).

Maheshwari, U., Vingralek, R., & Shapiro, W. (2000). How to build a trusted database system on untrusted storage.*Proceedings of the 4th USENIX Symposium: Operating System Design and Implementation*, Berkeley, CA, USA.

Mambo, M., Usuda, K., & Okamoto, E. (1996). Proxy Signatures for Delegating Signing Operation. *Proceedings of Third ACM Conference: Computer and Communication Security CCS '96* (pp. 48-57). doi:10.1145/238168.238185

Merkle, R. C. (1980). Protocols for Public Key Cryptosystems.*Proceedings of IEEE Symptoms: Security and Privacy* (pp. 122-133).

More, S., & Chaudhari, S. (2016). Third Party Public Auditing scheme for Cloud Storage. *Proceedings of theInternational Conference on Communication, Computing and Virtualization* (pp. 69-76). Elsevier. doi:10.1016/j.procs.2016.03.010

Muthitacharoen, A., Morris, R., Gil, T., & Chen, B. (2002). Ivy: A read/write peer-to-peer file system. *Proceedings of the 5th symposium on Operating Systems Design and Implementation: ACM SIGOPS Operating Systems Review OSDI '02* (pp. 31–44).

Naor, M., & Nissim, K. (1998). *Certificate revocation and certificate update*. USENIX Security.

Naor, M., & Rothblum, G. N. (2005). The complexity of online memory checking. *Proceedings of the 46th Annual IEEE Symposium on Foundations of Computer Science FOCS* (pp. 573–584). doi:10.1109/SFCS.2005.71

Network Technology Group. (2007). DataVault Offsite Data Backup to Completely Secure Critical Computer Data. Retrieved from http://www.ntg.com/datavault.asp

Pack, S., Rutagemwa, H., Shen, X., Mark, J., & Park, K. (2008). Proxy-Based Wireless Data Access Algorithms in Mobile Hotspots. *IEEE Transactions on Vehicular Technology*, *57*(5), 3165-3177.

Papamanthou, C., Tamassia, R., & Triandopoulos, N. (2008). Authenticated hash tables.*Proceedings of the 15th ACM Conference on Computer and Communications Security CCS '08* (pp. 437–448).

Rabin, M. (1989). Efficient dispersal of information for security, load balancing, and fault tolerance. *Journal of the ACM*, *36*(2), 335–348. doi:10.1145/62044.62050

Rivest, R. (2007). The pure crypto project's hash function. Cryptography Mailing List Posting. Retrieved from http://diswww.mit.edu/bloompicayune/crypto/13190

Ryoo, J, Rizvi, S. Aiken, W & Kissell, J. (2014). Cloud Security Auditing: Challenges and Emerging Approaches. *IEEE Security & Privacy*, *12*(6), 68-74.

Schwarz, T., & Miller, E. L. Store, Forget, and Check: Using Algebraic Signatures to Check Remotely Administered Storage. *Proceedings of 26th IEEE International Conference on Distributed Computing Systems ICDCS'06* (pp. 12). doi:10.1109/ICDCS.2006.80

Sebé, F., Domingo-Ferrer, J., Martínez-Ballesté, A., Deswarte, Y., & Quisquater, J. J. (2008). Efficient Remote Data Possession Checking in Critical Information Infrastructures. *IEEE Transactions on Knowledge and Data Engineering*, *20*(8), 1034–1038. doi:10.1109/TKDE.2007.190647

Shacham, H., & Waters, B. (2008). Compact proofs of retrievability. *Proceedings of the 14th International Conference on the Theory and Application of Cryptology and Information Security Asiacrypt '08* (Vol. 5350, pp. 90–107). doi:10.1007/978-3-540-89255-7_7

Shah, M. A. Baker, M. Mogul, J. C. & Swaminathan, R. Auditing to Keep Online Storage Services Honest. *Proceedings of the 11th USENIX Workshop Hot Topics in Operating Systems HotOS '07* (pp. 1-6).

Shah, M. A., Swaminathan, R., & Baker, M. (2008). Privacy-Preserving Audit and Extraction of Digital Contents. Cryptology ePrint Archive.

Shamir, A. (1979). How to share a secret. *Communications of the ACM*, *22*(11), 612–613. doi:10.1145/359168.359176

Tamassia, R. (2003). Authenticated data structures.Proceedings of ESA '05, LNCS (Vol. 2832, pp. 2–5). Springer.

104. th United States Congress. (1996). Health Insurance Portability and Accountability Act of 1996 (HIPAA). Retrieved from http://aspe.hhs.gov/admnsimp/pl104191.html

Tian, H. Chen, Y. Cheng, C. Jiang, H. Huang, Y. Chen, Y. & Liu, J. (2016). Dynamic-Hash-Table Based Public Auditing for Secure Cloud Storage. *IEEE Transactions on service computing*.

Valdes, A., Almgren, M., Cheung, S., Deswarte, Y., Dutertre, B., Levy, J., & Uribe, T. E. et al. (2003). An Architecture for Adaptive Intrusion-Tolerant Server.*Proceedings of Security Protocols Workshop* (pp. 158-178).

Wang, B., Baochun, L., & Hui, L. (2013). Public auditing for shared data with efficient user revocation in the cloud.*Proceedings of the 32nd IEEE International Conference on Computer Communications INFOCOM '13* (pp. 2904–2912). doi:10.1109/INFCOM.2013.6567101

Wang, B., Li, B., & Li, H. (2012). Oruta: Privacy-preserving public auditing for shared data in the cloud.*Proceedings of the IEEE Fifth International Conference on Cloud Computing CLOUD '12* (pp. 295–302). doi:10.1109/CLOUD.2012.46

Wang, C. Chow, S. M. Wang, Q. Ren, K. & Lou, W. (2013). Privacy-Preserving Public Auditing for Secure Cloud Storage. *IEEE Transactions on Computers*, *62*(2), 362-375.

Wang, C., Ren, K., Lou, W., & Li, J. (2010). Towards Publicly Auditable Secure Cloud Data Storage Services.IEEE Network Magazine, 24(4), 19-24.

Wang, C. Wang, Q. Ren, K. Cao, N. & Lou, W. (2012). Toward Secure and Dependable Storage Services in Cloud Computing. *IEEE Transactions on services computing*, *5*(2), 220-232.

Wang, C., Wang, Q., Ren, K., & Lou, W. (2009). Ensuring Data Storage Security in Cloud Computing.*Proceedings of 17th International Workshop on Quality of Service IWQoS '09* doi:10.1109/ IWQoS.2009.5201385

Wang, C., Wang, Q., Ren, K., & Lou, W. (2010). Privacy-Preserving Public Auditing for Data Storage Security in Cloud Computing. Proceedings of IEEE INFOCOM (pp. 1-9). doi:10.1109/INFCOM.2010.5462173

Wang, H. (2013). Proxy Provable Data Possession in Public Clouds. *IEEE Transactions on Services Computing*, 6(4), 551-559.

Wang, H. Wu, Q. Qin, B. & Domingo-Ferrer, J. (2014). Identity-based remote data possession checking in public clouds. *IET Information Security*, 8(2), 114- 121.

Wang, J., Chen, X., Huang, X., You, I., & Xiang, Y. (2015). Verifiable Auditing for Outsourced Database in Cloud Computing. *IEEE Transactions on Computers*, 64(11), 3293–3303. doi:10.1109/TC.2015.2401036

Wang, Q., Wang, C., Ren, K., Lou, W., & Li, J. (2011). Enabling Public Verifiability and Data Dynamics for Storage Security in Cloud Computing. *IEEE Transactions on Parallel and Distributed Systems*, 22(2/5), 847–859. doi:10.1109/TPDS.2010.183

Webopedia. (2007). Data Vaulting. http://www.webopedia.com/TERM/D/data_vaulting.html

Wikipedia. Cyclic Redundancy Check. 2007. http://en.wikipedia.org/wiki/Cyclic_redundancy_check

Worku, S. G., Xu, C., Zhao, J., & He, X. (2013). Secure and efficient privacy-preserving public auditing scheme for cloud storage. In Computers and Electrical Engineering (pp. 1703 – 1713). Elsevier.

Yuan, J., & Yu, S. (2013). Proofs of retrievability with public verifiability and constant communication cost in cloud. *Proceedings of the International Workshop on Security in Cloud Computing: Cloud Computing '13* (pp. 19–26). doi:10.1145/2484402.2484408

Yuan, J. & Yu, S. (2015). Public Integrity Auditing for Dynamic Data Sharing with Multi-User Modification. *IEEE Transactions on Information Forensics and Security*, 10(8), 1717-1726.

Zheng, & Xu, Q. (2011). Fair and dynamic proofs of Retrievability. *Proceedings of the first ACM conference on Data and Application Security & Privac: CODASPY'11* (pp. 237–248)

Zhu, Y. Hu, H. Ahn, G. & Yu, M. (2012). Cooperative Provable Data Possession for Integrity Verification in Multi-Cloud Storage. *IEEE Transactions on Parallel and Distributed Systems*, 23(12), 2231-2244.

Zhu, Y. Wang, H. Hu, Z. Ahn, G.J. & Hu, H. (2011). Zero-knowledge proofs of Retrievability. *Science China Information Sciences*, 54(8), 1608–1617.

Zhu, Y. Wang, H. Hu, Z. Ahn, G. J. Hu, H and Yau, S. (2013). Dynamic Audit Services for Outsourced Storage in Clouds. *IEEE Transactions on Services Computing*, 6(2), 227–238.

Zhu, Y., Wang, H., Hu, Z., Ahn, G. J., Hu, H., & Yau, S. S. (2011). Dynamic audit services for integrity verification of outsourced storages in clouds. *Proceedings of the 2011 ACM Symposium on Applied Computing SAC '11* (pp. 1550–1557). doi:10.1145/1982185.1982514

KEY TERMS AND DEFINITIONS

Public Auditing: Verifying the outsourced data correctness which is located at the cloud data storage.
Integrity Verification: Verifying the correctness of the outsourced data.

Third Party Auditor: A person who is performing the auditing task or integrity verification of outsourced data based on cost or agreement.

Privacy Preservation: Preserving the privacy of data after outsourced into the public storage.

Merkle Hash Tree: It is based on the binary tree data structure in which each non-leaf nodes are constructed by the leaf nodes with hash values to construct the root node.

Proxy: A computer or a machine to perform some automated tasks.

Signature: It is generated for a file or data block by the user using any cryptographic signature generation algorithms.

Chapter 7

Resource Management in Sensor Cloud

Prashant Sangulagi
BKIT, India

Ashok V Sutagundar
Basaveshwar Engineering College, India

ABSTRACT

Sensor Cloud is one of the attractive trend in present world. Sensor cloud is a combination of wireless sensor network and cloud computing. Due to the lack of battery energy and bandwidth the sensor nodes are incapable to store and process large data. Hence storing raw data is a challenging task. The sensor cloud comes into existence to accomplish multiple tasks that are not possible with existing sensor network. In sensor cloud the sensed data are processed and stored in the clouds and data can be accessed anywhere and anytime. Maintaining the resources and providing the resources to end users is a challenging task in sensor cloud. This chapter will brief the architecture of sensor cloud, application of sensor cloud in various sector, advantages of using sensor cloud compared to existing networks and management of resources in sensor cloud.

INTRODUCTION

Sensor cloud is a new model for cloud computing that uses the physical sensors to gather its data and transmit all sensory data into a cloud computing infrastructure. Sensor cloud is a well-designed sensor data storage, visualization and remote management platform that support powerful cloud computing technologies to provide great data scalability, rapid visualization, and user programmable analysis (Kian Tee Lan, 2010; R. Shea, 2013). In other words, sensor cloud can be defined as, an infrastructure that allows truly pervasive computation using sensors as interface between physical and cyber worlds, the data-compute clusters as the cyber backbone and the internet as the communication medium (Intellisys, 2014; David Irwin, 2010).

A sensor cloud collects and processes information from several sensor networks enables information sharing on big-scale and collaborate the applications on cloud among users. It integrates several networks with number of sensing applications and cloud computing platform by allowing applications to be cross-disciplinary that may traverse over organizational varieties. Sensor cloud enables users to

DOI: 10.4018/978-1-5225-2013-9.ch007

easily gather, access, processing, visualizing and analyzing, storing, sharing and searching large number of sensor data from several types of applications. These huge quantities of data are stored, processed, analyzed and then visualized by using the computational information technology and storage resources of the cloud (Doukas, 2011).

The main objective for going through the resource management in sensor cloud is to preserve the scarce resources and enhance the network lifetime. Physical sensor node can't give enough storage to store the raw data sensed by the sensor node. Cloud computing has huge storage and very good processing capability at different platforms. Hence combining these two will be beneficial one. Resource Management will provide a good platform to store the data in clouds as well as providing the data to end user at any time.

BACKGROUND

Wireless Sensor Network

Wireless sensor networks are used for monitoring environmental conditions like temperature, pressure, humidity, sound etc. in recent year wireless sensor networks are most widely used in military and many more applications. Wireless sensor network consists of set of sensor nodes and these sensor nodes sense the environmental parameters and updates the user/controller. The lifetime of sensor nodes depends on battery capacity and energy efficiency. Sensor nodes perform several functions hence these nodes are known as multifunctional. Sensor nodes are small in size, low cost and low power. Sensor nodes are capable of communicating wirelessly with each other in small distance. Energy efficiency is a critical issue in wireless sensor network as it depicts the lifetime of the network. Microcontroller, transreceiver, external memory, ADC, sensing unit, processing unit and power source are the components of sensor nodes (Heinzelman, 1999) as shown in Figure 1. Microcontroller is used for controlling functionality of other components in the sensor node. Microcontroller is low cost and low power consumption. Transreceiver combines the functions of both transmitter and receiver into single device. Sensor nodes use power supply for sensing, communicating and processing data. ADC is used for digitizing analog signal produced by the sensor. The work of sensing unit is to sense the environmental parameters and sensed information will be sent to processing unit for processing of data and storage is used to store the data with time.

Issues in Wireless Sensor Network

Some of the issues of wireless sensor network are listed below (Akyildiz, 1999):

- Node deployment
- Energy Consumption without losing accuracy
- Node/Link Heterogeneity
- Fault Tolerance
- Scalability
- Transmission media
- Coverage
- Data Aggregation

Figure 1. Wireless sensor network architecture

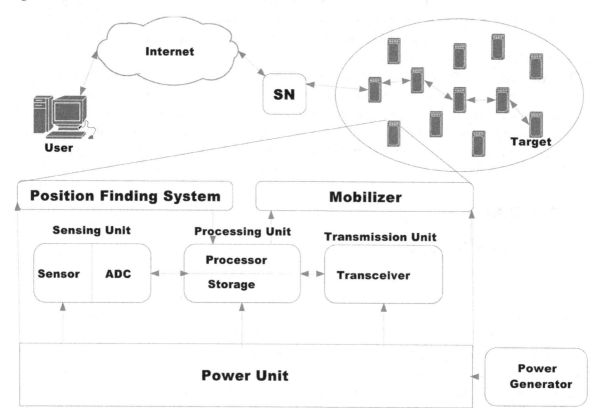

Advantages of Wireless Sensor Network (WSN)

The advantages of wireless sensor network are huge and some of the important one are listed below:

- Nodes communicate wirelessly. Hence free from wire complexity
- Network can be setup without infrastructure
- Size of the sensor node is very small and they can be of fixed type or have mobility property
- Low cost
- Easy integration with the systems
- Node can be deployed anywhere where human can't reach
- It can accommodate new devices at any time

Applications of Wireless Sensor Network (Akyildiz, 1999)

Sensor nodes can be used for continuous sensing, event detection, event ID, location sensing, and local control of actuators. Some of the popular applications of sensor network are listed below:

- Process management
- Health care monitoring

- Environmental/Earth sensing
- Industrial monitoring
- Forest Applications
- Military Applications
- Traffic Monitoring

Disadvantages of Wireless Sensor Network

- Sensor nodes are operated by battery power and they are more prone to failure due to lack of energy
- Less bandwidth
- Network lifetime depends on the number of transaction done by the node and its battery energy.
- Low speed compared to wired networks
- Less security
- Replacing of sensor when it is moving out of energy is a tedious job

Cloud Computing

Cloud computing involves deploying groups of remote servers and software networked that allow centralized data storage and online access to computer services or resources.

Cloud computing can be defined as "A model for conveying information technology facilities in which resources are regained from the internet through web-based tools and applications, rather than a direct link to a server" or "The storing and accessing of applications and computer data often through a web browser rather than running installed software on your personal computer or office server". the cloud computing is the set of hardware, software, networks, storage, services and interfaces that combine to deliver phases of computing as a service. Cloud computing allows people to do things they want to do on a computer without the need for them to purchase and form an IT infrastructure or to understand the fundamental technology. Cloud computing technology helps to do more with less expenses, higher quality services, reduced risk, less complexity and more importantly scalability.

The general cloud architecture is as shown below in Figure 2. The cloud providers actually have the physical data centers to provide virtualized services to their users through Internet. The cloud providers habitually provide parting between application and data. This situation is shown in the Figure 1. The primary physical machines are usually ordered in grids and they are usually geographically dispersed. Virtualization plays an important part in the cloud scenario. The data center hosts offer the physical hardware on which virtual machines exist in. User hypothetically can use any OS supported by the virtual machines used.

Some of the popular cloud characteristic includes, on-demand service, ubiquitous network access, location independent resource pooling and rapid elasticity (Weiss, 2007). Models of the cloud computing are mainly classified into three types, public clouds, private clouds and hybrid clouds. In public clouds, service provider makes resources, such as applications and storage, available to the general public over the Internet. Public cloud services may be free or offered on a pay-per-usage model. In a private cloud is a particular model of cloud computing that involves a distinct and secure cloud based environment in which only the specified client can operate. As with other cloud models, private clouds will provide computing power as a service within a virtualized environment using an underlying pool of physical

Figure 2. Architecture of cloud computing

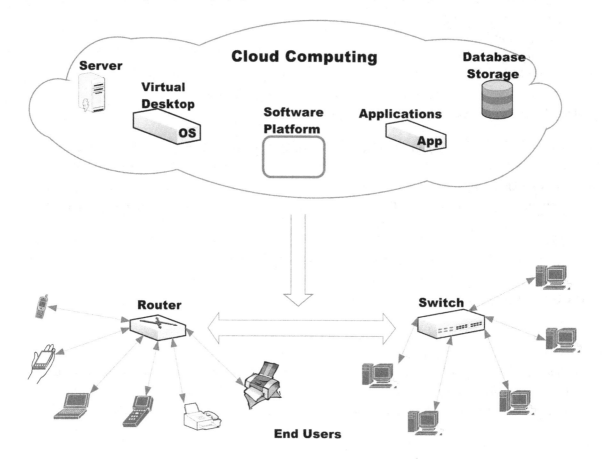

computing resource. However, under the private cloud model, the cloud (the pool of resource) is only accessible by a single organization providing that organization with greater control and privacy. Hybrid cloud combine elements of public and private clouds (Felici, 2013).

The service models of cloud computing are categorized into three types, Software as a service (SaaS), Infrastructure as a Service (IaaS), most basic cloud service model and lastly Platform as a Service (PaaS) (Felici, 2013).

Advantages of Cloud Computing

- Cloud computing exists to earn money while keeping principal and operational expenses to a minimum (Less costly).
- Cloud computing is more reliable and consistent than house side IT infrastructure. Cloud computing have quick failover mechanisms.
- Cloud is the flexible ability that can be twisted up, down or off depending upon situations.
- Cloud computing will eliminate the numbers of servers, the software cost, and the number of staff can considerably decrease IT costs without impacting an organization's IT proficiencies.

- With cloud computing the data can be accessed at anytime and anywhere. Helpful for those who works off-site.
- Cloud can handle multiple customers on share infrastructure. Hence efficient utilization of scarce resources.

Disadvantages of Cloud Computing

- Cloud service providers implement the best security, privacy standards and industry certifications, storing data and important files on external service providers continually unwraps up risks.
- Cloud infrastructure is wholly preserved, managed and supervised by the service provider, it handovers nominal control over to the clients. The client can only control and manage the applications, data and services functioned on top of that, not the backend infrastructure itself.
- Cloud computing is still a rapidly varying field, and there's always the risk that a new company might go out of business or drastically change its service.
- There is a need of continuous internet service with proper bandwidth
- Lack of support. Most of the service providers can't provide the user manuals to their clients.

ARCHITECTURE OF SENSOR CLOUD

The general architecture of cloud computing is as shown below in Figure 3:
    The architecture of the sensor cloud has the following components:

- **Physical Sensor Network:** It is the actual sensor network, where physical sensors are deployed either manually or random way. Sensor may have homogenous or heterogeneous property. All the sensors will sense the required information and transfer to sink node using one of the energy optical routing techniques.
- **Sink Node:** All the nodes in the sensor network will finally send the information to sink node. Sink node has control over all the sensing nodes in the network. Sink node maintains the database of all the sensor nodes and it will be updated always.
- **Gateway:** It is the middleware between physical sensor network and the cloud server. The sensed information can be sent to cloud server using basic networking technologies like wired or wireless networks. Wireless networking is preferred for data transmission i.e. Bluetooth technology.
- **Cloud Server:** It is the endpoint where all the sensed data are stored. Different users can access the data based on their interest.
- **Users:** Users are the end people who utilizes the services provided by the sensor cloud. User can also inject the query into the network and he/she waits for the results. Users can access any kind of data, if data is public then there will be no cost to view/access data and if data is secured then user need a password to access the data.
- **Virtual Sensors Group:** It is the virtual network of actual physical sensor network available at the cloud. It gives the actual status of the physical network and also updates the database all time. If any node is moving out of battery energy or if the node is about to die, then virtual network removes that node from the network and reform the routing table once again.

Figure 3. Sensor cloud architecture

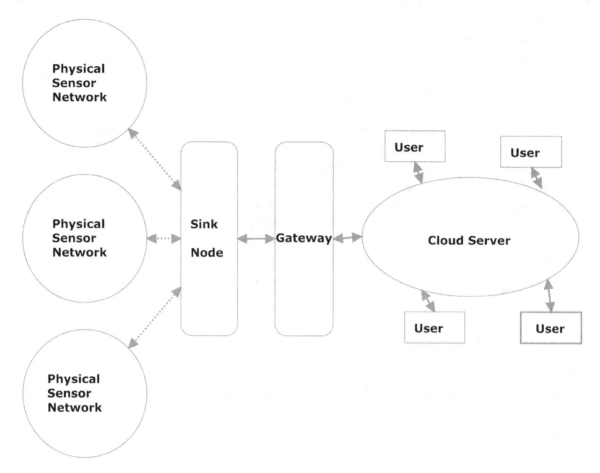

Advantages of Sensor Cloud

In this section, some of the major advantages of the sensor cloud are depicted.

1. **Scalability:** If the number of resources are increased then it can be possible to add extra services into cloud computing without paying extra money. Hence huge sensory raw data can be processed easily using sensor cloud.
2. **Increased Data Storage and Processing Power:** Date can be stored in servers and hence avoiding storage of information in personal computer and information can be accessed by many applications. Need of processing power also becomes less.
3. **Dynamic Provisioning of Services:** Services provided by the sensor cloud can be accessed anywhere anytime. Users no need to stick to their own computers.
4. **Multi-Tenancy:** Multi services from multiple service providers can be integrated onto a single network. Sensor cloud allows the accessibility of data anywhere anytime.
5. **Collaboration:** Sensor cloud enables collaborations among several users and applications, hence huge sensor data can be processed easily.

6. **Analyze:** Data analyzing from huge sensory data and distribution of data according to user requirement is very quick in sensor cloud.
7. **Visualization:** Through sensor cloud platform information from multimedia sensors can easily be visualized in the form of pictures or diagrams and future trend can be predicted (Ansari, 2013; Dinh, 2011).
8. **Resource Optimization:** Sensor-Cloud enables resource sharing capability to many number of applications.

Disadvantages of Sensor Cloud

The disadvantages of sensor cloud are listed below (Gul, 2011):

1. Structure doesn't give to a great degree precise statistics as in case of conventional allocation of physical sensors statistics.
2. The operations provided are not rapid adequate as assessed to amenities agreed by straight exchange of human projections.
3. Sensor-Cloud required enormously extensive organization pattern in order to follow the clients.
4. Cloud-Sensor architecture is susceptible and additional level to complicated share outer interruption attacks.

Issues in Sensor Cloud

Sensor cloud focuses on following issues like, power authorization, network management, energy, security, pricing, resource management, fault tolerance, routing, clock synchronization and programming. The issues are described on by one:

1. **Power Issues:** Power plays an important role in almost all networking sectors. Sensor nodes are operated by battery power. During processing and transmission of sensory data energy requirement becomes more which leads the node to move out of battery energy very soon. Likewise cloud computing also needs more power to process the data as well as store the data in database. Thus, an alternative power supply to sensor nodes becomes a major requirement also an arrangement should be made so that processing and storage of data at cloud server should consume less power.
2. **Authorization Issues:** Delivering the data to desired person is a one of the issues in sensor cloud. Cloud computing is operated by many platform and multiple users accessing the data at a time. Transferring the data to the right person plays important role as sometimes the authors are not authenticated and forcibly wants to access the data. A proper authentication technique should be adopted so that only authorized users access the data from the cloud server.
3. **Network Access Management:** There are many cloud computing platform at the cloud server so there is a need of proper and access management schemes for several networks which will optimize the bandwidth usage and overall performance is increased.
4. **Energy Efficiency Issues:** An algorithm should be prepared at the physical sensor network side so that the overall energy consumption should be as low as possible. Data transmission and processing requires large amount of energy at both platforms hence preparing a suitable algorithm cloud server and sensor network is an important requirement.

5. **Security:** Security is playing a vital issue in many platforms. The data transmitted should reach the desired destination without being leakage. Standard security approach should be adopted in order to avoid the accessibility of data by the third party at both physical network and cloud server side.

6. **Pricing Issues:** Pricing is a major issue in sensor cloud. If nodes are heterogeneous then cost of the overall system increases. The platform of the sensor cloud should be arranged in such a way that the performance of the system should be high with minimum cost. Cost of the system increases with increasing in bandwidth and if more platforms are included.

7. **Resource Management:** Raw sensed information from sensor nodes are classified in many ways like information may be regarding the physical signal which is usually represented in text format or the information may be represented in multimedia format. Sensing the data and transferring the data into the cloud from sensor nodes is challenging task where data are coming from different platforms and have different format. Arranging the data at the cloud server is tedious work in sensor cloud. The resource allocator should be selected in such a way that it should complete the task within the time and allocation should be error free and cost optimized.

8. **Fault Tolerance:** Fault tolerant is the important issue in sensor cloud as nodes may move out of battery energy and predefined path may not be used to transfer the data. Hence while designing the sensor cloud scenario one must design the dynamic routing table and if the node is moving out of battery energy then alternative route should be found without effecting the overall network. Fault tolerance can also be an important issue if the sensor devices and gateway for the cloud are out of reach. The important information may not reach the destination within the time if both are not within the communication range

9. **Routing Issues:** Routing the information from physical sensor nodes to a server is a critical issues. Initially sensed information has to be routed to sink node and through gateway the information from sink node has to be routed to cloud server. Nodes are operated by battery power and have small amount of energy hence finding the energy efficient path from source to destination is critical issue.

Applications of Sensor Cloud

Sensor cloud can be used in many application because of its attractive features (Barker, 2010). Using conventional WSN leads too many drawbacks like data processing and storage. In WSN nodes are operated by battery power and have limited energy & bandwidth hence inclusion of cloud is a mandatory option to broaden the applications of sensor network. In this section, we will discuss some of the important applications of sensor cloud.

1. **Agriculture Applications:** In this the sensor cloud is used to monitor the information of harvesting, work management, growth of crops and prevention of crop diseases. Initially sensor nodes will collect the information (in the form of text or images) of the crop and field. Later the information is stored in cloud computing. The former can collect the data from anywhere and further appropriate actions will be taken.

2. **Healthcare Applications:** Monitoring the patient activity is a major concern in hospitals even sometimes we need to monitor the patient activity in home or other areas. Several types of sensors are used in the hospital (such as heart rate sensor, blood pressure sensor and sensor for oxygen saturation in the blood). These sensors are used by the hospital services for supporting daily medical cares, for refining the service level, and for avoiding faults. There is an issue with respect to the

communication range, that is sometimes patient may not be in the communication range to monitor his/her activity. Hence a cloud is introduced and all sensed data from the patient are stored in the cloud so that doctor/controller will get the continuous update irrespective of communication range.

3. **Weather Applications:** In monitoring the weather condition sensor cloud infrastructure can be employed. In traditional sensor network one can get info regarding the existing area only. Cloud platform is employed along with sensor network to update all the weather-related information into the server so that anyone can get the information regarding the weather status of a particular area. Physical sensors will sense the environmental parameters and using the gateway all the sensed information are stores in cloud server. Now through cloud server anyone can get information regarding the weather. The weather service will be able to use the virtual sensors, analyze multiple sensors' data timely, give rapid warning, and control traffic effectively.

4. **Military Applications:** Sensor cloud can be used in military applications to detect the enemy and their weapons as well as to monitor their activity. Through cloud sever militants will access information by sitting far away from the target region. It's an important upgrade in the traditional WSN which was earlier used in military applications. Traditional WSN methodology had many drawbacks and usage of cloud computing will eliminate all problems and network lifetime will enhances.

Sensor cloud can also be used for many others applications also like, transportation and vehicle traffic applications, earth observation, telemetric etc. (Dinh, 2011).

RESOURCE MANAGEMENT IN SENSOR CLOUD

Physical sensor nodes have limited battery power, limited bandwidth and less memory storage. Data sensed by the sensor can't be stored for long period and processing of such a huge data is a tedious job. Cloud computing provides scalable processing power and numerous classes of connectable services. Through cloud computing huge amount of data can be stored and processed easily hence problems with sensor nodes can be solved easily. Managing the resources at the cloud server is a research issue in sensor cloud where huge data from different sensor networks comes and stored here. Raw sensed information from sensor nodes are classified in many ways like information may be regarding the physical signal which is usually represented in text format or the information may be represented in multimedia format. Sensing the data and transferring the data into the cloud from sensor nodes is challenging task where data are coming from different platforms and have different format. Arranging the data at the cloud server is tedious work in sensor cloud. The resource allocator should be selected in such a way that it should complete the task within the time and allocation should be error free and cost optimized. In this section, we are discussing some of the platforms which helps in allocating the sensory resources into the sensor cloud server and it is be accessible for all users.

There are different models for data storage in cloud server namely, file repository, database module, service module, resource configuration module (Jiang, 2014).

- **File Repository:** File repository makes use of hadoop distributed file system (HDFS) to store unstructured files in a distributed environment. We also add a version manager and a multitenant manager to implement the management of the versioned model files and the isolation of tenants' data. A file processor is used to improve the file repository's ability for handling small files.

- **Database Module:** Database module combines numerous databases and uses both NoSQL database and relational database for dealing organized data. This module also delivers integrated API and object–entity mapping for multiple databases to hide their changes in executing and interfacing so that the development of data access modules and the application migration of databases can be simplified.
- **Service Module:** Service module is built to create RESTful service automatically. This module removes the metadata through formation, then mapping to the data objects and files deposited in the databases and file repository rendering to the mined metadata and finally producing corresponding RESTful service.
- **Resource Configuration Module:** Resource configuration module supports static and dynamic data management in terms of predefined meta-model. Thus, data resource and related services can be configured based on occupant necessities. Additionally, data disposing mechanism such as load balanced and isolated preferences can also be carried out.

The Date storage operator will perform following operations (Khanna, 2014):

1. Precisely measure real-time energy depletion and estimate power usage effectiveness.
2. Deduce temperature, humidity, and subfloor pressure difference data from several sensor nodes by live-imaging maps.
3. Truthfully measure server specific performance features and drifts for evolving statistical models that can predict resource utilization and energy consumption.
4. Perfect association between server performance characteristics, energy consumption, and environmental parameters (temperature, humidity, subfloor pressure, etc.).
5. Establish baseline energy consumption and detect improvement chances by efficient provisioning and filling of server resources.
6. Using monitoring infrastructure, improve automation policy that achieves adaptive workload provisioning, air-flow control, and air-conditioning control.
7. Monitor environmental situations to confirm agreement as per the American Society of Heating, Refrigerating, and Air-Conditioning Engineers and convey alerts if the ranges are surpassed.

Few mathematical models were proposed for the selection of cloud service provider which satisfy the consumer need at maximum level and few data allocation problems which select the best storage systems which meet the user's data necessities and optimize cost and/or access latency/bandwidth.

Utility Based Model

This methodology customs utility functions in a QoS management framework with the goals to encounter the least requirements and maximize the entire utility for the consumer. By calculating the utility value related to each provider, the best provider will be the one with the highest utility value which is given in Equation 1 (Maria Salama, 2013).

$$f(U_i) = \sum_{j=1}^{m} \left(\sum_{l=1}^{aj} P_{ijl} * w_{jl} \right) * W_j \tag{1}$$

Where the calculation of the utility value u_{ij} is addressed as follows. Any class dimension j, where $j \in \{1,.....,m\}$, is defined by a group of measurable parameters P_{jl}, where $j \in \{1,.....,q_i\}$, and q_j is the size of this group. For example; a quality dimension like the performance is defined in terms of measurable parameters like response time, worst-case execution time, and throughput. Each of these parameter P_{jl} is further associated with a weight w_{jl}, where for $w_{jl} \in [0,1]$, and $\sum_{l=1}^{aj} w_{jl} = 1$. Varying P_{jl}, different parameters can be considered for one QoS dimension.

Resource Allocation Model

In this case the inputs are a list of user's requirements and the storage services' capabilities. The output of this first stage is a list of compatible storage services for each dataset in the application; these lists constitute the input for our data allocation problem. We use integer linear programming to model this problem. The general idea is to include the cost, latency, and bandwidth as parameters in the objective function that needs to be minimized.

Let us consider the dataset $(x_{i,j})$, an integer variable is introduced that represents the amount of computation required per month and an assignment of computation to cloud sites. Additional linear constraints are used to enforce different restrictions. For example, that each dataset is stored in at least one storage system and that each site can support the computations that access each dataset.

The objective function is the following one, where each wi is the combination of a weight assigned by the user and a normalizing factor which is depicted in Equation 2:

$$\min \begin{pmatrix} w1 * AvgStoragC\,os\,t \\ +w2 * AvgCompute\,Cos\,t \\ +w3 * AvgLatency \\ +w4 * AvgBandwidth \end{pmatrix} \tag{2}$$

It needs to be combined every term in order to evaluate cost, latency and bandwidth. In this case all parameters have been normalized.

Using game theory, grid computing and parallel computing the resources are managed in a better way along with that data aggregation techniques can also be employed to minimize large data into small one.

METHODS FOR RESOURCE MANAGEMENT IN SENSOR CLOUDS

Following are the methodologies used for resource management in sensor cloud.

1. Adding data in priority wise
2. Saving data on types of cloud
3. Saving data in cubes (Multidimensional)
4. Aggregating the data
5. Saving data based on organization modes
6. Grid computing

Adding Data in Priority Wise

The sensed information from the physical sensor are processed and sent to the sensor cloud using gateway. At the server side the management is done in such a way that, based on the importance of the data (Resource), the data is stored inside the database. The resources are classified in-terms of priority of the data.

If the information is very critical and need to be transferred/processed immediately to the end users, then it is labeled as high priority information.

If the information is moderately critical, then it is labeled as nominally prioritized information. This information is sent when high priority information is empty.

If the information is non-critical or general data then it is labeled as non-priority information. The information available in this section is sent to required users when both priority & nominally priority are empty.

Examples for priority, nominal priority and non-priority information are as follows.

- **Priority Information:** Military data, Accident information, Emergency data like fire in forest, leakage in power plants.
- **Nominally Priority Information:** Traffic Analysis, Product information.
- **Non-Priority Information:** Temperature, Humidity, Pressure information.

Saving Data on Types of Cloud

Generally, cloud computing is classified into three types namely, public cloud, private cloud and hybrid clouds.

Based on the data coming from the physical sensor, the data will be stored either in public, private or hybrid clouds. The classification is done based on the data type.

If the data is private then, it should be stored in private cloud. If any users want to access such data, then they need a valid user id and password to access the information. There is a need of security algorithms in order to protect the private data. Some of the popular encryption algorithms are Data Encryption System (DES), Advanced Encryption System (AES), RSA or cipher key management.

If the sensed information from the physical sensor is general (non-private) then such information is stored in the public clouds at the sensor cloud server. Any information which don't require encryption or non-private information can be stored here. There is no requirement of user id and password to access the information. If any user request information then they can connect to the server and they can access the data. Only authenticated users are allowed to access the information. No standard security approaches are required.

In case of hybrid clouds, the physical information from the sensors is stored in the server where users can access data it in two ways. Firstly, User need valid user id and password to access few data which are stored with security approaches. Secondly, some other data which can be accessed by the users without used id and password. In the second case security is not the important aspect.

Based on the importance of the data, it can be either stored privately or publically. Encryption algorithms can be applied to few data if they important and can't be accessed by the third party or unwanted users/systems.

The filtering techniques are included to divide the data. That's is private data and public data.

Saving Data in Cubes (Multidimensional)

Multidimensional cubes are the latest and easy way to store the sensed data from sensors. Each multidimensional cube is used to store sensory information. Based on the number of sensors the dimensionality can be increased. It is easy to store the updated data into the cubes and also useful for end users to retrieve from the cubes.

A label is provided to each of the sensed information and users will retrieve by providing proper label. Admin can update, edit and delete the data available inside the cubes.

The above Figure 4 shows the multidimensional cubes for storing physical sensor information into the sensor cloud server. In this case A is having set of data coming from one set of sensor group. Whenever there is an update then updated data is saved inside the cube at different dimensionality. Similarly different data are stored at different locations inside the cube. It's easy to find the location of the stored data and easy to retrieve.

Figure 4. Multidimensional cubes for sensor cloud server

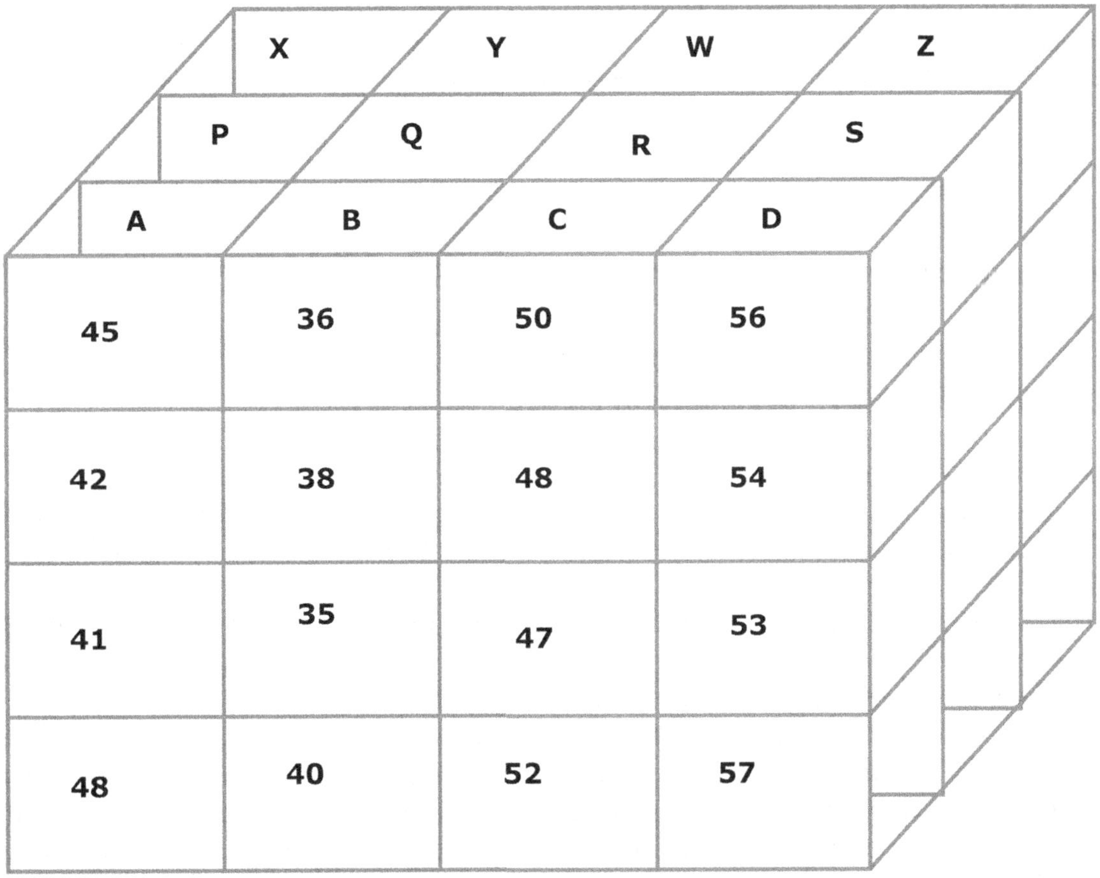

Aggregating the Data

Data aggregation is one of the data saving method in resource management for sensor cloud. The sensor may send duplicate information or multiple copies of same information. If we store such data then it consumes more space and effects the throughput of the overall system. Hence, in this case the data cross check is being done and it will be verified that server contains no duplicates data (J. Hill, 2003).

An algorithm/ filtering technology is employed before storing the data into the sensor cloud. This approach will store only required information inside the serve and removes redundant information.

The techniques used for data aggregation are minimum, maximum, summation, average or fusion. If similar information appears at the sensor cloud server then above mentioned techniques are used and it will give the unique information which reflects the similarity between the data appears at the output and same is being stored in the senor cloud server.

Data aggregation reduces the memory used by the sensory data. Hence information from other resource can also be stored in left space, hence the resources are managed (J. Johnson, 1999).

Example

If sensor1 and sensor2 sends the temperature information 42^0C and 43^0C respectively then, instead of keeping both sensory information at the server side. The data aggregation technique is employed to eliminate duplicate/redundant data and store only one data which reflects both the information's at the sensor cloud server. Different techniques produces different results and all results reflects the inputs are as shown below.

Maximum : $Max(42,43) = 43^0C$

Minimum : $Min(42,43) = 42^0C$

Average : $Avg(42,43) = 42.5^0C$

Saving Data Based on Organization Modes

In this case of resource management in sensor cloud, instead of keeping all data at one server, the server is subdivided into few categories based on the data coming from different organizations. The data coming from different organizations are stored separately in the sub server. The large bandwidth is divided and assigned to each organizations.

If data is coming from one of the organization, then it will be stored in a server which is assigned to it. Some of the organizations are operated with huge amount of data, in this case two or more servers are assigned for storage of data.

Different sectors have different kinds of applications running on it. Hence to work out their applications a particular operating system is employed and output data is stored inside the servers. Allotment of bandwidth is done based on the type of organizations. Few organizations requires encryption and they are provided with proper encryption techniques to provided security along with authentication process. If organization doesn't require any encryption technique, then only authentication process is acquired.

Grid Computing

Grid computing is one of the popular resource management technique, where data from different administrator are stores at one place. The size of the server may vary from small entity size to large hub servers. The data type can be anything. A unique ID has been assigned to each of the data incoming to the main server.

Grid computing alarms the application of the resources of several computers in a network to a single problem at the same time - typically to a scientific or technical problem that necessitates a great number of computer processing cycles or entree to large quantities of data (Amarnath, 2009). Grid computing seems to be a favorable trend in Resource Sharing for three reasons:

1. Its capability to mark more cost-effective use of a specified volume of computer resources,
2. It is a technique to reaction difficulties that can't be advanced without a massive extent of computing power.
3. It proposes that the resources of several computers can be supportively and possibly synergistically attached and managed as collaboration toward a collective objective.

The data can be properly utilized by using proper data fetching technologies i.e providing location of the data or unique ID provided to information.

Multiple data can be stored by using grid computing, different data from different clusters are taken and stored inside the large server calling as grid computation. Inside the server, the data may be of homogenous or heterogeneous property. In homogenous, all data of same type. In heterogeneous, all data are not same type.

Grid computing can also be used to fulfill the communication task using multiple resources. The grid computing is also responsible for aggregation of data incoming from clusters.

CONCLUSION

The main objective for going through the resource management in sensor cloud is to preserve the scarce resources and enhance the network lifetime. Physical sensor node can't give enough storage space to store the raw data sensed by the sensor node. Cloud computing has huge storage and very good processing capability at different platforms. Hence, combining these two will be beneficial. Resource Management facilitates a better platform to store the data in clouds as well as providing the data to end user at any time. Different resource management techniques for sensor cloud environment have been depicted in this chapter namely, adding data in priority wise, saving data on types of cloud, saving data in cubes (Multidimensional) aggregating the data, saving data based on organization modes, grid computing. All methods have their own methodology to manage the resources.

REFERENCES

Lan, K. T. (2010). What's next? Sensor+Cloud? *Proceeding of 7th International workshop on Data Management for Sensor networks.*

Intellisys. (2014). Retrieved from http://www.ntu.edu.sg/intellisys

Alamri, A., Ansari, W. S., Hassan, M. M., Hossain, M. S., Alelaiwi, A., & Hossain, M. A. (2013). A Survey on Sensor-Cloud.International Journal of Distributed Sensor Networks, 2013, 18–24.

Dinh, H.T., Lee, C., Niyato, D., & Wang, P. (2011). A Survey of Mobile Cloud Computing: Architecture, Applications, and Approaches. Wireless Communications and Mobile Computing, 13(18), 1587-1611.

Doukas, C., & Maglogiannis, I. (2011). Managing wearable sensor data through cloud computing. *Proceedings of theThird IEEE International Conference on Cloud Computing Technology and Science* (pp. 440-445). IEEE. doi:10.1109/CloudCom.2011.65

Shea, R., Liu, J., Ngai, E.-H., & Cui, Y. (2013). Cloud gaming: architecture and performance. IEEE Network, 27(4), 16–21. doi:10.1109/MNET.2013.6574660

Irwin, D., Sharma, N., Shenoy, P., & Zink, M. (2010). Towards a virtualized sensing environment. *Proceedings of the 6th International Conference on Test beds and Research Infrastructures for the Development of Networks and Communities.*

Barker, S., & Shenoy, P. (2010). Empirical evaluation of latency sensitive application performance in the cloud.*Proceedings of the 1st ACM Multimedia Systems Conference*, Scottsdale, AZ, USA. ACM. doi:10.1145/1730836.1730842

Hill, J., & Chang, K. C. (2003). Improved Representation of Sensor Exploitation for Automatic Sensor Management.*Proc. Sixth Int. Conf. Information Fusion*, Cairns, Queensland, Australia (pp. 688–694).

Johnson, J., & Chaney, R. (1999). Recursive Composition Inference for Force Aggregation.*Proc. of the Second Int. Conf. Information Fusion.*

Jiang, L., Da Xu, L., Cai, H., Jiang, Z., Bu, F., & Xu, B. (2014). An IoT-Oriented Data Storage Framework in Cloud Computing Platform. IEEE Transactions on Industrial Informatics, 10(2), 1443-1451.

Khanna, R., Liu, H., & Rangarajan, T. (2014). Wireless data center management. *IEEE Microwave Magazine, 15*(7), S45–S60. doi:10.1109/MMM.2014.2356151

Amarnath, B. R., Somasundaram, T. S., Ellappan, M., & Buyya, R. (2009). Ontology-based Grid resource management. *Software: Practice and Experience, 39*(17), 1419-1438.

Salama, M., Shawish, A., & Zeid, A. (2013). A Generic Framework for Modeling and Simulation of Cloud Computing Services. *International Journal of Computer Applications, 77*(17), 33-38.

Heinzelman, W., Kulik, J., & Balakrishnan, H. (1999). Adaptive protocols for information dissemination in wireless sensor networks.*Proc. Fifth Annual ACM/IEEE International Conference on Mobile Computing and Networking (MobiCom)* (pp. 174-185) ACM. doi:10.1145/313451.313529

Akyildiz, I. F., Su, W., Sankarasubramaniam, Y., & Cayirci, E. (2002). A survey on sensor networks. IEEE Communications Magazine, 40(8), 102-114.

Gul, I., & Hussain, M. (2011). Distributed Cloud Intrusion Detection Model. International Journal of advanced science and technology, 34(38), 71-82.

Weiss, A. (2007). Computing in the Clouds.netWorker, 11(4), 16-25.

Felici, M., Koulouris, T., & Pearson, S. (2013). Accountability for Data Governance in Cloud Ecosystems. *Proceedings of the 2013 IEEE International Conference on Cloud Computing Technology and Science.* . IEEE. doi:10.1109/CloudCom.2013.157

Chapter 8
Challenges and Issues in Web–Based Information Retrieval System

Sathiyamoorthi V.
Sona College of Technology, India

ABSTRACT

It is generally observed throughout the world that in the last two decades, while the average speed of computers has almost doubled in a span of around eighteen months, the average speed of the network has doubled merely in a span of just eight months! In order to improve the performance, more and more researchers are focusing their research in the field of computers and its related technologies. Internet is one such technology that plays a major role in simplifying the information sharing and retrieval. World Wide Web (WWW) is one such service provided by the Internet. It acts as a medium for sharing of information. As a result, millions of applications run on the Internet and cause increased network traffic and put a great demand on the available network infrastructure.

INTRODUCTION

The rapid growth of the World Wide Web (WWW) and web development are the result for many innovative advances in Web technologies. WWW works with arrays of technologies for better communication with the Internet user, but the inconveniences to users persists. A possible solution for this problem is adding a new resource and distributes the network traffic across one or more resources. Web caching is method that is commonly used, to reduce the network traffic by storing webpages to a location nearer the client site (Pallis et al., 2008). A proxy server is responsible for web caching which acts as a mediator between the Web server and the web client and thus reduces latency in retrieving the pages. This proxy-based web caching system can be improved further to control the performance of the web. This chapter thus focuses on a method for improving the proxy-based web caching system. It uses Web Usage Mining (WUM) to optimize the performance of the proxy-based web caching system.

DOI: 10.4018/978-1-5225-2013-9.ch008

BACKGROUND

As the Internet continues to nurture in size and popularity, web traffic and network problems are the major issues in the Internet world. Sustained increase in demand for objects on the Internet causes ruthless overloads on many websites and network links. The Internet users have no patience to wait even for few seconds to download a desired webpage. Web traffic reduction techniques are necessary for accessing the websites efficiently with the existing network facility. There are many factors that affect the performances of web: variations in network connectivity distance between nodes and congestion in networks or servers. This is due to unpredicted market or service demands. Hence, web caching with web pre-fetching techniques reduce the web latency that we normally face on the Internet.

Also, WWW is an evolving system and consists of interlinked objects like audio, images, videos and so on. Here, web caching and pre-fetching is found as an important strategy to enhance performance of web-based system. Recently WWW is most widely used by many users to distribute information across the world. Therefore, it leads to increased network traffic over the Internet and web server. As a result, web becomes one of the primary areas to hold up network performance.

Transferring of web objects over the Internet increases the network traffic; thus, reducing bandwidth for competing requests and increasing latencies for web users while accessing the webpages. In order to reduce such access delay, it is desirable to store popular web objects closer to the user so that they can access them. Hence, proxy-based pre-fetching technique has been used. Thus, web caching and web pre-fetching has become an important research topic to reduce the noticeable response latency incurred by the end users (Sathiyamoorthi & Murali Bhaskaran 2010a).

Moreover, research in web caching is considered very important due to the issues and challenges exist and arise in the following dimensions (Wessels & Duane 2001):

- Bandwidth cost
- Non-uniform bandwidth
- Non-uniform latencies across network
- Increase in Network distances
- High bandwidth demands

Therefore, web caching and web pre-fetching are methods needed for the increase of web performance (Sathiyamoorthi & Murali Bhaskaran 2013).

Further improvement in the web application often is achieved through data mining techniques (Bamshad 2007). These techniques are generally known as web mining. The following sections provide an overview of some of ascertained techniques.

DATA MINING

Data Mining(DM) also known as Knowledge Discovery in Databases (KDD), is the process of extracting nontrivial, implicit, previously unknown and potentially useful information from the raw data present in the large database. Data mining techniques can be applied upon various data sources to improve the value of existing information system. When implemented on high performance client and server system, data mining tools analyze large databases required to deliver highly reliable results. It is also described that the data mining techniques can be coupled with relational database engines (Jiawei et al, 2006).

Data mining differs from the conventional database retrieval in the fact, that it extracts hidden information or knowledge that is not explicitly available in database, whereas database retrieval extracts the data that is explicitly available in the databases. Based on the fact that, a certain degree of intelligence is incorporated in the system, data mining could further be viewed as a branch of artificial intelligence and thus, data mining could be treated as an intelligent database manipulation system. Dunham et al (2006) have explained that data mining is an interdisciplinary field that incorporates concepts from several disciplines such as statistics, neural networks and machine learning in the process of knowledge discovery.

Basic Steps in Data Mining

It is clear that data mining can be viewed as a crucial step in knowledge discovery process. It is composed of various phases such as:

- Pre-processing
- Data Mining
- Pattern Extraction
- Pattern Evaluation
- Knowledge Presentation

The data preprocessing phase devises the data to be in a format suitable for further data mining operations. Data cleaning removes noise, inconsistent data, and irrelevant data that are present in the data sources. Since the input database could be composed of data that arrives from multiple sources, data integration is employed to integrate data from those sources. Data mining phase identifies the specific data mining tasks that employs intelligent methods and extracts knowledge. The resulting knowledge or patterns are evaluated for usability in the pattern evaluation phase. The last step of KDD process is the presentation of discovered knowledge in a user friendly and user understandable format referred to as the knowledge presentation phase (Jiawei et al., 2006). The basic steps involved in KDD process is shown in below Figure 1.

Knowledge Types That Can Be Mined

The authors Jiawei et al. (2006) and Dunham et al. (2006) have suggested that the extraction of hidden predictive information from large database is a powerful new technology. Data mining helps research industry and business organization with the focus on most important information in their database. Data mining tools predict future trends and behaviors that allows user to make proactive, knowledge-driven decisions.

Data mining system could be categorized based on the following information (Jiawei et al., 2006):

- **Kinds of Databases to be Mined**
  - This includes relational, transactional, object-oriented, object-relational, active, spatial, time-series, text, multi-media, heterogeneous, legacy, WWW and so on.
- **Kinds of Knowledge to be Discovered**

Figure 1. Steps in KDD process

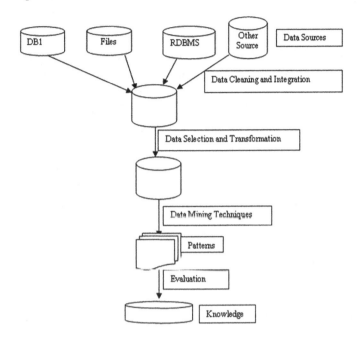

- ○ This includes characterization, discrimination, association, classification, clustering, and trend, deviation and outlier analysis and so on.
- **Kinds of Techniques Utilized**
  - ○ This includes database oriented, data warehouse, machine learning, statistics, visualization, neural network and so on.
- **Kinds of Applications Adapted**
  - ○ This includes retail, telecommunication, banking, fraud analysis, stock market analysis; web mining, web log analysis and so on.

In general, data mining tasks can be classified into descriptive and predictive (Jiawei et al 2006). Descriptive data mining tasks are those that provide description or characterization of objects present in the input database. Predictive data mining tasks are those that provide inference on input data to arrive at hidden knowledge and to make interesting predictions. Some of the data mining tasks and its categorization are given below.

- Classification [Predictive]
- Clustering [Descriptive]
- Association Rule Mining [Descriptive]
- Sequential Pattern Discovery [Descriptive]
- Regression [Predictive]
- Deviation Detection [Predictive]

Data Mining Techniques

Data mining is an interdisciplinary field that uses algorithms and techniques from various fields such as statistics, machine learning, artificial intelligence, neural networks and database technology. The most commonly used methods that assist in data mining tasks are (Jiawei et al., 2006) as below:

- **Artificial Neural Networks (ANN):** A non-linear predictive model comprises of different layers namely input, hidden and output layers that learn through training and resemble biological neural network in a structure.
- **Decision Tree:** A tree structure comprises of nodes and branches and represents a set of decisions. A node in decision tree represents conditions and branches of outcome. These decisions generate rules for the classifications of a dataset. Specific decision tree method includes classification and regression trees.
- **Genetic Algorithm (GA):** This Evolutionary optimization technique uses operators such as genetic combination, mutation, and natural selection in a design-based concept of evolution. This can be applied to optimization problem that either maximize or minimize the given objective function.
- **Nearest Neighbor Method:** A technique that classifies each record in a dataset based on a combination of the classes of 'k' records that are most similar to its historical dataset. Sometimes called as the K-Nearest Neighbor (KNN) technique.
- **Rule Induction:** This is the extraction of useful if-then rules from the dataset.

Data mining techniques such as classification, prediction, association rule mining, trend analysis, etc. are present so as to choose the suitable technique depending upon the nature of data mining application. The following sections provide an overview of various data mining techniques. Also, it discusses web caching and web pre-fetching to improve the performance of a web based system.

Association Rule Mining

As defined by (Jiawei et al 2006), an association rule identifies the collection of data attributes that are statistically related to one another. The association rule mining problem can be defined as follows: Given a database of related transactions, a minimal support and confidence value, find all association rules whose confidence and support are above the given threshold. In general, it produces a dependency rule that predicts an object based on the occurrences of other objects.

An association rule is of the form X->Y where X is called antecedent and Y is called consequent. There are two measures that assist in identification of frequent items and generate rules from it. One such measure is confidence which is the conditional probability of Y given X, Pr(Y|X), and the other is support which is the prior probability of X and Y, Pr(X and Y) (Jiawei et al., 2006). It can be classified into either single dimensional association rule or multidimensional association rule based on number of predicates it contains (Jiawei et al., 2006). It can be extended to better fit in the application domains like genetic analysis and electronic commerce and so on. Aprior algorithm, FP growth algorithm and vertical data format are some of the standard algorithm used to identify the frequent items present in the large data set (Jiawei et al., 2006).

Classification

It is the task of building a model that describe and distinguish data class of an object. This is used to predict class label for an object where class label information is not available (Jiawei et al., 2006). It is an example of learning from samples. The first phase called model construction is also referred to as training phase, where a model is built based on the features present in the training data. This model is then used to predict class labels for the testing data, where class label information is not available. A test set is used to determine the accuracy of the model. Usually, the given data set is divided into training and test sets, with training set used to construct the model and test set used to validate it.

Decision trees are commonly used to represent classification models. A decision tree is similar to a flowchart like structure where every node represents a test on an attribute value and branches denote a test outcome and tree leaves represent actual classes. Other standard representation techniques include K-nearest neighbor, Bayesians classification algorithm, if-then rules and neural networks (Jiawei et al., 2006). It is also known as supervised learning process. Effectiveness of prediction depends on training dataset used to train the model.

Prediction

Data Mining is an analytic process designed to explore data for consistent patterns or systematic relationships among variables and then to validate the findings by applying the detected patterns to new subsets of data. (Jiawei et al., 2006) uncover that the predictive data mining is the most common type of data mining and it has the most direct business applications. The process of predictive data mining task consists of three stages:

- Data Exploration
- Model Building
- Deployment

Data exploration usually starts with data preparation which may involve data cleaning, data transformations, selecting subsets of records and feature selection. Feature selection is one of the important operations in the exploration process. It is defined as reducing the numbers of variables to a manageable range if the datasets are with large number of variables performing some preliminary feature selection operations. Then, a simple choice of straightforward predictors for a regression model is used to elaborate exploratory analyses. The most widely used graphical and statistical method is exploratory data analysis. Model building and validation steps involve considering various models and choosing the best one based on their predictive performance. Deployment is the final step which involves selecting the best model in the previous step and applying it to a new data in order to generate predictions or estimates of the expected outcome.

Clustering

Dunham et al. (2006) highlight in their work that clustering is a process of dividing the given objects into groups of similar objects based on some similarity. It is also known as unsupervised learning process. In general it is described as follows: Given a set of data objects, each having a set of attributes and a similarity measure among them, find clusters such that objects within the clusters are highly similar to one another and dissimilar to objects of other clusters. Different similarity measure can be employed based on the type of attributes involved in distance calculation. For example, if attributes are continuous in nature then the distance calculated is a Euclidean distance. The ultimate goal of clustering is to segregate objects into k-subsets called clusters. Usually, subsets do not intersect and their union is equal to a full data set. Representing data by fewer clusters necessarily loses at least some fine details, but achieves simplification or reduction. Clustering represents many data objects into fewer clusters. K-Means and K-Medoids are some of the standard algorithms used in clustering (Jiawei et al 2006).

WEB MINING

In today's Internet scenario, WWW plays a significant role in retrieving and sharing information. Hence, WWW becomes a huge repository of data. As a result, it is difficult for data analyst or end users to analyze the entire data and to discover some useful information. To overcome these troubles, data mining can be applied for knowledge discovery in WWW. To discover knowledge from web, web mining is used. Web mining is broadly categorized into three major areas such as web Content Mining (WCM); Web Structure Mining (WSM) and Web Log Mining (WLM) or Web Usage Mining(WUM) (Srivastava et al., 2000; Zaiane, 2000).

Web content mining is the part of web mining which focuses on the raw information available in webpages (Kosala & Blockeel, 2000). Data source mainly consists of textual data present in the webpages. Mining is based on content categorization and content ranking of web pages. Web structure mining is a web mining task which deals with the structure of the Websites. The data source consists of structural information present in webpages that are hyperlinks. The mining includes link-based categorization of webpages, ranking of webpages through a combination of content and structure (Brin & Pange, 1998), and reverse engineering of website models. Web usage mining (WUM) is another web mining task which describes knowledge discovery from web server log files. The source data mainly consist of the raw text file that is stored in web server when a user accesses the webpage. It might be represented either in Common Log Format (CLF) or in Extended Common Log Format (ECLF). It includes Web personalization, adaptive websites, and user modeling. This chapter focuses on WUM to optimize the existing proxy based web caching system. The following section gives an overview of WUM and its application in Web based information retrieval and management system.

Web Usage Mining

It is noted that research in web usage mining started in late 1990's according to Srivastava et al. (2000), Mobasher et al. (2002), Cyrus et al. (1997) and Feng et al. (2009). Web usage mining is also known as web log mining wherein it relies on the information present in the web log file produced by the web servers. Web log files are raw text file which needs certain preprocessing methods before applying the data mining techniques (Sathiyamoorthi & Bhaskaran, 2011a).

The basic steps involved in WUM are:

1. Data Collection

2. Data Preprocessing
3. Pattern Extraction
4. Pattern Analysis and Visualization
5. Pattern Applications

Data Sources for Web Usage Mining

Data sources used for WUM can be collected from three different locations (Srivastva et al., 2000) as is shown in Figure 2.

- **Server-Level:** It stores data about the requests that are activated by different clients. It keeps track of multiple users' interest on a single website. The main drawback is that log files must be secured since it contains some sensitive information about the users. Further, it does not contain information about cached pages.
- **Client-Level**: The browser itself will send some information to a repository regarding the user's access. This is achieved by using an adhoc browsing application or through client-side applications that can run on standard web browsers. It requires the design team to develop special software and deploy it along with the end users' browsers.
- **Proxy-Level**: It collects the information about user's browsing behavior and recorded at proxy server log. It keeps track of multiple users' interest on several websites. It is used only by the users whose requests are passed through the proxy (Sathiyamoorthi & Murali Bhaskaran, 2011b).

The following information can be gathered from the Web log file:

- General summary information regarding user and page access
- Statistical information about web pages hit
- From where user is accessing the web pages
- Is Browser used by the users to access the webpages
- Success or failure code for each page access
- Report based on page size, type and so on
- How often user's visit each webpage
- When a web page has been accessed
- Who is interested in which pages
- What is the access frequency of each webpage
- Which pages are accessed frequently and recently

Web usage mining has been considered with great importance and hence many researchers have started focusing on this for better web utilization. The significance of this research work can be better realized through the following research scope and findings.

Web usage mining is well explained by Facca and Lanzi (2005) and Srivastava et al. (2000). Both of them have described it in their research and business communities' perspective.

Web personalization is a technique which delivers personalized web content depending on the user profile or user needs. It includes, a recommender system explained (Jaczynski & Trousse, 1998; Mobasher et al., 2000) and an adaptive website (Velasquez et al., 2004; De et al., 2004).

Figure 2. Data sources for web usage mining

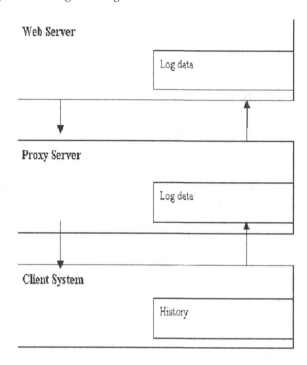

A recommender system suggests possible links to the user based on the access history. The adaptive website is the one which adapts itself for each user visiting the website in order to deliver the personalized content. Personalization is achieved by keeping track of the previously accessed webpages for E-Commerce applications (Pirolli et al., 1996).

The appearance of a website, in terms of both content and structure, is the most important factor to be considered in many applications like product catalog for E-Commerce. Web usage mining provides detailed information regarding user behavior and it can help website designers to redesign their website based on it. In adaptive website (Anderson, 2002; Perkowitz & Etzioni, 1998), the structure of a website changes dynamically based on the user access patterns discovered from server logs. Site improvement may be achieved either by modifying the logical structure or the physical structure of the website depending on the access patterns of the website users.

Response time and performance are the two important factors that play major role in determining user satisfaction (Sathiyamoorthi & Bhaskaran, 2012). This is mainly helpful for services like web-based applications, databases and networks, etc. Similar qualities have been expected from the users of web services. To enhance the performance, web log mining could provide the key to understand web traffic behavior by developing policies for web caching and network transmission (Anderson et al., 2002).

Web caching represents another possibility for improving the quality of a website as the pages are delivered to the users in a faster way (Podlipnig & Boszormenyi, 2003). Users are less likely to spend time on a slow website. By using the results of a WUM system, a web caching system turns capable to predict the user's next request by loading it into a cache. Thus, the speed of page retrieval from a website is improved as the user will not wait for the page to be loaded from the server. Information about how customers use a website is central for the marketers of retailing business. Alex and Mulvenna (1998) and Srivastava et al. (2000) have discussed a knowledge discovery process to discover marketing intelligence from web data.

The following section gives some of the research works and applications of web log mining in web caching and web pre-fetching.

There are many factors that affect the performance of a web-based system which includes diversity of network connectivity, real world distances, and congestion in networks or servers due to unpredicted demand. As a result, many research works have focused on the problem of improving web response times. Some of the researchers want to improve the performance either by increasing the bandwidth or improvement through alternate communication technologies. The Internet has evolved from a system that deliver a simple and static HTML page to one that provides higher end services like e-learning, video conferencing, e-commerce, etc. (Pallis et al., 2008). The probable solutions to reduce network traffic are given below (Sathiyamoorthi, 2016):

- Web caching
- Web pre-fetching

Web caching is a technique used to reduce the user perceived latency when user is accessing the webpages. Web pre-fetching is another scheme where webpages are pre-fetched into the intermediate server (proxy server) cache before the user accesses it. When combined, these techniques would complement each other.

Thus, a clustering-based pre-fetching technique has been introduced which will pre-fetch web objects for group of users having similar access behavior instead of single user interest.

WEB CACHING

As discussed, web caching is a technique which is used for caching as many webpages in the cache to improve the network performance. The main component is its page replacement policy. When a new document arrives, the replacement policy has to make critical decision in replacing an existing webpage from the cache. In this research work, WUM is used to modify the existing web cache page replacement policy for better performance.

Most of the traditional algorithms like Least Frequently Used (LFU), Least Recently Used (LRU) and First in First out (FIFO) employ simple statistical techniques in decision making process resulting in poor performance. From that it is inferred that Greedy-Dual-Size (GDS) algorithm outperforms when cache size is small. In (Martin et al., 1997) the authors discussed that SIZE outperforms than LFU, LRU and several other LRU variations in terms of different performance measures. In their experiments, they fail to consider the object frequency in decision making process. The authors (Pei and Irani, 1997) discussed that caching algorithms should address the network cost. As a result, they have introduced GDS and Greedy-Dual-Size-Frequency (GDSF) policy for web caching.

Most of the cache algorithms discussed here performs better if we go for a single object pre-fetching technique. In the case of clustering-based pre-fetching technique, as multiple objects are pre-fetched, there is a need for an efficient algorithm which can provide higher hit rate; reduce the number of objects to be pre-fetched and thereby save the bandwidth. On the basis of location, Web caching system is classified into:

Figure 3. Web caching location

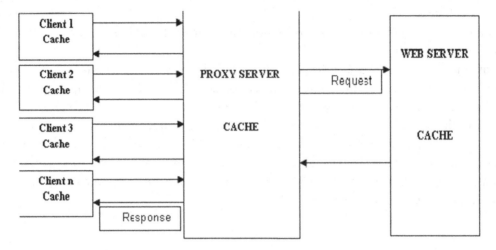

1. Browser cache
2. Proxy cache
3. Server cache as in Figure 3

WEB PRE-FETCHING

As discusses, web pre-fetching or pre-loading is a technique which pre-fetches webpages into the cache before the actual request for that page arrives. There are two approaches namely short-term pre-fetching and long-term pre-fetching is used.

- **Short-Term Pre-Fetching:** In short-term pre-fetching, webpages are pre-fetched into the cache by analyzing the recent access history of the web cache (Chen et al., 2002).
- **Long-Term Pre-Fetching:** In this technique, the probability of accessing webpages are identified and pre-fetched by analyzing the global access pattern (Lee et al., 2009).

The authors Loon and Bhargavan (1997) have presented a pre-fetching technique based on user profiles which are represented through a weighted directed graph where the nodes represent Uniform Resource Locators (URL) and the edges represent the access paths. The weight of a node represents the access frequency of URLs and the weight of an edge represents the access frequency of one URL after another. Ibrahim and Xu (2000) have presented a technique that uses an artificial neural network for predicting the next user request. Fan et al. (1999) investigated an approach to reduce web latency, by pre-fetching between caching proxies and browsers. This approach has used the Prediction by Partial Match (PPM) algorithm for pre-fetching. The authors Markatos et al. (1998) have presented a Top-10 approach for pre-fetching. In their approach, the ten most popular webpages are pre-fetched and cached. Also, Padmanabhan and Mogul (1996) have presented a pre-fetching scheme in which the server computes the likelihood that a particular webpage will be accessed and conveys the information to the client.

INTEGRATION OF WEB CACHING AND WEB PRE-FETCHING

Web caching and web pre-fetching schemes have been presented in (Podlipnig & Boszormenyi, 2003; Teng et al., 2005; Balamash & Krunz, 2004). It is stated that integration of these two techniques would perform better. An additional improvement to traditional cache replacement policies used in the proxy server's cache is explained in Pallis et al. (2008) which are based on the clustering-based pre-fetching scheme using dependency graph. In this work, the authors have used traditional algorithm to measure the performance of pre-fetching technique.

Web caching and pre-fetching have often been studied as separate tools for reducing the latency observed by the users in accessing the web. Less work has been done on integration of caching and pre-fetching techniques. Kroeger et al. (1997) have studied the combined effect of caching and pre-fetching on end user latency. Lan et al. (2000) have proposed a rule-assisted pre-fetching in web server caching. Yang et al. (2004) have proposed a method for mining web logs to obtain a prediction model and then using the model to extend the well known GDSF caching policy.

PROBLEM FORMULATION AND SCOPE OF RESEARCH

The speed of data transfer plays a vital role in the Internet technology. The slow retrieval of webpages may lessen the user's interest in accessing them. The bandwidth and speed has a great impact in the performance of accessing a webpage. In order to have efficient information distribution, web caching and web pre-fetching are used. Web caching is a technique used for storing as many webpages in a location nearer to the client, so that it can be accessed faster. Web pre-fetching is used to preload webpages into the cache before the actual request arrives. Thus, users can access the webpages with much higher speed. When these techniques are combined, it would complement each other. Web caching technique makes use of temporal locality (recently accessed items may be accessed in the near future), whereas web pre-fetching technique makes use of the spatial locality (items which are closer to each other may be accessed in the near future) of Web objects (Pallis et al., 2008).

In this background, a proxy-based web caching plays a major role in reducing latency in accessing webpages. The familiar web caching technique is the most commonly used method for improving performance of web-based system whereas web pre-fetching is a topic narrow to research. Currently deployed systems utilize a very simple pre-fetching strategy where it pre-fetches all hyperlinked objects present in the current page (Wessels & Duane, 2001). Therefore, there is a need to improve web caching systems as they can control the performance of the web today.

The problem with pre-fetching is to identify the webpages that are to be pre-fetched and then to be cached. This is forced by the fact that there are wide spectrums of users, and each of them has got their own preferences. Hence, research work can address the above problem using some novel algorithm for pre-fetching, by clustering the users based on their access patterns. Due to the grouping of users, the task of going into the individual's preferences is avoided. Deficiency in generation of cluster prototype and the similarity measure used are the challenges with traditional clustering technique. Moreover, most of the existing pre-fetching approach will predict only one object at a time which will increase network traffics when users increase. To overcome this, a research work can focus on proposing a novel clustering-based pre-fetching technique.

It is likely to group all the requests made from the IP addresses and assign the most popular webpages in a cluster for each IP address. Chen et al. (2003) states that the popularity of each Web objects vary significantly. It is difficult to choose the popular objects early and also to predict the popularity threshold. Therefore, Pallis et al. (2008) argues that a graph-based approach to cluster the webpages would be more effective. It is based on association rule mining and it is controlled by the threshold value. Jyoti et al. (2008) have adopted an approach that predicts the next page to be accessed based on higher-order Markov model.

Rangarajan et al. (2004) has presented an approach to group users based on their web access patterns using ART1 by grouping users and then pre-fetching. They have compared the quality of clustering produced by ART1 with K-Means clustering algorithm in terms of inter-cluster and intra-cluster distances. The result shows that ART1 performs better by providing high hit rate and better average inter- and intra-cluster distance than the clusters formed by K-Means algorithm. Hence they concluded that ART1 provides high quality of clusters.

Ramya and Shreedhara (2012) have presented a complete preprocessing methodology and pre-fetching system using ART1 and compared the quality of clustering of ART1 based clustering technique with that of traditional K-Means and Self Organization Map clustering algorithms. The results show that the average inter-cluster distance of ART1 is high when compared to K-Means and SOM when there are fewer clusters. As the number of clusters increase, average inter-cluster distance of ART1 is low compared to K-Means and SOM which indicates the high quality of clusters formed using ART1.

Most of the research work discussed for pre-fetching concentrates on pre-fetching individual users' requests according to their past access patterns. Although these methods are efficient for pre-fetching, they may considerably overload the network with unnecessary traffic when pre-fetching for a large number of users. To reduce such an effect of pre-fetching, it presents a pre-fetching scheme that uses MART1 clustering technique to

pre-fetch requests for a large community of users instead of pre-fetching individual users' requests. Moreover, the conventional replacement policies provide reduced network performance in terms of bandwidth utilization when multiple objects are

pre-fetched. In addition, the main problem associated with Web pre-fetching is that users may not request some of these pre-fetched objects. Therefore, web pre-fetching increases the network traffic as well as the web server load; thereby it offers reduced bandwidth utilization (Huang & Hsu, 2008). Thus, efficient integration of web pre-fetching and caching is the need of the hour to overcome the above said limitations (Pallis et al., 2008; Feng et al., 2009).

Based on the above discussion, the research objectives can be framed as follows. The main objectives of a research work are for improving the performance of proxy-based web caching system by integrating the web pre-fetching system into web caching system. This integrated system is arrived at after attaining the following objectives, namely:

1.   To prepare the data using data preprocessing techniques such as data cleaning so as to apply data mining tasks on the data.
2.   To experiment the optimized web caching with clustering-based web pre-fetching technique using sample datasets.

3. To identify and experiment web caching replacement algorithms.
4. To integrate the two-proposed works:
   a. clustering-based web pre-fetching
   b. web caching
5. To test the optimized web page retrieval speed that has reduced the latency in accessing a Web page.

FUTURE SCOPE AND PROBLEM FORMULATION

The vast amount of literature studied and reported so far in this paper has yielded the proposal of new web caching and pre-fetching approach to improve the scalability of the web-based system. The literature also points out the importance of web caching and pre-fetching using web mining techniques as important findings which stood as the base for the formulation of research problem, which are tabulated and presented in Table 1.

Table 1. Literature support for formulation of research problem

Base papers	Authors	Issue and Inference
1. Web user clustering and its application to pre-fetching using ART neural networks	Rangarajan et al (2004)	It presents a pre-fetching approach based on ART1 neural network. It does not address the issues while integrating web caching and web pre-fetching
2. Integrating Web caching and Web pre-fetching in Client-Side Proxies	Teng et al (2005)	Have proposed pre-fetching approach based on association rule. They have proposed an innovative cache replacement policy called (Integration of Web Caching and Pre-fetching (IWCP). They have categorized web objects into implied and non-implied objects.
3. A clustering-based pre-fetching scheme on a Web cache environment	Pallis et al (2008)	They have proposed a graph-based pre-fetching technique and have used DG for pre-fetching. It is based on association rule and it is controlled by support and confidence. Moreover they have used traditional policies in Web cache environment and didn't address issues while integrating these two.
4. Intelligent Client-side Web Caching Scheme Based on Least Recently Used Algorithm and Neuro-Fuzzy System	Ali & Shamsuddin (2009)	It uses the neuro-fuzzy system to classify a Web object into cacheable or un-cacheable objects. It has LRU algorithm in cache to predict Web objects that may be re-accessed later. Training process requires long time and extra computational cost. It ignored the factors such as cost and size of the objects in the cache replacement policy
5. A survey of Web cache replacement strategies	Podlipnig & Böszörmenyi (2003)	The authors have reviewed and presented an overview of various page replacement policies. It is observed that GDSF perform better in Web cache environment. They also have presented merits and demerits of various page replacement policies.
6. A Keyword-Based Semantic Pre-fetching Approach in Internet News Services	Ibrahim & Xu (2004)	It predicts users' future access based on semantic preferences of past retrieved Web documents. It is implemented on Internet news services. The semantic preferences are identified by analyzing keywords present in the URL of previously accessed Web. It employs a neural network model over the keyword set to predict user future requests.
7. A Survey of Web Caching and Pre-fetching	Waleed et al (2011)	The authors have discussed and reviewed various web caching and Web pre-fetching techniques. It is observed that most of the pre-fetching techniques discussed here were focusing on single user which will ultimately reduce server performance if number of users increase. Moreover, in recent year's data mining plays a major role in web pre-fetching areas and most of the data mining-based approach uses association rule mining.

Figure 4. Architecture of the proposed system

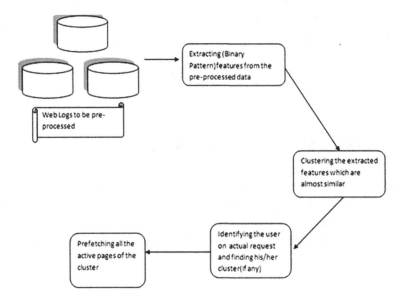

From this, it is also observed that both the techniques would improve the performance by reducing server load and latency in accessing webpages. However, if the web caching and pre-fetching approaches are integrated inefficiently then this might causes huge network traffic; increase in web server load in addition to the inefficient use of cache space (Waleed et al., 2011). Hence, the pre-fetching approach should be designed carefully in order to overcome the above said limitations. Therefore, the proposed system uses web usage mining to optimize the existing web cache performance which is shown in Figure 4.

Traditional cache replacement policies are not suitable for clustering-based pre-fetching technique since it increases the number of objects pre-fetched and hence poor bandwidth utilization. Hence, the web caching policy should be designed carefully in order to overcome the above said limitations. A new cache replacement policy is designed in such a way that it should provide better performance in terms of hit rate and it also reduces the number of objects pre-fetched and thereby saving the bandwidth.

CONCLUSION

From the entire explanations and discussions, it is understood that web caching and web pre-fetching are two important techniques used for improving the performance of a web based information retrieval system. However, the poor integration of these two techniques can lead to increased latency and poor bandwidth utilization. Hence, care must be taken while integrating these two techniques. This chapter also reviews and summarizes the work related to web caching and pre-fetching techniques. It is also observed that both the techniques would improve the performance by reducing server load and latency in accessing webpages since web caching exploits temporal locality whereas web pre-fetching exploits spatial locality of web objects. However, if the web caching and pre-fetching approaches are integrated inefficiently then this might cause huge network traffic; increase in web server load in addition to the inefficient use of cache space (Waleed et al., 2011). Hence, the pre-fetching approach should be designed carefully in order to overcome the above said limitations. Therefore, the importance of web usage mining to optimize the existing web cache performance has been realized.

REFERENCES

Alex, B., & Mulvenna, M. D. (1998). Discovering Internet Marketing Intelligence through Online Analytical Web Usage Mining. *SIGMOD Record*, *27*(4), 54–61. doi:10.1145/306101.306124

Anderson, C.R. (2002). A Machine Learning Approach to Web Personalization [Ph.D. Thesis]. University of Washington.

Balamash, A., & Krunz, M. (2004). An Overview of Web Caching Replacement Algorithms. *IEEE Communications Surveys and Tutorials*, *6*(2), 44–56. doi:10.1109/COMST.2004.5342239

Bamshad, M. (2007). *Data Mining for Web Personalization*. Heidelberg: Springer.

Brin, S., & Pange, L. (1998). The Anatomy of a Large-scale Hyper Textual Web Search Engine. *Computer Networks and ISDN Systems*, *30*(1-7), 107–117. doi:10.1016/S0169-7552(98)00110-X

Chen, X., & Zhang, X. (2002). Popularity-based PPM: An effective Web pre-fetching technique for high accuracy and low storage.*Proceedings of the International Conference on Parallel Processing* (pp. 296-304). doi:10.1109/ICPP.2002.1040885

Cyrus, S., Zarkessh, A. M., Jafar, A., & Vishal, S. (1997). Knowledge discovery from Users Web Page Navigation. *Proceedings of theWorkshop on Research Issues in Data Engineering*, Birmingham, England.

De, P. B., Aroyo, L., & Chepegin, V. (2004). The Next Big Thing: Adaptive Web Based Systems. *Journal of Digital Information*, *5*(1). http://jodi.ecs.soton.ac.uk/Articles/v05/ i01/DeBra/

Dunham, M. H. (2006). *Data Mining Introductory and Advanced Topics* (1st ed.). Pearson Education.

Facca, F. M., & Lanzi, P. L. (2005). Mining Interesting Knowledge from Web logs: A Survey. *Data & Knowledge Engineering*, *53*(3), 225–241. doi:10.1016/j.datak.2004.08.001

Feng, W., Man, S., & Hu, G. (2009). *Markov Tree Prediction on Web Cache Pre-fetching. Software Engineering, Artificial Intelligence, SCI* (Vol. 209, pp. 105–120). Berlin, Heidelberg: Springer.

Ibrahim, T. I., & Xu, C. Z. (2000). Neural Nets based Predictive Pre-fetching to Tolerate WWW Latency. *Proceedings of the 20th International Conference on Distributed Computing Systems,* Taipei, Taiwan.

Jaczynski, M., & Trousse, B. (1998). WWW Assisted Browsing by Reusing Past Navigations of a Group of Users. *Proceedings of the Advances in Case-Based Reasoning, Fourth European Workshop*, Dublin, Ireland, Springer LNCS (Vol. 1488, pp. 160-171).

Jiawei, H., Micheline, K., & Jian, P. (2006). *Data Mining Concepts and Techniques*. Pearson Education.

Kosala, R. & Blockeel, H. (2000). Web Mining Research: A Survey. *SIGKDD explorations, 2*(1), 1-15.

Koskela, T.J., Heikkonen, J., & Kaski, K. (2003). Web cache optimization with nonlinear model using object feature. *Computer Networks journal, 43*(6), 805-817.

Kroeger, T. M., Long, D. D. E., & Mogul, J. C. (1997). Exploring the Bounds of Web Latency Reduction from Caching and Pre-fetching. *Proceedings of the USENDC Symposium on Internet Technology and Systems* (pp. 13-22).

Lan, B., Bressan, S., Ooi, B. C., & Tan, K. L. (2000). Rule-Assisted Pre-fetching in Web-Server Caching.*Proceedings of the 9th International Conference on Information and Knowledge Management,* Washington DC, USA (pp. 504-511).

Lee, H. K., An, B. S., & Kim, E. J. (2009). Adaptive Pre-fetching Scheme Using Web Log Mining in Cluster-Based Web Systems. *Proceedings of theIEEE International Conference on Web Services (ICWS)* (pp. 903-910).

Loon, T. S., & Bharghavan, V. (1997). Alleviating the Latency and Bandwidth Problems in WWW Browsing.*Proceedings of the USENIX Symposium on Internet Technologies and Systems (USITS).*

Markatos, E.P., & Chronaki, C. E. (1998). A Top-10 Approach to Pre-fetching on the Web.*Proceedings of INET Geneva*, Switzerland (pp. 276-290).

Mobasher, B., Dai, H., Luo, T., & Nakagawa, M. (2002). Discovery and Evaluation of Aggregate Usage Profiles for Web Personalization. *Data Mining and Knowledge Discovery, 6*(1), 61–82. doi:10.1023/A:1013232803866

Padmanabhan, V. N., & Mogul, J. C. (1996). Using Predictive Pre-fetching to Improve World Wide Web Latency. *ACM Computer Communication Review, 26*(3), 23–36. doi:10.1145/235160.235164

Pallis, G., Vakali, A., & Pokorny, J. (2008). A Clustering-Based Pre-Fetching Scheme on A Web Cache Environment. ACM Journal Computers and Electrical Engineering, 34(4).

Pei, C., & Irani, S. (1997). Cost-Aware WWW Proxy Caching Algorithms.*Proceedings of the USENIX Symposium on Internet Technologies and Systems* (pp. 193-206).

Pirolli, P., Pitkow, J., & Ramna, R. (1996). Extracting Usable Structure from the Web. Proceedings of CHI '96, Vancouver (pp. 118-125).

Podlipnig, S., & Boszormenyi, L. (2003). A Survey of Web Cache Replacement Strategies. *ACM Computing Surveys, 35*(4), 374–398. doi:10.1145/954339.954341

Sathiyamoorthi, V. (2016). A Novel Cache Replacement Policy for Web Proxy Caching System Using Web Usage Mining. *International Journal of Information Technology and Web Engineering, 11*(2), 1–12. doi:10.4018/IJITWE.2016040101

Sathiyamoorthi, V., & Murali Bhaskaran, V. (2010a). Data Preparation Techniques for Mining World Wide Web through Web Usage Mining-An Approach. *International Journal of Recent Trends in Engineering, 2*(4), 1–4.

Sathiyamoorthi, V., & Murali Bhaskaran, V. (2010b). Data mining for intelligent enterprise resource planning system. *International Journal of Recent Trends in Engineering*, *2*(3), 1–4.

Sathiyamoorthi, V., & Murali Bhaskaran, V. (2011a). Improving the Performance of Web Page Retrieval through Pre-Fetching and Caching. *European Journal of Scientific Research*, *66*(2), 207–217.

Sathiyamoorthi, V., & Murali Bhaskaran, V. (2011b). Data Pre-Processing Techniques for Pre-Fetching and Caching of Web Data through Proxy Server. *International journal of Computer Science and Network security*, *11*(11), 92-98.

Sathiyamoorthi, V., & Murali Bhaskaran, V. (2012). Optimizing the Web Cache performance by Clustering Based Pre-Fetching Technique Using Modified ART1. *International Journal of Computers and Applications*, *44*(1), 51–60.

Sathiyamoorthi, V., & Murali Bhaskaran, V. (2013). Novel Approaches for Integrating MART1 Clustering Based Pre-Fetching Technique with Web Caching. *International Journal of Information Technology and Web Engineering*, *8*(2), 18–32. doi:10.4018/Jitwe.2013040102

Srivastava, J., Cooley, R., Deshpande, M., & Tan, P. N. (2000). Web Usage Mining: Discovery and Applications of Usage Patterns from Web Data. *SIGKDD Explorations*, *1*(2), 12–23. doi:10.1145/846183.846188

Teng, W., Chang, C., & Chen, M. (2005). Integrating Web Caching and Web Pre-fetching in Client-Side Proxies. *IEEE Transactions on Parallel and Distributed Systems*, *16*(5), 444–455. doi:10.1109/TPDS.2005.56

Velasquez, J., Bassi, A., Yasuda, H., & Aoki, T. (2004). Mining Web Data to Create Online Navigation Recommendations. *Proceedings of the Fourth IEEE International Conference on Data Mining* (ICDM), Brighton, United Kingdom (pp. 551-554).

Waleed, A., Siti M.S. & Abdul S.I. (2011). A Survey of Web Caching and Prefetching. *Int. J. Advance. Soft Comput. Appl.*, *3*(1).

Wessels, D. (2001). Web Caching. Sebastopol, CA: O'Reilly publication.

Yang, Q., Li, T., & Wang, K. (2004). Building Association-Rule Based Sequential Classifiers for Web-Document Prediction. *Journal of Data Mining and Knowledge Discovery*, *8*(3), 253–273. doi:10.1023/B:DAMI.0000023675.04946.f1

Zaiane, O. (2000). Web Mining: Concepts, Practices and Research. *Proc. SDBD, Conference Tutorial Notes*.

KEY TERMS AND DEFINITIONS

Bandwidth: Amount of data transferred per unit time or Capacity of the communication link that is used for transferring data between client and Server.

Clustering: It is the process of grouping objects based on similarity between them. It is also known as unsupervised learning. Each cluster contains objects that are similar to each other and highly dissimilar with objects present in the other cluster.

Data Mining: it is also known as knowledge discovery in database. It is the process of discovering novel, previously unknown and implicit information present in the database.

Internet: Interconnection of computers across the world is called as Internet. Each computer is identified using URL accessed through HTTP protocol.

Proxy Server: It acts as an inter-mediatory between client and server and contains caching mechanism for storing web objects for future access.

Web Caching: It provides temporal locality of a Web object i.e. most popular web objects are stored here for future access.

Web Client: Client is a machine that request some information from web server through HTTP Request protocol.

Web Pre-Fetching: It provides spatial locality of a Web object i.e. Pages that are closer to each other are considered for future reference.

Web Server: It is a machine that processes the user request and provides resources to the client machine through HTTP Response protocol.

Chapter 9
Big Data Optimization for Customer Discounts in Cloud Computing Environment

Raghvendra Kumar
LNCT College, India

Prasant Kumar Pattnaik
KIIT University, India

Priyanka Pandey
LNCT, India

ABSTRACT

Large companies have different methods of doing this, one of which is to run sales simulations. Such simulation systems often need to perform complex calculations over large amounts of data, which in turn requires efficient models and algorithms. This chapter intends to evaluate whether it is possible to optimize and extend an existing sales system called PCT, which is currently suffering from unacceptably high running times in its simulation process. This is done through analysis of the current implementation, followed by optimization of its models and development of efficient algorithms. The performances of these optimized and extended models are compared to the existing one in order to evaluate their improvement. The conclusion of this chapter is that the simulation process in PCT can indeed be optimized and extended. The optimized models serve as a proof of concept, which shows that results identical to the original system's can be calculated within < 1% of the original running time for the largest customers.

INTRODUCTION

Big data is a slightly abstract phrase which describes the relation between data size and data processing speed in a system. A comprehensible definition of the concept is data whose size forces us to look beyond the tried-and-true methods that are prevalent at that time. This means that a scenario where innovative optimization of both models and algorithms is required to handle large amounts of data might well be

DOI: 10.4018/978-1-5225-2013-9.ch009

classified as a big data problem. In PCT, the big data challenge arises from the huge amounts of data needed in order to run simulations for large customers. In some cases more than thousand historical order rows may have to be handled, with multiple possible conditions and discount rates applied to every single one of them. While the data set itself is not extremely large by today's standards, the complex operations and calculations which have to be performed on each one of them adds new dimensions to the simulation procedure. Discounts are for example inherited through a large tree structure containing tens of thousands of nodes and the results must be presented to the user within a reasonable amount of time. The reasonable time limit has been defined as ten seconds for the simulation procedure in PCT. This value is based on research showing that a system user who has to wait even further for results of complex calculations will lose focus something which could prove devastating during a negotiation with a customer. An ideal simulation procedure would always return the results within just a few seconds, since this would mean that simulations could take place during normal conversation without requiring any waiting at all.

DEFINING BIG DATA

Today, innovative era of technology, everywhere that are visible or not visible to us its only technology, everyone are using different-different technology for their daily uses, like if we are taking example of human being daily routine, when the person is wake up at early morning that the person uses different technology like mobile phone, laptop, notebook etc. And also uses the internet connection for checking any updates from their friends at one single time, for that they are transferring or uses huge amount of data in single seconds. Like that if we are taking an example of India there are internet users are increasing very rapidly, now everyone are using the smart phone, laptop and many other digital devices for connecting the different users at a single time, when the different users are connecting through internet at that time they are transferring the huge amount of data to the internet, that data size in the form of zeta bytes, peta bytes etc., this huge amount of data is known as Big data. That contains three main properties Volume, Variety and Velocity. Variety or Volume mainly focuses on the leads to the question of how to process big data analytics and velocity is mainly focuses on the possibilities rather than technologies, about performance and about business impact that we are using. As we already know that data processing for the large amount of unstructured data is very crucial, because consumers and citizens want the immediate response from the server or service providers. If they tweet their massage about what in their own mind and they want that massage served by the web care teams for their immediate response. As we know that today technology are growing very fast and rapidly. Everyone are using high speed electronic devices and they all wants the high processing and accessing speeds. Time is money and acceleration is synonymous with reasonable advantage. Real time analysis is not fast enough but for predicting what will happen in future is real ambition, if we are moving from the predictive to prescriptive analysis. Most of the data scientists are working on the prescriptive analysis for predicting the future analysis and some of the agencies are using the mobile phone data for statistical analysis. Insight from location data and people are moving around have proven to be an excellent alternative for charting the consumer behavior.

In big data we are analyzing the different data like location data and the people moving around have proven to be an excellent alternative for charting the consumer's behavior. There are many institute that have team of experts in the field of data analytics they are analyzed the problem and solve it what they have. This is an era of the big data time bomb there are many big data initiatives like consumers and citizens, who rule their own data. Big data time bomb scenario was discussed by the two international groups' cios and doc searls. The cios was submitted in the year of 2012 by the different international experts. And the doc searls, author of intention economy, the team of the intention economy take charges and hosted the meeting. The searls argues that individuals are themselves in the best position to analyze their personal data, which might be overthrowing the relationship with different organizations. Lastly the vendor relationship management (VRM) would replace the customer relationship management (CRM).

One of the most famous authors in the field of big data jaronlanier said that people should make money from their own personal data that they are using. He gives the solution for analyzing their personal data namely as big data analytics. But the big drawback of smart technology is that, they reduced the number of jobs of the people because use of the smart devices and technology. Privacy play an important role when are talking about the personal data, that are distributed or stored in the distributed environment, because no any person want to disclose their personal or secrete information to others. For preserving the privacy to our personal data we are following great privacy debate on a daily basis in the media as we are painfully aware to the fact that no secret information are safe since agencies and organizations have access to much more information that we would like.

How do we deal with privacy or what is left of it? When The Guardian started publishing Edward Snowden's revelations about the Big Data practices of secret services, it was fuel to an existing fire. The privacy issue always has been top of mind when personal data were involved. We now follow the great privacy debate on a daily basis in the media as we are painfully aware of the fact that no secrets are safe since agencies and organizations have access to much more information than we would like. Organizations and governments of course have been collecting enormous amounts of data that can be related to an individual, but this kind of Personally Identifiable Information (pii) is protected throughout the world by privacy laws. However, in the digital age, legislation alone is insufficient by far and thanks to Big Data Analytics non personal data also easily can lead to the right prospects. Few organizations seem to master the Privacy by Design maxim but the best advice to be trusted is: be transparent, comply and explain as much as you can.

The question remains how much the Big Data future is influenced by the Snowden revelations which have put data protection and privacy at the center of our attention. All major U.S. online services were persuaded to participate in the largest ever monitoring of data traffic: Big Data Analytics to the max. Friendly powers and foreign companies were tapped as smart phones and tablets were shamelessly searched. Encryption and other security systems were cracked or had loopholes to circumvent them.

In 2012, approximately forty years after the beginning of the information era, all eyes are now on its basis: digital data. This may not seem very exciting, but the influx of various data types, plus the speed with which the trend will continue, probably into infinity, is certainly striking. Data, data and more data: we are at the center of an expanding data universe, full of undiscovered connections. This is not abstract and general, but rather specific and concrete, as each new insight may be the entrance to a gold mine. This data explosion is so simple and fundamental that Joe Heller stein of Berkeley University speaks of 'a new industrial revolution': a revolution on the basis of digital data that form the engine of completely new business-operational and societal opportunities.

At the beginning of May 2012, at the Cloud Computing Conference arranged by Goldman Sachs, Shaun Connolly from Horton works presented data as "The New Competitive Advantage." Connolly articulated seven reasons for this statement, two of which were business-oriented, three were technological, and two were financial:

1. Business Reasons
   a. New innovative business models become possible
   b. New insights arise that give competitive advantages
2. Technological Reasons
   a. The generation and storage of data continue to grow exponentially
   b. We find data in various forms everywhere
   c. Traditional solutions do not meet new demands regarding complexity
3. Financial Reasons
   a. The costs of data systems continue to rise as a percentage of the it budget
   b. New standard hardware and open-source software offer cost benefits Connolly believes that, as a consequence of this combination, the traditional data world of business transactions is now beginning to merge with that of interactions and observations. Applying the formula Big Data = Transactions + Interactions +Observations, the goal is now: more business, higher productivity and new commercial opportunities.

Big Data = Transactions + Interactions + Observations Increasing Data Variety and Complexity

Ten Big Data Management Challenges

1. How are you coping with the growing quantities of semi-structured and unstructured data? It has been estimated that 80 per cent of the data most valuable to organizations are located outside the traditional relational data-warehousing and data-mining to which Business Intelligence has been primarily oriented until now.
2. Those new valuable data come from a range of different data types and data sources. Do you know which of these are important for your business and do you have a plan to apply them strategically?
3. Do you have an overall view of the complexity of your data, either independently or in combination? And do you know what exactly you want to know in which order of sequence.
4. New insights obtained from the combination of structured and unstructured data may have an imminent expiry date. Are you aware of the desired speed of processing and analyzing various data and data combinations? Which issues that you might wish to solve require a real-time approach? Please keep in mind that real time processes are needed to enable real-time decisions.
5. Have you thought about the costs of your new data management? How are they structured: according to data domains, technology and expertise, for instance?
6. The storage of all data that you wish to analyze and stockpile will probably make new demands upon your it infrastructure. Do you have any kind of plan to deal with this, and are you also watching performance?
7. What is the state of your data security system?
8. The storage and security of Big Data is of major importance with regard to your data governance, risk management and compliance. Are you involving the appropriate departments and people in your Big Data activities?

9. Generating new business insights from large quantities of data requires an organization-wide approach. New knowledge and expertise are needed for this. Are they available in your organization and how can these be guaranteed and further developed?

10. Do you know what your Big or Total Data efforts mean for your energy use?

THE IMPORTANCE OF BIG DATA

The reason why we should wish to have and examine all that data is evident. Social media, web analytics, log files, sensors, and suchlike all provide valuable information, while the cost of it solutions continues to drop and computer-processing power is increasing. With developments like these, the surplus of information seems to have largely vanished: in principle, organizations are now capable of managing the flood of data and to use it to their own advantage. Those who excel in acquiring, processing, and managing valuable data, says Gartner, will be able to realize a 20% better result, in financial terms, than their competitors.

Within organizations, the share of unstructured data, such as documents, e-mail and images, is around 60 to 80 per cent. Of all data analyses that currently take place in organizations, 5 to 15 per cent contain a social component that enriches the structured data. This number must increase, not least because of all the external data that can be included in the analyses.

Big Data is Extreme Information Management

Gartner has now elaborated the basic model of Volume, Variety and Velocity into three interactive layers, each with four dimensions. The resulting twelve factors dovetail together and must all be purposefully addressed in the information management of the 21st century: separately and as a whole. In short, here we have, moving from the bottom to the top, the following: departing from the variety and complexity, in particular, of an increasing amount of data – often also in real-time – it is very possible to express validated statements and to establish connections on the basis of correct technological applications in combination with intensive input of all data, in order to elevate business decision making to a qualitatively higher level. If we take Big Data as the point of departure, we find ourselves on the volume side, as the name indicates. Variety and speed are the other dimensions at that level. An extra addition is the complexity of not only the data but also of the 'use cases': the way in which all data is brought into association by means of relevant and constructive questioning. We have already presented a concrete typology on the basis of the formula:

Big Data = Transactions + Interactions + Observations

The intermediate level is concerned with access and control. To start with, there are always agreements about which information precisely should be recorded and how it can be used. Social media and cloud computing provide splendid opportunities, but new technology is needed to ensure that the data can be used everywhere and at any time. The top layer covers the reliability of information. It must be not only relevant and accurate when acquired, but also in the use case. It is also important whether or not enrichment occurs in combination with other information.

Altogether, in a Big Data context, organizations must respond to the six well-known standard questions: what, when, why, where, who and how? The first four cover the structure of your Enterprise Information Architecture and the last two that of your Enterprise Information Management.

Data Science Rules

Despite such indicative initiatives, the Big Data concept is most closely related to what we call Big Science. There, the Volume, Variety and Velocity aspects, in combination with state-of-the-art hardware and software, are most obviously present, although some people may contest scientific Relevance and Value, certainly in times of crisis. Moreover, the particle accelerator and hypermodern telescopes are somewhat larger than what we have to deal with businesswise, and they are of a completely different order in terms of data techniques. So, how does Big Data bring us from Big Science to Big Business? The heart of the answer is Data Science, the art of transforming existing data to new insights by means of which an organization can or will take action. Without mentioning the currently much-discussed concept of Data Science, Chirag Metha, the former Technology, Design & Innovation Strategist for the sap Office of the ceo, emphasized above all the importance of the tools and the corresponding collaboration, as Big Data is certainly not only for experts. On the contrary, it is imperative to involve as many people as possible in the data chain. Without self-service tools, most people will likely be cut off from the data chain even if they have access to data they want to analyze. I cannot overemphasize how important the tools are in the Big Data value chain. They make it an inclusive system where more people can participate in data discovery, exploration, and analysis. Unusual insights rarely come from experts; they invariably come from people who were always fascinated by data but analyzing data was never part of their day-to-day job. Big Data is about enabling these people to participate – all information accessible to all people.

Next in Big Data

No More Secrets, Big Social, offers a multi-faceted orientation to the promising Big Data development with regard to Social Analytics and Social Media. Some of these are indeed very promising, others only promise a lot. The more confident you are in your own judgment, the more able you will be to give a personal assessment and act in accordance with your observations. The crucial question for now is simply what's next in Big Data? Many organizations are finding that they have been waiting too long for concrete solutions. These should be easy to implement, of course, and should amply repay the effort expended. Nervous eagerness and skepticism now mark the start of business practices that more and more will confidently build upon Big Data. Large Big Data projects and strategies are yet to come but the current emerging next practices that already can be discerned surely will find their place in daily operations everywhere. In that context, please carefully consider the following observations, and see them primarily as central to the dynamic Big Data discussion that is currently in full swing:

1. Qualified best practices are under construction
2. Technology is making a breakthrough
3. Big Social will fulfill the promise of hyper targeting
4. Big Data runs the risk of becoming an out-of-control party
5. Clearly determine your actual needs
6. Behavior is often predictable without Big Data

7.   Big Data builds upon traditional data centricity
8.   Big Data is simmering through
9.   Social Analytics is the current Big Data pet topic

TOTAL DATA MANAGEMENT: THE 'BIG FIVE' SOCIAL SOURCES

Numerous data may form the basis of behavior analyses, such as client cards, search terms on internet, purchases, and responses to discount vouchers. In addition to the traditional enterprise applications as a data source, there are currently at least four other data categories that nourish the 'emerging next Big Data practices' of Social Analytics in widest sense of the word 'social'. These are: mobile data and app data, search-engine data, sensor data, and semantic data and, of course, social media data. Each of these 'Big Five' data sources has its own interesting characteristics. One is related to the way people perform searches on internet, another reveals the patterns behind purchasing. One type of data comes from one's own system, while another may come from an external system. Social Media Data concern the motives behind actions. We listen to these by means of 'listening platforms' and perform yet other analyses:

The 'Big Five' of Social Data, featuring the current Social Analytics practice for social media It is essential to look at the whole picture and have a Total Data Management view, taking into account the strengths and weaknesses of data sets and the strength of smart combinations in the context of our three-stage rocket Understand, Predict & Act. But let us first examine each of the 'Big Five'.

1.   **Sensor Data:** These are data from sensors, such as smart meters, which record the energy consumption and energy production of each household and neighborhood. The network consists of appliances that use energy, cars for the storage of energy in batteries, and people. This sort of 'neighborhood analytics' is a component of new production systems: a kind of 'Social erp'. But other data, too, such as the tracking of purchasing behavior in shops, as well as numerous data from human-machine interaction also fit into this category.

2.   **Enterprise Application Data:** Enterprise application data is traditionally used to recognize social patterns, such as purchasing behavior. It sits in structured databases of systems for Customer Relationship Management, Supply Chain Management, and Enterprise Resource Management or belongs to the data on a company's own website. In this context, we refer for example to on-site Web Analytics: the pages that people visit, the options that people click on, which 'landing page' is best in terms of leading to purchases, etcetera. There are also the so-called Cross Channel Attribution tools, which analyze great amounts of data from diverse sources. Enterprise application data are the building blocks of Business Intelligence, hrm applications, of production and commercial processes.

3.   **Social Media Data:** This is all about data, often unstructured, that comes from individuals who are engaged in 'ego-broadcasting' on social media. This data is accessible to organizations. Corporate data from internal micro blogs or company-based innovation platforms may also be an important source. So-called 'social listening tools' are applied in the analysis, enabling the subsequent steps of marketing and hrm.

4.   **Mobile Data:** This includes data from mobile applications, such as the popular apps category. Flurry and other players supply tools for App Analytics and make use of the same sort of metrics as those applied in web use. Mobile data may form the basis of location-based services that are

supplied in real-time. Social media on mobile devices often also transmit location data. Social and mobile data together can be said to be a marriage made in marketing heaven.

5. **Search Data and External Internet Data (Off-Site):** Search data may come from search engines, such as Google Trends or Google Insights, from other suppliers that 'scrape' the search engines, from 'phoning home' software or isps. The data is used for trend analysis, Search Engine Optimization and Search Engine Marketing, by making use of keyword monitoring and services of Google Ad words, for example. Off-site web data offers better insight into the popularity of websites, into where the buzz is, or where comments are given. Such data may come from the log files of web servers or from page-tagging with Java scripts. This also is likely to occur of course on a company's own website: 'on-site internet data'.

Privacy

Assuming that privacy is a fundamental human right, that there are different flavors, that privacy is a matter of human civilization, as some say, and essential to the economy, is it not a downright shame that there is so much fear, uncertainty and doubt at the moment? This is all the more true for digital privacy and the value of Personally Identifiable Information: in commercial transactions, in health care, for energy management, in the relationship between citizens and authority etc. Making personal and behavioral data available in exchange for efficient tailor-made service provision can engender an excellent deal with institutions, companies and authorities, as long as we know what is happening to our data and what the risks are. If this is known and arranged with a view to the future, we can then make deliberations and agreements and, as it were, take our Vendor Relationship Management (vrm) into our own hands or tender it out. To some extent, fear, uncertainty and doubt are just part of our nature, as privacy is typical of the fragile individual who has to stand his ground in the vortex of modern society with all the conflicts of interest that are part and parcel of it. In this digital era of more and more Privacy-Invasive Technologies and data surveillance, no efforts must be spared to remove the sting of fear.

Privacy is a Fundamental Human Right

No-one should be subjected to arbitrary interference with his privacy, family, home or correspondence, nor to attacks on his honor or reputation. Universal Declaration of Human Rights, 1948, section 12 In the Universal Declaration of Human Rights of the United Nations, privacy is an unalienable human right and is mentioned as such in charters, constitutions, regular laws and treaties throughout the world. Resolution A/hrc/20/L.13 of July 2012 of the United Nations Human Rights Committee – about "promoting, protecting and having human rights on the Internet" states that all human rights need to be protected offline and online, particularly freedom of speech. Moreover, this is conducive and even vital to economic transactions.

Privacy Comes in Different Flavors

The first privacy act dates from 1361, when peeping and eavesdropping were made punishable in England. Modern views with regard to privacy distinguish different categories such as personal, informational, organizational, and spiritual and intellectual of "bodily privacy (private parts), territorial privacy (private places), communications privacy (private messages), and information privacy." Our online privacy is usually called e-Privacy. Digital privacy is not necessarily online and, according to the letter, informational privacy need not necessarily be digital. An indication of what the term "digital Personally Identifiable Information" nowadays means.

Privacy is a Matter of Human Civilization

The well-known and even somewhat controversial Russian-American writer Ayn Rand equated our social civilization concisely with optimal privacy: Civilization is the progress toward a society of privacy. The savage's whole existence is public, ruled by the laws of his tribe. Civilization is the process of setting man free from men.

Privacy Is Essential to the Economy

The article "Privacy: Its Origin, Function, and Future" (1979) in which the American economist and professor Jack Hirschleifer emphasizes the economic dimension of privacy, starts with Rousscau's view. The economic dimension explicitly manifests itself in the influential Framework for Global Electronic Commerce (1997) by the Clinton administration, Hirschleifer said in 1979, is nowadays not so much a traditional matter of "secrecy" of withdrawal and of keeping things under cover. It is rather the "autonomy within society" that is central. This autonomy of individuals and groups is synonymous with active economic action. The way in which this could be related to uncertainty and information was something Hirschleifer was specialized in: what does it mean when people do not really know and cannot assess what is known about them? Privacy was "a way of organizing society" rather than of "withdrawal," as Hirschleifer literally underlined it in his article.

Privacy is Personal Total Data Management

According to the writer Gabriel García Márquez, each individual has three kinds of lives: a public life, a private life and a secret life. As early as 1948, George Orwell described in his book 1984 what devices and the Internet could do in this context: It was terribly dangerous to let your thoughts wander when you were in any public place or within range of a tele screen. The smallest thing could give you away. In those days that was a gross exaggeration and it still is in our time, fortunately, but it certainly reflects the fear with which we experience the present surveillance & data veillance society. In the street and online, all conceivable data flows can be monitored on a permanent basis. It seems that the only place where we have some privacy is in the toilet at home. It is not without reason that privy is related to privacy and private. The title of this Digital Life e-Guide plays with that relationship in meaning. The difference between public, private and secret is the essence of the privacy theme, not in the least in the context of private data and other personal information. The current European Data Protection Directive will be changed into a binding law for all member-states, and is meant to become effective as of 2015. With all the digital activity that we have today, the distinction between public, private and secret is more fluid and fuzzier than ever. Kaliya Hamlin, also known online as Identity Woman, made the mindmap below showing the cloud with personal digital data or Personally Identifiable Information (pii) that is hanging around us all to a greater or lesser extent: partly public, partly private and partly secret. All in all, this provides a complete picture at any time of who we are, what we think, and what we find interesting; in other words, what we might be ready to pay for or what we might be blackmailed with one way or another.

Privacy is a Matter of Trade-Offs

When we say that privacy or simply feeling free or good is essential to a welloiled digital economy, the economic concept of trade-off immediately comes to mind. Situation-wise and individually we make different choices as to what we will or will not be prepared to allow when it comes to collecting, sharing and using information. After all: Privacy is "the subjective condition that people experience when they have power to control information about themselves and when they exercise that power consistent with their interests and values." There is no free lunch: We cannot escape the trade-off between locking down information and the many benefits for consumers of the free flow of information. There are various kinds of privacy trade-offs, for instance:

1. Privacy versus upbringing
2. Privacy versus health
3. Privacy versus the fight against fraud
4. Privacy versus better service
5. Privacy versus efficient energy systems
6. Privacy versus self-expression
7. Privacy versus security

Privacy is Fear, Uncertainty and Doubt

As early as 1966, William Douglas, the longest serving member of the Supreme Court of the United States, said the following about uncertainty with regard to technology related privacy: We are rapidly entering the age of no privacy, where everyone is open to surveillance at all times; where there are no secrets from government. Nowadays living in a surveillance and data veillance society is considered acceptable. On the one hand, we have to cope with pits (Privacy-Invasive Technologies) and, on the other, with pets (Privacy-Enhancing Technologies). The American National Security Agency is currently building a quantum supercomputer, named Vesuvius, to enable constant monitoring of digital data flows of literally everything and everyone in the world.

PRIVACY AND BIG DATA

Ever since the development of media technology such as photography, telephony and telegraphy in the nineteenth century, privacy has become an increasingly important point of interest. The maxim Privacy Is the Right to Be Left Alone originated in the America of the 1890s. This is when the development of technology and our need of privacy were seriously at odds for the first time: Recent inventions and business methods call attention to the next step which must be taken for the protection of the person, and for securing to the individual what Judge Cooley calls the right "to be left alone." Numerous devices threaten to make good the prediction that "what is whispered in the closet shall be proclaimed from the rooftops." To date, the validity of this quotation still stands. Without the photography, the newspapers and the word "mechanical," which we have deliberately omitted from the quotation, no one could have suspected that these words date from 1890, and have been taken from the article "The Right to Privacy" by Samuel Warren and Louis Brandeis in the Harvard Law Review. In fact, this is what primed the entire modern debate on privacy. And even today, photography and paparazzi occupy center stage when it comes to privacy issues.

Technology and Privacy in a Nutshell

The Technology and Privacy: The New Landscape, which was published over fifteen years ago, contains an apt definition of digital privacy. The ensuing fear and hope are also touched upon, and the concept of Privacy by Design is also put forward from converging perspectives, albeit before the term truly existed: Privacy is the capacity to negotiate social relationships by controlling access to personal information. As laws, policies, and technological design increasingly structure people's relationships with social institutions, individual privacy faces new threats and new opportunities. The authors are international experts in the technical, economic, and political aspects of privacy; the chapter's strength is its synthesis of the three. Here we give a brief explanation:

1. **Privacy-Enhancing Technologies:** Technology and Privacy: The New Landscape contains a chapter by Herbert Burkert entitled "Privacy-Enhancing Technologies (pets): Typology, Vision, and Critique." This emeritus professor is currently in charge of the research center for Information Law at the University of Sankt Gallen, Switzerland.

2. **Privacy-Invasive Technologies:** One year later, in 1998, the Australian e-business consultant Roger Clarke placed the abbreviation pits – Privacy-Invasive Technologies – opposite pets. An up-to-date overview can be found on the pet wiki of the Center for Internet and Society.

3. **Data Veillance:** The Data Veillance & Information Privacy pages of Roger Clarke provide an interesting overview of pits, pets and their context. The term data Veillance was coined by Clarke. He discussed the concept in the article "Information Technology and Data Veillance" in the Communications of the acm magazine of May 1988. In addition to surveillance and data Veillance you may nowadays also come across the terms surveillance and uber veillance.

4. **Pets and Privacy by Design:** Recent literature on pets and Privacy by Design:
   a. The Privacy and Privacy-Enhancing Technologies (2003), devoted to intelligent software agents
   b. Privacy-Enhancing Technologies: A Review by hp Laboratories (2011)
   c. Privacy by Design in the Age of Big Data by the Canadian Information and Privacy Commissioner Ann Cavoukian and ibm's Big Data guru Jeff Jonas (June 2012)
   d. The report Operation alizing Privacy by Design: A Guide to Implementing Strong Privacy practices by Ann Cavoukian (December 2012).

5. **Privacy by Design and Pets:** The relation between Personally Identifiable Information (pii), pits, pets and Privacy by Design is very much in the making. A critical view is provided by the article "Regulating Privacy By Design" (2011) written by Ira Rubinstein, a Senior Fellow in the Information Law Institute of the Center for Democracy and Technology, among other things. Rubinstein has doubts about the worldwide enthusiasm with which Privacy by Design and pets have been greeted in recent years. The thing is that new worlds are hidden behind these concepts and this is where the work really begins, amidst rapidly developing technologies and data flows.

Privacy Challenge of Big Data

Data are of great value to the world economy as the raw material for innovation, productivity, efficiency and growth. At the same time, the flood of data poses privacy issues that may result in regulations that bring the data economy and innovations to a standstill.

To find a balance, policy makers need to address a number of the most fundamental privacy concepts, such as the definition of Personally Identifiable Information (pii), the way it can be controlled by the individual, and the principles of minimal and effective use of data.

Privacy Impact Assessment (PIA)

To keep the theme of privacy and security practical, a Privacy Impact Assessment can be made to clarify in advance the risks inherent in the implementation of plans. The British Information Commissioner's Office, for example, has such a pia and distinguishes the following nine steps:

- Identifying interested parties
- Initial assessment of privacy risks
- Decision as to the extent of pia
- Mapping out privacy risks
- Consulting interested parties
- Making proposals for acceptance
- Moderating or avoiding risks
- Checking compliance
- Planning a review

THE BIG DATA REALITY

The amount of information at the disposal of organizations and authorities has expanded, due to developments in data mining and analytics, and the enormous increase in computing power and data storage.

Raw data can now be analyzed without the help of structured databases. This way, it is much easier to demonstrate interrelationships, while new unthought-of applications for existing information are beginning to emerge.

At the same time, the growing numbers of people, devices and sensors that are linked by means of digital networks have caused a revolution in creating, communicating, sharing and accessing data.

Big Data Technologies

The processing stages that apply to Business Intelligence applications also apply to Big Data, but demand extra technological effort to enable the complete process of data capturing, storage, search, sharing, analytics and visualization to occur smoothly. In his book entitled Big Data Glossary, Pete Warden discusses a total of sixty technological innovations and provides the following concise overview of Big Data concepts and tools.

- **Data Acquisition:** For accessing various data sources, internal or external, structured or unstructured. Most interesting public data sources are poorly structured, full of contamination and difficult to open.
- **Serialization:** At various points during processing, the data will be stored in files. These operations all require some sort of ranking.
- **Storage:** Traditional file systems are unsuited to large-scale, distributed data processing, but nevertheless the Hadoop Distributed File System is actually suited to this function.
- **Cloud:** Hiring computers as virtual machines in a cloud environment is increasingly, Your Big Data Potentiating standard procedure. In this way, you can make use of large processing capacity for Big Data applications at relatively low cost.
- **NOSQL:** Nosql (Not only sql) is a broad class of management systems that deviates from the classical relational model.
- **Map Reduce:** In traditional relational database environments, all processing takes place via a special query language after the structured information has been loaded. In contrast, Map Reduce reads and writes unstructured data to all sorts of file formats. The interim results are passed on as files, and the processing is divided among many machines.
- **Processing:** Filtering concise, valuable information from an ocean of data is a challenge, but there are already many solutions that can help with such tasks.
- **Natural Language Processing (NLP):** Natural Language Processing extracts meaningful information from untidy, human based language.
- **Machine Learning:** Machine Learning systems automate and optimize decision-making. The recommendations given by Amazon, for instance, are well-know applications of this function.
- **Visualization:** This is one of the best ways to extract significance from data. Thanks to interactive graphics, the presentation and exploration of information blend together.

BIG DATA SECURITY WITHIN THE CLOUD

Defining Cloud Computing

Many experts from industry and academic spheres have made many attempts to define the basic definition of Cloud and its computing features. There are many researchers who have given Cloud definitions which we are going to discuss. Buyya et al. have explained the cloud as follows: "Cloud is a parallel and distributed computing system consisting of a collection of inter-connected and virtualized computers that are dynamically provisioned and presented as one or more unified computing resources based on service-level agreements (SLA) by Malis, A. (1993) established through negotiation between the service provider and consumers." A McKinsey and Co. have stated that "Clouds are hardware-based services offering compute, network, and storage capacity where: Hardware management is highly abstracted from the buyer, buyers incur infrastructure costs as variable OP EX, and infrastructure capacity is highly elastic.". According to Vaquero et al. "clouds are a large pool of easily usable and accessible virtualized resources (such as hardware, development platforms and/ or services). These resources can be dynamically reconfigured to adjust to a variable load (scale), allowing also for an optimum resource utilization. This pool of resources is typically exploited by a pay-per -use model in which guarantees are offered by the Infrastructure Provider by means of customized Service Level Agreements."New York

Times (2001). The National Institute of Standards and Technology (NIST) defines cloud computing as " a pay-per-use model for enabling available, convenient, on-demand network access to a shared pool of configurable computing resources (e.g. networks, servers, storage, applications, services) that can be rapidly provisioned and released with minimal management effort or service provider interaction." Armbrust et al. have termed cloud as the "data center hardware and software that provide services" Barr, J. (2006). The basic aim of Cloud Computing is to combine the physical and computing resources and to distribute the computing tasks to multiple distributed computers. In surge of rapid usage of Internet, Cloud Computing has become key interface in IT industry as well as in academia. Cloud computing is an enhancement of distributed and parallel computing, Cluster Computing and Grid computing. In this advanced era, not only user able to use a particular web based application but also that may be in active participation in its computational procedure by either adopting , demanding or pay per use basis by Sutter, H. (2005).

Characteristics of Cloud

In the previous section, from different definitions of cloud we can categorize some common and fundamental characteristics of cloud. Here we discuss some basic characteristics of cloud services, which make cloud concept so popular and desirable in surge of rapid growth of Internet.

Elasticity and Scalability

Cloud computing provides the illusion of infinite physical and computing resources which is available on-demand basis suggested by Toffler, A. (1980) & Wikipedia. Hence, from the user-point of view, computing and physical resources can be provisioned at any time how much they require the resources. A cloud infrastructure should be capable of providing enough computing resources in an elastic way when number of users or application load is increased and it can release the resources when it is of no use. Scalability also defines that an application is capable of scaling itself when more users and more applications are added and also when the configuration of application or application requirements change. It should be capable of releasing the resources when the users or applications are freed from the service. Therefore, we can say that cloud infrastructure is able to scale up and scale down according to the requirements of the applications.

Measured Metering and Billing of Service

While using a cloud infrastructure, cloud users need to not know the underlying architecture or the set-up capabilities. They have not to maintain the hardware and system resources. But they are using all those hardware or system or computation resources and services. Of course, these are not at all free. Cloud technology allows the users to request and facilitates them to use only the required amounts. Services must be termed and priced based on short-term basis like by the days or by the hours-basis, allowing them to free these resources when they are not required suggested by Wikinomics & Golden; B. (2009). Therefore, Clouds should have the features to allow competent trading services which include accounting, pricing and billing services suggested by Fellows, W. (2009). Metering should be categorized according to types of their required services such as processing resources, storage, hardware and system resources. Hence, how much the users are using the resources and services, they have to pay according to their usage; this is the concept of "pay-per-use" or "Pay-as-you-go". That is how metering of usage is promptly reported and billing service is concerned with that metering service.

Self-Service Provisioning of Resources

Consumers or Cloud subscribers of Cloud services is expecting instant access of resources while they are in need of the required resources. The cloud users are simply requesting for a certain amount of services, storage, processing capabilities, computing services from the CSPs. And for servicing that request, CSPs must provide an atmosphere for getting self-service access. This self-service provisioning of resources can facilitate the users to request, customize, pay per usage and use the resources and services without any interference of human operators by author Sims, K. (2009). Suppose, an organization is working on an application using a cloud and that organization wants to implement new application or add more features to the existing application; it has to request to the CSPs for new computing and hardware resources. And data centers within CSPs have to configure itself according to need of the request. So on-demand resource provisioning capabilities of services reduce the time delays and users nearly instantly get the cloud services on-demand basis.

Application Programming Interface (APIs)

Cloud services need to build a standardized interface which would facilitate the customers to manage the relationships among financial management system, accounting management system and renewal management system. Standard is meant by a set of common, configurable and repeatable protocols which are determined and shared by some organizations. So these standardized platforms or interfaces help the cloud users to avail the common instructions on how multiple applications or different data sources can able to interact with each other.

Performance Measurement Service

Service providers should have the capabilities to maintain a management system that monitors the accesses of data centers and IT services. For example, an organization is using a cloud service from a service provider and this organization has integrated its own data and services with the cloud. So it needs some privacy so that the internal data of the organization must be kept safely. When the organization needs some more resources for maintenance of the additional features and applications, it requests to the data centers, and service provider runs a monitoring system which monitors the availability of the resources and the resources are provisioned according to the need of the user. The management system monitors the services, measure the performance, reduce the time delays, and optimize the services.

Device and Location Independency

Cloud service facilitates the users to access the computation and hardware resources using only a web browser without any dependency of their location or what kind of device they are using. A cloud infrastructure is situated offsite and accessed for resources via the Internet by the cloud users. They can easily connect with the infrastructure and resources from anywhere regardless of their location.

Customization

The system and computation resources must be extremely customizable when the cloud users rented the resources from the providers. Customization leads to an atmosphere where users are allowed to deploy their applications onto cloud and resources are customized and configured according to the requirement of the users. For example, when an organization deploys more features and more clients for a certain amount of time, it needs more resources like more processing, bandwidth, computing resources and more CPU cores for that period time. And all the resources are configured and customized consequently with the features and the clients for that time span.

Security

When security is concerned, it improves security due to centralization of data. But it is concerned when loss of control over certain sensitive data. If we look at the network level of security, we have to ensure the confidentiality and integrity of the transmitting data to and from the cloud provider. But in a cloud infrastructure, Privacy is concerned because cloud providers have the access over the sensitive and private data of its client.

Need for Cloud

From business point of view, every cloud management is thinking about the reduction of cost complexity. Cloud providers must fulfill the satisfaction level of both the external or internal customers by minimizing the cost estimation.

Prompt Access for Supporting Business Agility

One of the most appreciable reimbursements of cloud infrastructure services is to append or add new infrastructure capacity swiftly with a minimal cost. As we discussed previously that self-service provisioning of resources allow the users to access the resources in a self-service manner without any human interaction. Hence, automated self-service leads to cloud infrastructure more flexible and reduce the cost complexity. A typical service provider has to maintain a cost-cutting edge to preserve the economies of the company that would help the organization to grow with enough capabilities.

Minimizing Investment Expenditures

An organization wants to build new business application, but it suffers from shortage of money. But the organization is in urgent need of computing and hardware resources for supporting its clients. Cloud Service providers is there to provide this type of facilities to that organization and the organization might rent the computing and system resources per-hour basis or per-storage unit basis. Company Management is getting pressured when more clients or more additional features is there to consume the service. To cover up the situation, the organization either may build up new infrastructure or may rent resources from some service provider pay-per-use basis. One cloud says that "it's smarter to rent than to buy". So, the organization can reduce its expenditures by renting the services from the cloud service providers.

Types of Cloud

While an organization is going to rent the cloud, cloud provider must ensure the security and privacy issues of their clients. There are different reasons to maintain different types of clouds for different particular purpose. In this section, we will explain different types of cloud and how the clouds interact with the customers in an efficient manner. Here we will elaborately discuss the fundamental concepts of four types of clouds, present in the current scenario, which is talked about below.

Public Cloud

According to Zimory GmbH (2009), public cloud has made the cloud available in pay-as-you-go manner to the general public. In this public cloud model, the hardware and computing resources and also same infrastructure is used by the multiple users. Public cloud has some basic criterion which makes it so popular.

- **Usable Standardize Workload for Application:** when more and more applications are deployed onto a cloud, physical resources should be provisioned in an efficient manner and the cloud infrastructure should be capable of maintaining the workload so that the users can get the service without any interruption.
- **High Scalability:** As we discussed previously that cloud has the property of being highly scalable. A huge number of users is using the public cloud at a same instance of time and public cloud is highly capable of providing all the services to the users.
- **Testing and Developing Application:** Public cloud facilitates the users for testing and developing the applications.
- **Collaborating Projects:** Public clouds are there to provide a platform where the users are facilitated to merge their projects and users collaborate them to build up a bigger and smarter project.

Public cloud or external cloud provides the users with traditional mainstream services where resources are dynamically provisioned and utilized based on fine-grained, self-service basis over the Internet, through web-application or web services. Email-system is a good example of public cloud. For example, when end-users use mail services say Yahoo or Gmail account, they need to have only a computer and internet connection. User need not to know about the underlying process. They are just using the Google cloud or Yahoo cloud. All the maintaining, testing and developing task are done by Yahoo or Google itself.

Private Cloud

When an organization wants to secure its own data but still need to gain cloud infrastructure, the organization feels the need for private cloud. Consider an example which makes you clear about Private cloud. Suppose an organization is maintaining a database of users and enables the users to submit their personal information to the database. And the organization wants to keep the database confidential and maintains its privacy. Hence, the organization has to put its important and private data in the private cloud which is kept inside the company's firewall. Some fundamental characteristics made the private cloud so usable.

- **Optimizing Usage of Computation Capability and Resource Provisioning**: It allows the IT industry to provide the users for resource provisioning and computation capability to the internal users of the organization in a self-service manner and in an optimized way for getting the maximum throughput.

- **Less Expensive:** Using a private cloud makes an organization more profitable. Considering a scenario, suppose an organization with huge data-center is using public cloud infrastructure; when it wants to add new features to the existing scheme, it has to rent the required resources from service provider and that is being much more expensive. Therefore, the organization can put a private cloud inside its firewall and that would more helpful to reduce the cost complexity than using a public cloud.

- **Supports Specific Workloads:** Private cloud is quiet capable of handle the specific workloads within the organization. Limited workload facilitates the private cloud to gain fast access over the resources.

- **Privacy:** In a private cloud, an organization can put all its own data within the organization's firewall which leads the company to maintain the security and privacy of its own data. The organization has to consider the aspects of data security such as data-in-transit (during transmission), data-at-rest (during storage), data provenance (data integrity with computationally accuracy), and data permanence (residual representation of data being nominally erased or removed) by authors of Right Scale Inc. (2009). Hence, Private cloud facilitates the organization as well as its clients to be relaxed about their data security.

- **Management Control:** As all the data reside inside the organization, it can capable to manage all the data itself. And it has the authority to put the rule and regulations over the accesses of the data. It helps the organization to control over all those issues.

For example, Amazon Virtual Private Cloud (VPC) is a private cloud, which offers clients isolated AWS (Amazon Work Space) and protection by Virtual Private Network (VPN) connections.

Hybrid Cloud

While public cloud deals with general clients and private cloud interacts with the customers dedicated to a particular organization, cloud giants think about mix of both cloud features to satisfy many business needs, which we can called hybrid cloud. A hybrid cloud can be organized when a private cloud is supplemented with resource and computing capability from public clouds. Hybrid cloud infrastructure comes up with a combination of public and private cloud. Hybrid cloud is a unique entity but both public and private clouds are bound together by standardized technology that facilitates an organization with application and data portability. An organization uses the physical resources from hybrid cloud on-demand basis and returns it when it is of no use.

Let us consider a scenario. Suppose a company wants to use a SaaS Application, which would meet the considerations of the company, i.e. Security, privacy and standardized usage throughout the company. The SaaS provider creates a private cloud for the particular company inside their firewall so that the entire company can use the cloud as a standard. Now they provide the company with a Virtual Private Network (VPN) for getting more security. Hybrid cloud has the characteristics of both private and public cloud. Hybrid cloud is quite capable of maintaining the privacy and security of the user-data and application of its clients. Considering another example, we can explain the concept behind hybrid cloud. Suppose, an organization offers services for different purposes in vertical markets. Different clients might tender to handle shipping services for manufacturers, payments for insurance brokers, credit checking services or any other services. The organization might want a public cloud for creating an online environment where each customer can get access to those services and can check their status. But the organization, for maintenance of privacy and security issues, wants to keep the data within its own private cloud to maintain and manage the user-data.

Community Cloud

In case of joint venture application, a same cloud infrastructure needs to be constructed and shared by several organizations jointly, so that they can use the same framework as well as policies, services, requirements, applications, and concerns. Hybrid cloud is highly scalable and reduces cost complexity. The third-party vendor or any one of the vendors within the community may host and maintain the community cloud infrastructure. When a large application or large project is to be carried out for a long period of time, the community cloud infrastructure is being very useful for that purpose and as one of the vendors is maintaining the cloud infrastructure, cost complexity is also being reduced.

Cloud Services

End-users or clients use the cloud services according to their needs. Cloud Service Providers (CSPs) deliver the service on-demand basis. In this section, we are going to discuss different types of services provided by the CSPs. Cloud providers are giving services through which cloud customers are accessing operating system, software application and data storage. In this section, we are just briefly explaining the services provided by a cloud service provider and will elaborately discuss later.

Resources as a Service (RAAS)

At the bottom-most layer of the cloud service stack, there would be a collection of physical Resources such as storage, servers, bandwidth, data center space, and networks, which may be accessed and shared by multiple CSPs. In the current scenario of IT industry, resource virtualization is the key feature of Cloud computing and fast growth of hardware and computing resource virtualization facilitates the service providers for using RAAS service when they are in need of the particular service. We will discuss later about virtualization techniques and different types of virtualization. In this surge of rapid growth of resources virtualization, from the pool of resources, computing and system resources are provisioned according to the requirement of the cloud user. As for example of RAAS, Amazon S3 may the best example.

Infrastructure as a Service

Infrastructure as a Service (IaaS) deals with infrastructure on which RaaS may get expanded itself due to resource virtualization. IaaS provides virtualization technology which involves the provisioning of infrastructure to the cloud users. Clients may rent infrastructure services rather than buying those services to reduce the cost complexity, and resource virtualization may facilitate to get those services. The capability to provision processing, networks, storage and other required computing resources, the subscribers are able to deploy their application and can run arbitrary software that includes operating systems and applications. The consumer of cloud services does not control or manage the underlying cloud infrastructure but has the control over deployed applications, operating systems, some networking components, bandwidth etc. The IaaS service model supports dynamic scaling and the resources are there in a distributed way. This cloud model is typically useful while the demand-type is volatile that means when the particular task is done, all the resources are return back to the resource pool. And this service is most fruitful when an organization wants to set up new business and it does not want to make much expenditure on investing in building up a new computing infrastructure. So, we can say that from business point view, IaaS is very useful for reducing the cost complexity. As for example, we can say, Amazon Elastic Cloud 2 (Amazon EC2) is the common example of IaaS. One of the most important functions of IaaS is Virtualization which mainly deals with network, storage and computation virtualization. The basic concept of Virtualization is to hide underlying infrastructure by creating a logical interface. Resources are virtualized and logically represented in this layer. We will discuss different types of virtualization in next phase of the book by Amrhein, D. & Willenborg, R. (2009).

Platform as a Service

Platform as a Service (PaaS) has the capability to provide independent platform having deployment capabilities and it may be capable of executing multiple application on single platform concurrently. The user may be free to create his applications which can be run over the service provider's infrastructure. PaaS provides the Interface to deploy consumer created or different acquired applications using different programming languages and various tools which is supported by the service provider. The users don't have the authority to control or manage the underlying Cloud infrastructure but have the control over their deployed applications. Platform services include device migration, device integration, session management, instrumentation and testing, environment configuration, content management, Universal Description Discovery and Integration (UDDI), Extensible Markup Language (XML)-based registry which provides a mechanism for registering and locating web service applications. Google Apps is the example of PaaS. PaaS is mostly used when a large software project is going on and when multiple developers and users are intend to collaborate different software modules and the deployment & testing services would be automated. In that case, cloud users need not to know the underlying infrastructure of the cloud but they are quite able to use the services and also customize the services.

Software as a Service

Software services are to use applications delivered by the service provider in a particular cloud infrastructure. The applications are accessible from various devices via a user-Interface like web-based mail. SaaS provides the platform for software usage. Clients just use the software service without the overhead of running, maintaining and updating the software. It helps to reduce the cost complexity because clients need not to be concerned about all those issues. Salesforce.com can be example of SaaS. This layer may provide ready-to-use software service and the clients need not to take any overhead for buying and maintaining the software. Cloud users need not to know the underlying architecture of cloud infrastructure; they just use and access the software. Basic blocks of software services may facilitate the creation, delivery and usage of the software. Software services offered to the clients include Enterprise services like workflow management, collaboration management, digital signature, supply chain, software delivery services, financial management, Customer Relationship Management (CRM) etc. Web 2.0 applications like metadata management, portal services, social networking, blogs etc. To support these three service delivery models, some necessary activities should be taken which includes:

- Service Management and resource provisioning, operations management, SLA management, QoS management, technical support and backups.
- Security management which includes authorization and authentication, intrusion prevention, certification, access control, audit, virus protection and firewalls.
- Customer services like online help or customer assistance, customer preference, reporting and personalization.
- Collaborating and integrating the services from heterogeneous field is also there for consideration.

Security Issues of Cloud Computing

Cloud computing is depending upon a paradigm shift with reflective implications on computing issues. Paradigms shift in cloud computing is the basic pillar of change in the traditional computing and there are various issues related data-security and privacy. There are multiple elements concerned with security and privacy related issues which we will discuss below.

User-Data is Controlled by Third Party Service

In the current scenario, the control is relinquished to the third party services; so different security and privacy issues are concerned like unauthorized access, data access control, data corruption, enhancing dynamic allocation strategies, controlling sensitive information flow etc. As third party service is concerned, users are keeping all their sensitive data to the database and storage service of the third party. So third party has the responsibility to maintain the security and privacy of the data and that's why third party has to enable auditing service. According to Information Systems Control and Audit, IT auditing can be defined as a process of aggregating and evaluating evidence to decide whether a computing information system safeguards resources, maintains data integrity and secure sensitive user data, attains organizational objectives effectively and consumes physical and computing resources efficiently.

How Third Party is Enabling Auditing Service

We are considering cloud data storage and database service involving four different entities, the cloud user, hosting machine in Cloud Service Provider (CSP), Cloud Database Server (CDS) and Third Party Auditing Service (TPAS). The cloud user, having a huge amount of data files which is to be stored in the cloud. The cloud user interacts with hosting machine in CSP through Cloud-based user Interface and deploys various applications. They may also dynamically communicate with CDS for storing and maintenance of their data files. While deploying their various applications onto host machine, the users may rely on TPAS in assuring the confidentiality, availability and integrity of their outsourced data to preserve the privacy of their own data. TPAS is quite expert and capable of maintaining the privacy of user-data and can be trusted as it may review the cloud database storage reliability in support of the cloud user upon request. An unauthorized user can put a set of intelligent queries to the database server, of which none of the query is forbidden. So the unauthorized user, combining the set of replies, may get the secret information which is forbidden. Hence TPAS has the responsibility to maintain the privacy of user data.

The Data is Stored on Various Sites Which are Administered by Multiple Organizations

Cloud services are provided by different service providers and the providers maintains the physical resources such as processors, memory, and storage at their respective places. As a result, the user-data has been stored on the multiple sites which are controlled by several organizations. Hence, the so-called problem "problem of many hands" would arise because the authority or ability of individuals to work out and control the management over the collection, use, share and disclose and reveal of their personal data by others. Unlimited and ubiquitous data usage, data sharing and pool of data storage among the organizations would become the problem in the complex organization of cloud services. It is quite difficult to determine that who will take the responsibility if something unwanted happens to data storage. In respect to data access, no controls have been implemented to restrict data modification and no logging events such as access, transmission, modification on data have not been monitored.

How Data can be in Safe in Cloud Computing Environment

This will be a serious concern about the ethics of cloud computing. For data-usage and data-storage, there should be a need for some rules and regulations which are to be maintained and governed by the service providers. The term "Governance" deals with the manner in which somewhat is regulated or governed, the system or criteria of regulations, the way management. These serious issues can be taken and explicit attention should be given by the governmental organizations. In the recent scenario, data is being stored, transferred and processed outside the company or organization. The raw data is not physically controlled by the organization and shared computing environments are also making it public. These kinds of loopholes need more security and privacy. Limited capabilities for change control and provider feasibility are also the drawbacks of cloud infrastructure. Governance is exceedingly concerned with the performance measurement & its strategies and risk management & its proper administration is also an important issue of an IT landscape. Different management laws and policies, priority & resources needed for the processes, alignment of customs are the basic functionalities of governing organizations.

Accountability is another component regarding privacy and security issues. Adequate information is required regarding how data is managed by the cloud providers so that they can maintain logging events like data access, data transmission or data modification. That's why, the governing organizations is enforcing the rules and regulations to maintain the accounting of accesses to the records.

CUSTOMER DISCOUNT

Customer discounts are currently fully implemented in PCT. By running an over the data described, sales representative will find out which would be gained if the customer bought the same articles as in the historical period but using current pricing conditions. Even more importantly, new discount rates can be applied to the simulation meaning that the sales representative can see which effects they will give and whether they seem pro table enough or not. The details of the simulation process are described, but reading the chapter in the presented order is highly recommended. Understanding of the under-lying concepts is a great advantage when trying to gain insight into the workings of the simulation process.

Data Needed for a Customer Discount

It is based on data from the following sources:

- **Article Tree:** A tree structure where branch nodes represent article categories and leaf nodes represent articles.
- **Sales History:** A set of aggregated order rows, containing information about previous sale history.
- **Existing Customer Conditions:** Agreed discount rates from existing contracts, which set a certain discount rate to a specific node in the article tree.
- **User Input:** Various parameters that specify which historical data and discount rates to use in the simulation.

The Article Tree

The article tree categorizes all of the company's articles into article groups. These are in turn grouped together into more general categories in three \price levels", where level 3 is the most specific and level 1 is the most general category. An example tree using this structure is presented in Figure 1.

As seen in Figure 1, leaf nodes contain articles while branch nodes represent article categories. The most general categories are stored in price level 1 (Clothes and Shoes), subcategories of these in price level 2 (Pants and Shirts are both subcategories of Clothes) and so on. In the current article database, each price level 3 nodes contains exactly one article group meaning that these two levels are equally specific.

Figure 1. An example article tree containing clothes and accessories

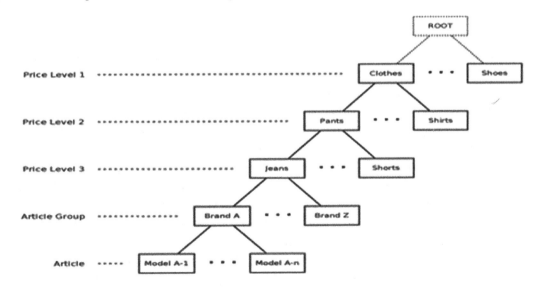

User Input

The final data needed for a simulation is provided by the user. This data consists of a customer, a path leading from the root down to an arbitrary node in the article tree, a time period and a set of discount rates for the nodes in the path. The customer is specified as a reference to the ID of a customer in the customer database. Each sales representative has a set of assigned customers whom he or she can choose from. The path is as a set of selected nodes in the article tree, where the first selected node lies on price level 1 and any node added afterwards must be a child of the last selected node. This means that there is always a price level 1 node in the path and that the sales representative may choose to add a price level 2 node as well. If a price level 2 node was added, the user can choose to proceed by adding a price level 3 node and so on. The shortest possible path has the length 1 (meaning that the path consists of a price level 1 node) and the longest possible path has the length 5 (containing one node each from price levels 1-3, an article group node and finally an article node), which is equal to the height of the article tree. The time period is represented by a start date and an end date, each represented as a combination of a year and a month. When a simulation is run, historical order data whose period parameter lies inside of this interval will be used and any data outside of the interval will be ignored. The end date must of course lie after the start date and the start date must lie within the last 13 months. This limit ensures that a full year's history can always be used, since the sale history database may not contain the current month's full history yet. Finally, the user will specify a discount rate for each node in the path. A discount rate is a decimal number between 0:0 and 99:9 with one decimal value, representing the discount percentage. It is also possible to let a node inherit its parent's value by not assigning a discount rate to it. Since the price level 1 node does not have a parent node to inherit from, its discount is set to 0:0% if no discount rate is entered on this level. The discount rates are typically modified multiple times during the simulation process, since the sales representative must simulate over multiple conjurations in order to find a suitable set of discount rates to add to a contract.

The Simulation Process

The sales representative starts by entering which customer he is negotiating with and selecting a path in the article tree for which discounts will be entered. Next up, a start and stop month is specified and now the system is ready to run the first simulation. Since no discount rates have been entered at this point, all nodes in the path will use their existing discount rates if any such exist in the active conditions and 0:0% otherwise. All price level 1 nodes which are not affected by the existing conditions will also have their discounts set to 0:0%. Due to the concept of discount inheritance all other nodes will inherit their parent's discount rate top-down if they do not have an existing condition. This means that the results of the first run will always show the economical results that will follow if the same item quantities are sold as in the historical data used for the simulation, taking only currently active conditions into account. Conditions may have been added or removed since the historical orders were handled, so it is not enough to just aggregate the values and proof from the history database. Instead, the \base value" (which one can think of as the price for the order rows if no discounts had been applied) must be calculated for each article. By applying discount rates from existing conditions to these base values, the system finds out how much the customer would have to pay for the same orders if they had been placed using current conditions. Sales representative sets discounts for the nodes in the selected path and runs another simulation over the same data. Any conditions affecting discount rates for the path nodes will be overrun by the discount rates set by the sales representative, while conditions affecting other nodes will still be taken into consideration. The user specified discount rates will then be inherited down through the article tree just like the ones from the conditions. The result will thereby correspond to the pro t which would be achieved if these new rates were added to the conditions database and the same orders as in the historical data were then placed again by the customer. This simulation step will typically be run multiple times with different discount rates for the nodes in the path, until they are balanced in such a way that both the customer and the sales representative are satisfied with the results. Running multiple simulations with different discount rates for the same time period and historical data until one gets satisfying results is referred to as going through a simulation process.

Simulation Output

So far, the output of simulations has been described in terms of \pro t" and \value". The actual values computed during a simulation are of course more specific than that and as such, the specification of requirements presents guidelines for the output data layout. The specification indicates that the output should be presented as a table, where each node in the selected path is represented as a row. There is also a top row labeled \Total", which shows the total simulation values of all articles in the whole article tree. A print screen showing how this looks in the current version of PCT is shown in Figure 2. The columns of each row are described in Table 1.

The five last columns are empty for the \Total" row, since these values are considered irrelevant to display for the whole article tree.

DISCOUNT INHERITANCE

Discounts can be applied to nodes on any level of the article tree - from price level 1 down to specific articles. It is intuitive that a discount which is set for a single article will only affect the price of that specific article. When it comes to discounts set on article groups or price level nodes, the system uses

Figure 2. A print screen from PCT showing how simulation output is presented in the current system

Customer Total	Volume (kg)	Value (EURO)	CD	CD%	Actual Discount	Agreed Discount				
Total	128,167	471,233	365,257	77.5	86.4					

Price Level 1	Volume (kg)	Value	CD	CD%	Actual Discount	Agreed Discount			Avg. Agreed	Target	Avg. Target
PL1_10	114,635	446,862	355,066	79.5	87.1	44.0	*0.0	0.0		58.5	66.2

Price Level 2	Volume (kg)	Value	CD	CD%	Actual Discount	Agreed Discount			Avg. Agreed	Target	Avg. Target
PL2_01	10,349	24,014	15,670	65.3	87.6	67.1	*0.0	0.0		66.9	66.9

Price Level 3	Volume (kg)	Value	CD	CD%	Actual Discount	Agreed Discount			Avg. Agreed	Target	Avg. Target
PL3_5751F1	26	187	161	86.0	78.1	12.4	*0.0	0.0		54.7	54.7

Table 1. The columns which are used to structure the output from a simulation

Field name	Unit	Type	Description
Node name	n/a	String	The name of the row's node
Volume	kg	Integer	The total volume of all orders for articles under the row's node in the article tree
Value	Euro	Integer	The total amount of money which the customer would have to pay if all historical orders for articles under the row's node were placed again, with the new discounts applied
C0	Euro	Integer	The pro t which the company would gain if all historical orders for articles under the row's node were placed again, with the new discounts applied
C0%	Percent	Decimal number	Shows how many percent of the row's value C0 corresponds to, i.e. (Value/C0)*100
Actual discount	Percent	Decimal number	The average historical discount for articles under the node in the simulation period
Above target	n/a	Boolean	A warning ag which shows whether the agreed discount is higher than the node's target discount
Agreed discount	Percent	Decimal number	The discount used for the row's node in the current simulation
Avg. Agreed	Percent	Decimal number	The average agreed discount for articles under the row's node in the article tree
Target discount	Percent	Decimal number	A recommended target discount for the node, based on the customer's pricing level
Avg. Target	Percent	Decimal number	The average historical target discount of articles under the row's node

a concept called discount inheritance" to let this affect underlying nodes. In order to determine which discount rate to apply to a given node, the method presented in algorithm is used.

Algorithm: Find Discount Rate (Node n)

```
Input: A node n from the article tree
Result: The discount rate which should be applied to n
if n is a node in the path for which a discount rate d is set then return d
Else if n is not a node in the path AND n has an active condition c then
Return the discount rate from condition c
Else if n is a price level 1 node then
Return 0:0%
Else
Parent:= n's parent node in the article tree
Return  findDiscountRate(parent)
End
```

The final result of the discount rate inheritance in the same tree can be seen in Figure 3 and Figure 4, where arrows show how discount rates are passed down through the tree.

Figure 3. An example article tree where discount rates have been set for four nodes

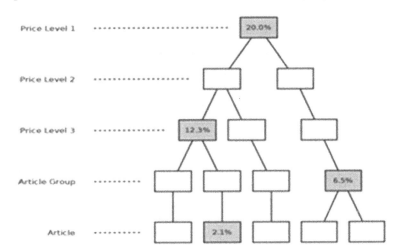

Figure 4. Discount inheritance in the example article tree

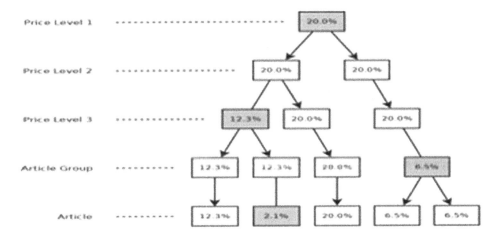

Current Implementation

The current implementation of PCT suffers from critical performance issues. Since the source code of this system is not allowed to be included in this report, the problems of its algorithm have to be explained in terms of bad structure choices and complexity rather than examples and excerpts from the actual code. While it does not motivate or explain the details of each step, it does provide enough information to analyze its complexity. To give the reader some sort of idea of the actual magnitude of the implementation of this algorithm, its Java source code takes up several hundred kilobytes (not including GUI, server connections, database handling and other parts which are not directly related to the algorithm). In other words, a line describing e.g. criteria matching means running a separate algorithm which in turn has a complexity worth mentioning.

Algorithm: Structure of the Simulation Process in PCT

```
If this is the first run of the simulation process then
Initialize connection to each input data element in the GUI [O(k)]
End
For each price level in the article tree [O(k)] do
Match condition level [O(k)]
Match price level [O(k)]
For each item in the customer's cache [O(n)] do
Match criteria [O(k)]
End
Retrieve target discount [O(k)]
For each article in the article tree [O(a)] do
For each article in the customer's cache [O(n)] do
Match criteria [O(k)]
For each price level in the article tree [O(k)] do
Retrieve data and calculate results
End
End
Retrieve agreed discounts [O(k)]
Compare discounts to target discounts [O(k)]
End
End
For each article in the customer's cache [O(n)] do
Calculate results for articles under price level 1 nodes 2= path
End
```

In the pseudo code above, the complexity has been included on each line where O notation is applicable. The total complexity of the implementation of the current simulation algorithm is $O(k+k(k+k+nk+k+a(n(k+k))+k+k)+n) = O(k+5k2+nk2+2ank2+n) = O(ank2)$.

It should also be noted that the complexity of repeated runs of the algorithm is $O(k(k + k + nk + k + a(n(k + k)) + k + k) + n) = O(5k2 + nk2 + 2ank2 + n) = O(ank2)$.

This is barely an improvement from the rst run at all - one single k term is removed since the initialization step on line 2 does not need to be run again. The total complexity of O(ank 2) is high in itself, since both a and n can hold quite large numbers and the k term is used at multiple places. However, this is not the only reason behind the high running times of the algorithm. Another big problem is the on-demand usage of database resources. Every time a set of values from the database is needed, a new connection to the database is opened. The sought values are then retrieved by an SQL query and afterwards the database connection is closed again. Repeatedly opening and closing database connections takes time and this is done in many parts of the algorithm, including the data retrieval methods mentioned in line 15. This means that O(ank2) database connections and SQL queries may have to be opened and run in the worst case. Some values are even retrieved from the database multiple times during a single execution, since they are used in multiple places in the code but are not saved after being retrieved the first time.

It should however be noted that some actions have been taken in order to reduce the amount of data retrieved from the database per simulation. Every customer's order history for the last year is stored as a list in a hash map indexed by the customer ID, which thereby works as an in-memory database. This makes retrieval of a customer's historical data (without direct database access) in O(1) time possible. Of course, iterating over the resulting list will still take O(n) time. This cache is created on server startup and updated regularly, so creation and updates of the cache do not affect the running time of the simulation algorithm. Some loops in PCT are still performed over all distinct values in certain database tables when information from this cache could have been used instead, leading to even more unnecessary database lookups.

CONCLUSION

This chapter has consisted of analysis, optimization and implementation of the algorithms in PCT as well as modeling and implementation of its upcoming scaling extension. The customer extension prove that implementation of the desired functionality in PCT is possible as well, as long as the big data issue is handled in an efficient way. Creating a new, optimized models and developing fast algorithms for these can prove far more efficient than optimization of existing algorithms based on models.

REFERENCES

Malis, A. (1993). Routing over Large Clouds (ROLC) Charter. Proceedings of the 32nd IETF meeting minutes.

Markoff, J. (2001). An Internet Critic Who Is Not Shy About Ruffling the Big Names in High Technology. *New York Times*.

Wikipedia. (n. d.). [computer scientist]. *John McCarthy*.

Barr, J. (2006). Amazon EC2 Beta.

Sutter, H. (2005). The Free Lunch Is Over: A Fundamental Turn Toward Concurrency in Software. *Dr. Dobb's Journal, 30*(3).

Toffler, A. (1980). *The Third Wave*. Pan Books.

Wikipedia. (n. d.). *Cloud Computing*.

Wikinomics. (n. d.). The Prosumers.

Golden; B. (2009). Capex vs. Opex: Most People Miss the Point About Cloud.

Fellows, W. (2009). *The State of Play: Grid*. Utility, Cloud.

Sims, K. (2009). IBM Blue Cloud Initiative Advances Enterprise Cloud Computing.

Zimory GmbH. (2009). Zimory Enterprise Cloud.

RightScale Inc. (2009). RightScale Cloud Management Features.

Amrhein, D., & Willenborg, R. (2009). Cloud computing for the enterprise, Part 3: Using WebSphere CloudBurst to create private clouds.

Chapter 10
Cloud Database Systems:
NoSQL, NewSQL, Hybrid:

Balamurugan Balusamy
VIT University, India

Sumalatha N
VIT University, India

Nadhlya S
VIT University, India

Malathi Velu
RGM College of Engineering and Technology, India

ABSTRACT

In earlier days, people ran their applications or programs on a physical computer or a server. Cloud computing is a kind of Internet-based computing, where shared resources, data and information are provided to computers and other devices on-demand. Many business organizations were moving towards cloud because it provides flexibility, disaster recovery, security, collaboration etc., Relational Databases ruled the IT Industries for almost 40 years. Limitations of relational database lead to the rise of cloud database. A cloud database is a database that typically runs on a cloud computing platform. Cloud databases are on the rise as more and more businesses look to capitalize on the advantages of cloud computing to power their business applications. Cloud databases are mainly used in data mining, data warehousing and business intelligence. This chapter deals with different types of cloud database and how database influence capacity planning.

INTRODUCTION

A Database is a collection of information that is organized so that it can easily be accessed, managed, and updated. Computer databases typically contain aggregations of data records or files. Such as sales transactions, product catalogue, inventories and customer profile. Database Manager provides users with the capabilities of controlling read or write access, to specify report generation and analyzing usage.

A Cloud database is a type of database service that is built, deployed and delivered through a cloud platform. It is primarily a cloud Platform as a Service (Pass) delivery model that allows an organization, end users and their applications to store, manage and retrieve data from the cloud. A cloud database typically works as a standard database solution that is generally implemented through the installation of

DOI: 10.4018/978-1-5225-2013-9.ch010

a database software on top of computing or infrastructure cloud. It may be directly accessed through a web browser or a vendor provided API for application and service integration. Unlike a typical database, a cloud database may be scaled at run time, in which additional resources of storage and computing may assign instantly. Moreover, a cloud database is also delivered as a service, where the vendor directly manages the back end processes of database installation deployment and resource assignment task.

LIMITATIONS OF TRADITIONAL DATABASE ARCHITECTURE

The two specific Areas where the traditional database architecture is particularly limiting is IO and Transaction management.

Let's start with IO. Bottom Line, there is simply too much of hit! The implicit disk synchronization requirements create bottlenecks. Given the constraints under which the original database architects worked, it was only natural for them to focus on maintaining strict data consistency through many of the locking and latching techniques. Despite recent advances in IO, these patterns simply no longer scale to meet today's demand patterns.

The limitation is transaction management. From the below data (Figure 1) it is clear that only 12% of the time goes for processing the data request. The remaining time is for managing the buffer, locks and the latches.

The information size has expanded enormously to the scope of petabytes—one petabyte = 1,024 terabytes. RDBMS thinks that it's testing to handle such enormous information volumes. To address this, RDBMS included more Central Processing Unit (or CPUs) or more memory to the database administration framework to scale up vertically. Most of the information arrives in a semi-organized or unstructured configuration from online networking, sound, video, messages, and messages. Be that as it may, the second issue identified by unstructured information is outside the domain of RDBMS because social databases can't sort unstructured information. They're outlined and organized to oblige organized information, for example, weblog sensor and budgetary information. Additionally, "huge information" is created at high speed. RDBMS needs in high speed since it's intended for relentless information maintenance as opposed to quick development. Regardless of the fact that RDBMS is utilized to handle and store "enormous information," it will end up being exceptionally costly. Subsequently, the failure of social databases to handle "huge information" prompted the development of innovations.

CLOUD DATABASE MANAGEMENT ARCHITECTURE

Five layered architecture for cloud database management is shown in Figure 2. The Five Layers are as follows:

1. External Layer
2. Conceptual Middleware Layer
3. Conceptual Layer
4. Physical Middleware Layer
5. Physical Layer

Figure 1. Percentage of computer cycles based on 3.5M samples

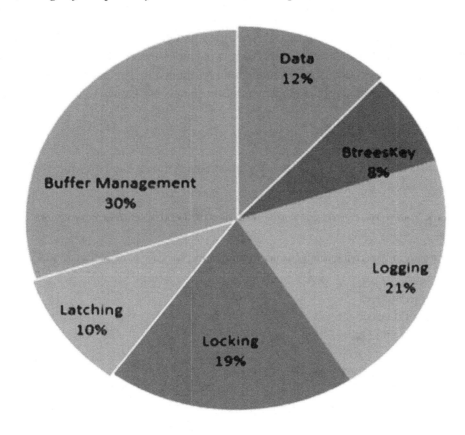

Figure 2. CDBMS

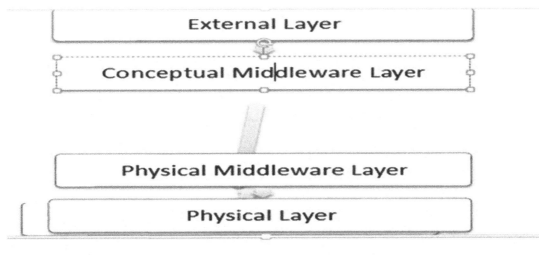

External Layer

External Layer manages various users. It records the time a particular user uses the CDBMS. Payment is based on this time only. It also creates the report for the payment history of the user and the use history of the user. Security is provided by using authentication mechanisms. The main function of this layer is providing transparency (i.e. the physical placement of the data is not known to the user).

Conceptual Middleware Layer

This layer hides the conceptual level heterogeneity among the different databases like SQL, db2, Oracle, MySQL, etc. as shown in Figure 3.

Conceptual Layer

The Conceptual Layer deals with

- Programming techniques
- Efficient Query Processing
- Query Processing and optimization

Physical Middleware Layer

This layer hides the heterogeneity across different platforms like Windows, Linux, and Mac OS.

Physical Layer

This layer is responsible for continuous monitoring and configuring the Database to achieve high scalability, high availability in the cloud. Various issues of this layer are given below:

Figure 3. Conceptual middleware layer

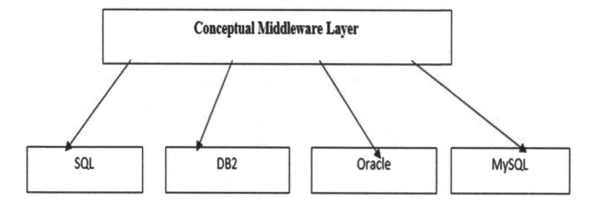

- **Backup and Replication:** Restoring and replication techniques should be used to avoid the data loss. Partitioning is used for balancing and sharing the load. Partitioning improves the scalability and availability.
- **Indexing:** Indexes must be created to the files which are stored in the database. Indexing helps to access the data easily.
- **Load Balancing:** It is a technique to move the load between the servers so that the hardware resources are utilized properly.
- **Fault Tolerant:** The system should have recovery techniques and the concurrency control techniques to handle the failures.
- **Security:** Security is provided by converting the data to unreadable format by using the encryption/decryption techniques.

CLOUD DATABASE DEPLOYMENT MODELS

There are two types of cloud database deployment models. The first type is that clients can run their databases on the cloud (i.e. using a virtual machine image). Another type is Purchasing database service access, maintained by a cloud database provider.

Cloud Database

A cloud database is a database that typically runs on a cloud computing platform.

A Recent study found that nearly one-third of organizations are currently using cloud database system. Cloud databases are mainly used in data mining, data warehousing and business intelligence. [Some of the cloud databases are relational databases (SQL). Postgre SQL, Microsoft SQL Server, NuoDB, Maria DB, MySQL, Oracle Database are relational databases which can run in the cloud. Apache Cassandra, Couch DB and Mongo DB, are another type of database (NoSQL) which can run on the cloud (Arora, 2012)

NoSQL database is more suited for cloud, because they can service heavy read/write loads and can be scaled up and down easily.

NOSQL Databases

NoSQL databases are non-structured databases in which each entity is considered as the independent unit of data. A NoSQL database is non-relational, horizontally scalable database without ACID guarantees. Data is stored as key-value pairs, which are written to the particular storage node(s), based on the hashed value of the primary key (Alam, 2013).

NoSQL database can store and retrieve:

- Unstructured Data,
- Semi-Structured Data, and
- Structured Data.

Implementations of NoSQL is classified as:

- Key-value store,
- Document store,
- Object store,
- Column store, and
- Graph store.

Data Models of NOSQL

Key-Value

Query speed is higher than the relational database. It supports high concurrency and mass storage. Simplest model among all. Using this model we can store data without the schema. Examples for key-value data model: Cassandra, Dynamo DB, Azure Table Storage (ATS), Riak, Berkeley DB.

Key-value databases are useful for storing session information, user profiles, preferences, shopping cart data. We would avoid using Key-value databases when we need to query data, have relationships between the data being stored or we need to operate on multiple keys at the same time.

Column-Store

The column-store data model is called as wide-column stores. It has high performance and highly scalable architecture. This model designed to store data table in the section of the column of data format instead of rows of data. Column families are groups of related data that are often accessed together. For a Customer, we would often access their Profile information at the same time, but not their Orders. Examples for Column-Store data model: HBase, Big Table and Hyper Table.

Column family databases are used for content management systems, blogging platforms, maintaining counters, expiring usage, heavy write volume such as log aggregation (Ramanathan, 2011). It would be better to avoid using column family databases for systems that are in early development, changing query patterns.

Graph-Store

Graph-store data model performs based on graph theory. This model suits for the application whose data can be easily represented as a graph and the elements of the graph are interconnected with undetermined number of relations between them. Examples for Graph-store data model: Neo4j and Titan.

Graph-store model well suited for the application which has problem spaces is interconnected data such as social networks, spatial data, routing information for goods and money, recommendation engines.

Document Database

Document database called as semi-structured data. It expands the concept of the key-value store. In this model, each document represented with the unique key, and we can easily retrieve the document using the key. It is used to store, retrieve and manage document-oriented information. Examples for Document Database Model: Mongo DB and Couch DB.

Document databases are useful for content management systems, blogging platforms, web analytics, real-time analytics, and e-commerce-applications (Peng, 2009). We would avoid using document databases for systems that need complex transactions spanning multiple operations or queries against varying aggregate structures

Comparison of NoSQL and RDBMS Databases

NoSQL

- Each entity is considered as the independent unit of data.
- Dynamically provisioned.
- Continuous Availability.
- Uses API to query the data.
- Structured, Semi/un structured Data.
- It is easy to scale.
- Simple transactions.
- Supports distributed architecture
- Decentralized application.
- Example: Web, mobile, IOT
- Amazon Simple DB, Couch DB, etc.

RDBMS

- Data in the database is treated as a whole.
- Statically Provisioned.
- Moderate to high availability.
- Uses SQL to query the data
- Structured Data.
- It is difficult to scale.
- Nested transactions.
- Supports centrally managed architecture
- Centralized applications. Example: ERP
- Example: Oracle, MySQL, SQL servers.

Features of NOSQL

- Reads and writes data quickly
- Easy to expand
- Supports mass storage
- Low cost

How to Implement NOSQL

How we would move to NoSQL from the RDBMS. There are three ways to implement the NoSQL database.

1. **New Applications:** When we start with new cloud application from the basis we can use NoSQL. This approach reduces the risk of data migrations, application rewrites, etc.
2. **Augmentation:** Some users choose to augment. This approach occurs when the user faces many problems in the applications due to the limitations of Relational databases.
3. **Full-Rip Replace:** The system becomes too costly to develop from the relational database perspective. To increases of user concurrency, data velocity, or data volume the whole system will replace by NoSQL.

Implementing a NoSQL Database at Your Organization

Regularly, associations will start with a substantial scale trial of a NoSQL database in their association, which gains it promising to ground a liberal of the innovation in a low-stakes way. Most NoSQL databases are likewise open-source, implying that they can be downloaded, executed and scaled at low cost. As you consider contrasting options to legacy foundations, you may have a few inspirations: to scale or perform past the abilities of your current framework, recognize reasonable other options to costly exclusive programming, while selecting the right database for your business and application, there are five critical measurements to consider (Cooper,2009).

Commonly Used NOSQL DB

Amazon Simple Storage Service (S3) and Databases

It is an internet-based storage service which stores up to 5GB of data along with 2KB of Meta data for each object. Buckets are used for organizing the objects and are identified by unique keys. Using REST/ SOAP interface, buckets and the objects are created. Amazon Simple Storage Service is a storage for the Internet. It is designed to make web-scale computing easier for developers. Amazon S3 has a pretentious web services interface that you can use to store and retrieve any amount of data, at any time, from anywhere on the web. It gives any designer access to the same exceptionally adaptable, dependable, quick, modest information stockpiling foundation that Amazon uses to run its particular worldwide system of sites. The administration plans to amplify advantages of scale and to pass those advantages on to engineers (Gonçalves2015). This controller explains the central concepts of Amazon S3, such as buckets and objects, and how to exertion with these resources using the Amazon S3 application programming interface (API).

Amazon Simple DB

Amazon Simple DB works closely with Amazon S3 and Amazon EC2 to provide the ability to store, process and query datasets in the cloud. It is highly available, scalable and non-relational data-store. It has a simple interface for Get, Post, Delete and Query to run the queries on structured data. It uses name-value-pair data model. It contains domains, fields, attributes, items and values. It allows the cells to contain multiple values per entry. Amazon Simple DB provides scalability by partitioning the work load across the multiple domains. Domains contain the items and the items are described by attribute-value pairs. It automatically manages indexing, performance tuning and replication.

Google App's Big Table

Google App's Big table is based on Google File System (GFS). It implements a replicating shared-nothing database. It is designed to handle heavy workloads at consistent low latency and high throughput. It handles millions of operations smoothly. Cloud Big table is an inadequately populated table that can scale to billions of lines and a large number of sections, permitting you to store terabytes or even petabytes of information. A solitary worth in every column is ordered; this quality is known as the line key. Cloud Big table is perfect for putting away a lot of single-keyed information with low idleness. It bolsters high read and composes throughput at low inertness, and it is a perfect information hotspot for Map-Reduce operations. Cloud Big table is presented to applications through numerous customers, including an up-held augmentation to the Apache HBase 1.x Java library. Accordingly, it incorporates with the current Apache biological community of open-source Big Data programming. Cloud Big table's capable back-end servers offer a few key preferences over a self-guided HBase establishment:

- **Incredible Scalability:** Cloud Big table scales in the direct extent to the quantity of machines in your group. A self-guided HBase establishment has a configuration bottleneck that restrains the execution after a specific QPS is come to. Cloud Big table does not have this bottleneck. Thus you can scale your bunch up to handle more inquiries by expanding your machine number.
- **Simple Administration:** Cloud Big table handles overhauls and restarts straightforwardly, and it naturally keeps up high information toughness. No all the more overseeing bosses, locales, nodes or hubs; you should simply outline your table mappings, and Cloud Big table will handle the rest for you.
- **The Cluster was Resizing Without Downtime:** You can build the extent of your Cloud Big Table bunch for a couple of hours to handle an expansive burden, then lessen the group's size once more all with no downtime. After you change a group's size, it commonly takes only a couple of minutes under burden for Cloud Big table to adjust execution over the greater nodes of the hubs in your hubs

Mongo DB

It is a document-oriented JSON database system. It supports dynamic schema design. This database uses document storage and data interchange format which provides a binary representation of JSON-like documents. Shading distributes the data in a collection across multiple systems for horizontal scalability.

Couch DB

It is a document-oriented database in which the documents are stored in JSON format. The documents are accessed through the HTTP interface. In Couch DB, views can be dynamically created by using JavaScript. Here scalability is achieved through asynchronous replication. It has the capability to serve as a self-contained application server and database. Couch DB is a database that totally grasps the web.

Store your information with JSON archives. Access your reports and inquiry your records with your web program, using HTTP. File, join, and change your archives with JavaScript. Couch DB functions admirably with cutting edge web and portable applications. You can even serve web applications specifically out of Couch DB. Furthermore, you can appropriate your information, or your applications, proficiently utilizing Couch DB's incremental replication. Couch DB bolsters expert setups with programmed strife identification. Couch DB accompanies a suite of components, for example, on-the-fly archive change and continuous change warnings, that makes web application improvement a breeze. It even accompanies a simple to utilize web organization console. You got it, served up specifically out of Couch DB. We think a considerable measure about circulated scaling. Couch DB is profoundly accessible and segment tolerant, but at the same time is in the long run steady. What's more, we think a considerable measure of your information. Couch DB has an issue tolerant capacity motor that puts the security of your information first.

Cassandra

Cassandra serves a large amount of data with high availability. It was developed to solve the inbox search storage problem. It is fault tolerant (i.e. the data in Cassandra is replicated on various nodes and spreads over various areas). So, that the data will be available even the node is down.

The Apache Cassandra database is the correct optimal when you need scalability and high availability without compromising performance. Linear scalability and proven fault-tolerance on commodity hardware or cloud infrastructure make it the perfect platform for mission-critical data Cassandra's support for replicating across multiple datacenters is best-in-class, providing lower latency for your users and the peace of mind of knowing that you can survive regional outages.

NEWSQL DATABASES

"NewSQL databases provides scalability and flexibility as in NoSQL while retaining the support for SQL queries and acid properties". NewSQL is a new database access language. It is easy, elegant, consistent, and well-defined. It is not an extension or subset of SQL, and not an Object database language. It is based on top of the cross-database library LDBC.

It is best for those enterprises interested in migrating existing applications to Big Data platforms, developing new applications on highly scalable online transaction processing systems, and wishing to use their existing knowledge of online transaction processing. NewSQL's focus appears to be on gaining performance and scalability for OLTP workload by supporting SQL as well as custom programming models(Doshi,2013).

NewSQL is a class of modern relational database management systems that seek to provide the same scalable performance of NoSQL systems for online transaction processing (OLTP) read-write workloads while still maintaining the ACID guarantees of a traditional database system.

Examples of NEWSQL Databases

Google Spanner, Clustrix, VoltDB, MemSQL, Pivotal's GemFire XD, SAP HANA, NuoDB, and Trafodion.

Features of NEWSQL Databases

- Uses SQL (structured query language) as a query language.
- Provides ACID support for the transactions.
- Has non-locking concurrency control Mechanism.
- Replication and Distributed Processing
- Dynamic Schemas
- Latency
- Transactional versus Analytic Applications
- Auto Sharing and Automatic Load Balancing:
- Integrated Caching

Comparison of NoSQL and NewSQL

NoSQL

- **DBMS Type:** Non-Relational
- **Schema:** Key-value, column store, document store.
- **Storage:** On disk + cache
- **OLTP:** Supported
- **Properties Support:** CAP through BASE
- **Query Complexity:** High
- **Horizontal Scalability:** Supported

NewSQL

- **DBMS Type:** Relational
- **Schema:** Table, Key-value, column store, document store.
- **Storage:** On disk + cache
- **OLTP:** Fully Supported
- **Properties Support:** ACID
- **Query Complexity:** Very High
- **Horizontal Scalability:** Supported

Common NEWSQL Databases

NuoDB

It divides data elements into software objects which are called as "atoms." It is built around a "durable distributed cache" design which uses a set of in-memory caches. In-memory caches support cloud-style elasticity and ensure that the data objects are safely stored. It also supports MVCC (multi-version concurrency control). MVCC is used for detecting data deadlocks and to resolve the access conflicts.

Clustrix DB

It is the matured NewSQL database used by the largest Internet websites for over three years. It was designed for large scale and fast-growing applications. It enables real-time analytics.

Clustrix DB handles massive data and transaction needs of application

- Without code changes
- Without replacing the database
- Without replacing hardware

Every node in the clustered database can receive the transaction and can process the transaction. It employs shared-nothing architecture (Marques,2006).

VoltDB

VoltDB is an in-memory SQL database. It combines streaming analytics with transaction processing. It is used to build applications that process streaming data. It delivers real-time transaction analytics and always produces correct results; it also enables the businesses to capture economic value.

NEWSQL Architecture

The three-tier model is divided into three layers namely:

- Administrative layer
- Transaction Layer
- Storage Layer

Transactional layer

This layer is responsible for:

- Atomicity
- Consistency
- Isolation

This layer is in memory. Hence it also acts as a caching layer.

Storage Layer

In this layer, durability is enforced. Even when there is a transactional miss, it provides access to the data. Durability is separate from the transaction processing. So that the failures can be handled independently.

Figure 4 Architecture of NewSQL database (NuoDB)

Administrative Layer

This layer supports on-demand scale out. Each host has management agent (local) and they form a peer-peer network. A collection of a connected host is called as the domain. Agents are responsible for the local host. Agents can also take the role of broker. Through brokers, databases can be migrated.

NuoDB provides a single, logical database view and scales across data centers. It also supports geographic distribution.

HYBRID DATABASES

Due to the growth of unstructured data, many companies are moving towards the NoSQL which can handle semi/un structured data in an efficient way. At the same time, most of the data is well defined in relational or perfectly relational. To rectify the gap between the two approaches, the hybrid database is used.

For example: If the Organization decides to use a particular database it may result in loss of data. For this problem, Hybrid Databases can be used.

Implementation

Hybrid Database, a piece of code which combines data from both relational and non-relational databases and final step would give the result. It serves as an abstraction layer on the top of SQL and NoSQL/NewSQL.

The features of abstraction layer:

- Retrieve required data from SQL and NoSQL databases.
- Combine the retrieved data from both database as a single query result.

Hence the result will be retrieved from the abstraction layer using a single query. The hybrid database acts as a common database with the help of the abstraction layer. Abstraction layer processes the user's query in a single step and returns the final result.

Disadvantages of Storing Data in Different Types of Databases

If the data is divided over SQL and NoSQL storage, uniform data access is hampered. There is no solution to bridge the gap.

CHALLENGES TO DEVELOP CLOUD DATABASE

1. Scalability
2. High Availability and Fault Tolerance
3. Heterogeneous Environment
4. Data Consistency and Integrity
5. Simplified Query Interface
6. Database Security and Privacy
7. Data Portability

Scalability

Resources should be dynamically scaled up/down. Developers must develop the database in such a way that a unlimited number of concurrent users should be supported by the database.

High Availability and Fault Tolerance

The database must run 365 days a year and 24 hours a day. Providing availability is one of the most challenging factors. Recovery techniques, deadlock detection techniques must be properly used to provide high availability.

Heterogeneous Environment

Providing support for accessing different applications from different locations using different devices like mobile phones, tablets and laptops are difficult.

Data Consistency and Integrity

Data integrity is the most critical requirement. Unexpected results or output will be produced due to the lack of integrity. It is difficult to manage the consistency if the update rate and request rates are too high.

Simplified Query Interface

Querying cloud databases is difficult since the query needs to access multiple nodes of the cloud database.

Data Security and Privacy

The risk is involved in storing the data on an un-trusted host. Hence data must be encrypted before uploading it to the cloud. The application should decrypt the data only at the time of data access.

Data Portability and Interoperability

Data portability can run the database components designed for a particular cloud provider in some other cloud provider. Cloud DB must have an interface with business intelligence tools.

Capacity Planning

"Capacity Planning is the process of predicting when future load levels will saturate the system and determining the most cost-effective way of delaying system saturation as much as possible". One of the main challenges in cloud computing is capacity planning. Capacity planning is adequately planning the resources, particularly virtual machines necessary to run the applications.

Cloud and Capacity Planning

Cloud computing offers much incredible flexibility and fantastic options compared to traditional computing and storage methods. Many cloud services operates with pay-as-you-go model which has no boundaries on usage or the capacity of the cloud. So here is the question is capacity planning is required in a cloud? The answer is "yes". Proper cloud capacity planning can reduce your budget and maximize the efficiency level.

One of the major advantages of cloud computing is the elastic usage of resources. Cloud has greater flexibility and lowers upfront cost, and we can easily and quickly purchase additional resources if required. Cloud has a possibility of elasticity, but it is up to the user to know how to use that power effectively.

Why Capacity Planning?

If capacity planning is not done, then at peak time the web pages may not be accessed by the users due to the heavy load. Figure 5 shows the connection reset problem.

Example: Consider at time T1; a thousand users are using the web application. Suddenly at time T2 ten thousand users are trying to access the web application. At this situation, if the capacity is not properly planned then the system may not be able to manage the sudden huge increase in the load. As a result, Connection reset problem occurs.

Another reason for capacity planning is cost. Proper capacity planning stops you from paying for resources that aren't being used effectively. Even though it seems fail-proof, in many cases the cloud is only cheaper when used properly. Pay-as-you-go services are fantastic but, they can be extremely expensive if you are paying for large amounts of capacity that are not being used. If we are implementing the cloud through a third-party vendor, it is necessary to have an understanding of the future usage needs. Another issue is the ability to properly managing the resources which we have acquired. While the cloud offers flexibility, it is extremely important to analyze the usage and plan accordingly. By analyzing company needs, cloud can save the company's IT budget and maximize the profit.

Figure 5 Connection reset problem

The connection was reset

The connection to the server was reset while the page was loading.

- The site could be temporarily unavailable or too busy. Try again in a few moments.
- If you are unable to load any pages, check your computer's network connection.
- If your computer or network is protected by a firewall or proxy, make sure that Firefox is permitted to access the Web.

Try Again

To Succeed in Capacity Planning

To succeed in capacity, planning requirements from the business must be known. Firstly business requirements must be analyzed. Secondly, understand the application needs. Then choose the hardware pattern. Thirdly identify how many machines are required. Finally, monitor to identify whether the growth is exceeding the current capacity.

Factors to Consider for Database Capacity Planning

- **Average Transaction Size:** To serve a transaction, how much of data does the system need?
- **Request Rate:** How many transactions are expected per second/minute/hour? Whether the demand is static or dynamic? For Example, in a search engine, 5-10 queries are expected over a period.
- **Update Rate:** It is a measure of how often the data is added, modified or deleted. If the update rate is high, then more priority should be given for database capacity planning.
- **Consistency:** How quickly an update spreads/reflects in the system? Consistency is a critical factor if the update rate is high. For Example, Social Networking Sites are expected to show the new comments immediately (i.e. within a second). Stock Trading system should reconcile in milliseconds.
- **Latency:** How quickly the transactions are expected to return the results (either success/ failure). The user will tolerate credit card transaction taking several milliseconds. But the user will not tolerate a web search taking few hundred milliseconds.
- **Computations:** What type of mathematical calculation is applied on the data? Whether the calculations are pre-computed and cached?

Capacity Planning in NOSQL (Cassandra) Database

Capacity planning is based on few factors such as row overhead, column overhead, indexes, transaction management, update rate, request rate, etc.

These factors are based on many parameters like some rows in the tables, some columns, the length of the primary key, etc. The capacity planning in the database is used for predicting the disk storage.

Steps to Predict Disk Storage

1. Determine the column overhead: Column overhead calculation: Column value size, column name size and 15 or 23 bytes are added depending on whether the column is expiring or not. A Non-Expiring column i.e. does not have time to live, takes fifteen bytes of overhead excluding the other factors. For Expiring column the overhead is twenty-three bytes.
2. Determine the row overhead: Row overhead calculation: In General, the overhead occurred in a row is 23 bytes. This overhead includes the indexes required for searching, cache for searching, etc. Hence 23 more bytes of disk space is needed to store the data (even the data is 3 or 4 bytes) in the row.
3. Calculate the size for the primary index of the table.
4. Add the calculated overheads and the indexes to the usable disk space.
5. Multiply with the replication factor: As the replication factor increases, the usable space for the disk also increases. For Example, if one node cluster has 50 GB of data, then a three node cluster requires 150GB of data approximately for the same amount of data.

Designing the Capacity Planning Model

1. The Cassandra Command Line Interface, obtain the column families.
2. Define the schema of the column families. Mention the data types, primary keys, expiring columns precisely.
3. Mention the number of rows for each of the column family.
4. Calculate the row and column overhead.
5. Determine the Bloom filter sizes: Formula for calculating Bloom Filter Sizes: Ceiling of ((# of rows * log (false-positive)) / log (1.0 / (POW (2.0, log (2.0)))))
6. Add the row overhead and the column overhead.
7. Usable disk space is calculated from the above step.
8. Calculate the index sizes and add it to the bloom filter size. Index size=rows*(10+average key size)
9. Add the sum obtained from step 6
10. Calculate the Format disk overhead.

The result obtained is the total space required for the deployment.

NOSQL vs. SQL Summary

Types

One type (SQL database) with minor variations. Many different types including key-value stores, document databases, wide-column stores, and graph databases.

Development History

Developed in the 1970s to deal with the first wave of data storage applications. Developed in the late 2000s to deal with limitations of SQL databases, especially scalability, multi-structured data, geo-distribution and agile development sprints (Doshi,2013)

Examples

MySQL, Postgre, Microsoft SQL Server, Oracle Database. SQL Example is Mongo DB, Cassandra, HBase, and Neo4j

Data Storage Model

Individual records (e.g., 'employees') are stored as rows in tables, with each column storing a specific piece of data about that record (e.g., 'manager,' 'date hired,' etc.), much like a spreadsheet. Related data is stored in separate tables, and then joined when more complex queries are executed. For example, 'offices' might be stored in one table, and 'employees' in another. When a user wants to find the work address of an employee, the database engine joins the 'employee' and 'office' tables together to get all the information necessary. For example, key-value stores function similarly to SQL databases, but have only two columns ('key' and 'value'), with more complex information sometimes stored as BLOBs within the 'value' columns. Document databases do away with the table-and-row model altogether, storing all relevant data together in single 'document' in JSON, XML, or another format, which can nest values hierarchically(Stahl,2013).

Schemas

Structure and data types are fixed in advance. To store information about a new data item, the entire database must be altered, during which time the database must be taken offline. Applications can add new fields on the fly, and unlike SQL table rows, dissimilar data can be stored together as necessary. For some databases (e.g., wide-column stores), it is somewhat more challenging to add new fields dynamically.

Scaling

Vertically, meaning a single server must be made increasingly powerful to deal with increased demand. It is possible to spread SQL databases over many servers, but significant additional engineering is generally required, and core relational features such as JOINs, referential integrity and transactions are typically lost. Horizontally, meaning that to add capacity, a database administrator can simply add more commodity servers or cloud instances. The database automatically spreads data across servers as necessary.

Development Model

Mix of open-source (e.g., Postgres, MySQL) and closed source (e.g., Oracle Database). Open-source

Supports Transactions

Yes, updates can be configured to complete entirely or not at all. In certain circumstances and at certain levels (e.g., document level vs. database level)

Data Manipulation

Specific language using Select, Insert, and Update statements, e.g. SELECT fields FROM table WHERE... Through object-oriented APIs.

Consistency

Can be configured for strong consistency. Some provide strong consistency (e.g., Mongo DB, with tunable consistency for reads) whereas others offer eventual consistency (e.g., Cassandra).

CONCLUSION

Thus, the chapter explored how the capacity can be planned for various types of cloud databases. This chapter deals with the different types of databases and their architecture. Factors affecting the capacity planning is also addressed. A capacity planning model for database and limitations of cloud database is also described.

REFERENCES

Lei, L., Sengupta, S., Pattanaik, T., & Gao, J. (2015, March). MCloudDB: A Mobile Cloud Database Service Framework. In *Mobile Cloud Computing, Services, and Engineering (MobileCloud), 2015 3rd IEEE International Conference on* (pp. 6-15). IEEE.

Chandra, Prakash, & Lamdharia. (2012). A study on Cloud database. *Bulletin of the IEEE Computer Society Technical Committee*. doi:10.1109/MobileCloud.2015.30

Ramanathan, S., Goel, S., & Alagumalai, S. (2011, December). Comparison of Cloud database: Amazon's SimpleDB and Google's Bigtable. In *Recent Trends in Information Systems (ReTIS), 2011 International Conference on* (pp. 165-168). IEEE.

Peng, B., Cui, B., & Li, X. (2009). Implementation Issues of A Cloud Computing Platform. *IEEE Data Eng. Bull., 32*(1), 59–66.

Cooper, B. F., Baldeschwieler, E., Fonseca, R., Kistler, J. J., Narayan, P. P. S., Neerdaels, C., & Stata, R. et al. (2009). Building a cloud for yahoo! *IEEE Data Eng. Bull., 32*(1), 36–43.

Alam, B., Doja, M. N., Alam, M., & Mongia, S. (2013). 5-Layered Architecture of Cloud Database Management System. *AASRI Procedia, 5*, 194–199. doi:10.1016/j.aasri.2013.10.078

Gonçalves, M., Cunha, M., Mendonça, N. C., & Sampaio, A. (2015, June). Performance inference: a novel approach for planning the capacity of IaaS cloud applications. In *2015 IEEE 8th International Conference on Cloud Computing* (pp. 813-820). IEEE. doi:10.1109/CLOUD.2015.112

Doshi, K. A., Zhong, T., Lu, Z., Tang, X., Lou, T., & Deng, G. (2013, October). Blending SQL and NewSQL approaches: reference architectures for enterprise big data challenges. In *Cyber-Enabled Distributed Computing and Knowledge Discovery (CyberC), 2013 International Conference on* (pp. 163-170). IEEE. doi:10.1109/CyberC.2013.34

Mahambre, S., Kulkarni, P., Bellur, U., Chafle, G., & Deshpande, D. (2012, October). Workload characterization for capacity planning and performance management in iaas cloud. In *Cloud Computing in Emerging Markets (CCEM), 2012 IEEE International Conference on* (pp. 1-7). IEEE. doi:10.1109/CCEM.2012.6354624

Lopes, R., Brasileiro, F., & Maciel, P. D. (2010, April). Business-driven capacity planning of a cloud-based it infrastructure for the execution of web applications. In *Parallel & Distributed Processing, Workshops and Phd Forum (IPDPSW), 2010 IEEE International Symposium on* (pp. 1-8). IEEE. doi:10.1109/IPDPSW.2010.5470726

Marques, F., Sauvé, J., & Moura, A. (2006, April). Business-oriented capacity planning of IT infrastructure to handle load surges. In *2006 IEEE/IFIP Network Operations and Management Symposium NOMS 2006* (pp. 1-4). IEEE. doi:10.1109/NOMS.2006.1687630

Liu, F., Makaroff, D., & Elnaffar, S. (2005, October). Classifying e-commerce workloads under dynamic caching. In *2005 IEEE International Conference on Systems, Man and Cybernetics* (Vol. 3, pp. 2819-2824). IEEE. doi:10.1109/ICSMC.2005.1571577

Usmani, Z., & Singh, S. (2016). A Survey of Virtual Machine Placement Techniques in a Cloud Data Center. *Procedia Computer Science*, 78, 491–498. doi:10.1016/j.procs.2016.02.093

Maurer, M., Brandic, I., & Sakellariou, R. (2013). Adaptive resource configuration for Cloud infrastructure management. *Future Generation Computer Systems*, 29(2), 472–487. doi:10.1016/j.future.2012.07.004

Stahl, E., Corona, A., De Gilio, F., Demuro, M., Dowling, A., Duijvestijn, L., & Mouleeswaran, C. (2013). *Performance and Capacity Themes for Cloud Computing*. Red Paper.

KEY TERMS AND DEFINITIONS

JSON: Stands for "JavaScript Object Notation". It is a language independent lightweight data interchange format.

Latch: A type of a lock which can be quickly acquired and released. It prevents more than one process executing the same code.

MVCC: (multi-version concurrency control):It is a concurrency control method used by DBMS.

REST: " Representational State Transfer (REST) is a style of architecture based on a set of principles that describe how networked resources are defined and addressed".

Sharing: It is a process of dividing a large database in to smaller parts.

SOAP: Stands for Simple Object Access protocol. Xml based protocol for exchanging information among the systems.

Update Rate: It is a measure of how often the data is added, modified or deleted. If the update rate is high then more priority should be given for database capacity planning.

Chapter 11
Security for Hybrid Mobile Development:
Challenges and Opportunities

Marcus Tanque
Independent Researcher, USA

ABSTRACT

In recent decades, vendors developed technology infrastructure solutions to integrate with enterprises and consumers' mobile devices. Hybrid development platforms are solution architecture designed to enhance developers' capabilities and provide organizations as well as customers the level of services to support mobile devices capabilities. Hybrid development platform solutions are easy to deploy at various enterprises. These capabilities can be distributed to/or integrated with mobile devices as agile applications and system interfaces. Hybrid mobile devices are designed to further provide users with enhanced technology solutions: cloud computing, big data, the Internet, physical and/or virtual network systems. The development of hybrid mobile platforms provides developers with advanced technology capabilities, necessary for supporting mobile devices once deployed to the marketplace. Technical and security features affecting the development and security of mobile devices are also discussed in this chapter.

INTRODUCTION

In recent years, vendors and information technology practitioners have researched on security solutions necessary, to prevent data breaches and protect user's privacy (Chess, & McGraw, 2004). For many years, mobile devices have been supported by a number of security applications. Thus technical constraints have contributed to organizations and consumer's confidence aimed at protecting user's privacy. Besides, homogeneity and heterogeneity capabilities for mobile devices are designed to support enterprises and consumer's requirements (Ubl, 2011; Rajapakse, 2008; Charland & LeRoux, 2011; Adam & Christ, 2011; Christ, 2011). In the modern time, the mobile industry has designed several technology product solutions to attract enterprises and consumers' business and market attention. Nearly a decade ago, vendors designed commodity hardware and software appliances with embedded capabilities to leverage

DOI: 10.4018/978-1-5225-2013-9.ch011

customer's specifications (Chess, & McGraw, 2004; Burns, 2009). These characteristics include, but are not limited to customized commodity hardware and software appliance, developed to satisfy the user's requirements (Ubl, 2011; Gartner, 2012; Mark, 2013). These features include: faster processing, improved memory and enough storage capacity designed to attract enterprises and consumers' business/market interests. The homogeneity and heterogeneity features mobile devices offer, focused on supporting the enterprises and consumer's business specifications (Fowler, & C. S., 2012; Burns, 2009; Christ, 2011).

BACKGROUND

For many years, securing mobile devices has been one of the challenging issues vendors and policy-makers have dealt with. This includes research on security solutions required, to address any gaps and/or challenges affecting the development of hybrid mobile devices (Thornycroft, 2016). Despite these efforts vendors such as Facebook have been skeptical, in complying with the federal laws, would put organizations/consumers' data protection and privacy policies at risk. Lacking these measures has raised greater concerns to federal and state legislators (Thornycroft, 2016; IBM, 2012). Aside from these policy disagreements between Apple and legislators, yet the U.S. government opted for an eccentric method also known as a "backdoor password solution". Apart from the U.S. government's decision vendors have expressed concerns on how federal laws, must be enforced without impacting on user's privacy. This comprises the development of mobile apps and how such laws must be applied to enterprises and consumers, who have existing contracts with various mobile carriers and providers (IBM, 2012). Despite any differences between Apple and the U.S. federal government, lawmakers vow to uphold the country's constitutional privileges such as national security's interests, and the protection of all citizens' rights. Vendors are confident any existing differences with the federal government must only be resolved through the implementation of suitable legislations to protect data and user's privacy. Apart from these progresses vendors such as Google are developing improved security solutions to protect subscribers' data and privacy. These security solutions are developed to afford users the ability to access and protect data stored on their mobile devices (Thornycroft, 2016; IBM, 2012). In recent years, vendors have developed improved encryption solutions to protect mobile devices, from being compromised by unauthorized personnel. These security tools are developed to protect data and user's privacy. Recently, Android and Apple deployed apps equipped with security capabilities for enterprises and consumers to have the ability to mask the Media Access Control (MAC) addresses stored on their mobile devices. Masking MAC address allows enterprises and consumers to limit any exploitation to mobile devices by unauthorized personnel i.e., attackers, hackers, intruders, via cyber domain sources (Thornycroft, 2016). These technology evolutions have afforded vendors the ability to anonymize requests made or generated from suspected sources, to users' mobile devices. Vendors argue that data and privacy are matters, which require improved security policies and procedures. In recent decade, the discovery of new cryptographic security solutions has significantly reduced the number of threats enterprises and consumers have always encountered from their adversaries (Thornycroft, 2016; Bloice & Wotawa, 2009). For that reason, IT managers and vendors must adopt new security measures to monitor, prevent, deny, moderate and reduce any threats launched against consumers' network resources (Fowler, & C. S., 2012; Chess & McGraw, 2004). Security for hybrid mobile development can be categorized into two different methods (Bloice & Wotawa, 2009; Dickson, 2012; Chess, & McGraw, 2004). These methods involve: single and multiple hybrid mobile development systems e.g., Apache Cordova. Cordova is an open source framework developed for mobile devices. This application structure was developed to guarantee mobile users, the access needed to standard-base web technologies i.e., HTML5, CSS3, JavaScript (Mark, 2013; Smutny, 2012; Ubl, 2011). These program apps are designed to separate data into small partitions or chunks when developing mobile platforms (Bloice & Wotawa, 2009; Gartner, 2012; Gavalas & Economou, 2010; Lyle & Monteleone, 2012; Fowler, & C. S., 2012; Thornycroft, 2016; Bloice & Wotawa, 2009).

MAIN FOCUS OF THE CHAPTER

In recent years, vendors have developed web application technologies such as Cordova, Xamarin, Ionic and React-native (Adam & Christ, 2011; Gavalas & Economou, 2010; Heitkötter, et al., 2012). These technologies are designed to perform as application programming interface modules needed for the day-to-day operations of mobile devices (Bloice & Wotawa, 2009; Heitkötter, et al., 2012). Such applications/systems are developed to provide vendors with standardized code-based capabilities required for developing integrated and hybrid mobile device solutions (Gavalas & Economou, 2010; Chess, & McGraw, 2004; Thornycroft, 2016). These code-based solutions/systems involve a wide range of applications i.e., *C#*, JavaScript programming languages (Fowler, & C. S., 2012; Chess, & McGraw, 2004; Mark, 2013; Smutny, 2012). These applications are also designed as versions of native code devices or systems required for replicating within mobile network environments (Bloice & Wotawa, 2009; Adam & Christ, 2011; Dickson, 2012; Fowler & C. S. T, 2012; Smutny, 2012; Mark, 2013; Christ, 2011). The lack of security solutions for protecting mobile devices has encouraged vendors to reassess existing processes and procedures needed, to prevent any system's vulnerability and emerging threats (Dickson, 2012; Lyle & Monteleone, 2012; Rajapakse, 2008). Such techniques are developed to deliver superior security features for supporting enterprises/consumers' data and privacy (Gavalas & Economou, 2010; Gartner, 2012). The need for adopting responsive security solutions is essential for balancing mobile applications and security solutions (Adam & Christ, 2011; Dickson, 2012; Chess, & McGraw, 2004). These solutions are critical for protecting enterprises and consumers' IT resources (Bloice & Wotawa, 2009; Adam & Christ, 2011; Lyle & Monteleone, 2012; Christ, 2011).

THE EVOLUTION AND TRENDS OF MOBILE DEVICES

Information technology/security experts and vendors view mobile devices: tablets, PDAs and smartphones as transforming high-tech systems designed with improved architecture and/or solution capabilities, to deliver sound performance (Heitkötter, et al., 2012; Rajapakse, 2008; Gartner, 2012; Heitkötter, et al., 2012). The adoption of tablets, smartphones and PDAs offers subscribers, key technology benefits (Bloice & Wotawa, 2009; Heitkötter et al., 2012; Gartner, 2012). Enterprises and consumers are extremely committed to deploy mobile solutions and apps designed to support their day to day business operations (Heitkötter, et al., 2012; Smutny, 2012). Hybrid apps such as *HTML5*, *CSS3* and *JavaScript* are designed for subscribers to integrate with mobile applications (Ubl, 2011; Mark, 2013; Andersson & Dan, 2012; Dickson, 2012; Gartner, 2012).

NATIVE, WEB AND HYBRID MOBILE APP SOLUTIONS

The implementation strategy of mobile devices and application solutions is complex and can be time consuming (Gartner, 2012; Bloice & Wotawa, 2009). Despite these strategies, vendors have adopted on consumers' specifications, identified issues affecting the development and/or security of mobile devices are paramount (Kaltofen, 2010). This phenomenon is a result of a lack of mechanisms for data protection and user's privacy (Fowler, & C. S., 2012). The developmental stage of mobile products such as apps, could be determined by the following classifications: native, web and hybrid ((Bloice & Wotawa, 2009; Fowler, & C. S., 2012; Fowler, & C. S., 2012). These segments are further categorized by the following controls: economics, project milestones, objectives, audience and app performance (Christ, 2011; Charland, & LeRoux, 2011; Bloice, & Wotawa, 2009). See Figure 1. Each production phase has its advantages and disadvantages (Kaltofen, 2010; Lakshman, & Thuijs, 2011; Bloice & Wotawa, 2009; Adam & Christ, 2011; Lyle & Monteleone, 2012; Fowler, & C. S., 2012). Figure 1 is a diagram which shows three different types of mobile apps development approaches: native, web and hybrid apps. First device from the left shows integrated characteristics of native apps; whereas the middle one describes the web apps; and finally the last one to the right illustrates the specifications for hybrid app configurations.

Native Apps

These apps consist of binary executable files. These apps can be downloaded directly from various vendor's web or Internet sources to mobile devices. The benefit of this process is that, once the download is complete the installation process begins allowing for mobile local repository/storage to processing its activities (Lakshman, & Thuijs, 2011). Mobile device users have the ability to install any of the selected apps/files onto the subscriber's device local drive (Bloice & Wotawa, 2009; Adam & Christ, 2011). Vendors encourage subscribers who are interested in downloading native apps, to visit their carrier's app stores for future inquiries (Fowler, & C. S., 2012; Burns, 2009). This process is only applicable for the following mobile applications: Apple's App Store, Android's Marketplace or Blackberry's App

Figure 1. Development methods for mobile apps (IBM, 2012)
Source: ftp://public.dhe.ibm.com/software/pdf/mobile-enterprise/WSW14182USEN.pdf

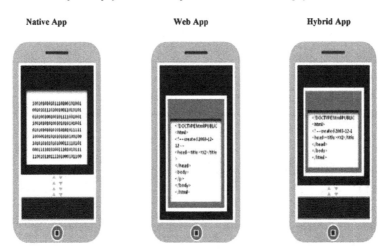

World. Mobile carriers have different perspectives on policies and procedures users must adhere to, when downloading apps from their respective websites. Vendors have developed apps allowing users to download on their mobile devices for free (Kaltofen, 2010; Ench, Ongtang, & McDaniel, 2009; Fowler, & C. S., 2012). Developers are required to write specific source code and compile for extractable binary programs. These source codes are developed to be integrated with the following application features: images, audio segments along with other OS specific declaration files stored on mobile devices (Kaltofen, 2010; Fowler, & C. S., 2012; Kapner, & Ziobro, 2014). Vendors are required to develop add-on and plug-in product application or specifications e.g., software development kit (Fowler, & C. S., 2012). Despite these technical parallels, the SDK provisions are different for each mobile device. Mobile OSs are equipped with their specific vendor's add-on and plug-in application tools (Kaltofen, 2010; Fowler, & C. S., 2012). Below is a list of add-on applications and/or tools which are commonly embedded into mobile devices: languages, formats and distribution channels (Lakshman & Thuijs, 2011). Every single mobile device is developed with add-on/plug-in application tools and capabilities. These tools/applications consist of: languages, operating systems, product names. Below is a list describing each of the mobile device's specifications (Kaltofen, 2010; Bloice & Wotawa, 2009; Adam & Christ, 2011; Fowler, & C. S., 2012):

- **Apple iOS:**
  - Languages
    - Objective-C, C++, Swift
  - Tools
    - Xcode
  - Packaging Format
    - . app
  - App Stores
    - Apple App Store
- **Android:**
  - Languages
    - Java (some C, C++)
  - Tools
    - Android SDK
  - Packaging Format
    - . apk
  - App Stores
    - Google Play
- **Blackberry OS:**
  - Languages
    - Java
  - Tools
    - BB Java Eclipse Plug-in
  - Packaging Format
    - . cod
  - App Stores
    - Blackberry App World

- **Windows Phone:**
  - Languages
    - C#, VB.Net
  - Tools
    - Visual Studio, Windows Phone Development Tools
  - Packaging Format
    - . xap
  - App Stores
    - Windows Phone Marketplace

BENEFITS AND LIMITATIONS

The three types of mobile apps discussed in this chapter are: native, web and hybrid. Each of these apps are epitomized by several operational benefits and limitations (Bloice & Wotawa, 2009; Christ, 2011; Lyle & Monteleone, 2012). The below list further describes the advantages and disadvantages each of the applications i.e., native, web and hybrid apps often provide to enterprises and/or consumers (Bloice & Wotawa, 2009; Adam & Christ, 2011; Dickson, 2012; Lyle & Monteleone, 2012; Christ, 2011):

- **Native App:**
  - **Benefits:**
    - Hybrid Graphical
    - App Store Distribution
    - Full Device Integration
  - **Limitations:**
    - No Portability
    - Platform Instability
    - Development Cost
    - Development Time
    - Maintenance Cost
    - Limited Control
- **Web App:**
  - **Benefits:**
    - Future Proof
    - Cross-platform
    - Low Development Cost
    - Simple Maintenance
    - Instant Updates
    - Complete Freedom
  - **Limitations:**
    - Moderate Device Integration
    - Limited Graphics
- **Hybrid App**
  - **Benefits:**

- Native Illustration e.g., look or feel (although native cost is not inclusive)
- App Store Distribution
- Full Device Integration
- Low Development Cost
  ○ **Limitations:**
    - Limited Graphs
    - Requires Familiarities with a Mobile Framework

CHALLENGES AND OPPORTUNITIES

According to the National Cybersecurity Center of Excellence (NCCE) developing mobile devices is a process, which requires vendors expertise as well as cooperation (Amatya & Kurti, 2014; Ramadath, 2012). Organizations and consumers deciding to adopt mobile devices, as platforms for supporting their day-to-day operations, must view security as a strategic factor aimed at determining threat levels affecting mobile platforms (Souppaya & Scarfone, 2013; Ramadath, 2012; Amatya & Kurti, 2014; Dickson, 2012; Fowler, & C. S., 2012; Howard, Pincus, & Wind, 2005; Bloice & Wotawa, 2009; Kaltofen, 2010). Organizations and consumers must determine whether any of these features are essential for providing: general policy; data-centricity communication and storage; user and device authentication or application features (Souppaya & Scarfone, 2013; Kaltofen, 2010). Granting these features are essential to day-to-day mobile devices performance, the following security characteristics are integral on how vendors could identify system security breaches: application functionality, managing solutions, loggings, system performance, authentication and protection (Souppaya & Scarfone, 2013; Kaltofen, 2010). Lacking these policies and procedures could result in major security concerns for mobile device vendors, enterprises and consumers (Fowler, & C. S., 2012). The lack of suitable security policies and/or procedures could undoubtedly allow unauthorized individuals: hackers, attackers or intruders, to gain utterly access to mobile devices (Gartner, 2012; Mark, 2013; Ramadath, 2012). Vendors have developed commercial-of-the-shelf applications and products to protect mobile devices (Amatya & Kurti, 2014; Dickson, 2012; Howard, Pincus, & Wind, 2005).

Challenges

Early studies pointed out that security solutions for hybrid mobile devices: smartphones, tablets, PDAs can be developed to provide appropriate policies and procedures to satisfy enterprises and consumer's needs (Ramadath, 2012; Mark, 2013; Gartner, 2012). Whereas recent industry survey has determined most consumers often lose/misplace mobile devices on a daily basis (IBM, 2012). As a result, any data stored on mobile devices could easily be compromised/ exposed to unauthorized personnel e.g., hackers, attackers and intruders. Despite this level of negligence that may involve various businesses or consumer, vendors have developed Enterprise Mobility Management (EMM) to mitigate, exploit, and prevent current/ emerging security breaches/vulnerabilities and/or emerging threats possibly launched against enterprise and consumers' mobile platforms. EMM was developed to inhibit unauthorized personnel from accessing enterprise applications stored on mobile devices (IBM, 2012). Secure mobile applications are developed with in-built features: password protection, encryption tools and software allowing vendors/carriers the ability to remotely sponge data stored on the mobile devices (IBM, 2012). In the corporate environment, system administrators are responsibility for taking on proper actions to guarantee that in the event any of mobile devices are lost, stolen or misplaced, the warehoused data can certainly be destroyed, before being access/compromised by unauthorized personnel (IBM, 2012). System administrators and security officers are also responsible for implementing policies/procedures designed for organization enterprise IT infrastructure. This process also ensures system administrators and security officers are able to centrally apply any techniques required for preventing system breaches/ spillages on the network. System administrators are responsible for centrally managing and configuring every mobile device synchronized with the server. This allows for computerized provisioning of mobile devices and servers to take place on the network (IBM, 2012). The process can be accomplished by programming any mobile device to synchronize its activities on the network in associate with application programming interfaces (APIs). System administrators are also responsible for ensuring all security/access controls are up-to-date by verifying any information being provisioned between mobile devices and servers is encrypted (IBM, 2012). Commonly organizations opt for virtual private network tunneling over SSL/HTTPS solutions with end-to-end authentication capabilities required to protect any flow of information (IBM, 2012).

Opportunities

Vendors have developed enhanced security solutions such as cryptographic algorithms to protect, prevent, mitigate and neutralize internal/external current or imminent threats affecting mobile network infrastructure solutions (Bloice & Wotawa, 2009; Dickson, 2012; Ramadath, 2012; Souppaya & Scarfone, 2013; Ballages, Rohs, Sheridan, & Borchers, 2008). The configuration of security features for hybrid mobile devices is required to preserve IT resources (Bloice & Wotawa, 2009; Dickson, 2012; Kaltofen, Milrad, & Kurti, 2010). The following are embedded features mobile devices must be equipped with when deployed to marketspace: display and interaction of application settings users would require (Bloice & Wotawa, 2009; Lakshman, & Thuijs, 2011; Burns, 2009). Enterprise and consumers have the ability to download user-friendly native apps with improved performance (Bloice & Wotawa, 2009; Ramadath, 2012; Ballages, Rohs, Sheridan, & Borchers, 2008; Souppaya & Scarfone, 2013; Thornycroft, 2016; Kaltofen, 2010). To prevent any spillages on corporate network, system administrators are responsible for arbitrarily conducting vulnerability scans, to ensure security patches are up-to-date e.g., checking for malwares, which could be embedded in mobile devices (IBM, 2012). Vendors are convinced that the integration of traditional solutions i.e., hardware and software applications is essential to the adoption of next-generation mobile devices (Bloice & Wotawa, 2009; Fowler, & C. S., 2012; Burns, 2009; Souppaya & Scarfone, 2013; Kaltofen, 2010). Lacking cryptographic security solutions, e.g., crypto algorithms, end-to-end encryption and protective security solutions are vital for protecting mobile devices. Thereby vendors must develop enhanced/agile cryptographic security solutions to protect mobile devices. These methods are often designed to provide end-to-end data encryption/protection amid mobile devices and network infrastructure solutions. Improved security features on mobile devices are needed minimize vulnerabilities or threats (Souppaya & Scarfone, 2013; Kaltofen, 2010).

ENTERPRISE MOBILE SECURITY

Vendors adopted the term 'mobile security' to analyze, exploit and mitigate any security vulnerabilities and/or emerging threats, affecting mobile platforms as well as wireless network infrastructure solutions

(Lakshman, & Thuijs, 2011; Livshits, & Larn, 2005; Howard, Pincus, & Wind, 2005; Ballages, Rohs, Sheridan, & Borchers, 2008; Kaltofen, 2010; Fowler, & C. S., 2012). Early studies underlined the term mobile security was firstly defined as wireless security solution. The nomenclature "mobile security" involves the following classifications (Zhu, Xiong, Ge, & Chen, 2014; Ballages, Rohs, Sheridan, & Borchers, 2008; Lakshman, & Thuijs, 2011; Bloice & Wotawa, 2009; Howard, Pincus, & Wind, 2005; Kaltofen, 2010):

- **Security of Mobile Devices:** A solution designed to guarantee the protection of enterprises and customers' mobile devices. The protection of security mobile systems is due to the increased presence of unauthorized personnel attempting to gain access to the network infrastructure solutions
- **Application Security:** Vendors view application security as one of the most ranked concerns in the adoption of mobile devices. The need for accessing more data sources on the mobile devices is observed as significant shift vendors must be concerned with when developing solutions required to synchronize their product with the next generation of wireless technology
- **IT Consumerization:** Despite these progresses mobile developers made in recent years, improved measures are being implemented to protect organizations data and user's privacy. As such, vendors argue that security will always be their main priority. Early researches concluded that vendors built advanced security solutions to deter, protect and mitigate any current/imminent threats.
- **Data Breaches:** A process that describes how hackers can simply gain access for protecting, sensitive / confidential data. Attackers are capable of exploiting mobile devices i.e., laptop, smartphones related wireless systems, to extract/steal any data stored in these systems. The personal health information, personal identifiable information and trade secrets and/or intellectual property is a factual example of data breaches. Individuals who are not authorized to access data stored in single/multiple devices opt for attacking network infrastructure solutions, where the data is stored. In present days, vendors have developed and improved security measures required to protect mobile devices. These applications are used to identify, prevent, mitigate, repudiate, and exploit any unauthorized access
- **Geolocation:** A process for identifying a wide range of geographic locations. Identifying these geographic locations can be supported by diverse technology layers. Radars, mobile devices and the Internet are common platforms designed to interface with geolocation systems in real-time. Enterprise, private citizens and any related research institutions frequently relies on geolocation methods to access, share and provision data among partners and stakeholders for future research
- **Cybercriminals:** Cybercriminals are progressively motivated by security issues affecting IT platforms and infrastructure. Increased information breaches on mobile systems are key resources for cybercriminals
- **Malware Attacks:** These type of attacks generally occurs on mobile devices/wireless systems. Hackers develop malware security solutions, which could be used to gain access to IT network infrastructure solutions/mobile platforms. Malware is software designed for hackers to gain access to single/multiple mobile systems. In recent years, vendors have developed the following types of malware: spyware, key loggers, true viruses, adware, scareware, Trojan horses, ransomware and worms. These malware applications can be cascaded to a modest or complex programing codes, then injected to mobile devices, computers and/or other type of wireless systems connected to the network via the Internet

- **Smartphone Thefts:** The theft of smartphones is on the rise, though some argue that in recent years such trends have reduced. Vendors are convinced that such decrease is conceivable to revised laws and policies the government has implemented for data protection and user's privacy. Aside from these trends employees and consumers are similarly responsible for protecting their mobile devices. The need for stronger password policies e.g., combination on smartphones can be an encouraging measure toward protecting mobile platforms.

Numerous market researchers have concluded that the development of mobile applications and/or solutions still a complex process to adopt. Vendors are researching on best practices to improve such a process (Kaltofen, 2010; Howard, Pincus, & Wind, 2005; Kaltofen, 2010). Mobile solutions are designed to interface with traditional/advanced platforms and network infrastructure systems (Kaltofen, 2010). The concept is not always easy to apply, due to the lack of IT expertise and/or resources required to support enterprises and consumer's requirements (Kaltofen, Milrad, & Kurti, 2010; Kaltofen, 2010). Vendors are responsible for developing cross-platforms and frameworks for mobile applications (Kaltofen, Milrad, & Kurti, 2010; Howard, Pincus, & Wind, 2005; Ballages, Rohs, Sheridan, & Borchers, 2008; Kaltofen, 2010).

Security Properties

The adoption of new IT security platforms and infrastructures is vital to the functionality, scalability and sustainability of hybrid mobile devices (Gartner, 2012). Mobile web apps are built with an integrated security layer (Ballages, Rohs, Sheridan, & Borchers, 2008; Howard, Pincus, & Wind, 2005). This security layer can be found on smartphones and tablet browser engines. In mobile devices and tablets the defense-in-depth security layer is often found in the back-end surface of the device. The layer is also designed to support application services, stored in the content delivery of mobile devices (Kaltofen, 2010; Howard, Pincus, & Wind, 2005; Kaltofen, 2010). The purpose of these activities is to establish an interface baseline with a micro app serving as entry points and/or gateways to web property(ies). Web properties consist of the traditional websites, web applications designed to interact with cloud, enterprise and software-as-a-service apps as well as backend mobile app interfaces. Mobile web properties encompass the following technologies: simple HTML and HTTP, web service definition language and eXtensible markup language/XML based interface (Lakshman, & Thuijs, 2011; Ballages, Rohs, Sheridan, & Borchers, 2008).

In supply chain management, web properties are regarded as integrated components designed to launch shared validation for securing socket layer/SSL (Kaltofen, 2010). Such security concept is designed to provide reliable interface with various APIs. Below is a diagram of mobile web properties (Kaltofen, 2010; Fowler, & C. S., 2012; Christ, 2011; Howard, Pincus, & Wind, 2005; Kaltofen, 2010):

- XML Weather Data
  - Weather Sensors and Stations
- Private, Public and Government Sources
  - Web Applications
- Weather App on Device Image
- NetScaler Web Optimization
- Social Media Links

- ○ Flickr
- ○ Facebook
- ○ Twitter

Even though enterprises and consumers adopt these solutions, privacy, data and location services must be respected all the time. These features are only provided through approved vendor's applications often procured by enterprises and consumers (Kaltofen, 2010; Fowler, & C. S., 2012). Nonetheless SSL and virtual private network capabilities are integrated in mobile devices, to provide extra security defense layer (Howard, Pincus, & Wind, 2005). Adequate functionality of these security layers often could be validated through a configuration of allocated applications generally known by the user (Kaltofen, 2010; Fowler, & C. S., 2012; Burns, 2009; Christ, 2011). Virtually a decade ago, Citrix launched WorxMail software designed to manage security of mobile enterprise and email application. As part of the dedicated security solutions, Citrix also developed XenMobile (Fowler, & C. S., 2012; Christ, 2011). This solution was designed to provide enterprises and consumers with improved security solutions: policy and provisioning controlled features (Kaltofen, 2010). On the gateway secure console, NetScaler is in the main deployed to provide micro VPN and WorxWeb and single sign-on/SSO access solutions. These solutions provide mobile devices the capability needed to interface with other enterprise managed web and software-as-a-service apps. The process of integrating web and native mobile technologies can easily generate other security issues: XSS/cross-site scripting types of attacks (Ballages, Rohs, Sheridan, & Borchers, 2008). Gaining access to a mobile system its via XSS, attackers could successfully bypass any existing access controls (Kaltofen, 2010; Fowler, & C. S., 2012). The security gap often allows attackers to conduct a code injection via web application, which could result of obstructive scenarios where intruders are able to arbitrarily launch malicious code(s) to a single or many mobile systems. Generally, the code injection is diffused in a form of a browser side script to protected websites (Kaltofen, 2010; Fowler, & C. S., 2012; Burns, 2009).

Firewalls for Mobile Devices

On mobile devices, the process of monitoring, regulating and complying with other security enabled practices/procedures is crucial for data protection and user's privacy. Mobile devices are designed with integrated web app firewalls (Bloice & Wotawa, 2009; Cheswick, Bellovin, & Rubin, 2003). NetScaler is a type of gateway or controller designed to reserve active content and session information (Cheswick, Bellovin, & Rubin, 2003; Burns, 2009). This key solution is also built to inhibit any pervasive threats, such as those launched from SQL injection and cross-site scripting attacks that could certainly influence the performance of enterprise mobile devices (Kaltofen, 2010; Ballages, Rohs, Sheridan, & Borchers, 2008; Bloice & Wotawa, 2009). These mechanisms are developed using private key modules. Such methods can only be managed through a small TCB - Trusted Computing Base (Howard, Pincus, & Wind, 2005; Cheswick, Bellovin, & Rubin, 2003). By and large private keys are held in a very inclusive storage area. These mechanisms are designed to transfer data to software module located on various mobile devices (Kaltofen, 2010; Howard, Pincus, & Wind, 2005; Burns, 2009). The tools are developed to protect mobile data and user's privacy (Howard, Pincus, & Wind, 2005). Each module is also assigned an encryption key required to generate or provide remote verification for single/multiple mobile devices (Burns, 2009). Mobile devices have the capability to send and receive encrypted information (Burns, 2009). This is attributable to sustained efforts vendors have made in developing robust security features for mobile devices (Kaltofen, 2010; Howard, Pincus, & Wind, 2005; Burns, 2009; Adam & Christ, 2011; Christ, 2011). These characteristics consist of (Bloice & Wotawa, 2009; Heitkötter, et al., 2012; Gartner, 2012):

- **Confidentiality:** A solution that provides mobile security applications with the capability needed for securing enterprises data and user's privacy. This feature is essentially designed to protect data being provisioned from various server applications to a single and/or mobile devices
- **Authentication:** Deployed applications are designed to authenticate employees and consumers' identity. This includes the adoption of enhanced mobile security controls required to provide enterprises and users with the capabilities needed to protect their mobile devices
- **Authorization:** A process designed to ensure mobile security applications are designed to protect consumer's information
- **Non-Repudiation:** A mobile security application/solution designed to maintain data integrity e.g., records events

Vendors accept that mobile core system applications are as complex as desktop operating applications (Howard, Pincus, & Wind, 2005). Whereas sandbox solution applications are developed to provide open source mobile software requests: Apple iOS jail-breaker can easily be compromised (Livshits, & Larn, 2005; Howard, Pincus, & Wind, 2005; Howard, Pincus, & Wind, 2005; Kaltofen, 2010). This process can be executed by a single click of a button affording web pages the ability to instantly react to all translated commands within the operating system. Mobile devices are designed to share scripting codes with open source OSs: GNU/Linux (Howard, Pincus, & Wind, 2005; Livshits, & Larn, 2005).

Original equipment manufacturer/OEM comprises the following items i.e., handset manufacturer, telecommunications benefactors/carriers, application designers, the device's proprietor as well as consumers (Kaltofen, 2010; Burns, 2009). In mobile devices these vendors or stakeholders e.g., carriers are responsible for the integration of platforms and customization of OEM handsets developed for interacting with other features e.g. firmware or custom applications (Kaltofen, 2010; Howard, Pincus, & Wind, 2005; Adam & Christ, 2011).

In present days, mobile devices are designed with improved security features to deter and attackers from accessing the network infrastructure systems. Google Wallet is an application designed to retain user's payment credentials (Howard, Pincus, & Wind, 2005). Many third party vendors have partnered with Google to develop a solution called Google Wallet. Thus Google also developed this application to provide consumers with the ability to configure their mobile devices and ensure these system act as a cybernetic wallet (Howard, Pincus, & Wind, 2005; Kaltofen, 2010). Mobile credentials are converted into contacts being processed via the Near Field Communication (NFC). NFC is a trusted protocol paired with point of sale (POS) devices. In order for the user's credentials to be stored securely, a coprocessor is assigned to Google Wallet to preserve all transactions (Howard, Pincus, & Wind, 2005). For successful completion of this transaction, Google Wallet must interface with secure element (SE). This application is also designed to interact with the secure storage and trusted path via the onboard NFC radio (Kaltofen, 2010; Howard, Pincus, & Wind, 2005; Burns, 2009).

Privacy

Vendors develop apps and/or related security solutions, to prevent existing/emerging threats from affecting mobile devices (Howard, Pincus, & Wind, 2005; Barker, Barker, Burr, Polk, & Smid, 2006). More security apps and mobile solutions are developed to prevent any changes on built-in applications stored in the operating system. This process can be initiated by using safer programing languages or sandboxing software appliances from third party apps (Barker, Barker, Burr, Polk, & Smid, 2006). As such, mechanism frequently can pose major challenges for mobile devices users as well as wireless network infrastructure systems (Howard, Pincus, & Wind, 2005; Livshits, & Larn, 2005; Burns, 2009). As a result of increased number of users: the number of employees and consumers, who own mobile devices has increased over the past decade (Burns, 2009). Lacking security best practices to protect mobile devices could result in continuous data breaches, loss of information i.e., individual/corporate contacts, calendar and possibly consumers and C-level executives' physical locations, which could easily put the user in a very precarious position (Burns, 2009; Barker, Barker, Burr, Polk, & Smid, 2006).

MANAGING MOBILE DEVICES

In recent years, vendors have developed mechanisms for securing mobile devices e.g., server's management capabilities, the use of commercial-of-the-shelf/COTS vendor's product and open source solutions. The need for adopting proper policies to address a range of critical issues affecting mobile devices is key to enhanced security measures (Souppaya & Scarfone, 2013; Souppaya & Scarfone, 2013; Kaltofen, 2010; Kaltofen, 2010). Managing mobile devices is a challenging responsibility Internet service providers, vendors, carriers and the general public "consumers" must continuously deal with. According to a vendor's recent survey the rapid shift in technology and new mobile apps gave developers to research on major issues affecting the performance of these systems once deployed to marketspace (Souppaya & Scarfone, 2013; Kaltofen, 2010). The adoption of wireless solutions ensures that all centralized mobile technologies are developed to mitigate any security challenges affecting organization and consumers (Souppaya & Scarfone, 2013; Kaltofen, 2010).

MOBILE DEVICE MODELING AND PLANNING

As part of mobile prototype, design and concept solutions, heterogeneity is a process developed to interact with development solutions: these processes do not draw parallelism with homogeneous solutions (Gartner, 2012; Burns, 2009; Kaltofen, Milrad, & Kurti, 2010). Due to these unique differentiators, the prices for mobile devices have increased significantly (Kaltofen, Milrad, & Kurti, 2010; Lakshman, & Thuijs, 2011). Lacking vendor's platform solutions and infrastructure capabilities is a major factor for degradation of mobile solutions in the enterprise (Kaltofen, 2010). These solutions are not always designed to satisfy neither the platform nor infrastructure capabilities (Gartner, 2012; Mark, 2013; Kaltofen, Milrad, & Kurti, 2010).

ENTERPRISE MOBILITY MANAGEMENT

Vendors describe Enterprise Mobility Management (EMM) a foundation stone of mobile devices operations. EMM consists of processes, consumers and technology fundamentals performing on mobile devices (IBM, 2012). These core areas in the telecommunications' domains are fundamental for determining how mobile devices and wireless network infrastructure systems frequently interface. The interoperability features of these mobile devices are designed to further guarantee that portable devices, for instance wireless systems and mobile computers can interface and share data, voice as well as video capabilities without any single point of failure. As a result of these technological evolutions, organizations and consumers can now synchronize their devices from anywhere at any time. These innovations allow most users to be reached via their handheld devices and offering them the option to execute any enterprise related activities from anywhere in the globe on condition that there is Internet/network services e.g., Wi-Fi, hotspot or any other types of connectivity, which consumers can lease from Internet Service Provider or carriers. Hybrid development solutions are part of the improved mobile device process (Mark, 2013; Kaltofen, Milrad, & Kurti, 2010; Charland & LeRoux, 2011; Mark, 2013; Gartner, 2012; Mark, 2013; Charland & LeRoux, 2011; Adam & Christ, 2011). Such systems are also designed to supplement the daily operations of mobile devices (Adam & Christ, 2011). Improved security standards e.g., best practices are discussed in this chapter, as prerequisite solutions for supporting the development of hybrid mobile devices. In this chapter other methods and techniques are explored (Charland & LeRoux, 2011; Adam & Christ, 2011; Barker, Barker, Burr, Polk, & Smid, 2006; Gartner, 2012; Mark, 2013; Charland & LeRoux, 2011; Adam & Christ, 2011; Souppaya & Scarfone, 2013; Kaltofen, 2010).

Asynchronous JavaScript and XML

The Asynchronous JavaScript and XML ("*AJAX*") is a technology used to support the synchronization between web-servers'/web pages and mobile devices. AJAX is a technology designed to interact with mobile solutions. The technology is also developed to simplify data alterations and updates on webpages without having to reload/resubmit a single or multiple new requests for the page to load. The following are characteristics that best describe the AJAX technology functions (Kaltofen, Milrad, & Kurti, 2010; jQuery Home Page, 2013):

- **Asynchronous:** A process through which web server responses are not submitted instantly. This method is different from the one performed whenever web pages are loaded. Vendors developed this feature to guarantee for a time delay between server response and reloading of web pages
- **JavaScript:** A client-side language used to initiate server requests. This process also guarantees that any request(s) made to the web server is/are seemingly dealt upon for consistency. JavaScript features are proven to be essential tools for the development and performance of mobile devices
- **XML:** eXtensible Markup Language is a format responsible for translating data between JavaScript and the web server

Asynchronous JavaScript and eXtensible Markup Language are unique terms vendors have developed to support any activities to be executed on webpages (Kaltofen, Milrad, & Kurti, 2010). This process is called dynamic concept that developers and vendors commonly upload to the servers by submitting new posts, purge users, etc. Activities can be executed without user's intervention on the link requested to be reloaded to a new page. Generally, developers describe AJAX as a dualistic model which consists of: JavaScript features designed to process requests to the web server (Kaltofen, Milrad, & Kurti, 2010; jQuery Home Page, 2013; Kaltofen, Milrad, & Kurti, 2010). This includes the dynamic page designed to accept requests, then processing as an output (Barker, Barker, Burr, Polk, & Smid, 2006). The following are programming languages developed to support dynamic requests: Hypertext Processor/PHP scripts, Microsoft active server pages/ASP, Ruby on Rails, *C++* or other related languages which could be running on webservers (Kaltofen, Milrad, & Kurti, 2010; jQuery Home Page, 2013).

APPLICATION PROGRAMMING INTERFACES

For many decades the Application Programming Interfaces (APIs) transformed the development of mobile device. The evolution of handheld devices consists of the Mobile First Approach (MFA) strategy and the API methods. In part, MFA strategy is developed to provide vendors the capabilities needed for designing websites/product applications to support Apple iOS (Bloice, & Wotawa, 2009; Fowler, & C. S., 2012). Such method can only be found in the United States market particularly built for Android product specifications (Bloice, & Wotawa, 2009; Fowler, & C. S., 2012). Aside from these technological trends, vendors argue that the final product of mobile development often can be sold in the U.S. and in Europe to fulfill consumer's demands. By and large, API first method was designed to support the development of API applications (Bloice, & Wotawa, 2009; Fowler, & C. S., 2012; Riggins, 2015; Riggins, 2015). This solution paradigm, allows vendors to deploy and manage the entire mobile lifecycle from a single framework. Developers rely on API backend as a Service (BaaS) to complete the any assigned task (Bloice, & Wotawa, 2009; Fowler, & C. S., 2012). By using BaaS model vendors are able to forecast the overall developmental lifecycle allowing for greater cost-savings. While using BaaS/MBaaS, developers often can establish a unified session between mobile devices and the back-end cloud storage (Bloice, & Wotawa, 2009; Fowler, & C. S., 2012). The link is also established to send out notifications, data and messaging queues between mobile devices and back-end cloud based storage systems (Riggins, 2015). The session also allows administrator to monitor, configure and integrate technology solutions. Most vendors view API backend as an integrated platform designed to deliver mobile products on time and under budget (Bloice, & Wotawa, 2009; Fowler, & C. S., 2012; Riggins, 2015). The benefits Baas/MBaaS afford both subscribers and developers the following benefits: elimination of redundant stack setup for apps, elimination of boilerplate code and the ability to integrate mobile applications using a unified model. The diagramin Figure 2 describes BaaS/MBaaS and cloud-based customer mobile architecture. Figure 2 is incorporated to provide a brief illustration of components, subcomponents as well as the relationship between each component (Barcia, Berardi, Kak, Kreger, & Schalk, 2015).

After user's effective installation of native app, immediately the system begins processing separable application stored on mobile devices. Consequently, an interactive function between the mobile device's OS and API applications is launched (Bloice, & Wotawa, 2009; Fowler, & C. S., 2012). This gives the APIs, the leverage to translate any tasks required for interacting with the OS operation. The provisioning process between OS and API consists of multiple sessions: low-level APIs and high-level APIs (Bloice, & Wotawa, 2009; Kaltofen, 2010; Fowler, & C. S., 2012):

- **Low-Level APIs:** APIs are developed to directly interface with the mobile device's touchscreen and/or keyboard features. This process also is designed to render graphical activities as well as connecting mobile devices to various networks such as processing audio activities received through the microphone, play sounds via the speaker/headphones (Bloice, & Wotawa, 2009). In this process, images and videos are projected through a fixed camera installed on the mobile device (Kaltofen, 2010; Fowler, & C. S., 2012). Once the session is activated, mobile applications are launched in real-time to support the functionality of these wireless systems. Low APIs are equipped with an integrated capability, to access the global positioning system, capturing any positioning data, read or write files to the solid-state disk (Fowler, & C. S., 2012). This includes, hardware utilities, which are made available for the consumer's immediate or future use

- **High-Level APIs:** Developed to interface with the low-level hardware access/ services. Vendors develop mobile OSs to interface other services being rendered by high-level APIs (Bloice, & Wotawa, 2009). These services involve application interfaces such as browser, web, calendar, contacts and photo applications. High-level APIs also provide consumer with the ability to generate and receive phone calls as well as text messaging (Bloice & Wotawa, 2009). Mobile devices are also built to support extra set of high-level APIs. Whereas native apps are designed with a set of high-level APIs. Vendors develop APIs to support various apps installed on mobile devices (Kaltofen, 2010; Fowler, & C. S., 2012; Burns, 2009)

Figure 2. Back-end as a service topology (Barcia et al., 2015)
Source: http://www.cloud-council.org/deliverables/CSCC-Cloud-Customer-Architecture-for-Mobile.pdf

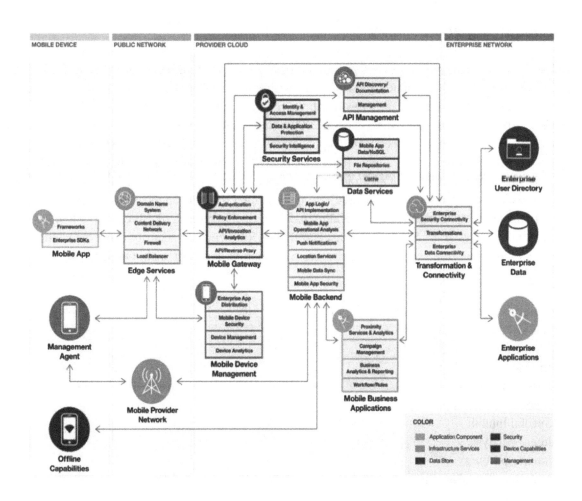

Android Application Development

The development of android apps is one of the key areas vendors have benefited from for many years (Burns, 2009). Early mobile devices had limited capabilities to support carriers' services or meet enterprises and consumers' requirements. In recent years, vendors have considered other development strategies to improve the functionality of mobile applications (Ench, Ongtang, & McDaniel, 2009). These capabilities involved: e-mail, pictures, mp3 files, and extra applications needed to interact with mobile operating system. Currently, there are nearly 1.2. billion mobile phones being used by many consumers (Fowler, & C. S., 2012; Burns, 2009). Apart from this surveyed number, in the world 14% percent of smartphone accounts, approximately 170 million subscribers are in use (Ballages, Rohs, Sheridan, & Borchers, 2008). In recent years, there has been a higher demand of mobile devices, services and new apps (Burns, 2009). These indices have prompted vendors to develop newer mobile development solutions: Java ME, Symbian (e.g., UIQ and S60), Android, Blackberry, OVI, Windows mobile, iPhone, LiMo, Angstrom distribution, Adobe flash light, BREW, OpenMoko, Plam OS (i.e., Garnet OS, Cobalt OS, Palm webOS (Mojo) et cetera. These mobile solutions are designed to interface with other vendors' wireless platforms (Kaltofen, 2010; Ench, Ongtang, & McDaniel, 2009; Burns, 2009).

Android Privacy and Security

Developing and securing mobile devices e.g., Android platforms is a complex process (Chess, & McGraw, 2004). Although most smartphones are developed with integrated security features, instead, Android devices are customized to meet user's specifications (Fowler, & C. S., 2012; Chess, & McGraw, 2004; Kaltofen, 2010; Ench, Ongtang, & McDaniel, 2009). Nevertheless, Android devices are built with integrated capabilities to support open source applications, subscribers are free to install add-on apps of their choice some of which are available free of charge (Kaltofen, 2010; Ench, Ongtang, & McDaniel, 2009; Livshits, & Larn, 2005). To Android or other mobile devices, hackers can easily send out an intent/alert, which is best described as a malicious application. Often the application is injected to create an obstruction activity on mobile device (Kaltofen, 2010; Ench, Ongtang, & McDaniel, 2009; Livshits, & Larn, 2005; Fowler, & C. S., 2012; Burns, 2009). The following are security concerns vendors and subscribers must take into account when dealing with mobile devices (Ench, Ongtang, & McDaniel, 2009; Burns, 2009):

- Unauthorized Intent Receipt,
- Activity Hijacking,
- Automated Analysis,
- Broadcast Theft,
- Service Hijacking,
- Manual Analysis,
- Special Intents,
- Intent Analysis,
- Intent Spoofing,
- Malicious Broadcasting Injection, and
- Malicious Activity Launch.

Vendors have developed and enhanced security tools to protect data and user's privacy. For instance, ComDroid is a mobile security tool vendors have developed to detect adversarial attackers' attempting to gain access to mobile platforms and network infrastructure systems (Ench, Ongtang, & McDaniel, 2009; Chess, & McGraw, 2004). In general, ComDroid is capable of exploiting and identifying any vulnerability/threats affecting Android mobile applications (Livshits, & Larn, 2005; Chess, & McGraw, 2004). Dalvik executable/DEX is another application solution developed by vendors to run on Android Dalvik Virtual Machine(s). This application is capable of intercepting any incoming traffic: Dedexer, potential logs components and the type of security vulnerabilities or emerging threats exploited over the Internet (Ench, Ongtang, & McDaniel, 2009; Livshits, & Larn, 2005; Livshits, & Larn, 2005; Burns, 2009; Fowler, & C. S., 2012). Recent studies confirmed that vendors have developed security applications to minimize and deter any vulnerability or threats affecting mobile devices. In spite of these advances in industry, there are still major security limitations vendors must address when developing and deploying mobile platforms (Ench, Ongtang, & McDaniel, 2009; Fowler, & C. S., 2012; Ballages, Rohs, Sheridan, & Borchers, 2008). Lacking human intervention in manual security reviews can potentially be observed as exploited weakness Android devices could display to enterprises and consumers. The need for enhanced security solutions to support the privilege delegation, Uniform Resource Locator (URL) read/write permissions, common application insertion also can be observed as a greater vulnerability or threats to Android mobile systems (Fowler, & C. S., 2012; Chess, & McGraw, 2004; Ballages, Rohs, Sheridan, & Borchers, 2008). In the event of any attack launched from unauthorized personnel against mobile platforms, Android developed extra security tool called ICE ("in case of emergency"). This security application can be launched even if the device is on lock screen mode. For instance, first responders such as paramedics have been using such a security feature to alert the law enforcement and the general public in the event of an emergency (Livshits, & Larn, 2005).

iOS Apps Development

iOS is an operating system developed for Apple mobile devices. iOS was first launched in 2007 as a mobile application for: iPhone, iPod Touch and Apple TV. Initially this operating system was developed as an OS X. The computer version of iOS is also called OS X. Recently, Apple designed Xcode 7 software as an integrated development environment/IDE. The software was initially designed to interface with other features such as source editor and graphical user interface editor. There are commercial off-the-shelf (COTS) software products used to develop iOS apps. Most iOS apps are developed using Xcode 7 application as well as add-ons: Swift 2 playgrounds, universal user interface design (Ballages, Rohs, Sheridan, & Borchers, 2008). Xcode 7 is a software product used to develop i.e., interface builder live views, embedded frameworks, cloudkit data storage, touchID authentication and apps extensions. Apple developers have now reached an advanced stage of iOS and OS X development using the Xcode 7 and iOS 9 SDK toolkit. Any vendors interested in Apple developer program can easily enroll in a program for an annual subscription of $99.00. Apple also offers a different subscription plan for subscribers who are interested to enroll in its developer program (Burns, 2009). Listed are some of the features Apple products offer to its clientele (Burns, 2009; Ballages, Rohs, Sheridan, & Borchers, 2008):

- **Software:**
  - Data Protection Class
  - App Sandbox

- ◦ User Partition (encryption)
- ◦ OS Partition
- ◦ File System
- **Hardware:**
  - ◦ Kernel
    - ▪ Secure Enclave
    - ▪ Secure Element
- **Hardware and Firmware:**
  - ◦ Crypto Engine
  - ◦ Device Key
  - ◦ Group Key
  - ◦ Apple Root Certificate

Apple system security is designed to guarantee for security of mobile device (hardware and software). These security solutions involve: boot-up process, software updates and secure enclave (Kaltofen, 2010; Ballages, Rohs, Sheridan, & Borchers, 2008).

Blackberry Apps Development

The development of mobile apps includes a number of specifications built to meet consumer's requirements (Burns, 2009; Kaltofen, 2010). The next-generation of mobile devices will be equipped with improved processors, applications, OS and add-on features e.g., user-interface built to interact with the traditional mobile platforms (Burns, 2009). The next evolution of mobile devices e.g., blackberry product will be defined by its market representation, comparative and competitive advantages e.g., core process mobilization (Burns, 2009; Kaltofen, 2010; Ballages, Rohs, Sheridan, & Borchers, 2008). Preceding investigations concluded that adaptive-integrated approaches in the development of new apps for blackberry mobile devices are key on how these systems often gain enterprise and consumer's market attention (Burns, 2009; Kaltofen, 2010; Ballages, Rohs, Sheridan, & Borchers, 2008).

Mobile Web Apps

Mobile web apps are standard-based web technologies e.g., HTML5 and JavaScript. These apps are developed with unified applications such as browser features. Mobile web apps are also developed to support HTML5 operational capabilities. These browsers are built to interface with all transactions of HTML5 services (Ballages, Rohs, Sheridan, & Borchers, 2008). In recent mobile devices application transactions are classified as CSS3 ("cascade style sheets"). In cross-platform environment, mobile web apps generally are developed to interact with the following smartphones: Android, iOS, Blackberry and Windows Phones (Kaltofen, 2010; Fowler, & C. S., 2012; Burns, 2009). Web apps are designed to provide distributed mobile solutions via the web (Kaltofen, 2010). Aside from these benefits, web apps are not installed on the smartphones, but rather are built to provide distributed services whenever requests are made for provisioning (Kaltofen, 2010; Ench, Ongtang, & McDaniel, 2009; Burns, 2009). There is a variance between mobile web apps and mobile web pages, though these two applications are often compatible. Mobile web pages are designed to support the functionality of web solutions i.e., HTML, CSS and JavaScript (Burns, 2009; Kaltofen, 2010). These applications are built to provide web pages with real-time solution configuration (Lakshman, & Thuijs, 2011; Kaltofen, 2010; Ench, Ongtang, & McDaniel, 2009). Below is a process, which illustrates side-by-side comparison for the three categories of mobile apps (i.e., native, web, and hybrid present for enterprises or consumers' benefits. Skills and tools required to support cross-platform app development (Ench, Ongtang, & McDaniel, 2009; Burns, 2009):

- **Native App:**
  - Objective-C
  - Java
  - C++
  - C#
  - Visual Basic. Net
  - **Apps Required to Interface with All Mobile Devices or Platforms**
    - Four
  - **Installed on Mobile Devices**
    - Yes
  - **Distribution**
    - App Store/Market
  - **Device Integration**
    - Provide Complete: camera, microphone, GPS, gyroscope, accelerometer, file, upload, contact list
  - **Best Used for**
    - Highly Graphical App
    - Apps that need to reach large enterprises and consumers
- **Web App:**
  - HTML
  - CSS
  - JavaScript
  - Web Programming Language e.g., Java
  - **Apps Required to Interact with All Mobile Devices or Platforms**
    - One
  - **Installed on Mobile Devices**
    - No
  - **Distribution**
    - Internet Based
  - **Partial Integration**
    - Partial Integration (e.g., GPS, gyroscope, accelerometer, file, upload)
  - **Best Used for**
    - Data-driven Apps
    - Business-to-Business Apps
    - Internal Business Apps
- **Hybrid App:**
  - HTML
  - CSS
  - JavaScript

- ○ Web Programming Language (e.g., Java)
- ○ Mobile Development Framework
- ○ **Apps Required to Interface with All Mobile Devices or Platforms**
  - ▪ One
- ○ **Installed on Mobile Devices**
  - ▪ Yes
- ○ **Distribution**
  - ▪ App Store/Market
- ○ **Full Integration**
  - ▪ Full Integration for (e.g., camera, microphone, GPS, gyroscope, accelerometer, file upload, contact list)
- ○ **Best Used for**
  - ▪ Cross-platform Apps, which require full device access
  - ▪ Business apps that require app store distribution

Almost a decade ago, vendors have built mobile devices to support cutting-edge integrated *JavaScript* apps (Bloice, & Wotawa, 2009; Adam & Christ, 2011; Kaltofen, 2010). These developments, resulted in the increase of new web application solutions i.e., *HTML5, CSS3 and JavaScript* (Bloice, & Wotawa, 2009). These mobile web applications also are designed to increase the translation of *HTML5* application(s) accessed from page-definition language. Such development is required to interface with browser-based requests (Adam & Christ, 2011; Kaltofen, 2010; Howard, Pincus, & Wind, 2005). Vendors view user interface components as integrated applications designed to support various requests: rich media types, geolocation services or offline user-friendliness applications (Kaltofen, 2010; Bloice, & Wotawa, 2009; Mark, 2013; Howard, Pincus, & Wind, 2005). There is difference between mobile browsing and mobile-optimized websites. These web-app methods are also developed to provide mobile devices with prime technology capabilities: smartphones, complete access to *HTML* pages (Kaltofen, 2010; Bloice, & Wotawa, 2009; Adam & Christ, 2011; Charland, & LeRoux, 2011; Bloice, & Wotawa, 2009). The shared applications displayed on the touch screen of smart devices often are designed to provide users with integrated solutions needed for business and operational requirements (Mark, 2013; Kaltofen, 2010; Fowler, & C. S., 2012). The following are web applications to support mobile browsers: *CSS3, HTML5* and *JavaScript* (Bloice, & Wotawa, 2009; Adam & Christ, 2011; Charland, & LeRoux, 2011; Bloice, & Wotawa, 2009). In mobile devices web apps are developed to support cross-organizational platforms (Kaltofen, 2010). Many vendors develop specific version(s) of web apps for specific browser engines. Webkit is an instance of mobile web browser developed by Apple and Google. This engine component was initially developed to protect and support the translation of electronic pages in web browsers (Adam & Christ, 2011; Kaltofen, 2010; Mark, 2013). Webkit is designed to interact with the following browsers (Bloice, & Wotawa, 2009; Kaltofen, 2010; Howard, Pincus, & Wind, 2005; Kaltofen, 2010):

- Apple's Safari,
- Google Chrome, and
- Opera.

In recent times vendors have developed newer browsers to interface with Amazon Kindle e-book, Apple iOS features, Blackberry browsers, OS6, Tizen mobile OSs and related applications. In Windows platform environment (Webkit *C++ APIs*) are designed as a set of software specifications needed to display other web contents (Christ, 2011; Fowler, & C. S., 2012; Howard, Pincus, & Wind, 2005). These features also are developed to support enterprise mobile infrastructures or platforms (Adam & Christ, 2011; Charland, & LeRoux, 2011; Bloice, & Wotawa, 2009):

- Apple,
- Google,
- Nokia,
- Bitstream,
- Blackberry, and
- Igalia.

Apple and Google are two most rated vendors whose features are developed to support HTML5 solutions. These specifications consist of: (Adam & Christ, 2011; Charland, & LeRoux, 2011; Bloice, & Wotawa, 2009; Howard, Pincus, & Wind, 2005)

- **Pure Mobile Web Apps:**
  - **Tools and Knowledge:**
    - Written entirely in HTML, CSS and JavaScript
  - **Execution:**
    - Installed, short, launched like a native app
  - **User Experience:**
    - Touch-friendly, interactive user interface
  - **Performance:**
    - User interface logic resides locally, making the app responsive and accessible offline
- **Pure Mobile Web:**
  - **Tools and Knowledge:**
    - Written entirely in HTML, CSS and JavaScript
  - **Execution:**
    - Reached by navigating to a website of a uniform resource locator aka URL
  - **User Experience:**
    - Navigational user interface between pages displaying static data
  - **Performance:**
    - All code executed from a server, resulting in network-dependent performance

Hybrid Apps

Integrated mobile applications are developed to provision native and web apps. These solutions are also known as web apps that are embedded in a specific platform shell (Fowler, & C. S., 2012; Howard, Pincus, & Wind, 2005). Hybrid apps consist of native and mobile integrated application solutions. In hybrid apps, applications are designed to support autonomous technologies. Specific plug-ins are designed to support vendor's requirements. This process comprises the access of mobile device features. The platform specific shell is generally designed to extract application native qualities: complete device consolidation, native setting up, and app store/market distribution (Fowler, & C. S., 2012; Burns, 2009; Kaltofen, 2010).

MOBILE DEVICES MODELING AND SOLUTIONS

Continuous demands of prime services among enterprises and consumers have motivated vendors to reassess their existing mobile strategies e.g., platform solutions (Barker, Barker, Burr, Polk, & Smid, 2006; Kaltofen, 2010). These are one of the key solutions vendors must focus on, while developing capabilities needed for enterprises and consumers' business operation requirements (Barker, Barker, Burr, Polk, & Smid, 2006). These solutions are defined by the need for developing better IT strategies and policies. The need for developing integrated mobile apps to support wireless platforms is also fundamental on how vendors and carriers redefine their marketing strategies (Barker, Barker, Burr, Polk, & Smid, 2006; Barker, Barker, Burr, Polk, & Smid, 2006; Ballages, Rohs, Sheridan, & Borchers, 2008). Most vendors are developing solutions to support enterprises and consumers' requirements (Barker, Barker, Burr, Polk, & Smid, 2006). When vendors develop apps for several mobile phones and tablets the following concept is considered. These solutions involve the development of web, native and hybrid apps. Table 1 describes each condition required for successful development of native, web and hybrid mobile apps (Oracle, 2015; Kaltofen, 2010).

The implementation of modern mobile prototypes such as, the centralized Mobile Management (CMM) is one of the key areas vendors continue to investigate (Barker, Barker, Burr, Polk, & Smid, 2006; Ballages, Rohs, Sheridan, & Borchers, 2008; Oracle, 2015; Kaltofen, 2010). CMM offers the customer wide-ranging integrated solutions compatible with most if not all mobile devices. CMM consists of: messaging server's management capabilities and centralized management functionality (Oracle, 2015). The need for developing more product strategy and security policies to ensure enterprises and consumers' data and privacy are protected is pervasive (Barker, Barker, Burr, Polk, & Smid, 2006; Aboba, Blunk, Vollbrecht, Carlson, & Levkowetz, 2004; Oracle, 2015; Kaltofen, 2010). More data communication and storage solutions are developed to provision enterprises and consumers' needs (Barker, Barker, Burr, Polk, & Smid, 2006). In recent decade, vendors have developed user/device authentication interface solutions e.g., mobile apps to meet customer's specifications (Barker, Barker, Burr, Polk, & Smid, 2006; Ballages, Rohs, Sheridan, & Borchers, 2008; Aboba, Blunk, Vollbrecht, Carlson, & Levkowetz, 2004; Kaltofen, 2010). The lack of security best practices and technical solutions has motivated developers to design more sophisticated wireless solutions to interact with the next-generation mobile platforms (Barker, Barker, Burr, Polk, & Smid, 2006; Aboba, Blunk, Vollbrecht, Carlson, & Levkowetz, 2004). When developing COTS or vendor's solutions the following are significant characteristics to be con-

Table 1. Model for developing mobile device apps (Oracle, 2015)

Mobile Web Apps	Native Mobile Apps	Hybrid Mobile Apps
• Online application regained through mobile device browsers • Browser administers access to native storage and device services e.g., camera, GPS • Extremely reusable code • Exceptionally portable	• Application installed and performed on the mobile device • Optimization of specific mobile platforms and form factors • Direct access to native storage and associated device services • Code reuse that often can be complexed • Transportability that requires extra work	• Application installed and performed on device with HTML5 User Interface • Optimization of specific mobile platforms and form factors • Undeviating access to native storages or service devices • Code reuse and simplified • Transferability simplified

Source: http://www.oracle.com/technetwork/middleware/id-mgmt/overview/omss-technical-wp-2104766.pdf

sidered in the development of security solutions: (Barker, Barker, Burr, Polk, & Smid, 2006; Ballages, Rohs, Sheridan, & Borchers, 2008; Kaltofen, 2010)

- Architecture
- Authentication
- Protection
- Performance
- User-friendly Default Settings
- Security of the Implementation
- Logging
- Management
- Connectivity or Paring
- Solution Implementation
- Cryptography
- Configuration Requirements
- Data/Device Provisioning
- Application Vetting
- Certification Requirements

MOBILE DEVICES FEATURES AND STANDARDS

HTML5 is a version five hypertext mark-up language developed to support the configuration and presentation of data stored on the World Wide Web (WWW). Vendors define HTML as a fifth generation web-based software standard (Ubl, 2011; Bloice & Wotawa, 2009; Mark, 2013; Dickson, 2012). Early adoption of *HTML5* generated the need for enterprises and consumers to reflect on altering the development concept for web services, to be compatible with other solutions e.g., cross-platform mobile applications. Web based solutions such as *HTML5* are developed to interact with other handheld devices: smartphones, tablets, PDAs (Bloice & Wotawa, 2009; Mark, 2013; Kaltofen, 2010; Burns, 2009; Dickson, 2012; Mark, 2013). In 2014 the World Wide Consortium (WWC) published HTML5. This software enhances language needed for supporting the newest multimedia application (Burns, 2009). The following are early adopters of HTML5: (Biolchini, et. El., 2005; Mark, 2013; Kaltofen, Milrad, & Kurti, 2010; Burns, 2009)

- Research-in-Motion Blackberry Torch
- iPhone version (4.0) and beyond
- iPad version (4.0) and above
- Android version (2.0) and beyond
- IE9 Browsers

Vendors developed HTML5 application to provide agile solutions to support user's readability of web addresses displayed in the browser section. Increased consumer needs have encouraged vendors to develop extra features for *HTML5* (Dickson, 2012; Burns, 2009). These solutions are designed to integrate, previous versions of markup language such as *HTML4, XHTML1.0* and related document object model L*evel2 HTML* (Bloice & Wotawa, 2009; Dickson, 2012; Mark, 2013; Ench, Ongtang, & McDaniel, 2009). Early and recent versions of common generic block schemes for markup language are embedded with the following features (Bloice & Wotawa, 2009; Dickson, 2012; Burns, 2009; Kaltofen, 2010):

- \<div\>
- \<span\>
- \<nav\>
- \<footer\>
- \<audio\>
- \<video\>
- \<object\>
- DOM Scripting
- JavaScript

INTEGRATED ARCHITECTURE FOR MOBILE DEVICES

For many years, vendors have developed apps and tools to strengthen security of mobile systems. Early researchers concluded that short message service apps are ideal solutions in emerging markets (Bloice & Wotawa, 2009; Dickson, 2012; Bloice, & Wotawa, 2009). In spite of these technology trends, native apps are still rated as the best solutions in the evolution of mobile systems. Irrespective of customers' preference for native applications over mobile web apps, either selections are suitable for enterprises and consumers (Bloice & Wotawa, 2009; Kaltofen, Milrad, & Kurti, 2010). This diagram (Figure 3) describes the mobile device integrated architecture framework most vendors have adopted for many years:

Figure 3. Mobile devices integrated architecture framework (Meier et al., 2008)
Source: http://robtiffany.com/wp-content/uploads/2012/08/Mobile_Architecture_Guide_v1.1.pdf

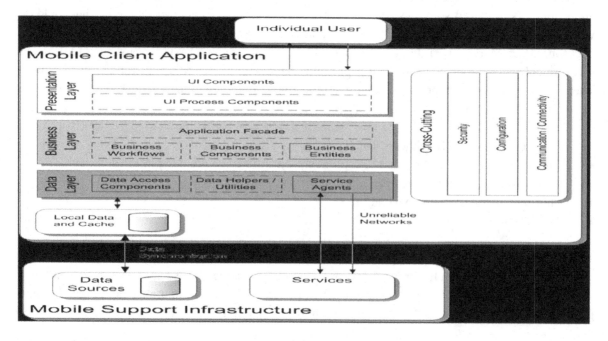

APPLICATION, DEVELOPMENT AND CONFIGURATION

When enterprises and consumers plan on acquiring and/or leasing mobile devices, the following specifications, must be considered: (Andersson & Dan, 2012; Bloice & Wotawa, 2009; Gartner, 2012; Kaltofen, 2010; Barker, Barker, Burr, Polk, & Smid, 2006)

- Type of applications designed to support graphics intensive performance.
- Select mobile applications are developed to support algorithmic based computation performances.
- Seek mobile device to support integrated apps specifications.
- Determine which app has high priority or security features integrated from the vendor.
- Decide whether the purchased apps must be stored on multiple platforms or on the device; what changes will the organization and consumers anticipate with the purchased app in the near term; knowing when the vendor plans to deploy new apps to the market.
- What are the key characteristics of new apps being deployed, if any; knowing if integrated web solutions into the app are compatible with the mobile device in use?
- Does the mobile device have supporting capabilities i.e., storage, bandwidth, performance, scalability to support new solutions vendors anticipate to deploy?
- Are the app solution capabilities compatible to the back-end system or data sources?
- What is the time frame for upgrading current apps to meet organization and consumer's business and operational requirements; be able to determine whether the app storefront or deployment strategy is compatible to the system requirements?

Vendors define dynamic data exchange/DDE as a standard container built to reduce, translate or filter any traffic content with no substance (Kaltofen, 2010; Burns, 2009; Bloice, & Wotawa, 2009). This function can also be used to group elements for stylistic and adaptive solutions. This function is frequently conceded through classic or identification attributes e.g., value(s) or language(s). Through this process syntaxes on mobile devices can easily be sustained. Vendors developed a AJAX toolkit to support embedded APIs calls or processes designed to interact with mobile devices platforms (Kaltofen, 2010; Andersson & Dan, 2012; Bloice & Wotawa, 2009).

Google Maps JavaScript APIs

Launching modern technologies encouraged vendors to reevaluate their current software strategy & solution concepts to accommodate enterprises and consumers' business and operation's requirements. These novelties in the cutting-edge technology solutions involve the development of mobile applications needed to interact with API functioning features. Aside from these business and operation demands vendors have upgraded API features to version three (3). This task requires that such codes be rewritten to satisfy user's system specifications and rendering the correct information when requested (Google Maps JavaScript, 2013). This includes, the upgrade of Google Maps JavaScript (GMJS) API version 2 to version 3. The process of migrating from version 2/3 of Google maps JavaScript is complex and requires that newer apps be developed to support any of the existing or future applications (GMJS, 2013; Ballages, Rohs, Sheridan, & Borchers, 2008). Google Maps JavaScript APIs are built to support the Google Developers Console. The console is also designed to manage the assigned keys: update the mobile device or user's API bootstrap, code, test and reiterated (GMJS, 2013). The new version of Google

Maps JavaScript API ver. 3 was designed with comprehensive capabilities required to support the modern JavaScript user interface design, procedures and/or concepts (GMJS, 2013). Google Developers Console is equipped with the following system capabilities: view usage reports, purchase extra quota as needed, allowing Google to have the ability to communicate with the mobile device subscriber regarding the warranted application (Stewart, & Wong, 2002; GMJS, 2013; Ballages, Rohs, Sheridan, & Borchers, 2008; GMJS, 2013). Recently, vendors pointed out that continued developments in software design are due to an increase in programming language systems/prototypes (GMJS, 2013). Google Maps JavaScript API ver. 3 was developed to provide complete interactive solution of libraries as well as streamlining API usability (GMJS, 2013; Ballages, Rohs, Sheridan, & Borchers, 2008). New features incorporated during the design phase include: simplified core library, enhanced concept for client-side usage limits, complete integration of modern browsers, removal of pointless general-purpose helper classes (i.e., GLog and/or GDownloadURL, Closure, jQuery). Whereas, HTML5 street view implementation is developed as a solution to be loaded on mobile devices, custom street view, styled maps customizations, elevation service and distance metrics, traveling salesman problem, bicycling layer, draggable directions the update of geocoding, integrated functionality concept for info window on a single map (GMJS, 2013; Ballages, Rohs, Sheridan, & Borchers, 2008; Kaltofen, 2010).

Secure Web Browser

Secure web browser(s) encompasses: Firefox, open source and preconfigured web applications developed to interact with other software deployed on the network (Aboba, Blunk, Vollbrecht, Carlson, & Levkowetz, 2004). For many years, vendors developed secure web browser(s) applications to protect the Internet from malicious software and unsolicited users' access (Aboba, Blunk, Vollbrecht, Carlson, & Levkowetz, 2004). These browsers are also developed to protect computer systems, data and other network infrastructure systems from any security breach posed by privacy and malware (Aboba, Blunk, Vollbrecht, Carlson, & Levkowetz, 2004). Attackers use JavaScript with cross-site scripting/ XSS to intercept secondary payloads functioning on adobe flash (Aboba, Blunk, Vollbrecht, Carlson, & Levkowetz, 2004). The use of numerous vulnerabilities and threats exploited by the following search engines: Mozilla firefox, google chrome, opera, microsoft explorer and safari potentially can be a path for platforms or infrastructure technical and operation shortcomings (Aboba, Blunk, Vollbrecht, Carlson, & Levkowetz, 2004; Kaltofen, 2010).

Cellular Phone Security

The lack of security best practices to protect mobile applications and malware software is the reason why enterprises and consumers' privacy/data is often compromised by unauthorized personnel. To properly mitigate some of these threats, enhanced policies and procedures must be developed to support enterprises and consumers' specifications (Ballages, Rohs, Sheridan, & Borchers, 2008; Kaltofen, 2010).

Model View Controllers

Model View Controllers (MVCs) are software application designed to support the translation ranges developers often view when implementing user interfaces on computers. In mobile devices, MVC is designed to capture or model any irregularity often identified by the application. This concept involves the problem domain dissimilar from a user interface. The complete functionality of user interface is very important in the development of mobile applications and platform (Barker, Barker, Burr, Polk, & Smid, 2006). Yet vendors have concluded that Swift and Objective-C programming languages continue to play an integral role in the design of mobile applications and platforms. Swift is a software designed to provide developers with an integrated approach required to develop mobile apps or related platforms. This software is frequently integrated with cocoa and Objective-C programing language (Barker, Barker, Burr, Polk, & Smid, 2006). Objective-C APIs are used to design user's custom code in Swift. In contrast, Swift can be used in APIs in Objective-C. The interactive solutions Swift APIs and Objective-C APIs display in the mobile apps and development stages have given developers a comparative and competitive advantage as well as opportunity to reach an iterative concept, when designing mobile app solutions. Whereas the interoperability interface is designed to ensure developers have the capability needed for Swift and Objective C codes to interface. This process allows the users to interface between Swift classes located in Objective-C and the Cocoa classes, while developers are preparing to Swift code (Barker, Barker, Burr, Polk, & Smid, 2006; Kaltofen, 2010).

UIView Screens

This concept is designed to support the iOS compatible applications and user interfaces. User Interface View/UIView is a process designed to support mobile device background screen with different colors. If a user needs to draw a rectangular area on the screen, along with any interfaces needed to manage contents in a particular dimension UIView offers prime features to support such activity. The interface is also developed to provide the user with the tool necessary to filling in a rectangular area with selected colors. The need for subclassing contents associated with such activity, allows UIView to implement accurate level of diagram and event management code (Barker, Barker, Burr, Polk, & Smid, 2006).

Bluetooth vs. Wi-Fi Security

Bluetooth and Wi-Fi solutions are key wireless/radio technologies introduced to the telephony industry (Barker, Barker, Burr, Polk, & Smid, 2006; Aboba, Blunk, Vollbrecht, Carlson, & Levkowetz, 2004). In mobile devices transactions are provided and/or processed through bluetooth or Wi-Fi technologies (Balfanz, Smetters, Stewart, & Wong, 2002; Barker, Barker, Burr, Polk, & Smid, 2006; Bluetooth SIG, 2006; Bluetooth SIG, 2006). Many enterprises and consumers have made use of significant features i.e., the encryption, wireless payment and file downloading (Barker, Barker, Burr, Polk, & Smid, 2006). These wireless radio solutions have provided enterprises and consumers with the following benefits (Aboba, Blunk, Vollbrecht, Carlson, & Levkowetz, 2004; Balfanz, Smetters, Stewart, & Wong, 2002; Barker, Barker, Burr, Polk, & Smid, 2006; Bluetooth SIG, 2006; Kaltofen, 2010):

- Enhanced Security
- Strong Radio Performance
- Data Transmission and Power Consumption
- Designed Network Use

Wireless solutions such as bluetooth and Wi-Fi are designed with enhanced security features for consumer's use. The wired equivalent privacy/WEP solution provides consumer with a level of security needed to protect the consumer's preferred activities (Aboba, Blunk, Vollbrecht, Carlson, & Levkowetz, 2004; Barker, Barker, Burr, Polk, & Smid, 2006). Bluetooth is equipped with a different level of security features. Bluetooth security is an integrated solution also named Diffie-Hellman key (Aboba, Blunk, Vollbrecht, Carlson, & Levkowetz, 2004). Through this key agreement protocol, enterprises and consumers are able to communicate with relevant parties via a two-way secure or dedicated network infrastructure systems (Aboba, Blunk, Vollbrecht, Carlson, & Levkowetz, 2004). Users are capable of synchronizing mobile devices with the designated servers through the use of robust Wi-Fi protected access solution. WPA is designed to provide an end-to-end authentication between two or more parties (Aboba, Blunk, Vollbrecht, Carlson, & Levkowetz, 2004; Balfanz, Smetters, Stewart, & Wong, 2002; Kaltofen, 2010).

Java Sandbox

Sandbox is a new security architecture designed to support the Java development toolkit/JDK. This application was developed to execute code injection from non-secure sources; while sandbox is originally an implemented security model developed to complement the JDK suite. The JDK security model consists of: remote code, local code, valuable resources, Java virtual machine and sandbox (Barker, Barker, Burr, Polk, & Smid, 2006). Developers designed JDK framework as an integrated platform to support the Java applications running in a secure environment. In a protected environment sandbox is deployed using JDK version 1.0X to interface with built-in applications designed to support JD toolkit (Stewart, & Wong, 2002; Kaltofen, 2010). Vendors developed machine-to-machine capabilities for mobile devices, as a parallel development strategy to support enterprises and consumers' requirements. This concept was initially developed to ensure that other mobile application products have the ability to interface with Java solutions through end-to-end portfolio or development conceptions (Barker, Barker, Burr, Polk, & Smid, 2006; Stewart, & Wong, 2002).

Unified Area of Security for Mobile Devices

Integrated security concepts for mobile devices are pervasive areas for vendors to develop enhanced security best practices (Aboba, Blunk, Vollbrecht, Carlson, & Levkowetz, 2004). Enterprises and consumers are concerned with the lack of best practices to protect data and user's privacy (Aboba, Blunk, Vollbrecht, Carlson, & Levkowetz, 2004). Proper integration of these security solutions could afford enterprises and consumers the ability to share corporate and/or personal data via the Internet without worrying about their information being compromised by unauthorized personnel (Aboba, Blunk, Vollbrecht, Carlson, & Levkowetz, 2004). The implementation of improved security best practices often requires trusted solutions; which vendors must develop to protect their subscribers' data from being accessed by unsolicited personnel. Presently, enterprises and consumers' platforms are converged through integrated solutions. These solutions are deployed to provide end-to-end encryption features, which are less exposed to attackers (Aboba, Blunk, Vollbrecht, Carlson, & Levkowetz, 2004; Kaltofen, 2010).

React-Native

For several years, vendors always relied on react-native as an efficient tool to build realistic and user-friendly apps for mobile devices. The software is designed to afford enterprises and consumers the ability world-class applications needed to support mobile device platforms. The use of JavaScript and React tools is key for the development of mobile apps, to be deployed on native mobile platforms. Facebook, Twitter use react-native tools in multiple production application environments (Aboba, Blunk, Vollbrecht, Carlson, & Levkowetz, 2004). Applications that support react-native framework are based on asynchronous execution of JavaScript application code and native platforms. The use of integrated solutions for mobile devices, yet provides enterprises and consumers with improved platform performance and sustainable capabilities. The following are native characteristics or components react-native offer to enterprises and consumers' mobile devices (Aboba, Blunk, Vollbrecht, Carlson, & Levkowetz, 2004):

- Asynchronous Execution
- Creating Android Views
- Creating Android Modules
- Creating iOS Views
- Creating iOS Modules
- Extensibility
- Polyfills
- Touch Handling
- Flexbox and Styling

React-native solutions are developed to support other standard platform components/tools. These tools consist of: UITabBar designed for iOS or Drawer t supports the Android environment. The ease-of-use features both TabBariOS and DrawerLayoutAndroid provide consumers with characteristics compatible with each platform service (Aboba, Blunk, Vollbrecht, Carlson, & Levkowetz, 2004; Kaltofen, 2010).

jQuery for Mobile Devices

Vendors define jQuery as a JavaScript collection and/or library. This programing language is comprised of functions, groups and subgroups of elements (Andersson & Dan, 2012; Bloice & Wotawa, 2009). Essentially, the jQuery main programming function is represented as a selector for $ feature (Kaltofen, 2010; Burns, 2009; Aboba, Blunk, Vollbrecht, Carlson, & Levkowetz, 2004). This feature is designed to interact with the following string $("#thisisanid"). Thereby the command/function is injected to ascertain any element associated with a particular id/identification. $("div") function is ascribed to render/ find divs tags or any selection found on HTML documents division element/HTLM-DDE (Kaltofen, 2010; Andersson & Dan, 2012; Bloice & Wotawa, 2009; Gartner, 2012; Burns, 2009; Ballages, Rohs, Sheridan, & Borchers, 2008; Kaltofen, 2010).

Graphical User Interface Toolkit

For the past decades, mobile devices evolved from being trial devices to full scale smart platforms (Ballages, Rohs, Sheridan, & Borchers, 2008). The need for an in-built graphical user interface/GUI tools, scheduling, addresses and personal details remains fundamental characteristics in the development of mobile devices (Kaltofen, 2010; Andersson & Dan, 2012; Bloice & Wotawa, 2009). The first generation of mobile devices provides basic connectivity for end-users, the development of innovative smart devices, giving mobile applications the capability needed to interface with web services (Ballages, Rohs, Sheridan, & Borchers, 2008). The integration of processes also gives vendors the ability to develop unified security solutions to support user's business requirements. Modern mobile devices are built to avert the following requirements: form factors, computing resources, network connectivity (Kaltofen, 2010; Andersson & Dan, 2012; Bloice & Wotawa, 2009). On the end-user side, vendors are devoted to develop solutions to support the enterprise or client's business requirements. These classifications encompass: personalization, usability and security. The integration of state-of-the-art APIs gives developers the capability needed to handle complex technical issues, consumers mostly encounter, while using their mobile devices (Kaltofen, 2010; Andersson & Dan, 2012; Bloice & Wotawa, 2009; Gartner, 2012; Ballages, Rohs, Sheridan, & Borchers, 2008; Ballages, Rohs, Sheridan, & Borchers, 2008). Launching web apps ensures enterprises have the ability to fulfill technical solutions and easily support the customer's operational capabilities. These capabilities consist of: intranets, VPNs, web services (Kaltofen, 2010; Andersson & Dan, 2012; Bloice & Wotawa, 2009). Mobile devices are equipped with a pool of features designed to support GUI services. For many years, GUI solutions have played a major role in guaranteeing that the end-state product is developed, tested and deployed efficaciously. The following are classifications of these differentiators (Kaltofen, 2010; Andersson & Dan, 2012; Bloice & Wotawa, 2009; Ballages, Rohs, Sheridan, & Borchers, 2008):

- **GUI:** Designed to support mobile devices, which do not have integrated features (e.g., network printer)
- **Propriety GUI:** Contain a simplified GUI displayed to display text or buttons
- **Raw Graphics Device:** Devices comprising raw graphics, which could require native GUI toolkit
- **Minimal GUI Toolkit:** GUI toolkit which does contain abstract window toolkit compatibility. This method is designed to be perfected by unambiguous lightweight toolkit
- **Applet Support for Web Browsers:** Comprises the functionality of web browsers, which commonly requires applet run-time capability
- **Rich GUI Toolkit:** This concept is designed to allow for basic graphics interface components/ contents. Rich GUI toolkit also is built to support robust graphs and/or imaging features

Data flow and hardware components are developed to read dynamic and static tags (Ballages, Rohs, Sheridan, & Borchers, 2008). This process allows for interactive data translation between the server and physical mobile devices, though tagging concept takes place between phones and designated servers (Ballages, Rohs, Sheridan, & Borchers, 2008; Ballages, Rohs, Sheridan, & Borchers, 2008). On the mobile device, tag graphic is displayed in a form of static illustration (e.g., button) used to provide the state output (Ballages, Rohs, Sheridan, & Borchers, 2008). Tag widgets are developed to support ecological assembling of user interface lagging process. On mobile devices, the classification of tag interface widgets is equivalent to those applications displayed in the desktop widget archives: radio buttons, drop down boxes (Ballages, Rohs, Sheridan, & Borchers, 2008; Kaltofen, 2010).

PhoneGap

An adobe acrobat application development framework designed by adobe system. The software was developed to support the development of mobile apps (Ballages, Rohs, Sheridan, & Borchers, 2008). PhoneGap is a user-friendly application, which means anyone with/without an in-depth knowledge of programming language must be able to interact using some built-in features PhoneGap offers. Users with basic concept in web development language or utilization i.e., HTML, CSS and JavaScript, must be able to execute any development activities (Ballages, Rohs, Sheridan, & Borchers, 2008). In the development process PhoneGap is deployed to provide developers with technical capabilities needed to scale performance of apps and mobile operating systems (Ballages, Rohs, Sheridan, & Borchers, 2008). These technical concepts involve: iOS, Android, Blackberry Windows Mobile OS. PhoneGap application has a capability to develop apps to execute on cross-platform interoperability i.e., Apple iOS, Android, Windows, Blackberry (Ballages, Rohs, Sheridan, & Borchers, 2008). Thus mobile device and desktop computers' architecture are developed to provide parallel features and improved application interface. These solutions encompass apps, OS, firmware and hardware capabilities. Each of these features are designed with core functionality based on proprietary, developed and engineered concepts; though some apps are designed by third party vendors, to support organization and consumer's specifications (Ballages, Rohs, Sheridan, & Borchers, 2008). Even with the proprietary of some mobile device OSs and vendors are developing open source software to interact with mobile platforms. The following are OSs are used by enterprises and consumers (Ballages, Rohs, Sheridan, & Borchers, 2008): Android, iOS, Windows, and Blackberry. Vendors design mobile applications to support a set of user's interactive capabilities or functionalities. This means apps must be designed to support vendor's specifications (Ballages, Rohs, Sheridan, & Borchers, 2008). Despite such limitations, vendors are developing apps to converge with carriers' services and/or solutions (Ballages, Rohs, Sheridan, & Borchers, 2008).

RhoMobile Suite

An open source framework developed for creating data-centric, cross-platform native mobile enterprise and consumer application (Avram, 2014; New RhoMobile Suite, 2014; Kapner, & Ziobro, 2014). The integrated application was developed by Adam Blum in 2008. The development was part of the Rhodes project designed to support the GitHub (New RhoMobile Suite, 2014). The application has integrated component that support enterprise API and the radio-frequency identification/RFID capture, tagging, bar code scanning as well as payment processing (Kapner, & Ziobro, 2014; Avram, 2014; New RhoMobile Suite, 2014; Avram, 2014). RhodeElements are built to support integrated security components: automatic data encryption. These elements include data at rest security, privacy protection and mitigation risks against existing and/or imminent vulnerabilities/threats (Kapner, & Ziobro, 2014; Avram, 2014). Vendors rely on RhoMobile suite when developing apps for mobile devices. This comprises the use of mobile web applications (New RhoMobile Suite, 2014; Kapner, & Ziobro, 2014): HTML5, Ruby, CSS3 and JavaScript. When writing apps to interface with mobile OSs i.e., Android, iOS, Windows phones, Windows mobile systems, Windows CE, Windows 8 and above; developers have the ability to manage and monitor apps behavior. On mobile devices there is a selection of tools RhoMobile suite support (Kapner, & Ziobro, 2014). RhoMobile suite product consists of (Kapner, & Ziobro, 2014; New RhoMobile Suite, 2014; Avram, 2014; Kaltofen, 2010):

- Rhodes
- RhoElement
- RhoStudio
- RhoConnect
- RhoGallary

Each of these products are developed to provide interactive mechanisms mobile devices require for performing diverse technical activities (Kapner, & Ziobro, 2014; Avram, 2014). RhoMobile solutions are designed to interact with other applications: built-in-view controller, object relational mapper, designed to support data intensive apps, granular API set of components, unified data synchronization (Kapner, & Ziobro, 2014; Avram, 2014; Kapner, & Ziobro, 2014; New RhoMobile Suite, 2014). RhoMobile suite is a mobile and/or computer cross-platform solution offered as part of cloud services. In the cloud, RhoMobile suite supports the hosted built synchronization or application management (Kapner, & Ziobro, 2014; New RhoMobile Suite, 2014; Avram, 2014). In 2014, the fifth-generation of RhoMobile also known as RhoMobile 5.0 was launched to organizations and consumer's needs (Avram, 2014; Kapner, & Ziobro, 2014; New RhoMobile Suite, 2014). In the same year, Zebra technologies that is, Motorola Solutions acquired RhoMobile suite (Kapner, & Ziobro, 2014; New RhoMobile Suite, 2014).

APPLICATION AND DEVICE SECURITY

Apple iOS and OS X products are built with enhanced security features to interact with the fundamental concept of related applications running on mobile devices. The architecture of Apple mobile platforms is a replica of several years of research that mobile developers put forth toward prototyping agile solutions (Souppaya & Scarfone, 2013). The combination of hardware, software and other services designed to interface with other mobile systems is what makes Apple products unique with competitive and comparative advantages, to consumers (Burns, 2009; Souppaya & Scarfone, 2013). Apple products are developed with unique key security features: non-configurable encrypted solutions. These solutions are non-configurable to prevent the user from attempting to disable any of the installed features by mistake (Burns, 2009). While the touchID feature is designed to improve user's experience and guarantees simplicity for each Apple device offer to subscribers (Burns, 2009; Souppaya & Scarfone, 2013; Kaltofen, 2010).

SERVICE ORIENTED ARCHITECTURE

Information technology experts and vendors are concerned with the lack of solutions for mobile devices (Adam & Christ, 2011). Adaptive-integrated implementation of *C#* programing language remains a cornerstone for the development of mobile devices. Experts and vendors continue to improve *JavaScript* apps to meet users, organizations' operation bearings and/or consumer's requirements (Bloice & Wotawa, 2009; Heitkötter, et al., 2012; Gartner, 2012; Kaltofen, Milrad, & Kurti, 2010). The implementation of security solutions, gives organizations and consumers an extra security layer to protect IT resources (Dickson, 2012; Lyle & Monteleone, 2012; Gartner, 2012). Despite these advances, these programming languages poses greater security implications to consumers. (Gartner, 2012; Heitkötter, et al., 2012; Kaltofen, Milrad, & Kurti, 2010; jQuery Home Page, 2013; Barker, Barker, Burr, Polk, & Smid, 2006).

Use Case

Many technical surveys conclude vendors must design agile and resilient solutions for mobile devices, seemly to support enterprises and consumers' requirements (Rajapakse, 2008; Gartner, 2012; Kaltofen, Milrad, & Kurti, 2010). Programming languages for mobile devices are complex solutions to adopt and/or implement (Adam & Christ, 2011; Dickson, 2012). Just as C# and JavaScript languages can be adopted/implemented to improve system performance (Bloice & Wotawa, 2009; Adam & Christ, 2011; Heitkötter, et al., 2012; Kaltofen, 2010).

ENTERPRISE MOBILE APPS

In modern times mobile apps have increased the enterprises and consumers' attention. Yet, there are billions of apps commonly subscribers download for use (Howard, Pincus, & Wind, 2005). Enterprises and consumers must determine which mobile device technology: apps, web-based solutions are viable to organizations and consumer's needs (Howard, Pincus, & Wind, 2005; Barker, Barker, Burr, Polk, & Smid, 2006). Such decision can be determined through a process of evaluating capital and operational expenditures. These expenditures are drives for economic growth opportunities (Dickson, 2012; Mark, 2013, Kaltofen, Milrad, & Kurti, 2010) As a result of increased number of users: mobile network solutions are relentlessly being inundated by user's unsystematic browser requests (Barker, Barker, Burr, Polk, & Smid, 2006). Lacking security best practices to protect mobile devices could result in data breaches i.e., leakage of information such as individual/corporate contacts, calendar and possibly consumers or C-level executives' physical locations (Kaltofen, Milrad, & Kurti, 2010; Kaltofen, 2010; IBM, 2012).

Apache Cordova Development

Cordova is a framework solution designed to support multiple-platform apps. This mobile device application is developed to interface with HTML5, JavaScript and native code solution. In recent years, these features increased popularity among developers (Kaltofen, 2010; Burns, 2009; Barker, Barker, Burr, Polk, & Smid, 2006). In Cordova application logic and user interface processes are executed using HTML5, CSS, and JavaScript language. This process can be executed by using extended webview. The plug-ins for Cordova mobile applications are developed in platform programming language (Java for Android). Below is a sequence of hyper-processing models that Android Cordova offers (Kaltofen, 2010; Burns, 2009; Barker, Barker, Burr, Polk, & Smid, 2006):

- **Web Architecture:**
  - HTML Android App
  - UI Layer (i.e., HTML, CSS, JavaScript)
  - Application Logic in JavaScript
  - Android WebView
  - Android Platform
- **Android Cordova Container:**
  - Cordova Plugins
  - Camera
  - Device Motion
  - In-App Browser
  - Network
  - Media

- ◦ File
- ◦ Geolocation
- ◦ Vibration
- **Android Platform:**
  - ◦ Android Webview
  - ◦ Android APIs
- **Custom Plug-Ins:**
  - ◦ Android APIs

In Android Cordova Architecture applications can execute and/or process activities at subscribers' requests, when connected to the carrier/provider's network. For many years, vendors have developed software capabilities, to protect mobile devices from unauthorized personnel (Kaltofen, Milrad, & Kurti, 2010; Burns, 2009; Bloice, & Wotawa, 2009). Lacking security features to support this JavaScript can simply compromise some of mobile device functions. Below is a set of JavaScript displaying the Cordova process for contact plugin (Thornycroft, 2016; Kaltofen, 2010):

```
Function showPhoneNumber (name) {
      var successCallback = function (contact) {
            alert ("phone  ("Phone number:   " + contacts . phone) ;
        }
        exec (successCallback, null, "ContactsPlugin", "find",
            [{"name" : name }]) ;
        }
Class ContactsPlugin     extends     CordovaPlugin  {
      boolean execute (String action, CordovaArgs  args,
                  CallbackContext     callbackContext)     {
          if ("find"  . equals (action))  {
              String name = args . get (0)  . name ;
              find (name, callbackContext) ;
      } else if ("create"  . equals (action))   ...
       }
        void find (String  name,  CallbackContext  callbackContext)
{
              Contact    contact  =  query ("SELECT   ...  where name = "
+  name) ;
              callbackContext . success (contact)  ;
        }
          }
```

The above strings/scripts demonstrate how JavaScript for contacts plugin is written in Apache Cordova programming language. These program functions are written to display a list of telephone numbers to be used for the Cordova app business logic application (Kaltofen, 2010). These functions consistently describe how Cordova foreign language interface, when mobile devices are in the developing/prototyping and testing phases (Thornycroft, 2016; Kaltofen, 2010).

In native mobile operational environment these program strings are written to identify the precise action developers/programmers require to execute any of the algorithm functions. In Apache Cordova developers/programmers usually develop agent structures needed to generate calls (Thornycroft, 2016; Kaltofen, 2010). When the Cordova framework delegates any call, a requested method is instantly executed from Java class ContactsPlugin. Once the call is made/initiated, at that juncture an action is initiated, as part of the find method. This method is also introduced to initiate any of the commands (Kaltofen, 2010). A SQL query is then executed to identify a requested contact information, which consequently is sent to the originated source, as a success callback. Once the information is received, the JavaScript method is responsible for transferring data to the corresponding destination (Ballages, Rohs, Sheridan, & Borchers, 2008; Thornycroft, 2016; Kaltofen, 2010).

Apache Cross-Language Flows

For many years, vendors have developed software solutions to support customer's requirements. Vendors describe these methods for developing mobile applications as a complex concept to adopt and/ or deploy (Ballages, Rohs, Sheridan, & Borchers, 2008). Developing solutions to satisfy the need for multiple mobile platforms is essential on how vendors can easily adapt to user's requirements. Lacking resources to support this mission could apparently elevate a degree of complexity for vendors. Sharing mobile applications i.e., social network content structure and advertisement selection gained enterprise and user's market attention (Ballages, Rohs, Sheridan, & Borchers, 2008). In Apache thrift the process of flow replication is applied as a basis for determined cross-language services execution and/or operation. Generally, this solution is deployed as the application layer, to act as a middleware (Slee, Agarwal, & Kwiatkowski, 2007). Vendors like Google have implemented request replications to gain immediate user's responses, in support of the company's online services. The following are characteristics the Apache thrift software model offers to organizations and consumers (Slee, Agarwal, & Kwiatkowski, 2007; Ballages, Rohs, Sheridan, & Borchers, 2008; Kaltofen, 2010):

- **Client Application:**
  - Client – Server
  - Processor – Processor
  - Protocol – Protocol
  - Transport – Transport
- **Server Application:**
  - Server – Client
  - Processor – Processor
  - Protocol – Protocol
  - Transport – Transport

The Apache Thrift is commonly developed as a model to support the replication process often taking place on mobile services (Slee, Agarwal, & Kwiatkowski, 2007; Ballages, Rohs, Sheridan, & Borchers, 2008; Kaltofen, 2010).

SOLUTIONS AND RECOMMENDATIONS

Mobile devices are unprotected to unauthorized personnel often attempting to gain access to these platforms (Howard, Pincus & Wind, 2005). Vendors must research on better solutions to deter, exploit, minimize or illuminate such identified vulnerabilities or threats, affecting mobile systems (i.e., smartphones, PDAs, tablets, and other wireless technologies). Vendors' failure to build software applications and hardware capabilities to easily interface with other solutions, may possibly be a key reason for mobile devices, to be less attractive to newer markets (Howard, Pincus, & Wind, 2005; Ench, Ongtang, & McDaniel, 2009; Kaltofen, 2010).

FUTURE RESEARCH DIRECTIONS

The need for reevaluating legacy mobile applications and lessons learned can be viable technical and strategic solutions for vendors, who seek to understand any security roots could affect the performance of mobile devices (Ench, Ongtang, & McDaniel, 2009; Kaltofen, Milrad, & Kurti, 2010). Improved web applications are designed to support all types of mobile platforms. This is important concept for how consumers its commonly invest in mobile devices and/or how carriers could provide first-rate hardware and software products. Integration of advanced features is a great tool for marketing current or the next-generation of mobile devices (Kaltofen, Milrad, & Kurti, 2010). Aside from many benefits and/or limitations, bluetooth and Wi-Fi solutions offer to diverse enterprises and consumers, Telecom vendors point out that the expansion of 'push button configuration' specifications, out of 'band, integrated pin features' and the 'lack of screen-based feedback' are designed to provide enhanced wireless capabilities needed to attractive consumers' interests (Bluetooth SIG, 2006).

CONCLUSION

Organizations business and/or corporate leaders must adopt practical application and development strategies required to determine best practices for mobile solutions spanning enterprise's business continuity operation/BCO and process improvement. Leaders and consumers, must also consider acquiring/leasing mobile devices, along with licenses needed to support add-on solutions. This includes the provision of 365x24x7 customer support as well as vendor's monthly or yearly subscription plan (Gartner, 2012; Mark, 2013; Howard, Pincus, & Wind, 2005).

According to vendors bluetooth and Wi-Fi solutions have provided a robust level of security to enterprises and consumers (Bluetooth SIG, 2006; Kaltofen, 2010; Bluetooth SIG, 2006). Despite these trends that industry has experienced over the course of years, mobile apps have transformed the way organizations and customers in the 21st century do business (IBM, 2012). Thus vendors are confident the next-generation of mobile devices will be equipped with faster processors, robust/enhanced security capabilities, applications compatible to all platforms. Aside from these industry advances, vendors are more optimistic that latest discoveries in technology are viewed as advancements made toward the next-generation of mobile devices. Even so the next-generation of mobile devices can be built with integrated cognitive analytics capabilities, allowing for decoding human language, other types of instructions and commands given by users (IBM, 2012). Developers forecast the next-generation of mobile devices will have built-in intelligent processors and autonomous security capabilities to warn users, of any existing or imminent cyber-attack in real-time (IBM, 2012).

REFERENCES

Aboba, B., Blunk, L., Vollbrecht, J., Carlson, J., & Levkowetz, H. (2004). *RFC 3748: Extensible Authentication Protocol.*

Adam, M., & Christ, B. (2011). The Mobile App Gap. *Sigma Journal: Inside the Digital Ecosystem, 11*(1), 28.

Amatya, S., & Kurti, A. (2014). Cross-Platform Mobile Development: Challenges and Opportunities. ICT Innovations, 231, 227-228.

Andersson, K., & Dan, J. (2012). Mobile e-Services Using HTML5. *2012 IEEE 37th Conference on Local Computer Networks Workshops*. doi:10.1109/LCNW.2012.6424068

Avram, A. (2014). *New in Motorola RhoMobile 5.0.* Licensing Model, Cloud Services and KitKat Support. InfoQ.

Balfanz, D., Durfee, G., Grinter, R. E., Smetters, D. K., & Stewart, P. (2004). Network-in-a-Box: How to set up a secure wireless network in under a minute. *Proceedings of the 13th USENIX Security Symposium*.

Balfanz, D., Smetters, D., Stewart, P., & Wong, H. C. (2002). Talking to Strangers: Authentication in ad-hoc wireless networks. *Proceedings of the Symposium on Network and Distributed Systems Security*.

Ballages, R., Rohs, M., Sheridan, J., & Borchers, J. (2008). *The Design space of mobile phone input techniques for ubiquitous computing. In Handbook of research on user interface design and evaluation for mobile technologies*. Hershey, PA: IGI Global.

Barcia, R., Berardi, T., Kak, A., Kreger, H., & Schalk, K. (2015). *Cloud Customer Architecture for Mobile*. Cloud Standards Customer Council. Retrieved from http://www.cloud-council.org/deliverables/CSCC-Cloud-Customer-Architecture-for-Mobile.pdf

Barker, E., Barker, W., Burr, W., Polk, W., & Smid, M. (2006). *National Institute of Standards and Technology (NIST) Special Publication 800-57 (Draft): Recommendation for Key Management - Part 1 General*. NIST.

Biolchini, J., Mian, G. P., Natali, A. C., & Travassos, H. G. (2005). *Systematic Review in Software Engineering*.Rio de Janeiro: Academic Press.

Bloice, D. M., & Wotawa, F. (2009). Java's Alternatives and the Limitations of Java when Writing Cross-Platform Applications for Mobile Devices in the Medical Domain. *Proceedings of the ITI 2009 31st International Conference on Information Technology Interfaces*. doi:10.1109/ITI.2009.5196053

Bluetooth, S. I. G. (2006). *Authorities raid Chinese factory suspected of infringing on Bluetooth SIG registered trademarks.* Retrieved from: http://www.bluetooth.com/Bluetooth/Press/SIG/AUTHORITIES RAID CHINESE FACTORY SUSPECTED OF INFRINGING ON BLUETOOTH SIG REGISTERED TRADEMARKS.htm

Burns, J. (2009). *Mobile application on Android.* Blackhat.

Charland, A., & LeRoux, B. (2011). Mobile Application Development: Web vs. Native. *Queue - Data, 9*(4), 4.

Chess, B., & McGraw, G. (2004). Static analysis for security. *Security & Privacy, IEEE, 2*(6), 76–79. doi:10.1109/MSP.2004.111

Cheswick, W., Bellovin, S., & Rubin, A. (2003). *Firewalls and Internet security: Repelling the wily hacker.* Boston, MA: Addison-Wesley Longman Publishing Co., Inc.

Christ, A. M. (2011). Bridging the Mobile App Gap. *Sigma Journal: Inside the Digital Ecosystem, 11*(1), 29.

Dickson, P. E. (2012). Cabana: A Cross-platform Mobile Development System. ACM Special Interest Group on Computer Science Education. doi:10.1145/2157136.2157290

Ench, W. (2009). Understanding Android security. *IEEE Security and Privacy, 7*(1), 50–57. doi:10.1109/MSP.2009.26

Fowler, M., & C. S., T. (2012). *Developing Software for Multiple Mobile Devices.* Thought Works, Inc. Retrieved from: http://martinfowler.com/articles/multiMobile/#ui-translate

Fuches, A. P., Chaudhuri, & Foster, J. S. (2009). ScanDroid: Automated security certification of Android applications. Technical report, University of Maryland.

Gartner. (2013). *Gartner recommends a hybrid approach for business-to-employee mobile apps* [Press release]. Retrieved from: http://www.gartner.com/newsroom/id/2429815

Gartner. (2014). *Gartner says more than 75 percent of mobile applications will fail basic security test through 2015* [Press release]. Retrieved from: http://www.gartner.com/newsroom/id/2846017

Gartner, Inc. (2012). *Gartner Says Free Apps Will Account for Nearly 90 Percent of Total Mobile App Store Downloads in 2012.* Retrieved from: http://www.gartner.com/DisplayDocument?ref=clientFriendlyUrl&id=2126015

Gavalas, D., & Economou, D. (2010). Development Platforms for Mobile Applications: Status and Trends. *Software, IEEE, 28*(1), 77–86. doi:10.1109/MS.2010.155

Google Maps JavaScript API v3. (2013). Google Inc. Retrieved from: https://developers.google.com/maps/documentation/javascript/

Heitkötter, H., Hanschke, S., & Majchrzak, T. A. (2012). *Comparing cross-platform development approaches for mobile applications.* Porto: WEBIST.

Hjärtström, D. (2012). *Utilizing web standards for cross platform mobile development Växjö*. Academic Press.

IBM. (2012). *Native, web or hybrid mobile-app development*. Somers. Retrieved from ftp://public.dhe. ibm.com/software/pdf/mobile-enterprise/WSW14182USEN.pdf

Jovanovic, N., Kirda, E., & Kruegel, C. (2006). Preventing cross site request forgery attacks. Securecomm and Workshops, 1-10. doi:10.1109/SECCOMW.2006.359531

jQuery Home Page. (2013). The jQuery Foundation. Retrieved from: http://jquery.com/

jQuery Mobile Home Page. (2013). The jQuery Foundation. Retrieved from: http://jquerymobile.com/

Juntunen, A., Jalonen, E., & Luukkainen, S. (2013). HTML 5 in Mobile Devices –Drivers and Restraints. *46th Hawaii International Conference on System Sciences*. doi:10.1109/HICSS.2013.253

Kaltofen, S. (2010). *Design and implementation of an end-user programming software system to create and deploy cross-platform mobile mashups*. Academic Press.

Kaltofen, S., Milrad, M., & Kurti, A. (2010). A Cross-Platform Software System to Create and Deploy Mobile Mashups. *ICWE'10 Proceedings of the 10th international conference on Web engineering*. doi:10.1007/978-3-642-13911-6_42

Kao, Y. W., & Lin, C. F. (2011). A Cross-Platform Runtime Environment for Mobile Widget- based Application. *2011 International Conference on Cyber-Enabled Distributed Computing and Knowledge Discovery*. doi:10.1109/CyberC.2011.20

Kapner, S., & Ziobro, P. (2014). Motorola Solutions Sells Scanner Business to Zebra Technologies. *Wall Street Journal*.

Krohn, M., Yip, A., & Brodsky, N. (2007). Information flow control for standard OS abstractions. *Proc. Of 21st ACM SIGOPS Symposium on Operating Systems Principles*, 321-334. doi:10.1145/1294261.1294293

Lafrance, A. (2016, May 16). Smartphones rule the internet. *The Atlantic*. Retrieved from: http://www. theatlantic.com/technology/archive/2016/05/smartphones-take-over/482880/

Lakshman, T., & Thuijs, X. (2011). Enhancing Enterprise Field Productivity via Cross Platform Mobile Cloud Apps. *MCS '11 Proceedings of the second international workshop on Mobile cloud computing and services*. doi:10.1145/1999732.1999741

Livshits, B. V., & Larn, M. S. (2005). Finding security vulnerabilities in Java applications with static analysis. *Proc. of the 14th Conference on USENIX Security Symposium*, 18-18.

Lyle, J., & Monteleone, S. (2012). Cross-platform access control for mobile web applications. *IEEE International Symposium on Policies for Distributed Systems and Networks*. doi:10.1109/POLICY.2012.9

Mark, P. (2013). *Geolocation - Dive Into HTML5*. Retrieved from: http://diveintohtml5.info/geolocation.html

Meier, J. D., Homer, A., Hill, D., Taylor, J., Bansode, P., Wall, L., . . . Bogwat, A. (2008). *Mobile Application Architecture Guide*. Retrieved from http://robtiffany.com/wp-content/uploads/2012/08/Mobile_Architecture_Guide_v1.1.pdf

New RhoMobile Suite 5.0 (2014). Offers developer-friendly pricing. *SD Times*.

Norris, C., & Soloway, E. (2011, November-December). Learning and schooling in the age of mobilism. *Educational Technology*, *51*(6), 3–10. Retrieved from http://cecs5580.pbworks.com/w/file/fetch/50304204/Soloway%20Ed%20Tech-Learning%20and%20Schooling%20in%20the%20Age%20of%20Mobilism.pdf

Oracle. (2015). *Oracle Mobile Security*. Retrieved from www.oracle.com: http://www.oracle.com/technetwork/middleware/id-mgmt/overview/omss-technical-wp-2104766.pdf

Pan, B., & Xiao, K. (2010). Component-based mobile web application of crossplatform. *10th IEEE International Conference on Computer and Information Technology (CIT)*.

Pincus & Wind. (2005). Measuring relative attack surfaces. Computer Security in the 21st Century, 109-137.

Qiu, Z., & Lou, L. (2012). *A Cross-platform Mobile Payment Solution Based on Web Technology. In 2012 Spring Congress on Engineering and Technology*. Xian: SCET.

Rajapakse, D. C. (2008). *Fragmentation of mobile applications*. National University of Singapore. Retrieved from: http://www.comp.nus.edu.sg/~damithch/df/device-fragmentation.htm

Ramadath, M. C. (2012). *Mobile Application Development: Challenges and Best Practices*. Accenture. Retrieved from: http://www.accenture.com/SiteCollectionDocuments/PDF/Accenture-Mobile- Application-Development-Challenges-Best-Practices.pdf

Riggins, J. (2015). *Why You Should Build Apps With API Backend - BaaS*. Retrieved from http://nordicapis.com/why-you-should-build-apps-with-an-api-backend-baas/

Sanneblad, J., & Holmquist, E. L. (2004). The GapiDraw Platform: High-Performance Cross-Platform Graphics on Mobile Devices. *MUM '04 Proceedings of the 3rd international conference on Mobile and ubiquitous multimedia*.

Schuermans, S., Vakulenko, M., & Voskoglou, C. (2015). *Developer megatrends hi 2015: Five key trends in the developer economy*. Retrieved from Vision Mobile: http://www.visionmobile.com/product/developer-megatrends-h1-2015/

Siegfried, B. (2011). *Enhanced Student Technology Support with Cross-Platform Mobile Apps. 39th annual ACM Special Interest Group on University and College Computing Services*, San Diego, CA.

Slee, M., Agarwal, A., & Kwiatkowski, M. (2007). *Thrift: Scalable Cross-Language Service Implementation. Technical report*. Facebook.

Smutny, P. (2012). Mobile development tools and cross-platform solutions. *13th International Carpathian Control Conference (ICCC)*.

Sun, X., & Du, Z., Z. (2011). A Secure Cross-platform Mobile IM System for Enterprise Applications. *International Conference on Uncertainty Reasoning and Knowledge Engineering.* doi:10.1109/URKE.2011.6007933

Thornycroft, P. (2016, March 31). What is the future of mobile communications app security. *Network-World from IDG.* Retrieved from http://www.networkworld.com/article/3050335/mobile-wireless/what-is-the-future-of-mobile-communications-app-security.html

Trice, A. (2012). *PhoneGap Blog.* Adobe Systems Inc. Retrieved from: http://phonegap.com/2012/05/02/phonegap-explained-visually/

Troy, M.A., & Vennon, T. (2010). *Android malware: Spyware in the Android Market.* Technical report, SMobile Systems.

Ubl, M. (2011). *Improving the Performance of your HTML5 App.* Retrieved from: http://www.html5rocks.com/en/tutorials/speed/html5/

Usage Statistics and Market Share of JavaScript Libraries for Websites. (2013). Retrieved from: http://w3techs.com/technologies/overview/javascript_library/all

Vogel, B. (2012). Architectural Concepts: Evolution of a Software System Across Design and Implementation Stages in Dynamically Changing Environments. *2012 IEEE 36th International Conference on Computer Software and Applications Workshops (COMPSACW).*

Wang, H. W., & Vick, C. (2004). Cross-Platform Multi-Network Mobile Application Architecture. *Proceedings of the IEEE 6th Circuits and Systems Symposium on Emerging Technologies: Frontiers of Mobile and Wireless Communication.*

Westin, A. F. (2003). Social and Political Dimensions of Privacy. *The Journal of Social Issues, 59*(2), 1–37. doi:10.1111/1540-4560.00072

Whinnery, K. (2012). *Comparing Titanium and PhoneGap.* Appcelerator Inc. Retrieved from: http://developer.appcelerator.com/blog/2012/05/comparing-titanium-andphonegap. html

Xin, C. (2009). Cross-Platform Mobile Phone Game Development Environment. *International Conference on Industrial and Information Systems.*

Yu, N., Liu, C., & Chen, J., J. (2011). The Development and Application of Cross-Platform Coal Mine Mobile Information System. *2011 International Conference on Computer Science and Network Technology.*

Zhang, B., & Wang, W. (2011). Research and Implementation of Cross-platform Development of Mobile Widget. *2011 IEEE 3rd International Conference on Communication Software and Networks (ICCSN).* doi:10.1109/ICCSN.2011.6014238

Zhu, H., Xiong, H., Ge, Y., & Chen, E. (2014). Mobile app recommendations with security and privacy awareness. *KDD '14 Proceedings of the 20th ACM SIGKDD international conference on Knowledge discovery and data mining,* 951-960. doi:10.1145/2623330.2623705

KEY TERMS AND DEFINITIONS

Business Continuity Planning: A theory covering operational and/or security risks, which could possibly affect the functionality of mobile devices. This concept, includes selecting security best practices to protect data and user's privacy.

Hybrid Apps: Multiple software applications i.e., native, web and hybrid solutions. These applications are designed to interface with the following web technologies: CSS, JavaScript and HTML5.

Mobile Applications; Software application developed to execute on various mobile devices/systems. By and large, vendors develop mobile devices with integrated apps designed to perform various functions.

Media Access Control: A single identifier component universally inserted on every computer and/ or mobile device. For instance, MAC address allows computer to launch communication activities on various networks. In a MAC environment, data link layer is responsible for launching a single or multiple sessions through network segmentation practices.

Mobile Devices: Handheld and/or portable wireless devices used for data processing or communication. Smartphones, PDAs, tablet computers, laptops are identified as mobile devices. Mobile devices frequently come with a built-in small screen and/or keyboard allowing for displaying and executing various functions/commands.

Mobile Networks: Communication networks designed to converge and/or provisioning data in simultaneous, to various destinations. Mobile networks comprise wireless, land hubs, etc. In mobile networks data is transported over dedicated/distributed network systems also known as wireless towers. Uplink signals are frequently transmitted from a base station via a wireless tower then to a downlink destination mobile device, or propagated to another base station via line of sight.

Mobile Technology: A technology used for mobile communication. In recent years, mobile technologies have evolved from providing a two-way signal transmission to multiple channel network propagation. In this day and age, mobile technologies are developed with integrated application interface i.e., APIs, web browsers, game console applications, GPS navigation features, instant messaging capabilities, camera capability, etc.

Native Apps: Application program developed for multiple mobile device usage. Commonly apps are developed to interact with a number of mobile applications or operating systems: iOS, blackberry, Android, etc.

Provisioning: A process of distributing data/services over many network media. In mobile devices, provisioning is regarded as a process through which users are able to receive, share and send data from/ to multiple destination devices in real-time. For such process to be implemented hardware and software are key resources for providing continuous abstraction and delivering of data packets between devices deployed on single and/or multiple networks.

Web Apps: A client-server software application designed to execute user and/or client interface activities. These apps consist of: retail sales applications, wikis, instant messaging services webmail, CSS, HTML5 and JavaScript applications. Each of these apps are developed to perform a single and/ or multiple activities.

Chapter 12
Denial of Service (DoS) Attacks Over Cloud Environment:
A Literature Survey

Thangavel M
Thiagarajar College of Engineering, India

Nithya S
Thiagarajar College of Engineering, India

Sindhuja R
Thiagarajar College of Engineering, India

ABSTRACT

Cloud computing is the fastest growing technology in today's world. Cloud services provide pay as go models on capacity or usage. For providing better cloud services, capacity planning is very important. Proper capacity planning will maximize efficiency and on the other side proper control over the resources will help to overcome from attacks. As the technology develops in one side, threats and vulnerabilities to security also increases on the other side. A complete analysis of Denial of Service (DOS) attacks in cloud computing and how are they done in the cloud environment and the impact of reduced capacity in cloud causes greater significance. Among all the cloud computing attacks, DOS is a major threat to the cloud environment. In this book chapter, we are going to discuss DOS attack in the cloud and its types, what are the tools used to perform DOS attack and how they are detected and prevented. Finally it deals with the measures to protect the cloud services from DOS attack and also penetration testing for DOS attack.

INTRODUCTION

Cloud computing is an emerging trend in the field of Information Technology. Cloud computing provides scalable and flexible resources for the end users on demand. The cloud offers three levels of services. They are Infrastructure as a service (Iaas), Platform as a service (Paas), and Software as a service (Saas). In Infrastructure as a service, the consumer (customer) have the capability of processing, storage and other computing resources. The consumer can deploy and run the software, like operating systems and applications (E.g. Host firewall). In platform as a service, the consumer can create the applications using

DOI: 10.4018/978-1-5225-2013-9.ch012

libraries, tools and programming languages offered by cloud service providers (cloud middleware's –E.g. Open nebula). The consumer cannot control the cloud infrastructure like operating systems, networks, and servers. In Software as a service, the consumer can make use of the applications that were created by the cloud service provider (E.g. Web based applications). Cloud characteristics include multi tenancy, device independence, resource pooling, measured services, resource allocation, scalability, use of third party services and energy efficiency.

Cloud computing provides the capabilities to store and process the data of the users and organizations in a third party (Cloud Service Provider) storage center. Cloud computing is one of the most innovative technologies in the present decade. In cloud computing, there are three types of cloud, namely, public cloud, private cloud and hybrid cloud. The advantages of cloud computing are cost saving, manageability and reliability. On the other side, there is a controversy in security and vendor lock in issue. In cloud computing, still some organizations cannot switch from one services to other services and it has not been completely evolved. This is called as vendor lock in. One of the major advantage of cloud computing is elasticity of the resources. The proper capacity planning is very necessary to manage the resources. Capacity planning means to plan the resources needed for the application in future. Pay as you go services is good as it needs to be paid only for the utilized resources. Capacity planning of resources will make us to handle multiple resources simultaneously.

In security aspect, there are so many attacks happening everyday like data theft, DOS attack and side channel attack, etc. Even though the cloud service providers provide the security standards, providing security in all aspects is quite difficult. In public cloud the vulnerable server or system and exploitation could happen easily. Other disadvantages are limited controls, technical difficulties, and downtime. Downtime is one of the disadvantages of the cloud service that affects the services when the internet connection goes down. In future, the security exploitation in cloud computing has to be managed effectively from the perspective of both providers and users.

COMMON ATTACKS ON CLOUD

Authentication Attack

Authentication is one of the vulnerable points in the cloud services. Generally authentication is provided for the users using username and password. Some of the developed organizations used site keys, virtual keyboards, and biometrics and shared secret questions. Most possible authentication attacks are i) brute force attack ii) shoulder surfing iii) Replay attack iv) Dictionary attack v) key loggers. We see in detail about all the above attacks. In a brute force attack, in order to break the username or password, we have to try all the possibilities (all possible combinations). In cloud, brute force attack is used to break the password which is in the encrypted form (encrypted text). In shoulder surfing, an attacker watches the employee or customer movements and tries to see the password when he/she types the password. This attack is also called spying. In Replay attack, an attacker intercept between the two valid users, capture the data and then retransmits the data frequently or in a delayed manner. This attack is also called Playback attack or reflection attack. Dictionary attack is to try out all the possible combinations of meaningful words in the dictionary to break the password (Ajey singh 2012). Key loggers is a software program and records the key pressed by the user. Key loggers monitor the user activities.

Denial of Service Attack

In DOS attacks, an attacker overloads the server by sending large number of requests and makes the server to un-respond to the valid users, at that time resource is not available to the user (Ramya 2015). DDOS attack which means many node systems attacking the one node systems at the same time by flooding the message.

Data Stealing Attack

Data stealing attack is similar to the authentication attack (Kumar 2014). In this attack, an attacker tries to break the username and passwords and steal the confidential information of the user.

Flooding Attack

An attacker can create an unwanted data, when the server is overloaded with the most number of requests and at that time attacker sends this unwanted request also. At that time the server will process both the legitimate requests and invalid requests (Kumar 2014). This leads to the more CPU utilization causing flooding attack or flooding of the systems.

Malware Injection Attack

An attacker injects the virtual machine or malicious services (like Saas or Paas) in the cloud. The attacker has to make believe the service as valid service among the valid instances in the cloud system. If an attacker is successful in that, the cloud automatically redirects the valid user to the malicious implementation services (Shikha Singh 2014). If the attacker takes control of the service, he/she can gain access to the victim's (user) data in the cloud.

Man in The Middle Attack

In man in the middle attack, the attacker tries to intercept between the two users. An attacker tries to make a communication path and modify the communications. There are several types of man in the middle attacks, important MITM is i) DNS spoofing ii) session hijacking. In DNS spoofing, for example, an attacker can create a fake website for a bank, a user visiting the his/her bank website for internet banking at that time user was redirected to the attacker's website, after that attacker will gain all the credentials of the user (Chouhan 2016). DNS spoofing is done to get the credentials of the user by creating fake information's or fake website.

Side Channel Attack

In Side channel attack, an attacker tries to compromise the cloud by placing the malicious virtual machine in the target server (cloud server) and doing a side channel attack. Side channel attack is one of the security threats in cloud. Side channel attacks can be done in two ways: VM CO-RESIDENCE AND PLACEMENT, VM EXTRACTION.VM CO-RESIDENCE AND PLACEMENT- an attacker is fixing his/her malicious instance on the same physical machine as a target *(Shikha Singh 2014)*. VM

EXTRACTION- the ability of malicious instance to utilize all the side channels and thus they are gaining information about the CO-RESIDENCE instances.

Wrapping Attack

In wrapping attack, attackers interrupt the process of the cloud server. This is done by a malicious SOAP (simple object access protocol) code element inserted in the TLS (Transport layer service) (Kumar 2014). After the code is inserted, the content is copied to the server; during the execution it interrupts the cloud server.

Attack on Hypervisor

Attacks in the hypervisor which lead to the compromise of security make whole cloud environment down. Hypervisor is the abstraction layer software between the virtual machine and hardware that comprise the cloud. If the attacker gains the control of operating systems, he/she can able to manipulate the data and even shut down or compromise the whole cloud services (Alani 2014). This attack on hypervisor is very low.

Resource Freeing Attack

Generally there are so many virtual machines are running on the same physical node in the cloud. The overall performance of the virtual machine will get down if another virtual machine over using the resources *(Alani 2014)*. So attack may done by the user to free up resources which are used in excess by the other user.

Attack on Confidentiality

In a cloud environment, security is the important aspect. Security is providing confidentiality (protect) the data from the unauthorized users. While we are concentrating on securing the data at the same time we have to think about providing security to the infrastructure as well. Attacks on confidentiality take place by social engineering, which an attacker eavesdrop or try to collect the encrypted passwords, keys, and identity of the cloud user (Alani 2014). Most of the time an attacker will impersonate the identity of the user and gain the access of the user to get the confidential data.

Denial of Service Attack

A cloud environment is vulnerable to denial of service attack because of the network resources are completely shared between the client and cloud service providers(CSP). In a distributed denial of service attack, requests are sent to the victim from different sources by an attacker. An attacker tries to prevent the usage of required computer resources by the legitimate user. For which an attacker will flood the packets and disrupt the service and thereby increasing the bandwidth usage, preventing the authorized user to access it. This is generally called as a DOS / DDOS attack in a cloud environment (Gunasekhar 2014). The denial of service attack in cloud is shown in Figure 1, involving the request and responses.

It is done as follows:

Figure 1. DOS attack in cloud

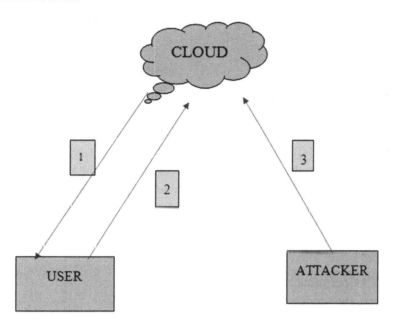

1. User's request to the cloud.
2. Cloud's response from the cloud.
3. The attacker tries to access the data from the cloud.

This DOS attack may cause to stop the service or shut down the service. It causes two kinds of impact in the cloud such as:

1. Direct denial of service, and
2. Indirect denial of service.

Direct Denial of Service

In the cloud environment, if the operating system faces large amount of workload in a particular service, at that time it provides more computational resource for that service like providing virtual machines in order to cope up with the assigned workload. Additional workload is given by the attacker to that particular service to stop or slow down the service.

Indirect Denial of Service

The indirect flooding attack causes the services provided on the same hardware servers to suffer severely from the workload. This is called as indirect denial of service. It depends upon the computational power under the control of the attacker.

Another important cause is accounting. The cloud service providers charge the user according to their resource usage. Because of the flooding attack, the service providers may raise the charge drastically for the cloud usage.

DDOS ATTACK IN CLOUD

DDOS attack in cloud in shown in Figure 2. In the above cloud network, so many servers are active and in each serving more than 10 computers or machines will run. An attacker targets any one of the machines, then the attacker sends the request from different sources along with the normal user (Somani 2015). Because of the overload of the request, the machine will slow down its performance.

SYMPTOMS OF DOS/DDOS ATTACK

1. Very slow network performance,
2. Inability to access the service, website, or network,
3. Unavailability of the website, and
4. Increase in a large number of spam mails.

The above factors contribute much towards denial of service attacks.

Figure 2. DDOS attack in cloud

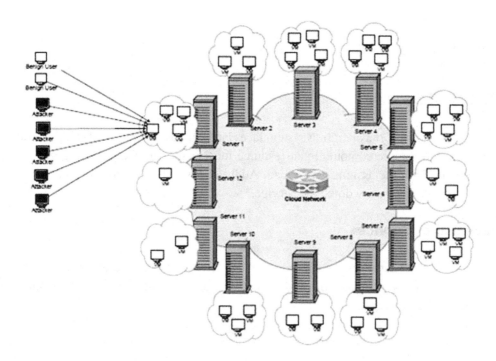

TERMINOLOGY IN DDOS ATTACK

- **Attacker:** An attacker is the root cause of the real attack in the cloud. To perform DOS attack, an attacker has to study the network topology clearly.
- **Agent/ Handler:** The agent program coordinates the attack through the Zombies. This is also called as Master program. The agent will carry out the attack to the target victim.
- **Zombies:** The agent carries out the attack to the victim. An attacker will gain access and the Zombies in the network will affect both the target as well as the host computer. This is also called as attack daemon agents.
- **Victim:** The victim or target receives the attack. It is shown in Figure 3.

The attacker will send the command to the Handler. The handler will receive the execute command and this command will propagate to the attack daemon agent or Zombie. Then the attack daemon agent will start attacking the victim and results in the slowdown of the service or unavailability of the service.

DDOS ATTACKS CLASSIFICATION

Volume based Attack

In this attack, an attacker sends more chunks of data to overload the victim machine. This is also called as Bandwidth based attack (Vidhya 2014). Eg. ICMP floods, UDP floods.

Figure 3. Elements of DOS attack in the cloud environment

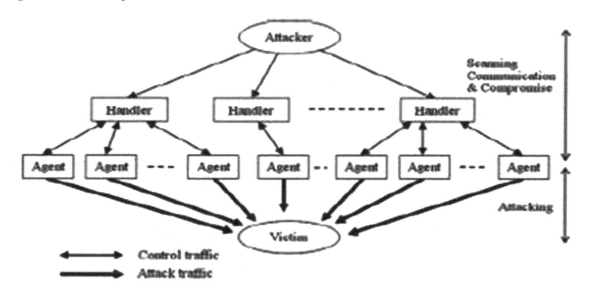

Protocol Attack

In this attack, an attacker use protocols to overload the resources of the victim. Eg. SYN floods, Smurf attack and Ping of Death.

Application based Attack

In this attack, an attacker will send a large amount request to the target. This can be done through web based applications. Eg. HTTP DOS and XML DDOS attack.

METHODOLODY IN DDOS ATTACK

There are several methodologies used in the DDOS or DOS attack (Nagaraju 2014), it is shown in Figure 4. Other than this methodology, there are so many different types of attacks possible.

Figure 4. Taxonomy of DDOS attack

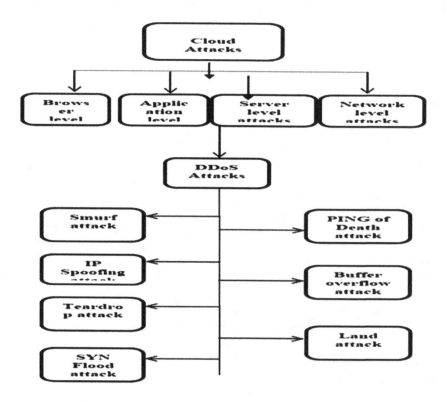

Smurf Attack

Smurf attack is the kind of distributed denial of service attack. In this, IP (Internet Protocol) and ICMP (Internet Control Message Protocol) protocols are used. ICMP packet is used to send the ECHO message and IP protocol is used to broadcast the messages. The Smurf attack is that the attacker sends large number ICMP packets as intended spoofed IP address (IP of victim's address is spoofed by the attacker), then these packets will broadcast in the cloud network by IP broadcast address. Normally the computer or machines in the network will reply to the source IP address, this will lead to the target machine flooded with traffic.

This will slow down the performance of the target machine and even it may stop the target from providing its services. This is generally called as Smurf attack. It is shown in Figure 5.

TOOL: HYENAE

Hyenae is a tool which we can use for Smurf attack. By using this tool we can perform man-in-the-middle attack, denial of service, distributed denial of service attack.

Features of Hyenae

1.   UDP flooding,
2.   TCP SYN flooding,
3.   LAND attack,
4.   DNS Query flooding,
5.   ICMP Smurf attack, and
6.   ICMP ECHO flooding.

The tool Hyenae screenshot is shown in Figure 6.

Figure 5. Smurf attack

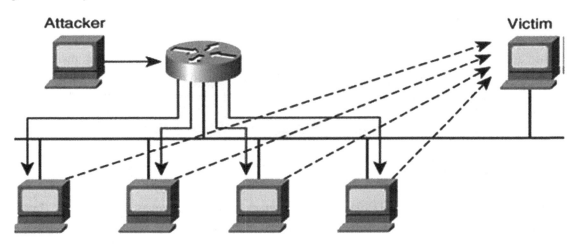

Figure 6. Screenshot for Hyena tool

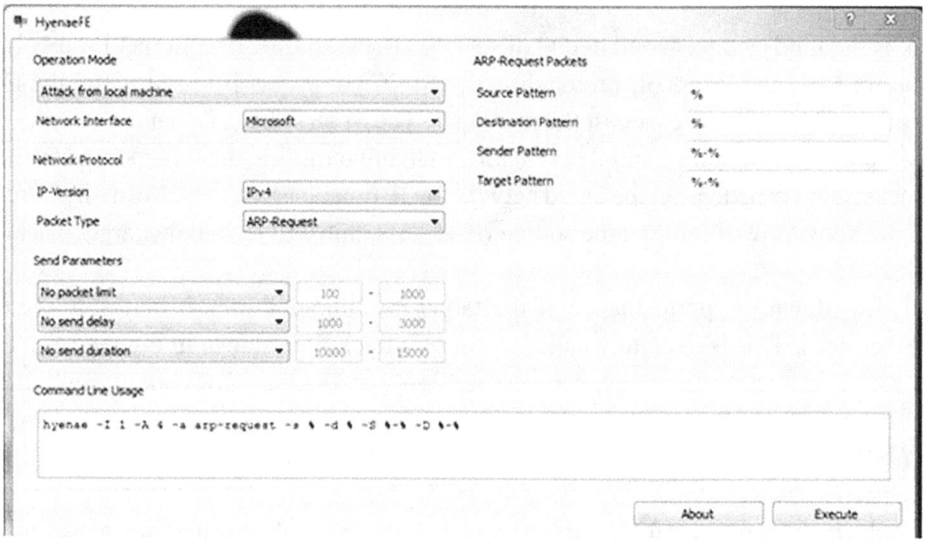

PING OF DEATH

Ping of death is one of the Denial of service attack. The IP (Internet Protocol) has the feature to send the IP packet into sub-packets. The attacker uses this feature of splitting the packets into sub-packets and sending the number of packets to the target. But In TCP/IP packet we can send only 65536 bytes of data. If an attacker tries to send more than 65536 bytes of data, it leads to PING OF DEATH attack.

Using Command Prompt

To perform ping of death attack, we can use command prompt of any operating system. In command prompt of windows OS, the attacker gives the command as ping –n 1000000 –l 65500, 216.58.220.361, where it is the IP address of www.google.com.

- **n:** Number of packets.
- **l:** Limitation of the packets.

When an attacker tries to send 1000000 numbers of packets which is more than the allowed bytes of data i.e 65536 at that time ping will not work and will not be able to give a reply from the IP address. This is called ping of death. It is shown in Figure 7. Ping of death is done by using the tool called CPU PING DEATH TOOL.

IP SPOOFING ATTACK

IP spoofing is generally used for Denial of service attack. Attacker changes the source IP (Internet Protocol) header field with the legitimate user IP address or an unreachable IP address. This causes the

Figure 7. Ping of Death using Command Prompt

```
Command Prompt - ping  -n 1000000 -l 65500 216.58.220.36
Microsoft Windows [Version 6.1.7601]
Copyright (c) 2009 Microsoft Corporation.  All rights reserved.

C:\Users\WIN7i> ping www.google.con

Pinging www.google.con [216.58.220.36] with 32 bytes of data:
Request tined out.
Reply from 216.58.220.36: bytes=32 tine=31ms TTL=57
Reply from 216.58.220.36: bytes=32 tine=31ms TTL=57
Reply from 216.58.220.36: bytes=32 tine=39ms TTL=57

Ping statistics for 216.58.220.36:
    Packets: Sent = 4, Received = 3, Lost = 1 (25% loss),
Approximate round trip tines in milli-seconds:
    Mininun = 31ms, Maximun = 39ms, Average = 33ms

C:\Users\WIN7i> ping   -n 1000000 -l 65500 216.58.220.36

Pinging 216.58.220.36 with 65500 bytes of data:
Request tined out.
Request tined out.
Request tined out.
Request tined out.
Request tined out.
Request tined out.
Request tined out.
Request tined out.
Request tined out.
Request tined out.
```

server in the cloud to wrongly lead to the legitimate user and server may unable to complete the task and affects the system performance. It is shown in Figure 8.

TOOL: NETWORK SPOOFER

This network spoofer is used in Android phone to spoof the network. It is used to break the Wi-Fi network. This tool shows that how the network is vulnerable to attacks like DOS attack etc.

Figure 8. IP spoofing

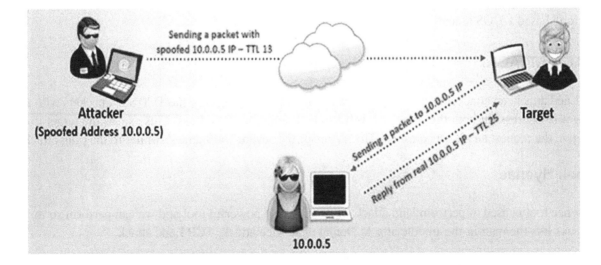

Figure 9. Tear Drop attack

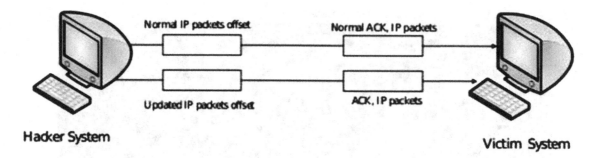

TEAR DROP ATTACK

In teardrop packet, the Internet protocol packets are divided into small chunks and sent as fragments along with the source IP address. The reason for sending the fragments along with source IP address, is that it is easy to reassemble at the destination side.

When TCP/IP stack is overlapped with fragments, it is difficult to reassemble and it easily fails. This is known as Teardrop attack. Because of this attack, the system may even crash. The attacker sends the invalid overlapping values along with the fragments in the offset field. This leads to the crash of the system, when the victim is trying to re-assemble the packet. It is shown in Figure 9.

TOOL: SCAPY

Scapy tool is used mostly for mobile devices. The scapy tool is used to perform tear drop attack.

BUFFER OVERFLOW ATTACK

In Buffer overflow attack, an attacker will write a code to perform the buffer overflow attack. Then the attacker will execute this code on the target machine. After the execution, the target machine will become fully under the control of the attacker. By using this target machine, the attacker will perform a cloud based DDOS attack.

LAND ATTACK

In Land attack, an attacker will write a program called land.c, to modify the TCP SYN packets with the target IP address for both the source as well as the destination IP address. This causes the target itself to give the request and it gets crashed. This is one of the severe DOS attack similar to the ping attack.

Tool: Hyenae

Hyenae tool is used to perform land attack. Hyenae is also powerful tool and we can perform so many attacks like the man-in-the-middle attack, Denial of service attack, TCP Land attack.

SYN Flood Attack

In SYN FLOOD attack, the attacker will flood the TCP/IP packet to the target machine from the fake IP address. In the TCP handshake process, the packets are considered as a request and this TCP will respond by giving TCP /SYN_ACK message.

The target machine will wait for the ACK, but it is never received because the request is coming from the fake IP address. This leads to a half open connection. Then the target machine will be no more able to accept any requests, even if it comes from the legitimate user.

By using Hyena tool we can perform TCP/SYN flood attack. Already we discussed about this tool in the previous attacks.

SYN flood attack can be classified into three types:

1. Direct attack,
2. Distributed attack, and
3. Spoof based attack.

Direct Attacks

The attacker will send the large amount of SYN REQ to the server without spoofing their IP address. Then the attacker prevents the operating system to reply to the SYN ACK. This task is done by using the firewall rules either we can allow only the outgoing packets which allow only SYN out or allow the incoming packets, such that any SYN ACK is denied before reaching the local TCP.

Distributed Attack

The attacker will use the many compromised machines and botnets through internet to do the Distributed SYN flood attack. Then the attacker will use each changeable machine for a spoofed attack and multiple spoofed addresses. This kind of attack is difficult to be blocked or stopped.

Spoof Based Attack

In this spoof based attacks, the attacker uses the spoofed IP address. In this attack, the client will not respond to the SYN ACKs send to them or at present there is no client system available for that spoofed IP address, this is happening because of the assumption of the spoofed address that does not respond.

OTHER POSSIBLE DOS/DDOS ATTACK IN CLOUD ENVIRONMENT

- UDP FLOOD,
- ICMP FLOOD,
- HTTP DOS ATTACK,
- XML DDOS ATTACK, and
- DNS REFLECTION ATTACK OR AMPLIFICATION ATTACK.

APPLICATION DOS ATTACK

Possible attacks in cloud (Wong 2014) are as follows,

UDP Flood

In UDP (User Datagram Protocol) flood, an attacker sends large number of UDP packets to the ports on the target machine using an attack Daemon agent (Zombie). As soon as the target identifies this request is coming from the unwanted source, the target will reply with the destination unreachable ICMP packet.

Because of the unwanted reply, the network bandwidth is used more and this bandwidth is not available for the legitimate users. The above is the overall scenario of UDP flood. Let's see, in detail, about the UDP flood attack.

UDP flood attack is also a kind of bandwidth attack. This uses the user datagram protocol, which is a stateless protocol, that means there is no need of an established session between the server and the client. The UDP flood attack starts by sending the largest amount of UDP packets to the target machine. As soon as the target machine determines that there is no application waiting on the port, it will send the ICMP unreachable message for each UDP to the forged source IP address. So the attacker uses the spoofed IP address to send UDP packets to the target, thus the target is overloaded with large UDP traffic responders. This UDP flood attack will create a weakness of CHARGEN and ECHO services (Exploit the services). The purpose of the CHARGEN is to continue generating some random characters and sent them to the correct source, this ECHO service continuously responds to the services by echoing the random characters back to the CHARGEN services. The attacker can pipe out the CHARGEN to ECHO. This situation creates an infinite loop between two UDP services. For example HOST B echoes a packet to HOST A, then HOST A responds to the echo packet of HOST B until the exhaustion of some shared resources.

Most of the UDP floods happens for larger bandwidth DDOS attack greater than 1Gbps(gigabytes per second) because we can easily generate UDP packets from various different languages.

ICMP Flood

In ICMP FLOOD, the target will be loaded with ICMP ECHO request packets by the attacker. When the target machine tries to reply to the attacker, because of the maximum bandwidth utilization, target couldn't reply, this leads to inaccessibility to the legitimate users. Let's see, in detail, about the ICMP flood attack. ICMP flood attack is often called as Ping attack or Smurf attack. This is often used for Ping based DDOS attack. The attacker will send a large number of ICMP packets to the server and try to crash the TCP/IP stack and stops response to the incoming TCP/IP requests to the server. Some times Hping and custom perl scripts are installed on the Zombie machine to do the ICMP flood. Sometimes the SYN flood attack is launched together with the ICMP flood.

HTTP (HYPER TEXT TRANSFER PROTOCOL) DOS ATTACK

HTTP DOS attack is a type of attack will occur in the application level. For this attack, the attacker will use HTTP GET and HTTP POST messages to the victim. An attacker will send the more number of

HTTP GET request to get some information and the server will load with get requests. This leads to the CPU and memory utilization and the victim will be unable to respond to other legitimate requests. The HTTP POST request is used to give input data (E.g. Forms). For this we require more computation from the server side. So, the HTTP POST DOS attack is complex than HTTP GET DOS attack.

There are three types of HTTP DOS attack:

- HTTP Malformed attack,
- HTTP Idle attack, and
- HTTP Request attack.

HTTP Malformed Attack

The attack happens when the Invalid HTTP packets are sent to the server and this results in the complete usage of the server resources. Eg. Zafi.B worm use malformed HTTP GET requests.

HTTP Idle Attack

HTTP connections are opened and left idle without sending the full request by the attacker. Eg. Slowloris. Slowloris means dribbling the small number of bytes or packets to keep the connection from timeout but it never completes the request.

HTTP Request Attack

HTTP request attack occur when a large number of legitimate requests are sent to the web server, which results in the consumption of server resources.

XML (EXTENSIBLE MARKUP LANGUAGE) DOS ATTACK

In X-DOS attack, the network is flooded with XML messages instead of packets inorder to prevent the legitimate users to access the network. The steps involved in X-DOS are,

- Exploit a known vulnerability.
- Flood the system with useless messages to exhaust.
- Attacker will try to hide their identities.
- Attacker will bypass a known defence that is in place to prevent it. This is also called as a REST based attack.

DNS (DOMAIN NAME SERVER) REFLECTION ATTACK

DNS reflection attack is also called as an amplification attack. It is a kind of distributed denial of service attack. An attacker sends a DNS name lookup request to the open DNS resolver from the spoofed source address (spoof the target address). The DNS server will send the DNS response to the spoofed source address. This response is larger than the DNS request. The attacker can amplify the traffic volume at the target. The attacker can use botnets to perform additional DNS queries, this results in overload of traffic. This type of attack is very difficult to block, because it is coming from the legitimate user from the authorized name servers.

The DNS reflection attack is possible by using the following:

- **Botnets:** In this DNS reflection attack, the attacker will compromise more numbers of online computers called as Botnets to send the DNS queries.
- **Source Address Spoofing:** When the attacker sends the DNS queries to open resolver, the source address of the DNS query is spoofed with target address rather than showing the real sender address. This is called as source address spoofing.
- **Malware:** This attack is triggered by botnets computer infected with malware EDNS0 (extension mechanism Domain name server). A 64 byte query is results in an 8x amplified 512 bytes UDP reply, if it's without EDNS0. EDNS0 will make the DNS requests to advertise their packet size and transfer the pack size larger than 512 bytes.
- **Open Recursion:** Open DNS resolvers which are generally called as servers on the internet, enables open recursion and provides the recursive DNS to response to anyone.

APPLICATION DOS ATTACK (ADOS)

Application DOS attack will use the vulnerability of the design, implementation and exploits it. Above all the attacks, the most recent and efficient attack is ADOS attack in recent times (Siva 2013). This prevents the access of the legitimate users to the services provided by CSP (Cloud Service Providers). This ADOS attack will disrupt the service rather than taking control of the service. This will happen mostly in the application layer.

The ADOS attack are broadly classified into four types:

1. Request Flooding Attack,
2. Repeated One shot Attack,
3. Application Exploit Attack, and
4. Asymmetric Attack,

Request Flooding Attack

The attacker tries to send heavy legitimate request to the server, the server will overload the session resources. Examples are HTTP, SIP INVITE'S, GET'S and DNS queries.

Repeated One Shot Attack

Repeated one shot attack occurs when high workload is sent to the server across many TCP sessions. This will slow down the service and shuts down the service on the server. This attack is similar to the asymmetric attack and request flooding attack.

Application Exploit Attack

Application exploit attack mainly focuses on the vulnerabilities of the application. It will exploit the application or server operating system by using the vulnerabilities of the application. Then it will allow the attacker to gain the control of the application in the cloud environment. Buffer overflow, SQL injection, Cookie poisoning, Hidden field manipulation and Scripting vulnerabilities are possible through this attack.

Asymmetric Attack

Asymmetric attack occurs when normal requests are in the need of large amount of computer resources, memory and disk space this leads to the degradation of the service.

THREATS OF DOS ATTACK IN CLOUD

X-DOS attack and H-DOS attack is one of the major threats of DOS in the cloud environment (Alotaibi 2015). There are three models in the cloud computing, they are Iaas, Paas, Saas. Cloud utilizes service oriented architecture (SOA) and web services to introduce the services.Web services and SOA are supported by Saas for many applications. When cloud users uses the web services in Saas, which leads to some vulnerabilities, by using this weakness an attacker tries to launch X-DOS and H-DOS attack in the cloud.

X-DOS attack uses the XML message to send to the web services or web server in the cloud. The message has the malicious content to exhaust all the resources and also exploits all the web service requests. When the attacker launches the X-DOS attack, this will flood the network with XML messages rather than packets, because of this the legitimate users are unable to use the network communication.

In H-DOS attack, the attacker uses HTTP Flooder to attack. The HTTP flooder starts up with 1500 threads. It has the capacity to send large number of HTTP requests to the web server to use all the communication channels. Till now there is no defined method to differentiate the legitimate and illegitimate packets.

SOLUTION TO THE X-DOS AND H-DOS ATTACK IN CLOUD

There are many approaches to mitigate X-DOS and H-DOS attack in the cloud environment. Using Cloud trace back method and Cloud protector (X-protector), can be implemented as discussed earlier in countermeasures of DOS. Another solution is a cloud defender system called cloud service queuing defender, that detects the X-DOS and H-DOS attack in an effective manner. Apart from X-DOS and H-DOS attack, there are so many types of DOS attack explained in the previous sections, which is also a severe threats to the cloud. To overcome the DOS attack, the detection and preventive methods are explained in the upcoming sections.

DETECTION OF DDOS ATTACK

In today's cloud environment all the DDOS/DOS attacks take place by using attack tool, malicious programs and botnets. There are so many detection techniques used to detect the DDOS attack. The detection techniques are used to identify and then discriminate the Unauthorized or Illegitimate packets.

The important detection techniques are:

1.   Signature based detection,
2.   Behaviour based detection,
3.   Active profiling,
4.   Wavelength based analysis, and
5.   Sequential change point.

Signature Based Detection

Signature based detection technique is useful only if the communication is not encrypted.This technique capture the traffic packets and compare with the existing attack patterns (Sendi 2015). It is useful to get the information,i.e how the communication takes place between the attacker and Zombie computer.

Behaviour Based Detection

Behaviour based detection technique concept is normal behaviour of the traffic is designed based on the traffic patterns. If there is any deviation from the normal traffic then it is consider as abnormal traffic (Sendi 2015). Generally the threshold value is set in order to differentiate the normal traffic(traffic is low than the threshold value) or abnormal traffic traffic is higher than the threshold value).

Active Profiling

Active profiling defines the average rate of the packet flow and it will monitor the header information of the packet. Average rating of the packet flow is calculated by the elapsed time between the consecutive packets. The sum of all inbound and outbound of the average packet rates gives the activity of the network.

Network activity is determined by an average rate of the packet flow. If we want to analyze one individual packet, we have to follow the order of 264 flows including the protocols such as TCP, IP, ICMP and SNMP. This leads to the high dimensionality problem. So we are clustering by exhibiting the similar characteristics.

By the above concept, attack is detected by an increase in the number of distinct clusters and an increase in the activity levels of the clusters.

Wavelet Signal based Analysis

The wavelet signal based analysis provides the description about a global frequency, but it will not provide any details about time localization. The wavelet signal based analysis gives the frequency detail and concurrent time. The input signal will be in the form of spectral components. The input signals have the time localization anomalous signals and background noise. It will detect the traffic by separating the time localized signals and noise. By analyzing each spectral windows, it is used to determine the presence of anomalies. The anomalies may represent a network failure or an attack such as DOS etc.

Sequential Change Point Detection

Sequential change point detection will separate, if there is an abnormal change in the traffic statistics. This technique will filter the target traffic such as port, address, flow of a time series and protocol. The time series states that, when there is a statistical change in the time the DOS attack starts. CUSUM is an algorithm used in the sequential change point detection. It is a change point detection algorithm. CUSUM will operate on continuous slamped data and it needs only a minimum computational resource and low memory.

It will identify the DOS attack by analyzing the deviations from the actual expected average in the time series. If the deviation is below the bound (normal flow condition), the cusum statistics will decrease. If the deviation is above the bound (abnormal traffic change), the cusum statistics will increase. This algorithm helps us to identify the appropriate DOS attack.

TOOLS

- Tools to perform the DOS / DDOS attack
- Tools to protect a DOS / DDOS attack

Tools to Perform the DOS / DDOS Attack

The following tools are available to perform denial of service or distributed denial of service attack.

LOIC (Low Orbit Ion Canon)

Low Orbit Ion Canon is the most famous tool. It is very easy to use for the beginners those who have basic knowledge about DOS attack. This tool will perform an attack by sending HTTP, TCP and UDP requests to the target.

XOIC (High Orbit Ion Canon)

The high orbit ion cannon is the most powerful tool. It is used to perform a DOS attack on target websites and servers.

HULK (HTTP Unbearable Load King)

HULK tool is also used to perform DOS attack by sending a distinct request and creating a complicate traffic on the server.

DDOSIM Layer-7 DOS Simulator

DDOSIM layer-7 DOS tool is used to perform DDOS attacks by generating Zombie hosts which are used to create TCP connection in the target. There are so many features available to perform in this tool, such as, HTTP DDOS, SMTP DDOS, Application layer DDOS attack.

R U Dead Yet

R U Dead Yet tool is also called as RUDY. RUDY is used for HTTP POST attack. This tool is used in long form submission field by using the POST method.

Tor's Hammer

Tor's hammer tool will perform slow post written in a language called python. During the attack, to act as anonymous, it can run in a TOR network. It can kill the IIS and Apache server in a few minutes.

OWASP DDOS HTTP POST

OWASP DDOS HTTP POST is a DOS checking tool. This will check your server, whether it can able to defend against DDOS attack or not.

PHP DOS

PHP DOS tool is used to perform the denial of service attack against the website or IP address. The script is written in PHP.

Sprut

Sprut is also used for DDOS/DOS attack. It will perform multisystem TCP denial of service attacks.

DOS HTTP

This tool is used to perform effective HTTP flood. It is also used as HTTP flood testing tool for windows operating system. Features of this tool are HTTP redirection, URL verification and monitoring the tracks.

Tools to Protect a DOS / DDOS Attack

The following tools are available to protect from denial of service or distributed denial of service attack.

D-Guard Anti DDOS Firewall Tool

D-Guard anti DDOS firewall will protect the cloud network system from DDOS attack. It protects against super DDOS, SYN flood, ICMP flood and UDP flood.

Forti DDOS Tool

Forti DDOS is a protection tool against Denial of service attack. After deploying the Forti DDOS we can analyze the network traffic behaviour.

DDOS Defend Tool

DDOS defend will protect against web exploits like real time DOS, SQL Injection and cross site scripting attacks. It also provides network level DDOS protection as it undergoes intense scrubbing, HTTP, ICMP, UDP and TCP defense.

DOS Arrest

DOS arrest's security service (DSS) provides the customized view for the client's website from both inside and outside. It is an online reporting tool with most important features like load balancing where real time traffic could be shown. It is a single point of access through which we can login, modify, view or add.

Defencepro

Defencepro is the famous DDOS protection service providing security for DDOS attack, login page attack, SSL based flood attacks.

METHODS TO PROTECT DDOS ATTACK

The various methods to protect DDOS attacks are as follows,

Cloud Trace Back Model and Cloud Protector

Cloud trace back model is based on the algorithm called Distributed Packet Marking (DPM) whereas the cloud protector is based on back propagation neural network. Cloud trace back is used to identify the DDOS attack source and cloud protector is used to separate or differentiate the illegal message patterns. To avoid direct DDOS attack, cloud trace back is placed before webserver.

CLASSIE Packet Marking Approach

CLASSIE Packet is an intrusion detection system and this uses a decision tree classification algorithm. CLASSIE is placed at one hop distance from the host and finds the malicious packets by defining its own rules (Vidhya 2014).

Thus, CLASSIE Packet is used to prevent the HDOS and XDOS attack in the cloud network. The malicious packet is marked and carried all the way through a router and switches. IN RAD (reconstruction and Drop) placed at one hop distance from the target makes the decision whether to allow the packet or deny the packet. This method will reduce the DDOS attack rates. The malicious packets will be marked at the attacker's side and dropped at the target's side.

Cooperative Intrusion Detection System

An Intrusion Detection System (IDS) is deployed in every cloud computing environment. The IDS maintains a Block table for monitoring and log activities. When the packets are received, a comparison is made for a match in the block table, if match is found it will immediately allow the packet and if there is no match found and detects it as a malicious packet, then it will send an alert to the other IDS in the network. The majority votes of the IDS decides whether it's a true or a false alert. If it is a true alert, then the block table is updated with the new rule for future reference and if it is a false alert, it will not update in the block table.

For this method IDS needs four elements namely,

1. Intrusion detection,
2. Alert clustering,
3. Intrusion response and block, and
4. Cooperative operation.

These kinds of IDS are used to detect the early DDOS attack.

Filtering Tree Approach

Filtering tree approach is generally used in the application level layers. The user (client) request is converted to XML format and this XML format is converted to SOAP (simple object access protocol) with user IP address, user puzzle and user solution which are twice signed. The SOAP message is forwarded to the IP trace back where the incoming packets are compared with the table maintained in the IP trace back. If match is found, the packet is denied, otherwise it is forwarded to the Cloud Defender. Cloud defender has five filters namely, sensor filter, Double signature filter, Hop count filter, Puzzle resolver and divergence filter. After passing this entire filter it allows the packet. This filtering tree approach prevents the HDOS and X-DOS attack, but fails to prevent network and transport layer DOS attack.

Confidence based Filtering Approach

In Confidence based filtering approach, there are two time periods, one is Attack period and another one is Normal period. In normal period, it finds the correlation pattern for legitimate packets by extracting the attribute pair in the TCP/IP header. This correlation between the attribute pair is used to calculate the Confidence values. The confidence value is calculated to identify the trust between the attribute pair. If the frequency of the attribute pair is high, the confidence level also goes high. This is stored in the log file and considered as a normal profile.

During the attack period, every packet is calculated by the weighted average of confidence values of the attribute pair and it is called as CBF (confidence based filtering) score. In CBF, all the packets are compared to the threshold value inorder to allow or deny the packet. If the CBF score is lower than the threshold, the packet will be considered as a malicious packet and so it would be discarded. If the CBF score is higher than the threshold, the packet will be allowed.

Information Theory based Metric Method

In Information theory based metric method there are two phases such as, behaviour monitoring and behaviour detection. In behaviour monitoring phase, it will monitor the web user behaviour and entropy value is calculated for requests and the trust score is given to each user. This is generally called as a Non-attack period.

In behaviour detection phase, the entropy value is compared with the threshold value and if it exceeds the value, it is considered as a malicious packet and the packet is denied. If the entropy value is lesser than the threshold value, based on the trusted score restricted access is provided to the user.

COUNTERMEASURES FOR DDOS ATTACK

The countermeasures for the distributed denial of service attack in the cloud are as follows,

1. Secondary victims should be protected,
2. Neutralize the handlers,
3. Prevent the potential attacks,
4. Deflect the attacks,
5. Mitigate the attacks, and
6. Forensic the post attacks.

The various countermeasures above are explained in detail (Countermeasure 2015).

Secondary Victims should be Protected (in the Cloud Network Systems)

The secondary victims should always be protected from security issues by prevention techniques. This can avoid secondary victims to become Zombies. The system should check their own security, and by checking it should ensure that there is no agent program installed. The system should also check their DDOS agent traffic. The following measures should be taken to check and monitor the secondary victims,

- Awareness should be increased among the internet users about the security issues and its prevention techniques.
- Licensed Antivirus and Anti Trojan virus should be installed and updated often.
- Regular updates and configuration of the core hardware and software should be done.
- Uninstall unnecessary as well as unused application and disable unwanted services.
- Scan all the files from the external source, outside the network.

Another important thing in the cloud environment is price. In cloud, pricing should be fixed according to the usage of the services provided by the CSP (cloud service providers). This will allow only the legitimate users to access and avoids the DDOS attack in the cloud.

Neutralize the Handlers

One of the ways to stop the DDOS attack is to neutralize the handlers. This can be done in the following ways,

- Analyze the communication protocols and traffic patterns in the network.
- The DDOS attack deployed are compared to the number of agents. When we neutralize the handlers, it possibly renders many numbers of agents useless.
- The attack can come from a spoofed source address, thus we can prevent by neutralizing the handlers.

Prevent the Potential Attacks

We can prevent the DDOS attack by:

- Ingress Filtering,
- Egress Filtering, and
- TCP Intercept.

Ingress Filtering

In ingress filtering it will prohibit the attack, where the attacker trying to launch an attack from the spoofed IP address that does not obey ingress filtering rules. Ingress filtering will not protect against flooding attacks on the network.

It will have the strict traffic rules and it will not allow the packets if it has not come from the legitimate users. Another major advantage of ingress filtering is, it will trace the originator and its true source address.

Egress Filtering

In this method of traffic filtering, the IP header is initially scanned and checked whether it meets the criteria. If it meets the criteria, it is allowed into the network, otherwise it gets rejected. Egress filtering assures that unauthorized or malicious traffic will never initiate from the internal network.

TCP Intercept

To avoid the SYN flood attack, TCP intercept is introduced. In TCP intercept mode, it will intercept the SYN packets which are sent by the client to the server and find matches with an extended access list. If match is found, the TCP intercept establishes the connection to the server on behalf of the client and also establishes the connection to the client on behalf of the server. After the two half connections are made, the TCP intercept combines the connections transparently. This TCP intercept act as mediator between the client and the server. This TCP intercept mode prevents fake connections trying to reach the server. If a match is found, it will deny the request.

Deflect the Attack

One of the ways to deflect the attack is by using honey pots. The system which acts as a lure(tempt an attaccker) for the attacker and provides partial security is called honey pots. Honey pots not only protect the systems in the cloud network, but also track the activities of the attacker what they are trying to accomplish. Honey pots were specially designed to attract the DDOS attackers. The installation of the agent code within the honeypot avoids the legitimate system being compromised.

There are two types of honey pots namely, High interaction honeypot and Low interaction honeypot.

High Interaction Honeypot

It will simulate the complete layout of the entire network of the computers and its main aim is to capture the attacks. This will track and control all the activities in the network. Example for high interaction honeypot is a Honeynet.

Low Interaction Honeypot

It will simulate only the services often requested by the attacker. Here, multiple virtual machines run on one physical system consuming only few resources. It reduces the complexity of the virtual machine security. Example for low interaction honeypot is Honeyd.

Mitigate the Attacks

In two ways we can stop the DOS/DDOS attack:

1. Load Balancing, and
2. Throttling.

Load Balancing

Cloud service providers can increase their bandwidth, which prevents the servers going down. The above scenario is done to prevent the DOS / DDOS attack from happening. Another important thing is the replication server model, if there is a replication server, we can provide better load management and minimize the risk. This will mitigate the effect of Denial of service attack.

Throttling

Throttling helps to avoid DDOS attack in the cloud. This method enable the routers to handle more number of traffic in the network. It can also be used to filter the legitimate user traffic from fake DDOS attack traffic.

This throttling method is in the experimental stage. The major disadvantage is that throttling may trigger false alarms. Sometimes it will allow the malicious traffic and deny the authorized traffic.

Forensic the Post Attack

Among all the countermeasures, one of the important factor that investigate is the post attacks. This can be done in two ways:

1. Traffic pattern analysis, and
2. Run Zombie Zapper tool.

Traffic Pattern Analysis

During the DDOS attack, traffic pattern analysis helps to store the post attack data to analyze the traffic. The post attack data is helpful in changing load balancing and enhancing the anti attack measures.

This traffic pattern analysis is helpful for the admin to create a new filtering technique to prevent DDOS attack, this will avoid the traffic entering into the network. By analyzing the IDS (Intrusion Detection System) logs, firewall helps to identify the source of the DOS traffic.

Run Zombie Zapper Tool

When the providers are unable to ensure the security for the server and when DDOS attack begins, the IDS realizes large amount of traffic. At that time, the target victim starts running the Zombie Zapper tool acts as defence against TRINOO, TFN, Shaft and Stacheldraht. TRINOO is a set of computer programs that conducts DDOS attack. The tribe flood network is also the computer programs used to conduct DDOS attack. Shaft and Stacheldraht belong to the family of train and tfn, which is used to perform DDOS attack. The various Defence mechanisms and the model in which it can be applied for different attacks are shown in Table 1.

PENETRATION TESTING

The penetration testing is done to identify the weakness and security loopholes in the cloud network. As a pen tester, we have to check the system have the ability to sustain for DOS attack or it gets crashed. To do a penetration testing, we have to do the following steps in the cloud network. It is shown in Figure 10 (Penetration 2015).

Define the Objective

As a penetration tester we have to define the objective. This helps the analyst to accomplish the goal of the test in the cloud.

Testing Heavy Loads on the Server

The Penetration tester, tests the server or the target by loading artificially to test the stability and performance of the cloud network. There are many tools available to test the heavy loads on the server.

Table 1. DDOS attack Defence mechanisms

ATTACK	DEFENCE MECHANISM	APPLIED MODEL
Smurf attack	i) Routers should configure to disable the IP broadcast address. ii) Operating system should be configured properly.	IAAS
Ping of Death	Ping of death can be avoided by using most recent operating systems and network devices	IAAS and PAAS
IP spoofing attack	To avoid IP spoofing attack, we have to implement Hop count filtering technique as well as the IP to Hop count filtering technique.	PAAS
Tear Drop attack	Tear Drop attack can be avoided by using most recent network devices and operating systems	IAAS and PAAS
Buffer overflow attack	To write the code to avoid overflow and to check for the array boundaries and time limit consumption	SAAS
Land attack	i) Use most recent network device and OS (updated versions). ii) Drop the packets which have same IP address for both source and destination	IAAS and PAAS
SYN flood attack	i) Firewall monitoring ii) Filtering techniques iii) SYN cache/SYN cookies approach	PAAS and IAAS
UDP flood	i) Rate limits on UDP traffic ii) Configure the router to disable the IP Broadcast transmission	IAAS and PAAS
ICMP flood	Configuring the routers to response only to legitimate ICMP packets	PAAS
HTTP DOS	i) We can provide defence by using IPS (Intrusion Prevention System). ii) We can use WAF (Web Application Firewall).	SAAS
XML DOS	Firewall monitoring and Intrusion Prevention System.	SAAS
DNS Reflection attack	i) Use Ingress filtering technique. ii) Limiting the DNS recursion by configuring the server to allow recursion for the list of authorized DNS servers.	SAAS and PAAS
A-DOS	To defence against DDOS attack we can use WAF (Web Application Firewall).	SAAS

Figure 10. Penetration testing

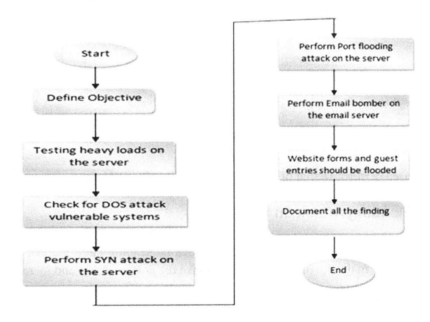

Web Server Test Tool

The web server test tool helps to perform a load test. It is a software tool to check the performance and stability of the web servers and web infrastructures.

Web Stress Tester Tool

This tool helps to check the stability of the proxy servers with SSL(secure socket layer)/TLS (transport layer security)enabled in the web servers.

Check for DOS Attack Vulnerable Systems

The penetration tester should check for the DOS attack vulnerable systems in the network by scanning the cloud network. To check the DOS attack vulnerable systems, several tools are available.

N-map Tool

N-map is the famous tool for port scanning. It is used to check the state of ports, services running on the port, operating system versions, firewall and filters.

Nessus Tool

Nessus is a vulnerability assessment tool. It is used for audit profiling, data discovery and vulnerability analysis.

Perform a SYN Attack on the Server

The penetration tester will try to do a SYN attack on the server. This can be done by bombarding the target by sending the request packets.

DOS HTTP tool

The DOS HTTP tool is used to perform SYN attacks on the server.

Sprut Tool

Sprut tool is also used perform Denial of service attack, especially SYN attack.

Perform Port Flooding Attack on the Server

The penetration tester should perform port flooding attack by sending large number of UDP or TCP packets to the target. The main aim of this attack is to make the port unusable and increase CPU utilization. To perform port flooding we can use the following tools.

Mutilate Tool

Mutilate is a tool which is used to see the open ports on the target. By using the open ports we can do the attack. This tool mainly concentrates on TCP/IP networks.

Pepsi5 Tool

Pepsi5 is a tool mainly focusing on UDP packets and it will show the size of the datagrams whereas it runs in the background.

Perform Email Bomber on the Email Server

The penetration tester will do an Email Bomber by sending a large number emails or bulk emails to the target server. If the target is withstanding enough, it will not crash. Otherwise the target would certainly crash. We can use the following tools to perform email bomber.

Mail Bomber

Mail Bomber is a tool to send a bulk amount of emails to the target server. These tools have the capability to hold separate mailing list. But it is not a free, open source tool requiring the payment of amount in dollars to use this tool.

Advanced Email Bomber

Advanced email bomber is able to send a personalized message (large amount of emails) to the subscriber using different predefined templates. This tool will deliver the message very fast and also tracks the feedback of the user.

Website Forms and Guest Entries should be Flooded

The penetration tester tests the online application forms by entering the lengthy entries to check causing it to crash. Generally DDOS attacker, try to enter the bogus entries to crash the website. To avoid this we are doing a penetration testing in the website forms.

Document all the Findings

The penetration tester should document the entire findings to report for future references.

CONCLUSION

In this chapter, we have analyzed that one of the major threat to the cloud environment is the denial of service attack. Most of the DOS attacks are performed to deprive resource utilization as the server would not be able to respond to the request. On preventing DOS attack, proper capacity planning will be achieved. When there is a proper capacity planning, we can easily manage the resources even though if there are massive amount of resources to be handled. To overcome the DOS attack, we need to follow some security techniques, mitigation strategies to overcome the attack. Thus, a detailed ananlysis of the impact, mitigation strategies, tools and the penetration testing is done for Denial of Service attack. Thus, the Denial of Service attack can be detected and prevented through the adherence of the DOS countermeasures.

REFERENCES

Alani. (2014). Securing the Cloud: Threats, Attacks, and Mitigation Techniques. *Journal of Advanced Computer Science and Technology*, 202-213.

Alotaibi. (2015). Threat in Cloud- Denial of Service (DoS) and Distributed Denial of Service (DDoS) Attack, and Security Measures. *Journal of Emerging Trends in Computing and Information Sciences, 6*(5).

Chouhan & Singh. (2016). Security Attacks on Cloud Computing with Possible Solution. *International Journal of Advanced Research in Computer Science and Software Engineering, 6*(1).

Gunasekhar, T., Thirupathi Rao, K., Saikiran, P., & Lakshmi, P. V. S. (2014). A Survey on Denial of Service Attacks. *International Journal of Computer Science and Information Technologies, 5*(2), 2373–2376.

Kilari & Sridaran. (n.d.). An Overview of DDoS Attacks in Cloud Environment. *International Journal of Advanced Networking Applications*.

Ramya, R., & Kesavaraj, G. (2015). A Survey on Denial of Service Attack in Cloud Computing Environment. *International Journal of Advanced Research in Education & Technology, 2*(3).

Shameli-Sendi, Pourzandi, Fekih-Ahmed, & Cheriet. (2015). Taxonomy of Distributed Denial of Service Mitigation Approaches for Cloud Computing. *Journal of Network and Computer Applications*, (October), 28.

Singh & Shrivastava. (2012). Overview of Attacks on Cloud Computing. *International Journal of Engineering and Innovative Technology, 1*(4).

Singh, S., Pandey, B. K., & Srivastava, R. (2014). Cloud Computing Attacks: A Discussion with Solutions. Open Journal of Mobile Computing and Cloud Computing, 1(1).

Siva, T., & Phalguna Krishna, E. S. (2013). Controlling various network based ADoS Attacks in cloud computing environment: By Using Port Hopping Technique. *International Journal of Engineering Trends and Technology, 4*(5).

Somani, G., Gaur, M. S., Sanghi, D., Conti, M., & Buyya, R. (2015). DDoS Attacks in Cloud Computing: Issues, Taxonomy, and Future Directions. ACM Comput. Surv., 1(1).

Venkatesa Kumar & Nithya. (2014). Improving security issues and security attacks in cloud computing. *International Journal of Advanced Research in Computer and Communication Engineering, 3*(10).

Vidhya, V. (2014). A Review of DOS Attacks in Cloud Computing. *IOSR Journal of Computer Engineering, 16*(5), 32-35.

Wong & Tan. (2014). A Survey of Trends in Massive DDOS Attacks and Cloud-based Mitigations. *International Journal of Network Security & Its Applications, 6*(3).

Chapter 13
Security Aspects in Cloud Computing

Tabassum N. Mujawar
Terna Engineering College, India

Ashok V. Sutagundar
Basaveshwar Engineering College, India

Lata L. Ragha
Terna Engineering College, India

ABSTRACT

Cloud computing is recently emerging technology, which provides a way to access computing resources over Internet on demand and pay per use basis. Cloud computing is a paradigm that enable access to shared pool of resources efficiently, which are managed by third party cloud service providers. Despite of various advantages of cloud computing security is the biggest threat. This chapter describes various security concerns in cloud computing. The clouds are subject to traditional data confidentiality, integrity, availability and various privacy issues. This chapter comprises various security issues at different levels in environment that includes infrastructure level security, data level and storage security. It also deals with the concept of Identity and Access Control mechanism.

INTRODUCTION

Cloud computing is a nascent and rapidly emerging computing paradigm with broad-ranging effects across IT Industry, Business, Software Engineering, and Data Storage. Cloud computing can be defined as a huge collection of distributed servers which provide on demand services to the users over Internet. It is a model which provides network access to shared computing resources such as data, servers, applications and services etc. Thus, users can access any resource from cloud on demand basis at a particular time and can pay only for their use.

A Cloud system consists of 3 major components such as clients, datacenter, and distributed servers (Velte A. T., Velte T.J. & Elsenpeter R., 2010), as shown in Figure 1.

DOI: 10.4018/978-1-5225-2013-9.ch013

Figure 1. Cloud computing components

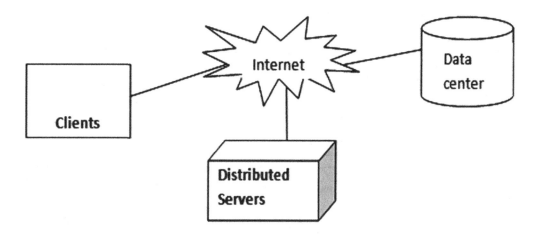

Clients

End users interact with the clients to access services provided by the cloud. Clients generally fall into various categories as thin client, thick client and mobile client.

Datacenter

In order to subscribe different applications, an end user connects to the datacenter which is a collection of servers hosting different applications.

Distributed Servers

Distributed servers are present throughout the Internet to host different applications.

Based on the domain or environment in which clouds are used, clouds can be divided into 3 categories as (Velte A. T.,Velte T.J. & Elsenpeter R., 2010) (See Figure 2):

- **Public Cloud:** It is available to the general public users in a pay-as-you-go manner irrespective of their origin or affiliation.
- **Private Cloud:** Its usage is restricted to members, employees, and trusted partners of the organization.
- **Hybrid Cloud:** It is combination of both the private and public clouds and enables the use of private and public Cloud in a seamless manner.

The services of cloud computing are categorized as (Velte A. T.,Velte T.J. & Elsenpeter R., 2010):

- **Software as a Service (SaaS):** In SaaS, the client uses different software applications from different servers through the Internet and pays for the time he uses the software.

Figure 2. Cloud computing deployment and deliver models

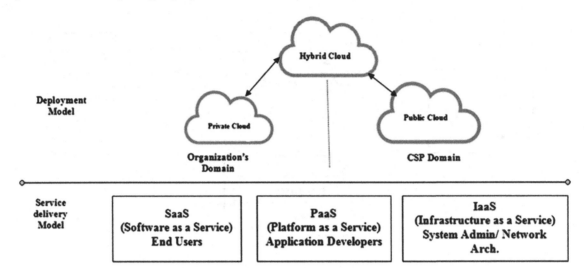

- **Platform as a Service (PaaS):** PaaS provides all the resources that are required for building applications and services completely from the Internet, without downloading or installing software.
- **Infrastructure as a Service (IaaS):** IaaS provides necessary infrastructure to develop and deploy applications. It is also known as Hardware as a Service (HaaS). It offers the hardware as a service to an organization so that it can put anything into the hardware according to its will.

Though cloud computing is the most promising technology, it faces many security challenges. The security concern arises because user's data and applications are present outside the administrative control in a shared environment and accessed by various other users. This shared and on-demand nature of cloud computing introduces the new security violations which limits the adoption of cloud computing. Therefore many users are reluctant in completely trusting the cloud computing environment (KPMG, 2010; Keiko H., Rosado D. G., Eduardo F. & Eduardo B.F., 2013).

The traditional security mechanisms such as identity management, authentication, and authorization are not sufficient for cloud computing in form they exist presently. The security risks associated with the organization by adoption of cloud are quite different than the traditional IT organizations (Li W., Ping L., 2009). Cloud computing security mechanism must address the security concerns from the perspective of end users and also for the cloud service providers. The security mechanism must include different standards and procedures to provide security assurance for all cloud service delivery models i.e. Software as a Service (SaaS), Platform as a Service (PaaS) and Infrastructure as a Service (IaaS). It should also take into consideration the different deployment models of cloud computing (public, private and hybrid cloud).

Organization of Chapter

The section II describes the security issues and threats in cloud computing. In section III we describe infrastructure security in detail. The section IV constitutes the data security aspects in cloud computing. The section V discusses the Identity and access management mechanism.

SECURITY ISSUES IN CLOUD COMPUTING

Security is the biggest barrier for adoption of cloud computing. The security challenges can be faced at different levels such as architectural level, communication level and contractual and legal level (Ali M., Khan S. U., Athanasios V. & Vasilakos, 2015). The challenges at communication level are similar to the challenges of conventional IT communication which include denial-of-service, man-in-the-middle, eavesdropping, IP-spoofing based flooding, and masquerading (Liu B., Bi J. & Vasilakos A, 2014; Sankar K., Kannan S. & Jennifer P., 2014). The security concerns at architecture level include various issues such as Virtualization, Data privacy, integrity, Identity management and access control. As organization's data and application is present under administrative control of cloud service provider various issues like legal, performance assurance, regulatory laws compliance, geographic jurisdictions, monitoring of contract enforcement come into picture.

The CSA (Cloud Security Alliance) has listed the following top 12 cloud computing threats in (Cloud Standards Customer Council, 2015; Infoworld, 2016; Cameron C., 2016, CSA,2012).

Data Breaches

The large amount of data is stored in cloud environment. This data is primary target of attackers and can be exposed in some unauthorized way. The data breaches include expose of any sensitive information such as health related records, financial information, trade secrets, intellectual property.

Compromised Credentials and Broken Authentication

The Data breaches generally occur due to poor authentication, week passwords or poor key management. The identity management must be done properly where credentials are assigned to users on basis of their roles and responsibilities. If user's access permissions are not added and removed properly then it results in unauthorized access to various resources.

Hacked Interfaces and APIs

The organizations use various APIs to interact with cloud services. If these APIs are not secure then the organization has to face security issues in terms of confidentiality, integrity, availability, and accountability.

System Vulnerabilities

Due to multitenancy feature of cloud computing different system vulnerabilities may occur. The shared resources like memory, database and other resources become the attractive targets for attacks.

Account Hijacking

Attackers can use cloud application to eavesdrop on activities, manipulate transactions, to modify data and to launch new threat.

Malicious Insiders

Along with the attacks from outside world, the huge risk for organization exists due to malicious insiders also. It includes threats due to current or former employee, business partner, system administrator, service provider.

The APT

The APT is advanced persistent threats which gain access to system to establish a foothold and then steal data and intellectual property over an extended period of time.

Permanent Data Loss

The malicious attackers can delete the cloud data permanently. The cloud data centers are vulnerable to natural disasters so adequate data backup measures are essential.

Inadequate Diligence

Organizations must clearly understand the cloud environment and the associated risk before adopting cloud technology. If any organizations fail to scrutinize a contract with the service provider then some operational or architectural issues may arise.

Cloud Service Abuses

The cloud services can be hijacked to perform malicious activities, such as launch an attack, send spam and phishing emails, and host malicious content. The new service providers should have some way to recognize types of abuses.

DoS (Denial of Service) Attacks

The DoS attacks affect the availability and accountability in cloud. Due to this system may slow down or may become unavailable for long time.

Shared Technology, Shared Dangers

Cloud service providers share infrastructure, platforms, and applications, and if a vulnerability arises in any of these layers, it affects everyone.

In this chapter we limit our discussion to infrastructure security, data security and Identity and access management in cloud computing.

Infrastructure Security

The infrastructure security standards are established at network, host and application level. The infrastructure security should take into account all service delivery models of cloud such as SaaS, PasS and

IaaS. It should also consider which deployment model is being used i.e. whether it is public cloud or private cloud (Mather T., Subra K., & Latif S., 2009; Reese G., 2009). The infrastructure security is implemented at different building levels such as the network, host and application levels (Mather T., Subra K., & Latif S., 2009; NetApp, 2009).

NETWORK LEVEL

The most important concern at network level infrastructure security is to differentiate between public and private cloud. The existing security tools and considerations without adoption of cloud computing are applicable to private cloud. Though the organization's architecture changes due to adoption of private cloud, the network topology remains same (Reese G., 2009). In case of public cloud architecture data and recourses previously bounded to a private network are now exposed to shared public network belonging to a third-party cloud provider. Thus the change in security requirements requires a significant change in network topology. The various factors that must be addressed for network level security are (Mather T., Subra K., & Latif S., 2009):

- Confidentiality and integrity of data
- Proper access control
- Availability of resources
- How existing topology interacts with cloud provider's network topology

Confidentiality and Integrity of Data

The data and resources are now exposed to the public network managed by some third party cloud service provider. Therefore a huge risk is present for the data and resources. In order to protect them against the un-trusted environment ensuring confidentiality and integrity is very important. Confidentiality ensures that data is protected from malicious user (Mather T., Subra K., & Latif S., 2009). Data confidentiality means keeping users data secret in the cloud. The two important aspects of confidentiality are access control mechanism and encryption of data. The cryptographic encryption techniques are used to ensure confidentiality (Mather T., Subra K., & Latif S., 2009).

Integrity of data ensures that data has not modified in any unauthorized way (Mather T., Subra K., & Latif S., 2009). The confidentiality only ensures the secrecy of data but it does not guarantee the integrity of data. Therefore to achieve strong security only confidentiality is not sufficient, data integrity is also important. The techniques used to provide integrity are the Message Authentication Code (MAC), digital signature etc.

Proper Access Control

In traditional model the access to various resources is under control of organization itself. Therefore it is possible to provide proper secure access to various resources. In cloud computing organization has to trust the cloud service provider as handling of resources is not under control of organization now.

The boundary is extended to service provider's domain. Thus in order to manage secure access to resources, organization has to follow some access control mechanism (Mather T., Subra K., & Latif S., 2009; Ronald L., Krutz & Russell D. V., 2012). Access control mechanism ensures that proper access privileges are assigned using some policy and all users and cloud services are properly authenticated, authorized and audited.

One of the risks associated with this is reassignment of IP addresses. Whenever any customer releases the IP addresses the cloud service provider reassigns these addresses to any other customer. This is beneficial for the service provider as IP addresses are valuable assets. Such kind of reassignment of IP addresses can increase risk to the customer resources. The release of IP addresses by customer never guarantees the termination of access to its resources. There exists some delay between changing IP address in DNS and clearing the address in DNS cache. Similar delay exists between changing addresses in ARP table and clearing them from ARP cache. It is possible that the addresses are modified in DNS and ARP table but are still present in cache. Due to this it is possible that the customer's resources are still accessible in an unauthorized way.

Another risk of unauthorized access to resources exists in cloud service provider's domain. It is possible that any resource is not directly accessible through internet but it is accessible within the cloud service provider's network through private addressing (Instance addressing and Network Security, 2008). Thus any customer may unintentionally access the resource owned by other customer.

Availability of Resources

Availability ensures that the data and resources are available and accessible to authorized users on demand at anytime and anywhere. The main threat for availability of data and resources is the network level attacks (Mather T., Subra K., & Latif S., 2009; Charanya R. et.al., 2013). The various network level attacks are discussed in the rest of this section.

BGP Prefix Hijacking

In this type of attack wrong announcement on IP address associated with an autonomous system is done. Autonomous system is a connected group of one or more IP prefixes managed by different network operators. This kind of announcement happens due to the miss-configuration of addresses and it affects the availability of resources. Thus the malicious users get access to the untraceable IP address. The actual traffic gets routed to some other IP than the intended one. Due to this the resources of that IP becomes unavailable in cloud environment.

DNS Attacks

In order to ensure the availability of resources through internet many organization allows external DNS queries. Due to this there is increase in DNS attacks at network level.

This attack includes redirecting the name server to another domain instead of the one asked. The sender and a receiver get rerouted through some evil connection. It also includes responding before the real name server which is referred as DNS forgery.

DoS (Denial of Service) Attack

This attack makes the services provided by cloud unavailable for long time. It forces the system component to limit or even halt the normal services. The attacker can flood, disrupt or jam the network so that the network becomes unavailable. DoS attacks can be prevented with use of a firewall if they have configured properly.

DDoS (Distributed Denial of Service Attack)

Distributed Denial of Service attack is a DoS attack that occurs from more than one source, and from more than one location at the same time. In case of IaaS the DDoS is not external always but it can be also an internal DDoS attack. The internal network of service provider is available to all of its customers so that customers can get access to various resources. Therefore any malicious customer can use this internal network and attack other customers or the provider's infrastructure. In this case the service provider has no way to prevent such attack. The only way to prevent this attack is that the customers have to properly manage the access to their resources.

Replay Attack and In Sybil Attack

The other possible attacks are Replay attack and In Sybil attack. In Replay attack the data transmission is maliciously repeated or delayed. Here the malicious user intercepts and save the old messages and later it sends to one of participants to gain access to unauthorized resources. In case of In Sybil attack the malicious user acts as a valid user by obtaining multiple identities. Then such user tries to communicate with some valid user and gain unauthorized privileges to attack the system.

How Existing Topology Interacts with Cloud Provider's Network Topology

In existing traditional model, there is clear cut separation between network zones and tiers. The entities with specific roles will gain access to resource in a particular zone. In the same way the entities within a specific tier have access permissions in or across the tier only. In case of clod environment such separation does not exists. Here the network zones and tiers are replaced by security domains, security groups or virtual data centers (Mather T., Subra K., & Latif S., 2009).

HOST LEVEL

The host level security considers the cloud service delivery models (SaaS, IaaS and PaaS) and deployment models (Public cloud, Private cloud) (Mather T., Subra K., & Latif S., 2009). The host level Infrastructure security comprises different virtualization security threats. Here, the major responsibility is securing the hosts present in the cloud.

SaaS and PaaS Host Security

In case of SaaS and PaaS the security of hosts is completely responsibility of cloud service provider. The customers do not have any information about the hosts which are located in service provider's domain and the customers do not have any physical control over these hosts. The cloud service providers do not reveal any information about the hosts, host operating system or various processes. Because this information can be used by any malicious user to gain unauthorized access. Thus the customers completely relay on service providers for the security of hosts. The only thing customers can do is to take appropriate level assurance that the cloud service provider is managing the host security (Mather T., Subra K., & Latif S., 2009). There are some third party assessment frameworks available to ensure that cloud service provider has properly managed the security of their hosts.

Another key technology is virtualization. The virtualization enables to have different operating systems running on the same underlying hardware. The next question is how cloud service providers secure the virtualization layer. In case of SaaS or PaaS the details about the host operating systems are hidden from the customers. So the customers rely on the cloud service provider to provide secure host platform on which the customer's applications are deployed and developed (Mather T., Subra K., & Latif S., 2009).

IaaS Host Security

In case of IaaS services the customers also play major role in securing the hosts. The main security aspects at this level are virtualization software security and virtual server security.

Virtualization Software Security

The virtualization technique allows running multiple guest operating systems on the same underlying hardware. It provides a way of proper hardware utilization. Thus the multiple virtual machines exist at the same time and run without interfering with each other. These multiple virtual machines are managed by the virtual machine monitor or hypervisor. The hypervisor sits between hardware and the virtual machines. This hypervisor forms the virtualization layer. This layer is completely managed by the cloud service provider and customers do not have access to this layer. Therefore cloud service providers must provide necessary security mechanisms to control and limit the access to the hypervisors.

Virtual Server Security

The customers have full access to virtual machines running in the system. The customers should take responsibility of securing these VMs. The different security threats for the hosts are: stealing of security keys, attacking vulnerable ports, attacking accounts and systems which are not secure, deploying viruses in the VMs.

APPLICATION LEVEL

Application level security includes security concerns for both single user applications and multi-user applications. This level deals with the Application-level security threats, End user security, managing application security for cloud service delivery models and Public cloud security limitations. Application security is most important part of information security.

There are various application level security threats such as: Cross site scripting, SQL injection, malicious file execution, Denial of Service attack, Distributed Denial of Service attack etc (Mather T., Subra K., & Latif S., 2009). DoS attacks can bring services of any organization down for long amount of time. Due to this there will be drastic increase in cloud utility bill of that organization. This type of attack is called as Economic denial of sustainability (EDoS). The proper security controls along with host and network level access control can be used to protect against these types of attack. In order to secure application deployed in cloud the security features must be embedded in software development life cycle.

The end users are responsible to protect their host connected to internet for accessing cloud services. The customers can use various antivirus software, firewalls, security patches, IPS-type software to protect their host.

The web browsers provide a way to access applications and services on cloud. Therefore security of browsers must be taken into consideration while designing application security. The web browsers are more vulnerable to end user attacks. It will be responsibility of customers to maintain proper security for the web browsers. Customers can do regular updates required to keep browser secure.

SaaS Application Security

The SaaS services provide different applications or software for the customers on demand. These applications are managed by the cloud service providers. Therefore managing security of applications is responsibility of service provider (Mather T., Subra K., & Latif S., 2009). The customers can only manage the operational security by applying proper access control. The service providers have to apply different security measures to protect the applications. The customers have to be dependent on service providers for the security of SaaS applications. The customers can request information related to security measures taken by cloud service provider. There are some third party security vendors who can perform necessary testing of security practices provided by cloud service provider. The customers can hire such vendors to get assurance about security policies provided by cloud service provider for the SaaS applications.

The access control and authentication are the most important security aspects for SaaS applications and must be implemented in proper way. The customers must implement cloud specific access control mechanism. A strong authentication and privilege management mechanisms must be implemented to protect the applications. Hence customers must provide strong passwords for authentication of the applications (Mather T., Subra K., & Latif S., 2009).

The next issue is related to how the service providers store customers' data. Generally the service providers use single multitenant data store to store data of all customers. The concept of data tagging is used to uniquely identify each customer's data and process it. This isolation among data can become vulnerable when any software updates are done by providers. Therefore customers must have knowledge about virtual data store architecture and the security measures provided by the service providers.

PaaS Application Security

The PaaS architecture provides the platform on which customers can build and deploy their applications. The application security in PaaS must consider two factors as: security of platform itself and security of applications deployed by customers (Mather T., Subra K., & Latif S., 2009). The cloud service providers are completely responsible for the security of platform. Some third party components, applications and services are also required while developing applications. These third party service providers will be responsible for maintaining security of their services and components.

The platform provided by service provider of PaaS acts as run time engine for the customer's applications. It is like sandbox architecture in which the applications of customers are executed. This sandbox is managed by the cloud service provider and so it is responsibility of service provider to provide necessary security measures for the applications running on cloud platform.

The cloud service providers are responsible for maintaining confidentiality and integrity of customer's data and applications. The customers can request necessary information from the service providers to get assurance about the security of their applications. The management of network and host level security is also the responsibility of cloud service provider.

There are specific APIs available to manage and deploy applications in PaaS environment. So it is necessary that platform specific security features must be provided by the service providers. These security features include authentication and authorization control, single sign-on, SSL support. The security features provided by each provider will be different.

IaaS Application Security

In the private cloud architecture, the application executes on the customer's virtual servers and completely managed by the customers. The customers are solely responsible for securing their applications. There is no any support provided by the service providers to secure customers applications other than some basic features like firewall.

The scenario is different for public cloud environment. In public cloud environment the applications run in service provider's domain and managed by the service provider. The necessary security measures to protect the applications against various vulnerabilities must be provided by the customers. In order to keep applications secure the necessary security measures must be embedded in software development life cycle. While developing applications the developers must implement necessary authentication and authorization features. These features must work in collaboration with the authentication control provided by the organization's identity provider system.

The comparison of security control at the three levels is depicted in Table 1 (Mather T., Subra K., & Latif S., 2009).

Table 1. Security controls

Sr. No.	Level	Preventive Control	Detective Control
1	Network level	Network access control available through service provider, encryption techniques	Intrusion detection/prevention system, Security event logs
2	Host level	Authentication, Firewall, Access Control, Patching	Security event logs, Host based IDS/IPS
3	Application Level	IAM, Access control assessment, antivirus, IPS, Multifactor authentication	Login History

DATA SECURITY AND STORAGE

The cloud is similar to a big black box where users have no knowledge about what is happening inside. The user's data and applications are present outside the administrative control of the organization in a shared environment and also accessed by various other users. Generally the user's data, applications and resources are located with the cloud service providers. All the security policies and enforcement are managed by the cloud service providers. Thus the users are completely dependent on service providers to ensure the security of their data. Due to such loss of control, lack of trust and multi-tenancy features the security concern arises in cloud computing. Hence the clouds are subject to traditional data confidentiality, integrity, availability, and privacy issues, plus some additional attacks (Rao R.V. & Selvamani K., 2015). Therefore many users are disinclined in completely trusting the cloud computing environment.

One of the important threats for cloud computing is data loss and leakage. Data loss and leakage occurs due to lack of security and privacy in both storage and transmission. Data security should take into account all service delivery models of cloud i.e. Software as a Service, Platform as a Service and Infrastructure as a Service (Mather T., Subra K., & Latif S., 2009).

The various data security aspects are:

Data-in-Transit

The term data-in-transit refers to the data during transmission (Jayalekshmi M. B. & Krishnaveni S. H. 2015). The data can be transmitted either from data owner to cloud service provider or from cloud service provider to data owner. While transmitting the data ensuring confidentiality of data is very important. In order to achieve confidentiality proper encryption algorithm must be used. Along with the maintaining confidentiality of data, ensuring data integrity is also important. The communication protocol used for transmission of data over internet must provide confidentiality as well as integrity. Thus transmitting encrypted data using non-secured protocol will only guarantee the confidentiality but it will not provide integrity of data.

Data-at-Rest

The next data security aspect is data-at-rest, which refers to the data in the storage (Jayalekshmi M. B. & Krishnaveni S. H. 2015). In conjunction with the data-in-transit it is equally important to ensure security for the stored data. In case of IaaS, encryption techniques are used to protect the data. The multi-tenancy is one of the important characteristics of cloud architecture.

All users' data is stored in some massive storage in combined fashion. Therefore though data is encrypted there are possibilities of unauthorized access to the data. This situation arises while using PaaS or SaaS cloud service model. Also for IaaS the encryption of data will prevent the searching and indexing operations on data. Thus it is very difficult to store entire data in encrypted form in cloud storage.

Processing of Data Including Multi-Tenancy

Another issue related to data security is processing of data, including multi-tenancy. While transmitting data to and from service provider it is in encrypted form. Also the data is stored in encrypted format in cloud storage. If any application wants to process the data then the data must be decrypted because it is not possible to perform any operation on encrypted form. Once the processing is done the data can be encrypted again and can be stored. In order to solve this issue in 2009 IBM has proposed homomorphic encryption technique (Gentry C. (2009). In this technique it is not necessary to decrypt the data to perform any operations on it. The data can be processed in encrypted form also. The only issue related to this technique is its computational complexity.

Data Lineage

The data lineage concept provides a way to follow the path of the data. It describes a lifecycle of data which includes source of data and the movement of data over the time. It specifies where the data is located and when it is processed. It provides complete path of what happened to data from its source through distinct applications (Jayalekshmi M. B. & Krishnaveni S. H. 2015). This kind of information is required by auditors. Generally by adoption of cloud computing organizations expose their data on public network. Therefore there is possibility of any kind of security breach and exposure of sensitive data. In this case data lineage technique helps organizations to keep track of how information is used for particular purpose. Data lineage is difficult for public clouds.

Data Provenance

Another most important requirement of data security is data provenance. In some applications data integrity alone is not sufficient but more specific provenance of the data is required. Data Integrity ensures that data has not been modified in an unauthorized manner. Data provenance ensures that the data has integrity and also it is computationally accurate. It provides more specific history of the data i.e., who created, modified and deleted the data, who has accessed the data, where it has processed, how it is processed in the cloud etc. Sometimes data provenance may reveal some sensitive information. Let us consider the example of healthcare data (Asghar M. R., Ion M., Giovanni R. & Bruno C., 2011). In this scenario necessary information about the patient's medical history, medical report is stored in cloud. This information can be used by doctor to give required treatment. It is also possible that the doctor forwards this data to another doctor for further diagnosis. In above scenario data provenance technique can answer various queries like who has generated the report? Where it is generated? How it is produced? Which doctor has worked on the report? and so on. Therefore it is possible that even if all medical data is available in protected form the data provenance still may reveal some sensitive information about a patient. Therefore, in addition to provide protection to the sensitive data, it is equally important to make the data provenance secure.

Data Remanence

The data remanence refers to the data left behind after deletion (Jayalekshmi M. B. & Krishnaveni S. H. 2015). The sensitive data of any organization must be protected from unauthorized access. At the same time it is also equally important to delete it after its processing gets over. Because if some data is left behind then there is risk of recovery of entire data by any unauthorized user. This problem is called as data remanence. In the example of healthcare record explained in previous section the data remanence must be properly managed, otherwise the patient's personal health related information can be revealed in unauthorized manner. Another examples where data remanence play important role are financial records, defense etc. The risk of such unauthorized disclosure of sensitive data is available for all cloud service models (SaaS, PaaS, or IaaS). Generally with SaaS or PaaS, this risk is almost certainly unintentional.

If all resources are under full control of organization then the recycling of storage resources is used to destroy all traces of data. But in cloud environment any clear standard does not exist to recycle memory or disk space. The users do not have any direct access to the physical devices so this responsibility is left to the cloud service provider. The service provider must offer secure deletion as a feature of his services.

In the present scenario very less attention is given to data remanence in the Cloud. The infrastructure level assumes that this problem will be solved by application level and application level consigns the responsibility to the infrastructure level. At the end the problem remains unsolved.

The only solution available at infrastructure level is to have strong encryption technique and secure deletion is achieved by simply destroying the key. At application level data encryption never solves the data remanence problem. The reason is, we can process encrypted data. If any processing of data is to be done then the data must be decrypted and then the data remanence problem is raised again. Thus at application level encrypting data is sufficient if data is only stored in cloud and any processing of data is not required.

Storage

In case of storage-as-a-service the major security concerns are confidentiality, integrity, and availability as depicted in Figure 3 below (Stallings W., 2011; Behrouz A., Fourouzan & Debdeep M., 2010).

Confidentiality

Confidentiality ensures that data is protected from malicious user. Data confidentiality means keeping users data secret in the cloud. The two important aspects of confidentiality are access control mechanism and encryption of data. The cryptographic encryption techniques are used to ensure confidentiality. Encryption is process of converting original data into some coded form. Generally the original data is

Figure 3. Major security concerns

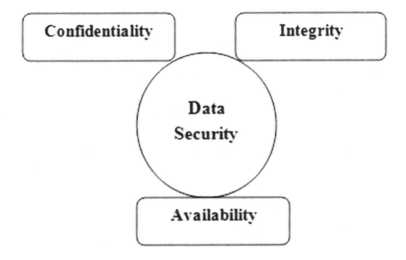

Figure 4. Encryption/ decryption process

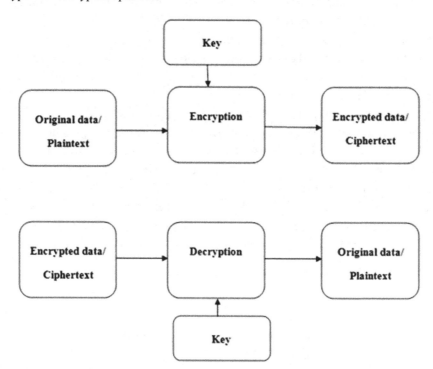

called as plaintext. The converted form is called as ciphertext. The process of converting ciphertext into plaintext is called as decryption. These processes are represented in Figure 4.

Some secret keys are used in encryption and decryption process. The cloud service provider encrypts the user data before storing and provides the keys only to the authorized persons. Sometimes user itself encrypts data before storing in cloud. There are some important concerns related to encryption such as: encryption algorithm, key length and key management. In order to ensure confidentiality a strong cryptographic encryption algorithm must be used. There are various encryption algorithms available. One such technique is symmetric key encryption. In symmetric key encryption one secret key is used for encryption and decryption. The same secrete key shared by sender and receiver as shown in Figure 5.

The various algorithms in this category are AES, DES, and BlowFish etc. The symmetric key encryption is simpler, faster and efficient approach but the only disadvantage is that same key is shared by sender and receiver.

Another encryption technique is Asymmetric key encryption which is also called as public key encryption. In this case two different keys are used for encryption and decryption. These keys are called as public key and private key. The public key of receiver is used for encryption by the sender and receiver uses its own private key for decryption. This process is shown in Figure 6.

The popular encryption algorithm in this category is RSA. In case of symmetric encryption the larger key length provides stronger security. Thus as much longer is the key length that much stronger encryption. But larger key length induces computational complexities.

The next important aspect is the key management: how the keys are managed and who will manage them. The security of the data is dependent on the security of the keys used for encryption. Therefore there must be a proper standard for key management which provides methods for the generation, ex-

Figure 5. Symmetric key encryption

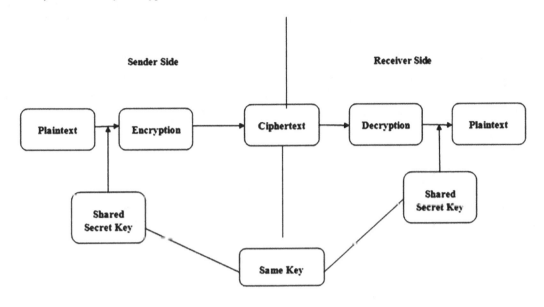

Figure 6. Asymmetric key encryption

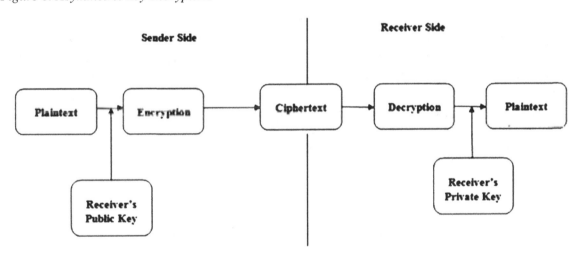

change, use, storage and destruction of the keys. The various standards for key management are ANSI X9.17 / ISO 8732, ANSI X9.24 ETEBACS, ISO 11166, ISO 11568 etc.

Integrity

Integrity of data ensures that data has not modified in any unauthorized way. The confidentiality only ensures the secrecy of data but it does not guarantee the integrity of data. Therefore to achieve strong security only confidentiality is not sufficient, data integrity is also important. The Message Authentication Code (MAC) is used to provide data integrity. Here a checksum is calculated using hash function and sent along with the message. At receiver side the checksum is again calculated from the received data. Finally the received checksum and recomputed checksum is compared to check integrity of data. If both are same then the data is not modified and if they are different then the data is modified by any unauthorized person. The data is present in massive amount in cloud storage.

The data integrity check must be done in cloud without need of download or upload of data. It is difficult task to check integrity of such massive storage in cloud because service provider has to perform this task without looking inside data. Another challenge for data integrity is that the data keeps changing frequently and therefore the traditional integrity assurance techniques are not adequate.

Availability

Availability ensures that the data is available and accessible to authorized users on demand at anytime and anywhere. The main threat for availability of data is the network level attacks. The next issue in this regard is the availability of cloud service provider. The next aspect of availability is whether the service provider maintains the backup of user's data or not. Some service providers do back up of data as an additional service for an additional cost.

IDENTITY AND ACCESS MANAGEMENT (IAM)

In traditional model the access to various resources is under control of organization itself. Therefore it is possible to provide proper secure access to various resources. In cloud computing organization has to trust the cloud service provider as handling of resources is not under control of organization now. The boundary is extended to service provider's domain. Thus in order to manage secure access to resources, organization has to follow some identity and access management (IAM) mechanism. IAM is used to manage user identities and their related access permissions in an automated way. See Figure 7. IAM ensures that proper access privileges are assigned using some policy and all users and cloud services are properly authenticated, authorized and audited.

Figure 7. IAM security aspects

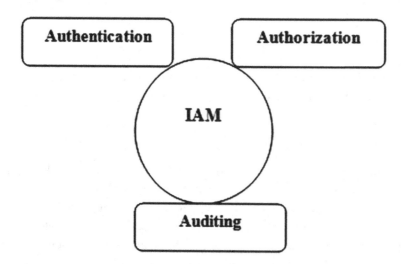

The basic concepts of IAM are authentication, authorization and auditing (Mather T., Subra K., & Latif S., 2009; Altice Lab, 2014; Cloud Security Alliance, 2012).

Authentication

Authentication process provides a way of identifying a user. It verifies user's identity. A very simple example of authentication is user having correct username and password will get access to particular services. Another example is service to service interaction in which authentication process verifies a network service which requests information from other service. In case of authentication each user will have certain set of criteria for gaining access.

Authorization

Authentication process proves the identity of user; the next step is to verify whether user has necessary privileges to do some task. Thus the authorization process determines whether user is authorized user to perform some operation or not using some predefined policies. The authorization process enforces various policies to determine what types of activities, resources, or services a user is permitted. Once a user is authenticated then that user becomes authorized for different types of access or activity.

Auditing

Auditing process reviews the authentication and authorization records to verify compliance with security policies. It also detects breaches in security services and suggest changes if required.

IAM Architecture

IAM framework is collection of various technologies, components, process and standard practices. The core service is the directory service. This service maintains repository of credentials, identities, and attributes of all users in an organization. This service interacts with other components of IAM architecture such as provisioning, authentication and user management. The components of IAM architecture are shown in Figure 8 (Mather T., Subra K., & Latif S., 2009; Altice Lab, 2014; Cloud Security Alliance, 2012).

The IAM processes are classified as:

1. **User Management:** This process provides a way to manage and control the identity of user.
2. **Authentication Management:** This process provides a way to verify identity of any entity.
3. **Authorization Management:** This process determines whether the entity has necessary access permissions for any resource or not.
4. **Access Management:** This process implements access control policies when any entity requests a resource.
5. **Data Management and Provisioning:** This process provides a way to disseminate identity and data for authorization of resources.
6. **Monitoring and Auditing:** This process monitors and audits the compliance of security policies by users while accessing the resources.

Figure 8. IAM architecture

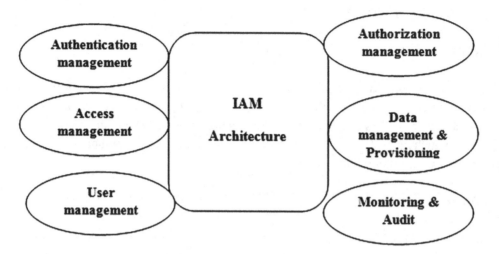

There are various activities of IAM as listed below:

1. **Provisioning:** This process combines the functionalities of human resources and IT infrastructure of organization in providing access to resources according to some identity of user. This process grants users access permission to various resources. The deprovisioning is completely opposite process. It deactivates the access privileges assigned to a particular user.
2. **Credential and Attribute Management:** This process creates, issues, manages and revokes the user's credentials and attributes. It involves activities like proper management of user attributes and credentials which follows the password standards, handling expiration of passwords, encryption of credentials and access policies of user attributes.
3. **Entitlement Management:** This process enables provisioning and deprovisioning of access privileges for users to access any resource. This process ensures that only necessary privileges are assigned to users. Thus this process manages the authorization policies for users.
4. **Compliance Management:** This process refers to the auditing functionality of IAM. This process reviews the access privileges to ensure compliance with security policies. It helps auditors to manage and track the access control policies and standards.
5. **Identity Federation Management:** This process enables organization to share information with other organization and allows collaboration among organizations. It manages the relationship between the administrative domains of different organization.
6. **Centralization of Authentication and Authorization:** In traditional method application developers must build authentication and authorization functionality in their applications. The centralized authentication and authorization process free application developers from this task. This approach separates authentication and authorization from the application development.

IAM Standards and Protocols

The identity and access management standards help organizations to implement effective and efficient user access management practices and processes in the cloud (Lightfoot J. 2016).There are following challenges for accessing and managing the user data in the cloud:

- How to avoid duplication of identity, attributes, and credentials?
- How to provide a single sign-on user experience for my users?
- How to automate the process of provisioning and deprovisioning?
- How to provision user accounts with appropriate privileges and manage entitlements for my users?
- How to authorize one cloud service to access user's data in another cloud service without disclosing credentials.

IAM Standards and Specifications for Organizations are:

- **SAML:** It stands for Security Assertion Markup Language. It is an open standard that provides both authentication and authorization (Mehta L., 2014).
- **SPML:** It is Service Provisioning Markup Language (SPML). It is the open standard for the integration and interoperation of service provisioning requests. SPML's goal is to allow organizations securely and quickly set-up user's provisioning for Web services and applications, by allowing enterprise platforms such as Web portals, application servers, and service centers generate provisioning requests within and across organizations. (Cloud Security Alliance, 2012).
- **XACML:** It stands for eXtensible Access Control Markup Language. It is an XML-based language, used to represent policies and to define how to evaluate them. (Cloud Security Alliance, 2012).
- **OAuth:** It stands for Open Authentication. OAuth provides a way for users to access their data hosted by another provider while protecting their account credentials. (Mehta L., 2014).

IAM Standards and Specifications for Consumers are (Relevant IAM Standards, 2010):

- **OpenID:** It is an open, decentralized standard for user authentication and access control. It provides a single sign-on user experience with services supporting OpenID, which allows users to log on to many services with the same digital identity.
- **Information Cards:** It is a standard, which provides a safe, consistent, phishing-resistant user interface that doesn't require a username and password. People can use an information card digital identity across multiple sites for convenience without compromising their login information.
- **Open Authenticate (OATH):** OATH provides strong authentication across all users and all devices over all networks. It includes Subscriber Identity Module (SIM)-based authentication, Public Key Infrastructure (PKI)-based authentication and One-Time Password (OTP)-based authentication.
- **Open Authentication API (OpenAuth):** It is an AOL-proprietary API that enables third-party websites and applications to authenticate AOL and AOL Instant Messenger (AIM) users through their websites and applications.

Table 2. Comparison of IAM standards

	OpenID	**OAuth**	**SAML**
Year	2005	2006	2001
Current Version	OpenId Connect	2.0	2.0
Purpose	Single Sign-on for consumers	API Authorization	Single Sign-on for enterprises
Protocol	JSON	JSON or SAML	XML
Authorization	No	Yes	Yes
Authentication	Yes	Pseudo-authentication	Yes
Security Risks	Phishing Some authentication flaws.	Vulnerable to session fixation attack. It does not have native encryption capabilities. It relies on the SSL/TLS.	XML signature wrapping vulnerability
Token Format	JSON	JSON or SAML2	XML
Mobile Apps	Both for Web Browser and Mobile Apps	Both for Web Browser and Mobile Apps	Only for Web Browser
Support for SSO	Yes	Yes	Web SSO only

The comparison of various IAM standards is shown in Table 2 (Mather T., Subra K., & Latif S., 2009; Altice Lab, 2014; Sherif K., 2013; Lightfoot J., 2016; Relevant IAM, 2010).

CONCLUSION

Cloud computing allows users to outsource sensitive data for sharing on cloud servers located in different un-trusted domain. In order to keep sensitive user data confidential against un-trusted servers, issues of security standards and compatibility must be addressed. The important aspects of security concern in cloud include strong authentication, delegated authorization, key management for encrypted data, data loss protections and regulatory reporting. These security aspects must be applied to all cloud service delivery models (IAAS, PAAS and SAAS) and all deployment models (private and public cloud).

Summary

This chapter explores the key aspects of cloud security. It includes infrastructure security, data security and Identity & access control mechanisms. The chapter addresses various issues, challenges and security requirements at each level.

REFERENCES

Ali, M., Khan, S. U., & Athanasios, V., & Vasilakos. (2015). Security in Cloud Computing: Opportunities and Challenges. *Information Sciences*.

Altice Lab. (2014). *Identity and Access Management*. Retrieved From http://www.alticelabs.com/content/WP-Information-Access-Control-Models.pdf

Asghar, M. R., Ion, M., Giovanni, R., & Bruno, C. (2011). *Securing Data Provenance in the Cloud. EU FP7 programme, Research Grant 257063*. Endorse.

Cameron, C. (2016). 9-cloud-computing-security-risks-every-company-faces. *Skyhighnetworks*. Retrieved From https://www.skyhighnetworks.com/cloud-security-blog/9-cloud-computing-security-risks-every-company-faces/

Charanya, R. (2013). Levels of Security Issues in Cloud Computing. IJET, 5(2).

Cloud Security Alliance. (2012). *Security guidance for critical areas of Mobile Computing*. Retrieved From https://downloads.cloudsecurityalliance.org/initiatives/ mobile/Mobile_Guidance_v1.pdf

Cloud Security Alliance. (2012). *Identity and Access Management*. Cloud Security Alliance: SecaaS Implementation Guidance, Category 1.

Cloud Standards Customer Council. (2015). *Security for Cloud Computing Ten Steps to Ensure Success Version 2.0*. Author.

Fourouzan & Mukhopadhyay. (2010). Cryptography and Network (2nd ed.). TMH.

Gentry, C. (2009). *A fully homomorphic encryption scheme* (PhD thesis). Stanford University. Retrieved from http://crypto.stanford.edu/craig

Infoworld. (2016). *The 12-cloud-security-threats*. Retrieved From http://www.infoworld.com/article/3041078/security/the-dirty-dozen-12-cloud-security-threats.html

Instance Addressing and Network Security. (2008). *Amazon Elastic Computer Cloud Developer Guide (API Version 2008-12-011)*. Author.

Jayalekshmi, M. B., & Krishnaveni, S. H. (2015). A Study of Data Storage Security Issues in Cloud Computing. *Indian Journal of Science and Technology*, 8(24), 1–5. doi:10.17485/ijst/2015/v8i1/84229

Keiko, H., Rosado, D. G., Eduardo, F., & Eduardo, B. F. (2013). An analysis of security issues for cloud computing. *Journal of Internet Services and Applications*.

KPMG. (2010). *From hype to future: KPMG's 2010 Cloud Computing survey*. Retrieved From http://www.techrepublic.com/whitepapers/from-hype-to-futurekpmgs

Krutz & Russell. (2012). *Cloud Security A comprehensive guide to secure cloud computing*. Wiley India Pvt. Ltd.

Li, W., & Ping, L. (2009). Trust model to enhance Security and interoperability of Cloud environment. *Proceedings of the 1st International conference on Cloud Computing*, 69–79. doi:10.1007/978-3-642-10665-1_7

Lightfoot, J. (2016). *Authentication and Authorization: OpenID vs OAuth2 vs SAML*. Retrieved from https://spin.atomicobject.com/2016/05/30/openid-oauth-saml/

Liu, B., Bi, J., & Vasilakos, A. (2014). Towards incentivizing anti-spoofing deployment. *IEEE Trans. Inform. Forensics Sec.*, 9(3), 436–450. doi:10.1109/TIFS.2013.2296437

Mather, T., Subra, K., & Latif, S. (2009). *Cloud security and Privacy* (1st ed.). O'Reilly.

Mehta, L. (2014). *SAML-OAuth –OpenID*. Retrieved from http://resources.infosecinstitute.com/saml-oauth-openid/

NetApp. (2009). *Secure Cloud Architecture*. WP-7083-0809. NetApp.

Rao, R. V., & Selvamani, K. (2015). Data Security Challenges and Its Solutions in Cloud Computing. *Proceedings of Conference International Conference on Intelligent Computing, Communication & Convergence*. doi:10.1016/j.procs.2015.04.171

Reese, G. (2009). *Cloud Application Architectures: Building Applications and Infrastructure in the Cloud*. O'Reilly Media, Inc.

Relevant IAM Standards and Protocols for Cloud Services. (2010). Retrieved from http://mscerts.programming4.us/programming/

Sankar, K., Kannan, S., & Jennifer, P. (2014). On-demand security architecture for cloud computing. *Middle-East J. Sci. Res., 20*(2), 241–246.

Sherif, K. (2013). *Federated Identities: OpenID Vs SAML Vs OAuth*. Authentication, Blog Posts, Federated Identities, Secure Coding, Securiy.

Stallings, W. (2011). *Cryptography and Network Security: Principles and Practice* (5th ed.). Pearson.

Velte, A. T., Velte, T. J., & Elsenpeter, R. (2010). *Cloud Computing: A Practical Approach*. Tata: McGraw-Hill.

Chapter 14

A User–Centered Log–Based Information Retrieval System Using Web Log Mining:
An Efficient Information Retrieval System

Sathiyamoorthi V
Sona College of Technology, India

ABSTRACT

It is generally observed throughout the world that in the last two decades, while the average speed of computers has almost doubled in a span of around eighteen months, the average speed of the network has doubled merely in a span of just eight months! In order to improve the performance, more and more researchers are focusing their research in the field of computers and its related technologies. Data Mining is also known as knowledge discovery in database (KDD) is one such research area. The discovered knowledge can be applied in various application areas such as marketing, fraud detection, customer retention and production control and marketing to improve their business. It discovers implicit, previously unknown and potentially useful information out of datasets. Recent trends in data mining include web mining where it discovers knowledge from web based information to improve the page layout, structure and its content thereby it reduces the user latency in accessing the web page and website performance.

INTRODUCTION

Internet technology has provided a lot of services for sharing and distributing information across the world. Among all the services, World Wide Web (WWW) plays a significant role. The slow retrieval of Web pages may subside the interest of users from accessing them. Therefore, in the present day Internet world, the speed of data transfer plays a vital role. Hence the speed of information retrieval from the Web must be addressed efficiently. To deal with this problem Web caching and Web pre-fetching are the two techniques used. Web proxy caching plays a key role in improving Web performance by keeping Web objects that are likely to be used in the near future in the proxy server which is closer to the end user.

DOI: 10.4018/978-1-5225-2013-9.ch014

It helps in reducing user perceived latency, network bandwidth utilization, and alleviating loads on the Web servers. Thus, it improves the efficiency and scalability of Web based system. Among these two, proxy- based Web caching has been widely used to reduce the network traffic by caching frequently requested Web pages. In this chapter, Web usage mining is used to optimize existing proxy-based Web caching system for better performance. The following sections narrate the importance of Web caching and Web pre-fetching system and propose a novel technique for integrating Web caching with Web pre-fetching system using Web usage mining.

BACKGROUD

There are many aspects which affect the performance of Web today, including discrepancies in network connectivity, real-world distances and overcrowding in networks or servers due to unforeseen demand. Some of the methodologies addressed here that help to increase the performance are Web caching, Web pre-fetching and integration of Web caching and Web pre-fetching (Waleed et al 2011).

Web caching is an intermediate storage between client and server and used to store the Web objects that are likely to be accessed in the near future. Web pre-fetching is used to load Webpages into the cache before the actual request arrives. When combined, these can complement each other where Web caching technique makes use of temporal locality, whereas Web pre-fetching technique use spatial locality of Web objects (Teng et al 2005). As a standard process, Web caching technique makes use of temporal locality and Web pre-fetching technique exploits the spatial locality of Web objects. When combined these techniques may complement each other. In this background, a Proxy-based Web caching and pre-fetching can be more efficient since it reduces the latency incurred while accessing Web pages.

Therefore, Web caching reduces the bandwidth utilization as well as the server load by temporarily storing the Web objects nearer to the *client*. This provides the benefits such as reducing the cost of connection to the Internet, the latency of WWW and server workload and network traffic (Kumar & Norris 2008).

Web caching can be positioned at different locations that are client side, server side and proxy side (Chen et al 2003). In these, proxy-based Web caching is widely used to reduce the latency problem of today's Webpages as it resides in between client and server. It plays a major role in dropping the response time and saves the bandwidth. The main element of Web caching is its page replacement policy (Chen 2007). When a new document arrives and if the cache is full, then the replacement policy has to make critical decision in replacing an existing Webpage from the cache. Hence, the following sections examine some of the existing research works on Web caching and Web pre-fetching techniques. Also, it integrates both Web caching and Web pre-fetching system using clustering based pre-fetching technique.

RELATED WORKS ON WEB CACHING

The traditional cache replacement algorithms used are FIFO, LRU and LFU. FIFO expels an object based on arrival time. The object which has entered first will be removed first regardless of its accessibility. LRU will evict the least recently used Web objects when cache is full. It is easy to implement but efficient only for uniform sized objects; it is not suitable for Web caching as it does not consider the object size or the download latency of Web objects and object access frequency in removal policy (Koskela et al 2003).

The LFU policy throws out an object with the least number of user accesses. LFU stores the often-accessed Web objects and evicts the rarely-accessed ones. The problem with LFU is that the objects with large reference count are never replaced, even if they are not re-accessed again. It fails to consider the recentness and size of a Web object in making decision.

SIZE is another Web caching policy that replaces the largest object from a fully filled cache when new object arrives. Thus, the cache contains large number of small-sized objects that are never requested again. To overcome the above problem, Pei and Irani (1997) have put-forward a new algorithm called GDS. GDS considers several factors such as cost, recency and size in decision making process and assigns priority value for each of the Web object present in the cache. Thus the object with least priority value is evicted first.

Mathematically, it is represented as in Equations (1) and (2) below. When the user requests a Web object 'o$_i$', GDS algorithm assigns priority value P(oi) to Web object 'oi' as shown in Equations (1) and (2) below.

$$P(O_i) = L + Cost(O_i) / Size(O_i) \tag{1}$$

where

$$Cost(O_i) = 2 + Size(O_i) / 536 \tag{2}$$

Here, Cost(oi) is the cost of fetching an object 'oi' from server that is calculated from Equation (2); Size(oi) is the size of an object 'oi'; L is an aging factor. L is initialized to 0 and is updated to the priority value of the recently replaced object. Thus, larger priority value is assigned to the recently visited object. The problem with GDS is that it fails to consider the object frequency in decision making process.

Therefore, in order to overcome the above situation, Cherkasova (1998) has proposed an enhanced GDS algorithm called Greedy Dual-Size-Frequency (GDSF) by considering the object access frequency and the priority value assigned P(oi) as in Equation (3).

$$P(O_i) = L + F(O_i) * (Cost(O_i) / Size(O_i)) \tag{3}$$

Here F(oi) is access frequency of an object 'oi'. When object is accessed for the first time then F(oi) is initialized to 1. If object is in the cache, its current frequency is updated by incrementing it by one. The problem with GDSF is that it fails to consider the objects popularity. Also, cost factor considered here is dynamic which changes on available network traffic and server load.

Therefore, the following are some of the important features of Web objects that must be considered while making decisions (Chen et al 2003; Podlipnig & Boszormenyi 2003).

- **Recency:** Last access time, on accessing a Web object;
- **Frequency:** Number of times an object is accessed since it is in the cache;
- **Size:** Size of an object in bytes; and
- **Cost:** Cost to fetch an object from server into the cache.

Ali and Shamsuddin (2009) have proposed an intelligent Web caching called Intelligent Client side Web Caching Scheme (ICWCS). The Web objects have been classified into either cacheable or un-cacheable objects. They have used neuro-fuzzy system to predict Web objects that are likely to be accessed in the near future. A trained neuro-fuzzy system with LRU has been employed. The simulation results show that ICWCS would provide better Hit Rate (HR) but it provides low Byte Hit Rate (BHR) since it ignored the factors such as cost and size of the objects in the cache replacement process. This client side implementation poses other issues like the training process which requires longer time and higher computational cost.

The Authors Cobb and ElAarag (2008), Elaarag and Romano (2009) have used an Artificial Neural Network (ANN) in making cache replacement decision which classifies Web objects into different classes. However, objects that belong to the same classes are removed without any precedence between them. Moreover they have considered only conventional algorithm. Tian et al (2002) have proposed an adaptive Web cache access predictor using neural network. They have presented an intelligent predictor design that uses back propagation neural network algorithm to improve the performance of Web catching by predicting the most likely re-accessed objects and then keeping these objects in the cache for future access.

However, they have ignored recency factor in Web objects removal policy. Even though the above methods are better than traditional algorithms, practically it is difficult as it is time consuming and moreover it does not consider the objects cost and size in the cache replacement process.

The authors in (Podlipnig & Boszormenyi 2003) have presented an overview of various replacement algorithms. They conclude that Greedy Dual-Size (GDS) outperform when cache size is small. The authors in (Jyoti et al 2008) has discussed that SIZE outperforms than LRU and several LRU variations in terms of different performance measures such as hit rate and byte hit rate. But in their experiments, they have failed to consider the object frequency in decision making process. From this it is observed that most of the Web cache replacement policies are suitable for memory caching since it involves fixed sized objects and not suitable for Web caching system where it involves varying sized objects called Web pages. Hence, there is a need for an algorithm which will increase hit rate and byte hit rate as well. So, the proposed work introduces a cache replacement policy which will consider all factors discussed above.

RESARCH PROGRESS IN WEB PRE-FETCHING

Web pre-fetching or pre-loading is a technique which pre-fetch Web pages into the cache before even the actual request arrive. There are two approaches namely,

- **Short-Term Pre-Fetching:** Where Web pages are pre-fetched into the cache by analyzing recent Web cache access history (Chen et al 2003).
- **Long-Term Pre-Fetching:** Where the probability of accessing Web pages are identified and pre-fetched by analyzing the global access pattern (Heung et al 2009).

Pre-fetching or Pre-loading is a technique adopted in order to reduce the latency problem and also to boost up the Web caching system performance. It uses intelligent algorithms to predict the Webpages expected to be accessed in the near future before the actual user request. Then, the predicted objects are fetched from the server and stored in a location close to the client. Thus, it helps in increasing the cache hit rate and reduces the latency in accessing Webpages.

Similar to Web caching, Web pre-fetching can also be implemented on server side, proxy side and client side. The client-based pre-fetching only deals with access behavior of a single user while sever-based pre-fetching deals with access behavior of all the users to a single Website. The proxy-based pre-fetching deals with access behavior of user group segments which reflect a common interest for user's community. Hence, proxy-based pre-fetching is the most widely used method as it is more and more useful and accurate to predict the pages of many Websites (Pallis et al 2008; Domenech et al 2010).

Web pre-fetching techniques can be categorized into two main classes (Zhijie et al 2009).

- Content-based approach, and
- History-based approach.

The content-based pre-fetching analyses the current Webpage contents and identifies hyperlinks that are likely to be visited. The prediction is carried out using ANN mechanism depending on keywords in URL (Ibrahim & Xu 2000). It is suitable for client side pre-fetching technique. At the server side, it negatively affects the server performance due to high overhead involved in parsing every Webpage by affecting the server service time with an increase in the server load (Domenech et al 2010).

According to Zhijie et al (2009), in history-based pre-fetching, prediction is done based on the historical page access recorded in the Web log file. It is mainly used in server side pre-fetching techniques where user's history of accesses is recorded in the form of server log. Pre-fetching can be done using any one of the approaches given below:

- Graph based approach,
- Markov model approach,
- Cost based approach, and
- Data mining approach.

Dependency Graph Based Pre-Fetching Approach

According to Padmanabhan and Mogul (1996), pre-fetching technique can be based on Dependency Graph (DG). The DG consists of nodes representing Webpages, and links representing access sequence from one page to other. Weight associated with each of the links represents the probability of accessing the target node from the current node. Domenech et al (2010) have presented a pre-fetching approach based on Double Dependency Graph (DDG). DDG is used to predict inter and intra Webpage access. The main drawbacks of DG are that it is controlled by the threshold value and it will predict only one page at a time which will increase the server load and the network traffic when multiple users are accessing the server (Nanopoulos et al 2003).

Markov Model Based Pre-Fetching Approach

Pre-fetching approach based on Markov model is more appropriate to predict user's next request by comparing the user's current access with the user's past access sequences that are recorded in Web log file (Pitkow & Pirolli 1999).

This approach follows different order that is either the first order Markov model or the higher order Markov model which are discussed below. A user access sequence consists of sequence of pages of the form:

$$x_1 \rightarrow x_2 \rightarrow \dots x_{k-1}$$

where

$k \geq 2$

(Palpanas & Mendelzon 1999).

In the first-order Markov model, also known as low-order Markov model, the next page access x_k depends only on current page x_{k-1}. If the access of x_k depends on consecutive two access of the form $x_{k-2} \rightarrow x_{k-1}$, then it is called a second-order Markov model. In general, if next page access depends on set of K previously accessed Webpages then it is called a Kth higher-order Markov model (Palpanas & Mendelzon 1999; Pitkow & Pirolli 1999).

In the low-order Markov model, the prediction accuracy is very low, since it considers only the current Web page access. Therefore, Pitkow and Pirolli (1999) have proposed higher-order Markov model to improve the prediction accuracy. In this, predictions are carried out first using the higher- order Markov model. If there is no match then predictions is done by using lower-order Markov model. The order of Markov is decreased until the state is covered. The problem with higher-order Markov model is that it involves higher complexity in constructing probability matrix.

Palpanas and Mendelzon (1999) have proposed pre-fetching based on Prediction-by-Partial-Match which depends on higher-order Markov model where prediction is done based on Markov decision tree that is constructed from the past access sequence of the users. The main drawback is, the tree size is increased based on number of past requests of user. The researchers Pitkow and Pirolli 1999, Chen et al (2002) have proposed different methods to control the tree size. The PPM based pre-fetching approach is not suitable for proxy side because proxy server can receive requests for pages on different server instead of a single Web server (Liu 2009).

Cost Based Pre-Fetching Approach

This approach uses a function to pre-fetch the Web objects into the cache based on some factors including page popularity and its lifetime. According to Markatos and Chronaki (1998), 'pre-fetch by popularity' predicts and keeps top ten popular Webpages in cache. It is also known as Top-10 approach. The other work presented by (Jiang et al 2002) is called 'pre-fetch by lifetime' where the 'n' objects are selected based on their lifetime minimizing the bandwidth consumption.

Data Mining Based Pre-Fetching Approach

The data mining based pre-fetching approach is classified based on the two data mining techniques namely, Association Rules and Clustering.

Association Rules Based Pre-Fetching Approach

In association rule, the prediction is done using the set of rules revealed from different user sessions which is segregated using Web log file. These sessions describe the sequence of Webpages accessed by a single user during some period of time. In association rules, support measure is used to identify frequent pages whereas confidence measure is used to discover rules from these frequent pages (Yang et al 2004). Yang et al (2001) have proposed an N-gram based pre-fetching approach which is based on association rule.

The problem in this approach is that too many useless rules are produced from the user's session which makes incorrect predictions, especially when the dataset is large. Hence, the predictions become inaccurate (Khalil et al 2009; Xiao et al 2001). The research progress in association rule mining is given below.

Jianhan (2002) has used the Markov model to predict the user's next access. In his work, he applied a transition matrix to predict Webpages based on past visitor behavior which makes the user find information more efficiently and accurately.

An improved Apriori algorithm proposed by Wang (1999) consumes less time and space complexity than the original algorithm. It adds an attribute called 'userid' during each and every step of producing the candidate set. It can decide whether an item in the candidate set should be added into the large set which will be used to produce the next candidate set or not. This makes the algorithm widely and aptly useful in Web mining.

Two common data mining approaches such as FP Growth and PrefixSpan in sequential data mining have been presented by Hengshan et al (2006). It helps in Web content personalization and user navigation through pre-fetching and caching. It also uses the Maximum Forward Path (MFP) in Web usage mining model.

Sandeep (2010) has proposed a custom-built Apriori algorithm based on the traditional Apriori algorithm, to find the effective pattern. He has tested the proposed work in educational log file. This algorithm helps the Website developer in making effective decisions to improve the efficiency of the Website.

Navin et al (2011) have proposed a recommendation methodology based on correlation rules where Association rules are generated from log data using FP Growth algorithm. Further the cosine measure is used for generating correlation rules.

Clustering Based Pre-Fetching Approach

All the methodologies employed in previous section covers only a single object pre-fetching which will increase network traffic and server load when multiple users are accessing the server. In order to overcome these problems clustering-based pre-fetching techniques have been proposed.

Clustering is the process of grouping the users based on similarity present in the user session. The objects present in the same clusters are highly similar whereas objects present in different clusters are highly dissimilar.

An effective clustering algorithm should minimize the intra-cluster distance and maximize inter-cluster distance. Many research works have been carried out related to clustering (Papadakis et al 2005; Cadez et al 2003; Adami et al 2003).

Clustering can be either Webpage clustering or user session clustering (Khalil et al 2009). The Webpage clustering is achieved by grouping the pages into different clusters based on the content similarity (Tang & Vemuri 2005; Xu et al 2006). In session-based clustering technique, users are grouped based on the similarity between different user sessions. Clustering-based approach is widely used in fields like Webpage prediction, personalization and Web pre-fetching. Pallis et al (2008) have proposed an algorithm called ClustWeb for clustering inter-site Webpages in proxy servers based on DG and association rule. The problem with this approach is that the high complexity involved in construction of DG and moreover it is pruned by support and confidence measures.

As per Paola (2007), Self Organized Maps (SOM) is a kind of artificial neural network, in the process of WUM to detect user patterns. The authors have stated that, in order to identify the common patterns in Websites, SOM is better than K-means.

Mehrdad (2008) has proposed an approach that was based on the graph partitioning for modeling user navigation patterns. In order to perform mining on user navigation patterns, he has established an undirected graph based on connectivity between each pair of the Webpages. He also proposed a novel formula for assigning weights to edges of the graph.

Another clustering-based pre-fetching approach has been proposed by Rangarajan et al (2004), based on ART1 neural network. It includes grouping the users' access patterns and pre-fetch the prototype vector of each group. In their experiment they have focused only on the pre-fetching and did not address the issues related to interaction between Web caching and pre-fetching. In recent years data mining approaches have been widely used in Web pre-fetching area (Huang and Hsu 2008, Pallis et al 2008).

Sujatha and Iyakutty (2010) have proposed a new framework to improve the cluster quality from k-means clustering using Genetic Algorithm.

The above discussed works were found to be inefficient because they use association rules for pre-fetching Web objects which ultimately leads to inaccuracy due to the prediction of a particular page depending on the patterns observed from all the user's preferences (Khalil et al 2009; Xiao et al 2001). Furthermore, these approaches employed traditional replacement algorithms that are not suitable for clustering-based pre-fetching environment. Both Web caching and Web pre-fetching schemes were presented in (Podlipnig & Boszormenyi 2003) and (Teng et al 2005). It is stated that integration of these two techniques would perform better. An additional improvement to traditional cache replacement policies used in the cache of proxy server is explained in (Pallis et al 2008). This is based on the clustering-based pre-fetching scheme using dependency graph. The authors state that a graph-based approach to cluster the Web pages would be more effective. But it is pruned by threshold value. The authors in (Jyoti et al 2008) also have arrived at an approach that predicts the page access before user accessing them. They have used higher order Markov model for predicting next user request. Most of the work discussed above will predict only one object at a time which will increase network traffic when the number of users gets increased. To overcome this, it is decided to propose a clustering-based pre-fetching technique using MART1 algorithm.

PERFORMANCE MEASURES

The most commonly used metrics to measure the performance of Web caching and Web pre-fetching systems are given below (Koskela et al 2003; Cobb & ElAarag 2008, Wong 2006).

- Hit Ratio (HR) also known as Hit Rate, and
- Byte Hit Ratio (BHR) also known as Byte Hit Rate.

HR is the percentage of user requests that are served from the cache. That is HR is the ratio of total number of cache hit to the total number of user requests while BHR is the ratio of total bytes served from the cache to the total bytes requested by user.

The mathematical representation is:

Let N be the total number of user requests (objects) and $\delta_i = 1$, if the requested object 'i' is in the cache (Cache Hit), and $\delta_i = 0$ otherwise (Cache Miss). Equation (4) mathematically represents HR while Equation (5) mathematically represents BHR

$$HR = \frac{1}{n} * \sum_{i=1}^{N} \delta_i \tag{4}$$

whereas BHR is as follows

$$BHR = \frac{\sum_{i=1}^{N} \delta_i * b_i}{\sum_{i=1}^{N} b_i} \tag{5}$$

Here b_i = size of the ith requested object.

The most commonly used metrics to measure the performance of Web pre-fetching (Huang & Hsu 2008; Domenech et al 2010) are given in Equations (6) and (7) below.

- **Precision (Pc):** The ratio of pre-fetch hits to the total number of objects pre-fetched.

$$Pc = \frac{No.of \; \Pr efetchHits}{No.ofObjects \; \Pr efetchHits} \tag{6}$$

- **Recall (Rc):** The ratio of pre-fetch hits to the total number of objects requested by users.

$$Rc = \frac{No.of \; \Pr efetchHits}{No.ofUser \; \mathrm{Re} \, quest} \tag{7}$$

SUMMARY AND PROBLEM FORMULATION

The vast amount of literature studied and reported so far in this chapter has yielded the proposal of new Web caching and pre-fetching approach to improve the scalability of the Web-based system. The literature also points out the importance of Web caching and pre-fetching using Web mining techniques as important findings which stood as the base for the formulation of research problem, which are tabulated and presented in Table 1.

Table 1. Literature support for formulation of research problem

S.No.	Base Papers	Authors	Issue and Inference
1	Web user clustering and its application to pre-fetching using ART neural networks	Rangarajan et al (2004)	It presents a pre-fetching approach based on ART1 neural network. It does not address the issues while integrating Web caching and Web pre-fetching
2	Integrating Web caching and Web pre-fetching in Client-Side Proxies	Teng et al (2005)	Have proposed pre-fetching approach based on association rule. They have proposed an innovative cache replacement policy called (Integration of Web Caching and Pre-fetching (IWCP). They have categorized Web objects into implied and non-implied objects.
3	A clustering-based pre-fetching scheme on a Web cache environment	Pallis et al (2008)	Proposed a graph-based pre-fetching technique. Have used DG for pre-fetching. It is based on association rule and it is controlled by support and confidence. Moreover they have used traditional policies in Web cache environment and didn't address issues while integrating these two.
4	Intelligent Client-side Web Caching Scheme Based on Least Recently Used Algorithm and Neuro-Fuzzy System	Ali & Shamsuddin (2009)	It uses the neuro-fuzzy system to classify a Web object into cacheable or un-cacheable objects. It has LRU algorithm in cache to predict Web objects that may be re-accessed later. Training process requires long time and extra computational cost. It ignored the factors such as cost and size of the objects in the cache replacement policy
5	A survey of Web cache replacement strategies	Podlipnig & Böszörmenyi (2003)	The authors have reviewed and presented an overview of various page replacement policies. It is observed that GDSF perform better in Web cache environment. They also have presented merits and demerits of various page replacement policies.
6	A Keyword-Based Semantic Pre-fetching Approach in Internet News Services	Ibrahim & Xu (2004)	It predicts users' future access based on semantic preferences of past retrieved Web documents. It is implemented on Internet news services. The semantic preferences are identified by analyzing keywords present in the URL of previously accessed Web. It employs a neural network model over the keyword set to predict user future requests.
7	A Survey of Web Caching and Pre-fetching	Waleed et al (2011)	The authors have discussed and reviewed various Web caching and Web pre-fetching techniques. It is observed that most of the pre-fetching techniques discussed here were focusing on single user which will ultimately reduce server performance if number of users increase. Moreover, in recent year's data mining plays a major role in Web pre-fetching areas and most of the data mining-based approach uses association rule mining.

From this, it is also observed that both the techniques would improve the performance by reducing server load and latency in accessing Webpages. However, if the Web caching and pre-fetching approaches are integrated inefficiently then this might causes huge network traffic; increase in Web server load in addition to the inefficient use of cache space (Waleed et al 2011). Hence, the pre-fetching approach should be designed carefully in order to overcome the above said limitations (Feng et al 2009). Hence, it is decided to propose a clustering based pre-fetching technique using Web usage mining.

Problems with Web Based Information Retrieval System

From this survey, it is understood that network congestion remains one of the main barriers to the continuing success of the internet and Web based services. In this background, proxy caching is one of the most successful solutions for civilizing the performance of Web since it reduce network traffic, Web server load and improves user perceived response time. Here, the most popular Web objects that are likely to be revisited in the near future are stored in the proxy server thereby it improves the Web response time and saves network bandwidth. The main component of Web caching is it cache replacement policy. It plays a key role in replacing existing objects when there is no room for new one especially when cache is full. Moreover, the conventional replacement policies are used in Web caching environments. These policies are suitable for memory caching since it involves fixed sized objects. But, Web caching which involves objects of varying size and hence there is a need for an efficient policy that works better in Web cache environment. Moreover, most of the existing Web caching policies have considered few factors and ignored the factors that have impact on the efficiency of Web proxy caching. Hence, it is decided to propose a novel policy for Web cache environment. The proposed policy includes size, cost, frequency, ageing and popularity of Web objects in cache removal policy. It uses the Web usage mining as a technique to improve Web caching policy. Also, empirical analyses shows that proposed policy performs better than existing policies in terms of various performance metrics such as hit rate and byte hit rate.

Moreover, the problem with Web pre-fetching is, to identify the pages that are to be pre-fetched and then to be cached. This is forced by the fact that there are wide spectrums of users and each one of them has their own preferences. Hence this research work tries to solve the above problem using Modified Adaptive Resonance Theory1 (MART1), a variation of ART1 algorithm, by clustering the users based on their access patterns. Deficiency in generation of cluster prototype vector and the similarity measure used are the challenges with traditional ART1 based clustering technique.

Also, the main problem associated with clustering-based pre-fetching is, users may not request some of these pre-fetched objects. In this case, the Web pre-fetching increases the network traffic as well as Web server load and hence lead to reduced bandwidth utilization. This makes traditional replacement algorithms end with reduced network performance and increased bandwidth consumption. Hence the need for an efficient integration of Web pre-fetching and Web caching to overcome the above said limitations.

Proposed Information Retrieval System

This work integrates Web caching and clustering-based pre-fetching technique using MART1. This work also introduces two replacement policies for better bandwidth utilization and to improve network performances. Due to the grouping of users, the task of going into the individual preferences is avoided. A clustering-based pre-fetching technique, namely MART1 has been proposed and compared with traditional ART1 technique. The MART1 would provide better inter-, intra-clusters distance and produce highly homogeneous clusters than the traditional ART1.

Cache replacement policies have been considered in the second work. This work proposes two different cache replacement policies namely Modified Least Frequently Used (MLFU) and Pre-fetching based Modified LFU (PMLFU) to address the issues while integrating clustering-based Pre-fetching technique with Web caching. Both MLFU and PMLFU provide better performance by reducing the number of objects to be pre-fetched and increases the byte hit rate thereby improving the bandwidth utilization. The MLFU combines the benefits of frequency, recency, popularity and the size of a Web document in removal policy while PMLFU updates priority dynamically after assigning the priority based on whether it is: i) an actual request or ii) a pre-fetching request. This automatic update of priorities enables the efficient utilization of cache both for actual and pre-fetching requests. The next section discusses the proposed system using MART1 algorithm.

Figure 1. Snapshot of sample proxy server log

```
1168300926.602 285938 103.7.55.59 TCP_MISS/504         1663
GEThttp://204.95.60.12/servlet/StorageGuard/update/updateclientversion=2.1andversion=99.99andlanguage=enuandoe
m=vsgandbannerDate=05/01/2010 - TIMEOUT_DIRECT/204.95.60.12 text/html
1168300927.853 1250 50.141.5.120 TCP_DENIED/407 1995 GET http://cdn5.tribalfusion.com/media/261216.gif -
NONE/- text/html
1168300928.348         1746         151.33.90.119         TCP_MISS/404         333         GET
http://info.ddcd.jp/ddcd3_info/fujitsu/Fujitsu_JPN_CD_News(421).txt - DIRECT/210.174.185.15 text/html
1168300928.351         1750         151.33.90.119         TCP_CLIENT_REFRESH_MISS/404         333         GET
http://info.ddcd.jp/ddcd3_info/fujitsu/Fujitsu_JPN_CD(421).txt - DIRECT/210.174.185.15 text/html
```

CLUSTERING BASED PRE-FETCHING SYSTEM USING MART1

The proposed system is based on the concept of Web log mining which deals with the web log file present in the Web server. Log files are raw text files which contain information about the user's access to a Web site. It keeps track of the information like who accessed, what was accessed from and when accessed a Web site. Figure 1 shows the example of actual log file generated by proxy server. Various fields included in this file are: time stamp of the request, time required to process the request in millisecond, IP address of the machine requesting the object, response code, requested item size in bytes, type of method used, requested object name, identity information, redirection information, whether the request was redirected to another server and content type.

Data Preparation

The raw proxy server log files are unsuitable for access pattern analysis. This log file requires efficient preprocessing to remove irrelevant, inconsistent and incomplete data from the proxy server log file for analysis. It is important to remove all the requests from the Web proxy log file that are not explicitly requested by the user.

Identification of user from a log file is a critical task in most web usage mining applications. Most of the log files provide only the computer IP address and the user agent for user identification. For Web sites requiring user registration, the log file also contains the user login that can be used for the user identification. In this work, to identify frequent users and frequent pages for pre-fetching, an individual IP address is identified as a user.

For each unique IP address identified in user identification process, the page identification process constructs tuple of the form $\{IP_i, Pages_j\}$. This helps in identifying the set of pages visited by the particular user from a particular machine. The most frequent visitors are identified and stored in a vector - users $\{u_1, u_2, u_3... u_n\}$. The most frequent pages visited are identified and stored in a vector - pages $\{p_1, p2...p_m\}$. In access pattern entries a_{ij} indicates the number of times user i has visited the page j. The vector gives information about the preferences of each user visiting the site. Figure 2 shows the Web access pattern.

Hence, the architecture of the proposed system includes the following modules:

1. Preprocessing component to extract relevant fields from Web log file.
2. Feature Extractor to extract the access pattern from the log file.
3. Clustering component to apply MART1 algorithm for grouping users based on the access pattern.
4. Pre-fetcher module to identify the pages to be pre-fetched.

Figure 2. Web access pattern

$$\begin{pmatrix} a_{11}\ a_{12}\ a_{13}\ ....a_{1m} \\ \\ a_{21}\ a_{22}\ a_{23}\ ....a_{2m} \end{pmatrix}$$

The major differences between ART1 (Rangarajan et al 2004) and MART1 techniques are given below:

- Using binary addition of the input pattern with winning column of the top down matrix instead of the usual multiplication (MART1).
- Using binary addition introduces a new problem – i.e., all the bits in the centroid of the cluster become '1'. To overcome this, the centroid (top down weight of the winning column) is chosen by performing the test between the current input pattern and all the input patterns of the users belonging to that cluster (MART1).
- The similarity between two binary vectors A and B is calculated as follows:
  ○ DAB= S / | B|

Where S refers to Number of 0's in A whose corresponding bit in B is 1. DAB is the distance between A and B, a conditional probability that defines object dissimilarity, that is, if A and B are similar then it should be assigned minimum DAB value.

Pre-Fetching

The steps involved in pre-fetching are given below.

- After the training of MART1 network, if a particular user request arrives, the previous access pattern of the user is searched from the database. If the access pattern is found, it is then fed into the MART1 network to identify the user cluster.
- After identifying the cluster, it outputs the prototype of the cluster. Based on this prototype, the pages are pre-fetched and cached. Once cached, they can be accessed at much higher speed.

RESULTS AND DISCUSSIONS

The datasets for testing the proposed system have been obtained from National Laboratory of Applied Network Research (NLANR) project that provides dataset for researchers and encourages research on Web caching. The datasets and its preprocessing details are shown in Table 2. The performance of the

Table 2. Testing datasets and it preprocessing details

S.No	Data source Name	Size of the Data Source	Size of the Data Source After Preprocessing	No. of Unique Users	No. of Unique Pages	No of Frequent Users	No of Frequent Pages
1	sv[1].sanitized-access.20070109	76.9 MB	1.18 MB	53	4157	44	986
2	uc[1].sanitized-access.20070110	76.0 MB	0.957 MB	99	5376	82	417
3	bo2[1].sanitized-access.20070110	66.5 MB	1.19 MB	53	4576	46	797
4	uc[1].sanitized-access.20070109	78.2 MB	1.35 MB	90	5046	75	372

MART1 clustering algorithm is observed better, than ART1 clustering algorithm in terms of the average inter- and intra-cluster distance. Through the experiment, the average inter-cluster distance shows that 97.5% of the pages pre-fetched by the clusters are different. Figure 3 depicts the difference in intra-cluster distance between ART1 and MART1. It is seen that the intra-cluster distance for the MART1 algorithm is zero since the center of each cluster is formed based on binary addition. Thus it pre-fetches all the frequent pages corresponding to all the frequent users belonging to that cluster. The difference in inter-cluster distance by ART1 and MART1 is shown Figure 4. From the graph, it is inferred that use of MART1 algorithm does not affect the inter-cluster similarity. The averages inter- cluster distance still lies above 0.975 which shows that 97.5 percent of the pages pre-fetched by the clusters are different. Figure 5 and Figure 6 compares the hit rate without pre-fetching, pre-fetching using ART1 and pre-fetching using MART1 for different cache sizes. From the graph, it is observed that the average hit rate increases as it moves from schemes ART1 to MART1.

Figure 3. ART1 vs modified ART1 intra cluster distance with first three datasets

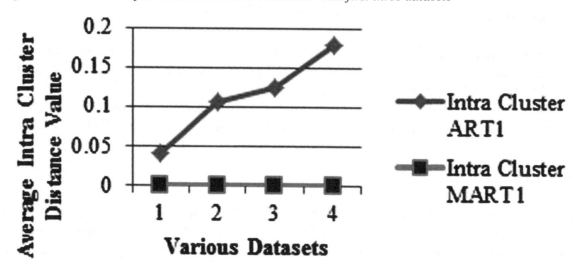

Figure 4. ART1 vs modified ART1 inter cluster distance with first three datasets

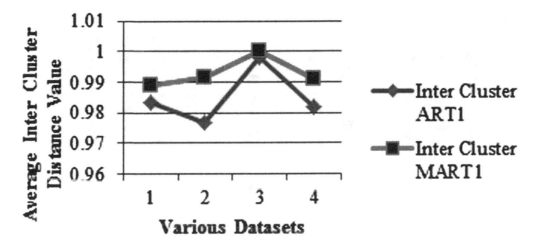

INTEGRATING WEB PRE-FETCHING AND WEB CACHING SYSTEM

Most of the existing pre-fetching techniques employ single object pre-fetching technique, which is handled by traditional cache replacement algorithms. However, using the clustering-based pre-fetching technique, multiple objects are pre-fetched that users may not request some of these objects but the server load is increased. So to overcome these problems, an efficient integration of Web pre-fetching and caching is challenged. The proposed replacement policies are compared with LFU, LRU, FIFO, GDS and GDSF for hit rate and byte hit rate. For the GDS and GDSG algorithms the cost function considered is one. Cache size considered, starts from 1 MB to 5 MB, because the size of the testing dataset is smaller than 1.5MB. In order to evaluate the performance, cache size has chosen smaller than testing datasets.

Figure 7 shows the performance of Modified Least Frequently Used (MLFU) algorithm in terms of hit rate under varying cache size. It is understood that MLFU performs much better than all other cache replacement policies. Graph plots show the performance of proposed work of MLFU in terms of hit rate with different cache size in dataset shown in Table 1. To increase the byte hit rate of LFU policy,

Figure 5. ART1 Vs modified ART1 using Data Set3 (sv [1].sanitized-access.20070110)

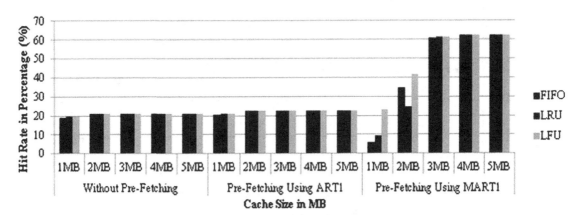

Figure 6. ART1 VS modified ART1 using dataset (uc[1].sanitized-access.20070110)

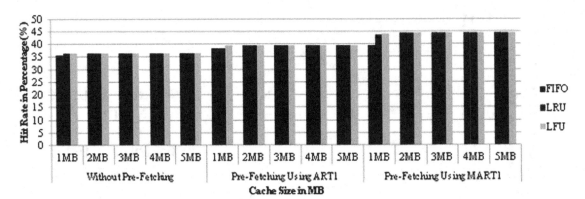

Figure 7. Comparision of hit rate by FIFO, LRU, LFU and MLFU on dataset (sv[1].sanitized-access.20070109)

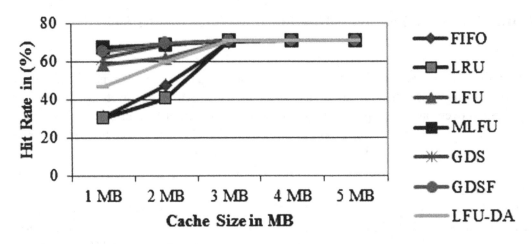

Figure 8. Byte hit rate of LRU Vs LFU Vs MPLFU on dataset (uc[1].sanitized-access.20070110)

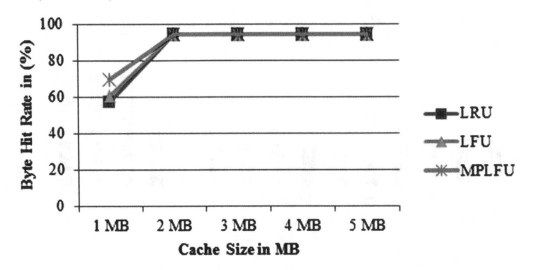

PMLFU policy has been proposed. Graph plots in Figure 8 shows the byte hit rate of Pre-fetching based Modified Least Frequently Used(MPLFU) policy compared with LRU and LFU policies. From Figure 8, it is seen that MPLFU algorithm provides better byte hit rate than LFU and LRU algorithm.

Figure 7 and Figure 8 shows the comparison of two proposed work MPLFU and MLFU polcies. These two policies are compared against hit rate and byte hit rate. It is inferred that MPLFU policy provides higher byte hit rate and low hit rate whereas MLFU policy provides mostly higher hit rate and byte hit rate. Hence it saves the bandwith .

While considering hit rate of MPLFU policy it provides only a moderate hit rate than LFU policies. However, MPLFU policy improves network performance by yielding higher byte hit rate. Hence it provides better bandwidth utilization. Graph given below gives the performance of MPLFU policy in terms of hit rate under varying cache size. From this it is observed that MPLFU policy provides moderate hit rate but provides higher byte hit rate. Hence network performance gets improved.

CONCLUSION AND FUTURE WORKS

The speed of information retrieval is very important while using the Internet. With the proposed system, the information providers can provide information at a faster rate to satisfy and retain their visitors. In this approach, frequently requested Web pages by the users are tracked and identified, in addition to the integration of the Web pre-fetching scheme and Web caching to achieve performance improvement for the proxy-based Web cache. It is evident that the proposed cache replacement policies suit the proposed system for improved network performance. It is expected that the user datasets containing the privacy information should not be exposed to the outside world. Therefore, privacy preserving data mining techniques can also be applied in order to hide personal information about the users. Further, it is also possible to apply the evolutionary optimization technique in MART1

REFERENCES

Ali, W., & Shamsuddin, S. M. (2009). Intelligent Client-Side Web Caching Scheme Based on Least Recently Used Algorithm and Neuro-Fuzzy System. *The Sixth International Symposium on Neural Networks (ISNN 2009)*, 70-79.

Chen, T. (2007). Obtaining the Optimal Cache Document Replacement Policy for the Caching System of an EC Website. *European Journal of Operational Research*, *181*(2), 828–835. doi:10.1016/j.ejor.2006.05.034

Chen, Y., Qiu, L., Chen, W., Nguyen, L., & Katz, R. H. (2003). Efficient and adaptive Web replication using content clustering. *Selected Areas in Communications. IEEE Journal on*, *21*(6), 979–994.

Cobb, J., & Elaarag, H. (2008). Web Proxy Cache Replacement Scheme based on Back-Propagation Neural Network. *Journal of Systems and Software*, *81*(9), 1539–1558. doi:10.1016/j.jss.2007.10.024

Domenech, J., Pont-Sanju, A., Sahuquillo, J., & Gil, J. A. (2010). *Evaluation, Analysis and Adaptation of Web Pre-fetching Techniques in Current Web. In Web-based Support Systems* (pp. 239–271). London: Springer.

Elaarag, H., & Romano, S. (2009). Improvement of the neural network proxy cache replacement strategy. *Proceedings of the 2009 Spring Simulation Multiconference*, 90-100.

Feng, W., Man, S. & Hu G. (2009). Markov Tree Prediction on Web Cache Pre-fetching. In *Software Engineering, Artificial Intelligence (SCI)*. Springer-Verlag.

Heung, K.L., Baik, S.A., & Kim, E.J. (2009). Adaptive Pre-fetching Scheme Using Web Log Mining in Cluster-based Web. *ICWS*, 1-8.

Huang, Y. F., & Hsu, J. M. (2008). Mining web logs to improve hit ratios of pre-fetching and caching. *Knowledge-Based Systems*, *21*(1), 62–69. doi:10.1016/j.knosys.2006.11.004

Ibrahim, T. I., & Xu, C. Z. (2004). A Keyword-Based Semantic Pre-fetching Approach in Internet News Services. *IEEE Transactions on Knowledge and Data Engineering*, *16*(5), 601–611. doi:10.1109/TKDE.2004.1277820

Jianhan, Z. (2002). Using Markov Chains for Link Prediction in Adaptive Web Sites. *SoftWare*, 60-73.

Jyoti, P., Goel, A., & Sharma, A. K. (2008). A Framework for Predictive Web Pre-fetching at the Proxy Level using Data Mining. *IJCSNS, 8*(6), 303–308.

Kaya, C. C., Zhang, G., Tan, Y., & Mookerjee, V. S. (2009). An Admission-Control Technique for Delay Reduction in Proxy Caching. *Decision Support Systems*, *46*(2), 594–603. doi:10.1016/j.dss.2008.10.004

Khalil, F., Li, A. J., & Wang, H. (2009). Integrated Model for Next Page Access Prediction. Int. *J. Knowledge and Web Intelligence*, *1*(2), 48–80. doi:10.1504/IJKWI.2009.027925

Koskela, T.J., Heikkonen, & Kaski, K. (2003). Web cache optimization with nonlinear model using object feature. *Computer Networks Journal, 43*(6), 805-817.

Kumar, C., & Norris, J. B. (2008). A New Approach for a Proxy-level Web Caching Mechanism. *Decision Support Systems, Elsevier, 46*(1), 52–60. doi:10.1016/j.dss.2008.05.001

Liu, Q. (2009). *Web Latency Reduction with Pre-fetching* (Ph.D Thesis). University of Western Ontario, London, Canada.

Markatos, E. P., & Chronaki, C. E. (1998). A Top-10 Approach to Pre-fetching on the Web. In *Proceedings of INET*, 276-290.

Mehrdad, J. (2008). Web User Navigation Pattern Mining Approach Based on Graph Partitioning Algorithm. *Journal of Theoretical and Applied Information Technology*.

Nanopoulos, A., Katsaros, D., & Manolopoulos, Y. (2003). A Data Mining Algorithm for Generalized Web Pre-fetching. *IEEE Transactions on Knowledge and Data Engineering*, *15*(5), 1155–1169. doi:10.1109/TKDE.2003.1232270

Navin, K., Tyagi, & Solanki, A.K. (2011). Analysis of Server Log by Web Usage Mining for Website Improvement. *International Journal of Computer Science Issues*, *7*(4).

Pallis, G., Vakali, A., & Pokorny, J. (2008). A Clustering-Based Pre-Fetching Scheme on A Web Cache Environment.ACM Journal Computers and Electrical Engineering, 34(4).

Palpanas, T., & Mendelzon, A. (1999). Web Pre-fetching using Partial Match Prediction. *Proceedings of the 4th International Web Caching Workshop*.

Paola, B. (2007). Web Usage Mining Using Self Organized Maps. *International Journal of Computer Science and Network Security, 7*(6).

Pei, C., & Irani, S. (1997). Cost-Aware WWW Proxy Caching Algorithms. *Proceedings of the USENIX Symposium on Internet Technologies and Systems*, 193-206.

Pitkow, J., & Pirolli, P. (1999). Mining Longest Repeating Subsequences to Predict World Wide Web Surfing. *Proceedings USENIX Symposium on Internet Technologies and Systems*.

Podlipnig, S., & Boszormenyi, L. (2003). Survey of Web Cache Replacement strategies. *ACM Computing Surveys, 35*(4), 374–398. doi:10.1145/954339.954341

Rangarajan, S. K., Phoha V.V., Balagani, K., Selmic, R. R. & Iyengar, S. S. (2004). Web user clustering and its application to pre-fetching using ART neural networks. *IEEE Computer*, 1-17.

Sandeep, S. (2010). Discovering Potential User Browsing Behaviors Using Custom-Built Apriori Algorithm. *International Journal of Computer Science & Information Technology, 2*(4).

Sathiyamoorthi, V. (2016). A Novel Cache Replacement Policy for Web Proxy Caching System Using Web Usage Mining. *International Journal of Information Technology and Web Engineering, 11*(2), 12–20. doi:10.4018/IJITWE.2016040101

Sujatha, N., & Iyakutty, K. (2010). Refinement of Web usage Data Clustering from K-means with Genetic Algorithm. *European Journal of Scientific Research, 42*(3), 464-476.

Tang, N., & Vemuri, R. (2005). An Artificial Immune System Approach to Document Clustering. *Proceedings of the Twentieth ACM Symposium on Applied Computing*, 918-922. doi:10.1145/1066677.1066889

Teng, W., Chang, C., & Chen, M. (2005). Integrating Web Caching and Web Pre-fetching in Client-Side Proxies. *IEEE Transactions on Parallel and Distributed Systems, 16*(5), 444–455. doi:10.1109/TPDS.2005.56

Teng, W., Chang, C. Y., & Chen, M. S. (2005). Integrating Web caching and Web pre-fetching in client-side proxies. *IEEE Transactions on Parallel and Distributed Systems, 16*(5), 444–455. doi:10.1109/TPDS.2005.56

Tian, W., Choi, B., & Phoha, V. V. (2002). An Adaptive Web Cache Access Predictor Using Neural Network. *Proceedings of the 15th international conference on Industrial and engineering applications of artificial intelligence and expert systems: developments in applied artificial intelligence, 2358*, 450-459. doi:10.1007/3-540-48035-8_44

Waleed, A., Siti, M.S., & Abdul, S.I. (2011). A Survey of Web Caching and Prefetching. *Int. J. Advance. Soft Comput. Appl., 3*(1).

Wang, J. (1999). A Survey of Web Caching Schemes for the Internet. *ACM Comp. Commun. Review, 29*(5), 36–46. doi:10.1145/505696.505701

Wong, A. K. Y. (2006). Web Cache Replacement Policies: A Pragmatic Approach. *IEEE Network, 20*(1), 28–34. doi:10.1109/MNET.2006.1580916

Xiao, J., Zhang, Y., Jia, X., & Li, T. (2001). Measuring Similarity of Interests for Clustering Web-users. *12th Australasian Database Conference (ADC)*, 107-114.

Xu, L., Mo, H., Wang, K., & Tang, N. (2006). Document Clustering Based on Modified Artificial Immune Network. Rough Sets and Knowledge Technology, 4062, 516-521.

Zhijie, B., Zhimin, G., & Yu, J. (2009). A Survey of Web Pre-fetching. *Journal of Computer Research and Development, 46*(2), 22–210.

KEY TERMS AND DEFINITIONS

Classification: It is the supervised learning process where data objects are classified into no. of groups based on some predefined groups.

Client: A client is a machine which makes some request to the Web server.

Clustering: Clustering is the process of grouping objects into clusters where objects within the clusters are highly similar and objects between clusters are highly dissimilar.

Database: It is the collection of interrelated data and software to manage those data.

Data Mining: It is also known as knowledge discovery in database (KDD). It is the process of extracting implicit, previously unknown and potentially useful information from database.

Data Preprocessing: It is the process of removing irrelevant, incomplete and inconsistent data from data source.

Proxy Server: It is widely used to reduce the latency problem of today's Webpages as it resides in between client and server. It plays a major role in dropping the response time and saves the bandwidth.

Server: A server is a machine which process the user request and sends the response to the client.

Web Caching: Web Caching is an intermediate storage between client and server and used to store the Web objects that are likely to be accessed in the near future.

Web Pre-Fetching: Web Pre-fetching is used to load Webpages into the cache before the actual request arrives.

Chapter 15
Session Hijacking over Cloud Environment:
A Literature Survey

Thangavel M
Thiagarajar College of Engineering, India

Pandiselvi K
Thiagarajar College of Engineering, India

Sindhuja R
Thiagarajar College of Engineering, India

ABSTRACT

Cloud computing is a technology that offers an enterprise model to provide resources made available to the client and network access to a shared pool of configurable computing resources and pay-for-peruse basis. Generally, a session is said to be the collective information of an ongoing transaction. This package is typically stored on the server as a temporary file and labeled with an ID, usually consisting of a random number, time and date the session was initiated. That session ID is sent to the client with the first response, and then presented back to the server with each subsequent request. This permits the server to access the stored data appropriate to that session. That, in turn allows each transaction to be logically related to the previous one. Session hijacking is the common problem that is experienced in the cloud environment in which the session id is gained and information is gathered using the session ID compromising its security. This chapter covers session hijacking and the countermeasures to prevent session hijacking.

INTRODUCTION

Cloud Computing is considered as a small or medium-sized data centers with computational power, as this technology equally rely on virtualization for management with large data or information processing requirements and it includes the combination of Software as a Service (SaaS) and utility computing.

DOI: 10.4018/978-1-5225-2013-9.ch015

Due to the innovative hacking techniques the risk in security has increased to a greater extent in the cloud environment. To safeguard security several security management and measures are followed such as Information Technology Infrastructure Library (ITIL) guidelines, ISO/IEC 27001/27002 standards and Open Virtualization Format (OVF) standards that focuses on security principles (Challa 2012). Despite having such measures researchers cannot promise cloud security is the dark side of this picture. Some of the hacking techniques are Heartbleed, ShellShock, Poodle, Rosetta Flash, Hacking PayPal Accounts with 1 Click, Google Two-Factor Authentication Bypass etc.,. There are two explanations in reality; 1) weaknesses in the security that is currently adopted all over the globe, 2) the innovative hacking techniques that are quickly becoming extraordinarily intelligent, sophisticated and hard to detect.

Clients are the user of the cloud where they store their valuable information and the communication between the clients are taken place. If the client can access the application from any location, then the privacy of the client could be compromised. Authentication techniques are used for securing privacy. While providing authentication the client should be aware of the assaults in cloud computing. The authentication attacks included in cloud computing are Eavesdropping, Man-in-the-Middle Attacks, Cookie Poisoning, Replay Attack, Session Hijacking, Shoulder Surfing, Cloud Malware Injection, Password Discovery Attacks, Reflection Attack, Customer Fraud Attack, Denial-of service Attack, Insider Attack, Wrapping Attack, Flooding Attack, Browser Attack, Impersonating Attack, SSL Attacks, Guessing Attack, Brute Force Attack, Dictionary Attack, Video Recording Attack, and Stolen Verifier Attack (Misbahuddin 2013).

The authentication attacks that are listed above are explained one after the other. Eavesdropping is the process of listening or monitoring the established communication between two authorized clients by which information are gathered. In Man in the middle attack, hacker impersonates as the authorized client and gains the information that is communicated between authorized users. Cookie poisoning is done where the attacker gains the access permission by modifying the credentials information of the authorized client that is stored in the cookies (Khare 2015) . Replay Attack is an attack where the communication between the authorized users is intruded by the attacker, the message from the sender is received then modified by the attacker and it is modified and sent back to the receiver. Shoulder Surfing is to gain the sensitive information by observing the clients entry of data via keyboard by the attacker. Cloud Malware Injection aims to inject a malicious service or virtual machine instance, which appears as the valid service instance running on the cloud platform. Password Discovery is an attack where various techniques are involved to gain the password of the authorized client. Reflection Attack is processed on mutual authentication schemes in which the attacker tricks the victim by revealing the secret to its own challenge. Customer Fraud Attack is where the client deliberately compromises its authentication token. Denial-of-service is harass in which the hacker sends the request to the target machines by which the legitimate clients request is not responded (Zunnurhain 2012; Dacosta 2012). Among these attacks the most powerful is the Session hijacking attack as the legitimate user is unaware of this attack that compromises his privacy and data security. In this chapter, author will discuss the methodology of session hijacking, its major risks and the countermeasures to prevent it from occurring in the cloud environment.

SESSION HIJACKING

Session hijacking is the process of knowing the session ID (SID) of an active client, so that his account can be impersonated or hijacked. The application tries to identify him based on his cookie value, which

Figure 1. Session hijacking

contains the SID (Clark 2005). SID value of any active client can be used and logged into the application by a victim. It is shown in Figure 1.

As Hyper Text Transfer Protocol (HTTP) 1.1 protocol is introduced the concern towards session hijacking became serious and in the former version 1.0 of HTTP protocol this kind of hijacking was not possible as these were inherently stateless. The connection exists between two entities for a limited amount of time in the prior versions of HTTP protocols. Only these connections are terminated as soon as the sender forwards the data packet and the receiver receives the packet.

According to the security perspective, it was a safer form of communication in which the illegitimate client cannot access or hack as the connection is no longer active. For example, when a client tries for online ticket booking first selects the destination, time and ticket category and further proceeds to the subsequent page to approve the ticket and then payment. An active session between the client and the server is required for such type of communication to display the output and activeness of the session was fulfilled with the introduction of session states to keep track of client's activities (sending, receiving) on the web. Session hijacking vulnerabilities are very simple to be exploited thus easily cause danger to the system. To overcome such vulnerability in most of the computers TCP/IP is used. By this TCP/IP the system can be protected against hijacking to a little extent unless another protocol is used to secure (Margaret 2014). Only when encryption is used the countermeasure that is explained in that section can be executed. Major dangers that are caused by hijacking are identity theft, information loss, fraud activities, etc.

Rather than to enter the system directly, the session hijacking process easily sneaks in as a genuine client. An established session is found by session hijacking process and that session can be taken over after a genuine client has accessed and authenticated. The attacker can stay connected for hours once the session has been hijacked. This session is the effective chance gained by the attacker to plant backdoors or to even gain an additional access privilege to a system. To identify an attacker who impersonates as a genuine client is difficult, thus it is one of the main reasons for which the session hijacking is complicated. All routed traffic sent to the client's IP address are redirected to the attacker's system (Chou 2013). The hijacking process can be broken down into three broad phases such as tracking the connection, desynchronizing the connection, injecting the attacker's packet. The Session hijacking techniques are brute force (attacker attempts different IDs until he succeeds), Stealing (attacker uses different techniques to steal session IDs) and calculating (using non-randomly generated IDs, an attacker tries to calculate the session IDs).

This section highlights various types of session hijacking attacks and the techniques used to perform those attacks. And methods that are involved to hijack the session are also briefly explained with examples. Tools that are needed to perform session hijacking attacks are also listed with the uses and procedures to handle the tools respectively.

Types of Attacks

Various types of session hijacking attacks are explained here (Bhaturkar 2014).

Active Session Hijacking

An active attacker searches for an active session and utilizes the session for communicating between the client and server. Here the active attacker impersonates as a genuine client / client where the client is being manipulated and the server is being fooled by the active attacker.

Passive Session Hijacking

An attacker hijacks a session in the traffic that is being sent onwards but sits back, watches and records all the traffic in the network. In a passive attack the traffic or communication taking place between the client and the server is being monitored. In this situation where the traffic is monitored and captured while going across the wire Sniffing software is utilized.

Session Hijacking in OSI model

Session hijacking attacks are classified based on the OSI model as application level session hijacking and network level session hijacking. The techniques that are involved for these attacks are explained in detail. It is shown in Figure 2.

Application-Level Session Hijacking

In the application level session hijacking attack, the unauthorized privileges to the web server is gained by forecasting a valid session token which is compromised to gain. Application-level hijacking is performed by gathering the information, which is provided through network-level hijacking. Therefore, in most of the cases network-level and application-level session hijacking occurs together. Application-level session hijacking involves either creating a new session using the stolen data or gaining control of an existing session. Application- level session hijacking transpires with HTTP sessions. By gaining the control of the respective session IDs and the unique identifiers of the HTTP sessions, HTTP sessions can be hijacked as it is defined by web application.

Figure 2. Session hijacking attacks

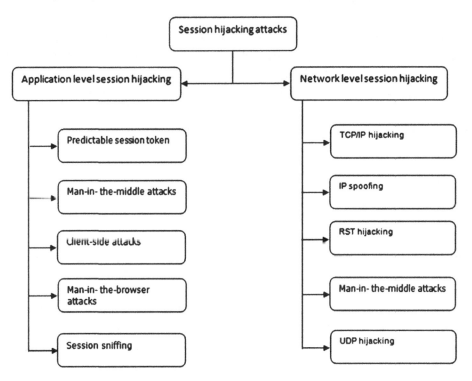

Various ways in which application-level session hijacking can be proficient by compromising the session tokens are mentioned below.

- Predictable session token,
- Man-in- the-middle attacks,
- Client-side attacks,
- Man-in- the-browser attacks, and
- Session sniffing.

Predictable Session Token

It is a method used for forecasting a session ID or impersonating a website client. Predicting or forecasting a session ID is also known as session hijacking. By negotiating the client's privileges, attacker gets the capability to ping the requests in website. The attacker accomplishes the attack, by forecasting the unique session value or guessing the session ID.

Session Fixation

The attacker tries with a known session ID to entice a client to authenticate himself and by the knowledge of the client session ID attacker hijacks the client-validated session. The vulnerability of a server which allows a client to use fixed Session ID is exploited by the attacker.

Network-Level Session Hijacking

Network-level session hijacking is implemented by the web applications through the data flow of the protocol which is shared. Critical information that is helpful to the attacker to attack the application - level sessions are provided by the attacks on network-level sessions.

Network-level session hijacking includes:

- TCP/IP hijacking,
- IP spoofing,
- RST hijacking,
- Blind hijacking,
- Man - in - the -middle, and
- UDP hijacking.

TCP/IP Hijacking

A TCP session hijacker tries to forge acceptable packets for both ends which acts as the real packets and creates a state where the client and server are unable to exchange data. Attacker is able to achieve control of the session. Wherein, the Server's Sequence Number (SSN) no longer matches the Client's Acknowledgement Number (ACK) and vice versa that is the reason why the client and server drop packets sent between them.

Blind Hijacking

Even if the source-routing is disabled, the attacker can introduce malevolent data or commands into the interrupted communication in the TCP session. The attacker has no access to see the response but can send the data or comments.

IP Spoofing

It is a host-file hijack or an IP address forgery, a hijacking technique which an attacker impersonates as a trusted host to obscure his distinctiveness, hijack browsers, spoof a website, or gain access to a network. The hijacker obtains the IP address of a genuine user and modifies the packet headers so that the genuine user appears to be the source.

Man in the Middle

It is one common method used to track what is being communicated using packet sniffing tools, between two systems.

RST Hijacking

Hijacker involves introducing an authentic-looking reset (RST) packet using spoofed source address and forecasting the acknowledgment number. By using a packet crafting tool such as Colasoft's Packet Builder and TCP/IP analysis tool such as tcpdump, RST Hijacking can be executed.

UDP Hijacking

UDP hijacker sends a counterfeit reply to the client´s UDP request before the server responds to it. To intercept server´s response to the client, attacker uses man-in-the-middle and sends its own forged reply. Managing sequence number and other TCP mechanisms is not yet needed to be worried by UDP attackers. As UDP are connectionless communications injecting data into session without being detected is extremely easy.

This network level hijacking process is done through three-way handshaking and sequence number.

Three-Way Handshake

A three -way handshake is performed by the two parties and thus the connection is established by using TCP. Once a three -way handshake starts the connection, it exchanges all the parameters needed for the communication between the two parties. Thus a new connection is established in TCP by using a three -way handshake. It is shown in Figure 3.

Initially client and server establish the connection. In which the connection is in the closed state on the client side and the connection is in the listening state on the server side. The Initial Sequence Number (ISN) is being sent initially by the client and setting the SYN flag. Now the state of the client is changed as the SYN-SENT state. The server acknowledges the client sequence number (ISN), and sends its own ISN with the SYN flag set on receipt of this packet. Now the state of the server is changed as SYN-RECEIVED state. The client acknowledges the server sequence number (ISN) by incrementing it and setting the ACK flag on receipt of this packet.

Now the client is in the established state. At this point, both the machines established a session or connection and can begin the communication. The server enters the established state and sends back the acknowledgment by incrementing the client's sequence number on receiving the client's acknowledgement. By either using the FIN or RST flag or by time out the connection can be closed or terminated. The receiving host enters the CLOSED state and frees all resources correlated with this occurrence of the connection if the RST flag of a packet is set. And any of the incoming packets which are additional for that connection will be dropped.

The receiving host closes the connection as it enters the CLOSE-WAIT mode if the packet is sent with the FIN flag turned on. If the sequence number is within the range and follows its predecessor, the packets sent by the client are accepted in an established connection. The packet is dropped and an ACK packet will be sent using the expected sequence number, if the sequence number is beyond the range of the acceptable sequence numbers.

Figure 3. Three-way handshake

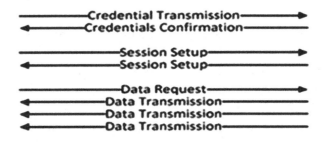

The required things for the three parties to communicate are as follows:

- The IP address,
- The port numbers, and
- The sequence numbers.

The IP address and the port number are listed in the IP packets thus finding out is easy, as it does not change throughout the session. After discovering the addresses, the information exchanged stays the same for the remainder of the session that are communicating with the ports.

The attacker must successfully guess the sequence numbers for a blind hijack since the sequence numbers change. The attacker can successfully hijack the session if the attacker can fool the server to receive his or her spoofed packets and to execute them.

For example:

- By sending a packet to the server with the SYN bit set Bob initiates a connection with the server.
- The server replies Bob by sending a packet with the SYN/ACK bit as it receives this packet and sends an ISN (Initial Sequence Number) for the server.
- Bob increments the sequence number by 1 and to acknowledge the receipt of the packet, sets the ACK bit.
- A session is established successfully between the two machines.

Sequence Number

In TCP the three-way handshake has been already discussed. Full duplex reliable stream connection is provided between two end points by TCP. Four elements which is used to define a connection is IP address of the sender, IP address of the receiver, TCP port number of the sender, and TCP port number of the receiver. In the three-way handshaking protocol sequence number has incremented for each step. A particular sequence number is carried by each byte which is sent by a sender that is acknowledged by the receiver at its end. With the same sequence number, the receiver responds to the sender. The sequence number is different for different connections, and each session of a TCP connection has a different sequence number for security purposes (Cappelli 2012).

These sequence numbers are fundamental for security; which makes it very difficult to guess them since they are 32 bits, and thus there are more than 4 billion possible combinations. They are also significant for an attacker to hijack a session. When the initial sequence number is predictable an attacker can send packets that are forged to appear to come from a trusted computer. Attackers gaining access to unauthorized information can also perform session hijacking.

The next step is to introduce randomness in the ISN and tighten the OS implementation of TCP. Pseudo random number generators (PRNGs) are used carry out this. Using PRNGs, ISNs are randomized which is used in TCP connections. However, adding a series of numbers provides insufficient variance in the range of ISN values because of the implications of the central limit theorem, thereby against vulnerable TCP/IP stack implementations which allows an attacker to disrupt or hijack existing TCP connections or spoof future connections. The insinuation is that systems that rely on haphazard increments to generate ISNs are still susceptible to statistical attack. In other words, as the haphazardness is based on an internal algorithm that a particular operating system uses over time, even computers choosing haphazard numbers will repeat them. All the packets that follow will be the ISN_1 and a sequence number has been agreed. Thus injecting data into the communication stream is made possible.

The following are some of the terms that are used to refer to ISN numbers:

- **SVR_SEQ:** The next byte to be sent by the server's Sequence number.
- **SVR_ACK:** In server, the Next byte to be received (the sequence number plus one of the last byte received).
- **SVR_WIND:** Receiving window of the server.
- **CLT_SEQ:** The next byte to be sent by the client's Sequence number.
- **CLT_ACK:** In client, the Next byte to be received.
- **CLT_WIND:** Receiving window of the client.
- Initially, SVR_SEQ _ CLT_ACK and CLT_SEQ _SVR_ACK has no data to be replaced.
- When the connection is in a quiet state (i.e., no data is being sent on each side, these equations are also true.
- When data is sent, these equations are not true during fleeting states.

The following are the header fields of the TCP packet: Source port (SP), Destination port (DP), Sequence number (Sequence number of the first byte in this packet), and Acknowledgment number (AN) Expected sequence number of the next byte to be received).

The following are some of the control bits URG (Urgent pointer), ACK (Acknowledgment), PSH (Push function), RST (Reset the connection), SYN (Synchronize sequence numbers), FIN (No more data from sender), Window (Window size of the sender), Checksum (TCP checksum of the header and data), Urgent pointer (TCP urgent pointer), Options (TCP options), SEG_SEQ (Refers to the packet sequence number), SEG_ACK (Refers to the packet acknowledgment number), SEG_FLAG (Refers to the control bits).

On a characteristic packet sent by the client (no retransmission), SEG_SEQ is set to CLT_SEQ, and SEG_ACK is set to CLT_ACK.

The following actions will take place if a client initiates a connection with the server:

- On the client side the connection is in the CLOSED state.
- On the server side the connection is in the LISTEN state.
- Initially the client sends its ISN and sets the SYN bit:
  ○ SEG_SEQ =CLT_SEQ_0, SEG_FLAG = SYN.
- Now SYN-SENT is its state.
- The server acknowledges the client sequence number, sends its own ISN, and sets the SYN bit when it receives this packet:
  ○ SEG_SEQ_SVR_SEQ_0
  ○ SEQ_ACK _ CLT_SEQ_0_1
  ○ SEG_FLAG _ SY N
- And in turn sets:
  ○ S V R_ A C K_C LT_S E Q_0_ 1
- Now SYN-RECEIVED is its state.
- The client acknowledges the server ISN on receipt of this packet:
  ○ SEG_SEQ _ CLT_SEQ_0_1

- ◦   SEQ_ACK _ SVR_SEQ_0_1
- •   And in turn sets:
- ◦   CLT_ACK_SVR_SEQ_0_1
- •   Now ESTABLISHED is its state
- •   The server enters the ESTABLISHED state on receipt of this packet:
  - ◦   C LT_S E Q_C LT_S E Q_0_ 1
  - ◦   C LT_ A C K_S V R_S E Q_0_ 1
  - ◦   SVR_SECLSVR_SEQ_0_1
  - ◦   S V R_ A C K_C LT_S E Q_0_ 1
- •   The next steps in the process are shown in Figure 4.

Any attacker can introduce data into the session stream if a sequence number within the receiving window is known, or if he or she knows the number of bytes, so far transmitted in the session (only applicable to a blind hijack) and terminate the connection.

With different sequence numbers that fall within the appropriate range the attacker sends out a number of packets and can guess a suitable range of sequence numbers into the network. To close a connection recalls that the FIN packet is used. It is likely that the server accepts at least one packet since the range is known. The attacker can resort to send an appropriate number of packets with sequence numbers a window size apart but does not send a packet for every sequence number.

The number of packets to be sent is known by the attacker by dividing the range of sequence numbers to be covered by the fraction of the window size used and increment, is obtained. This randomization is

Figure 4. Connection establishment

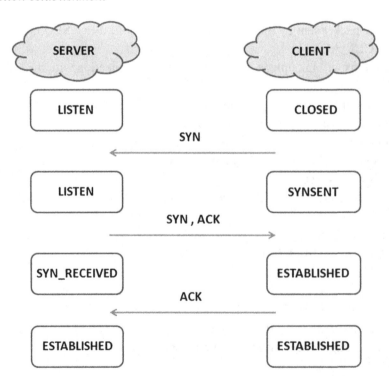

taken care by PRNG. The randomness of the ISNs is directly proportional to the difficulty of carrying out such attacks. To these attacks, the more random the ISN, the more difficult it is.

Sequence Number Prediction

The server responds (SYN/ACK) with a sequence number, once a client sends a connection request (SYN) packet to the server which then the client must acknowledge (ACK). The attacker connects to a service first with its own IP address, records the sequence number chosen, and then opens a second connection from the counterfeit IP address since sequence number is predictable. The attacker can guess the correct response though he does not see the SYN/ACK (or any other packet) from the server. The attacker can use one-sided communication to break into the server if the source IP address is used for authentication.

METHODS

Reverse-proxies, cross-site scripting, network sniffing and source-routed IP packet method are the methods which are currently in use to steal active sessions. By employing strong encryption algorithms, regeneration of cookies after successful login process and the use of long random session IDs are different measures used to reduce the likelihood of session hijacking.

Due to the various technical impurities it was also noticed that the problem still exists. For the whole client area, by using the Secure Socket Layer/Secure Hyper Text Transfer Protocol (SSL/HTTPS) communication mechanism this problem can be solved. Not all pages that are being sent to the cloud clients are protected by SSL. It is also an evident that it will sufficiently reduce the network speed, so to address this issue, HTTPS protocols can be used, if all pages are needed to be protected by SSL. In this case, the cookies will be sent to the client through a SSL link along with the regular cookies and the client will be logged into the system by using a page protected by HTTPS. Despite successful session hijacking, the adversary would not be able to, because once the client again tries to access the client area; the client browser needs to send the secure cookie along with the regular cookie. If it is not possible to protect the whole client area with SSL this remedy will work best. It will protect the cloud clients even if their valid session cookie has been hijacked by disallowing the multiple active sessions at the same time, but this will work only when the real client is still logged in. This problem can be solved to a great extent by checking the IP address of the cloud client for a safer way of communication and where the cloud clients have a static IP address, on every new HTTP request made by the client. From a remote location the possibility of session hijacking will rule out. Even in case of successful cookie theft, the cloud client can still remain secure since the encryption should also be applied on the session value itself (Cheng 2010).

One of the ways of session hijacking is source-routed IP packet method. To commence data transfer between the two victims through its machine an invader, which usually is an anonymous cloud client, places him between two clients X and Y. When the intruder comes into power to send any command to obtain control over the victim's machine, the connection is established. A network sniffing program of session hijacking is using to monitor the conversation between the two nodes is another famed approach where once it gets the packet and decrypts it the hacker can get the control over victim's machine. This type of attack is called middleman attack (Misbahuddin 2013). A HTTP request is modified and a client data is transmitted to a malicious code in which there are the methods of Reverse-proxies but this way of session hijacking is not an important worry for cloud security as clients of a cloud are not using the same local area network. An attacker uses a sniffing tool to sniff the communication between the nodes to steal cookies is yet another widespread technique of session hijacking called Session side-jacking. It is probable that not all the pages are supported with a secure form of communication though cloud providers use the protected way of communication such as SSL. A malicious code is run on the client system to obtain access to the cookies is still a threat to cloud security in which it is Cross-site scripting. Filtering techniques can play an essential role to filter-out the merely concerned data packets (i.e., packets containing the text login and afterward those packets can be analyzed though it is fairly impractical to inspect and examine each and every data packet (Larry 2009).

These techniques are in fact not a work of the cloud service providers and they have developed diverse solutions to undertake such attacks. A few examples of procedures in use to safeguard a cloud from such bots are the encryption algorithms, regeneration of cookies after successful login and the use of long haphazard session IDs to prevent the likelihood of session hijacking.

To safeguard their client's communication almost every major cloud enterprise is using the secure socket layers such as SSL or Transport Layer Security (TLS). Session state timeout has created outstanding results with the use of strong encryption/decryption algorithms. Session hijacking still has a lucid anxiety in 2013 as evidences of successful hijacking are constantly being reported in the IT news at present regardless of all the measures taken by the cloud vendors. Firesheep, extension of Mozilla Firefox exaggerated clients of Facebook and Twitter they were using it and Firesheep extension of Mozilla Firefox came under this type of attack in October 2010. A fresh attack is experimented on a Google mobile messaging application, WhatsApp in May 2012 in which clients connected to the same network were able to gain the right to enter and view the WhatsApp messages of each other (Al-Nemrat 2015).

SESSION HIJACKING TOOLS

Zaproxy Tool

Zed Attack Proxy is an open-source web application security scanner. It is planned to be used by both those who are new to professional penetration testing as well as application security. In OWASP projects ZAP is one of the most active projects that have been given Flagship status. It is being interpret into over 25 languages and is also completely internationalized. It permits the user to manipulate all of the traffic that passes through it, including traffic using https when it is used as a proxy server (Baishya 2014).

REST Application programming interface is used to control when ZAP tool run in a "daemon" mode. It is offered in all of the admired operating systems such as Microsoft Windows, Linux and Mac OS X This cross-platform tool is written in Java and in the Thought Works Technology Radar ZAP was added in May 2015 in the trial ring (Larry 2009).

Burp Suite Tool

In the web applications for performing security testing Burp Suite tool acts as an integrated platform. Its diverse tools work flawlessly together, from initial mapping and analysis of an application's attack surface, through which the security vulnerabilities are found and exploited. Burp provides the full control, hiring by the combination of highly developed manual techniques with state-of-the-art mechanisms, to create the work faster and more effectual (Baishya 2014).

J-Hijack Tool

A Java Hijacking tool is used for web application session security assessment. An easy Java Fuzzer that can mostly be used for parameter enumeration and numeric session hijacking.

In addition to Zaproxy, Burp Suite, and J-hijack, numerous other session hijacking tools exists. These session hijacking tools permit attacker to hijack a TCP session. These tools even hijack HTTP connections to steal cookies (Al-Nemrat 2015).

Hamster Tool

Hamster is a tool or it is "side-jacking". It replaces your cookies with session cookies stolen from somebody else, allowing you to hijack their sessions by acting as a proxy server. Using the Ferret program, the cookies are sniffed. The attacker only needs a copy of the cookies sniffed.

Surf Jack Tool

A Surf Jack tool is the tool which is used to permit the attacker to hijack HTTP connections to steal cookies and even on HTTPS sites. It works on both Ethernet and Wi-Fi (monitor mode). It requires Python 2.4 and Scapy (Baishya 2014).

Ettercap Tool

Ettercap is an open source network security tool which is used for man-in-the-middle attacks on LAN. It can also be used for security auditing and computer network protocol analysis. It works on a variety of Unix-like operating systems which includes Linux, Mac OS X, BSD and Solaris, and on Microsoft Windows. It is accomplished by interrupting the traffic on a network segment through active eavesdropping and capturing passwords (Long 2010).

Hunt Tool

Hunt tool is the hijacking software that has the following functionality features (Baishya 2014):

- **Connection Management:** Sets what are the connections that the users are interested in. Not alone the start of SYN, noticing all the continuing connection. The detection of the ACK storm is used to perform active hijacking. With the detection of successful ARP spoof, ARP spoofed/ normal hijacking is performed. After hijacking, the true client is synchronized with the server thus the connection does not reset.
- **Daemons:** For automatic connection, reset the daemon. ARP spoof or relay daemon has the capability to transmit all packets from spoofed hosts for ARP spoofing of the hosts. For gathering the MAC addresses, MAC discovery daemon is used. Sniff daemon has the capability to investigate for a particular string for logging TCP traffic.
- **Host Resolving:** Delayed host is decided through DNS helper servers.
- **Packet Engine:** For watching ARP, TCP, UDP, and ICMP traffic, extensible packet engine is used. With sequence numbers and the ACK storm detection, TCP connections are gathered.

PerJack Tool

PerJack is a tool which is used to hijack the session in TCP and it is written in Perl language. It exhibits all active sessions, takes over the chosen TCP session and performs a man-in-the-middle attack (Baishya 2014).

Whatssup Gold Engineer's Toolkit

The Whatsup Gold Engineer's Toolkit was intended to make easy for the attacker to act as a network administrator. Three new tools are there for helping to increase the capability to manage the network quickly and easily. Syslog Server tool permits the attacker to collect, save, view and forward Syslog messages in the network. Interface Bandwidth tool affords with one interface from which they can read, gather and understand traffic information. TFTP Server is the service-based tool which can help to transfer system and configuration files such as operating system software, device configuration files securely through the network (Baishya 2014).

Juggernaut Tool

Juggernaut is fundamentally a network sniffer which can also be used in TCP sessions hijacking. It works on Linux as well as, has a Trinux module. Juggernaut tool can be made active to monitor all the network traffic on the local network, or can set to pay attention for an extraordinary token. For example, Juggernaut tool remains until the login prompt, and then collects evidence of the password.

It can be used for traditionally capturing certain types of network traffic by merely leaving the tool running for a few days, and then the attacker has to take the log file that has the recorded traffic. Comparing to regular network sniffers this tool is different which records all network traffic and makes a log file tremendously huge. But its capability to preserve a connection is the main feature of this tool. This means that an attacker can monitor the entire local network TCP based connection and probably "hijack" that session. Attacker can monitor the entire session only when the connection is made.

Cookie Cadger Tool

Cookie Cadger tool helps to recognize the information that leaked from application using HTTP GET requests, which is insecure.

Cookie Cadger is the first open-source pen-testing tool which is used for interrupting and repeating particular insecure HTTP GET requirements into a browser.

Compatibility and Use

Cookie Cadger operates on Windows, Linux, or Mac, and it needs Java 7. For using Cookie Cadger, it requires having "tshark" which has the utility to act as a part of the Wireshark that needs to be installed.

Capturing Wi-Fi traffic needs hardware proficient of monitor mode, and the information of placing the device into monitor mode.

SESSION HIJACKING USING WIRESHARK

- Wireshark is a packet sniffer in which cookies can also be captured.
- Open wireshark and click on interface list and select LAN and then start. Once it is started wireshark would capture all the packets as shown in Figure 5.
- The credential of the given website is captured using wireshark as shown in Figure 6.
- Cookie is tracked as shown in Figure 7.

Figure 5. Capturing the packets using wireshark

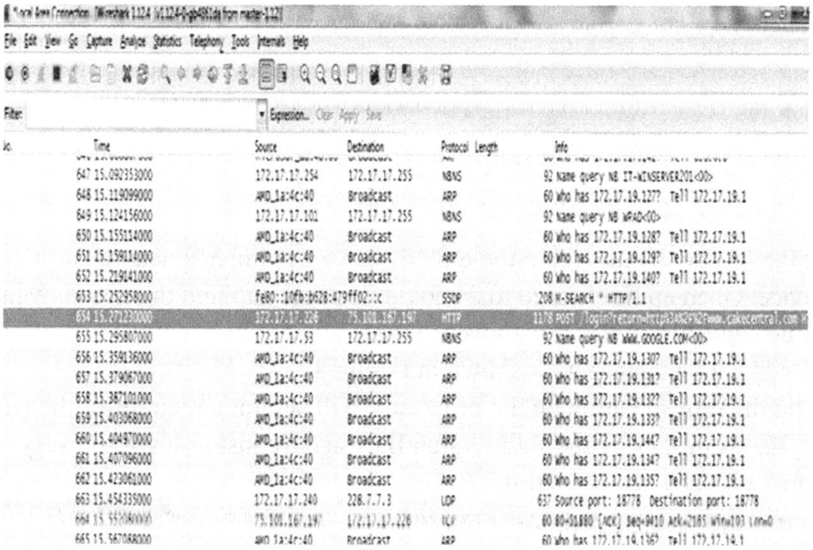

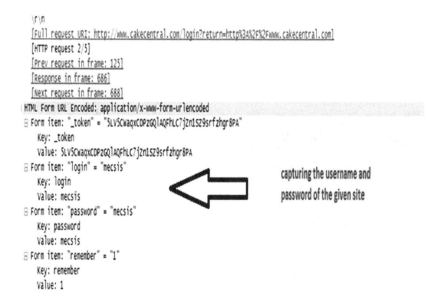

Figure 6. Capturing the credentials of the given site

Figure 7. Tracking the cookies

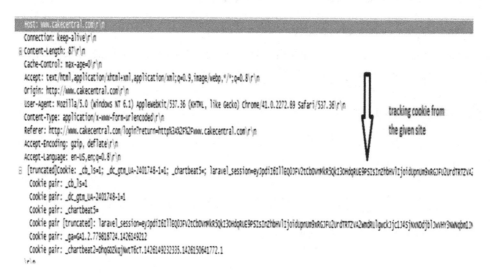

- Now insert the session ID into our cookie field, so we can impersonate the user currently logged-in to his device. Open up Firefox, go to a cookie manager and find the session value. Replace this with the value copied from the step above and save it.
- In Chrome, edit cookie manager, as shown in Figure 8.
- When you hit the refresh button on the browser it will submit a request for the page but this time it will make the request using the new session ID you have just inserted. If every step is followed, you will now be logged in as a victim.

Figure 8. Cookie is replaced

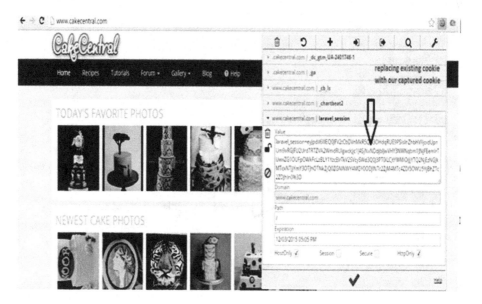

THREATS OF SESSION HIJACKING

Man-in-the-Middle Attack

It is used to interrupt the messages that are being replaced between the end users in a network. Attacker split the TCP connection into two connections (attacker-to-server and client-to-attacker) and uses different techniques.

An attacker can read, modify, and insert fraudulent data into the interrupted communication after the interception of TCP connection is successful. The TCP connection between the client and the server becomes the target in case of an http transaction (Zunnurhain 2012).

Client-Side Attack

The attacker can negotiate the session token by sending malicious activities such as malwares to the client-side programs (Cheng 2010).

Man-in-the-Browser Attack

In this attack the calls between the browser and its security mechanisms or libraries are intercepted by using Trojans. To cause financial dishonesties by influencing transactions of Internet banking systems is its main objective (Kavitha 2011).

Session Sniffing

In this attack, the attacker uses a sniffer tool to capture a valid or correct session token called session ID. Attacker then uses the session ID to get authenticated as a genuine user to the web server (Cappelli 2012).

SOLUTIONS FOR SESSION HIJACKING THREATS

Protecting against Session Hijacking

The following are the ways that are used to protect against session hijacking (Nikiforakis 2011).

Use Secure Shell (SSL) to Create a Secure Communication Channel

Communication security over the internet is provided by SSL protocol. At the transport layer the SSL encrypts the segments of network connections. An attacker can send any confidential information such as credit card numbers, addresses, and other payment details through the internet with SSL configured on the attacker's network (Jayaram 2008).

Pass the Authenticated Cookies over HTTPS Connection

On adding the security capabilities or SSL to the standard HTTP communication, it then results to HTTPS. HTTPS offers protection for cookies transferred over it similar to SSL.

Implement the Log-Out Functionality for Client to end the Session

To avoid session hijacking is to implement the log-out functionality as one of the most defensive steps. When a session is started, it forces to authenticate (Danish 2011).

Generate the Session ID after Successful Login

As the attacker will not be aware of the session ID generated after login, this prevents the session fixation attacks (Nikiforakis 2011).

Pass the Encrypted Data between the Client and the Web Server

Before transmitting it over the Internet encrypts victim's data so that the attackers stealing the data are unable to understand the message or data.

Use String or Long Random Number as a Session Key

A very important factor in communication is session keys. A string or a long random number can be used as a session key to avoid risk.

Use Different Client Names and Passwords for Different Accounts

Longer passwords make it tricky for attackers to deduct or manipulate. When the attacker succeeds in compromising one account using different client names and passwords for different accounts avoids the risk of compromising all the accounts.

Minimize Remote Access

The injection by attackers in the communication session of the legitimate client with the remote server is avoided by minimizing remote access.

Educate Employees

The employees must be educated about the various kinds of session hijacking attacks, signs, and defenses against attacks, to prevent session hijacking attacks.

Do Not Transport Session ID in Query String

Through referrer, the Session IDs in query strings or form fields are being leaked. Session IDs in the query string is recommended not to transport.

Limit Incoming Connections

When the IP ranges are finite and predictable, the incoming connection works well. Example is an intranet of such an environment.

Use Switches Rather than Hubs

In a network, hubs transfer data to all the systems connected which in turn makes the attacker's job easy to encroach. Switches send data only to the destined host. Hence, prefer switches over hubs to avoid session hijacking attacks.

Use Encrypted Protocols That are Available at OpenSSH Suite

Collection of SSH connectivity tools are known as OpenSSH. In OpenSSH all the encrypted protocols are available and the encrypted passwords would transmit across the Internet. The risk of connection hijacking, eavesdropping, and other attacks are eliminated by encrypting all the traffic in the internet by OpenSSH.

Configure the Appropriate Internal and External Spoof Rules on Gateways

On the border gateway suitable internal and external spoof rules are needed to be configured by the user to avoid blind spoofing or Remote Network Session Hijacking (RNSH). Similarly, ARP cache poisoning is monitored by using ARP watch or IDS products. It also uses peer- to-peer VPNs or strong authentication "like Kerberos" (Seltzer 2009).

To avert network intrusions a practice of using multiple security systems or technologies is called as Defense-in-depth. A comprehensive security plan's key component is the defense-in-depth and particularly the network is protected from session hijacking attacks. If one countermeasure fails to safeguard the network, there are additional levels of protection to provide security which is the central idea behind this concept. While the attacker tries to penetrate through abundant layers of security, performing an attack the speed is slowed down by defense-in-depth. Thus for the security administrators, it gives additional time to detect and defend against the attack. A good example of the defense-in-depth strategy is a new firewall configuration strategy. Highly secure networks are implemented by several types of firewall to achieve a defense-in-depth strategy (Larry 2009).

Web Developer's Countermeasures

By exploiting the vulnerabilities that are caused when the session is established session hijacking can be frequently performed, where security is focused often by Web developers (Nair 2013). The risk of session hijacking can be avoided to an extent if the web developers follow the below measures during the development process (Adi 2012):

- Generate session keys with random number or lengthy string in order that it is difficult for an attacker to detect a legitimate session key.
- Encrypt the session key and the data that is transmitted between the web server and the client.
- Prevent eavesdropping technique within the network.
- After a successful login regenerate the session ID to prevent from session fixation attack.
- As soon as the client logs out of the session, it has to be expired.
- A session's or a cookie's life span must be reduced.

Web Client's Countermeasures

Ensure that the attacker's applications are locked when attacker uses the Internet, and select only authorized sites for browsing. While browsing the Internet some of the measures to be followed are:

- Links that are received through emails should not be clicked.
- Prevent malevolent content from entering the network using firewalls.
- Restrict cookies by using firewall and browser settings.
- The websites are to be ensured for verified certificates.
- After every sensitive and confidential transaction from the browser make sure to clear all such as history, offline content, and cookies.
- Rather than using HTTP protocol for transmitting confidential and sensitive data, prefer a secure transmission protocol like HTTPS.
- Instead of closing the browser, logout from the browser by clicking on the Logout option.

Safeguarding Cloud from Session Hijacking

Prior to the HTTP 1.1 protocols, session hijacking was not an issue because the previous versions of HTTP protocols were intrinsically stateless. This problem is experienced by the cloud clients in various forms (Ahmed 2014). For example, reverse-proxy's method by using a HTTP request, network sniffing and cross-site scripting are the variants of account hijacking techniques. It can also be reduced by using Secure Socket Layer (SSL), antivirus, firewalls and code scanners (Larry 2009).

IPSec

IP Security is the expansion of IPSec. At the IP layer a collection of protocols is referred to support secure exchange of packets. It is the VPN technology which is deployed broadly to address confidentiality, integrity, authentication, and key management in the IP networks. IPSec with the help of security services in cryptography, it protects the communication.

Both the sending and receiving devices must share a public key for proper functionality of IPSec. Characteristically, by using Internet Security Association and Key Management Protocol /Oakley

(ISAKMP/Oakley) it is achieved. The receiver is allowed to authenticate the sender based on the digital certificates and to obtain a public key by this protocol (Jayaram 2008).

The benefits that are offered by IPSec include:

- Replay protection,
- Data confidentiality,
- Data integrity,
- Data origin authentication, and
- Network-level peer authentication.

IP Sec Architecture

At the network layer, IPSec offers its services as shown in Figure 9. This reduces the restrictions of selecting the necessary security protocols, for the services. The corresponding cryptographic keys are requested to make the available services based on its requirement. IPSec uses two traffic security protocols to such as Authentication Header (AH) and Encapsulating Security Payload (ESP) and cryptographic key management protocols and procedures to assure confidentiality, integrity and authenticity (Long 2010).

Figure 9. IPSec

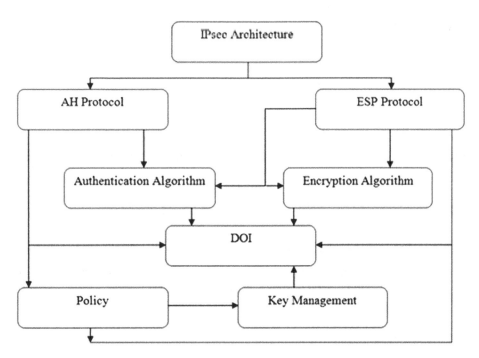

Encapsulating Security Payload (ESP)

It is essentially used for providing encryption and authentication services.

Authentication Header (AH)

Only datagram authentication service is provided in this mode and it does not provide encryption.

Domain of Interpretation (DOI)

For security information it characterizes the payload formats, types of exchange, and naming conventions such as security policies or cryptographic algorithms. The ISAKMP is intended to support security services at all layers in addition to the IP layer. Exactness of the DOI is needed for IP Security.

ISAKMP (Internet Security Association and Key Management Protocol)

In the IPSec architecture, ISAKMP is a key protocol. The required security is provided for a variety of internet communications by combining the security concepts of authentication, key management and security association, such as government, private and commercial.

Policy

Policy establishes whether the two entities can communicate with each other or not thus it is also the key element. If the entities can communicate, then the transformation is predicted. If the policy is not defined appropriately, then those entities may not be able to communicate with each other.

Modes of IPSec

IPSec modes are linked by the two core protocols namely, Authentication Header (AH) and Encapsulating Security Payload (ESP). By adding a datagram to the header, both these protocols offer protection. The difference between these two protocols is in terms of the parts of protected IP datagram and headers arrangement (Halton 2014). Two modes of encryption supported by IPSec are transport mode and the tunnel mode.

Transport Mode

In the transport mode, leaving the header untouched each packet of the payload is encrypted by IPSec. ESP authenticates two linked computers and also has an alternative to encrypt data transfer. It is compatible with NAT. So far, NAT can be used to make available VPN services.

Tunnel Mode

In tunnel mode, both the payload and the header are encrypted by using IPSec thus tunnel mode is highly secure. AH is also called in the Tunnel mode. By the IPSec-compliant device the encrypted data will be decrypted on the receiver's side. NAT is not capable of rewriting the encrypted IP header and it is not capable of providing VPN services as the tunnel mode encrypts the header of the IP packet.

IPSec Authentication and Confidentiality

In IPSec the data authentication includes two concepts, data integrity and data origin authentication. Even though origin authentication is reliant upon data integrity, data authentication refers either to integrity alone or to both of these concepts.

- Data integrity makes sure that the data has not been distorted.
- Data origin authentication makes sure that the data was sent only by the claimed sender.
- ESP affords confidentiality (encryption) in addition to integrity, authentication, and protection against replay attack. It can be used along with AH. On default setting, it protects only the payload of the IP data but otherwise, it protects both the IP header and the payload in tunnel mode.

Components of IPSec

IPSec consists of the components as follows,

- IPSec Driver is the software that achieves protocol-level function necessary to encrypt, decrypt, authenticate, and verify the packet (Halton 2014).
- Internet Key Exchange (IKE) is an IPSec protocol in which it fabricates the security keys for IPSec and other protocols.
- Internet Security Association Key Management Protocol (ISAKMP) is an IPSec protocol that permits encryption of data using frequent security settings to communicate between two computers. The exchange of keys is also secured.
- Oakley is an IPSec protocol that generates a master key and a key that is particular to each session in IPSec data transfer by using the Diffie-Hellman algorithm.
- IPSec Policy Agent is a windows 2000 series from Active Directory that gathers IPSec policy settings and then it sets the configuration.

IPSec Implementation

Based on the platform the IPSec implementation varies. Here platform-independent IPSec implementations are discussed. The main set of components in IPSec implementation is as follows:

- IPSec base protocols,
- SADB,
- SPD,
- Manual keying,
- ISAKMP/IKE,
- SA management, and
- Policy management.

IPSec base protocols implement both ESP and AH. By interacting with the SPD and SADB, it processes the headers and determines the security of the packet. Fragmentation and PMTU is also handled by it.

SADB maintains a list of active SAs for both inbound and outbound processing. Either manually or with the help of an automatic key management system such as IKE it supports the population of SAs.

SPD mainly determines the security of a packet. For both inbound and outbound processing of the packet it is referred. The IPSec base protocol component consults the SPD in order to check whether the security afforded to the packet meets the security configuration of the policy. The IPSec base protocol consults SPD to decide whether outbound packet needs any security which is similar for outbound processing.

Internet Key Exchange is considered as a client-level process in most of the operating systems but it does not support in embedded operating systems. In embedded operating systems with routers (example of node in a network), there is no difference between the client space and kernel space. The policy either mandates an SA or when the SA bundle is present, the policy engine invokes IKE but the SA is not established. Peer invokes IKE when the nodes are needed to be communicated securely.

PENETRATION TESTING

In Session hijacking, penetration testing involves the same steps as that of the session hijacking attack. First the penetration tester locates a session. Various possibilities to hijack a session are then checked by the penetration tester. Depending on the network and the mechanisms which are used for the communication, the possibilities may vary but still there exists standard procedures for session hijacking penetration testing (Whitaker 2005). See Figure 10.

Figure 10. Penetration testing

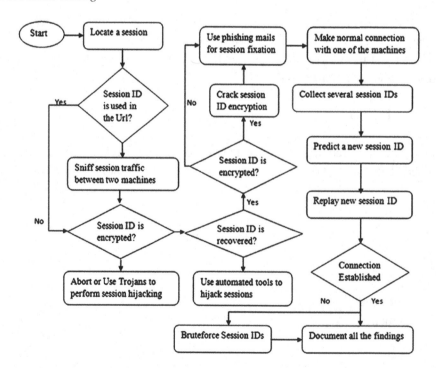

Step 1: Locating a Session

As it is mentioned early, the first step of hijacking is to locate a target active session in order to take control over it through packet sniffing. Check whether the session ID is used in the URL after locating a session. If session ID is used in the URL, check whether the session is encrypted. If session ID is not used in the URL, sniff session traffic between two machines (Clark 2005).

Step 2: Sniffing the Session Traffic Between Two Machines

Using various available tools such as CACE pilot, Wireshark, Capsa network analyzer, Win dump, etc. between two machines, the session traffic is sniffed. The victim's network traffic is watched and a session is grabbed. Next, the session is checked for whether it is encrypted or not. Recover the session ID if the session is not encrypted otherwise either abort or use Trojans to perform session hijacking.

Step 3: Recuperate the Session ID

Automated tools such as Paros proxy, Burp Suite, Web scarab, etc are used to hijack the session if the session IDs are unable to be recovered. The session hijacking process is made easy by using these tools. Using various algorithms, the Session IDs are created whereas if the attacker is able to predict the algorithm he can easily recover or regenerate the session IDs. The attacker can also perform session fixation by sending phishing mails to the victim in case of an encrypted Session ID .

Step 4: Crack Session ID's Encryption

Usually the client authentication process is carried out by using session IDs. If the URL is encoded such as, HTML encoded, Unicode encoded, Base64 encoded, or hex encoded, and then original session IDs of the victim is obtained by cracking the encrypted session IDs. If the attackers are able to recuperate the Session IDs of an authentic client, then the attacker can introduce a malicious activity in between the victim's machine and the remote machine as well as the unauthorized connection can be used for attacking purposes. Session fixation with the help of phishing mails later can be done by the attacker later, if he succeeds in cracking the encrypted Session ID.

Step 5: Make Normal Connection with One of the Machines in the Network

A normal connection can be executed with one of the machine targeted in the network traffic and can gain the entry to the remote machine by impersonating as the authorized client of the network after performing session attacks.

Step 6: Collection of Several Session IDs

Attacker can collect several session IDs of the machines that are connected in the network, once the attacker gets connected to one of its machines. For retrieving the session IDs there are two different techniques available. First technique is to retrieve the session ID from a cookie in the response headers, and next technique is to match a usual expression against the response body. Attacker must make sure that the "from message body" check box is not selected, while collecting session IDs from the cookies, thought the above option is selected while collecting the session IDs from the message body.

Step 7: Prediction of a New Session ID

To predict or guess the new session ID investigate the collected session IDs. To perform replay attack and in order to find the current session ID attacker should forecast a new session ID.

Step 8: Replay New Session ID

When an attacker copies a stream of messages (session IDs) between two parties in the network and repeat the stream to one or more of the parties replay attack occurs.

Now the connection establishment of the machine is checked and when the connection is established the penetration tester should document all the findings of the penetration testing. If the connection establishment is not done, then establish the connection by brute forcing technique to find the current valid session ID.

Step 9: Brute Force Session IDs

Brute forcing the session ID is the process in which all the possible range of values are tried for the session ID, until the correct session ID is obtained. SessionIDs are randomly generated and while brute forcing thousands of requests are involved by these session IDs. This is the most inclusive technique but still this process requires more time.

Step 10: Document all the Findings

The last step of penetration testing is to document all the findings that are obtained through each and every step that are tested for the analysis.

FUTURE RESEARCH

In the web application session hijacking is a severe issue and thus hijacker implements various methods to capture the cookies and to perform session hijacking in the web application. Because of the developing technology the need to access information from web application has its greater significance.

In WLAN, new intrusion detection techniques are needed to be developed to attain low false positive rate and misdetection ratio whereas the packet delivery ratio is to be increased. These detection techniques can also be developed to Mobile Ad-hoc Networks (MANET) and Wireless Sensor Network (WSN). The scope of wired networks execution lies on investigating the likelihood of executing intrusion detection techniques for diverse standards of IEEE 802.11X. Networks and applications must be monitored and tested to ensure that it is no more vulnerable to the tricks that are carried out by the hijacker.

The IN-Network approach can be executed with diverse and many more common approaches appropriate to numerous platforms. Some of the restrictions in executing these methods on a fabricated network are: The server value is not common. In the Windows machine, the detect ability rate can be enhanced.

In the Out-Network approach the significant constraint used to distinguish and compose a resolution, is the IP address, but for the potential values to augment the security: User agent string, Session created time, and Session ID must be used always.

CONCLUSION

Cloud computing faces serious issues regarding account hijacking as the attackers can fortify secret information, infringe data integrity and can perform monetary transactions. The significant factor that security analysts should be apprehensive with this is that the interface and the authentication layer must not be combined into a single layer because it causes risk to the authentication system as the interface is already uncovered to the world. For helping the cloud users to protect the devices, login-aiding along with secret keys other than passwords can be used. This method can be additionally enhanced by executing a few rational security measures.

Thus the severe issues of session hijacking particularly after introducing HTTP 1.1 protocols are solved by using the SSL/HTTP communication mechanism. The optimal merge of HTTPS and SSL protocols can solve many problems of hijacking. The session hijacking can also be prevented from the attacker by using various tools in the cloud environment. Thus, the major issue of session hijacking can be handled effectively thereby protecting the information by following the countermeasures and penetration testing steps in the right sequence.

REFERENCES

Adi, P., Bhavesh, B., Chirag, M., Dhiren, P., & Muttukrishnan, R. (2012). *A survey on security issues and solutions at different layers of Cloud computing*. Springer.

Ahmed, M., & Ashraf Hossain, M. (2014). Cloud computing and security issues in the cloud. *International Journal of Network Security & Its Applications*, 6(1), 25–36. doi:10.5121/ijnsa.2014.6103

Al-Nemrat, Tawil, Mangut, & Benza. (2015). ARP Cache Poisoning Mitigation and Forensics Investigation. *IEEE Trustcom/BigDataSE/ISPA*.

Baishya, R. C., Bhattacharyya, D. K., Hoque, N., Kalita, J. K., & Monowar, H. (2014). Network attacks: Taxonomy, tools and systems. *Journal of Network and Computer Applications*, 40, 307–324. doi:10.1016/j.jnca.2013.08.001

Bhaturkar, K. P., & Bagde, K. G. (2014). Prevention of Session Hijacking and IP Spoofing With Sensor Nodes and Cryptographic Approach. *International Journal of Computer Science and Mobile Computing*, 3(Issue.5), 1198–1206.

Cappelli, D., Moore, A., & Trzeciak, R. (2012). *The CERT Guide to Insider Threats: How to prevent, Detect and Respond to Information Technology Crimes (Theft, Sabotage, and Fraud)*. Addison-Wesley Professional.

Challa, K. A., & Meena, B. (2012). Cloud Computing Security Issues with possible solution. *International Journal of Computer Science and Technology*, 2(1).

Cheng, K., Gao, M., & Guo, R. (2010). Analysis and Research on HTTPS Hijacking Attacks. *Networks Security Wireless Communication and Trusted Computing (NSWCTC), 2010 Second International Conference*, 223-226.

Chou, T.-S. (2013). Security threats on Cloud Computing vulnerabilities. *International Journal of Computer Science & Information Technology, 5*(3), 79–88. doi:10.5121/ijcsit.2013.5306

Clark, Smith, Looi, & Gill. (2005). *Passive techniques for detecting session hijacking attacks in IEEE 802.11 wireless networks*. Academic Press.

Dacosta, I., Chakradeo, S., Ahamad, M., & Traynor, P. (2012). One-time cookies: Preventing session hijacking attacks with stateless authentication tokens. *ACM Transactions on Internet Technology, 12*(1), 1–24. doi:10.1145/2220352.2220353

Danish, J., & Hassan, Z. (2011). Security Measures in Cloud computing and Countermeasures. *International Journal of Engineering Science and Technology, 3*(4).

Halton, W. (2014). *Security Issues and Solutions in Cloud Computing*. Wolf Halton Open Source Security.

Jayaram, K. R., & Mathur. (2008). On the Adequacy of Statecharts as a Source of Tests for Cryptographic Protocols. *Annual IEEE International Computer Software and Applications Conference*. doi:10.1109/COMPSAC.2008.203

Kavitha, V., & Subashini, S. (2011). A Survey on Security Issues in Service Delivery Models of Cloud Computing. *Journal of Network and Computer Applications, 34*(1), 1–11. doi:10.1016/j.jnca.2010.07.006

Kazi, Z., & Vrbsky. (2012). Security Attacks and Solutions in Clouds. The University of Alabama.

Khare & Verma. (2015). A Strong Authentication Technique in Cloud Environment Using: SMTP OTP and MD5. *International Journal of Innovative Research in Computer and Communication Engineering, 3*(12).

Larry, S. (2009). *Spoofing Server-Server communication: How can you prevent it?* Retrieved from https://otalliance.org/resources/EV/SSLStrip_Whitepaper.pdf

Long, X. & Sikdar, B. (2010). A mechanism for detecting session hijacking in wireless networks. *Wireless Communication, IEEE Transactions*, 1380-1389.

Margaret, R. (2014). *Session Hijacking (TCP Session Hijacking).What is it?* Academic Press.

Misbahuddin, M., & Sumitra, B. (2013). A Survey of Traditional and Cloud Specific Security Issues, Security in Computing and Communications. *Communications in Computation and Information Science, Springer, 377*, 110–129. doi:10.1007/978-3-642-40576-1_12

Nair, S. (2013). *How to Avoid Session Hijacking in Web Applications*. TechNet. Microsoft.

Nikiforakis, Meert, Younan, Johns. & Joosen. (2011). Session Shield: Lightweight protection against session hijacking. In *Engineering Secure Software and Systems*. Springer Berlin Heidelberg.

Whitaker, A., & Newman, D. P. (2005). *Penetration testing and network defense*. Pearson Education.

KEY TERMS AND DEFINITIONS

Active Session Hijacking: An active attacker searches for an active session and utilizes the session for communicating between the client and server. Here the active attacker impersonates as a genuine client where the client is being manipulated and the server is being fooled by the active attacker.

Application-Level Session Hijacking: It is performed by gathering the information, which is provided through network-level hijacking.

Client-Side Attack: The attacker can negotiate the session token by sending malicious activities such as malwares to the client-side programs.

IPSec: At the IP layer a collection of protocols is referred to support secure exchange of packets.

Man-in-the-Browser Attack: In this the calls between the browser and its security mechanisms or libraries are intercepted by using Trojans. To cause financial dishonesties by influencing transactions of Internet banking systems is its main objective.

Man-in-the-Middle attack: To interrupt the messages that is being transferred between the end users in a network. Attacker split the TCP connection into two connections (attacker-to-server and client-to-attacker) and uses different techniques to impersonate the users.

Network-Level Session Hijacking: It is implemented by the web applications through the data flow of the protocol which is shared. Critical information that is helpful to the attacker to attack the application - level sessions are provided by the attacks on network-level sessions.

Passive Session Hijacking: An attacker hijacks a session in the traffic that is being sent onwards but sits back, watches and records all the traffic in the network.

Session Hijacking: Session hijacking is the process of knowing the session ID (SID) of an active client, so that his account can be impersonated or hijacked.

Session Sniffing: In this the attacker uses a sniffer tool to capture a valid session token called session ID. Attacker then uses the session ID to get authenticated as a legitimate user to the web server.

Compilation of References

104. th United States Congress. (1996). Health Insurance Portability and Accountability Act of 1996 (HIPAA). Retrieved from http://aspe.hhs.gov/admnsimp/pl104191.html

Aboba, B., Blunk, L., Vollbrecht, J., Carlson, J., & Levkowetz, H. (2004). *RFC 3748: Extensible Authentication Protocol.*

Adam, M., & Christ, B. (2011). The Mobile App Gap. *Sigma Journal: Inside the Digital Ecosystem, 11*(1), 28.

Adi, P., Bhavesh, B., Chirag, M., Dhiren, P., & Muttukrishnan, R. (2012). *A survey on security issues and solutions at different layers of Cloud computing.* Springer.

Ahmed, M., & Ashraf Hossain, M. (2014). Cloud computing and security issues in the cloud. *International Journal of Network Security & Its Applications, 6*(1), 25–36. doi:10.5121/ijnsa.2014.6103

Akoush, S., Sohan, R., Rice, A. C., Moore, A. W., & Hopper, A. (2011). Free Lunch: Exploiting Renewable Energy for Computing. HotOS, 13, 17.

Aksanli, B., Venkatesh, J., Zhang, L., & Rosing, T. (2012). Utilizing green energy prediction to schedule mixed batch and service jobs in data centers. *SIGOPS Operating Systems Review, ACM, 45*(3), 53–57. doi:10.1145/2094091.2094105

Akyildiz, I. F., Su, W., Sankarasubramaniam, Y., & Cayirci, E. (2002). A survey on sensor networks. IEEE Communications Magazine, 40(8), 102-114.

Alam, B., Doja, M. N., Alam, M., & Mongia, S. (2013). 5-Layered Architecture of Cloud Database Management System. *AASRI Procedia, 5*, 194–199. doi:10.1016/j.aasri.2013.10.078

Alamri, A., Ansari, W. S., Hassan, M. M., Hossain, M. S., Alelaiwi, A., & Hossain, M. A. (2013). A Survey on Sensor-Cloud.International Journal of Distributed Sensor Networks, 2013, 18–24.

Alani. (2014). Securing the Cloud: Threats, Attacks, and Mitigation Techniques. *Journal of Advanced Computer Science and Technology*, 202-213.

Alex, B., & Mulvenna, M. D. (1998). Discovering Internet Marketing Intelligence through Online Analytical Web Usage Mining. *SIGMOD Record, 27*(4), 54–61. doi:10.1145/306101.306124

Alhazmi, K. M. (2014). *Online Virtual Network Provisioning in Distributed Cloud Computing Data Centers.* Electronic Thesis and Dissertation Repository. Paper 2319. Retrieved from: http://ir.lib.uwo.ca/cgi/viewcontent.cgi?article=3713&context=etd

Alhazmi, K., & Shami, A. (2014). *A Greener Cloud: Energy Efficient Provisioning for Online Virtual Network Requests in Cloud Data Centers.* IEEE International Conference on Communications (ICC).

Alhazmi, K., Abusharkh, M., Ban, D., & Shami, A. (2014). A map of the clouds: Virtual network mapping in cloud computing data centers. *IEEE Canadian Conference on Electrical and Computer Engineering*. doi:10.1109/CCECE.2014.6901053

Alhazmi, K., Abusharkh, M., Ban, D., & Shami, A. (2014). *Drawing the Cloud Map: Virtual network embedding in cloud computing Environment. IEEE Systems Journal.*

Ali, W., & Shamsuddin, S. M. (2009). Intelligent Client-Side Web Caching Scheme Based on Least Recently Used Algorithm and Neuro-Fuzzy System. In *sixth International Symposium on Neural Networks, Lecture Notes in Computer Science (LNCS)*. Springer-Verlag Berlin Heidelberg. doi:10.1007/978-3-642-01510-6_9

Ali, W., & Shamsuddin, S. M. (2009). Intelligent Client-Side Web Caching Scheme Based on Least Recently Used Algorithm and Neuro-Fuzzy System. *The Sixth International Symposium on Neural Networks (ISNN 2009)*, 70-79.

Ali, M., Khan, S. U., & Athanasios, V., & Vasilakos. (2015). Security in Cloud Computing: Opportunities and Challenges. *Information Sciences.*

Alliance for Telecommunications Industry Solutions. (n.d.). Retrieved from: http://www.atis.org

Allmydata Inc. (2001). Unlimited Online Storage and Backup. Retrieved from http://allmydata.com

Al-Nemrat, Tawil, Mangut, & Benza. (2015). ARP Cache Poisoning Mitigation and Forensics Investigation. *IEEE Trustcom/BigDataSE/ISPA.*

Alotaibi. (2015). Threat in Cloud- Denial of Service (DoS) and Distributed Denial of Service (DDoS) Attack, and Security Measures. *Journal of Emerging Trends in Computing and Information Sciences, 6*(5).

Altice Lab. (2014). *Identity and Access Management.* Retrieved From http://www.alticelabs.com/content/WP-Information-Access-Control-Models.pdf

Amarnath, B. R., Somasundaram, T. S., Ellappan, M., & Buyya, R. (2009). Ontology-based Grid resource management. *Software: Practice and Experience, 39*(17), 1419-1438.

Amatya, S., & Kurti, A. (2014). Cross-Platform Mobile Development: Challenges and Opportunities. ICT Innovations, 231, 227-228.

Amazon Auto Scaling. (n.d.). Retrieved from: http://aws.amazon.com/autoscaling/

Amazon S3 Availability Event. (2008). Retrieved from: http://status.aws.amazon.com/s3-20080720.html

Amazon.com. 2009. Amazon Web Services (AWS). http://aws.amazon.com

Amrhein, D., & Willenborg, R. (2009). Cloud computing for the enterprise, Part 3: Using WebSphere CloudBurst to create private clouds.

Anderson, C. R. (2002). *A Machine Learning Approach to Web Personalization* (Ph. D. Thesis). University of Washington.

Anderson, C.R. (2002). A Machine Learning Approach to Web Personalization [Ph.D. Thesis]. University of Washington.

Andersson, K., & Dan, J. (2012). Mobile e-Services Using HTML5. *2012 IEEE 37th Conference on Local Computer Networks Workshops*. doi:10.1109/LCNW.2012.6424068

Armbrust, M., Fox, A., Griffith, R., Joseph, A. D., Katz, R. H., Konwinsky, A., . . . Zaharia, M. (2009). *Above the Clouds: A Berkley View of Cloud Computing.* Technical Report No. UCB/EECS-2009-28, Department of Electrical Engineering and Computer Sciences, University of California at Berkley. Retrieved from: http://www.eecs.berkeley.edu/Pubs/TechRpts/2009/EECS-2009-28.pdf

Armbrust, M., Stoica, I., Zaharia, M., Fox, A., Griffith, R., Joseph, A. D., & Rabkin, A. et al. (2010). A View of Cloud Computing. *Communications of the ACM*, *53*(4), 50–58. doi:10.1145/1721654.1721672

Asghar, M. R., Ion, M., Giovanni, R., & Bruno, C. (2011). *Securing Data Provenance in the Cloud. EU FP7 programme, Research Grant 257063*. Endorse.

Association for Retail Technology Standards (ARTS). (n.d.). Retrieved from: http://www.nrf-arts.org

Ateniese, G., Burns, R., Curtmola, R., Herring, J., Kissner, L., Peterson, Z., & Song, D. (2007). Provable data possession at untrusted stores. Cryptology ePrint Archive. Retrieved from http://eprint.iacr.org/

Ateniese, G., Pietro, R.D., Mancini, L.V., & Tsudik, G. (2008). Scalable and Efficient Provable Data Possession. *Proceedings of Fourth International Conference on. Security and Privacy in Communication Networks SecureComm '08* (pp. 1-10). doi:10.1145/1460877.1460889

Avram, A. (2014). *New in Motorola RhoMobile 5.0*. Licensing Model, Cloud Services and KitKat Support. InfoQ.

Badger, L., Grance, T., Patt-Corner, R., & Voas, J. (2011). *Draft Cloud Computing Synopsis and Recommendations*. National Institute of Standards and Technology (NIST) Special Publication 800-146. US Department of Commerce. Retrieved from: http://csrc.nist.gov/publications/drafts/800-146/Draft-NIST-SP800-146.pdf

Baer, P. (2008). *Exploring the 2020 global emissions mitigation gap. Analysis for the Global Climate Network*. Stanford University, Woods Institute for the Environment.

Baishya, R. C., Bhattacharyya, D. K., Hoque, N., Kalita, J. K., & Monowar, H. (2014). Network attacks: Taxonomy, tools and systems. *Journal of Network and Computer Applications*, *40*, 307–324. doi:10.1016/j.jnca.2013.08.001

Balamash, A., & Krunz, M. (2004). An Overview of Web Caching Replacement Algorithms. *IEEE Communications Surveys and Tutorials*, *6*(2), 44–56. doi:10.1109/COMST.2004.5342239

Balfanz, D., Durfee, G., Grinter, R. E., Smetters, D. K., & Stewart, P. (2004). Network-in-a-Box: How to set up a secure wireless network in under a minute. *Proceedings of the 13th USENIX Security Symposium.*

Balfanz, D., Smetters, D., Stewart, P., & Wong, H. C. (2002). Talking to Strangers: Authentication in ad-hoc wireless networks.*Proceedings of the Symposium on Network and Distributed Systems Security.*

Ballages, R., Rohs, M., Sheridan, J., & Borchers, J. (2008). *The Design space of mobile phone input techniques for ubiquitous computing. In Handbook of research on user interface design and evaluation for mobile technologies.* Hershey, PA: IGI Global.

Bamshad, M. (2007). *Data Mining for Web Personalization.* Heidelberg: Springer.

Barcia, R., Berardi, T., Kak, A., Kreger, H., & Schalk, K. (2015). *Cloud Customer Architecture for Mobile.* Cloud Standards Customer Council. Retrieved from http://www.cloud-council.org/deliverables/CSCC-Cloud-Customer-Architecture-for-Mobile.pdf

Barker, E., Barker, W., Burr, W., Polk, W., & Smid, M. (2006). *National Institute of Standards and Technology (NIST) Special Publication 800-57 (Draft): Recommendation for Key Management - Part 1 General.* NIST.

Barker, S., & Shenoy, P. (2010). Empirical evaluation of latency sensitive application performance in the cloud.*Proceedings of the 1st ACM Multimedia Systems Conference*, Scottsdale, AZ, USA. ACM. doi:10.1145/1730836.1730842

Barr, J. (2006). Amazon EC2 Beta.

Barroso, L. A., & Holzle, U. (2007). The case for energy-proportional computing. *IEEE Computer, 40*(12), 33–37. doi:10.1109/MC.2007.443

Bellare, M., & Goldreich, O. (1992). On defining proofs of knowledge. In E.F. Brickell (Ed.), Advances in Cryptology – CRYPTO '92, (pp. 390–420). Springer.

Bellare, M., & Miner, S. (1999). A forward-secure digital signature scheme. In Advances in Cryptology CRYPTO'99 (pp. 431-448). doi:10.1007/3-540-48405-1_28

Bellare, M., Goldreich, O., & Goldwasser, S. (1994). Incremental Cryptography: The Case of Hashing and Signing. *Proceedings of 14th Annual International Cryptology Conference: Advances in Cryptology CRYPTO '94* (pp. 216-233).

Beloglazov, A. (2013). Energy-efficient management of virtual machines in data centers for cloud computing.

Beloglazov, A., Abawajy, J., & Buyya, R. (2012). Energy-aware resource allocation heuristics for efficient management of data centers for Cloud computing. *Future generation computer systems, 28*(5), 755–768.

Beloglazov, A., Buyya, R., Lee, Y. C., & Zomaya, A. (2011). A taxonomy and survey of energy-efficient data centers and cloud computing systems. *Advances in Computers, 82*(2), 47-111.

Beloglazov, A., & Buyya, R. (2012). Optimal online deterministic algorithms and adaptive heuristics for energy and performance efficient dynamic consolidation of virtual machines in cloud data centers. *Concurrency and Computation, 24*(13), 1397–1420. doi:10.1002/cpe.1867

Berendt, B., Mobasher, B., Nakagawa, M., & Spiliopoulou, M. (2002). The Impact of Site Structure and User Environment and Session Reconstruction in Web usage analysis. *Proceedings of the forth Web KDD 2002 Workshop at the ACM – SIGKDD Conference on Knowledge Discovery in Databases (KDD 2002),* 159-179.

Berral, J. L., Goiri, Í., Nguyen, T. D., Gavalda, R., Torres, J., & Bianchini, R. (2014). Building green cloud services at low cost. *34th International Conference on Distributed Computing Systems (ICDCS),* 449-460. doi:10.1109/ICDCS.2014.53

Bertion, E., Paci, F., & Ferrini, R. (2009). *Privacy-preserving digital identity management for cloud computing IEEE Computer Society Data Engineering Bulletin.*

Bhaturkar, K. P., & Bagde, K. G. (2014). Prevention of Session Hijacking and IP Spoofing With Sensor Nodes and Cryptographic Approach. *International Journal of Computer Science and Mobile Computing, 3*(Issue.5), 1198–1206.

Bichler, M., Setzer, T., & Speitkamp, B. (2006). Capacity Planning for Virtualized Servers. *Proceedings of theWorkshop on Information Technologies and Systems (WITS),* Milwaukee, Wisconsin, USA. Social Science Network.

Biggs & Vidalis. (2009). Cloud Computing: The Impact on Digital Forensic Investigations. *Proceedings of the 7th International Conference for Internet Technology and Secured Transactions* (ICITST'09), 1-6.

Bilal, K., Manzano, M., Khan, S.U., Calle, E., Li, K., & Zomaya, A.Y. (2013). On the Characterization of the Structural Robustness of Data Center Networks. *IEEE Transactions on* Cloud Computing, *1*(1), 1–1.

Bila, N., & Lara, E. D. et al.. (2012). Jettison: efficient idle desktop consolidation with partial VM migration. *Proceeding EuroSys'12 proceedings of the 7th ACM European conference on computer systems (*pp. 211–224). New York: ACM. doi:10.1145/2168836.2168858

Biolchini, J., Mian, G. P., Natali, A. C., & Travassos, H. G. (2005). *Systematic Review in Software Engineering.*Rio de Janeiro: Academic Press.

Blaze, M., Kannan, S., Lee, I., Sokolsky, O., Smith, J. M., Keromytis, A. D., & Lee, W. (2009). Dynamic Trust Management. *IEEE Computer, 42*(2), 44–52. doi:10.1109/MC.2009.51

Bloice, D. M., & Wotawa, F. (2009). Java's Alternatives and the Limitations of Java when Writing Cross-Platform Applications for Mobile Devices in the Medical Domain. *Proceedings of the ITI 2009 31st International Conference on Information Technology Interfaces*. doi:10.1109/ITI.2009.5196053

Bluetooth, S. I. G. (2006). *Authorities raid Chinese factory suspected of infringing on Bluetooth SIG registered trademarks*. Retrieved from: http://www.bluetooth.com/Bluetooth/Press/SIG/AUTHORITIES RAID CHINESE FACTORY SUSPECTED OF INFRINGING ON BLUETOOTH SIG REGISTERED TRADEMARKS.htm

Blum, M., Evans, W. S., Gemmell, P., Kannan, S., & Naor, M. (1994). Checking the correctness of Memories. *Algorithmica*, *12*(2/3), 225–244. doi:10.1007/BF01185212

Bobroff, N., Kochut, A., & Beaty, K. (2007) Dynamic placement of virtual machines for managing SLA violations. *Proceedings of the 10th IFIP/IEEE international symposium on integrated network management IM '07*, Munich (pp. 119–128).

Boneh, D., Lynn, B., & Shacham, H. (2001). Short Signatures from the Weil Pairing. *Proceedings of Seventh International Conference on Theory and Application of Cryptology and Information Security: Advances in Cryptology ASIACRYPT '01* (pp. 514-532). doi:10.1007/3-540-45682-1_30

Boneh, D., Gentry, C., Lynn, B., & Shacham, H. (2003). Aggregate and Verifiably Encrypted Signatures from Bilinear Maps.*Proceedings of 22nd International Conference on Theory and Applications of Cryptographic techniques Eurocrypt'03* (pp. 416-432). doi:10.1007/3-540-39200-9_26

Borgetto, D., Casanova, H., Da Costa, G., & Pierson, J. M. (2012). Energy-aware service allocation.Future Generation Computer Systems, 28(5), 769–779.

Bowers, K.D. Juels, A. & Oprea, A. (2008). Proofs of Retrievability: Theory and Implementation. Cryptology ePrint Archive.

Box, G. E., Jenkins, G. M., Reinsel, G. C., & Ljung, G. M. (2015). *Time series analysis: forecasting and control*. John Wiley & Sons.

Brey, T., & Lamers, L. (2009). Using virtualization to improve data center efficiency. *The Green Grid, Whitepaper, 19*.

Brin, S., & Pange, L. (1998). The Anatomy of a Large-scale Hyper Textual Web Search Engine. *Computer Networks and ISDN Systems, 30*(1-7), 107–117. doi:10.1016/S0169-7552(98)00110-X

Brooks, S. P., & Morgan, B. J. (1995). Optimization using simulated annealing. *The Statistician, 44*(2), 241–257. doi:10.2307/2348448

Bruening, P. J., & Treacy, B. C. (2009). *Cloud Computing: Privacy, Security Challenges*. Bureau of National Affairs.

Buchbinder, N., Jain, N., & Menache, I. (2011). Online job-migration for reducing the electricity bill in the cloud.*International Conference on Research in Networking*, 172-185. doi:10.1007/978-3-642-20757-0_14

Burns, J. (2009). *Mobile application on Android*. Blackhat.

Buyya, R., Calheiros, R.N., Li, X., & Computing, A.C. (2012). Open Challenges and Architectural Elements. *Proceedings of theThird International Conference on Emerging Applications of Information Technology (EAIT)*. doi:10.1109/EAIT.2012.6407847

Buyya, R., Ramamohanarao, K., Leckie, C., Calhieros, N., Dastjerdi, A., & Versteeg, S. (2015). *Big Data Analytics-Enhanced Cloud Computing: Challenges, Architectural Elements, and Future Directions*. Retrieved from: http://arxiv.org/abs/1510.06486

Buyya, R., Ranjan, R., Rodrigo, N., & Calheiros, R. N. (2010). InterCloud: Utility-oriented federation of cloud computing environments for scaling of application services. In *Proceedings of the 10th International Conference on Algorithms and Architectures for Parallel Processing*, *6081*, 13–31.

Calheiros, R. N., & Buyya, R. (2014). Meeting deadlines of scientific workflows in public clouds with tasks replication. *IEEE Transactions on Parallel and Distributed Systems*, *25*(7), 1787–1796. doi:10.1109/TPDS.2013.238

Cameron, C. (2016). 9-cloud-computing-security-risks-every-company-faces. *Skyhighnetworks*. Retrieved From https://www.skyhighnetworks.com/cloud-security-blog/9-cloud-computing-security-risks- every-company-faces/

Cappelli, D., Moore, A., & Trzeciak, R. (2012). *The CERT Guide to Insider Threats: How to prevent, Detect and Respond to Information Technology Crimes (Theft, Sabotage, and Fraud)*. Addison-Wesley Professional.

Cardosa, M., Korupolu, M.R., & Singh, A. (2009). Shares and utilities based power consolidation in virtualized server environments. Proceedings of the IFIP/IEEE international symposium on integrated network management, Long Island (pp. 327–334).

Cash, D., Kp, A., & Wichs, D. (2013). *Dynamic proofs of retrievability via oblivious ram. In Advances in Cryptology: EUROCRYPT 2013, LNCS* (pp. 279–295). Springer. doi:10.1007/978-3-642-38348-9_17

Castro, M., & Liskov, B. (2002). Practical Byzantine Fault Tolerance and Proactive Recovery. *ACM Transactions on Computer Systems*, *20*(4), 398–461. doi:10.1145/571637.571640

Celesti, A., Puliafito, A., Tusa, F., & Villari, M. (2013). Energy Sustainability in Cooperating Clouds. CLOSER, 83-89.

Center for the Protection of Natural Infrastructure. (2010). *Information Security Briefing on Cloud Computing, March 2010*. Retrieved from: http://www.cpni.gov.uk/Documents/Publications/2010/2010007-ISB_cloud_computing.pdf

Challa, K. A., & Meena, B. (2012). Cloud Computing Security Issues with possible solution. *International Journal of Computer Science and Technology*, *2*(1).

Chandra, Prakash, & Lamdharia. (2012). A study on Cloud database. *Bulletin of the IEEE Computer Society Technical Committee*. doi:10.1109/MobileCloud.2015.30

Chang, E. C., & Xu, J. (2008). Remote Integrity Check with Dishonest Storage Server.*Proceedings of 13th European Symposium on Research in Computer Security ESORICS '08* (pp. 223-237). doi:10.1007/978-3-540-88313-5_15

Charanya, R. (2013). Levels of Security Issues in Cloud Computing. IJET, 5(2).

Charland, A., & LeRoux, B. (2011). Mobile Application Development: Web vs. Native. *Queue - Data, 9*(4), 4.

Chen, Y., Paxson, V., & Katz, R. H. (2010). What's New About Cloud Computing Security? Technical Report UCB/EECS-2010-5. Berkeley, CA: EECS Department, University of California. Retrieved from http://www.eecs.berkeley.edu/Pubs/TechRpts/2010/EECS-2010-5.html

Chen, Z., Dong, W., Li, H., Cao, L., Zhang, P., & Chen, X. (n.d.). *Collaborative network security in multi-tenant data center for cloud computing*. Retrieved from: http://www.mit.edu/~caoj/pub/doc/jcao_j_netsec.pdf

Chen, C., He, B., & Tang, X. (2012). Green-aware workload scheduling in geographically distributed data centers.*4th International Conference on Cloud Computing Technology and Science (CloudCom)*, 82-89. doi:10.1109/CloudCom.2012.6427545

Cheng, K., Gao, M., & Guo, R. (2010). Analysis and Research on HTTPS Hijacking Attacks. *Networks Security Wireless Communication and Trusted Computing (NSWCTC), 2010 Second International Conference*, 223-226.

Chen, K. Y., Xu, Y., Xi, K., & Chao, H. J. (2013). Intelligent virtual machine placement for cost efficiency in geo-distributed cloud systems.*International Conference on Communications (ICC)*, 3498-3503. doi:10.1109/ICC.2013.6655092

Chen, T. (2007). Obtaining the Optimal Cache Document Replacement Policy for the Caching System of an EC Website. *European Journal of Operational Research*, *181*(2), 828–835. doi:10.1016/j.ejor.2006.05.034

Chen, X., & Zhang, X. (2002). Popularity-based PPM: An effective Web pre-fetching technique for high accuracy and low storage.*Proceedings of the International Conference on Parallel Processing* (pp. 296-304). doi:10.1109/ICPP.2002.1040885

Chen, Y., Qiu, L., Chen, W., Nguyen, L., & Katz, R. H. (2003). Efficient and adaptive Web replication using content clustering. *Selected Areas in Communications. IEEE Journal on*, *21*(6), 979–994.

Chess, B., & McGraw, G. (2004). Static analysis for security. *Security & Privacy, IEEE*, *2*(6), 76–79. doi:10.1109/MSP.2004.111

Cheswick, W., Bellovin, S., & Rubin, A. (2003). *Firewalls and Internet security: Repelling the wily hacker*. Boston, MA: Addison-Wesley Longman Publishing Co., Inc.

Chor, B., Kushilevitz, E., Goldreich, O., & Sudan, M. (1998). Private Information Retrieval. *Journal of the ACM*, *45*(9), 965–981. doi:10.1145/293347.293350

Chouhan & Singh. (2016). Security Attacks on Cloud Computing with Possible Solution. *International Journal of Advanced Research in Computer Science and Software Engineering, 6*(1).

Chou, T.-S. (2013). Security threats on Cloud Computing vulnerabilities. *International Journal of Computer Science & Information Technology*, *5*(3), 79–88. doi:10.5121/ijcsit.2013.5306

Chowdhury, M., Rahman, R. M, & Boutaba, R. (2012). Vineyard: Virtual network embedding algorithms with coordinated node and link mapping. *IEEE/ACM Transactions on Networking, 20*(99), 206–219.

Chow, R., Golle, P., Jakobsson, M., Shi, E., Staddon, J., Masuoka, R., & Molina, J. (2009). Controlling Data in the Cloud: Outsourcing Computation without Outsourcing Control. In *Proceedings of the ACM Workshop on Cloud Computing Security (CCSW'09)*. ACM Press. doi:10.1145/1655008.1655020

Christ, A. M. (2011). Bridging the Mobile App Gap. *Sigma Journal: Inside the Digital Ecosystem, 11*(1), 29.

Cisco. (2011). Cisco Global Cloud Index "Growth in data center electricity use 2005 to 2010." (Tech. Report). Analytics Press.

Cisco. (2011). *Virtual Machine Networking: Standards and Solutions*. San Jose, CA: Cisco.

Cisco. (n. d.). Cisco Global Cloud Index: Forecast and Methodology, 2013–2018 (whitepaper).

Clark, Smith, Looi, & Gill. (2005). *Passive techniques for detecting session hijacking attacks in IEEE 802.11 wireless networks*. Academic Press.

Clarke, D. E., Suh, G. E., Gassend, B., Sudan, A., vanDijk, M., & Devadas, S. (2005). Towards constant bandwidth overhead integrity checking of untrusted data. *Proceedings of theIEEE Symposium on Security and Privacy'05* (pp. 139–153). doi:10.1109/SP.2005.24

Cloud Security Alliance (CSA)'s Security Guidance for Critical area of Cloud Computing. (2009). CSA. Retrieved from: https://cloudsecurityalliance.org/csaguide.pdf

Cloud Security Alliance. (2012). *Identity and Access Management*. Cloud Security Alliance: SecaaS Implementation Guidance, Category 1.

Cloud Security Alliance. (2012). *Security guidance for critical areas of Mobile Computing*. Retrieved From https://downloads.cloudsecurityalliance.org/initiatives/ mobile/Mobile_Guidance_v1.pdf

Cloud Standards Customer Council. (2015). *Security for Cloud Computing Ten Steps to Ensure Success Version 2.0*. Author.

Cobb, J., & Elaarag, H. (2008). Web Proxy Cache Replacement Scheme based on Back-Propagation Neural Network. *Journal of Systems and Software, 81*(9), 1539–1558. doi:10.1016/j.jss.2007.10.024

Cooley, R., Mobasher, B., & Srinivastaa, J. (1999). Data Preparation for Mining World Wide Web Browsing Patterns. *Journal of knowledge and Information Systems,* 78-85.

Cooley, R., Bamshed, M., & Srinivastava, J. (1997). Web Mining: Information and Pattern Discovery on the World Wide Web. In *International conference on Tools with Artificial Intelligence*. IEEE. doi:10.1109/TAI.1997.632303

Cooper, B. F., Baldeschwieler, E., Fonseca, R., Kistler, J. J., Narayan, P. P. S., Neerdaels, C., & Stata, R. et al. (2009). Building a cloud for yahoo! *IEEE Data Eng. Bull., 32*(1), 36–43.

Curtmola, R., Khan, O., Burns, R., & Atoniooo, G. (2008). MR-PDP: Multiple-Replica Provable Data Possession *Proceedings of IEEE 28th International Conference on Distributed Computing Systems ICDCS '08* (pp. 411-420).

Cyrus, S., Zarkessh, A. M., Jafar, A., & Vishal, S. (1997). Knowledge discovery from Users Web Page Navigation. In *Workshop on Research Issues in Data Engineering*. Data mining tutorial retrieved from www.tutorialspoint.com/data_mining/notes

Cyrus, S., Zarkessh, A. M., Jafar, A., & Vishal, S. (1997). Knowledge discovery from Users Web Page Navigation. *Proceedings of theWorkshop on Research Issues in Data Engineering*, Birmingham, England.

Dacosta, I., Chakradeo, S., Ahamad, M., & Traynor, P. (2012). One-time cookies: Preventing session hijacking attacks with stateless authentication tokens. *ACM Transactions on Internet Technology, 12*(1), 1–24. doi:10.1145/2220352.2220353

Danish, J., & Hassan, Z. (2011). Security Measures in Cloud computing and Countermeasures. *International Journal of Engineering Science and Technology, 3*(4).

DeCandia, G., Hastorun, D., Jampani, M., Kakulapati, G., Lakshman, A., Pilchin, A., & Vogels, W. et al. (2007). Dynamo: Amazon's Highly Available Key-Value Store.*Proceedings of the 21st ACM SIGOPS Symposium on Operating Systems Principles,* 205-220. doi:10.1145/1294261.1294281

De, P. B., Aroyo, L., & Chepegin, V. (2004). The Next Big Thing: Adaptive Web-Based Systems. *Journal of Digital Information, 5*(1), 22–30.

Desisto, R. P., Plummer, D. C., & Smith, D. M. (2008). *Tutorial for Understanding the Relationship between Cloud Computing and SaaS*. Stamford, CT: Gartner.

Deswarte, Y., Quisquater, J. J., & Saidane, A. (2003). Remote Integrity Checking. *Integrity and Internal Control in Information Systems, 6*, 1–11.

Dickson, P. E. (2012). Cabana: A Cross-platform Mobile Development System. ACM Special Interest Group on Computer Science Education. doi:10.1145/2157136.2157290

Dinh, H.T., Lee, C., Niyato, D., & Wang, P. (2011). A Survey of Mobile Cloud Computing: Architecture, Applications, and Approaches. Wireless Communications and Mobile Computing, 13(18), 1587-1611.

Di, S., Kondo, D., & Wang, C. L. (2015). Optimization of composite cloud service processing with virtual machine. *IEEE Transactions on Computers, 64*(6), 1755–1768.

Dodis, Y., Vadhan, S., & Wichs, S. (2009). Proofs of Retrievability via Hardness Amplification.*Proceedings of the Sixth Theory of Cryptography Conference on Theory of Cryptography TCC '09* (pp. 109-127).

Domenech, J., Pont-Sanju, A., Sahuquillo, J., & Gil, J. A. (2010). *Evaluation, Analysis and Adaptation of Web Pre-fetching Techniques in Current Web. In Web-based Support Systems* (pp. 239–271). London: Springer.

Doshi, K. A., Zhong, T., Lu, Z., Tang, X., Lou, T., & Deng, G. (2013, October). Blending SQL and NewSQL approaches: reference architectures for enterprise big data challenges. In *Cyber-Enabled Distributed Computing and Knowledge Discovery (CyberC), 2013 International Conference on* (pp. 163-170). IEEE. doi:10.1109/CyberC.2013.34

Doukas, C., & Maglogiannis, I. (2011). Managing wearable sensor data through cloud computing. *Proceedings of theThird IEEE International Conference on Cloud Computing Technology and Science* (pp. 440-445). IEEE. doi:10.1109/CloudCom.2011.65

Dunham, M. H. (2006). *Data Mining Introductory and Advanced Topics* (1st ed.). Pearson Education.

Dupont, C., & Schulze, T., Giuliani, G., Somov, A., & Hermenier, F. (2012). An energy aware framework for virtual machine placement in cloud federated data centres. *Proceedings of the 3rd international conference on future energy systems: where energy, computing and communication meet e-Energy'12*. New York: ACM.

Duy, T. V. T., Sato, Y., & Inoguchi, Y. (2010). *Performance evaluation of a green scheduling algorithm for energy savings in Cloud computing. Proceedings of the 2010 IEEE international symposium on parallel and distributed processing, workshops and Phd forum* (pp. 1–8). Atlanta: IPDPSW. doi:10.1109/IPDPSW.2010.5470908

Dwork, C., Goldberg, D., & Naor, M. (2003). On memory-bound functions for fighting spam. In D. Boneh, (Ed.), CRYPTO '03 (pp. 426–444). Springer. doi:10.1007/978-3-540-45146-4_25

Elaarag, H., & Romano, S. (2009). Improvement of the neural network proxy cache replacement strategy.*Proceedings of the 2009 Spring Simulation Multiconference*, 90-100.

Emig, C., Brandt, F., Kreuzer, S., & Abeck, S. (2007). Identity as a Service- Towards a Service-Oriented Identity Management Architecture. *Proceedings of the 13th Open European Summer School and IFIP TC6.6 Conference on Dependable and Adaptable Network and Services*, 1-8.

Ench, W. (2009). Understanding Android security. *IEEE Security and Privacy*, 7(1), 50–57. doi:10.1109/MSP.2009.26

Erway, C., Kupcu, A., Papamanthou, C., & Tamassia, R. (2009). Dynamic provable data possession.*Proceedings of the 16th ACM conference on Computer and Communications Security: CCS'09* (pp. 213-222).

Etizoni, O. (1996). The World Wide Web: Quagmire or Gold Mine. *Communications of the ACM*, 39(2), 65–68. doi:10.1145/240455.240473

Everett, C. (2009). Cloud Computing- A Question of Trust. *Computer Fraud & Security,* (6), 5-7.

Facca, F.M., & Lanzi, P. L. (2005). Mining Interesting Knowledge from Web logs: A Survey. *International Journal of Data and Knowledge Engineering, 53*(3), 225-241.

Facca, F. M., & Lanzi, P. L. (2005). Mining Interesting Knowledge from Web logs: A Survey. *Data & Knowledge Engineering, 53*(3), 225–241. doi:10.1016/j.datak.2004.08.001

Feitelson, D. (2007). *Parallel workloads archive*. Academic Press.

Feitelson, D.G. (2001, June). Utilization and Predictability in Scheduling the IBM SP2 with backfilling 1 Introduction. *IEEE Trans. Parallel & Distributed Syst., 12*(6), 529-543.

Felici, M., Koulouris, T., & Pearson, S. (2013). Accountability for Data Governance in Cloud Ecosystems.*Proceedings of the 2013 IEEE International Conference on Cloud Computing Technology and Science*. . IEEE. doi:10.1109/CloudCom.2013.157

Feller, E., Rilling, L., & Morin, C. (2011). Energy-aware ant colony based workload placement in Clouds.*Proceeding GRID'11 proceedings of the 2011 IEEE/ACM 12th international conference on grid computing* (pp. 26–33). IEEE Computer Society, Washington, DC, doi:10.1109/Grid.2011.13

Fellows, W. (2009). *The State of Play: Grid*. Utility, Cloud.

Feng, W., Man, S. & Hu G. (2009). Markov Tree Prediction on Web Cache Pre-fetching. In *Software Engineering, Artificial Intelligence (SCI)*. Springer-Verlag.

Feng, W., Man, S., & Hu, G. (2009). *Markov Tree Prediction on Web Cache Pre-fetching. Software Engineering, Artificial Intelligence (SCI)* (Vol. 209, pp. 105–120). Berlin. Springer-Verlag.

Feng, W., Man, S., & Hu, G. (2009). *Markov Tree Prediction on Web Cache Pre-fetching. Software Engineering, Artificial Intelligence, SCI* (Vol. 209, pp. 105–120). Berlin, Heidelberg: Springer.

Ferrara, A. L., Greeny, M., Hohenberger, S., & Pedersen, M. (2009). Practical short signature batch verification.*Proceedings of CT-RSA, LNCS* (pp. 309–324). Springer. doi:10.1007/978-3-642-00862-7_21

Filho, D.L.G., & Barreto, P.S.L.M. (2006). Demonstrating Data Possession and Uncheatable Data Transfer. IACR Eprint archive.

Foster, I., Zhao, Y., Raicu, I., & Lu, S. (2008). Cloud computing and grid computing 360-degree compared. *Proceedings of the Grid Computing Environments Workshop GCE'08*. IEEE.

Fourouzan & Mukhopadhyay. (2010). Cryptography and Network (2nd ed.). TMH.

Fowler, M., & C. S., T. (2012). *Developing Software for Multiple Mobile Devices*. Thought Works, Inc. Retrieved from: http://martinfowler.com/articles/multiMobile/#ui-translate

Fu, Y., Sandhu, K., & Shih, M. (2000). A Generalization-Based Approach to Clustering of Web Usage Sessions. *Proceedings of the KDD Workshop on Web Mining, 1836*, 21-38.

Fuches, A. P., Chaudhuri, & Foster, J. S. (2009). ScanDroid: Automated security certification of Android applications. Technical report, University of Maryland.

Gajek, S., Jensen, M., Liao, L., & Schwenk, J. (2009). Analysis of Signature Wrapping Attacks and Countermeasures. *Proceedings of the IEEE International Conference on Web Services*, 575-582. doi:10.1109/ICWS.2009.12

Garfinkel, S., & Shelat, A. (2003). Remembrance of Data Passed: A Study of Disk Sanitization Practices. *IEEE Security and Privacy, 1*(1), 17–27. doi:10.1109/MSECP.2003.1176992

Garg, S. K., Yeo, C. S., Anandasivam, A., & Buyya, R. (2011). Environment-conscious scheduling of HPC applications on distributed Cloud-oriented data centers. *Journal of Parallel and Distributed Computing, 71*(6), 732–749. doi:10.1016/j.jpdc.2010.04.004

Garg, S. K., Yeo, C. S., & Buyya, R. (2011). Green cloud framework for improving carbon efficiency of clouds.*European Conference on Parallel Processing*, 491-502. doi:10.1007/978-3-642-23400-2_45

Gartner Hype-Cycle. (2012). *Cloud computing and Big data*. Retrieved from http://www.gartner.com/technology/research/hype-cycles/

Gartner, Inc. (2012). *Gartner Says Free Apps Will Account for Nearly 90 Percent of Total Mobile App Store Downloads in 2012.* Retrieved from: http://www.gartner.com/DisplayDocument?ref=clientFriendlyUrl&id=2126015

Gartner. (2009). *Gartner Says Cloud Consumers Need Brokerages to Unlock the Potential of Cloud Services.* Retrieved from http://www.gartner.com/it/page.jsp?id=1064712

Gartner. (2013). *Gartner recommends a hybrid approach for business-to-employee mobile apps* [Press release]. Retrieved from: http://www.gartner.com/newsroom/id/2429815

Gartner. (2014). *Gartner says more than 75 percent of mobile applications will fail basic security test through 2015* [Press release]. Retrieved from: http://www.gartner.com/newsroom/id/2846017

Gavalas, D., & Economou, D. (2010). Development Platforms for Mobile Applications: Status and Trends. *Software, IEEE, 28*(1), 77–86. doi:10.1109/MS.2010.155

Gellman, R. (2009). *Privacy in the Clouds: Risks to Privacy and Confidentiality from Cloud Computing.* World Privacy Forum (WPF) Report. Retrieved from: http://www.worldprivacyforum.org/cloudprivacy.html

Gen, M., & Cheng, R. (2000). *Genetic algorithms and engineering optimization.* John Wiley & Sons.

Gentry, C. (2009). *A fully homomorphic encryption scheme* (PhD thesis). Stanford University. Retrieved from http://crypto.stanford.edu/craig

Gentry, C. (2009). Fully Homomorphic Encryption Using Ideal Lattices.*Proceedings of the 41st Annual ACM Symposium on Theory of Computing,* 169-178. doi:10.1145/1536414.1536440

Goiri, I., Le, K., Guitart, J., Torres, J., & Bianchini, R. (2011). Intelligent placement of datacenters for internet services.*31st International Conference on Distributed Computing Systems (ICDCS),* 131-142. doi:10.1109/ICDCS.2011.19

Goiri, Í., Le, K., Haque, M. E., Beauchea, R., Nguyen, T. D., Guitart, J., & Bianchini, R. (2011). GreenSlot: scheduling energy consumption in green datacenters.*Proceedings of International Conference for High Performance Computing, Networking, Storage and Analysis,* 20. doi:10.1145/2063384.2063411

Goiri, Í., Le, K., Nguyen, T. D., Guitart, J., Torres, J., & Bianchini, R. (2012). GreenHadoop: leveraging green energy in data-processing frameworks.*Proceedings of the 7th ACM european conference on Computer Systems,* 57-70. doi:10.1145/2168836.2168843

Golden, B. (2009). *Capex vs. Opex: Most People Miss the Point about Cloud Economics.* Retrieved from: http://www.cio.com/article/484429/Capex_vs._Opex_Most_People_Miss_the_point_About_Cloud_Economic

Golden; B. (2009). Capex vs. Opex: Most People Miss the Point About Cloud.

Golle, P., & Mironov, I. (2001). Uncheatable distributed computations. In D. Naccache (Ed.), CT-RSA '01 (pp. 425–440). Springer. doi:10.1007/3-540-45353-9_31

Golle, P., Jarecki, S., & Mironov, I. (2002). Cryptographic primitives enforcing communication and storage complexity. In M. Blaze (Ed.), Financial Cryptography '02 (pp. 120–135). Springer.

Gonçalves, M., Cunha, M., Mendonça, N. C., & Sampaio, A. (2015, June). Performance inference: a novel approach for planning the capacity of IaaS cloud applications. In *2015 IEEE 8th International Conference on Cloud Computing* (pp. 813-820). IEEE. doi:10.1109/CLOUD.2015.112

Gong, Z.H., & Gu, X.H. (2010). PAC: pattern-driven application consolidation for efficient Cloud computing. *Proceeding MASCOTS' 10 proceedings of the 2010 IEEE international symposium on modeling, analysis and simulation of computer and telecommunication systems* (pp. 24–33). doi:10.1109/MASCOTS.2010.12

Google Maps JavaScript API v3. (2013). Google Inc. Retrieved from: https://developers.google.com/maps/documentation/javascript/

Gorelik, E. (2013). *Cloud computing models* (Master's Thesis). Massachusetts Institute of Technology, MIT Sloan School of Management. Retrieved from: http://web.mit.edu/smadnick/www/wp/2013-01.pdf

Goudarzi, H., & Pedram, M. (2012). Energy-efficient virtual machine replication and placement in a cloud computing system.*5th International Conference on Cloud Computing (CLOUD)*, 750-757. doi:10.1109/CLOUD.2012.107

Grance, T., & Mell, P. (2011). The NIST definition of cloud computing. (NIST Publication No. NIST SP- 800-145). Washington, DC: US Department of Commerce. Retrieved from http://csrc.nist.gov/publications/drafts/800-146/Draft-NIST-SP800-146.pdfhttp://www.nist.gov/manuscript-publicationsearch.cfm?pub_id=909616

Gruschka, N., & Iacono, L. L. (2009). Vulnerable Cloud: SOAP Message Security Validation Revisited.*Proceedings of IEEE International Conference on Web Services, 625-631*. doi:10.1109/ICWS.2009.70

Gul, I., & Hussain, M. (2011). Distributed Cloud Intrusion Detection Model. International Journal of advanced science and technology, 34(38), 71-82.

Gunasekhar, T., Thirupathi Rao, K., Saikiran, P., & Lakshmi, P. V. S. (2014). A Survey on Denial of Service Attacks. *International Journal of Computer Science and Information Technologies*, 5(2), 2373–2376.

Halton, W. (2014). *Security Issues and Solutions in Cloud Computing*. Wolf Halton Open Source Security.

Haque, M. E., Le, K., Goiri, Í., Bianchini, R., & Nguyen, T. D. (2013). Providing green SLAs in high performance computing clouds.*International Green Computing Conference (IGCC)*, 1-11. doi:10.1109/IGCC.2013.6604503

Harney, E., Goasguen, S., Martin, J., Murphy, M., & Westall, M. (2007). The efficacy of live virtual machine migrations over the internet.*Proceedings of the 2nd international workshop on Virtualization technology in distributed computing*, 8. doi:10.1145/1408654.1408662

Harris, T. (n.d.). *Cloud computing. An Overview*. Retrieved from: http://www.thbs.com/downloads/Cloud-Computing-Overview.pdf

Heinzelman, W., Kulik, J., & Balakrishnan, H. (1999). Adaptive protocols for information dissemination in wireless sensor networks.*Proc. Fifth Annual ACM/IEEE International Conference on Mobile Computing and Networking (MobiCom)* (pp. 174-185) ACM. doi:10.1145/313451.313529

Heitkötter, H., Hanschke, S., & Majchrzak, T. A. (2012). *Comparing cross-platform development approaches for mobile applications*. Porto: WEBIST.

Hendricks, J., Ganger, G., & Reiter, M. (2007). Verifying Distributed Erasure-Coded Data.*Proceedings of 26th ACM Symposium on Principles of Distributed Computing PODC '07* (pp. 139-146).

Heung, K.L., Baik, S.A., & Kim, E.J. (2009). Adaptive Pre-fetching Scheme Using Web Log Mining in Cluster-based Web. *ICWS*, 1-8.

Hill, J., & Chang, K. C. (2003). Improved Representation of Sensor Exploitation for Automatic Sensor Management. *Proc. Sixth Int. Conf. Information Fusion*, Cairns, Queensland, Australia (pp. 688–694).

Hjärtström, D. (2012). *Utilizing web standards for cross platform mobile development Växjö*. Academic Press.

Holland, J. H. (1992). *Adaptation in Natural and Artificial Systems*. Cambridge, MA, USA: MIT Press.

Houidi, I., Louati, W., Zeghlache, D., Papadimitriou, P., & Mathy, L. (2010). *Adaptive virtual network provisioning.* Retrieved from: https://orbi.ulg.ac.be/bitstream/2268/126822/1/adaptive_embedding_VISA10.pdf

Huang, Y. F., & Hsu, J. M. (2008). Mining web logs to improve hit ratios of pre-fetching and caching. *Knowledge-Based Systems*, *21*(1), 62–69. doi:10.1016/j.knosys.2006.11.004

Huanliu. (2012, March 13). Amazon data centre size. Retrieved from http://huanliu.wordpress.com/2012/03/13/amazondata-center-size/

Hwang, M., Lu, J., & Lin, E. (2003). A Practical (t, n) Threshold Proxy Signature Scheme Based on the RSA Cryptosystem. *IEEE Transactions on Knowledge and Data Engineering*, *15*(6), 1552–1560. doi:10.1109/TKDE.2003.1245292

IBM. (2012). *Native, web or hybrid mobile-app development.* Somers. Retrieved from ftp://public.dhe.ibm.com/software/pdf/mobile-enterprise/WSW14182USEN.pdf

Ibrahim, T. I., & Xu, C. Z. (2000). Neural Nets based Predictive Pre-fetching to Tolerate WWW Latency. *Proceedings of the 20th International Conference on Distributed Computing Systems,* Taipei, Taiwan.

Ibrahim, T. I., & Xu, C. Z. (2004). A Keyword-Based Semantic Pre-fetching Approach in Internet News Services. *IEEE Transactions on Knowledge and Data Engineering*, *16*(5), 601–611. doi:10.1109/TKDE.2004.1277820

Infoworld. (2016). *The 12-cloud-security-threats.* Retrieved From http://www.infoworld.com/article/3041078/security/the-dirty-dozen-12-cloud-security-threats.html

Instance Addressing and Network Security. (2008). *Amazon Elastic Computer Cloud Developer Guide (API Version 2008-12-011).* Author.

Intellisys. (2014). Retrieved from http://www.ntu.edu.sg/intellisys

Irwin, D., Sharma, N., Shenoy, P., & Zink, M. (2010). Towards a virtualized sensing environment.*Proceedings of the 6th International Conference on Test beds and Research Infrastructures for the Development of Networks and Communities.*

Itani, W., Kayssi, A., & Chehab, A. (2009). Privacy as a Service: Privacy-Aware Data Storage and Processing in Cloud Computing Architectures.*Proceedings of the 8th IEEE International Conference on Dependable, Automatic and Secure Computing,* 711-716. doi:10.1109/DASC.2009.139

Jaczynski, M., & Trousse, B. (1998). WWW Assisted Browsing by Reusing Past Navigations of a Group of Users. *Proceedings of the Advances in Case-Based Reasoning, Forth European Workshop*, *1488*, 160-171.

Jaczynski, M., & Trousse, B. (1998). WWW Assisted Browsing by Reusing Past Navigations of a Group of Users. *Proceedings of the Advances in Case-Based Reasoning, Fourth European Workshop*, Dublin, Ireland, Springer LNCS (Vol. 1488, pp. 160-171).

Jakobsson, M., & Juels, A. (1999). Proofs of work and bread pudding protocols. In B. Preneel (Ed.), *Communications and Multimedia Security* (pp. 258–272). Kluwer.

Jayalekshmi, M. B., & Krishnaveni, S. H. (2015). A Study of Data Storage Security Issues in Cloud Computing. *Indian Journal of Science and Technology*, *8*(24), 1–5. doi:10.17485/ijst/2015/v8i1/84229

Jayaram, K. R., & Mathur. (2008). On the Adequacy of Statecharts as a Source of Tests for Cryptographic Protocols. *Annual IEEE International Computer Software and Applications Conference.* doi:10.1109/COMPSAC.2008.203

Jiang, L., Da Xu, L., Cai, H., Jiang, Z., Bu, F., & Xu, B. (2014). An IoT-Oriented Data Storage Framework in Cloud Computing Platform. IEEE Transactions on Industrial Informatics, 10(2), 1443-1451.

Jianhan, Z. (2002). Using Markov Chains for Link Prediction in Adaptive Web Sites. *SoftWare*, 60-73.

Jiawei, H., Micheline, K., & Jian, P. (2006). *Data Mining Concepts and Techniques*. Pearson Education.

Johnson, J., & Chaney, R. (1999). Recursive Composition Inference for Force Aggregation.*Proc. of the Second Int. Conf. Information Fusion.*

Joshi, A., & Krishnapuram, R. (2000). On Mining Web Access Logs.*ACM SIGMOD Workshop on Research Issues in Data Mining and Knowledge Discovery*, 63- 69.

Joshi, J. B. D., Bhatti, R., Bertino, E., & Ghafoor, A. (2004). Access Control Language for Multi-domain Environments. *IEEE Internet Computing*, *8*(6), 40–50. doi:10.1109/MIC.2004.53

Jovanovic, N., Kirda, E., & Kruegel, C. (2006). Preventing cross site request forgery attacks. Securecomm and Workshops, 1-10. doi:10.1109/SECCOMW.2006.359531

jQuery Home Page. (2013). The jQuery Foundation. Retrieved from: http://jquery.com/

jQuery Mobile Home Page. (2013). The jQuery Foundation. Retrieved from: http://jquerymobile.com/

Juels, A., & Kaliski, J. S. (2007). PoRs: Proofs of Retrievability for Large Files.*Proceedings of 14th ACM Conference Computer and Communication Security CCS '07* (pp. 584-597) doi:10.1145/1315245.1315317

Juntunen, A., Jalonen, E., & Luukkainen, S. (2013). HTML 5 in Mobile Devices –Drivers and Restraints. *46th Hawaii International Conference on System Sciences*. doi:10.1109/HICSS.2013.253

Jyoti, P., Goel, A., & Sharma, A. K. (2008). A Framework for Predictive Web Pre-fetching at the Proxy Level using Data Mining. *IJCSNS*, *8*(6), 303–308.

Kallahalla, M., Riedel, E., Swaminathan, R., Wang, Q., & Fu, K. (2003). Plutus: Scalable secure file sharing on untrusted storage. *Proceedings of the 2nd USENIX conference on File and Storage Technologies FAST' 03* (pp. 29–42).

Kaltofen, S. (2010). *Design and implementation of an end-user programming software system to create and deploy cross-platform mobile mashups*. Academic Press.

Kaltofen, S., Milrad, M., & Kurti, A. (2010). A Cross-Platform Software System to Create and Deploy Mobile Mashups. *ICWE'10 Proceedings of the 10th international conference on Web engineering*. doi:10.1007/978-3-642-13911-6_42

Kansal, A., Zhao, F., Liu, J., Kothari, N., & Bhattacharya, A.A. (2010). Virtual machine power metering and provisioning. *Proceeding SoCC'10 proceedings of the 1st ACM symposium on Cloud computing* (pp. 39–50). New York: ACM. doi:10.1145/1807128.1807136

Kant, K. (2009). *Data center evolution. A tutorial on state of the art, issues, and challenges*. Intel Corporation. Retrieved from: http://bnrg.cs.berkeley.edu/~randy/Courses/CS294.S13/1.3.pdf

Kao, Y. W., & Lin, C. F. (2011). A Cross-Platform Runtime Environment for Mobile Widget- based Application. *2011 International Conference on Cyber-Enabled Distributed Computing and Knowledge Discovery*. doi:10.1109/CyberC.2011.20

Kapner, S., & Ziobro, P. (2014). Motorola Solutions Sells Scanner Business to Zebra Technologies. *Wall Street Journal*.

Kaufman, L. M. (2009). Data Security in the World of Cloud Computing. *IEEE Security and Privacy*, *7*(4), 61–64. doi:10.1109/MSP.2009.87

Kavitha, V., & Subashini, S. (2011). A Survey on Security Issues in Service Delivery Models of Cloud Computing. *Journal of Network and Computer Applications*, *34*(1), 1–11. doi:10.1016/j.jnca.2010.07.006

Kaya, C. C., Zhang, G., Tan, Y., & Mookerjee, V. S. (2009). An Admission-Control Technique for Delay Reduction in Proxy Caching. *Decision Support Systems, 46*(2), 594–603. doi:10.1016/j.dss.2008.10.004

Kazi, Z., & Vrbsky. (2012). Security Attacks and Solutions in Clouds. The University of Alabama.

Keiko, H., Rosado, D. G., Eduardo, F., & Eduardo, B. F. (2013). An analysis of security issues for cloud computing. *Journal of Internet Services and Applications*.

Kephart, J. O., & Das, R. (2007). Achieving self-management via utility functions. *IEEE Internet Computing, 11*(1), 40–48. doi:10.1109/MIC.2007.2

Khalil, F., Li, A. J., & Wang, H. (2009). Integrated Model for Next Page Access Prediction. Int. *J. Knowledge and Web Intelligence, 1*(2), 48–80. doi:10.1504/IJKWI.2009.027925

Khanna, R., Liu, H., & Rangarajan, T. (2014). Wireless data center management. *IEEE Microwave Magazine, 15*(7), S45–S60. doi:10.1109/MMM.2014.2356151

Khare & Verma. (2015). A Strong Authentication Technique in Cloud Environment Using: SMTP OTP and MD5. *International Journal of Innovative Research in Computer and Communication Engineering, 3*(12).

Kher, V., & Kim, Y. (2005). Securing distributed storage: Challenges, techniques, and systems.*Proceedings of the ACM Workshop on Storage security and survivability StorageSS '05* (pp 9–25). doi:10.1145/1103780.1103783

Khosravi, A., Garg, S. K., & Buyya, R. (2013). Energy and carbon-efficient placement of virtual machines in distributed cloud data centers.*European Conference on Parallel Processing*, 317-328. doi:10.1007/978-3-642-40047-6_33

Kilari & Sridaran. (n.d.). An Overview of DDoS Attacks in Cloud Environment. *International Journal of Advanced Networking Applications*.

Ko, M., Ahn, G.-J., & Shehab, M. (2009). Privacy-Enhanced User-Centric Identity Management.*Proceedings of IEEE International Conference on Communications*, 998-1002.

Koomey, J. G. (2007). *Estimating total power consumption by servers in the US and the world*. Academic Press.

Koomey, J. G. (2007). *Estimating total power consumption by servers in the US and the world*. Lawrence Berkeley National Laboratory, Tech. Rep.

Koomey, J. G. (2008). Worldwide electricity used in data centers. *Environmental Research Letters. IOP Publishing, 3*(3), 034008.

Kosala, R. & Blockeel, H. (2000). Web Mining Research: A Survey. *SIGKDD explorations, 2*(1), 1-15.

Koskela, T.J., Heikkonen, & Kaski, K. (2003). Web cache optimization with nonlinear model using object feature. *Computer Networks Journal, 43*(6), 805-817.

Koskela, T.J., Heikkonen, J., & Kaski, K. (2003). Web cache optimization with nonlinear model using object feature. *Computer Networks journal, 43*(6), 805-817.

KPMG. (2010). *From hype to future: KPMG's 2010 Cloud Computing survey*. Retrieved From http://www.techrepublic.com/whitepapers/from-hype-to-futurekpmgs

Kroeger, T. M., Long, D. D. E., & Mogul, J. C. (1997). Exploring the Bounds of Web Latency Reduction from Caching and Pre-fetching. *Proceedings of the USENDC Symposium on Internet Technology and Systems* (pp. 13-22).

Krohn, M., Yip, A., & Brodsky, N. (2007). Information flow control for standard OS abstractions.*Proc. Of 21st ACM SIGOPS Symposium on Operating Systems Principles*, 321-334. doi:10.1145/1294261.1294293

Krutz & Russell. (2012). *Cloud Security A comprehensive guide to secure cloud computing.* Wiley India Pvt. Ltd.

Kubiatowicz, J., Bindel, D., Chen, Y., Czerwinski, S., Eaton, P., Geels, D., & Zhao, B. et al. (2000). Oceanstore: An architecture for global-scale persistent storage. *SIG PLAN Notices., 35*(11), 190–201. doi:10.1145/356989.357007

Kumar, C., & Norris, J. B. (2008). A New Approach for a Proxy-level Web Caching Mechanism. *Decision Support Systems, Elsevier, 46*(1), 52–60. doi:10.1016/j.dss.2008.05.001

Kumbhare, A. G., Simmhan, Y., Frincu, M., & Prasanna, V. K. (2015). Reactive Resource Provisioning Heuristics for Dynamic Dataflows on Cloud Infrastructure. *IEEE Transactions on Cloud Computing, 3*(2), 105–118. doi:10.1109/TCC.2015.2394316

Kumbhare, A. G., Simmhan, Y., Frincu, M., & Prasanna, V. K. (2015). Reactive Resource Provisioning Heuristics for Dynamic Dataflows on Cloud Infrastructure. *IEEE Transactions on Cloud Computing, 3*(2), 105–118.

Kwon, W., & Pearson, A. (1977). A modified quadratic cost problem and feedback stabilization of a linear system. *IEEE Transactions on Automatic Control, 22*(5), 838–842. doi:10.1109/TAC.1977.1101619

Lafrance, A. (2016, May 16). Smartphones rule the internet. *The Atlantic.* Retrieved from: http://www.theatlantic.com/technology/archive/2016/05/smartphones-take-over/482880/

Lai, J. K. 2013. Truthful and Fair Resource Allocation [Doctoral dissertation]. Harvard University. Retrieved from http://nrs.harvard.edu/urn-3:HUL.InstRepos:11108713

Lakshman, T., & Thuijs, X. (2011). Enhancing Enterprise Field Productivity via Cross Platform Mobile Cloud Apps. *MCS '11 Proceedings of the second international workshop on Mobile cloud computing and services.* doi:10.1145/1999732.1999741

Lan, K. T. (2010). What's next? Sensor+Cloud? *Proceeding of 7th International workshop on Data Management for Sensor networks.*

Lan, B., Bressan, S., Ooi, B. C., & Tan, K. L. (2000). Rule-Assisted Pre-fetching in Web-Server Caching. *Proceedings of the 9th International Conference on Information and Knowledge Management,* Washington DC, USA (pp. 504-511).

Larry, S. (2009). *Spoofing Server-Server communication: How can you prevent it?* Retrieved from https://otalliance.org/resources/EV/SSLStrip_Whitepaper.pdf

Lawson, B. G., & Smirni, E. (2002, March). Multiple-queue Backfilling Scheduling with Priorities and Reservations for Parallel Systems. *Performance Evaluation Review, 29*(4), 40–47. doi:10.1145/512840.512846

Le, K., Bianchini, R., Martonosi, M., & Nguyen, T. D. (2009). Cost-and energy-aware load distribution across data centers. Proceedings of HotPower, 1-5.

Lease, D. R. (2005). Factors influencing the adoption of biometric security technologies by decision-making information technology and security managers (Capella University). ProQuest Dissertations and Theses. Retrieved from http://search.proquest.com/docview/305359883?accountid=27965

Leavitt, N. (2009). Is Cloud Computing Really Ready for Prime Time? *IEEE Computer, 42*(1), 15–20. doi:10.1109/MC.2009.20

Lee, H. K., An, B. S., & Kim, E. J. (2009). Adaptive Pre-fetching Scheme Using Web Log Mining in Cluster-Based Web Systems. *Proceedings of theIEEE International Conference on Web Services (ICWS)* (pp. 903-910).

Lefèvre, L., & Orgerie, A. C. (2010). Designing and evaluating an energy efficient cloud. *The Journal of Supercomputing, 51*(3), 352–373. doi:10.1007/s11227-010-0414-2

Lei, L., Sengupta, S., Pattanaik, T., & Gao, J. (2015, March). MCloudDB: A Mobile Cloud Database Service Framework. In *Mobile Cloud Computing, Services, and Engineering (MobileCloud), 2015 3rd IEEE International Conference on* (pp. 6-15). IEEE.

Leighon, T. (2009). *Akamai and Cloud Computing: A Perspective from the Edge of the Cloud.* White Paper. Akamai Technologies. Retrieved from http://www.essextec.com/assets/cloud/akamai/cloudcomputing-perspective-wp.pdf

Le, K., Bianchini, R., Nguyen, T. D., Bilgir, O., & Martonosi, M. (2010). Capping the brown energy consumption of internet services at low cost. *International Green Computing Conference*, 3-14. doi:10.1109/GREENCOMP.2010.5598305

Le, K., Bianchini, R., Zhang, J., Jaluria, Y., Meng, J., & Nguyen, T. D. (2011). Reducing electricity cost through virtual machine placement in high performance computing clouds. *Proceedings of International Conference for High Performance Computing, Networking, Storage and Analysis*, 22. doi:10.1145/2063384.2063413

Li, B., Li, Y., He, M., Wu, H., & Yang, J. (2011). Scheduling of a Relaxed Backfill Strategy with Multiple Reservations. *Proceedings of the Parallel and Distributed Computing, Applications and Technologies (PDCAT)International Conference.* IEEE.

Li, J., Krohn, M., Mazieres, D., & Shasha, D. (2004). Secure untrusted data repository (SUNDR). *Proceedings of 6th conference on symposium on Operating System Design & Implementation OSDI '04* (pp. 121–136).

Li, W., & Ping, L. (2009). Trust model to enhance Security and interoperability of Cloud environment. *Proceedings of the 1st International conference on Cloud Computing*, 69–79. doi:10.1007/978-3-642-10665-1_7

Libert, B & Vergnaud, D. (2011). Unidirectional Chosen-Ciphertext Secure Proxy Re-Encryption. *IEEE Transactions on Information Theory, 57*(3), 1786-1802.

Lightfoot, J. (2016). *Authentication and Authorization: OpenID vs OAuth2 vs SAML.* Retrieved from https://spin.atomicobject.com/2016/05/30/openid-oauth-saml/

Li, J., Zhang, L., Liu, J. K., Qian, H., & Dong, Z. (2016). Privacy-Preserving Public Auditing Protocol for Low-Performance End Devices in Cloud. *IEEE Transactions on Information Forensics and Security, 11*(11), 2572–2583. doi:10.1109/TIFS.2016.2587242

Lillibridge, M., Elnikety, S., Birrell, A., Burrows, M., & Isard, M. (2003). A Cooperative Internet Backup Scheme. *Proceedings of USENIX Annual Technical Conference: General Track* (pp. 29-41)

Lin, M., Wierman, A., Andrew, L. L., & Thereska, E. (2013). Dynamic right-sizing for power-proportional data centers. *Transactions on Networking (TON), IEEE/ACM, 21*(5), 1378-1391.

Lindsay, A. M., Galloway-Carson, M., Johnson, C.R., Bunde, D.P., & Leung, V.J. (2011). Backfilling with guarantees granted upon job submission. In *Euro-Par'11 Parallel Processing* (pp. 142-153). Springer. doi:10.1007/978-3-642-23400-2_14

Lin, M., Liu, Z., Wierman, A., & Andrew, L. L. (2012). Online algorithms for geographical load balancing. *International Green Computing Conference (IGCC)*, 1-10.

Liu, C., Ranjian, R., Zhang, X., Yang, C., Georgakopoulos, D., & Chen, J. (2013). Public Auditing for Big Data Storage in Cloud Computing - A Survey. *Proceedings of 16th IEEE International Conference on Computational Science and Engineering CSE* (pp. 1128-1135).

Liu, Q. (2009). *Web Latency Reduction with Pre-fetching* (Ph.D Thesis). University of Western Ontario, London, Canada.

Liu, B., Bi, J., & Vasilakos, A. (2014). Towards incentivizing anti-spoofing deployment. *IEEE Trans. Inform. Forensics Sec.*, 9(3), 436–450. doi:10.1109/TIFS.2013.2296437

Liu, C., Ranjan, R., Yang, C., Zhang, X., Wang, L., & Chen, J. (2015). Mur-DPA: Top-Down Levelled Multi-Replica Merkle Hash Tree Based Secure Public Auditing for Dynamic Big Data Storage on Cloud. *IEEE Transactions on Computers*, 64(9), 2609–2622. doi:10.1109/TC.2014.2375190

Liu, F., Makaroff, D., & Elnaffar, S. (2005, October). Classifying e-commerce workloads under dynamic caching. In *2005 IEEE International Conference on Systems, Man and Cybernetics* (Vol. 3, pp. 2819-2824). IEEE. doi:10.1109/ICSMC.2005.1571577

Liu, Z., Lin, M., Wierman, A., Low, S. H., & Andrew, L. L. (2011). Geographical load balancing with renewables. *Performance Evaluation Review*, 39(3), 62–66. doi:10.1145/2160803.2160862

Livshits, B. V., & Larn, M. S. (2005). Finding security vulnerabilities in Java applications with static analysis. *Proc. of the 14th Conference onUSENIX Security Symposium*, 18-18.

Long, X. & Sikdar, B. (2010). A mechanism for detecting session hijacking in wireless networks. *Wireless Communication, IEEE Transactions*, 1380-1389.

Loon, T. S., & Bharghavan, V. (1997). Alleviating the Latency and Bandwidth Problems in WWW Browsing.*Proceedings of the USENIX Symposium on Internet Technologies and Systems (USITS)*.

Lopes, R., Brasileiro, F., & Maciel, P. D. (2010, April). Business-driven capacity planning of a cloud-based it infrastructure for the execution of web applications. In *Parallel & Distributed Processing, Workshops and Phd Forum (IPDPSW), 2010 IEEE International Symposium on* (pp. 1-8). IEEE. doi:10.1109/IPDPSW.2010.5470726

Lovsz, G., Niedermeier, F., & Meer, H. D. (2012). Performance tradeoffs of energy-aware virtual machine consolidation. *Cluster Computing*.

Lowensohn, J., & McCarthy, C. (2009). *Lessons from Twitter's Security Breach*. Retrieved from: http://news.cnet.com/8301-17939_109-10287558-2.html

Luo, J., Rao, L., & Liu, X. (2015). Spatio-Temporal Load Balancing for Energy Cost Optimization in Distributed Internet Data Centers. *IEEE Transactions on Cloud Computing*, 3(3), 387–397. doi:10.1109/TCC.2015.2415798

Lyle, J., & Monteleone, S. (2012). Cross-platform access control for mobile web applications. *IEEE International Symposium on Policies for Distributed Systems and Networks*. doi:10.1109/POLICY.2012.9

Mahambre, S., Kulkarni, P., Bellur, U., Chafle, G., & Deshpande, D. (2012, October). Workload characterization for capacity planning and performance management in iaas cloud. In *Cloud Computing in Emerging Markets (CCEM), 2012 IEEE International Conference on* (pp. 1-7). IEEE. doi:10.1109/CCEM.2012.6354624

Maheshwari, U., Vingralek, R., & Shapiro, W. (2000). How to build a trusted database system on untrusted storage. *Proceedings of the 4th USENIX Symposium: Operating System Design and Implementation*, Berkeley, CA, USA.

Malis, A. (1993). Routing over Large Clouds (ROLC) Charter. Proceedings of the 32nd IETF meeting minutes.

Mambo, M., Usuda, K., & Okamoto, E. (1996). Proxy Signatures for Delegating Signing Operation. *Proceedings of Third ACM Conference: Computer and Communication Security CCS '96* (pp. 48-57). doi:10.1145/238168.238185

Margaret, R. (2014). *Session Hijacking (TCP Session Hijacking).What is it?* Academic Press.

Mark, P. (2013). *Geolocation - Dive Into HTML5*. Retrieved from: http://diveintohtml5.info/geolocation.html

Markatos, E. P., & Chronaki, C. E. (1998). A Top-10 Approach to Pre-fetching on the Web. In *Proceedings of INET*, 276-290.

Markatos, E.P., & Chronaki, C. E. (1998). A Top-10 Approach to Pre-fetching on the Web.*Proceedings of INET Geneva*, Switzerland (pp. 276-290).

Markoff, J. (2001). An Internet Critic Who Is Not Shy About Ruffling the Big Names in High Technology. *New York Times*.

Marquardt, C., Becker, K., & Ruiz, D. (2004). A Pre-processing Tool for Web Usage Mining in the Distance Education Domain. *Proceedings of the International Database Engineering and Application Symposium (IDEAS)*, 78-87.

Marques, F., Sauvé, J., & Moura, A. (2006, April). Business-oriented capacity planning of IT infrastructure to handle load surges. In *2006 IEEE/IFIP Network Operations and Management Symposium NOMS 2006*(pp. 1-4). IEEE. doi:10.1109/NOMS.2006.1687630

Mather, T., Subra, K., & Latif, S. (2009). *Cloud security and Privacy* (1st ed.). O'Reilly.

Maurer, M., Brandic, I., & Sakellariou, R. (2013). Adaptive resource configuration for Cloud infrastructure management. *Future Generation Computer Systems*, 29(2), 472–487. doi:10.1016/j.future.2012.07.004

Mehrdad, J. (2008). Web User Navigation Pattern Mining Approach Based on Graph Partitioning Algorithm. *Journal of Theoretical and Applied Information Technology*.

Mehta, L. (2014). *SAML-OAuth –OpenID*. Retrieved from http://resources.infosecinstitute.com/saml-oauth-openid/

Meier, J. D., Homer, A., Hill, D., Taylor, J., Bansode, P., Wall, L., . . . Bogwat, A. (2008). *Mobile Application Architecture Guide*. Retrieved from http://robtiffany.com/wp-content/uploads/2012/08/Mobile_Architecture_Guide_v1.1.pdf

Mell, P., & Grance, T. (2009). Effectively and Securely Using the Cloud Computing Paradigm. NIST, Information Technology Laboratory. Retrieved from https://www.cs.purdue.edu/homes/bb/cs590/handouts/Cloud_NIST.pdf

Mell, P., & Grance, T. (2011). *The NIST definition of cloud computing*. NIST special publication, 800, 145.

Merkle, R. C. (1980). Protocols for Public Key Cryptosystems.*Proceedings of IEEE Symptoms: Security and Privacy* (pp. 122-133).

Messmer, E. (2009, October 21). Gartner on Cloud Security: 'Our Nightmare Scenario is Here Now'. *Network World*. Retrieved from: http://www.networkworld.com/news/2009/102109-gartner-cloud-security.html

Metzler, J. (2011). *Virtualization: Benefits, Challenges and Solutions*. Riverbed Technology. Retrieved from: http://www.stotthoare.com.au/sites/default/files/files/1_16100_WhitePaper_VirtualizationBenefits_by_Webtorials.pdf

Mills, K., Filliben, J., & Dabrowski, C. (2011). Comparing VM-placement algorithms for on-demand Clouds. *Proceedings of the2011 IEEE third international conference on Cloud computing technology and science (CloudCom)*, Athens (pp. 91–98). doi:10.1109/CloudCom.2011.22

Misbahuddin, M., & Sumitra, B. (2013). A Survey of Traditional and Cloud Specific Security Issues, Security in Computing and Communications. *Communications in Computation and Information Science, Springer*, 377, 110–129. doi:10.1007/978-3-642-40576-1_12

Mobasher, B., Dai, H., Luo, T., & Nakagawa, M. (2002). Discovery and Evaluation of Aggregate Usage Profiles for Web Personalization. *Data Mining and Knowledge Discovery*, 6(1), 61–82. doi:10.1023/A:1013232803866

Molnar, D., & Schechter, S. (2010). Self-Hosting vs. Cloud Hosting: Accounting for the Security Impact of Hosting in the Cloud. *Proceedings of the Workshop on the Economics of Information Security*. Retrieved from: http://weis2010. econinfosec.org/papers/session5/weis2010_schechter.pdf

More, S., & Chaudhari, S. (2016). Third Party Public Auditing scheme for Cloud Storage. *Proceedings of theInternational Conference on Communication, Computing and Virtualization* (pp. 69-76). Elsevier. doi:10.1016/j.procs.2016.03.010

Mualem, A. W., & Feitelson, D. G. (2001). Utilization, predictability, workloads, and user runtime estimates in scheduling the IBM SP2 with backfilling. *IEEE Transactions on Parallel and Distributed Systems*, *12*(6), 529–543. doi:10.1109/71.932708

Muthitacharoen, A., Morris, R., Gil, T., & Chen, B. (2002). Ivy: A read/write peer-to-peer file system. *Proceedings of the 5th symposium on Operating Systems Design and Implementation: ACM SIGOPS Operating Systems Review OSDI '02* (pp. 31–44)

MYPVDATA Energy Recommerce. (n.d.). Retrieved from https://www.mypvdata.com/

Nair, S. (2013). *How to Avoid Session Hijacking in Web Applications*. TechNet. Microsoft.

Nanopoulos, A., Katsaros, D., & Manolopoulos, Y. (2003). A Data Mining Algorithm for Generalized Web Pre-fetching. *IEEE Transactions on Knowledge and Data Engineering*, *15*(5), 1155–1169. doi:10.1109/TKDE.2003.1232270

Naor, M., & Rothblum, G. N. (2005). The complexity of online memory checking. *Proceedings of the 46th Annual IEEE Symposium on Foundations of Computer Science FOCS* (pp. 573–584). doi:10.1109/SFCS.2005.71

Naor, M., & Nissim, K. (1998). *Certificate revocation and certificate update*. USENIX Security.

Nathani, A., Chaudhary, S. & Somani, G. (2012). Policy based resource allocation in IaaS cloud. *Future Generation Computer Systems*, *28*(1), 94–103. Retrieved from at:.10.1016/j.future.2011.05.016

Nathuji, R., & Schwan, K. (2007). Virtualpower: coordinated power management in virtualized enterprise systems. *ACM SIGOPS Oper. Syst. Rev.*, *41*(6).

National Renewable Energy Laboratory (NREL). (n.d.). Retrieved from http://www.nrel.gov/

Navin, K., Tyagi, & Solanki, A.K. (2011). Analysis of Server Log by Web Usage Mining for Website Improvement. *International Journal of Computer Science Issues*, *7*(4).

Nayak, S. C., & Tripathy, C. (2016). Deadline sensitive lease scheduling in cloud computing environment using AHP. *Journal of King Saud University - Computer and Information Sciences*. doi:10.1016/j.jksuci.2016.05.00

NetApp. (2009). *Secure Cloud Architecture*. WP-7083-0809. NetApp.

Network Technology Group. (2007). DataVault Offsite Data Backup to Completely Secure Critical Computer Data. Retrieved from http://www.ntg.com/datavault.asp

New RhoMobile Suite 5.0 (2014). Offers developer-friendly pricing. *SD Times*.

Nikiforakis, Meert, Younan, Johns. & Joosen. (2011). Session Shield: Lightweight protection against session hijacking. In *Engineering Secure Software and Systems*. Springer Berlin Heidelberg.

Norris, C., & Soloway, E. (2011, November-December). Learning and schooling in the age of mobilism. *Educational Technology*, *51*(6), 3–10. Retrieved from http://cecs5580.pbworks.com/w/file/fetch/50304204/Soloway%20Ed%20Tech-Learning%20and%20Schooling%20in%20the%20Age%20of%20Mobilism.pdf

Oh, F.Y.K., Kim, H.S., Eom, H., & Yeom, H.Y. (2011). Enabling consolidation and scaling down to provide power management for Cloud computing. *Proceeding HotCloud'11 proceedings of the 3rd USENIX conference on hot topics in Cloud computing.*

Open Compute Project. (n. d.). Energy efficiency. Retrieved from http://opencompute.org/about/energy-efficiency/

Oracle. (2015). *Oracle Mobile Security.* Retrieved from www.oracle.com: http://www.oracle.com/technetwork/middleware/id-mgmt/overview/omss-technical-wp-2104766.pdf

Oracle. (2016). *Management Network Virtualization and Network Resources in Oracle Solaris* (11.3 ed.). Reston, VA: Oracle.

Pack, S., Rutagemwa, H., Shen, X., Mark, J., & Park, K. (2008). Proxy-Based Wireless Data Access Algorithms in Mobile Hotspots. *IEEE Transactions on Vehicular Technology, 57*(5), 3165-3177.

Padmanabhan, V. N., & Mogul, J. C. (1996). Using Predictive Pre-fetching to Improve World Wide Web Latency. *ACM Computer Communication Review, 26*(3), 23–36. doi:10.1145/235160.235164

Pallis, G., Vakali, A., & Pokorny, J. (2008). A Clustering-Based Pre-Fetching Scheme on A Web Cache Environment. ACM Journal Computers and Electrical Engineering, 34(4).

Pallis, G., Vakali, A., & Pokorny, J. (2008). A Clustering-Based Pre-Fetching Scheme on A Web Cache Environment. ACM Journal Computers and Electrical Engineering, 34(4).

Palpanas, T., & Mendelzon, A. (1999). Web Pre-fetching using Partial Match Prediction.*Proceedings of the 4th International Web Caching Workshop.*

Pan, B., & Xiao, K. (2010). Component-based mobile web application of crossplatform. *10th IEEE International Conference on Computer and Information Technology (CIT).*

Paola, B. (2007). Web Usage Mining Using Self Organized Maps. *International Journal of Computer Science and Network Security, 7*(6).

Papamanthou, C., Tamassia, R., & Triandopoulos, N. (2008). Authenticated hash tables.*Proceedings of the 15th ACM Conference on Computer and Communications Security CCS '08* (pp. 437–448).

Parida, S., & Nayak, S. C. (2013). An algorithm that earning users' trust on cloud. *Proceedings of the2013 Fifth International Conference*Advanced Computing (ICoAC*). IEEE.

Pearson, S. (2009). Taking Account of Privacy when Designing Cloud Computing Services.*Proceedings of the ICSE Workshop on Software Engineering Challenges of Cloud Computing,* 44-52. doi:10.1109/CLOUD.2009.5071532

Pearson, S., & Charlesworth, A. (2009). Accountability as a Way Forward for Privacy Protection in the Cloud.*Proceedings of the 1st International Conference on Cloud Computing,* 131-144. doi:10.1007/978-3-642-10665-1_12

Pei, C., & Irani, S. (1997). Cost-Aware WWW Proxy Caching Algorithms.*Proceedings of the USENIX Symposium on Internet Technologies and Systems* (pp. 193-206).

Pelley, S., Meisner, D., Wenisch, T. F., & VanGilder, J. W. (2009). Understanding and abstracting total data center power. *Workshop on Energy-Efficient Design.*

Peng, B., Cui, B., & Li, X. (2009). Implementation Issues of A Cloud Computing Platform. *IEEE Data Eng. Bull., 32*(1), 59–66.

Perkowitz, M., & Etzioni, O. (1998). Adaptive Web Sites: Automatically Synthesizing Web Pages. *AAAI '98/IAAI '98: Proceedings of the Fifteenth National/Tenth International Conference on Artificial Intelligence/Innovative Applications of Artificial Intelligence*, 727-732.

Petry, A. (2007). *Design and Implementation of a Xen-Based Execution Environment* (Diploma Thesis). Technische Universitat Kaiserslautern.

Pincus & Wind. (2005). Measuring relative attack surfaces. Computer Security in the 21st Century, 109-137.

Pirolli, P., Pitkow, J., & Ramna, R. (1996). Extracting Usable Structure from the Web. CHI – 96, 118-125.

Pirolli, P., Pitkow, J., & Ramna, R. (1996). Extracting Usable Structure from the Web. Proceedings of CHI '96, Vancouver (pp. 118-125).

Pitkow, J., & Pirolli, P. (1999). Mining Longest Repeating Subsequences to Predict World Wide Web Surfing. *Proceedings USENIX Symposium on Internet Technologies and Systems*.

Podlipnig, S., & Böszörmenyi, L. (2003). A Survey of Web Cache Replacement Strategies. *ACM Computing Surveys*, *35*(4), 374–398. doi:10.1145/954339.954341

Price, M. (2008). The Paradox of Security in Virtual Environments. *IEEE Computer*, *41*(11), 22–38. doi:10.1109/MC.2008.472

Qiu, Z., & Lou, L. (2012). *A Cross-platform Mobile Payment Solution Based on Web Technology. In 2012 Spring Congress on Engineering and Technology*. Xian: SCET.

Qureshi, A., Weber, R., Balakrishnan, H., Guttag, J., & Maggs, B. (2009). Cutting the electric bill for internet-scale systems. ACM SIGCOMM Computer Communication Review, 39(4), 123-134. doi:10.1145/1592568.1592584

Rabin, M. (1989). Efficient dispersal of information for security, load balancing, and fault tolerance. *Journal of the ACM*, *36*(2), 335–348. doi:10.1145/62044.62050

Rajalakshmi, A., Srinandhini, S., & Uma, R. (2015). *A technical review on virtualization technology*. Retrieved from: http://www.ijircce.com/upload/2015/october/69_A%20Technical.pdf

Rajapakse, D. C. (2008). *Fragmentation of mobile applications*. National University of Singapore. Retrieved from: http://www.comp.nus.edu.sg/~damithch/df/device-fragmentation.htm

Rajbhandary, A., Bunde, D. P., & Leung, V. J. (2013). Variations of Conservative to improve fairness. *Proceedings of the17th Workshop on Job Scheduling Strategies for Parallel Processing (JSSPP)*. Springer.

Ramadath, M. C. (2012). *Mobile Application Development: Challenges and Best Practices*. Accenture. Retrieved from: http://www.accenture.com/SiteCollectionDocuments/PDF/Accenture-Mobile- Application-Development-Challenges-Best-Practices.pdf

Ramanathan, S., Goel, S., & Alagumalai, S. (2011, December). Comparison of Cloud database: Amazon's SimpleDB and Google's Bigtable. In *Recent Trends in Information Systems (ReTIS), 2011 International Conference on* (pp. 165-168). IEEE.

Ramya, R., & Kesavaraj, G. (2015). A Survey on Denial of Service Attack in Cloud Computing Environment. *International Journal of Advanced Research in Education & Technology, 2*(3).

Rangarajan, S. K., Phoha V.V., Balagani, K., Selmic, R. R. & Iyengar, S. S. (2004). Web user clustering and its application to pre-fetching using ART neural networks. *IEEE Computer*, 1-17.

Rangarajan, S.K., Phoha, V.V., Balagani, K., Selmic, R.R., & Iyengar S.S. (2004). Web User Clustering and its Application to Pre-fetching using ART Neural Networks. *IEEE Computer*, 45-62.

Ranjan, R., Buyya, R., & Parashar, M. (2012, June). Autonomic Cloud Computing: Technologies, Services, and Applications. *Concurrency and Computation: Practice and Experience, 24*(9), 935-937.

Rao, R. V., & Selvamani, K. (2015). Data Security Challenges and Its Solutions in Cloud Computing.*Proceedings of Conference International Conference on Intelligent Computing, Communication & Convergence.* doi:10.1016/j.procs.2015.04.171

Rasmussen, N. (2007). Electrical efficiency measurement for data centers. *White paper, 154.*

RedHat. (2016). *Advantages and Misconceptions of Virtualization.* Raleigh, NC: RedHat.

Reese, G. (2009). *Cloud Application Architectures: Building Applications and Infrastructure in the Cloud.* O'Reilly Media, Inc.

Relevant IAM Standards and Protocols for Cloud Services. (2010). Retrieved from http://mscerts.programming4.us/programming/

Ren, S., He, Y., & Xu, F. (2012). Provably-efficient job scheduling for energy and fairness in geographically distributed data centers.*32nd International Conference on Distributed Computing Systems (ICDCS)*, 22-31. doi:10.1109/ICDCS.2012.77

Riggins, J. (2015). *Why You Should Build Apps With API Backend - BaaS.* Retrieved from http://nordicapis.com/why-you-should-build-apps-with-an-api-backend-baas/

RightScale Inc. (2009). RightScale Cloud Management Features.

Ristenpart, T., Tromer, E., Shacham, H., & Savage, S. (2009). Hey, You, Get Off of My Cloud: Exploring Information Leakage in Third-Party Compute Clouds.*Proceedings of the 16th ACM Conference on Computer and Communications Security,* 199-212. doi:10.1145/1653662.1653687

Rivest, R. (2007). The pure crypto project's hash function. Cryptography Mailing List Posting. Retrieved from http://diswww.mit.edu/bloompicayune/crypto/13190

Rochwerger, R., Caceres, J., Montero, R. S., Breitgand, D., & Elmroth, E. (2009). The RESERVOIR Model and Architecture for Open Federated Cloud Computing. *IBM Systems Journal, 53*(4), 4:1–4:11. doi:10.1147/JRD.2009.5429058

Ross, V. W. (2010). *Factors influencing the adoption of cloud computing by Decision making manager.* (Capella University). ProQuest Dissertations and Theses. Retrieved from http://search.proquest.com/docview/305262031?accountid=27965

Ryoo, J, Rizvi, S. Aiken, W & Kissell, J. (2014). Cloud Security Auditing: Challenges and Emerging Approaches. *IEEE Security & Privacy, 12*(6), 68-74.

Salama, M., Shawish, A., & Zeid, A. (2013). A Generic Framework for Modeling and Simulation of Cloud Computing Services. *International Journal of Computer Applications, 77*(17), 33-38.

Sandeep, S. (2010). Discovering Potential User Browsing Behaviors Using Custom-Built Apriori Algorithm. *International Journal of Computer Science & Information Technology, 2*(4).

Sankar, K., Kannan, S., & Jennifer, P. (2014). On-demand security architecture for cloud computing. *Middle-East J. Sci. Res., 20*(2), 241–246.

Sanneblad, J., & Holmquist, E. L. (2004). The GapiDraw Platform: High-Performance Cross-Platform Graphics on Mobile Devices. *MUM '04 Proceedings of the 3rd international conference on Mobile and ubiquitous multimedia.*

Sathiyamoorthi, V., & Murali Bhaskaran, V. (2011b). Data Pre-Processing Techniques for Pre-Fetching and Caching of Web Data through Proxy Server. *International journal of Computer Science and Network security, 11*(11), 92-98.

Sathiyamoorthi, V., & Murali Bhaskaran, V. (2011b). Data Pre-Processing Techniques for Pre-Fetching and Caching of Web Data through Proxy Server. *International Journal of Computer Science and Network Security, 11*(11), 92-98.

Sathiyamoorthi, V. (2016). A Novel Cache Replacement Policy for Web Proxy Caching System Using Web Usage Mining. *International Journal of Information Technology and Web Engineering, 11*(2), 12–20. doi:10.4018/IJITWE.2016040101

Sathiyamoorthi, V., & Murali Bhaskaran, V. (2010a). Data Preparation Techniques for Mining World Wide Web through Web Usage Mining-An Approach. *International Journal of Recent Trends in Engineering, 2*(4), 1–4.

Sathiyamoorthi, V., & Murali Bhaskaran, V. (2010b). Data mining for intelligent enterprise resource planning system. *International Journal of Recent Trends in Engineering, 2*(3), 1–4.

Sathiyamoorthi, V., & Murali Bhaskaran, V. (2010b). Data Mining for Intelligent Enterprise Resource Planning System. *International Journal of Recent Trends in Engineering, 2*(3), 1–4.

Sathiyamoorthi, V., & Murali Bhaskaran, V. (2011a). Improving the Performance of Web Page Retrieval through Pre-Fetching and Caching. *European Journal of Scientific Research, 66*(2), 207–217.

Sathiyamoorthi, V., & Murali Bhaskaran, V. (2012). Optimizing the Web Cache performance by Clustering Based Pre-Fetching Technique Using Modified ART1. *International Journal of Computers and Applications, 44*(1), 51–60.

Sathiyamoorthi, V., & Murali Bhaskaran, V. (2012a). A Novel Approach for Web Caching through Modified Cache Replacement Algorithm. *International Journal of Engineering Research and Industrial Applications, 5*(1), 241–254.

Sathiyamoorthi, V., & Murali Bhaskaran, V. (2012b). Optimizing the Web Cache Performance by Clustering Based Pre-Fetching Technique Using Modified ART1. *International Journal of Computers and Applications, 44*(1), 51–60.

Sathiyamoorthi, V., & Murali Bhaskaran, V. (2013). Novel Approaches for Integrating MART1 Clustering based Pre-Fetching Technique with Web Caching. *International Journal of Information Technology and Web Engineering, 8*(2), 18–32. doi:10.4018/jitwe.2013040102

Schubert, L., Kipp, A., & Wesner, S. (2009). Above the Clouds: From Grids to Service- Oriented Operating Systems. In Towards the Future Internet- A European Research Perspective (pp. 238-249). Amsterdam: IOS Press.

Schuermans, S., Vakulenko, M., & Voskoglou, C. (2015). *Developer megatrends hi 2015: Five key trends in the developer economy.* Retrieved from Vision Mobile: http://www.visionmobile.com/product/developer-megatrends-h1-2015/

Schwarz, T., & Miller, E. L. Store, Forget, and Check: Using Algebraic Signatures to Check Remotely Administered Storage. *Proceedings of 26th IEEE International Conference on Distributed Computing Systems ICDCS'06* (pp. 12). doi:10.1109/ICDCS.2006.80

Sebé, F., Domingo-Ferrer, J., Martínez-Ballesté, A., Deswarte, Y., & Quisquater, J. J. (2008). Efficient Remote Data Possession Checking in Critical Information Infrastructures. *IEEE Transactions on Knowledge and Data Engineering, 20*(8), 1034–1038. doi:10.1109/TKDE.2007.190647

Sen, J. (2010b). An Intrusion Detection Architecture for Clustered Wireless Ad Hoc Networks.*Proceedings of the 2nd IEEE International Conference on Intelligence in Communication Systems and Networks*, 202-207. doi:10.1109/CIC-SyN.2010.51

Sen, J. (2010c). A Robust and Fault-Tolerant Distributed Intrusion Detection System.*Proceedings of the 1st International Conference on Parallel, Distributed and Grid Computing*, 123-128. doi:10.1109/PDGC.2010.5679879

Sen, J., Chowdhury, P. R., & Sengupta, I. (2006c). A Distributed Trust Mechanism for Mobile Ad Hoc Networks.*Proceedings of the International Symposium on Ad Hoc and Ubiquitous Computing,* 62-67. doi:10.1109/ISAHUC.2006.4290649

Sen, J., Chowdhury, P. R., & Sengupta, I. (2007). A Distributed Trust Establishment Scheme for Mobile Ad Hoc Networks. *Proceedings of the International Conference on Computation: Theory and Applications,* 51-57. doi:10.1109/ICCTA.2007.3

Sen, J., & Sengupta, I. (2005). Autonomous Agent-Based Distributed Fault-Tolerant Intrusion Detection System.*Proceedings of the 2nd International Conference on Distributed Computing and Internet,* 125-131. doi:10.1007/11604655_16

Sen, J., Sengupta, I., & Chowdhury, P. R. (2006a). A Mechanism for Detection and Prevention of Distributed Denial of Service Attacks.*Proceedings of the 8th International Conference on Distributed Computing and Networking,* 139-144. doi:10.1007/11947950_16

Sen, J., Sengupta, I., & Chowdhury, P. R. (2006b). An Architecture of a Distributed Intrusion Detection System Using Cooperating Agents.*Proceedings of the International Conference on Computing and Informatics,* 1-6. doi:10.1109/ICOCI.2006.5276474

Sen, J., Ukil, A., Bera, D., & Pal, A. (2008). A Distributed Intrusion Detection System for Wireless Ad Hoc Networks. *Proceedings of the 16th IEEE International Conference on Networking,* 1-5. doi:10.1109/ICON.2008.4772624

Shacham, H., & Waters, B. (2008). Compact Proofs of Retrievability. *Proceedings of the 14th International Conference on the Theory and Application of Cryptology and Information Security, 5350,* 90-107. doi:10.1007/978-3-540-89255-7_7

Shah, M. A., Swaminathan, R., & Baker, M. (2008). Privacy-Preserving Audit and Extraction of Digital Contents. Cryptology ePrint Archive.

Shah, M. A. Baker, M. Mogul, J. C. & Swaminathan, R. Auditing to Keep Online Storage Services Honest. *Proceedings of the 11th USENIX Workshop Hot Topics in Operating Systems HotOS '07* (pp. 1-6).

Shameli-Sendi, Pourzandi, Fekih-Ahmed, & Cheriet. (2015). Taxonomy of Distributed Denial of Service Mitigation Approaches for Cloud Computing. *Journal of Network and Computer Applications,* (October), 28.

Shamir, A. (1979). How to share a secret. *Communications of the ACM, 22*(11), 612–613. doi:10.1145/359168.359176

Shea, R., Liu, J., Ngai, E.-H., & Cui, Y. (2013). Cloud gaming: architecture and performance. IEEE Network, 27(4), 16–21. doi:10.1109/MNET.2013.6574660

Sherif, K. (2013). *Federated Identities: OpenID Vs SAML Vs OAuth.* Authentication, Blog Posts, Federated Identities, Secure Coding, Securiy.

Shin, D., & Ahn, G.-J. (2005). Role-Based Privilege and Trust Management. *Computer Systems Science and Engineering, 20*(6), 401–410.

Shmueli, E. (2003, June). Backfilling with Lookahead to Optimize the Packing of Parallel Jobs.

Siegfried, B. (2011). *Enhanced Student Technology Support with Cross-Platform Mobile Apps. 39th annual ACM Special Interest Group on University and College Computing Services,* San Diego, CA.

Sims, K. (2009). IBM Blue Cloud Initiative Advances Enterprise Cloud Computing.

Sims, K. (2009). *IBM Blue Cloud Initiative Advances Enterprise Cloud Computing.* Retrieved from: http://www-03.ibm.com/press/us/en/pressrelease/26642.wss

Sinclair, S., & Smith, S. W. (2008). Preventive Directions for Insider Threat Mitigation Using Access Control. In Insider Attack and Cyber Security: Beyond the Hacker. Springer.

Singh & Shrivastava. (2012). Overview of Attacks on Cloud Computing. *International Journal of Engineering and Innovative Technology, 1*(4).

Singh, S., Pandey, B. K., & Srivastava, R. (2014). Cloud Computing Attacks: A Discussion with Solutions. Open Journal of Mobile Computing and Cloud Computing, 1(1).

Siva, T., & Phalguna Krishna, E. S. (2013). Controlling various network based ADoS Attacks in cloud computing environment: By Using Port Hopping Technique. *International Journal of Engineering Trends and Technology, 4*(5).

Slee, M., Agarwal, A., & Kwiatkowski, M. (2007). *Thrift: Scalable Cross-Language Service Implementation. Technical report.* Facebook.

Smutny, P. (2012). Mobile development tools and cross-platform solutions. *13th International Carpathian Control Conference (ICCC).*

Somani, G., Gaur, M. S., Sanghi, D., Conti, M., & Buyya, R. (2015). DDoS Attacks in Cloud Computing: Issues, Taxonomy, and Future Directions. ACM Comput. Surv, 1(1)

Song, D., Wagner, D., & Perrig, A. (2000). Practical Techniques for Searches on Encrypted Data. *Proceedings of the IEEE Symposium on Research in Security and Privacy*, 44-55.

Sotomayor, B. 2009. The Haizea Manual. Retrieved from http://haizea.cs.uchicago.edu/haizea_manual.pdf

Sotomayor, B., Montero, R.S., Llorente, I.M., & Foster, I. (2009). Resource Leasing and the Art of Suspending Virtual Machines. *Proceedings of the 2009 11th IEEE International Conference on High Performance Computing and Communications* (pp. 59–68).

Sotomayor, B., Montero, R. S., Llorente, I. M., & Foster, I. (2009). Virtual Infrastructure Management in Private and Hybrid Cloud. *IEEE Internet Computing, 13*(5), 14–22. doi:10.1109/MIC.2009.119

Srikantaiah, S., Kansal, A., & Zhao, F. (2008). Energy aware consolidation for Cloud computing. *Proceedings of the 2008 conference on power aware computing and systems*, San Diego (p. 10).

Srikantaiah, S., Kansal, A., & Zhao, F. (2008). Energy aware consolidation for cloud computing. *Proceedings of the conference on Power aware computing and systems*, 10, 1-5.

Srinivasan, S. (2002). Selective Reservation Strategies for Backfill Job Scheduling £ 2 Background and Workload Characterization. *Proceedings of the 8th International Workshop, JSSPP* (pp. 55-71). Springer.

Srivastava, J., Cooley, R., Deshpande, M., & Tan, P. N. (2000). Web Usage Mining: Discovery and Applications of Usage Patterns from Web Data. *SIGKDD Explorations, 1*(2), 12–23. doi:10.1145/846183.846188

Stahl, E., Corona, A., De Gilio, F., Demuro, M., Dowling, A., Duijvestijn, L., & Mouleeswaran, C. (2013). *Performance and Capacity Themes for Cloud Computing.* Red Paper.

Stallings, W. (2011). *Cryptography and Network Security: Principles and Practice* (5th ed.). Pearson.

Standard Performance Evaluation Corporation. (2012). SPECpower_ssj2008 Results res2012q1. Retrieved from http://www.spec.org/power_ssj2008/results/res2012q1/power_ssj2008-20120306-00434.html

Stanton, J. M., Stam, K. R., Mastrangelo, P., & Jolton, J. (2005). Analysis of end user security behaviors. *Computers & Security, 24*(2), 124–133. doi:10.1016/j.cose.2004.07.001

Stoess, J., Lang, C., & Bellosa, F. (2007). Energy management for hypervisor-based virtual machines. *Proceeding ATC'07 USENIX annual technical conference on proceedings of the USENIX annual technical conference.*

Sujatha, N., & Iyakutty, K. (2010). Refinement of Web usage Data Clustering from K-means with Genetic Algorithm. *European Journal of Scientific Research, 42*(3), 464-476.

Sun, X., & Du, Z., Z. (2011). A Secure Cross-platform Mobile IM System for Enterprise Applications. *International Conference on Uncertainty Reasoning and Knowledge Engineering.* doi:10.1109/URKE.2011.6007933

Sutter, H. (2005). The Free Lunch Is Over: A Fundamental Turn Toward Concurrency in Software. *Dr. Dobb's Journal, 30*(3).

Takabi, H., Joshi, J. B. D., & Ahn, G.-J. (2010). Security and Privacy Challenges in Cloud Computing Environments. *IEEE Security and Privacy, 8*(6), 24–31. doi:10.1109/MSP.2010.186

Tamassia, R. (2003). Authenticated data structures.Proceedings of ESA '05, LNCS (Vol. 2832, pp. 2–5). Springer.

Tang, N., & Vemuri, R. (2005). An Artificial Immune System Approach to Document Clustering.*Proceedings of the Twentieth ACM Symposium on Applied Computing*, 918-922. doi:10.1145/1066677.1066889

Teng, W., Chang, C., & Chen, M. (2005). Integrating Web Caching and Web Pre-fetching in Client-Side Proxies. *IEEE Transactions on Parallel and Distributed Systems, 16*(5), 444–455. doi:10.1109/TPDS.2005.56

Thornycroft, P. (2016, March 31). What is the future of mobile communications app security. *NetworkWorld from IDG*. Retrieved from http://www.networkworld.com/article/3050335/mobile-wireless/what-is-the-future-of-mobile-communications-app-security.html

Tian, H. Chen, Y. Cheng, C. Jiang, H. Huang, Y. Chen, Y. & Liu, J. (2016). Dynamic-Hash-Table Based Public Auditing for Secure Cloud Storage. *IEEE Transactions on service computing*.

Tian, W., Choi, B., & Phoha, V. V. (2002). An Adaptive Web Cache Access Predictor Using Neural Network.*Proceedings of the 15th international conference on Industrial and engineering applications of artificial intelligence and expert systems: developments in applied artificial intelligence, 2358*, 450-459. doi:10.1007/3-540-48035-8_44

Toffler, A. (1980). *The Third Wave*. Pan Books.

Toosi, A. N., Calheiros, R. N., & Buyya, R. (2014). Interconnected Cloud Computing Environments: Challenges, Taxonomy, and Survey. *ACM Comput. Surv., 47*(1), Article 7.

Trice, A. (2012). *PhoneGap Blog*. Adobe Systems Inc. Retrieved from: http://phonegap.com/2012/05/02/phonegap-explained-visually/

Troy, M.A., & Vennon, T. (2010). *Android malware: Spyware in the Android Market*. Technical report, SMobile Systems.

Tsafrir, D., Etsion, Y., & Feitelson, D. G. (2005). Backfilling using runtime predictions rather than user estimates (tech. report). Hebrew University of Jerusalem. Retrieved from http://leibniz.cs.huji.ac.il/tr/acc/2005/HUJI-CSE-LTR-2005-5_pred+schedulers.pdf

Tsafrir, D., & Feitelson, D. G. 2006. The dynamics of backfilling: Solving the mystery of why increased inaccuracy may help.*Proceedings of the 2006 IEEE International Symposium on Workload Characterization IISWC '06* (pp. 131–141). doi:10.1109/IISWC.2006.302737

Ubl, M. (2011). *Improving the Performance of your HTML5 App*. Retrieved from: http://www.html5rocks.com/en/tutorials/speed/html5/

Usage Statistics and Market Share of JavaScript Libraries for Websites. (2013). Retrieved from: http://w3techs.com/technologies/overview/javascript_library/all

Usmani, Z., & Singh, S. (2016). A Survey of Virtual Machine Placement Techniques in a Cloud Data Center. *Procedia Computer Science*, *78*, 491–498. doi:10.1016/j.procs.2016.02.093

Valdes, A., Almgren, M., Cheung, S., Deswarte, Y., Dutertre, B., Levy, J., & Uribe, T. E. et al. (2003). An Architecture for Adaptive Intrusion-Tolerant Server.*Proceedings of Security Protocols Workshop* (pp. 158-178).

Vaquero, L. M., Rodero-Merino, L., Caceres, J., & Linder, M. (2009). A Break in the Clouds: Towards a Cloud Definition. *Computer Communication Review*, *39*(1), 50–55. doi:10.1145/1496091.1496100

Velasquez, J., Bassi, A., Yasuda, H., & Aoki, T. (2004). Mining Web Data to Create Online Navigation Recommendations. *Proceedings of the Fourth IEEE International Conference on Data Mining* (ICDM), Brighton, United Kingdom (pp. 551-554).

Velasquez, J., Bassi, A., Yasuda, H., & Aoki, T. (2004) Mining Web Data to Create Online Navigation Recommendations.*Proceedings of the Fourth IEEE International Conference on Data Mining (ICDM)*, 551-554. doi:10.1109/ICDM.2004.10019

Velte, A. T., Velte, T. J., & Elsenpeter, R. (2010). *Cloud Computing: A Practical Approach*. Tata: McGraw-Hill.

Venkatesa Kumar & Nithya. (2014). Improving security issues and security attacks in cloud computing. *International Journal of Advanced Research in Computer and Communication Engineering, 3*(10).

Venkatesan, S., Basha, M.S.S., Vaish, A., & Bhavachelvan, P. (2013). Analysis of accounting models for the detection of duplicate requests in web services. Journal of King Saud University - Computer and Information Sciences, 25(1), 7–24. doi:10.1016/j.jksuci.2012.05.003

Verman, A., Ahuja, P., & Neogi, A. (2008). pMapper: power and migration cost aware application placement in virtualized systems. *Proceeding middleware '08 proceedings of the 9th ACM/IFIP/USENIX international conference on middleware* (pp. 243–264). New York: Springer.

Vidhya, V. (2014). A Review of DOS Attacks in Cloud Computing. *IOSR Journal of Computer Engineering, 16*(5), 32-35.

Vogel, B. (2012). Architectural Concepts: Evolution of a Software System Across Design and Implementation Stages in Dynamically Changing Environments. *2012 IEEE 36th International Conference on Computer Software and Applications Workshops (COMPSACW)*.

Vouk, M. A. (2008). Cloud Computing – Issues, Research and Implementations.*Proceedings of the 30th International Conference on Information Technology Interfaces*, 31-40.

Vozmediano, R. M., Montero, R. S., & Llorente, I. M. (2011). Multi-Cloud Deployment of Computing Clusters for Loosely-Coupled MTC Applications.*IEEE Transactions on Parallel and Distributed Systems, 22*(6), 924–930. doi:10.1109/TPDS.2010.186

Waleed, A., Siti M.S. & Abdul S.I. (2011). A Survey of Web Caching and Prefetching. Int. *J. Advance. Soft Comput. Appl.*, *3*(1).

Waleed, A., Siti, M.S., & Abdul, S.I. (2011). A Survey of Web Caching and Prefetching. *Int. J. Advance. Soft Comput. Appl.*, *3*(1).

Waleed, A., Siti, M. S., & Abdul, S. I. (2011). A Survey of Web Caching and Pre--fetching. *International Journal on Advances in Soft Computing and Application*, *3*(1).

Wang, C. Chow, S. M. Wang, Q. Ren, K. & Lou, W. (2013). Privacy-Preserving Public Auditing for Secure Cloud Storage. *IEEE Transactions on Computers, 62*(2), 362-375.

Wang, C. Wang, Q. Ren, K. Cao, N. & Lou, W. (2012). Toward Secure and Dependable Storage Services in Cloud Computing. *IEEE Transactions on services computing, 5*(2), 220-232.

Wang, C., Ren, K., Lou, W., & Li, J. (2010). Towards Publicly Auditable Secure Cloud Data Storage Services.IEEE Network Magazine, 24(4), 19-24.

Wang, C., Wang, Q., Ren, K., & Lou, W. (2010). Privacy-Preserving Public Auditing for Data Storage Security in Cloud Computing. Proceedings of IEEE INFOCOM (pp. 1-9). doi:10.1109/INFCOM.2010.5462173

Wang, H. (2013). Proxy Provable Data Possession in Public Clouds. *IEEE Transactions on Services Computing, 6*(4), 551-559.

Wang, H. W., & Vick, C. (2004). Cross-Platform Multi-Network Mobile Application Architecture. *Proceedings of the IEEE 6th Circuits and SystemsSymposium on Emerging Technologies: Frontiers of Mobile and Wireless Communication.*

Wang, H. Wu, Q. Qin, B. & Domingo-Ferrer, J. (2014). Identity-based remote data possession checking in public clouds. *IET Information Security, 8*(2), 114- 121.

Wang, B., Baochun, L., & Hui, L. (2013). Public auditing for shared data with efficient user revocation in the cloud. *Proceedings of the 32nd IEEE International Conference on Computer Communications INFOCOM '13* (pp. 2904–2912). doi:10.1109/INFCOM.2013.6567101

Wang, B., Li, B., & Li, H. (2012). Oruta: Privacy-preserving public auditing for shared data in the cloud.*Proceedings of the IEEE Fifth International Conference on Cloud Computing CLOUD '12* (pp. 295–302). doi:10.1109/CLOUD.2012.46

Wang, C., Wang, Q., Ren, K., & Lou, W. (2009). Ensuring Data Storage Security in Cloud Computing.*Proceedings of 17th International Workshop on Quality of Service IWQoS '09* doi:10.1109/IWQoS.2009.5201385

Wang, J. (1999). A Survey of Web Caching Schemes for the Internet. *ACM Comp. Commun. Review, 29*(5), 36–46. doi:10.1145/505696.505701

Wang, J., Chen, X., Huang, X., You, I., & Xiang, Y. (2015). Verifiable Auditing for Outsourced Database in Cloud Computing. *IEEE Transactions on Computers, 64*(11), 3293–3303. doi:10.1109/TC.2015.2401036

Wang, Q., Wang, C., Ren, K., Lou, W., & Li, J. (2011). Enabling Public Verifiability and Data Dynamics for Storage Security in Cloud Computing. *IEEE Transactions on Parallel and Distributed Systems, 22*(2/5), 847–859. doi:10.1109/TPDS.2010.183

Ward, W.A., Jr., Mahood, C.L., & West, J.E. (2002). Scheduling Jobs on Parallel Systems Using a Relaxed Backfill Strategy. *Proceedings of the8th International Workshop JSSPP* (pp. 88-102). Springer. doi:10.1007/3-540-36180-4_6

Webopedia. (2007). Data Vaulting. http://www.webopedia.com/TERM/D/data_vaulting.html

Weiss, A. (2007). Computing in the Clouds.netWorker, 11(4), 16-25.

Wessels, D. (2001). Web Caching. Sebastopol, CA: O'Reilly publication.

Westin, A. F. (2003). Social and Political Dimensions of Privacy. *The Journal of Social Issues, 59*(2), 1–37. doi:10.1111/1540-4560.00072

Whinnery, K. (2012). *Comparing Titanium and PhoneGap*. Appcelerator Inc. Retrieved from: http://developer.appcelerator.com/blog/2012/05/comparing-titanium-andphonegap. html

Whitaker, A., & Newman, D. P. (2005). *Penetration testing and network defense*. Pearson Education.

Wikinomics. (n. d.). The Prosumers.

Wikipedia. (n. d.). [computer scientist]. *John McCarthy.*

Wikipedia. (n. d.). *Cloud Computing.*

Wikipedia. Cyclic Redundancy Check. 2007. http://en.wikipedia.org/wiki/Cyclic_redundancy_check

Wong & Tan. (2014). A Survey of Trends in Massive DDOS Attacks and Cloud-based Mitigations. *International Journal of Network Security & Its Applications, 6*(3).

Wong, A.K.L., & Goscinski, A.M. (2007). Evaluating the EASY-Backfill Job Scheduling of Static Workloads on Clusters. *Proceedings of the 2007 IEEE International Conference on Cluster Computing.*

Wong, A. K. Y. (2006). Web Cache Replacement Policies: A Pragmatic Approach. *IEEE Network, 20*(1), 28–34. doi:10.1109/MNET.2006.1580916

Worku, S. G., Xu, C., Zhao, J., & He, X. (2013). Secure and efficient privacy-preserving public auditing scheme for cloud storage. In Computers and Electrical Engineering (pp. 1703 – 1713). Elsevier.

Xiao, J., Zhang, Y., Jia, X., & Li, T. (2001). Measuring Similarity of Interests for Clustering Web-users. *12th Australasian Database Conference (ADC)*, 107-114.

Xin, C. (2009). Cross-Platform Mobile Phone Game Development Environment. *International Conference on Industrial and Information Systems.*

Xu, L., Mo, H., Wang, K., & Tang, N. (2006). Document Clustering Based on Modified Artificial Immune Network. Rough Sets and Knowledge Technology, 4062, 516-521.

Xu, H., Feng, C., & Li, B. (2013). Temperature aware workload management in geo-distributed datacenters. *Proceedings of the 10th International Conference on Autonomic Computing (ICAC)*, 303-314. doi:10.1145/2465529.2465539

Xu, J., & Fortes, J. A. (2010). Multi-objective virtual machine placement in virtualized data center environments. *Int'l Conference on Green Computing and Communications (GreenCom) & Int'l Conference on Cyber, Physical and Social Computing (CPSCom), IEEE/ACM*, 179-188. doi:10.1109/GreenCom-CPSCom.2010.137

Yang, Q., Li, T., & Wang, K. (2004). Building Association-Rule Based Sequential Classifiers for Web-Document Prediction. *Journal of Data Mining and Knowledge Discovery, 8*(3), 253–273. doi:10.1023/B:DAMI.0000023675.04946.f1

Yu, N., Liu, C., & Chen, J., J. (2011). The Development and Application of Cross-Platform Coal Mine Mobile Information System. *2011 International Conference on Computer Science and Network Technology.*

Yuan, J. & Yu, S. (2015). Public Integrity Auditing for Dynamic Data Sharing with Multi-User Modification. *IEEE Transactions on Information Forensics and Security, 10*(8), 1717-1726.

Yuan, J., & Yu, S. (2013). Proofs of retrievability with public verifiability and constant communication cost in cloud. *Proceedings of the International Workshop on Security in Cloud Computing: Cloud Computing '13* (pp. 19–26). doi:10.1145/2484402.2484408

Zaiane, O. (2000). Web Mining: Concepts, Practices and Research. *Proc. SDBD, Conference Tutorial Notes.*

Zetter, K. (2010). Google hackers Targeted Source Code of More Than 30 Companies. *Wired Threat Level.* Retrieved from: http://www.wired.com/threatlevel/2010/01/google-hackattack/

Zhang, B., & Wang, W. (2011). Research and Implementation of Cross-platform Development of Mobile Widget. *2011 IEEE 3rd International Conference on Communication Software and Networks (ICCSN)*. doi:10.1109/ICCSN.2011.6014238

Zhang, Y., & Joshi, J. (2009). *Access Control and Trust Management for Emerging Multidomain Environments.* In S. Upadhyay & R. O. Rao (Eds.), *Annals of Emerging Research in Information Assurance, Security and Privacy Services* (pp. 421–452). Emerald Group Publishing.

Zhang, Y., Wang, Y., & Wang, X. (2011). Greenware: Greening cloud-scale data centers to maximize the use of renewable energy.*International Conference on Distributed Systems Platforms and Open Distributed Processing, ACM/IFIP/ USENIX*, 143-164. doi:10.1007/978-3-642-25821-3_8

Zheng, & Xu, Q. (2011). Fair and dynamic proofs of Retrievability. *Proceedings of the first ACM conference on Data and Application Security & Privac: CODASPY'11* (pp. 237–248)

Zhijie, B., Zhimin, G., & Yu, J. (2009). A Survey of Web Pre-fetching. *Journal of Computer Research and Development*, *46*(2), 22–210.

Zhou, R., Wang, Z., McReynolds, A., Bash, C. E., Christian, T. W., & Shih, R. (2012). Optimization and control of cooling microgrids for data centers.*13th Intersociety Conference on Thermal and Thermomechanical Phenomena in Electronic Systems (ITherm)*, 338-343. doi:10.1109/ITHERM.2012.6231449

Zhu, H., Xiong, H., Ge, Y., & Chen, E. (2014). Mobile app recommendations with security and privacy awareness. *KDD '14 Proceedings of the 20th ACM SIGKDD international conference on Knowledge discovery and data mining*, 951-960. doi:10.1145/2623330.2623705

Zhu, Y. Hu, H. Ahn, G. & Yu, M. (2012). Cooperative Provable Data Possession for Integrity Verification in Multi-Cloud Storage. *IEEE Transactions on Parallel and Distributed Systems*, *23*(12), 2231-2244.

Zhu, Y. Wang, H. Hu, Z. Ahn, G. J. Hu, H and Yau, S. (2013). Dynamic Audit Services for Outsourced Storage in Clouds. *IEEE Transactions on Services Computing*, *6*(2), 227–238.

Zhu, Y. Wang, H. Hu, Z. Ahn, G.J. & Hu, H. (2011). Zero-knowledge proofs of Retrievability. *Science China Information Sciences*, *54*(8), 1608–1617.

Zhu, Y., Wang, H., Hu, Z., Ahn, G. J., Hu, H., & Yau, S. S. (2011). Dynamic audit services for integrity verification of outsourced storages in clouds.*Proceedings of the 2011 ACM Symposium on Applied Computing SAC '11* (pp. 1550–1557). doi:10.1145/1982185.1982514

Zimory Gmb, H. (2009). *Zimory Distributed Cloud-Whitepaper.* Retrieved from: http://www.zimory.de/index.php?eID=tx_ nawsecuredl&u=0&file=fileadmin/user_upload/pdf/Distributed_Clouds_Whitepaper.pdf&t=1359027268&hash=93c5 f42f8c91817a746f7b8cff55fbdc68ae7379

Zimory GmbH. (2009). Zimory Enterprise Cloud.

About the Contributors

Narendra Kumar Kamila is presently working as Professor and Head, Department of Computer Science and Engineering, C V Raman College of Engineering, Bhubaneswar, Odisha, India. He received his master degree from Indian Institute of Technology, Kharagpur and subsequently obtained his Ph. D. degree from Utkal University, Bhubaneswar in the year 2000. Prof. Kamila was also post doctoral fellow to University of Arkansas, USA. He has published several research papers in the national/international journal of repute in the field of wireless sensor networking, Adhoc-networking, Image processing, meta cognition, data privacy/security. He has served as program committee members in many international conferences. He has also conducted staff development programs under the financial support of All Indian Council for Technical Education as chief-coordinator. However, he had organized "International Conference on Computer Technology (ICCT-2010)" from 3rd Dec. to 5th Dec. 2010 at C V Raman College of Engineering successfully as General/Local Organizing Chair with financial assistance from AICTE, CSIR and Biju Patnaik University of Technology. He was also Guest Editor of International Journal of Computer and Communication Technology, Vol. 2, Issues 2, 3 and 4, 2010. He has completed many projects sponsored by various sponsoring agencies. He has guided many M.Tech. and Ph.D. students under different universities. However Dr. Kamila has been appointed as DSC member of Biju Patnaik University of Technology, Dr. Kamila has been rendering his best services as editorial board member to American Journal of Intelligent System, American Journal of Advances in Networks, American journal of Networks and Communications, Reviewer of International journal of Intelligent Information System(USA), Reviewer of International journal of Automation Control and Intelligent Systems(USA), Reviewer of Elsevier Publication, Reviewer of AMSE, modelling simulation(France), editor-in-chief of International Journal of Advanced Computer Engineering and Communication Technology, former editor-in-chief of International Journal of Communication Network and Security(IJCNS) and editor-in-chief of many international conference proceedings.

* * *

Balamurugan Balusamy had completed his B.E. (Computer Science) from Bharathidasan University and M.E. (Computer Science) from Anna University. He completed his Ph.D. in cloud security domain specifically on access control techniques. He has published papers and chapters in several renowned journals and conferences.

Phillip G. Bradford is a Computer Scientist with extensive experience in academia and industry. Phil was a post-doctoral fellow at the Max-Planck-Institut für Informatik, he earned his PhD at Indiana

University, an MS form the University of Kansas, and a BA from Rutgers University. He was on the faculty at Rutgers Business School and the University of Alabama in the School of Engineering. He has worked for BlackRock, Reuters Analytics, founded a firm and both consulted and worked with a number of early stage firms. Currently he works for GE Asset Management.

Rajkumar Buyya is a Fellow of IEEE, Professor of Computer Science and Software Engineering, Future Fellow of the Australian Research Council, and Director of the Cloud Computing and Distributed Systems (CLOUDS) Laboratory at the University of Melbourne, Australia. He is also serving as the founding CEO of Manjrasoft, a spin-off company of the University, commercializing its innovations in Cloud Computing. He has authored over 525 publications and seven text books including "Mastering Cloud Computing" published by McGraw Hill, China Machine Press, and Morgan Kaufmann for Indian, Chinese and international markets respectively. He also edited several books including "Cloud Computing: Principles and Paradigms" (Wiley Press, USA, Feb 2011). He is one of the highly cited authors in computer science and software engineering worldwide (h-index=105, g-index=216, 51,600+ citations). Microsoft Academic Search Index ranked Dr. Buyya as #1 author in the world (2005-2016) for both field rating and citations evaluations in the area of Distributed and Parallel Computing. "A Scientometric Analysis of Cloud Computing Literature" by German scientists ranked Dr. Buyya as the World's Top-Cited (#1) Author and the World's Most-Productive (#1) Author in Cloud Computing. Recently, Dr. Buyya is recognized as "2016 Web of Science Highly Cited Researcher" by Thomson Reuters.

Harry J. Foxwell is a principal consultant at Oracle's Public Sector division in the Washington, DC area, where he is responsible for solutions consulting and customer education on Cloud Computing, Big Data, Operating Systems, and virtualization technologies. Harry has worked for Oracle and for Sun Microsystems (acquired by Oracle in 2009) since 1995. Prior to that, he worked as a UNIX and Internet specialist for Digital Equipment Corporation; he has worked with UNIX systems since 1979 and with Linux systems since 1995. Harry is coauthor of two Sun BluePrints: "Slicing and Dicing Servers: A Guide to Virtualization and Containment Technologies" (Sun BluePrints Online, October 2005), and "The Sun BluePrints Guide to Solaris Containers: Virtualization in the Solaris Operating System" (Sun BluePrints Online, October 2006). He coauthored Pro OpenSolaris (Apress, 2009), Oracle Solaris 11 System Administration: The Complete Reference (Oracle Press, 2012), and Oracle Solaris 11.2 System Administration Handbook (Oracle Press, 2015). He blogs about Cloud Computing and other technologies at http://http://blogs.oracle.com/drcloud/. He earned his doctorate in information technology in 2003 from George Mason University (Fairfax, VA), and has since taught graduate courses there in operating systems, computer architecture and security, and electronic commerce. Harry is a Vietnam veteran; he served as a platoon sergeant in the US Army's 1st Infantry Division in 1968-1969. He was awarded an Air Medal and a Bronze Star. He is also an amateur astronomer and member of the Northern Virginia Astronomy Club. In addition, Harry is a USA Table Tennis (USATT) member and competitive table tennis player, and is also a US Soccer Federation (USSF) soccer referee. For additional information about Harry, please visit his home page: http://cs.gmu.edu/~hfoxwell.

Atefeh Khosravi is a PhD candidate at Cloud Computing and Distributed Systems (CLOUDS) Laboratory within the Department of Computing and Information Systems at the University of Melbourne. She received her M.Sc. degree of Computer Engineering in 2011 and B.Sc. degree of Information Technology Engineering in 2008, both from the Amirkabir University of Technology (Tehran Polytechnic),

Iran. Atefeh's PhD research is on energy and carbon-aware resource management across distributed cloud data centers. It is mainly focused on the development of policies and algorithms for placement and migration of virtual machines by considering data centers energy sources, carbon footprint, and power consumption. Atefeh is also a Research Scientist at Amazon Web Services (AWS).

Pandiselvi K, Student of II Year M.E. Computer Science and Information Security at Thiagarajar College of Engineering. Her research interest includes Cryptography and Cloud Computing.

Thangavel M is an Assistant Professor, Department of Information Technology at Thiagarajar college of Engineering, Madurai. He is pursuing Ph.D under the faculty of Information and Communication, Anna University. He completed his M.E in Computer Science & Engineering at J.J College of Engineering. His research interests include Cryptography &Network security, Compiler Design and Data Structures.

Sumalatha N is a PG scholar in VIT University and her area of interests are cloud computing and data science.

Suvendu Chandan Nayak is currently working as an Asst. Prof in the Dept.of Computer Science and Engineering, C V Raman College of Engineering, Bhubaneswar, India. Also pursuing PhD in Computer Science and Engg. in Veer Surendra Sai University of Technology (VSSUT), Burla, India. He has completed BTech, MTech in Computer Science and Engg. from BPUT, India. He has published more than twelve number of research papers in different International journals and conferences. His area of research is Cloud Computing and IoT.

Sindhuja R, Student of II Year M.E. Computer Science and Information Security at Thiagarajar College of Engineering. Her research interest includes Cryptography and Cloud Computing.

Rashmi Rai is a full time researcher with focus in cloud technology specifically energy efficiency in cloud data centers.

Nadhiya S is a PG scholar in VIT University and her area of interests are cloud computing and data science.

Nithya S, Student of II Year M.E. Computer Science and Information Security at Thiagarajar College of Engineering. Her research interest includes Data Mining and Cloud Computing.

Prashant Sangulagi received B.E in Electronics and Communication Engineering in the year 2009. Completed M.Tech in Digital Communication in the year 2011. Now he is perusing Ph.D. in the area of sensor cloud. Presently He is working as an Asst. Prof in ECE Dept. BKIT, Bhalki INDIA. He has Published 10 journal papers, 3 international conference papers and 10 national papers. His Area of interest are, WSN, Ad-Hoc Network, Agent Technology, Cloud Computing, IOT and Network Security. He is a member of IETE INDIA, IACSIT and reviewer / editorial board member of many journals.

S. Sridhar received his B.Tech - Information Technology degree under the faculty of Information & Communication Engineering from Thiagarajar college of Engineering, Affiliated to Anna University,

Chennai.His research interests include Cloud Security and Network Security. He completed his M.E. Computer Science and Information Security degree under the Department of Information Technology, Thiagarajar college of Engineering, Madurai. Now, he is working as an assistant professor in the department of Information Technology in M.Kumarasamy College of Engineering, Karur.

Ashok V. Sutagundar completed his B. E in Electronics and Communication Engineering from Karnatak University Dharwad, India and M.Tech from Visvesvaraya Technological University Belgaum, India. Completed his Ph.D in the area of Wireless Sensor Networks (WSNs). Presently, he is working as Faculty in Department of Electronics and Communication Engineering, Basaveshwar Engineering College, Bagalkot, Karnataka, India. He has published 32 national and international conference papers and 10 national and international journals. His area of interest is a wireless network, Image processing Video Processing, especially and Multimedia Networks. He is a member of IETE, India.

Marcus Tanque is an experienced professional, thought-leader and adjunct professor with demonstrated expertise in business analyses, corporate marketing strategies, cyber security practices, enterprise infrastructure management, IT management consulting practices, and technical expertise. Dr. Tanque's consultative functions with several leaders in the public-private sector resulted in outstanding achievements. His natural entrepreneurial flair coupled with his unparalleled contribution to academic, federal, and industry customers, has led to exceptional accomplishments. In recent years, Dr. Tanque has been involved in several business and IT technology projects encompassing IT engineering, program/ project management, systems security, cyber security operations, health IT, mechatronics, data science/ analytics, telecommunications, big data/predictive analytics, cloud-based and cyber security products convergence of legacy and leading-edge technical solutions not to mention a few. His management and engineering expertise has been remarkably rewarding to him and the stakeholders. As an adept in research and development, research and technology, management, research and engineering, strategies/ policies, and business theories, Marcus always has been enthusiastic in taking upon complex missions that require critical-thinking and in-depth analytical methodologies on varied IT practices in support of many government customers and the industry stakeholders. Dr. Tanque is a distinguished recipient of a Ph.D. degree in Information Technology with a dual specialization in Information Assurance/Security; and he also holds a Master of Science degree in Information Systems Engineering.

Sathiyamoorthi V is currently working as an Associate Professor in Computer Science and Engineering Department at Sona College of Technology, Salem, Tamil Nadu, India. He was born on June 21, 1983, at Omalur in Salem District, Tamil Nadu, India. He received his Bachelor of Engineering degree in Information Technology from Periyar University, Salem with First Class. He obtained his Master of Engineering degree in Computer Science and Engineering from Anna University, Chennai with Distinction and secured 30th University Rank. He received his Ph.D degree from Anna University, Chennai in Web Mining. His areas of specialization include Web Usage Mining, Data Structures, Design and Analysis of Algorithm and Operating System. He has published five papers in International Journals and eight papers in various National and International conferences. He has also participated in various National level Workshops and Seminars conducted by various reputed institutions.

P. Varalakshmi is an Associate Professor at the Department of Computer Technology, Madras Institute of Technology, Anna University, Chennai, Tamilnadu, India. She received her PhD under Information and Communication Engineering-Trust Management in Grid Computing at the Anna University, Chennai, Tamilnadu, India. Her research interests include compiler design, network security in grid and cloud computing.

Malathi Velu has completed B.E. (Computer Science) from Panimalar and M.E. (Information Technology) from VIT University.

Index

A

B

C

D

   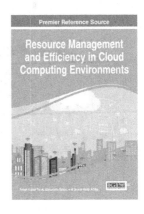

Printed in the United States
By Bookmasters